READINGS IN
AMERICAN
POLITICS

Second Edition

READINGS IN AMERICAN POLITICS

Analysis and Perspectives

Second Edition

Ken Kollman

UNIVERSITY OF MICHIGAN

W. W. Norton & Company ■ New York ■ London

W. W. Norton & Company has been independent since its founding in 1923, when William Warder Norton and Mary D. Herter Norton first published lectures delivered at the People's Institute, the adult education division of New York City's Cooper Union. The firm soon expanded its program beyond the Institute, publishing books by celebrated academics from America and abroad. By mid-century, the two major pillars of Norton's publishing program—trade books and college texts—were firmly established. In the 1950s, the Norton family transferred control of the company to its employees, and today—with a staff of four hundred and a comparable number of trade, college, and professional titles published each year—W. W. Norton & Company stands as the largest and oldest publishing house owned wholly by its employees.

Editor: Ann Shin
Associate editor: Jake Schindel
Production manager: Eric Pier-Hocking
Project supervised by Westchester Book Group/Debbie Masi
Composition by Westchester Book Group
Manufacturing by RR Donnelley—Crawfordsville

Library of Congress Cataloging-in-Publication Data

Kollman, Ken, 1966–
Readings in American politics : analysis and perspectives / Ken Kollman.—2nd ed.
p. cm.
Includes bibliographical references.
ISBN 978-0-393-91282-1 (pbk.)
1. United States—Politics and government.   I. Title.
JK21.K65 2011
320.473—dc23

2011028354

W. W. Norton & Company, Inc , 500 Fifth Avenue, New York, N.Y. 10110-0017

www.wwnorton.com

W. W. Norton & Company Ltd., Castle House, 75/76 Wells Street, London W1T 3QT

1 2 3 4 5 6 7 8 9 0

CONTENTS

17 FOREIGN POLICY

PREFACE

This reader makes some of the most important work in political science and the subfield of American politics easily accessible to students in introductory courses. The selections included in this second edition have been chosen to help accomplish several things in a college classroom: introduce students to fundamental concepts in political science and the study of American politics, such as collective-action problems, agenda-setting power, ideologies, and the median voter; provide specific insights into the workings of the major institutions and processes of American government; spur discussion on controversial topics, such as gun control, gay rights, campaign finance, and contemporary American foreign policy; and improve students' abilities to digest official government documents like Supreme Court cases.

The opening Fundamentals section introduces students to four crucial problems for understanding politics:

1. *the problem of maintaining individual liberty* under any form of government based on laws that constrain behavior;
2. *collective-action problems* among groups of people and how organizers and leaders of institutions can try to overcome such problems;
3. *common–resource problems*, which are variants of the standard collective-action problem but refer specifically to allocating scarce resources;
4. and *delegation (or principal-agent) problems*, which are ubiquitous in modern, democratic government and that require contract-like arrangements to solve.

The material in the Fundamentals section is a good foundation for students approaching the rest of the readings. Students reading the classic selections can approach them fresh with knowledge of the "problems" discussed in Chapter 1. One can read Madison's *Federalist*, No. 10, for instance, with an eye toward common–resource problems. Madison was concerned that an overpowering majority interest would oppress other groups, and he favored having many different groups represented in a single government. It is worth discussing the question: Was Madison naïve about collective-action problems inherent when many groups compete for common resources? The selection from Robert Dahl offers criticisms of the solutions and compromises Madison and his fellow Founders made when crafting the Constitution.

Many of the contemporary selections also have one or more of the "problems" from Chapter 1 as their backdrop. To take an example from Chapter 5 on Congress, the delegation problem is at the root of the arguments by Cox and McCubbins on how (and why) partisan majorities grant agenda control to party leaders in Congress. And Burns, Schlozman, and Verba's arguments in Chapter 10 focus attention on the ways men and women differ in their costs and benefits of participation in the face of collective-action problems. Students benefit greatly from seeing these theoretical threads in contemporary political science scholarship.

Quite a few of the readings provide grist for lively discussion of current events and policy controversies. Students will gain knowledge of legal arguments about gay marriage, elections, education, and gun control, and will confront arguments about the sustainability of recent trends in American foreign policy.

I use these readings when I teach. In preparing this second edition, I have paid close attention to the suggestions of my own students and of other professors who assigned the first edition. I hope you find these readings as useful as I do in understanding politics and, specifically, the American political system.

I owe special thanks to several people. Reviewers of the first edition provided wonderful feedback leading to this second edition. Erin Ackerman and Ann Shin made possible the first edition, and Hannah Bozian helped with this second edition. Jake Schindel was also instrumental in helping me pull together this second edition.

ABOUT THE EDITOR

KEN KOLLMAN is professor in the Department of Political Science and research professor in the Center for Political Studies in the Institute for Social Research at the University of Michigan, Ann Arbor. His research and teaching focus on political parties, elections, lobbying, and federal systems. He also regularly teaches the introductory American politics course at the University of Michigan. In addition to numerous articles, he has written *The Formation of National Party Systems: Federalism and Party Competition in Canada, Great Britain, India, and the United States* (with Pradeep Chhibber, 2004) and *Outside Lobbying: Public Opinion and Interest Group Strategies* (1998). Professor Kollman is also the author of a new American government textbook published by W. W. Norton, *The American Political System*.

1

FUNDAMENTALS

1.1

JOHN LOCKE

From *The Second Treatise of Government*

Locke's treatise forms part of the intellectual foundations of the American and French Revolutions, and of all modern democracies and democratic movements. He argues that people are born free and equal but that oppressive government tramples this "natural liberty." However, Locke explains, people can freely consent to having a government inhibit this liberty, and because they consent to being constrained, such a government can lead to "peace, safety, and public good."

OF THE BEGINNING OF POLITICAL SOCIETIES

95. Men being . . . by nature all free, equal, and independent, no one can be put out of this estate and subjected to the political power of another without his own consent. The only way whereby any one divests himself of his natural liberty and puts on the bonds of civil society is by agreeing with other men to join and unite into a community for their comfortable, safe, and peaceable living one amongst another, in a secure enjoyment of their properties and a greater security against any that are not of it. This any number of men may do, because it injures not the freedom of the rest; they are left as they were in the liberty of the state of nature. When any number of men have so consented to make one community or government, they are thereby presently incorporated and make one body politic wherein the majority have a right to act and conclude the rest.

96. For when any number of men have, by the consent of every individual, made a community, they have thereby made that community one body, with a

power to act as one body, which is only by the will and determination of the majority; for that which acts any community being only the consent of the individuals of it, and it being necessary to that which is one body to move one way, it is necessary the body should move that way whither the greater force carries it, which is the consent of the majority; or else it is impossible it should act or continue one body, one community, which the consent of every individual that united into it agreed that it should; and so every one is bound by that consent to be concluded by the majority. And therefore we see that in assemblies impowered to act by positive laws, where no number is set by that positive law which impowers them, the act of the majority passes for the act of the whole and, of course, determines, as having by the law of nature and reason the power of the whole.

97. And thus every man, by consenting with others to make one body politic under one government, puts himself under an obligation to every one of that society to submit to the determination of the majority and to be concluded by it; or else this original compact, whereby he with others incorporates into one society, would signify nothing, and be no compact, if he be left free and under no other ties than he was in before in the state of nature. For what appearance would there be of any compact? What new engagement if he were no further tied by any decrees of the society than he himself thought fit and did actually consent to? This would be still as great a liberty as he himself had before his compact, or any one else in the state of nature has who may submit himself and consent to any acts of it if he thinks fit.

98. For if the consent of the majority shall not in reason be received as the act of the whole and conclude every individual, nothing but the consent of every individual can make anything to be the act of the whole; but such a consent is next to impossible ever to be had if we consider the infirmities of health and avocations of business which in a number, though much less than that of a commonwealth, will necessarily keep many away from the public assembly. To which, if we add the variety of opinions and contrariety of interests which unavoidably happen in all collections of men, the coming into society upon such terms would be only like Cato's coming into the theatre only to go out again. Such a constitution as this would make the mighty leviathan of a shorter duration than the feeblest creatures, and not let it outlast the day it was born in; which cannot be supposed till we can think that rational creatures should desire and constitute societies only to be dissolved; for where the majority cannot conclude the rest, there they cannot act as one body, and consequently will be immediately dissolved again.

99. Whosoever, therefore, out of a state of nature unite into a community must be understood to give up all the power necessary to the ends for which they unite into society to the majority of the community, unless they expressly agreed in any number greater than the majority. And this is done by barely agreeing to unite into one political society, which is all the compact that is, or needs be, between the individuals that enter into or make up a commonwealth. And thus that which begins and actually constitutes any political soci-

ety is nothing but the consent of any number of freemen capable of a majority to unite and incorporate into such a society. And this is that, and that only, which did or could give beginning to any lawful government in the world.

▪ ▪ ▪

OF THE ENDS OF POLITICAL SOCIETY AND GOVERNMENT

123. If man in the state of nature be so free, . . . if he be absolute lord of his own person and possessions, equal to the greatest, and subject to nobody, why will he part with his freedom, why will he give up his empire and subject himself to the dominion and control of any other power? To which it is obvious to answer that though in the state of nature he has such a right, yet the enjoyment of it is very uncertain and constantly exposed to the invasion of others; for all being kings as much as he, every man his equal, and the greater part no strict observers of equity and justice, the enjoyment of the property he has in this state is very unsafe, very unsecure. This makes him willing to quit a condition which, however free, is full of fears and continual dangers; and it is not without reason that he seeks out and is willing to join in society with others who are already united, or have a mind to unite, for the mutual preservation of their lives, liberties, and estates, which I call by the general name 'property.'

124. The great and chief end, therefore, of men's uniting into commonwealths and putting themselves under government is the preservation of their property. To which in the state of nature there are many things wanting:

First, there wants an established, settled, known law, received and allowed by common consent to be the standard of right and wrong and the common measure to decide all controversies between them; for though the law of nature be plain and intelligible to all rational creatures, yet men, being biased by their interest as well as ignorant for want of studying it, are not apt to allow of it as a law binding to them in the application of it to their particular cases.

125. Secondly, in the state of nature there wants a known and indifferent judge with authority to determine all differences according to the established law; for every one in that state being both judge and executioner of the law of nature, men being partial to themselves, passion and revenge is very apt to carry them too far and with too much heat in their own cases, as well as negligence and unconcernedness to make them too remiss in other men's.

126. Thirdly, in the state of nature there often wants power to back and support the sentence when right, and to give it due execution. They who by any injustice offend will seldom fail, where they are able, by force, to make good their injustice; such resistance many times makes the punishment dangerous and frequently destructive to those who attempt it.

127. Thus mankind, notwithstanding all the privileges of the state of nature, being but in an ill condition while they remain in it, are quickly driven into society. Hence it comes to pass that we seldom find any number of men live

any time together in this state. The inconveniences that they are therein exposed to by the irregular and uncertain exercise of the power every man has of punishing the transgressions of others make them take sanctuary under the established laws of government and therein seek the preservation of their property. It is this makes them so willingly give up every one his single power of punishing, to be exercised by such alone as shall be appointed to it amongst them; and by such rules as the community, or those authorized by them to that purpose, shall agree on. And in this we have the original right of both the legislative and executive power, as well as of the governments and societies themselves.

128. For in the state of nature, to omit the liberty he has of innocent delights, a man has two powers:

The first is to do whatsoever he thinks fit for the preservation of himself and others within the permission of the law of nature, by which law, common to them all, he and all the rest of mankind are one community, make up one society, distinct from all other creatures. And, were it not for the corruption and viciousness of degenerate men, there would be no need of any other, no necessity that men should separate from this great and natural community and by positive agreements combine into smaller and divided associations.

The other power a man has in the state of nature is the power to punish the crimes committed against that law. Both these he gives up when he joins in a private, if I may so call it, or particular politic society and incorporates into any commonwealth separate from the rest of mankind.

129. The first power, viz., of doing whatsoever he thought fit for the preservation of himself and the rest of mankind, he gives up to be regulated by laws made by the society, so far forth as the preservation of himself and the rest of that society shall require; which laws of the society in many things confine the liberty he had by the law of nature.

130. Secondly, the power of punishing he wholly gives up, and engages his natural force—which he might before employ in tne execution of the law of nature by his own single authority, as he thought fit—to assist the executive power of the society, as the law thereof shall require; for being now in a new state, wherein he is to enjoy many conveniences from the labor, assistance, and society of others in the same community as well as protection from its whole strength, he is to part also with as much of his natural liberty, in providing for himself, as the good, prosperity, and safety of the society shall require, which is not only necessary, but just, since the other members of the society do the like.

131. But though men when they enter into society give up the equality, liberty, and executive power they had in the state of nature into the hands of the society, to be so far disposed of by the legislative as the good of the society shall require, yet it being only with an intention in every one the better to preserve himself, his liberty and property—for no rational creature can be supposed to change his condition with an intention to be worse—the power of the

society, or legislative constituted by them, can never be supposed to extend farther than the common good, but is obliged to secure every one's property by providing against those three defects above-mentioned that made the state of nature so unsafe and uneasy. And so whoever has the legislative or supreme power of any commonwealth is bound to govern by established standing laws, promulgated and known to the people, and not by extemporary decrees; by indifferent and upright judges who are to decide controversies by those laws; and to employ the force of the community at home only in the execution of such laws, or abroad to prevent or redress foreign injuries, and secure the community from inroads and invasion. And all this to be directed to no other end but the peace, safety, and public good of the people.

1.2

MANCUR OLSON, JR.

From *The Logic of Collective Action: Public Goods and the Theory of Groups*

Olson introduces us to the concept of the collective action problem. This "problem" arises when individuals have incentives to free-ride off the contributions of others, reaping the benefits of some action without paying any of the costs. In describing the collective action problem and how groups or organizations can overcome it, Olson strongly challenges the widely held notion that having common interests is a sufficient condition for a political group to form.

I. A THEORY OF GROUPS AND ORGANIZATIONS

A. The Purpose of Organization

Since most (though by no means all) of the action taken by or on behalf of groups of individuals is taken through organizations, it will be helpful to consider organizations in a general or theoretical way.[1] The logical place to begin any systematic study of organizations is with their purpose. But there are all types and shapes and sizes of organizations, even of economic organizations, and there is then some question whether there is any single purpose that would be characteristic of organizations generally. One purpose that is nonetheless characteristic of most organizations, and surely of practically all organizations with an important economic aspect, is the furtherance of the interests of their members. That would seem obvious, at least from the economist's perspective. To be sure, some organizations may out of ignorance fail to further their members' interests, and others may be enticed into serving only the ends of the leadership.[2] But organizations often perish if they do nothing to further the interests of their members, and this factor must severely limit the number of organizations that fail to serve their members.

The idea that organizations or associations exist to further the interests of their members is hardly novel, nor peculiar to economics; it goes back at least to Aristotle, who wrote, "Men journey together with a view to particular advantage, and by way of providing some particular thing needed for the purposes of life, and similarly the political association seems to have come together originally, and to continue in existence, for the sake of the *general* advantages it brings."[3] More recently Professor Leon Festinger, a social psychologist, pointed out that "the attraction of group membership is not so much in sheer belonging, but rather in attaining something by means of this membership."[4] The late Harold Laski, a political scientist, took it for granted that "associations exist to fulfill purposes which a group of men have in common."[5]

The kinds of organizations that are the focus of this study are *expected* to further the interests of their members.[6] Labor unions are expected to strive for higher wages and better working conditions for their members; farm organizations are expected to strive for favorable legislation for their members; cartels are expected to strive for higher prices for participating firms; the corporation is expected to further the interests of its stockholders;[7] and the state is expected to further the common interests of its citizens (though in this nationalistic age the state often has interests and ambitions apart from those of its citizens).

Notice that the interests that all of these diverse types of organizations are expected to further are for the most part *common* interests: the union members' common interest in higher wages, the farmers' common interest in favorable legislation, the cartel members' common interest in higher prices, the stockholders' common interest in higher dividends and stock prices, the citizens' common interest in good government. It is not an accident that the diverse types of organizations listed are all supposed to work primarily for the *common* interests of their members. Purely personal or individual interests can be advanced, and usually advanced most efficiently, by individual, unorganized action. There is obviously no purpose in having an organization when individual, unorganized action can serve the interests of the individual as well as or better than an organization; there would, for example, be no point in forming an organization simply to play solitaire. But when a number of individuals have a common or collective interest—when they share a single purpose or objective—individual, unorganized action (as we shall soon see) will either not be able to advance that common interest at all, or will not be able to advance that interest adequately. Organizations can therefore perform a function when there are common or group interests, and though organizations often also serve purely personal, individual interests, their characteristic and primary function is to advance the common interests of groups of individuals.

The assumption that organizations typically exist to further the common interests of groups of people is implicit in most of the literature about organizations, and two of the writers already cited make this assumption explicit: Harold Laski emphasized that organizations exist to achieve purposes or interests which "a group of men have in common," and Aristotle apparently had a similar notion in mind when he argued that political associations are created and maintained because of the "general advantages" they bring. R. M. MacIver also made this point explicitly when he said that "every organization presupposes an interest which its members all share."[8]

Even when unorganized groups are discussed, at least in treatments of "pressure groups" and "group theory," the word "group" is used in such a way that it means "a number of individuals with a common interest." It would of course be reasonable to label even a number of people selected at random (and thus without any common interest or unifying characteristic) as a "group"; but most discussions of group behavior seem to deal mainly with groups that do have common interests. As Arthur Bentley, the founder of the "group theory" of modern political science, put it, "there is no group without its interest."[9] The social psychologist Raymond Cattell was equally explicit, and stated that "every group has its interest."[10] This is also the way the word "group" will be used here.

Just as those who belong to an organization or a group can be presumed to have a common interest,[11] so they obviously also have purely individual interests, different from those of the others in the organization or group. All of the members of a labor union, for example, have a common interest in higher wages, but at the same time each worker has a unique interest in his personal income, which depends not only on the rate of wages but also on the length of time that he works.

B. Public Goods and Large Groups

The combination of individual interests and common interests in an organization suggests an analogy with a competitive market. The firms in a perfectly competitive industry, for example, have a common interest in a higher price for the industry's product. Since a uniform price must prevail in such a market, a firm cannot expect a higher price for itself unless all of the other firms in the industry also have this higher price. But a firm in a competitive market also has an interest in selling as much as it can, until the cost of producing another unit exceeds the price of that unit. In this there is no common interest; each firm's interest is directly opposed to that of every other firm, for the more other firms sell, the lower the price and income for any given firm. In short, while all firms have a common interest in a higher price, they have antagonistic interests where output is concerned. This can be illustrated with a simple supply-and-demand model. For the sake of a simple argument, assume that a perfectly competitive industry is momentarily in a disequilibrium position, with price exceeding marginal cost for all firms at their present output. Suppose, too, that all of the adjustments will be made by the firms already in the industry rather than by new entrants, and that the industry is on an inelastic portion of its demand curve. Since price exceeds marginal cost for all firms, output will increase. But as all firms increase production, the price falls; indeed, since the industry demand curve is by assumption inelastic, the total revenue of the industry will decline. Apparently each firm finds that with price exceeding marginal cost, it pays to increase its output, but the result is that each firm gets a smaller profit. Some economists in an earlier day may have questioned this result,[12] but the fact that profit-maximizing firms in a perfectly competitive industry can act contrary to their interests as a group is now widely understood and accepted.[13] A group of profit-maximizing firms can act to reduce their aggregate profits because in perfect competition each firm is, by definition, so small that it can ignore the effect of its output on price. Each firm finds it to its advantage to increase output to the point where marginal cost equals price and to ignore the effects of its extra output on the position of the industry. It is true that the net result is that all firms are worse off, but this does not mean that every firm has not maximized its profits. If a firm, foreseeing the fall in price resulting from the increase in industry output, were to restrict its own output, it would lose more than ever, for its price would fall quite as much in any case and it would have a smaller output as well. A firm in a perfectly competitive market gets only a small part of the benefit (of a small share of the industry's extra revenue) resulting from a reduction in that firm's output.

For these reasons it is now generally understood that if the firms in an industry are maximizing profits, the profits for the industry as a whole will be less than they might otherwise be.[14] And almost everyone would agree that this theoretical conclusion fits the facts for markets characterized by pure competition. The important point is that this is true because, though all the firms have a common interest in a higher price for the industry's product, it is in the interest of each firm that the other firms pay the cost—in terms of the necessary reduction in output—needed to obtain a higher price.

About the only thing that keeps prices from falling in accordance with the process just described in perfectly competitive markets is outside intervention. Government price supports, tariffs, cartel agreements, and the like may keep the firms in a competitive market from acting contrary to their interests. Such aid or intervention is quite common. It is then important to ask how it comes about. How does a competitive industry obtain government assistance in maintaining the price of its product?

Consider a hypothetical, competitive industry, and suppose that most of the producers in that industry desire a tariff, a price-support program, or some other government intervention to increase the price for their product. To obtain any such assistance from the government the producers in this industry will presumably have to organize a lobbying organization; they will have to become an active pressure group.[15] This lobbying organization may have to conduct a considerable campaign. If significant resistance is encountered, a great amount of money will be required.[16] Public relations experts will be needed to influence the newspapers, and some advertising may be necessary. Professional organizers will probably be needed to organize "spontaneous grass roots" meetings among the distressed producers in the industry, and to get those in the industry to write letters to their congressmen.[17] The campaign for the government assistance will take the time of some of the producers in the industry, as well as their money.

There is a striking parallel between the problem the perfectly competitive industry faces as it strives to obtain government assistance, and the problem it faces in the marketplace when the firms increase output and bring about a fall in price. *Just as it was not rational for a particular producer to restrict his output in order that there might be a higher price for the product of his industry, so it would not be rational for him to sacrifice his time and money to support a lobbying organization to obtain government assistance for the industry. In neither case would it be in the interest of the individual producer to assume any of the costs himself. A lobbying organization, or indeed a labor union or any other organization, working in the interest of a large group of firms or workers in some industry, would get no assistance from the rational, self-interested individuals in that industry.* This would be true even if everyone in the industry were absolutely convinced that the proposed program was in their interest (though in fact some might think otherwise and make the organization's task yet more difficult).[18]

Although the lobbying organization is only one example of the logical analogy between the organization and the market, it is of some practical importance. There are many powerful and well-financed lobbies with mass support in existence now, but these lobbying organizations do not get that support because of their legislative achievements. The most powerful lobbying organizations now obtain their funds and their following for other reasons.

Some critics may argue that the rational person will, indeed support a large organization, like a lobbying organization, that works in his interest, because he knows that if he does not, others will not do so either, and then the organization will fail, and he will be without the benefit that the organization could have provided. This argument shows the need for the analogy with the perfectly competitive market. For it would be quite as reasonable to argue that prices will never fall below the levels a monopoly would have charged in a perfectly competitive market, because if one firm increased its output, other firms would also, and the price would fall; but each firm could foresee this, so it would not start a chain of price-destroying increases in output. In fact, it does not work out this way in a competitive market; nor in a large organization. When the number of firms involved is large, no one will notice the effect on price if one firm increases its output, and so no one will change his plans because of it. Similarly, in a large organization, the loss of one dues payer will not noticeably increase the burden for any other one dues payer, and so a rational person would not believe that if he were to withdraw from an organization he would drive others to do so.

The foregoing argument must at the least have some relevance to economic organizations that are mainly means through which individuals attempt to obtain the same things they obtain through their activities in the market. Labor unions, for example, are organizations through which workers strive to get the same things they get with their individual efforts in the market—higher wages, better working conditions, and the like. It would be strange indeed if the workers did not confront some of the same problems in the union that they meet in the market, since their efforts in both places have some of the same purposes.

However similar the purposes may be, critics may object that attitudes in organizations are not at all like those in markets. In organizations, an emotional or ideological element is often also involved. Does this make the argument offered here practically irrelevant?

A most important type of organization—the national state—will serve to test this objection. Patriotism is probably the strongest non-economic motive for organizational allegiance in modern times. This age is sometimes called the age of nationalism. Many nations draw additional strength and unity from some powerful ideology, such as democracy or communism, as well as from a common religion, language, or cultural inheritance. The state not only has many such powerful sources of support; it also is very important economically. Almost any government is economically beneficial to its citizens, in that the law and order it provides is a prerequisite of all civilized economic activity. But despite the force of patriotism, the appeal of the national ideology, the bond of a common culture, and the indispensability of the system of law and order, no major state in modern history has been able to support itself through voluntary dues or contributions. Philanthropic contributions are not even a significant source of revenue for most countries. Taxes, *compulsory* payments by definition, are needed. Indeed, as the old saying indicates, their necessity is as certain as death itself.

If the state, with all of the emotional resources at its command, cannot finance its most basic and vital activities without resort to compulsion, it would seem that large private organizations might also have difficulty in getting the individuals in the groups whose interests they attempt to advance to make the necessary contributions voluntarily.[19]

The reason the state cannot survive on voluntary dues or payments, but must rely on taxation, is that the most fundamental services a nation-state provides are, in one important respect, like the higher price in a competitive market: they must be available to everyone if they are available to anyone. The basic and most elementary goods or services provided by government, like defense and police protection, and the system of law and order generally, are such that they go to everyone or practically everyone in the nation. It would obviously not be feasible, if indeed it were possible, to deny the protection provided by the military services, the police, and the courts to those who did not voluntarily pay their share of the costs of government, and taxation is accordingly necessary. The common or collective benefits provided by governments are usually called "public goods" by economists, and the concept of public goods is one of the oldest and most important ideas in the study of public finance. A common, collective, or public good is here defined as any good such that, if any person X_i in a group $X_1, \ldots, X_i, \ldots, X_n$ consumes if, it cannot feasibly be withheld from the others in that group.[20] In other words, those who do not purchase or pay for any of the public or collective good cannot be excluded or kept from sharing in the consumption of the good, as they can where noncollective goods are concerned.

Students of public finance have, however, neglected the fact that *the achievement of any common goal or the satisfaction of any common interest means that a public or collective good has been provided for that group.*[21] The very fact that a goal or purpose is *common* to a group means that no one in the group is excluded from the benefit or satisfaction brought about by its achievement. As the opening paragraphs of this chapter indicated, almost all groups and organizations have the purpose of serving the common interests of their members. As R. M. MacIver puts it, "Persons . . . have common interests in the degree to which they participate in a cause . . . which indivisibly embraces them all."[22] It is of the essence of an organization that it provides an inseparable, generalized benefit. It follows that the provision of public or collective goods is the fundamental function of organizations generally. A state is first of all an organization that provides public goods for its members, the citizens; and other types of organizations similarly provide collective goods for their members.

And just as a state cannot support itself by voluntary contributions, or by selling its basic services on the market, neither can other large organizations support themselves without providing some sanction, or some attraction distinct from the public good itself, that will lead individuals to help bear the burdens of maintaining the organization. The individual member of the typical large organization is in a position analogous to that of the firm in a perfectly competitive market, or the taxpayer in the state: his own efforts will not have a noticeable effect on the situation of his organization, and he can enjoy any improvements brought about by others whether or not he has worked in support of his organization.

There is no suggestion here that states or other organizations provide *only* public or collective goods. Governments often provide noncollective goods like electric power, for example, and they usually sell such goods on the market much as private firms would do. Moreover, as later parts of this study will argue, large organizations that are not able to make membership compulsory *must also* provide some noncollective goods in order to give potential members an incentive to join. Still, collective goods are the characteristic organizational goods, for ordinary noncollective goods can always be provided by individual action, and only where common purposes of collective goods are concerned is organization or group action ever indispensable.[23]

▪   ▪   ▪

Nontechnical summary of section D
The technical part of this section has shown that certain small groups can provide themselves with collective goods without relying on coercion or any positive inducements apart from the collective good itself.[24] This is because in some small groups each of the members, or at least one of them, will find that his personal gain from having the collective good exceeds the total cost of providing some amount of that collective good; there are members who would be better off if the collective good were provided, even if they had to pay the entire cost of providing it themselves, than they would be if it were not provided. In such situations there is a presumption that the collective good will be

provided. Such a situation will exist only when the benefit to the group from having the collective good exceeds the total cost by more than it exceeds the gain to one or more individuals in the group. Thus, in a very small group, where each member gets a substantial proportion of the total gain simply because there are few others in the group, a collective good can often be provided by the voluntary, self-interested action of the members of the group. In smaller groups marked by considerable degrees of inequality—that is, in groups of members of unequal "size" or extent of interest in the collective good—there is the greatest likelihood that a collective good will be provided; for the greater the interest in the collective good of any single member, the greater the likelihood that that member will get such a significant proportion of the total benefit from the collective good that he will gain from seeing that the good is provided, even if he has to pay all of the cost himself.

Even in the smallest groups, however, the collective good will not ordinarily be provided on an optimal scale. That is to say, the members of the group will not provide as much of the good as it would be in their common interest to provide. Only certain special institutional arrangements will give the individual members an incentive to purchase the amounts of the collective good that would add up to the amount that would be in the best interest of the group as a whole. This tendency toward suboptimality is due to the fact that a collective good is, by definition, such that other individuals in the group cannot be kept from consuming it once any individual in the group has provided it for himself. Since an individual member thus gets only part of the benefit of any expenditure he makes to obtain more of the collective good, he will discontinue his purchase of the collective good before the optimal amount for the group as a whole has been obtained. In addition, the amounts of the collective good that a member of the group receives free from other members will further reduce his incentive to provide more of that good at his own expense. Accordingly, *the larger the group, the farther it will fall short of providing an optimal amount of a collective good.*

This suboptimality or inefficiency will be somewhat less serious in groups composed of members of greatly different size or interest in the collective good. In such unequal groups, on the other hand, there is a tendency toward an arbitrary sharing of the burden of providing the collective good. The largest member, the member who would on his own provide the largest amount of the collective good, bears a disproportionate share of the burden of providing the collective good. The smaller member by definition gets a smaller fraction of the benefit of any amount of the collective good he provides than a larger member, and therefore has less incentive to provide additional amounts of the collective good. Once a smaller member has the amount of the collective good he gets free from the largest member, he has more than he would have purchased for himself, and has no incentive to obtain any of the collective good at his own expense. In small groups with common interests there is accordingly *a surprising tendency for the "exploitation" of the great by the small.*

The argument that small groups providing themselves with collective goods tend to provide suboptimal quantities of these goods, and that the burdens of providing them are borne in an arbitrary and disproportionate way, does not hold in all logically possible situations. Certain institutional or procedural arrangements can lead to different outcomes. The subject cannot be analyzed adequately in any brief discussion. For this reason, and because the main focus of this reading is on large groups, many of the complexities of small-group behavior have been neglected in this study. An argument of the kind just outlined could, however, fit some important practical situations rather well, and may serve the purpose of suggesting that a more detailed analysis of the kind outlined above could help to explain the apparent tendency for large countries to bear disproportionate shares of the burdens of multinational organizations, like the United Nations and NATO, and could help to explain some of the popularity of neutralism among smaller countries. Such an analysis would also tend to explain the continual complaints that international organizations and alliances are not given adequate (optimal) amounts of resources.[25] It would also suggest that neighboring local governments in metropolitan areas that provide collective goods (like commuter roads and education) that benefit individuals in two or more local government jurisdictions would tend to provide inadequate amounts of these services, and that the largest local government (e.g., the one representing the central city) would bear disproportionate shares of the burdens of providing them.[26] An analysis of the foregoing type might, finally, provide some additional insight into the phenomenon of price leadership, and particularly the possible disadvantages involved in being the largest firm in an industry.

The most important single point about small groups in the present context, however, is that they may very well be able to provide themselves with a collective good simply because of the attraction of the collective good to the individual members. In this, small groups differ from larger ones. The larger a group is, the farther it will fall short of obtaining an optimal supply of any collective good, and the less likely that it will act to obtain even a minimal amount of such a good. In short, the larger the group, the less it will further its common interests.

■   ■   ■

F. A Taxonomy of Groups

To be sure, there can also be many instances in inclusive or non-market groups in which individual members do take into account the reactions of other members to their actions when they decide what action to take—that is, instances in which there is the strategic interaction among members characteristic of oligopolistic industries in which mutual dependence is recognized. In groups of one size range at least, such strategic interaction must be relatively important. That is the size range where the group is not so small that one individual would find it profitable to purchase some of the collective good himself, but where the number in the group is nonetheless sufficiently small that each member's attempts or lack of attempts to obtain the collective good would bring about noticeable differences in the welfare of some, or all, of the others in the group. This can best be understood by assuming for a moment that an inclusive collective good is already being provided in such a group through a formal organization, and then asking what would happen if one member of the group were to cease paying his share of the cost of the good. If, in a reasonably small organization, a particular person stops paying for the collective good he enjoys, the costs will rise noticeably for each of the others in the group; accordingly, they may then refuse to continue making their contributions, and the collective good may no longer be provided. However, the first person could realize that this might be the result of his refusal to pay anything for the collective good, and that he would be worse off when the collective good is not provided than when it was provided and he met part of the cost. Accordingly he might continue making a contribution toward the purchase of the collective good. He might; or he might not. As in oligopoly in a market situation, the result is indeterminate. The rational member of such a group faces a strategic problem and while the Theory of Games and other types of analyses might prove very helpful, there seems to be no way at present of getting a general, valid, and determinate solution at the level of abstraction of this chapter.[27]

What is the range of this indeterminateness? In a small group in which a member gets such a large fraction of the total benefit that he would be better off if he paid the entire cost himself, rather than go without the good, there is some presumption that the collective good will be provided. In a group in which no one member got such a large benefit from the collective good that he had an interest in providing it even if he had to pay all of the cost, but in which the individual was still so important in terms of the whole group that his contribution or lack of contribution to the group objective had a noticeable effect on the costs or benefits of others in the group, the result is indeterminate.[28] By contrast, in a large group in which no single individual's contribution makes a perceptible difference to the group as a whole, or the burden or benefit of any single member of the group, it is certain that a collective good will *not* be provided unless there is coercion or some outside inducements that will lead the members of the large group to act in their common interest.[29]

The last distinction, between the group so large it definitely cannot provide itself with a collective good, and the oligopoly-sized group which may provide itself with a collective good, is particularly important. It depends upon whether any two or more members of the group have a perceptible interdependence, that is, on whether the contribution or lack of contribution of any one individual in the group will have a perceptible effect on the burden or benefit of any other individual or individuals in the group. Whether a group will have the possibility of providing itself with a collective good without coercion or outside inducements therefore depends to a striking degree upon the number of individuals in the group, since the larger the group, the less the likelihood that the contribution of any one will be perceptible. It is not, however, strictly accurate to say that it depends solely on the number of individuals in the group. The relation between the size of the group and the significance of an individual member cannot be defined quite that simply. A group which has members with highly unequal degrees of interest in a collective good, and which wants a collective good that is (at some level of provision) extremely valuable in relation to its cost, will be more apt to provide itself with a collective good than other groups with the same number of members. The same situation prevails in the study of market structure, where again the number of firms an industry can have and still remain oligopolistic (and have the possibility of supracompetitive returns) varies somewhat from case to case. The standard for determining whether a group will have the capacity to act, without coercion or outside inducements, in its group interest is (as it should be) the same for market and non-market groups: it depends on whether the individual actions of any one or more members in a group are noticeable to any other individuals in the group.[30] This is most obviously, but not exclusively, a function of the number in the group.

It is now possible to specify when either informal coordination or formal organization will be necessary to obtain a collective good. The smallest type of group—the group in which one or more members get such a large fraction of the total benefit that they find it worthwhile to see that the collective good is provided, even if they have to pay the entire cost—may get along without any group agreement or organization. A group agreement might be set up to spread the costs more widely or to step up the level of provision of the collective good. But since there is an incentive for unilateral and individual action to obtain the collective good, neither a formal organization nor even an informal group agreement is indispensable to obtain a collective good. In any group larger than this, on the other hand, no collective good can be obtained without some group agreement, coordination, or organization. In the intermediate or oligopoly-sized group, where two or more members must act simultaneously before a collective good can be obtained, there must be at least tacit coordination or organization. Moreover, the larger a group is, the more agreement and organization it will need. The larger the group, the greater the number that will usually have to be included in the group agreement or organization. It may not be necessary that the entire group be organized, since some subset of the whole group may be able to provide the collective good. But to establish a group agreement or organization will nonetheless always tend to be more difficult the larger the size of the group, for the larger the group the more difficult it will be to locate and organize even a subset of the group, and those in the subset will have an incentive to continue bargaining with the others in the group until the burden is widely shared, thereby adding to the expense of bargaining. In short, costs of organization are an increasing function of the number of individuals in the group. (Though the more members in the group the greater the total costs of organization, the costs of organization per person need not rise, for there are surely economies of scale in organization.) In certain cases a group will already be organized for some other purpose, and then these costs of organization are already being met. In such a case a group's capacity to provide itself with a collective good will be explained in part by whatever it was that originally enabled it to organize and maintain itself. This brings attention back again to the costs of organization and shows that these costs cannot be left out of the model, except for the smallest type of group in which unilateral action can provide a collective good. The costs of organization must be clearly distinguished from the type of cost that has previously been considered. The cost functions considered before involved only the direct resource costs of obtaining various levels of provision of a collective good. When there is no pre-existing organization of a group, and when the direct resource costs of a collective good it wants are more than any single individual could profitably bear, additional costs must be incurred to obtain an agreement about how the burden will be shared and to coordinate or organize the effort to obtain the collective good. These are the costs of communication among group members, the costs of any bargaining among them, and the costs of creating, staffing, and maintaining any formal group organization.

A group cannot get infinitesimally small quantities of a formal organization, or even of an informal group agreement; a group with a given number of members must have a certain minimal amount of organization or agreement if it is to have any at all. Thus there are significant initial or minimal costs of organization for each group. Any group that must organize to obtain a collective good, then, will find that it has a certain minimum organization cost that must be met, however little of the collective good it obtains. The greater the number in the group, the greater these minimal costs will be. When this minimal organizational cost is added to the other initial or minimal costs of a collective good, which arise from its previously mentioned technical characteristics, it is evident that the cost of the first unit of a collective good will be quite high in relation to the cost of some subsequent units. However immense the benefits of a collective good, the higher the absolute total costs of getting any amount of that good, the less likely it is that even a minimal amount of that good could be obtained without coercion or separate, outside incentives.

This means that there are now three separate but cumulative factors that keep larger groups from furthering their own interest. First, the larger the group, the smaller the fraction of the total group benefit any person acting in the group interest receives, and the less adequate the reward for any group-oriented action, and the farther the group falls short of getting an optimal supply of the collective good, even if it should get some. Second, since the larger the group, the smaller the share of the total benefit going to any individual, or to any (absolutely) small subset of members of the group, the less the likelihood that any small subset of the group, much less any single individual, will gain enough from getting the collective good to bear the burden of providing even a small amount of it; in other words, the larger the group the smaller the likelihood of oligopolistic interaction that might help obtain the good. Third, the larger the number of members in the group the greater the organization costs, and thus the higher the hurdle that must be jumped before any of the collective good at all can be obtained. For these reasons, the larger the group the farther it will fall short of providing an optimal supply of a collective good, and very large groups normally will not, in the absence of coercion or separate, outside incentives, provide themselves with even minimal amounts of a collective good.[31]

NOTES

1. Economists have for the most part neglected to develop theories of organizations, but there are a few works from an economic point of view on the subject. See, for example, three papers by Jacob Marschak, "Elements for a Theory of Teams," *Management Science*, I (January 1955), 127–137, "Towards an Economic Theory of Organization and Information," in *Decision Processes*, ed. R. M. Thrall, C. H. Combs, and R. L. Davis (New York: John Wiley, 1954), pp. 187–220, and "Efficient and Viable Organization Forms," in *Modern Organization Theory*, ed. Mason Haire (New York: John Wiley, 1959), pp. 307–320; two papers by R. Radner, "Application of Linear Programming to Team Decision Problems," *Management Science*, V (January 1959), 143–150, and "Team Decision Problems," *Annals of Mathematical Statistics*, XXXIII (September 1962), 857–881; C. B. McGuire, "Some Team Models of a Sales Organization," *Management Science*, VII (January 1961), 101–130; Oskar Morgenstern, *Prolegomena to a Theory of Organization* (Santa Monica, Calif.: RAND Research Memorandum 734, 1951); James G. March and Herbert A. Simon, *Organizations* (New York: John Wiley, 1958); Kenneth Boulding, *The Organizational Revolution* (New York: Harper, 1953).

2. Max Weber called attention to the case where an organization continues to exist for some time after it has become meaningless because some official is making a living out of it. See his *Theory of Social and Economic Organization*, trans. Talcott Parsons and A. M. Henderson (New York: Oxford University Press, 1947), p. 318.

3. Aristotle, *Ethics* viii.9.1160a.

4. Leon Festinger, "Group Attraction and Membership," in *Group Dynamics*, ed. Dorwin Cartwright and Alvin Zander (Evanston, Ill.: Row, Peterson, 1953), p. 93.

5. *A Grammar of Politics*, 4th ed. (London: George Allen & Unwin, 1939), p. 67.

6. Philanthropic and religious organizations are not necessarily expected to serve only the interests of their members; such organizations have other purposes that are considered more important, however much their members "need" to belong, or are improved or helped by belonging. But the complexity of such organizations need not be debated at length here, because this study will focus on organizations with a significant economic aspect. The emphasis here will have something in common with what Max Weber called the "associative group"; he called a group associative if "the orientation of social action with it rests on a rationally motivated agreement." Weber contrasted his "associative group" with the "communal group" which was centered on personal affection, erotic relationships, etc., like the family. (See Weber, pp. 136–139, and Grace Coyle, *Social Process in Organized Groups*, New York: Richard Smith, Inc., 1930, pp. 7–9.) The logic of the theory developed here can be extended to cover communal, religious, and

philanthropic organizations, but the theory is not particularly useful in studying such groups.

7. That is, its members. This study does not follow the terminological usage of those organization theorists who describe employees as "members" of the organization for which they work. Here it is more convenient to follow the language of everyday usage instead, and to distinguish the members of, say, a union from the employees of that union. Similarly, the members of the union will be considered employees of the corporation for which they work, whereas the members of the corporation are the common stockholders.

8. R. M. MacIver, "Interests," *Encyclopaedia of the Social Sciences,* VII (New York: Macmillan, 1932), p. 147.

9. Arthur Bentley, *The Process of Government* (Evanston, Ill.: Principia Press, 1949), p. 211. David B. Truman takes a similar approach; see his *The Governmental Process* (New York: Alfred A. Knopf, 1958), pp. 33–35. See also Sidney Verba, *Small Groups and Political Behavior* (Princeton, N.J.: Princeton University Press, 1961), pp. 12–13.

10. Raymond Cattell, "Concepts and Methods in the Measurement of Group Syntality," in *Small Groups,* ed. A. Paul Hare, Edgard F. Borgatta, and Robert F. Bales (New York: Alfred A. Knopf, 1955), p. 115.

11. Any organization or group will of course usually be divided into subgroups or factions that are opposed to one another. This fact does not weaken the assumption made here that organizations exist to serve the common interests of members, for the assumption does not imply that intragroup conflict is neglected. The opposing groups within an organization ordinarily have some interest in common (if not, why would they maintain the organization?), and the members of any subgroup or faction also have a separate common interest of their own. They will indeed often have a common purpose in defeating some other subgroup or faction. The approach used here does not neglect the conflict within groups and organizations, then, because it considers each organization as a unit only to the extent that it does in fact attempt to serve a common interest, and considers the various subgroups as the relevant units with common interests to analyze the factional strife.

12. See J. M. Clark, *The Economics of Overhead Costs* (Chicago: University of Chicago Press, 1923), p. 417, and Frank H. Knight, *Risk, Uncertainty and Profit* (Boston: Houghton Mifflin, 1921), p. 193.

13. Edward H. Chamberlin, *Monopolistic Competition,* 6th ed. (Cambridge, Mass.: Harvard University Press, 1950), p. 4.

14. For a fuller discussion of this question see Mancur Olson, Jr., and David McFarland, "The Restoration of Pure Monopoly and the Concept of the Industry, *Quarterly Journal of Economics,* LXXVI (November 1962), 613–631.

15. Robert Michels contends in his classic study that "democracy is inconceivable without organization," and that "the principle of organization is an absolutely essential condition for the political struggle of the masses." See his *Political Parties,* trans. Eden and Cedar Paul (New York: Dover Publications, 1959), pp. 21–22. See also Robert A. Brady, *Business as a System of Power* (New York: Columbia University Press, 1943), p. 193.

16. Alexander Heard, *The Costs of Democracy* (Chapel Hill: University of North Carolina Press, 1960), especially note 1, pp. 95–96. For example, in 1947 the National Association of Manufacturers spent over $4.6 million, and over a somewhat longer period the American Medical Association spent as much on a campaign against compulsory health insurance.

17. "If the full truth were ever known . . . lobbying, in all its ramifications, would prove to be a billion dollar industry." U.S. Congress, House, Select Committee on Lobbying Activities, *Report*, 81st Cong., 2nd Sess. (1950), as quoted in the *Congressional Quarterly Almanac*, 81st Cong., 2nd Sess., VI, 764–765.

18. For a logically possible but practically meaningless exception to the conclusion of this paragraph.

19. Sociologists as well as economists have observed that ideological motives alone are not sufficient to bring forth the continuing effort of large masses of people. Max Weber provides a notable example:

"All economic activity in a market economy is undertaken and carried through by individuals for their own ideal or material interests. This is naturally just as true when economic activity is oriented to the patterns of order of corporate groups . . .

"Even if an economic system were organized on a socialistic basis, there would be no fundamental difference in this respect . . . The structure of interests and the relevant situation might change; there would be other means of pursuing interests, but this fundamental factor would remain just as relevant as before. It is of course true that economic action which is oriented on purely ideological grounds to the interest of others does exist. But it is even more certain that the mass of men do not act in this way, and it is an induction from experience that they cannot do so and never will . . .

"In a market economy the interest in the maximization of income is necessarily the driving force of all economic activity." (Weber, pp. 319–320.)

Talcott Parsons and Neil Smelser go even further in postulating that "performance" throughout society is proportional to the "rewards" and "sanctions" involved. See their *Economy and Society* (Glencoe, Ill.: Free Press, 1954), pp. 50–69.

20. This simple definition focuses upon two points that are important in the present context. The first point is that most collective goods can only be defined with respect to some specific group. One collective good goes to one group of people, another collective good to another group; one may benefit the whole world, another only two specific people. Moreover, some goods are collective goods to those in one group and at the same time private goods to those in another, because some individuals can be kept from consuming them and others can't. Take for example the parade that is a collective good to all those who live in tall buildings overlooking the parade route, but which appears to be a private good to those who can see it only by buying ticket, for a seat in the stands along the way. The second point is that once the relevant group has been defined, the definition used here, like Musgrave's, distinguishes collective good in terms of infeasibility of excluding potential consumers of the good. This approach is used because collective goods produced by organizations of all kinds seem to be such that exclusion is normally not feasible. To be sure, for some collective goods it is physically possible to practice exclusion. But, as Head has shown, it is not necessary that exclusion be technically impossible; it is only necessary that it be infeasible or uneconomic. Head has also shown most clearly that nonexcludability is only one of two basic elements in the traditional understanding of public goods. The other, he points out, is "jointness of supply." A good has "jointness" if making it available to one individual means that it can be easily or freely supplied to others as well. The polar case of jointness would be Samuelson's pure public good, which is a good such that additional consumption of it by one individual does not diminish the amount available to others. By the definition used here, jointness is not a necessary attribute of a public good. At least one type of collective good considered here exhibits no jointness whatever, and few if any would have the degree of jointness needed to qualify as pure public goods. Nonetheless, most

of the collective goods to be studied here do display a large measure of jointness. On the definition and importance of public goods, see John G. Head, "Public Goods and Public Policy," *Public Finance,* vol. XVII, no. 3 (1962), 197–219; Richard Musgrave, *The Theory of Public Finance* (New York: McGraw-Hill, 1959); Paul A. Samuelson, "The Pure Theory of Public Expenditure," "Diagrammatic Exposition of A Theory of Public Expenditure," and "Aspects of Public Expenditure Theories," in *Review of Economics and Statistics,* XXXVI (November 1954), 387–390, XXXVII (November 1955), 350–356, and XL (November 1958), 332–338. For somewhat different opinions about the usefulness of the concept of public goods, see Julius Margolis, "A Comment on the Pure Theory of Public Expenditure," *Review of Economics and Statistics,* XXXVII (November 1955), 347–349, and Gerhard Colm, "Theory of Public Expenditures," *Annals of the American Academy of Political and Social Science,* CLXXXIII (January 1936), 1–11.

21. There is no necessity that a public good to one group in a society is necessarily in the interest of the society as a whole. Just as a tariff could be a public good to the industry that sought it, so the removal of the tariff could be a public good to those who consumed the industry's product. This is equally true when the public-good concept is applied only to governments; for a military expenditure, or a tariff, or an immigration restriction that is a public good to one country could be a "public bad" to another country, and harmful to world society as a whole.

22. R. M. MacIver in *Encyclopaedia of the Social Sciences,* VII, 147.

23. It does not, however, follow that organized or coordinated group action is *always* necessary to obtain a collective good.

24. I am indebted to Professor John Rawls of the Department of Philosophy at Harvard University for reminding me of the fact that the philosopher David Hume sensed that small groups could achieve common purposes but large groups could not. Hume's argument is however somewhat different from my own. In A *Treatise of Human Nature,* Everyman edition (London: J. M. Dent, 1952), II, 239, Hume wrote: "There is no quality in human nature which causes more fatal errors in our conduct, than that which leads us to prefer whatever is present to the distant and remote, and makes us desire objects more according to their situation than their intrinsic value. Two neighbours may agree to drain a meadow, which they possess in common: because it is easy for them to know each other's mind; and each must perceive, that the immediate consequence of his failing in his part, is the abandoning of the whole project. But it is very difficult, and indeed impossible, that a thousand persons should agree in any such action; it being difficult for them to concert so complicated a design, and still more difficult for them to execute it; while each seeks a pretext to free himself of the trouble and expense, and would lay the whole burden on others. Political society easily remedies both these inconveniences. Magistrates find an immediate interest in the interest of any considerable part of their subjects. They need consult nobody but themselves to form any scheme for promoting that interest. And as the failure of any one piece in the execution is connected, though not immediately, with the failure of the whole, they prevent that failure, because they find no interest in it, either immediate or remote. Thus, bridges are built, harbours opened, ramparts raised, canals formed, fleets equipped, and armies disciplined everywhere, by the care of government, which, though composed of men subject to all human infirmities, becomes, by one of the finest and most subtle inventions imaginable, a composition which is in some measure exempted from all these infirmities."

25. Some of the complexities of behavior in small groups are treated in Mancur Olson, Jr., and Richard Zeckhauser, "An Economic Theory of Alliances," *Review of Economics and Statistics,* XLVIII (August 1966), 266–279, and in "Collective Goods,

Comparative Advantage, and Alliance Efficiency," in *Issues of Defense Economics* (A Conference of the Universities-National Bureau-Committee for Economics Research), ed. Roland McKean (New York: National Bureau of Economic Research, 1967), pp. 25–48. [Footnote added in 1970.]

26. I am indebted to Alan Williams of York University in England, whose study of local government brought the importance of these sorts of spillovers among local govenments to my attention.

27. It is of incidental interest here to note also that oligopoly in the marketplace is in some respects akin to logrolling in the organization. If the "majority" that various interests in a legislature need is viewed as a collective good—something that a particular interest cannot obtain unless other interests also share it—then the parallel is quite close. The cost each special-interest legislator would like to avoid is the passage of the legislation desired by the other special-interest legislators, for if these interests gain from their legislation, often others, including his own constituents, may lose. But unless he is willing to vote for the legislation desired by the others, the particular special-interest legislator in question will not be able to get his own legislation passed. So his goal would be to work out a coalition with other special-interest legislators in which they would vote for exactly the legislation he wanted, and he in turn would give them as little in return as possible, by insisting that they moderate their legislative demands. But since every potential logroller has this same strategy, the result is indeterminate: the logs may be rolled or they may not. Every one of the interests will be better off if the logrolling is done than if it is not, but as individual interests strive for better legislative bargains the result of the competing strategies may be that no agreement is reached. This is quite similar to the situation oligopolistic groups are in, as they all desire a higher price and will all gain if they restrict output to get it, but they may not be able to agree on market shares.

28. The result is clearly indeterminate when F_4 is less than C/V_g at every point and it is also true that the group is not so large that no one member's actions have a noticeable effect.

29. One friendly critic has suggested that even a large pre-existing organization could continue providing a collective good simply by conducting a kind of plebiscite among its members, with the understanding that if there were not a unanimous or nearly unanimous pledge to contribute toward providing the collective good, this good would no longer be provided. This argument, if I understand it correctly, is mistaken. In such a situation, an individual would know that if others provided the collective good he would get the benefits whether he made any contribution or not. He would therefore have no incentive to make a pledge unless a completely unanimous set of pledges was required, or for some other reason his one pledge would decide whether or not the good would be provided. But if a pledge were required of every single member, or if for any other reason any one member could decide whether or not the group would get a collective good, this one member could deprive all of the others in the group of great gains. He would therefore be in a position to bargain for bribes. But since any other members of the group might gain just as much from the same holdout strategy, there is no likelihood that the collective good would be provided. See Buchanan and Tullock, pp. 96–116.

30. The noticeability of the actions of a single member of a group may be influenced by the arrangements the group itself sets up. A previously organized group, for example, might ensure that the contributions or lack of contributions of any member of the group, and the effect of each such member's course on the burden and benefit for others, would be advertised, thus ensuring that the group effort would not collapse from

imperfect knowledge. I therefore define "noticeability" in terms of the degree of knowledge, and the institutional arrangements, that actually exist in any given group, insetad of assuming a "natural noticeability" unaffected by any group advertising or other arrangements. This point, along with many other valuable comments, has been brought to my attention by Professor Jerome Rothenberg, who does, however, make much more of a group's assumed capacity to create "artificial noticeability" than I would want to do. I know of no practical example of a group or organization that has done much of anything, apart from improve information, to enhance the noticeability of an individual's actions in striving for a collective good.

31. There is one logically conceivable, but surely empirically trivial, case in which a large group could be provided with a very small amount of a collective good without coercion or outside incentives. If some very small group enjoyed a collective good so inexpensive that any one of the members would benefit by making sure that it was provided, even if he had to pay all of the cost, and if millions of people then entered the group, with the cost of the good nonetheless remaining constant, the large group could be provided with a little of this collective good. This is because by hypothesis in this example the costs have remained unchanged, so that one person still has an incentive to see that the good is provided. Even in such a case as this, however, it would still not be quite right to say that the large group was acting in its group interest, since the output of the collective good would be incredibly suboptimal. The optimal level of provision of the public good would increase each time an individual entered the group, since the unit cost of the collective good by hypothesis is constant, while the benefit from an additional unit of it increases with every entrant. Yet the original provider would have no incentive to provide more as the group expanded, unless he formed an organization to share costs with the others in this (now large) group. But that would entail incurring the considerable costs of a large organization, and there would be no way these costs could be covered through the voluntary and rational action of the individuals in the group. Thus, if the total benefit from a collective good exceeded its costs by the thousandfold or millionfold, it is logically possible that a large group could provide itself with some amount of that collective good, but the level of provision of the collective good in such a case would be only a minute fraction of the optimal level. It is not easy to think of practical examples of groups that would fit this description, but one possible example is discussed on page 161, note 94. It would be easy to rule out even any such exceptional cases, however, simply by defining *all* groups that could provide themselves with some amount of a collective good as "small groups" (or by giving them other names), while putting all groups that could not provide themselves with a collective good in another class. But this easy route must be rejected, for that would make this part of the theory tautologous and thus incapable of refutation. Therefore the approach here has been to make the (surely reasonable) empirical hypothesis that the total costs of the collective goods wanted by large groups are large enough to exceed the value of the small fraction of the total benefit that an individual in a large group would get, so that he will not provide the good. There may be exceptions to this, as to any other empirical statement, and thus there may be instances in which large groups could provide themselves with (at most minute amounts of) collective goods through the voluntary and rational action of one of their members.

1.3

GARRETT HARDIN

"The Tragedy of the Commons"

In this powerful reading, Hardin builds on Olson's ideas to show the negative consequences that may ensue when people are not constrained in their acquisition of food, energy, land, water, minerals, and other natural resources. People pursuing their own interests can overdraw publicly owned resources, leading to a depletion of those resources. This argument is significant in the study of politics because many governmental institutions not only prevent the overdrawing of fixed resources, but also determine who *has access to those resources.*

The population problem has no technical solution; it requires a fundamental extension in morality.

At the end of a thoughtful article on the future of nuclear war, Wiesner and York[1] concluded that: "Both sides in the arms race are . . . confronted by the dilemma of steadily increasing military power and steadily decreasing national security. *It is our considered professional judgment that this dilemma has no technical solution.* If the great powers continue to look for solutions in the area of science and technology only, the result will be to worsen the situation."

I would like to focus your attention not on the subject of the article (national security in a nuclear world) but on the kind of conclusion they reached, namely that there is no technical solution to the problem. An implicit and almost universal assumption of discussions published in professional and semipopular scientific journals is that the problem under discussion has a technical solution. A technical solution may be defined as one that requires a change only in the techniques of the natural sciences, demanding little or nothing in the way of change in human values or ideas of morality.

In our day (though not in earlier times) technical solutions are always welcome. Because of previous failures in prophecy, it takes courage to assert that a desired technical solution is not possible. Wiesner and York exhibited this courage; publishing in a science journal, they insisted that the solution to the problem was not to be found in the natural sciences. They cautiously qualified their statement with the phrase, "It is our considered professional judgment. . . ." Whether they were right or not is not the concern of the present article. Rather, the concern here is with the important concept of a class of human problems which can be called "no technical solution problems," and, more specifically, with the identification and discussion of one of these.

It is easy to show that the class is not a null class. Recall the game of tick-tack-toe. Consider the problem, "How can I win the game of tick-tack-toe?" It is well known that I cannot, if I assume (in keeping with the conventions of game theory) that my opponent understands the game perfectly. Put another way, there is no "technical solution" to the problem. I can win only by giving a radical meaning to the word "win." I can hit my opponent over the head; or I can drug him; or I can falsify the records. Every way in which I "win" involves, in some sense, an abandonment of the game, as we intuitively understand it. (I can also, of course, openly abandon the game—refuse to play it. This is what most adults do.)

The class of "No technical solution problems" has members. My thesis is that the "population problem," as conventionally conceived, is a member of this class. How it is conventionally conceived needs some comment. It is fair to say that most people who anguish over the population problem are trying to find a way to avoid the evils of overpopulation without relinquishing any of the privileges they now enjoy. They think that farming the seas or developing new strains of wheat will solve the problem—technologically. I try to show here that the solution they seek cannot be found. The population problem cannot be solved in a technical way, any more than can the problem of winning the game of tick-tack-toe.

WHAT SHALL WE MAXIMIZE?

Population, as Malthus said, naturally tends to grow "geometrically," or, as we would now say, exponentially. In a finite world this means that the per capita share of the world's goods must steadily decrease. Is ours a finite world?

A fair defense can be put forward for the view that the world is infinite; or that we do not know that it is not. But, in terms of the practical problems that we must face in the next few generations with the foreseeable technology, it is clear that we will greatly increase human misery if we do not, during the immediate future, assume that the world available to the terrestrial human population is finite. "Space" is no escape.[2]

A finite world can support only a finite population; therefore, population growth must eventually equal zero. (The case of perpetual wide fluctuations above and below zero is a trivial variant that need not be discussed.) When this condition is met, what will be the situation of mankind? Specifically, can Bentham's goal of "the greatest good for the greatest number" be realized?

No—for two reasons, each sufficient by itself. The first is a theoretical one. It is not mathematically possible to maximize for two (or more) variables at the same time. This was clearly stated by von Neumann and Morgenstern,[3] but the principle is implicit in the theory of partial differential equations, dating back at least to D'Alembert (1717–1783).

The second reason springs directly from biological facts. To live, any organism must have a source of energy (for example, food). This energy is utilized for two purposes: mere maintenance and work. For man, maintenance of life requires about 1600 kilocalories a day ("maintenance calories"). Anything that he does over and above merely staying alive will be defined as work, and is supported by "work calories" which he takes in. Work calories are used not only for what we call work in common speech; they are also required for all forms of enjoyment, from swimming and automobile racing to playing music and writing poetry. If our goal is to maximize population it is obvious what we must do: We must make the work calories per person approach as close to zero as possible. No gourmet meals, no vacations, no sports, no music, no literature, no art. . . . I think that everyone will grant, without argument or proof, that maximizing population does not maximize goods. Bentham's goal is impossible.

In reaching this conclusion I have made the usual assumption that it is the acquisition of energy that is the problem. The appearance of atomic energy has led some to question this assumption. However, given an infinite source of energy, population growth still produces an inescapable problem. The problem of the acquisition of energy is replaced by the problem of its dissipation, as J. H. Fremlin has so wittily shown.[4] The arithmetic signs in the analysis are, as it were, reversed; but Bentham's goal is still unobtainable.

The optimum population is, then, less than the maximum. The difficulty of defining the optimum is enormous; so far as I know, no one has seriously tackled this problem. Reaching an acceptable and stable solution will surely require more than one generation of hard analytical work—and much persuasion.

We want the maximum good per person; but what is good? To one person it is wilderness, to another it is ski lodges for thousands. To one it is estuaries to nourish ducks for hunters to shoot; to another it is factory land. Comparing one good with another is, we usually say, impossible because goods are incommensurable. Incommensurables cannot be compared.

Theoretically this may be true; but in real life incommensurables *are* commensurable. Only a criterion of judgment and a system of weighting are needed. In nature the criterion is survival. Is it better for a species to be small and hideable, or large and powerful? Natural selection commensurates the incommensurables. The compromise achieved depends on a natural weighting of the values of the variables.

Man must imitate this process. There is no doubt that in fact he already does, but unconsciously. It is when the hidden decisions are made explicit that the arguments begin. The problem for the years ahead is to work out an acceptable theory of weighting. Synergistic effects, nonlinear variation, and difficulties in discounting the future make the intellectual problem difficult, but not (in principle) insoluble.

Has any cultural group solved this practical problem at the present time, even on an intuitive level? One simple fact proves that none has: there is no prosperous population in the world today that has, and has had for some time, a growth rate of zero. Any people that has intuitively identified its optimum point will soon reach it, after which its growth rate becomes and remains zero.

Of course, a positive growth rate might be taken as evidence that a population is below its optimum. However, by any reasonable standards, the most rapidly growing populations on earth today are (in general) the most miserable. This association (which need not be invariable) casts doubt on the optimistic assumption that the positive growth rate of a population is evidence that it has yet to reach its optimum.

We can make little progress in working toward optimum population size until we explicitly exorcize the spirit of Adam Smith in the field of practical demography. In economic affairs, *The Wealth of Nations* (1776) popularized the "invisible hand," the idea that an individual who "intends only his own gain," is, as it were, "led by an invisible hand to promote . . . the public interest."[5] Adam Smith did not assert that this was invariably true, and perhaps neither did any of his followers. But he contributed to a dominant tendency of thought that has ever since interfered with positive action based on rational analysis, namely, the tendency to assume that decisions reached individually will, in fact, be the best decisions for an entire society. If this assumption is correct it justifies the continuance of our present policy of laissez-faire in reproduction. If it is correct we can assume that men will control their individual fecundity so as to produce the optimum population. If the assumption is not correct, we need to reexamine our individual freedoms to see which ones are defensible.

TRAGEDY OF FREEDOM IN A COMMONS

The rebuttal to the invisible hand in population control is to be found in a scenario first sketched in a little-known pamphlet[6] in 1833 by a mathematical amateur named William Forster Lloyd (1794–1852). We may well call it "the tragedy of the commons," using the word "tragedy" as the philosopher Whitehead used it:[7] "The essence of dramatic tragedy is not unhappiness. It resides in the solemnity of the remorseless working of things." He then goes on to say, "This inevitableness of destiny can only be illustrated in terms of human life by incidents which in fact involve unhappiness. For it is only by them that the futility of escape can be made evident in the drama."

The tragedy of the commons develops in this way. Picture a pasture open to all. It is to be expected that each herdsman will try to keep as many cattle as possible on the commons. Such an arrangement may work reasonably satisfactorily for centuries because tribal wars, poaching, and disease keep the numbers of both man and beast well below the carrying capacity of the land. Finally, however, comes the day of reckoning, that is, the day when the long-desired goal of social stability becomes a reality. At this point, the inherent logic of the commons remorselessly generates tragedy.

As a rational being, each herdsman seeks to maximize his gain. Explicitly or implicitly, more or less consciously, he asks, "What is the utility *to me* of adding one more animal to my herd?" This utility has one negative and one positive component.

1. The positive component is a function of the increment of one animal. Since the herdsman receives all the proceeds from the sale of the additional animal, the positive utility is nearly +1.
2. The negative component is a function of the additional overgrazing created by one more animal. Since, however, the effects of overgrazing are shared by all the herdsmen, the negative utility for any particular decision-making herdsman is only a fraction of –1.

Adding together the component partial utilities, the rational herdsman concludes that the only sensible course for him to pursue is to add another animal to his herd. And another; and another. . . . But this is the conclusion reached by each and every rational herdsman sharing a commons. Therein is the tragedy. Each man is locked into a system that compels him to increase his herd without limit—in a world that is limited. Ruin is the destination toward which all men rush, each pursuing his own best interest in a society that believes in the freedom of the commons. Freedom in a commons brings ruin to all.

Some would say that this is a platitude. Would that it were! In a sense, it was learned thousands of years ago, but natural selection favors the forces of psychological denial.[8] The individual benefits as an individual from his ability to deny the truth even though society as a whole, of which he is a part, suffers. Education can counteract the natural tendency to do the wrong thing, but the inexorable succession of generations requires that the basis for this knowledge be constantly refreshed.

A simple incident that occurred a few years ago in Leominster, Massachusetts, shows how perishable the knowledge is. During the Christmas shopping season the parking meters downtown were covered with plastic bags that bore tags reading: "Do not open until after Christmas. Free parking courtesy of the mayor and city council." In other words, facing the prospect of an increased demand for already scarce space, the city fathers reinstituted the system of the commons. (Cynically, we suspect that they gained more votes than they lost by this retrogressive act.)

In an approximate way, the logic of the commons has been understood for a long time, perhaps since the discovery of agriculture or the invention of private property in real estate. But it is understood mostly only in special cases which are not sufficiently generalized. Even at this late date, cattlemen leasing national land on the western ranges demonstrate no more than an ambivalent understanding, in constantly pressuring federal authorities to increase the head count to the point where overgrazing produces erosion and weed-dominance. Likewise, the oceans of the world continue to suffer from the survival of the philosophy of the commons. Maritime nations still respond automatically to the shibboleth of the "freedom of the seas." Professing to believe in the "inexhaustible resources of the oceans," they bring species after species of fish and whales closer to extinction.[9]

The National Parks present another instance of the working out of the tragedy of the commons. At present, they are open to all, without limit. The parks themselves are limited in extent—there is only one Yosemite Valley—whereas population seems to grow without limit. The values that visitors seek in the parks are steadily eroded. Plainly, we must soon cease to treat the parks as commons or they will be of no value to anyone.

What shall we do? We have several options. We might sell them off as private property. We might keep them as public property, but allocate the right to enter them. The allocation might be on the basis of wealth, by the use of an auction system. It might be on the basis of merit, as defined by some agreed-upon standards. It might be by lottery. Or it might be on a first-come, first-served basis, administered to long queues. These, I think, are all the reasonable possibilities. They are all objectionable. But we must choose—or acquiesce in the destruction of the commons that we call our National Parks.

POLLUTION

In a reverse way, the tragedy of the commons reappears in problems of pollution. Here it is not a question of taking something out of the commons, but of putting something in—sewage, or chemical, radioactive, and heat wastes into water; noxious and dangerous fumes into the air; and distracting and unpleasant advertising signs into the line of sight. The calculations of utility are much the same as before. The rational man finds that his share of the cost of the wastes he discharges into the commons is less than the cost of purifying his wastes before releasing them. Since this is true for everyone, we are locked into a system of "fouling our own nest," so long as we behave only as independent, rational, free-enterprisers.

The tragedy of the commons as a food basket is averted by private property, or something formally like it. But the air and waters surrounding us cannot readily be fenced, and so the tragedy of the commons as a cesspool must be prevented by different means, by coercive laws or taxing devices that make it cheaper for the polluter to treat his pollutants than to discharge them untreated. We have not progressed as far with the solution of this problem as we have with the first. Indeed, our particular concept of private property, which deters us from exhausting the positive resources of the earth, favors pollution. The owner of a factory on the bank of a stream—whose property extends to the middle of the stream—often has difficulty seeing why it is not his natural right to muddy the waters flowing past his door. The law, always behind the times, requires elaborate stitching and fitting to adapt it to this newly perceived aspect of the commons.

The pollution problem is a consequence of population. It did not much matter how a lonely American frontiersman disposed of his waste. "Flowing water purifies itself every 10 miles," my grandfather used to say, and the myth was near enough to the truth when he was a boy, for there were not too many people. But as population became denser, the natural chemical and biological recycling processes became overloaded, calling for a redefinition of property rights.

HOW TO LEGISLATE TEMPERANCE?

Analysis of the pollution problem as a function of population density uncovers a not generally recognized principle of morality, namely: *the morality of an act is a function of the state of the system at the time it is performed*.[10] Using the commons as a cesspool does not harm the general public under frontier conditions, because there is no public; the same behavior in a metropolis is unbearable. A hundred and fifty years ago a plainsman could kill an American bison, cut out only the tongue for his dinner, and discard the rest of the animal. He was not in any important sense being wasteful. Today, with only a few thousand bison left, we would be appalled at such behavior.

In passing, it is worth noting that the morality of an act cannot be determined from a photograph. One does not know whether a man killing an elephant or setting fire to the grassland is harming others until one knows the total system in which his act appears. "One picture is worth a thousand words," said an ancient Chinese; but it may take 10,000 words to validate it. It is as tempting to ecologists as it is to reformers in general to try to persuade others by way of the photographic shortcut. But the essense of an argument cannot be photographed: it must be presented rationally—in words.

That morality is system-sensitive escaped the attention of most codifiers of ethics in the past. "Thou shalt not . . ." is the form of traditional ethical directives which make no allowance for particular circumstances. The laws of our society follow the pattern of ancient ethics, and therefore are poorly suited to governing a complex, crowded, changeable world. Our epicyclic solution is to augment statutory law with administrative law. Since it is practically impossible to spell out all the conditions under which it is safe to burn trash in the back yard or to run an automobile without smog-control, by law we delegate the details to bureaus. The result is administrative law, which is rightly feared for an ancient reason—*Quis custodiet ipsos custodes?*—"Who shall watch the watchers themselves?" John Adams said that we must have "a government of laws and not men." Bureau administrators, trying to evaluate the morality of acts in the total system, are singularly liable to corruption, producing a government by men, not laws.

Prohibition is easy to legislate (though not necessarily to enforce); but how do we legislate temperance? Experience indicates that it can be accomplished best through the mediation of administrative law. We limit possibilities unnecessarily if we suppose that the sentiment of *Quis custodiet* denies us the use of administrative law. We should rather retain the phrase as a perpetual reminder of fearful dangers we cannot avoid. The great challenge facing us now is to invent the corrective feedbacks that are needed to keep custodians honest. We must find ways to legitimate the needed authority of both the custodians and the corrective feedbacks.

FREEDOM TO BREED IS INTOLERABLE

The tragedy of the commons is involved in population problems in another way. In a world governed solely by the principle of "dog eat dog"—if indeed there ever was such a world—how many children a family had would not be a matter of public concern. Parents who bred too exuberantly would leave fewer descendants, not more, because they would be unable to care adequately for their children. David Lack and others have found that such a negative feedback demonstrably controls the fecundity of birds.[11] But men are not birds, and have not acted like them for millenniums, at least.

If each human family were dependent only on its own resources; *if* the children of improvident parents starved to death; *if*, thus, overbreeding brought its own "punishment" to the germ line—*then* there would be no public interest in controlling the breeding of families. But our society is deeply committed to the welfare state,[12] and hence is confronted with another aspect of the tragedy of the commons.

In a welfare state, how shall we deal with the family, the religion, the race, or the class (or indeed any distinguishable and cohesive group) that adopts overbreeding as a policy to secure its own aggrandizement?[13] To couple the concept of freedom to breed with the belief that everyone born has an equal right to the commons is to lock the world into a tragic course of action.

Unfortunately this is just the course of action that is being pursued by the United Nations. In late 1967, some 30 nations agreed to the following:[14]

> The Universal Declaration of Human Rights describes the family as the natural and fundamental unit of society. It follows that any choice and decision with regard to the size of the family must irrevocably rest with the family itself, and cannot be made by anyone else.

It is painful to have to deny categorically the validity of this right; denying it, one feels as uncomfortable as a resident of Salem, Massachusetts, who denied the reality of witches in the 17th century. At the present time, in liberal quarters, something like a taboo acts to inhibit criticism of the United Nations. There is a feeling that the United Nations is "our last and best hope," that we shouldn't find fault with it; we shouldn't play into the hands of the archconservatives. However, let us not forget what Robert Louis Stevenson said: "The truth that is suppressed by friends is the readiest weapon of the enemy." If we love the truth we must openly deny the validity of the Universal Declaration of Human Rights, even though it is promoted by the United Nations. We should also join with Kingsley Davis[15] in attempting to get Planned Parenthood-World Population to see the error of its ways in embracing the same tragic ideal.

CONSCIENCE IS SELF-ELIMINATING

It is a mistake to think that we can control the breeding of mankind in the long run by an appeal to conscience. Charles Galton Darwin made this point when he spoke on the centennial of the publication of his grandfather's great book. The argument is straightforward and Darwinian.

People vary. Confronted with appeals to limit breeding, some people will undoubtedly respond to the plea more than others. Those who have more children will produce a larger fraction of the next generation than those with more susceptible consciences. The difference will be accentuated, generation by generation.

In C. G. Darwin's words: "It may well be that it would take hundreds of generations for the progenitive instinct to develop in this way, but if it should do so, nature would have taken her revenge, and the variety *Homo contracipiens* would become extinct and would be replaced by the variety *Homo progenitivus*."[16]

The argument assumes that conscience or the desire for children (no matter which) is hereditary—but hereditary only in the most general formal sense. The result will be the same whether the attitude is transmitted through germ cells, or exosomatically, to use A. J. Lotka's term. (If one denies the latter possibility as well as the former, then what's the point of education?) The argument has here been stated in the context of the population problem, but it applies equally well to any instance in which society appeals to an individual exploiting a commons to restrain himself for the general good—by means of his conscience. To make such an appeal is to set up a selective system that works toward the elimination of conscience from the race.

PATHOGENIC EFFECTS OF CONSCIENCE

The long-term disadvantage of an appeal to conscience should be enough to condemn it; but has serious short-term disadvantages as well. If we ask a man who is exploiting a commons to desist "in the name of conscience," what are we saying to him? What does he hear?—not only at the moment but also in the wee small hours of the night when, half asleep, he remembers not merely the words we used but also the nonverbal communication cues we gave him unawares? Sooner or later, consciously or subconsciously, he senses that he has received two communications, and that they are contradictory: (i) (intended communication) "If you don't do as we ask, we will openly condemn you for not acting like a responsible citizen"; (ii) (the unintended communication) "If you *do* behave as we ask, we will secretly condemn you for a simpleton who can be shamed into standing aside while the rest of us exploit the commons."

Everyman then is caught in what Bateson has called a "double bind." Bateson and his co-workers have made a plausible case for viewing the double bind as an important causative factor in the genesis of schizophrenia.[17] The double bind may not always be so damaging, but it always endangers the mental health of anyone to whom it is applied. "A bad conscience," said Nietzsche, "is a kind of illness."

To conjure up a conscience in others is tempting to anyone who wishes to extend his control beyond the legal limits. Leaders at the highest level succumb to this temptation. Has any President during the past generation failed to call on labor unions to moderate voluntarily their demands for higher wages, or to steel companies to honor voluntary guidelines on prices? I can recall none. The rhetoric used on such occasions is designed to produce feelings of guilt in non-cooperators.

For centuries it was assumed without proof that guilt was a valuable, perhaps even an indispensable, ingredient of the civilized life. Now, in this post-Freudian world, we doubt it.

Paul Goodman speaks from the modern point of view when he says: "No good has ever come from feeling guilty, neither intelligence, policy, nor compassion. The guilty do not pay attention to the object but only to themselves, and not even to their own interests, which might make sense, but to their anxieties."[18]

One does not have to be a professional psychiatrist to see the consequences of anxiety. We in the Western world are just emerging from a dreadful two-centuries-long Dark Ages of Eros that was sustained partly by prohibition laws, but perhaps more effectively by the anxiety-generating mechanisms of education. Alex Comfort has told the story well in *The Anxiety Makers*;[19] it is not a pretty one.

Since proof is difficult, we may even concede that the results of anxiety may sometimes, from certain points of view, be desirable. The larger question we should ask is whether, as a matter of policy, we should ever encourage the use of a technique the tendency (if not the intention) of which is psychologically pathogenic. We hear much talk these days of responsible parenthood; the coupled words are incorporated into the titles of some organizations devoted to birth control. Some people have proposed massive propaganda campaigns to instill responsibility into the nation's (or the world's) breeders. But what is the meaning of the word responsibility in this context? Is it not merely a synonym for the word conscience? When we use the word responsibility in the absence of substantial sanctions are we not trying to browbeat a free man in a commons into acting against his own interest? Responsibility is a verbal counterfeit for a substantial *quid pro quo*. It is an attempt to get something for nothing.

If the word responsibility is to be used at all, I suggest that it be in the sense Charles Frankel uses it.[20] "Responsibility," says this philosopher, "is the product of definite social arrangements." Notice that Frankel calls for social arrangements—not propaganda.

MUTUAL COERCION MUTUALLY AGREED UPON

The social arrangements that produce responsibility are arrangements that create coercion, of some sort. Consider bank-robbing. The man who takes money from a bank acts as if the bank were a commons. How do we prevent such action? Certainly not by trying to control his behavior solely by a verbal appeal to his sense of responsibility. Rather than rely on propaganda we follow Frankel's lead and insist that a bank is not a commons; we seek the definite social arrangements that will keep it from becoming a commons. That we thereby infringe on the freedom of would-be robbers we neither deny nor regret.

The morality of bank-robbing is particularly easy to understand because we accept complete prohibition of this activity. We are willing to say "Thou shalt not rob banks," without providing for exceptions. But temperance also can be created by coercion. Taxing is a good coercive device. To keep downtown shoppers temperate in their use of parking space we introduce parking meters for short periods, and traffic fines for longer ones. We need not actually forbid a citizen to park as long as he wants to; we need merely make it increasingly expensive for him to do so. Not prohibition, but carefully biased options are what we offer him. A Madison Avenue man might call this persuasion; I prefer the greater candor of the word coercion.

Coercion is a dirty word to most liberals now, but it need not forever be so. As with the four-letter words, its dirtiness can be cleansed away by exposure to the light, by saying it over and over without apology or embarrassment. To many, the word coercion implies arbitrary decisions of distant and irresponsible bureaucrats; but this is not a necessary part of its meaning. The only kind of coercion I recommend is mutual coercion, mutually agreed upon by the majority of the people affected.

To say that we mutually agree to coercion is not to say that we are required to enjoy it, or even to pretend we enjoy it. Who enjoys taxes? We all grumble about them. But we accept compulsory taxes because we recognize that voluntary taxes would favor the conscienceless. We institute and (grumblingly) support taxes and other coercive devices to escape the horror of the commons.

An alternative to the commons need not be perfectly just to be preferable. With real estate and other material goods, the alternative we have chosen is the institution of private property coupled with legal inheritance. Is this system perfectly just? As a genetically trained biologist I deny that it is. It seems to me that, if there are to be differences in individual inheritance, legal possession should be perfectly correlated with biological inheritance—that those who are biologically more fit to be the custodians of property and power should legally inherit more. But genetic recombination continually makes a mockery of the doctrine of "like father, like son" implicit in our laws of legal inheritance. An idiot can inherit millions, and a trust fund can keep his estate intact. We must admit that our legal system of private property plus inheritance is unjust—but we put up with it because we are not convinced, at the moment, that anyone has invented a better system. The alternative of the commons is too horrifying to contemplate. Injustice is preferable to total ruin.

It is one of the peculiarities of the warfare between reform and the status quo that it is thoughtlessly governed by a double standard. Whenever a reform measure is proposed it is often defeated when its opponents triumphantly discover a flaw in it. As Kingsley Davis has pointed out,[21] worshippers of the status quo sometimes imply that no reform is possible without unanimous agreement, an implication contrary to historical fact. As nearly as I can make out, automatic rejection of proposed reforms is based on one of two unconscious assumptions: (i) that the status quo is perfect; or (ii) that the choice we face is between reform and no action; if the proposed reform is imperfect, we presumably should take no action at all, while we wait for a perfect proposal.

But we can never do nothing. That which we have done for thousands of years is also action. It also produces evils. Once we are aware that the status quo is action, we can then compare its discoverable advantages and disadvantages with the predicted advantages and disadvantages of the proposed reform, discounting as best we can for our lack of experience. On the basis of such a comparison, we can make a rational decision which will not involve the unworkable assumption that only perfect systems are tolerable.

RECOGNITION OF NECESSITY

Perhaps the simplest summary of this analysis of man's population problems is this: the commons, if justifiable at all, is justifiable only under conditions of low-population density. As the human population has increased, the commons has had to be abandoned in one aspect after another.

First we abandoned the commons in food gathering, enclosing farm land and restricting pastures and hunting and fishing areas. These restrictions are still not complete throughout the world.

Somewhat later we saw that the commons as a place for waste disposal would also have to be abandoned. Restrictions on the disposal of domestic sewage are widely accepted in the Western world; we are still struggling to close the commons to pollution by automobiles, factories, insecticide sprayers, fertilizing operations, and atomic energy installations.

In a still more embryonic state is our recognition of the evils of the commons in matters of pleasure. There is almost no restriction on the propagation of sound waves in the public medium. The shopping public is assaulted with mindless music, without its consent. Our government is paying out billions of dollars to create supersonic transport which will disturb 50,000 people for every one person who is whisked from coast to coast 3 hours faster. Advertisers muddy the airwaves of radio and television and pollute the view of travelers. We are a long way from outlawing the commons in matters of pleasure. Is this because our Puritan inheritance makes us view pleasure as something of a sin, and plain (that is, the pollution of advertising) as the sign of virtue?

Every new enclosure of the commons involves the infringement of some-body's personal liberty. Infringements made in the distant past are accepted because no contemporary complains of a loss. It is the newly proposed infringements that we vigorously oppose; cries of "rights" and "freedom" fill the air. But what does "freedom" mean? When men mutually agreed to pass laws against robbing, mankind became more free, not less so. Individuals locked into the logic of the commons are free only to bring on universal ruin; once they see the necessity of mutual coercion, they become free to pursue other goals. I believe it was Hegel who said, "Freedom is the recognition of necessity."

The most important aspect of necessity that we must now recognize, is the necessity of abandoning the commons in breeding. No technical solution can rescue us from the misery of overpopulation. Freedom to breed will bring ruin to all. At the moment, to avoid hard decisions many of us are tempted to propa-gandize for conscience and responsible parenthood. The temptation must be resisted, because an appeal to independently acting consciences selects for the disappearance of all conscience in the long run, and an increase in anxiety in the short.

The only way we can preserve and nurture other and more precious free-doms is by relinquishing the freedom to breed, and that very soon. "Freedom is the recognition of necessity"—and it is the role of education to reveal to all the necessity of abandoning the freedom to breed. Only so, can we put an end to this aspect of the tragedy of the commons.

NOTES

1. J. B. Wiesner and H. F. York. *Sci. Amer.* 211 (No. 4), 27 (1964).

2. G. Hardin, *J. Hered.* 50, 68 (1959); S. von Hoernor, *Science* 137, 18 (1962).

3. J. von Neumann and O. Morgenstern, *Theory of Games and Economic Behavior* (Princeton Univ. Press, Princeton, N.J., 1947), p. 11.

4. J. H. Fremlin, *New Sci.*, No. 415 (1964), p. 285.

5. A. Smith, *The Wealth of Nations* (Modern Library, New York, 1937), p. 423.

6. W. F. Lloyd, *Two Lectures on the Checks to Population* (Oxford Univ. Press, Oxford, England, 1833), reprinted (in part) in *Population, Evolution, and Birth Control*, G. Har-din, Ed. (Freeman, San Francisco, 1964), p. 37.

7. A. N. Whitehead, *Science and the Modern World* (Mentor, New York, 1948), p. 17.

8. G. Hardin, Ed. *Population, Evolution, and Birth Control* (Freeman, San Fran-cisco, 1964), p. 56.

9. S. McVay, *Sci. Amer.* 216 (No. 8), 13 (1966).

10. J. Fletcher, *Situation Ethics* (Westminster, Philadelphia, 1966).

11. D. Lack, *The Natural Regulation of Animal Numbers* (Clarendon Press, Oxford, 1954).

12. H. Girvetz, *From Wealth to Welfare* (Stanford Univ. Press, Stanford, Calif., 1950).

13. G. Hardin, *Perspec. Biol. Med.* 6, 366 (1963).

14. U. Thant, *Int. Planned Parenthood News*, No. 168 (February 1968), p. 3.

15. K. Davis, *Science* 158, 730 (1967).

16. S. Tax, Ed., *Evolution after Darwin* (Univ. of Chicago Press, Chicago, 1960), vol. 2, p. 469.

17. G. Bateson, D. D. Jackson, J. Haley, J. Weakland, *Behav. Sci.* 1, 251 (1956).

18. P. Goodman, *New York Rev. Books* 10 (No. 8), 22 (23 May 1968).

19. A. Comfort, *The Anxiety Makers* (Nelson, London, 1967).

20. C. Frankel, *The Case for Modern Man* (Harper, New York, 1955), p. 203.

21. J. D. Roslansky, *Genetics and the Future of Man* (Appleton-Century-Crofts, New York, 1966), p. 177.

1.4

D. RODERICK KIEWIET AND MATHEW McCUBBINS

From *The Logic of Delegation: Congressional Parties and the Appropriations Process*

Kiewiet and McCubbins describe the pervasive problem of delegation, sometimes called the principal-agent problem. This common "problem" occurs when there is a conflict of interest between the people who make decisions (principals) and the people hired by principals to carry out the decisions (agents). A key task of modern representative government is to ensure that decision makers have the means to manage the behavior of those implementing policies. For example, elected representatives rely on government agencies and bureaucrats to implement policies. How do elected officials control what government bureaucrats do?

COLLECTIVE ACTION AND DELEGATION

. . . The most familiar collective action problem is the prisoner's dilemma. It takes its name from the simple two-person game, but the social contexts in which most human interaction takes place tend to make n-person prisoners' dilemmas the more pervasive phenomenon. The crux of the dilemma is that individuals, in seeking to maximize their self-interest, have incentives to behave in ways that are inimical to the interests of the community as a whole (Hardin 1968). A good example of the dilemma is that of public goods (Olson 1965). The community would on net benefit from such a good, but those who do not contribute to its provision cannot be excluded from enjoying it. Everyone therefore has an incentive to free ride on the contributions of others. Even though the community may unanimously favor acquisition of the public good, little or no effort is expended to supply it. Rational individual choices produce irrational collective outcomes.

Collective action may also be stymied by a lack of coordination. In contrast to the prisoner's dilemma, where dominant strategies yield an inefficient equilibrium, other situations confront the community with multiple efficient equilibria. Members of the community are uncertain as to which strategies other members will pursue, and coordination may never be achieved. A simple coordination problem occurs when two cars enter an intersection simultaneously. Neither driver cares particularly who goes first; both are far more concerned about avoiding a collision. What frequently occurs, however, is a nerve-wracking *pas de deux* of false starts and sudden stops as the drivers make their way through the crossing. Even if everyone in the community would benefit from all alternatives under consideration, problems of coordination are exacerbated when different alternatives benefit some members relative to others.

■ ■ ■

According to property rights theorists, the best response to collective action problems is to minimize their occurrence, something that is accomplished by relegating as much human activity as possible to the realm of the marketplace. Adam Smith argued long ago that the well-being of a community is better realized through individual market transactions than through the schemes of even the most benevolent planner. Much social benefit can also be derived from simple patterns of reciprocity. But there are limits to what can be achieved through voluntary trade and cooperation; uncoordinated, unorganized activity will get a community only so far. In most cases, the benefits of collective action are realized through organizations. It is in the context of organizations that collective action is most effectively coordinated, that prisoners' dilemmas are most readily overcome, and that stable social decisions are most likely to be reached.

The organizational bases of collective action are many—firms, bureaucracies, associations, committees, leagues, representative assemblies, to name a few. What the most prominent forms of organization have in common, however, is the delegation of authority to take action from the individual or individuals to whom it was originally endowed—the principal—to one or more agents. One major organizational theorist, in fact, defines organizations as "networks of overlapping or nested principal/agent relationships" (Tirole 1986, p. 181). Delegation from principals to agents is the key to the division of labor and development of specialization; tremendous gains accrue if tasks are delegated to those with the talent, training, and inclination to do them. This, when all is said and done, is what allows firms to profit, economies to grow, and governments to govern.

The underlings in an organization are obviously agents of their superiors, but the heads of organizations, such as coaches, firm managers, party leaders, are agents, too. Indeed, it is the delegation of authority to a central agent to lead or manage the organization that is the key to overcoming problems of collective action. Agents performing as leaders or managers must be endowed with the resources they need to discharge their duties effectively. In the case of congressional parties, leaders can exploit the prominence of their position to identify a focal point, thus solving problems of coordination by rallying support around one of possibly many acceptable alternatives. Their ability to structure the voting agenda, moreover, can overcome social choice instability.

In such a relationship the agent seeks to maximize his or her return subject to the constraints and incentives offered by the principal. The principal, conversely, seeks to structure the relationship with the agent so that the outcomes produced through the agent's efforts are the best the principal can achieve, given the choice to delegate in the first place. There is, then, a natural conflict of interest between the two. In economic settings this conflict is often over the amount of effort expended by the agent. In political settings it is more likely to be over the course of action the agent is to pursue. The policy agenda of agency bureaucrats, for example, can be quite at odds with the preferences of the elected officials who oversee them. As a consequence of this conflict of interest, the principal always experiences some reduction in welfare. First, he suffers agency losses that result from the agent behaving in ways other than those that best serve his interests. Second, the principal incurs agency costs in undertaking efforts to mitigate agency losses. Agency problems may be so great that they exceed the benefits to be derived from collection action, in which case the delegation should not occur.

The opportunistic behavior that is at the root of agency problems is by no means confined to principal/agent relationships. Individuals involved in market transactions have similar incentives to behave in a less than noble manner. Certain conditions that are generally present in principal/agent relationships, however, make it a particularly congenial environment for opportunism. These are the conditions of hidden action, hidden information, and a form of strategic vulnerability on the part of the principal that we refer to as Madison's dilemma.

Hidden Action and Hidden Information

In a wide variety of agency relationships, the agent possesses or acquires information that is either unavailable to the principal or prohibitively costly to obtain. The agent has incentives to use this information strategically or to simply keep it hidden—a situation referred to variously as the problem of truthful revelation or incentive incompatibility. In a firm, workers have information that is not available to management, such as how fast the assembly line can run before quality is compromised. They would prefer not to reveal this information, however, because they would rather not work at a breakneck pace. Another type of information that agents often have and principals do not is the agent's type (for example, knowledge of whether the agent is hardworking or lazy, talented or untalented, risk-averse or risk-acceptant). This variation on the hidden information problem is referred to as adverse selection.

Situations in which agents acquire information that is unavailable to the principal pervade public policy-making. The basis of Niskanen's (1971) argument as to how bureaus maximize the size of their budgets is that bureaucrats are privy to information about service delivery costs that is not available to elected politicians. Through their investigations, congressional committees uncover information that is not available to other members of the chamber. Individual members, similarly, have better information than do congressional party leaders as to whether or not supporting the party's position might cause them trouble back home.

The second problem, that of hidden action, manifests itself in a variety of situations. Stockholders cannot observe whether the actions that firm managers take are in their best interest. Voters cannot observe whether the actions of elected representatives—their agents—are in their best interest. Hidden action is especially problematic when the agent's actions only partially determine outcomes, as in the case of team production or committee decisions, or when outcomes are partially determined by chance. In such cases, the principal is unable to infer the appropriateness of the agent's actions even from observed results.

Madison's Dilemma

Arguing for the separation of powers specified under the new Constitution, Madison wrote in *Federalist 51*, "In framing a government to be administered by men over men, the great difficulty lies in this: you must first enable the government to control the governed; and in the next place oblige it to control itself." Whatever their views about the document that was ultimately produced, members of the Constitutional Convention were keenly appreciative of Madison's observation. They had seen that under the Articles of Confederation the federal government had not been delegated enough authority to accomplish much of anything. Yet they feared that a government powerful enough to govern effectively would necessarily be powerful enough to oppress them.

In addition to problems of hidden action and hidden information, this third problem, one we call Madison's dilemma, is a potential pitfall in all institutions that rely upon delegation. The essence of the problem is that resources or authority granted to an agent for the purpose of advancing the interests of the principal can be turned against the principal. Although the problem is a general one of agency, it has long been recognized in liberal political theory as being of paramount importance when the agents involved are those in a position of leadership. Madison's dilemma is not a consequence of agents taking hidden action or acquiring hidden information, although these conditions can certainly make matters worse. Rather, it arises from agents exploiting the favorable strategic situation in which they have been placed.

In seeking to solve collective action problems, members of the community must be prescient in their delegation of authority to a central agent. If not, they may find that that they would have been better off continuing to endure their problems than they are living with the solution their agent has achieved.

Collective Principals and Collective Agents

Problems of hidden action, hidden information, and Madison's dilemma are endemic to all agency relationships. There are additional hazards to delegation, however, when either collective principals or collective agents are involved. Specifically, the very same collective action problems that delegation is intended to overcome—prisoners' dilemmas, lack of coordination, and social choice instability—can reemerge to afflict either the collective agent or a collective principal. A collective principal may be unable to announce a single preference over its agent's actions or to offer a single contract governing compensation for the agent. A subset of the membership may strategically manipulate the decision-making process of the collective principal. Similarly, agents who are delegated management or leadership roles may use their agenda powers to do the same thing, thus leaving the collective principal vulnerable to a form of Madison's dilemma. A related consideration is that in appointing a new individual to a collective agent, such as a production team or a committee, that person's abilities and preferences cannot be evaluated in isolation. The principal must consider instead how the new agent will interact with existing members of the team or committee.

Distinct from the problems of collective principals and agents are problems specific to multiple principals and agents. An agent attempting to serve multiple principals often finds that any action he or she might take to benefit one principal injures another. Federal agencies are buffeted by conflicting pressures from their departments, the president, the courts, their interest group clients, as well as several congressional committees and subcommittees. Second, when there are multiple agents it is possible that they will collude against the principal. This can occur in a number of ways. Workers who break the curve, for example, are likely to be castigated by their fellow workers. The essence of "iron triangle" or "subgovernment" theories of public policy formation is that collusion between two sets of agents—federal agencies and the congressional committees that ostensibly oversee them—serves to undermine the welfare of the general public (their ultimate principal) rather than to promote it.

OVERCOMING AGENCY PROBLEMS

Agency losses can be contained, but only by undertaking measures that are themselves costly. There are are four major classes of such measures: (1) contract design, (2) screening and selection mechanisms, (3) monitoring and reporting requirements, and (4) institutional checks.

Contract Design

Any contract between a principal and agent must satisfy the participation constraint. The agent's compensation must be at least as great as his or her opportunity costs, but less than the marginal benefit the principal derives from the actions of the agent. If this condition is not met, one side or the other will not be made better off by entering into the relationship and will decline to do so. Assuming that the participation constraint is satisfied, the principal's goal is to delegate tasks and responsibilities and to specify a corresponding schedule of compensation in such a way that the agent is motivated to best serve the principal's interests. Such contracts may specify negative rewards, or sanctions, particularly when the agent is capable of taking actions that are very harmful to the principal. In some situations, particularly when noncompliance with the principal's directives is hard to detect, the sanctions required to effect compliance are far greater in magnitude than the benefits that the principal derives from compliance.

Under conditions that usually exist in principal/agent relationships—hidden information and hidden action—designing compensation schedules is a tricky business. Examples abound of compensation schemes that create incentives for agent behavior other than that intended by the principal. If not otherwise constrained, brokers receiving a commission on trades churn through their clients' portfolios. Ford factory managers, no less creative than their celebrated Soviet counterparts, often met their quotas by surreptitiously building large numbers of automobiles prior to the official start of the production run (Halberstam 1986). Governmental agencies have an especially difficult time designing appropriate compensation schedules. Medicare administrators, for example, came to realize that simply reimbursing hospitals for all "reasonable" costs incurred in treating patients contributed to rapidly escalating claims. In 1982 they won congressional approval for a new system under which hospitals receive a fixed fee for treatment based upon the diagnosis related group (DRG) to which the patient has been assigned. In short order the system began to experience "DRG creep"; elderly Americans were succumbing to increasingly expensive diseases that often could be diagnosed only with the most advanced (and expensive) medical technology.

The problem of inappropriate incentives in compensation schemes can be mitigated by giving agents a residual claim on output. The compensation received by corporate executives, for example, is often in the form of profit sharing or other bonuses linked to the performance of the firm. Another example of this arrangement is sharecropping. Instead of charging a fixed rent, the landlord leases land to a tenant in return for a percentage of the crop. Compensation contracts of this form can be used in the public sector as well. In previous centuries, the king of France and other European monarchs garnered much of their revenue from "tax farmers," that is, individuals who were given the right to collect taxes in a particular geographic area so long as they surrendered an agreed-upon amount of the proceeds to the crown. The state of Ohio actually implemented this method for garnering revenue at the end of the Civil War; counties and cities were permitted to engage "tax inquisitors" who were empowered to find concealed taxable holdings (usually stocks and bank deposits) in return for a percentage of the proceeds.

Although such profit-sharing arrangements can help mitigate agency losses, they are hardly a panacea. They can be very expensive to the principal and do not necessarily remove all inappropriate incentives. In the realm of public policy, awarding agents a residual claim on output can have particularly obnoxious consequences; the interested student should be able to surmise why the institution of tax farming fell out of favor. Even if it were desirable to motivate public servants with a piece of the action, most important policy outputs are impossible to measure. How, for example, could the military establishment be awarded an incentive bonus that hinged upon whether or not they had had a good year?

Given the difficulties involved in designing optimal contracts prior to the establishment of an agency relationship, an alternative strategy for the principal may be to simply offer a compensation contract and, conditioned on the agent accepting it, to see how well he or she works out. There is, after all, no better information about how well an agent performs than his or her actual performance. Most employment contracts specify an initial probationary period (ranging from three or four days for waiters to three or four years for professors) and provide for periodic reviews after that. The principal can minimize the risk associated with this strategy by initially assigning an agent a modest set of tasks and responsibilities at a modest level of compensation. Those who perform well are rewarded by increasing the range of their authority and responsibility and, concommitantly, the level of their compensation. Agents who perform poorly will not similarly advance, or may even be demoted or dismissed. Like other strategies available to the principal, this one works best when agents can be induced to compete with each other. One of the major rationales for hierarchy in organizations is that it means there are more people seeking promotion to the next level than there are opportunities available.

Screening and Selection Mechanisms

A policy of hiring first and adjusting compensation later does nothing to address the problem of adverse selection discussed earlier; the offer of a given level of compensation attracts only those applicants whose opportunity costs are lower than the offer. This is not a damaging critique, however, because there is little that can be done about adverse selection simply by altering the terms of the compensation contract. The more telling problem is that information revealed by the agent's on-the-job performance, as valuable as it is, can be exceedingly expensive to obtain. Spence (1974) details several reasons why it can be so costly to sort out good agents from bad after they have been hired and why it pays both principals and agents to invest time and effort into avoiding bad matches in the first place:

> One might ask why the employer would not simply hire the person, determine his productivity, and then either fire him or adjust his wage or salary accordingly. There are several reasons why he will not do this. Frequently, he cannot. It may take time (even a long time) for the individual's real capabilities to become apparent. There may be a specific training required before the individual can handle certain kinds of jobs. There may be a contract and a contract period within which the individual cannot be fired and his salary cannot be adjusted. All of these factors tend to make the hiring decision an investment decision for the employer. Certain costs incurred in hiring and in the early period of employment are sunk and cannot be recovered if the investment turns out badly. (p. 14)

To the extent they share in the benefits of minimizing agency losses and agency costs, both sides are better off if principals are able to identify those individuals who possess the appropriate talents, skills, and other personal characteristics prior to the establishment of the principal/agent relationship. The greater the investment entailed in the hiring decision, the more critical screening and selection mechanisms become. Thus Spence's arguments apply with even more force in the public sector than in the private. Congressional members appointed to committees do not serve a probationary period to see how well they work out. Civil Service employees, for all practical purposes, cannot be fired. And as incumbent presidents typically point out when running for reelection, the Oval Office is no place for on-the-job training.

But how are principals and agents able to find suitable matches when they lack the requisite information? Principals cannot observe agents' actual performance until after the commitment to hire them has been made. Potential agents, similarly, cannot know exactly what the job is like until they start doing it. This problem is compounded by the fact that both potential principals and potential agents frequently have an incentive to misrepresent their abilities and preferences. According to Spence, this informational gap is bridged by observing properties of each other that are reliable signals of the underlying qualities of interest. Many signals that employers attend to in the labor market are beyond the applicants' control, such as race, age, or gender, and for that reason can be illegitimate sources of discrimination. Other signals, however, the applicant has at least partial control over, such as appearing on time for the job interview, presenting a neat personal appearance, and expressing enthusiasm for the job.

Signaling is an important phenomenon in the political world as well. Congressional candidates who have served in an elected office before are far more likely to get elected than those who have not. A major reason for this is that their previous success signals to potential contributors that they are high-quality candidates. Congressional parties also tend not to name freshmen to the House Appropriations Committee. This is because freshmen have not been around long enough to demonstrate that they are the type of *homme sérieux* who has traditionally served on the committee– hardworking, respectful, and, whatever their ideological predilections, responsive to the needs of the party.

Monitoring and Reporting Requirements

Once a principal and agent have entered into a relationship, the most straightforward way to eliminate the conditions of hidden action and information would seem to be to institute procedures requiring agents to report whatever relevant information they have obtained and whatever actions they have taken. After all, hidden information is no longer hidden if you make the agent reveal it. On the basis of information provided by the agent, the principal can presumably tie the agent's compensation more directly to his or her actual conduct. As before, to the extent both sides share in a reduction in agency losses and agency costs, both principal and agent can be made better off.

In fact, reporting requirements are ubiquitous in both the private and public sectors. Employees fill out weekly progress reports for their supervisors, who in turn report to their supervisors on the status of their operations. Every year congressional committees, regulatory agencies, and executive departments report millions of pages of material on their hearings, investigations, and policy recommendations.

There are, however, costs entailed both in the agent's provision and in the principal's consumption of information. If nothing else, the transfer of information deflects time and attention away from tasks that they would otherwise be performing. Rather than require agents to report all relevant information, their reports should be at an optimal level of "coarsification." Unfortunately, this is difficult to modulate; a principal can either be starving for information or, more often, drowning in a sea of it. That hundreds of millions of dollars are invested annually in the design of management information systems attests to the difficulty of this problem.

The more serious drawback to reporting requirements, however, has already been broached, and that is the problem of truthful revelation or incentive incompatibility. The agent has incentives to shade things, to make reports that reflect favorably upon himself, or to reveal information in some other strategic manner. Employees may discover that energy, skill, and creativity applied to their weekly progress reports pays off much more handsomely than actually doing the job. Even if agents can somehow be constrained to be truthful in their reports, the principal will still not know what they are not reporting. For that reason principals typically supplement these requirements with what McCubbins and Schwartz (1984) have dubbed "police patrol" oversight— audits, investigations, and other direct methods of monitoring. To be effective, monitoring policies should be applied stochastically so as to preserve the element of surprise. Direct monitoring can cost the principal a great deal of time and effort. Anyone who has ever worked on a factory floor can attest to the fact that constant supervision is also demeaning and corrosive to the morale of both supervisor and supervisee.

Frequently an agent's actions affect individuals who are not a party to the original principal/agent contract. These individuals may be the intended beneficiaries of the agent's actions, as when an employee supplies a service to a customer on behalf of the firm's owners, or when bureaucrats deliver benefits to constituents on behalf of members of Congress or the president. Because affected third parties have an incentive to observe and to influence the actions of the agent, opportunities arise for oversight that is potentially less costly and more reliable than "police patrols." Instead of examining a sample of the agent's activities (or, more typically, the agent's reports about his or her activities), looking for inappropriate actions or improper use of information, the principal instead obtains information from the affected third parties. This McCubbins and Schwartz refer to as "fire alarm" oversight.

Fire alarm oversight offers several advantages. First, it allows the principal to gather information at lower cost; even when it is as costly as police patrol oversight, much of the cost is borne by the affected third parties. Second, it can yield better information. Under a realistic police patrol policy the principal examines only a small sample of the agent's actions and is therefore likely to miss violations. Under a well-designed fire alarm system, third parties can bring to the principal's attention any serious violation by the agent. More important, the affected third parties have incentives that are in accord with the principal's interests and not, as in the case of the agent, in conflict with them. Third, it is usually difficult to specify a priori a contract with the agent that unambiguously covers all contingencies, and consequently it is hard to tell whether an agent has violated the contract. In this situation, complaints by the affected third parties give principals the opportunity to spell out their goals more clearly.

Often it is no easier for affected third parties to oversee the agent's actions than it is for the principal. In such cases the principal can provide third parties with the means and the incentive to gather information and to report it to him. One common example is that of companies who post on the rear of their trucks an 800 number that motorists can call to report reckless driving by the vehicle's operator. Until 1874 the federal government awarded 25 percent of the fines and forfeitures collected to those who informed on fraudulent valuations by customs officers (Studenski and Krooss 1952, p. 170). Today several agencies of the federal government, including the Department of Defense, the Internal Revenue Service, and the Security and Exchange Commission, have taken similar measures by setting up fraud "hotlines" and advertising rewards for whistle-blowers. Although such programs have a number of operational problems, their deterrent effect may be substantial.

Alternatively, principals can set up a fire alarm system by requiring agents to notify third parties of any actions that affect them. According to McCubbins, Noll, and Weingast (1987), this requirement is a key feature of the Administrative Procedures Act of 1946. To comply with this legislation, an administrative agency must announce its intention to consider an issue well in advance of any decision. It must solicit comments and allow all interested parties to communicate their views. The agency must explicitly address any and all evidence presented and provide a rationalizable link between the evidence and its decisions. Such procedures, of course, do not necessarily remove inherent biases in agency decision making. But the mandated sequence of notice, comment, collection of evidence, and deliberation affords numerous opportunities for members of Congress to respond when an agency seeks to move in a direction that a key constituency group finds objectionable. This makes it very difficult for agencies to strategically manipulate congressional decisions by presenting a fait accompli, that is, a new policy with already mobilized supporters.

Institutional Checks

Most applications of the principal/agent framework in economics characterize the principal's problem as one of seeking to induce the agent to expend more effort. The assumption is that the harder they work, the more they produce. But agents are often in a position to do more harm to the principal than to simply withhold effort; embezzlement, insider trading, official corruption, abuse of authority, and coups d'etat are all testaments to this fact. Whenever an agent can take actions that might seriously jeopardize the principal's interests, the principal needs to thwart the agent's ability to pursue such courses of action unilaterally.

We refer to various countermeasures the principal may take in this regard as institutional checks. Operationally, institutional checks require that when authority has been delegated to an agent, there is at least one other agent with the authority to veto or to block the actions of that agent. The framers of the Constitution established many interlocking checks with the intention of constraining the more powerful central government they had created. Most firms also employ systems of checks. Large expenditures, for example, typically require the approval of both management and the comptroller. Some of the most check-laden institutions are universities. Granting tenure usually requires an overwhelmingly favorable vote in the department, the approval of the dean, the acquiescence of a university-wide ad hoc committee, and ratification by the trustees.

As Madison observed, ambition is best checked by ambition—agents positioned against each other should have countervailing interests. This is most readily accomplished by making the agents' compensation contingent on different standards, such as rewarding managers for increasing production but rewarding comptrollers for cutting costs. Checks can also be applied in information acquisition. Rather than striving for an unbiased source of information, a principal may do better obtaining biased reports from different agents who have conflicting incentives. The view that legal proceedings should be adversarial rather than administrative is based on the same logic. Conversely, checks are disabled when agents' incentives cease to be in conflict.

Checks are equivalent to what social choice theorists refer to as the presence of veto subgroups. The major theoretical results concerning the effects of veto subgroups are generally intuitive. First, the more veto subgroups (checks) there are, the harder it is to change the status quo. The status quo also becomes more difficult to change as preferences within veto subgroups become more homogeneous and as preferences between veto subgroups become more diverse. Checks, then, inhibit the ability of agents to take actions that the principal considers undesirable, but necessarily retard agents from taking desirable actions as well; security comes at the price of flexibility. The desirability of imposing checks on delegated authority thus increases with the utility the principal derives from the status quo and with the amount of danger posed by inappropriate agency actions.

REFERENCES

Halberstam, David. 1986. *The Reckoning*. New York, NY: William Morrow and Company.

Hardin, Garrett. 1968. "The Tragedy of the Commons." *Science* 162:1243–48.

McCubbins, Mathew, Roger Noll, and Barry Weingast. 1987. "Administrative Procedures as an Instrument of Political Control." *Journal of Law, Economics, and Organization* 3:243–77.

———, and Thomas Schwartz. 1984. "Congressional Oversight Overlooked: Police Patrols versus Fire Alarms." *American Journal of Political Science* 28:165–79.

Niskanen, William A. 1971. *Bureaucracy and Representative Government*. Chicago, IL: Aldine-Atherton.

Olson, Mancur, 1965. *The Logic of Collective Action*. Cambridge, MA: Harvard University Press.

Spence, A. Michael. 1974. *Market Signalling: Informational Transfer in Hiring and Related Screening Processes*. Cambridge, MA: Harvard University Press.

Studenski, Paul, and Herman Krooss. 1952. *Financial History of the United States*. New York, NY: McGraw-Hill.

Tirole, Jean. 1986. "Hierarchies and Bureaucracies: On the Role of Coercion in Organizations." *Journal of Law, Economics, and Organization* 2:181–214.

2

THE CONSTITUTION
AND THE FOUNDING

2.1

JAMES MADISON

The Federalist, No. 10

In this famous reading first published in 1787, James Madison promotes the view that a large republic will be better than a small republic. He argues that a large republic will have multiple, competing interest groups, none of which will be able to form a majority on its own. A small republic would likely be dominated by powerful interests.

Among the numerous advantages promised by a well constructed Union, none deserves to be more accurately developed than its tendency to break and control the violence of faction. The friend of popular governments never finds himself so much alarmed for their character and fate, as when he contemplates their propensity to this dangerous vice. He will not fail, therefore, to set a due value on any plan which, without violating the principles to which he is attached, provides a proper cure for it. The instability, injustice, and confusion introduced into the public councils, have, in truth, been the mortal diseases under which popular governments have everywhere perished; as they continue to be the favorite and fruitful topics from which the adversaries to liberty derive their most specious declamations. The valuable improvements made by the American constitutions on the popular models, both ancient and modern, cannot certainly be too much admired; but it would be an unwarrantable partiality, to contend that they have as effectually obviated the danger on this side, as was wished and expected. Complaints are everywhere heard from our most considerate and virtuous citizens, equally the friends of public and private faith, and of public and personal liberty, that our governments are too unstable, that the public good is disregarded in the conflicts of rival parties, and that measures are too often decided, not according to the rules of justice and the rights of the minor party, but by the superior force of an interested and overbearing majority. However anxiously we may wish that these complaints had no foundation, the evidence, of known facts will not permit us to deny that they are in some degree true. It will be found, indeed, on a candid review of our situation, that some of the distresses under which we labor have been erroneously charged on the operation of our governments; but it will be found, at the same time, that other causes will not alone account for many of our heaviest misfortunes; and, particularly, for that prevailing and increasing distrust of public engagements, and alarm for private rights, which are echoed from one end of the continent to the other. These must be chiefly, if not wholly, effects of the unsteadiness and injustice with which a factious spirit has tainted our public administrations.

By a faction, I understand a number of citizens, whether amounting to a majority or a minority of the whole, who are united and actuated by some common impulse of passion, or of interest, adversed to the rights of other citizens, or to the permanent and aggregate interests of the community.

There are two methods of curing the mischiefs of faction: the one, by removing its causes; the other, by controlling its effects.

There are again two methods of removing the causes of faction: the one, by destroying the liberty which is essential to its existence; the other, by giving to every citizen the same opinions, the same passions, and the same interests.

It could never be more truly said than of the first remedy, that it was worse than the disease. Liberty is to faction what air is to fire, an aliment without which it instantly expires. But it could not be less folly to abolish liberty, which is essential to political life, because it nourishes faction, than it would be to wish the annihilation of air, which is essential to animal life, because it imparts to fire its destructive agency.

The second expedient is as impracticable as the first would be unwise. As long as the reason of man continues fallible, and he is at liberty to exercise it, different opinions will be formed. As long as the connection subsists between his reason and his self-love, his opinions and his passions will have a reciprocal influence on each other; and the former will be objects to which the latter will attach themselves. The diversity in the faculties of men, from which the rights of property originate, is not less an insuperable obstacle to a uniformity of interests. The protection of these faculties is the first object of government. From the protection of different and unequal faculties of acquiring property, the possession of different degrees and kinds of property immediately results; and from the influence of these on the sentiments and views of the respective proprietors, ensues a division of the society into different interests and parties.

The latent causes of faction are thus sown in the nature of man; and we see them everywhere brought into different degrees of activity, according to the different circumstances of civil society. A zeal for different opinions concerning religion, concerning government, and many other points, as well of speculation as of practice; an attachment to different leaders ambitiously contending for pre-eminence and power; or to persons of other descriptions whose fortunes have been interesting to the human passions, have, in turn, divided mankind into parties, inflamed them with mutual animosity, and rendered them much more disposed to vex and oppress each other than to co-operate for their common good. So strong is this propensity of mankind to fall into mutual animosities, that where no substantial occasion presents itself, the most frivolous and fanciful distinctions have been sufficient to kindle their unfriendly passions and excite their most violent conflicts. But the most common and durable source of factions has been the various and unequal distribution of property. Those who hold and those who are without property have ever formed distinct interests in society. Those who are creditors, and those who are debtors, fall under a like discrimination. A landed interest, a manufacturing interest, a mercantile interest, a moneyed interest, with many lesser interests, grow up of necessity in civilized nations, and divide them into different classes, actuated by different sentiments and views. The regulation of these various and interfering interests forms the principal task of modern legislation, and involves the spirit of party and faction in the necessary and ordinary operations of the government.

No man is allowed to be a judge in his own cause, because his interest would certainly bias his judgment, and, not improbably, corrupt his integrity. With equal, nay with greater reason, a body of men are unfit to be both judges and parties at the same time; yet what are many of the most important acts of legislation, but so many judicial determinations, not indeed concerning the rights of single persons, but concerning the rights of large bodies of citizens? And what are the different classes of legislators but advocates and parties to the causes which they determine? Is a law proposed concerning private debts? It is a question to which the creditors are parties on one side and the debtors on the other. Justice ought to hold the balance between them. Yet the parties are, and must be, themselves the judges; and the most numerous party, or, in other words, the most powerful faction must be expected to prevail. Shall domestic manufactures be encouraged, and in what degree, by restrictions on foreign manufactures? are questions which would be differently decided by the landed and the manufacturing classes, and probably by neither with a sole regard to justice and the public good. The apportionment of taxes on the various descriptions of property is an act which seems to require the most exact impartiality; yet there is, perhaps, no legislative act in which greater opportunity and temptation are given to a predominant party to trample on the rules of justice. Every shilling with which they overburden the inferior number, is a shilling saved to their own pockets.

It is in vain to say that enlightened statesmen will be able to adjust these clashing interests, and render them all subservient to the public good. Enlightened statesmen will not always be at the helm. Nor, in many cases, can such an adjustment be made at all without taking into view indirect and remote considerations, which will rarely prevail over the immediate interest which one party may find in disregarding the rights of another or the good of the whole.

The inference to which we are brought is, that the *causes* of faction cannot be removed, and that relief is only to be sought in the means of controlling its *effects*.

If a faction consists of less than a majority, relief is supplied by the republican principle, which enables the majority to defeat its sinister views by regular vote. It may clog the administration, it may convulse the society; but it will be unable to execute and mask its violence under the forms of the Constitution. When a majority is included in a faction, the form of popular government, on the other hand, enables it to sacrifice to its ruling passion or interest both the public good and the rights of other citizens. To secure the public good and private rights against the danger of such a faction, and at the same time to preserve the spirit and the form of popular government, is then the great object to which our inquiries are directed. Let me add that it is the great desideratum by which this form of government can be rescued from the opprobrium under which it has so long labored, and be recommended to the esteem and adoption of mankind.

By what means is this object attainable? Evidently by one of two only. Either the existence of the same passion or interest in a majority at the same time must be prevented, or the majority, having such coexistent passion or interest, must be rendered, by their number and local situation, unable to concert and carry into effect schemes of oppression. If the impulse and the opportunity be suffered to coincide, we well know that neither moral nor religious motives can be relied on as an adequate control. They are not found to be such on the injustice and violence of individuals, and lose their efficacy in proportion to the number combined together, that is, in proportion as their efficacy becomes needful.

From this view of the subject it may be concluded that a pure democracy, by which I mean a society consisting of a small number of citizens, who assemble and administer the government in person, can admit of no cure for the mischiefs of faction. A common passion or interest will, in almost every case, be felt by a majority of the whole; a communication and concert result from the form of government itself; and there is nothing to check the inducements to sacrifice the weaker party or an obnoxious individual. Hence it is that such democracies have ever been spectacles of turbulence and contention; have ever been found incompatible with personal security or the rights of property; and have in general been as short in their lives as they have been violent in their deaths. Theoretic politicians, who have patronized this species of government, have erroneously supposed that by reducing mankind to a perfect equality in their political rights, they would, at the same time, be perfectly equalized and assimilated in their possessions, their opinions, and their passions.

A republic, by which I mean a government in which the scheme of representation takes place, opens a different prospect, and promises the cure for which we are seeking. Let us examine the points in which it varies from pure democracy, and we shall comprehend both the nature of the cure and the efficacy which it must derive from the Union.

The two great points of difference between a democracy and a republic are: first, the delegation of the government, in the latter, to a small number of citizens elected by the rest; secondly, the greater number of citizens, and greater sphere of country, over which the latter may be extended.

The effect of the first difference is, on the one hand, to refine and enlarge the public views, by passing them through the medium of a chosen body of citizens, whose wisdom may best discern the true interest of their country, and whose patriotism and love of justice will be least likely to sacrifice it to temporary or partial considerations. Under such a regulation, it may well happen that the public voice, pronounced by the representatives of the people, will be more consonant to the public good than if pronounced by the people themselves, convened for the purpose. On the other hand, the effect may be inverted. Men of factious tempers, of local prejudices, or of sinister designs, may, by intrigue, by corruption, or by other means, first obtain the suffrages, and then betray the interests, of the people. The question resulting is, whether small or extensive republics are more favorable to the election of proper guardians of the public weal; and it is clearly decided in favor of the latter by two obvious considerations:

In the first place, it is to be remarked that, however small the republic may be, the representatives must be raised to a certain number, in order to guard against the cabals of a few; and that, however large it may be, they must be limited to a certain number, in order to guard against the confusion of a multitude. Hence, the number of representatives in the two cases not being in proportion to that of the two constituents, and being proportionally greater in the small republic, it follows that, if the proportion of fit characters be not less in the large than in the small republic, the former will present a greater option, and consequently a greater probability of a fit choice.

In the next place, as each representative will be chosen by a greater number of citizens in the large than in the small republic, it will be more difficult for unworthy candidates to practice with success the vicious arts by which elections are too often carried; and the suffrages of the people being more free, will be more likely to centre in men who possess the most attractive merit and the most diffusive and established characters.

It must be confessed that in this, as in most other cases, there is a mean, on both sides of which inconveniences will be found to lie. By enlarging too much the number of electors, you render the representatives too little acquainted with all their local circumstances and lesser interests; as by reducing it too much, you render him unduly attached to these, and too little fit to comprehend and pursue great and national objects. The federal Constitution forms a happy combination in this respect; the great and aggregate interests being referred to the national, the local and particular to the State legislatures.

The other point of difference is, the greater number of citizens and extent of territory which may be brought within the compass of republican than of democratic government; and it is this circumstance principally which renders factious combinations less to be dreaded in the former than in the latter. The smaller the society, the fewer probably will be the distinct parties and interests composing it; the fewer the distinct parties and interests, the more frequently will a majority be found of the same party; and the smaller the number of individuals composing a majority, and the smaller the compass within which they are placed, the more easily will they concert and execute their plans of oppression. Extend the sphere, and you take in a greater variety of parties and interests; you make it less probable that a majority of the whole will have a common motive to invade the rights of other citizens; or if such a common motive exists, it will be more difficult for all who feel it to discover their own strength, and to act in unison with each other. Besides other impediments, it may be remarked that, where there is a consciousness of unjust or dishonorable purposes, communication is always checked by distrust in proportion to the number whose concurrence is necessary.

Hence, it clearly appears, that the same advantage which a republic has over a democracy, in controlling the effects of faction, is enjoyed by a large over a small republic,—is enjoyed by the Union over the States composing it. Does the advantage consist in the substitution of representatives whose enlightened views and virtuous sentiments render them superior to local prejudices and schemes of injustice? It will not be denied that the representation of the Union will be most likely to possess these requisite endowments. Does it consist in the greater security afforded by a greater variety of parties, against the event of any one party being able to outnumber and oppress the rest? In an equal degree does the increased variety of parties comprised within the Union, increase this security. Does it, in fine, consist in the greater obstacles opposed to the concert and accomplishment of the secret wishes of an unjust and interested majority? Here, again, the extent of the Union gives it the most palpable advantage.

The influence of factious leaders may kindle a flame within their particular States, but will be unable to spread a general conflagration through the other States. A religious sect may degenerate into a political faction in a part of the Confederacy; but the variety of sects dispersed over the entire face of it must secure the national councils against any danger from that source. A rage for paper money, for an abolition of debts, for an equal division of property, or for any other improper or wicked project, will be less apt to pervade the whole body of the Union than a particular member of it; in the same proportion as such a malady is more likely to taint a particular county or district, than an entire State.

In the extent and proper structure of the Union, therefore, we behold a republican remedy for the diseases most incident to republican government. And according to the degree of pleasure and pride we feel in being republicans, ought to be our zeal in cherishing the spirit and supporting the character of Federalists.

PUBLIUS

2.2

JAMES MADISON

The Federalist, No. 51

Here, James Madison offers a clear justification for having a form of government that fragments power among different branches and across different levels of government, arguing, "Ambition must be made to counteract ambition." This famous reading lays out the theoretical basis for three core features of the U.S. Constitution: separation of powers, checks and balances, and federalism.

To what expedient, then, shall we finally resort, for maintaining in practice the necessary partition of power among the several departments, as laid down in the Constitution? The only answer that can be given is, that as all these exterior provisions are found to be inadequate, the defect must be supplied, by so contriving the interior structure of the government as that its several constituent parts may, by their mutual relations, be the means of keeping each other in their proper places. Without presuming to undertake a full development of this important idea, I will hazard a few general observations, which may perhaps place it in a clearer light, and enable us to form a more correct judgment of the principles and structure of the government planned by the convention.

In order to lay a due foundation for that separate and distinct exercise of the different powers of government, which to a certain extent is admitted on all hands to be essential to the preservation of liberty, it is evident that each department should have a will of its own; and consequently should be so constituted that the members of each should have as little agency as possible in the appointment of the members of the others. Were this principle rigorously adhered to, it would require that all the appointments for the supreme executive, legislative, and judiciary magistracies should be drawn from the same fountain of authority, the people, through channels having no communication whatever with one another. Perhaps such a plan of constructing the several departments would be less difficult in practice than it may in contemplation appear. Some difficulties, however, and some additional expense would attend the execution of it. Some deviations, therefore, from the principle must be admitted. In the constitution of the judiciary department in particular, it might be inexpedient to insist rigorously on the principle: first, because peculiar qualifications being essential in the members, the primary consideration ought to be to select that mode of choice which best secures these qualifications; secondly, because the permanent tenure by which the appointments are held in that department, must soon destroy all sense of dependence on the authority conferring them.

It is equally evident, that the members of each department should be as little dependent as possible on those of the others, for the emoluments annexed to their offices. Were the executive magistrate, or the judges, not independent of the legislature in this particular, their independence in every other would be merely nominal. But the great security against a gradual concentration of the several powers in the same department, consists in giving to those who administer each department the necessary constitutional means and personal motives to resist encroachments of the others. The provision for defense must in this, as in all other cases, be made commensurate to the danger of attack. Ambition must be made to counteract ambition. The interest of the man must be connected with the constitutional rights of the place. It may be a reflection on human nature, that such devices should be necessary to control the abuses of government. But what is government itself, but the greatest of all reflections on human nature? If men were angels, no government would be necessary. If angels were to govern men, neither external nor internal controls on government would be necessary. In framing a government which is to be administered by men over men, the great difficulty lies in this: you must first enable the government to control the governed; and in the next place oblige it to control itself.

A dependence on the people is, no doubt, the primary control on the government; but experience has taught mankind the necessity of auxiliary precautions. This policy of supplying, by opposite and rival interests, the defect of better motives, might be traced through the whole system of human affairs, private as well as public. We see it particularly displayed in all the subordinate distributions of power, where the constant aim is to divide and arrange the several offices in such a manner as that each may be a check on the other that the private interest of every individual may be a sentinel over the public rights. These inventions of prudence cannot be less requisite in the distribution of the supreme powers of the State. But it is not possible to give to each department an equal power of self-defense. In republican government, the legislative authority necessarily predominates. The remedy for this inconveniency is to divide the legislature into different branches; and to render them, by different modes of election and different principles of action, as little connected with each other as the nature of their common functions and their common dependence on the society will admit. It may even be necessary to guard against dangerous encroachments by still further precautions. As the weight of the legislative authority requires that it should be thus divided, the weakness of the executive may require, on the other hand, that it should be fortified.

An absolute negative on the legislature appears, at first view, to be the natural defense with which the executive magistrate should be armed. But perhaps it would be neither altogether safe nor alone sufficient. On ordinary occasions it might not be exerted with the requisite firmness, and on extraordinary occasions it might be perfidiously abused. May not this defect of an absolute negative be supplied by some qualified connection between this weaker department and the weaker branch of the stronger department, by which the latter may be led to support the constitutional rights of the former, without being too much detached from the rights of its own department? If the principles on which these observations are founded be just, as I persuade myself they are, and they be applied as a criterion to the several State constitutions, and to the federal Constitution it will be found that if the latter does not perfectly correspond with them, the former are infinitely less able to bear such a test.

There are, moreover, two considerations particularly applicable to the federal system of America, which place that system in a very interesting point of view. First. In a single republic, all the power surrendered by the people is submitted to the administration of a single government; and the usurpations are guarded against by a division of the government into distinct and separate departments. In the compound republic of America, the power surrendered by the people is first divided between two distinct governments, and then the portion allotted to each subdivided among distinct and separate departments. Hence a double security arises to the rights of the people. The different governments will control each other, at the same time that each will be controlled by itself. Second. It is of great importance in a republic not only to guard the society against the oppression of its rulers, but to guard one part of the society against the injustice of the other part. Different interests necessarily exist in different classes of citizens. If a majority be united by a common interest, the rights of the minority will be insecure.

There are but two methods of providing against this evil: the one by creating a will in the community independent of the majority that is, of the society itself; the other, by comprehending in the society so many separate descriptions of citizens as will render an unjust combination of a majority of the whole very improbable, if not impracticable. The first method prevails in all governments possessing an hereditary or self-appointed authority. This, at best, is but a precarious security; because a power independent of the society may as well espouse the unjust views of the major, as the rightful interests of the minor party, and may possibly be turned against both parties. The second method will be exemplified in the federal republic of the United States. Whilst all authority in it will be derived from and dependent on the society, the society itself will be broken into so many parts, interests, and classes of citizens, that the rights of individuals, or of the minority, will be in little danger from interested combinations of the majority.

In a free government the security for civil rights must be the same as that for religious rights. It consists in the one case in the multiplicity of interests, and in the other in the multiplicity of sects. The degree of security in both cases will depend on the number of interests and sects; and this may be presumed to depend on the extent of country and number of people comprehended under the same government. This view of the subject must particularly recommend a proper federal system to all the sincere and considerate friends of republican government, since it shows that in exact proportion as the territory of the Union may be formed into more circumscribed Confederacies, or States oppressive combinations of a majority will be facilitated: the best security, under the republican forms, for the rights of every class of citizens, will be diminished: and consequently the stability and independence of some member of the government, the only other security, must be proportionately increased. Justice is the end of government. It is the end of civil society. It ever has been and ever will be pursued until it be obtained, or until liberty be lost in the pursuit. In a society under the forms of which the stronger faction can readily unite and oppress the weaker, anarchy may as truly be said to reign as in a state of nature, where the weaker individual is not secured against the violence of the stronger; and as, in the latter state, even the stronger individuals are prompted, by the uncertainty of their condition, to submit to a government which may protect the weak as well as themselves; so, in the former state, will the more powerful factions or parties be gradually induced, by a like motive, to wish for a government which will protect all parties, the weaker as well as the more powerful.

It can be little doubted that if the State of Rhode Island was separated from the Confederacy and left to itself, the insecurity of rights under the popular form of government within such narrow limits would be displayed by such reiterated oppressions of factious majorities that some power altogether independent of the people would soon be called for by the voice of the very factions whose misrule had proved the necessity of it. In the extended republic of the United States, and among the great variety of interests, parties, and sects which it embraces, a coalition of a majority of the whole society could seldom take place on any other principles than those of justice and the general good; whilst there being thus less danger to a minor from the will of a major party, there must be less pretext, also, to provide for the security of the former, by introducing into the government a will not dependent on the latter, or, in other words, a will independent of the society itself. It is no less certain than it is important, notwithstanding the contrary opinions which have been entertained, that the larger the society, provided it lie within a practical sphere, the more duly capable it will be of self-government. And happily for the REPUBLICAN CAUSE, the practicable sphere may be carried to a very great extent, by a judicious modification and mixture of the FEDERAL PRINCIPLE.

PUBLIUS

2.3

BRUTUS

The Antifederalist, No. 1

Brutus (a pseudonym used by an anonymous Antifederalist author or authors) argues against the Constitution, saying that it will grant too much power to the central, national government. In this essay, Brutus warns that if the national government were granted the powers described in the Constitution, it would eventually come to dominate the states and oppress the people.

To the Citizens of the State of New-York.

When the public is called to investigate and decide upon a question in which not only the present members of the community are deeply interested, but upon which the happiness and misery of generations yet unborn is in great measure suspended, the benevolent mind cannot help feeling itself peculiarly interested in the result.

In this situation, I trust the feeble efforts of an individual, to lead the minds of the people to a wise and prudent determination, cannot fail of being acceptable to the candid and dispassionate part of the community. Encouraged by this consideration, I have been induced to offer my thoughts upon the present important crisis of our public affairs.

Perhaps this country never saw so critical a period in their political concerns. We have felt the feebleness of the ties by which these United-States are held together, and the want of sufficient energy in our present confederation, to manage, in some instances, our general concerns. Various expedients have been proposed to remedy these evils, but none have succeeded. At length a Convention of the states has been assembled, they have formed a constitution which will now, probably, be submitted to the people to ratify or reject, who are the fountain of all power, to whom alone it of right belongs to make or unmake constitutions, or forms of government, at their pleasure. The most important question that was ever proposed to your decision, or to the decision of any people under heaven, is before you, and you are to decide upon it by men of your own election, chosen specially for this purpose. If the constitution, offered to your acceptance, be a wise one, calculated to preserve the invaluable blessings of liberty, to secure the inestimable rights of mankind, and promote human happiness, then, if you accept it, you will lay a lasting foundation of happiness for millions yet unborn; generations to come will rise up and call you blessed. You may rejoice in the prospects of this vast extended continent becoming filled with freemen, who will assert the dignity of human nature. You may solace yourselves with the idea, that society, in this favoured land, will fast advance to the highest point of perfection; the human mind will expand in knowledge and virtue, and the golden age be, in some measure, realised. But if, on the other hand, this form of government contains principles that will lead to the subversion of liberty—if it tends to establish a despotism, or, what is worse, a tyrannic aristocracy; then, if you adopt it, this only remaining assylum for liberty will be shut up, and posterity will execrate your memory.

Momentous then is the question you have to determine, and you are called upon by every motive which should influence a noble and virtuous mind, to examine it well, and to make up a wise judgment. It is insisted, indeed, that this constitution must be received, be it ever so imperfect. If it has its defects, it is said, they can be best amended when they are experienced. But remember, when the people once part with power, they can seldom or never resume it again but by force. Many instances can be produced in which the people have voluntarily increased the powers of their rulers; but few, if any, in which rulers have willingly abridged their authority. This is a sufficient reason to induce you to be careful, in the first instance, how you deposit the powers of government.

With these few introductory remarks, I shall proceed to a consideration of this constitution:

The first question that presents itself on the subject is, whether a confederated government be the best for the United States or not? Or in other words, whether the thirteen United States should be reduced to one great republic, governed by one legislature, and under the direction of one executive and judicial; or whether they should continue thirteen confederated republics, under the direction and controul of a supreme federal head for certain defined national purposes only?

This enquiry is important, because, although the government reported by the convention does not go to a perfect and entire consolidation, yet it approaches so near to it, that it must, if executed, certainly and infallibly terminate in it.

This government is to possess absolute and uncontroulable power, legislative, executive and judicial, with respect to every object to which it extends, for by the last clause of section 8th, article 1st, it is declared "that the Congress shall have power to make all laws which shall be necessary and proper for carrying into execution the foregoing powers, and all other powers vested by this constitution, in the government of the United States; or in any department or office thereof." And by the 6th article, it is declared "that this constitution, and the laws of the United States, which shall be made in pursuance thereof, and the treaties made, or which shall be made, under the authority of the United States, shall be the supreme law of the land; and the judges in every state shall be bound thereby, any thing in the constitution, or law of any state to the contrary notwithstanding." It appears from these articles that there is no need of any intervention of the state governments, between the Congress and the people, to execute any one power vested in the general government, and that the constitution and laws of every state are nullified and declared void, so far as they are or shall be inconsistent with this constitution, or the laws made in pursuance of it, or with treaties made under the authority of the United States.—The government then, so far as it extends, is a complete one, and not a confederation. It is as much one complete government as that of New-York or Massachusetts, has as absolute and perfect powers to make and execute all laws, to appoint officers, institute courts, declare offences, and annex penalties, with respect to every object to which it extends, as any other in the world. So far therefore as its powers reach, all ideas of confederation are given up and lost. It is true this government is limited to certain objects, or to speak more properly, some small degree of power is still left to the states, but a little attention to the powers vested in the general government, will convince every candid man, that if it is capable of being executed, all that is reserved for the individual states must very soon be annihilated, except so far as they are barely necessary to the organization of the general government. The powers of the general legislature extend to every case that is of the least importance—there is nothing valuable to human nature, nothing dear to freemen, but what is within its power. It has authority to make laws which will affect the lives, the liberty, and property of every man in the United States; nor can the constitution or laws of any state, in any way prevent or impede the full and complete execution of every power given. The legislative power is competent to lay taxes, duties, imposts, and excises;—there is no limitation to this power, unless it be said that the clause which directs the use to which those taxes, and duties shall be applied, may be said to be a limitation: but this is no restriction of the power at all, for by this clause they are to be applied to pay the debts and provide for the common defence and general welfare of the United States; but the legislature have authority to contract debts at their discretion; they are the sole judges of what is necessary to provide for the common defence, and they only are to determine what is for the general welfare; this power therefore is neither more nor less, than a power to lay and collect taxes, imposts, and excises, at their pleasure; not only [is] the power to lay taxes unlimited, as to the amount they may require, but it is perfect and absolute to raise them in any mode they please. No state legislature, or any power in the state governments, have any more to do in carrying this into effect, than the authority of one state has to do with that of another. In the business therefore of laying and collecting taxes, the idea of confederation is totally lost, and that of one entire republic is embraced. It is proper here to remark, that the authority to lay and collect taxes is the most important of any power that can be granted; it connects with it almost all other powers, or at least will in process of time draw all other after it; it is the great mean of protection, security, and defence, in a good government, and the great engine of oppression and tyranny in a bad one. This cannot fail of being the case, if we consider the

contracted limits which are set by this constitution, to the late [state?] governments, on this article of raising money. No state can emit paper money—lay
any duties, or imposts, on imports, or exports, but by consent of the Congress;
and then the net produce shall be for the benefit of the United States: the only
mean therefore left, for any state to support its government and discharge its
debts, is by direct taxation; and the United States have also power to lay and
collect taxes, in any way they please. Every one who has thought on the subject, must be convinced that but small sums of money can be collected in any
country, by direct taxe[s], when the foederal government begins to exercise the
right of taxation in all its parts, the legislatures of the several states will find it
impossible to raise monies to support their governments. Without money they
cannot be supported, and they must dwindle away, and, as before observed,
their powers absorbed in that of the general government.

It might be here shewn, that the power in the federal legislative, to raise
and support armies at pleasure, as well in peace as in war, and their controul
over the militia, tend, not only to a consolidation of the government, but the
destruction of liberty.—I shall not, however, dwell upon these, as a few observations upon the judicial power of this government, in addition to the preceding, will fully evince the truth of the position.

The judicial power of the United States is to be vested in a supreme court,
and in such inferior courts as Congress may from time to time ordain and
establish. The powers of these courts are very extensive; their jurisdiction
comprehends all civil causes, except such as arise between citizens of the
same state; and it extends to all cases in law and equity arising under the constitution. One inferior court must be established, I presume, in each state, at
least, with the necessary executive officers appendant thereto. It is easy to see,
that in the common course of things, these courts will eclipse the dignity, and
take away from the respectability, of the state courts. These courts will be, in
themselves, totally independent of the states, deriving their authority from the
United States, and receiving from them fixed salaries; and in the course of
human events it is to be expected, that they will swallow up all the powers of
the courts in the respective states.

How far the clause in the 8th section of the 1st article may operate to do
away all idea of confederated states, and to effect an entire consolidation of
the whole into one general government, it is impossible to say. The powers
given by this article are very general and comprehensive, and it may receive
a construction to justify the passing almost any law. A power to make all laws,
which shall be *necessary and proper*, for carrying into execution, all powers
vested by the constitution in the government of the United States, or any
department or officer thereof, is a power very comprehensive and definite
[indefinite?], and may, for ought I know, be exercised in a such manner as
entirely to abolish the state legislatures. Suppose the legislature of a state
should pass a law to raise money to support their government and pay the state
debt, may the Congress repeal this law, because it may prevent the collection

of a tax which they may think proper and necessary to lay, to provide for the general welfare of the United States? For all laws made, in pursuance of this constitution, are the supreme lay of the land, and the judges in every state shall be bound thereby, any thing in the constitution or laws of the different states to the contrary notwithstanding.—By such a law, the government of a particular state might be overturned at one stroke, and thereby be deprived of every means of its support.

It is not meant, by stating this case, to insinuate that the constitution would warrant a law of this kind; or unnecessarily to alarm the fears of the people, by suggesting, that the federal legislature would be more likely to pass the limits assigned them by the constitution, than that of an individual state, further than they are less responsible to the people. But what is meant is, that the legislature of the United States are vested with the great and uncontroulable powers, of laying and collecting taxes, duties, imposts, and excises; of regulating trade, raising and supporting armies, organizing, arming, and disciplining the militia, instituting courts, and other general powers. And are by this clause invested with the power of making all laws, *proper and necessary*, for carrying all these into execution; and they may so exercise this power as entirely to annihilate all the state governments, and reduce this country to one single government. And if they may do it, it is pretty certain they will; for it will be found that the power retained by individual states, small as it is, will be a clog upon the wheels of the government of the United States; the latter therefore will be naturally inclined to remove it out of the way. Besides, it is a truth confirmed by the unerring experience of ages, that every man, and every body of men, invested with power, are ever disposed to increase it, and to acquire a superiority over every thing that stands in their way. This disposition, which is implanted in human nature, will operate in the federal legislature to lessen and ultimately to subvert the state authority, and having such advantages, will most certainly succeed, if the federal government succeeds at all. It must be very evident then, that what this constitution wants of being a complete consolidation of the several parts of the union into one complete government, possessed of perfect legislative, judicial, and executive powers, to all intents and purposes, it will necessarily acquire in its exercise and operation.

Let us now proceed to enquire, as I at first proposed, whether it be best the thirteen United States should be reduced to one great republic, or not? It is here taken for granted, that all agree in this, that whatever government we adopt, it ought to be a free one; that it should be so framed as to secure the liberty of the citizens of America, and such an one as to admit of a full, fair, and equal representation of the people. The question then will be, whether a government thus constituted, and founded on such principles, is practicable, and can be exercised over the whole United States, reduced into one state?

If respect is to be paid to the opinion of the greatest and wisest men who have ever thought or wrote on the science of government, we shall be constrained to conclude, that a free republic cannot succeed over a country of such immense extent, containing such a number of inhabitants, and these encreasing in such rapid progression as that of the whole United States. Among the many illustrious authorities which might be produced to this point, I shall content myself with quoting only two. The one is the baron de Montesquieu, spirit of laws, chap. xvi. vol. I [book VIII]. "It is natural to a republic to have only a small territory, otherwise it cannot long subsist. In a large republic there are men of large fortunes, and consequently of less moderation; there are trusts too great to be placed in any single subject; he has interest of his own; he soon begins to think that he may be happy, great and glorious, by oppressing his fellow citizens; and that he may raise himself to grandeur on the ruins of his country. In a large republic, the public good is sacrificed to a thousand views; it is subordinate to exceptions, and depends on accidents. In a small one, the interest of the public is easier perceived, better understood, and more within the reach of every citizen; abuses are of less extent, and of course are less protected." Of the same opinion is the marquis Beccarari.

History furnishes no example of a free republic, any thing like the extent of the United States. The Grecian republics were of small extent; so also was that of the Romans. Both of these, it is true, in process of time, extended their conquests over large territories of country; and the consequence was, that their governments were changed from that of free governments to those of the most tyrannical that ever existed in the world.

Not only the opinion of the greatest men, and the experience of mankind, are against the idea of an extensive republic, but a variety of reasons may be drawn from the reason and nature of things, against it. In every government, the will of the sovereign is the law. In despotic governments, the supreme authority being lodged in one, his will is law, and can be as easily expressed to a large extensive territory as to a small one. In a pure democracy the people are the sovereign, and their will is declared by themselves; for this purpose they must all come together to deliberate, and decide. This kind of government cannot be exercised, therefore, over a country of any considerable extent; it must be confined to a single city, or at least limited to such bounds as that the people can conveniently assemble, be able to debate, understand the subject submitted to them, and declare their opinion concerning it.

In a free republic, although all laws are derived from the consent of the people, yet the people do not declare their consent by themselves in person, but by representatives, chosen by them, who are supposed to know the minds of their constituents, and to be possessed of integrity to declare this mind.

In every free government, the people must give their assent to the laws by which they are governed. This is the true criterion between a free government and an arbitrary one. The former are ruled by the will of the whole, expressed in any manner they may agree upon; the latter by the will of one, or a few. If the people are to give their assent to the laws, by persons chosen and appointed by them, the manner of the choice and the number chosen, must be such, as to possess, be disposed, and consequently qualified to declare the sentiments of the people; for if they do not know, or are not disposed to speak the sentiments of the people, the people do not govern, but the sovereignty is in a few. Now, in a large extended country, it is impossible to have a representation, possessing the sentiments, and of integrity, to declare the minds of the people, without having it so numerous and unwieldly, as to be subject in great measure to the inconveniency of a democratic government.

The territory of the United States is of vast extent; it now contains near three millions of souls, and is capable of containing much more than ten times that number. Is it practicable for a country, so large and so numerous as they will soon become, to elect a representation, that will speak their sentiments, without their becoming so numerous as to be incapable of transacting public business? It certainly is not.

In a republic, the manners, sentiments, and interests of the people should be similar. If this be not the case, there will be a constant clashing of opinions; and the representatives of one part will be continually striving against those of the other. This will retard the operations of government, and prevent such conclusions as will promote the public good. If we apply this remark to the condition of the United States, we shall be convinced that it forbids that we should be one government. The United States includes a variety of climates. The productions of the different parts of the union are very variant, and their interests, of consequence, diverse. Their manners and habits differ as much as their climates and productions; and their sentiments are by no means coincident. The laws and customs of the several states are, in many respects, very diverse, and in some opposite; each would be in favor of its own interests and customs, and, of consequence, a legislature, formed of representatives from the respective parts, would not only be too numerous to act with any care or decision, but would be composed of such heterogenous and discordant principles, as would constantly be contending with each other.

The laws cannot be executed in a republic, of an extent equal to that of the United States, with promptitude.

The magistrates in every government must be supported in the execution of the laws, either by an armed force, maintained at the public expence for that purpose; or by the people turning out to aid the magistrate upon his command, in case of resistance.

In despotic governments, as well as in all the monarchies of Europe, standing armies are kept up to execute the commands of the prince or the magistrate, and are employed for this purpose when occasion requires: But they have always proved the destruction of liberty, and [are] abhorrent to the spirit of a free republic. In England, where they depend upon the parliament for their annual support, they have always been complained of as oppressive and unconstitutional, and are seldom employed in executing of the laws; never except on extraordinary occasions, and then under the direction of a civil magistrate.

A free republic will never keep a standing army to execute its laws. It must depend upon the support of its citizens. But when a government is to receive its support from the aid of the citizens, it must be so constructed as to have the confidence, respect, and affection of the people." Men who, upon the call of the magistrate, offer themselves to execute the laws, are influenced to do it either by affection to the government, or from fear; where a standing army is at hand to punish offenders, every man is actuated by the latter principle, and therefore, when the magistrate calls, will obey: but, where this is not the case, the government must rest for its support upon the confidence and respect which the people have for their government and laws. The body of the people being attached, the government will always be sufficient to support and execute its laws, and to operate upon the fears of any faction which may be opposed to it, not only to prevent an opposition to the execution of the laws themselves, but also to compel the most of them to aid the magistrate; but the people will not be likely to have such confidence in their rulers, in a republic so extensive as the United States, as necessary for these purposes. The confidence which the people have in their rulers, in a free republic, arises from their knowing them, from their being responsible to them for their conduct, and from the power they have of displacing them when they misbehave: but in a republic of the extent of this continent, the people in general would be acquainted with very few of their rulers: the people at large would know little of their proceedings, and it would be extremely difficult to change them. The people in Georgia and New-Hampshire would not know one another's mind, and therefore could not act in concert to enable them to effect a general change of representatives. The different parts of so extensive a country could not possibly be made acquainted with the conduct of their representatives, nor be informed of the reasons upon which measures were founded. The consequence will be, they will have no confidence in their legislature, suspect them of ambitious views, be jealous of every measure they adopt, and will not support the laws they pass. Hence the government will be nerveless and inefficient, and no way will be left to render it otherwise, but by establishing an armed force to execute the laws at the point of the bayonet—a government of all others the most to be dreaded.

In a republic of such vast extent as the United-States, the legislature cannot attend to the various concerns and wants of its different parts. It cannot be sufficiently numerous to be acquainted with the local condition and wants of the different districts, and if it could, it is impossible it should have sufficient time to attend to and provide for all the variety of cases of this nature, that would be continually arising.

In so extensive a republic, the great officers of government would soon become above the controul of the people, and abuse their power to the purpose of aggrandizing themselves, and oppressing them. The trust committed to the executive offices, in a country of the extent of the United-States, must be various and of magnitude. The command of all the troops and navy of the republic, the appointment of officers, the power of pardoning offences, the collecting of all the public revenues, and the power of expending them, with a number of other powers, must be lodged and exercised in every state, in the hands of a few. When these are attended with great honor and emolument, as they always will be in large states, so as greatly to interest men to pursue them, and to be proper objects for ambitious and designing men, such men will be ever restless in their pursuit after them. They will use the power, when they have acquired it, to the purposes of gratifying their own interest and ambition, and it is scarcely possible, in a very large republic, to call them to account for their misconduct, or to prevent their abuse of power.

These are some of the reasons by which it appears, that a free republic cannot long subsist over a country of the great extent of these states. If then this new constitution is calculated to consolidate the thirteen states into one, as it evidently is, it ought not to be adopted.

Though I am of opinion, that it is a sufficient objection to this government, to reject it, that it creates the whole union into one government, under the form of a republic, yet if this objection was obviated, there are exceptions to it, which are so material and fundamental, that they ought to determine every man, who is a friend to the liberty and happiness of mankind, not to adopt it. I beg the candid and dispassionate attention of my countrymen while I state these objections—they are such as have obtruded themselves upon my mind upon a careful attention to the matter, and such as I sincerely believe are well founded. There are many objections, of small moment, of which I shall take no notice—perfection is not to be expected in any thing that is the production of man—and if I did not in my conscience believe that this scheme was defective in the fundamental principles—in the foundation upon which a free and equal government must rest—I would hold my peace.

2.4

ROBERT A. DAHL

From *How Democratic Is the American Constitution?*

Dahl casts a critical eye on the American Constitution. He lists numerous problems with the document. Most important, it implicitly sanctioned slavery and set up two undemocratic institutions: the Supreme Court and the Senate. He concludes that it survived by allowing for mass elections to determine who controlled the national government, and thus was "democratic" enough to overcome its weaknesses.

UNDEMOCRATIC ELEMENTS IN THE FRAMERS' CONSTITUTION

. . . Judged from later, more democratic perspectives, the Constitution of the Framers contained at least seven important shortcomings.

Slavery. First, it neither forbade slavery nor empowered Congress to do so. In fact, the compromise on slavery not only denied Congress the effective power to prohibit the importation of slaves before 1808[1] but it gave constitutional sanction to one of the most morally objectionable byproducts of a morally repulsive institution: the Fugitive Slave laws, according to which a slave who managed to escape to a free state had to be returned to the slaveholder, whose property the slave remained.[2] That it took three-quarters of a century and a sanguinary civil war before slavery was abolished should at the least make us doubt whether the document of the Framers ought to be regarded as holy writ.

Suffrage. Second, the constitution failed to guarantee the right of suffrage, leaving the qualifications of suffrage to the states.[3] It implicitly left in place the exclusion of half the population—women—as well as African Americans and Native Americans.[4] As we know, it took a century and a half before women were constitutionally guaranteed the right to vote, and nearly two centuries before a president and Congress could overcome the effective veto of a minority of states in order to pass legislation intended to guarantee the voting rights of African Americans.

Election of the president. Third, the executive power was vested in a president whose selection, according to the intentions and design of the Framers, was to be insulated from both popular majorities and congressional control. As we'll see, the Framers' main design for achieving that purpose—a body of presidential electors composed of men of exceptional wisdom and virtue who would choose the chief executive unswayed by popular opinion—was almost immediately cast into the dustbin of history by leaders sympathetic with the growing democratic impulses of the American people, among them James Madison himself. Probably nothing the Framers did illustrates more sharply their inability to foresee the shape that politics would assume in a democratic republic. . . .

Choosing senators. Fourth, senators were to be chosen not by the people but by the state legislatures, for a term of six years.[5] Although this arrangement fell short of the ambitions of delegates like Gouverneur Morris who wanted to construct an aristocratic upper house, it would help to ensure that senators would be less responsive to popular majorities and perhaps more sensitive to the needs of property holders. Members of the Senate would thus serve as a check on the Representatives, who were all subject to popular elections every two years.[6]

Equal representation in the Senate. The attempt to create a Senate that would be a republican version of the aristocratic House of Lords was derailed, as we have seen, by a prolonged and bitter dispute over an entirely different question: Should the states be equally represented in Congress or should members of both houses be allocated according to population? This question not only gave rise to one of the most disruptive issues of the Convention, but it resulted in a fifth undemocratic feature of the constitution. As a consequence of the famous—or from a democratic point of view, infamous—"Connecticut Compromise" each state was, as we have seen, awarded the same number of senators, without respect to population. Although this arrangement failed to protect the fundamental rights and interests of the most deprived minorities, some strategically placed and highly privileged minorities—slaveholders, for example—gained disproportionate power over government polices at the expense of less privileged minorities. . . .

Judicial power. Sixth, the constitution of the Framers failed to limit the powers of the judiciary to declare as unconstitutional laws that had been properly passed by Congress and signed by the president. What the delegates intended in the way of judicial review will remain forever unclear; probably many delegates were unclear in their own minds, and to the extent that they discussed the question at all, they were not in full agreement. But probably a majority accepted the view that the federal courts should rule on the constitutionality of state and federal laws in cases brought before them. Nevertheless, it is likely that a substantial majority intended that federal judges should not participate in making government laws and policies, a responsibility that clearly belonged not to the judiciary but to the legislative branch. Their opposition to any policy-making role for the judiciary is strongly indicated by their response to a proposal in the Virginia Plan that "the Executive and a convenient number of the National Judiciary, ought to compose a council of revision" empowered to veto acts of the National Legislature. Though this provision was vigorously defended by Madison and Mason, it was voted down, 6 states to 3.[7]

A judicial veto is one thing; judicial legislation is quite another. Whatever some of the delegates may have thought about the advisability of justices sharing with the executive the authority to veto laws passed by Congress, I am fairly certain that none would have given the slightest support to a proposal that judges should themselves have the power to legislate, to make national policy. However, the upshot of their work was that in the guise of reviewing the constitutionality of state and congressional actions or inactions, the federal judiciary would later engage in what in some instances could only be called judicial policy-making—or, if you like, judicial legislation.[8]

Congressional power. Finally, the powers of Congress were limited in ways that could, and at times did, prevent the federal government from regulating or controlling the economy by means that all modern democratic governments have adopted. Without the power to tax incomes, for example, fiscal policy, not to say measures like Social Security, would be impossible. And regulatory actions—over railroad rates, air safety, food and drugs, banking, minimum wages, and many other policies—had no clear constitutional authorization. Although it would be anachronistic to charge the Framers with lack of foresight in these matters,[9] unless the constitution could be altered by amendment or by heroic reinterpretation of its provisions—presumably by what I have just called judicial legislation—it would prevent representatives of later majorities from adopting the policies they believed were necessary to achieve efficiency, fairness, and security in a complex post-agrarian society.

Enlightened as the Framers' constitution may have been by the standards of the eighteenth century, future generations with more democratic aspirations would find some of its undemocratic features objectionable— and even unacceptable. The public expression of these growing democratic aspirations was not long in coming.

Even Madison did not, and probably could not, predict the peaceful democratic revolution that was about to begin. For the American revolution was soon to enter into a new and unforeseen phase.

THE FRAMERS' CONSTITUTION MEETS EMERGENT DEMOCRATIC BELIEFS

We may tend to think of the American republic and its constitution as solely the product of leaders inspired by extraordinary wisdom and virtue. Yet without a citizenry committed to republican principles of government and capable of governing themselves in accordance with those principles, the constitution would soon have been little more than a piece of paper. As historical experience would reveal, in countries where democratic beliefs were fragile or absent, constitutions did indeed become little more than pieces of paper— soon violated, soon forgotten.

The American democratic republic was not created nor could it have been long maintained by leaders alone, gifted as they may have been. It was they, to be sure, who designed a framework suitable, as they thought, for a republic. But it was the American people, and the leaders responsive to them, who ensured that the new republic would rapidly become a *democratic* republic.

▪   ▪   ▪

I have little doubt that if the American Constitutional Convention had been held in 1820, a very different constitution would have emerged from the deliberations—although, I hasten to add, we can never know what shape that constitution might have taken. We can be reasonably sure, however, that the delegates would have attempted to provide more support for, and fewer barriers to, a democratic republic.

As to the undemocratic features of the constitution created in 1787, let me suggest four conclusions.

First, the aspects of the constitution that are most defective from a democratic point of view do not necessarily all reflect the intentions of the Framers, insofar as we may surmise them. Though the flaws are traceable to their handiwork, they are in some cases flaws resulting from the inability of these superbly talented craftsmen to foresee how their carefully crafted instrument of government would work under the changing conditions that were to follow—and most of all, under the impact of the democratic revolution in which Americans were, and I hope still are, engaged.

Second, some of the undemocratic aspects of the original design also resulted from the logrolling and compromises that were necessary to achieve agreement. The Framers were not philosophers searching for a description of an ideal system. Nor—and we may be forever grateful to them for this—were they philosopher kings entrusted with the power to rule. They were practical men, eager to achieve a stronger national government, and as practical men they made compromises. Would the country have been better off if they had refused to do so? I doubt it. But in any case, they did compromise, and even today the constitution bears the results of some of their concessions. I'll have more to say on that point in my next chapter.

Third, undemocratic aspects that were more or less deliberately built into the constitution overestimated the dangers of popular majorities—American popular majorities, at any rate—and underestimated the strength of the developing democratic commitment among Americans. As a result, in order to adapt the original framework more closely to the requirements of the emerging democratic republic, with the passage of time some of these aspects of the original constitution were changed, sometimes by amendment, sometimes, as with political parties, by new institutions and practices.

Finally, though the defects seem to me serious and may grow even more serious with time, Americans are not much predisposed to consider another constitution, nor is it clear what alternative arrangements would serve them better.

As a result, the beliefs of Americans in the legitimacy of their constitution will remain, I think, in constant tension with their beliefs in the legitimacy of democracy.

For my part, I believe that the legitimacy of the constitution ought to derive solely from its utility as an instrument of democratic government—nothing more, nothing less.

NOTES

1. Article I, Section 9. For an excellent account of the only full public debate over the slavery issue, see Joseph J. Ellis, *Founding Brothers: The Revolutionary Generation* (New York: Alfred A. Knopf, 2000), 81–119. The debate took place in the House of Representatives in March 1790 in response to petitions from Quakers in New York and Philadelphia "calling for the federal government to put an immediate end to the African slave trade." (81).

2. Article IV, Section 2.

3. Article I, Sections 2, 3.

4. For a magisterial study of the evolution of American citizenship, see Rogers Smith, *Civic Ideals: Conflicting Visions of Citizenship in U.S. History* (New Haven: Yale University Press, 1997). On the constitution's omission of citizenship for women, Native Americans, and African Americans, see 130–34.

5. Article I, Section 3.

6. By the same electorate as that for "the most numerous branch of the state legislature," (Article I, Section 2).

7. *Records*, 2: 83.

8. For evidence that the Supreme Court sometimes plays such a role, see my "Decision-Making in a Democracy: The Supreme Court as a National Policy-Maker," *Journal of Public Law 6*, no. 2, 279–95.

9. It is only fair to point out that given the political opposition to any increase in federal powers, the Framers may well have gone as far as they could go. Their major opponents, the Anti-Federalists, who saw the constitution as a threat to popular government at the state level, objected that the powers of Congress to regulate interstate commerce were excessive. Richard L. Perry, ed., *The Sources of Our Liberties: Documentary Origins of Individual Liberties in the United States Constitution and Bill of Rights* (New York: American Bar Association, 1959), 240.

3

FEDERALISM

3.1

JAMES MADISON

The Federalist, No. 39

James Madison portrays the American government as having a dual nature. He uses the terminology of national versus federal to describe the underlying tensions in the constitutional design. Some institutional features (national) represent the entire people, while others (federal) represent the states.

The last paper having concluded the observations which were meant to introduce a candid survey of the plan of government reported by the convention, we now proceed to the execution of that part of our undertaking.

The first question that offers itself is, whether the general form and aspect of the government be strictly republican. It is evident that no other form would be reconcilable with the genius of the people of America; with the fundamental principles of the Revolution; or with that honorable determination which animates every votary of freedom, to rest all our political experiments on the capacity of mankind for self-government. If the plan of the convention, therefore, be found to depart from the republican character, its advocates must abandon it as no longer defensible.

What, then, are the distinctive characters of the republican form? Were an answer to this question to be sought, not by recurring to principles, but in the application of the term by political writers, to the constitution of different States, no satisfactory one would ever be found. Holland, in which no particle of the supreme authority is derived from the people, has passed almost universally under the denomination of a republic. The same title has been bestowed on Venice, where absolute power over the great body of the people is exercised, in the most absolute manner, by a small body of hereditary nobles. Poland, which is a mixture of aristocracy and of monarchy in their worst forms, has been dignified with the same appellation. The government of England, which has one republican branch only, combined with an hereditary aristocracy and monarchy, has, with equal impropriety, been frequently placed on the list of republics. These examples, which are nearly as dissimilar to each other as to a genuine republic, show the extreme inaccuracy with which the term has been used in political disquisitions.

If we resort for a criterion to the different principles on which different forms of government are established, we may define a republic to be, or at least may bestow that name on, a government which derives all its powers directly or indirectly from the great body of the people, and is administered by persons holding their offices during pleasure, for a limited period, or during good behavior. It is ESSENTIAL to such a government that it be derived from the great body of the society, not from an inconsiderable proportion, or a favored class of it; otherwise a handful of tyrannical nobles, exercising their oppressions by a delegation of their powers, might aspire to the rank of republicans, and claim for their government the honorable title of republic. It is SUFFI-CIENT for such a government that the persons administering it be appointed, either directly or indirectly, by the people; and that they hold their appointments by either of the tenures just specified; otherwise every government in the United States, as well as every other popular government that has been or can be well organized or well executed, would be degraded from the republican character. According to the constitution of every State in the Union, some or other of the officers of government are appointed indirectly only by the people. According to most of them, the chief magistrate himself is so appointed. And according to one, this mode of appointment is extended to one of the co-ordinate branches of the legislature. According to all the constitutions, also, the tenure of the highest offices is extended to a definite period, and in many instances, both within the legislative and executive departments, to a period of years. According to the provisions of most of the constitutions, again, as well as according to the most respectable and received opinions on the subject, the members of the judiciary department are to retain their offices by the firm tenure of good behavior.

On comparing the Constitution planned by the convention with the standard here fixed, we perceive at once that it is, in the most rigid sense, conformable to it. The House of Representatives, like that of one branch at least of all the State legislatures, is elected immediately by the great body of the people. The Senate, like the present Congress, and the Senate of Maryland, derives its appointment indirectly from the people. The President is indirectly derived from the choice of the people, according to the example in most of the States. Even the judges, with all other officers of the Union, will, as in the several States, be the choice, though a remote choice, of the people themselves, the duration of the appointments is equally conformable to the republican standard, and to the model of

State constitutions The House of Representatives is periodically elective, as in all the States; and for the period of two years, as in the State of South Carolina. The Senate is elective, for the period of six years; which is but one year more than the period of the Senate of Maryland, and but two more than that of the Senates of New York and Virginia. The President is to continue in office for the period of four years; as in New York and Delaware, the chief magistrate is elected for three years, and in South Carolina for two years. In the other States the election is annual. In several of the States, however, no constitutional provision is made for the impeachment of the chief magistrate. And in Delaware and Virginia he is not impeachable till out of office. The President of the United States is impeachable at any time during his continuance in office. The tenure by which the judges are to hold their places, is, as it unquestionably ought to be, that of good behavior. The tenure of the ministerial offices generally, will be a subject of legal regulation, conformably to the reason of the case and the example of the State constitutions.

Could any further proof be required of the republican complexion of this system, the most decisive one might be found in its absolute prohibition of titles of nobility, both under the federal and the State governments; and in its express guaranty of the republican form to each of the latter.

"But it was not sufficient," say the adversaries of the proposed Constitution, "for the convention to adhere to the republican form. They ought, with equal care, to have preserved the FEDERAL form, which regards the Union as a CONFEDERACY of sovereign states; instead of which, they have framed a NATIONAL government, which regards the Union as a CONSOLIDATION of the States." And it is asked by what authority this bold and radical innovation was undertaken? The handle which has been made of this objection requires that it should be examined with some precision.

Without inquiring into the accuracy of the distinction on which the objection is founded, it will be necessary to a just estimate of its force, first, to ascertain the real character of the government in question; secondly, to inquire how far the convention were authorized to propose such a government; and thirdly, how far the duty they owed to their country could supply any defect of regular authority.

First. In order to ascertain the real character of the government, it may be considered in relation to the foundation on which it is to be established; to the sources from which its ordinary powers are to be drawn; to the operation of those powers; to the extent of them; and to the authority by which future changes in the government are to be introduced.

On examining the first relation, it appears, on one hand, that the Constitution is to be founded on the assent and ratification of the people of America, given by deputies elected for the special purpose; but, on the other, that this assent and ratification is to be given by the people, not as individuals composing one entire nation, but as composing the distinct and independent States to which they respectively belong. It is to be the assent and ratification of the several States, derived from the supreme authority in each State, the authority of the people themselves. The act, therefore, establishing the Constitution, will not be a NATIONAL, but a FEDERAL act.

That it will be a federal and not a national act, as these terms are understood by the objectors; the act of the people, as forming so many independent States, not as forming one aggregate nation, is obvious from this single consideration, that it is to result neither from the decision of a MAJORITY of the people of the Union, nor from that of a MAJORITY of the States. It must result from the UNANIMOUS assent of the several States that are parties to it, differing no otherwise from their ordinary assent than in its being expressed, not by the legislative authority, but by that of the people themselves. Were the people regarded in this transaction as forming one nation, the will of the majority of the whole people of the United States would bind the minority, in the same manner as the majority in each State must bind the minority; and the will of the majority must be determined either by a comparison of the individual votes, or by considering the will of the majority of the States as evidence of the will of a majority of the people of the United States. Neither of these rules have been adopted. Each State, in ratifying the Constitution, is considered as a sovereign body, independent of all others, and only to be bound by its own voluntary act. In this relation, then, the new Constitution will, if established, be a FEDERAL, and not a NATIONAL constitution.

The next relation is, to the sources from which the ordinary powers of government are to be derived. The House of Representatives will derive its powers from the people of America; and the people will be represented in the same proportion, and on the same principle, as they are in the legislature of a particular State. So far the government is NATIONAL, not FEDERAL. The Senate, on the other hand, will derive its powers from the States, as political and coequal societies; and these will be represented on the principle of equality in the Senate, as they now are in the existing Congress. So far the government is FEDERAL, not NATIONAL. The executive power will be derived from a very compound source. The immediate election of the President is to be made by the States in their political characters. The votes allotted to them are in a compound ratio, which considers them partly as distinct and coequal societies, partly as unequal members of the same society. The eventual election, again, is to be made by that branch of the legislature which consists of the national representatives; but in this particular act they are to be thrown into the form of individual delegations, from so many distinct and coequal bodies politic. From this aspect of the government it appears to be of a mixed character, presenting at least as many FEDERAL as NATIONAL features.

The difference between a federal and national government, as it relates to the OPERATION OF THE GOVERNMENT, is supposed to consist in this, that in the former the powers operate on the political bodies composing the Confederacy, in their political capacities; in the latter, on the individual citizens composing the nation, in their individual capacities. On trying the Constitution by this criterion, it falls under the NATIONAL, not the FEDERAL character; though perhaps not so completely as has been understood. In several cases, and particularly in the trial of controversies to which States may be parties, they must be viewed and proceeded against in their collective and political capacities only. So far the national countenance of the government on this side seems to be disfigured by a few federal features. But this blemish is perhaps unavoidable in any plan; and the operation of the government on the people, in their individual capacities, in its ordinary and most essential proceedings, may, on the whole, designate it, in this relation, a NATIONAL government.

But if the government be national with regard to the OPERATION of its powers, it changes its aspect again when we contemplate it in relation to the EXTENT of its powers. The idea of a national government involves in it, not only an authority over the individual citizens, but an indefinite supremacy over all persons and things, so far as they are objects of lawful government. Among a people consolidated into one nation, this supremacy is completely vested in the national legislature. Among communities united for particular purposes, it is vested partly in the general and partly in the municipal legislatures. In the former case, all local authorities are subordinate to the supreme; and may be controlled, directed, or abolished by it at pleasure. In the latter, the local or municipal authorities form distinct and independent portions of the supremacy, no more subject, within their respective spheres, to the general authority, than the general authority is subject to them, within its own sphere. In this relation, then, the proposed government cannot be deemed a NATIONAL one; since its jurisdiction extends to certain enumerated objects only, and leaves to the several States a residuary and inviolable sovereignty over all other objects. It is true that in controversies relating to the boundary between the two jurisdictions, the tribunal which is ultimately to decide, is to be established under the general government. But this does not change the principle of the case. The decision is to be impartially made, according to the rules of the Constitution; and all the usual and most effectual precautions are taken to secure this impartiality. Some such tribunal is clearly essential to prevent an appeal to the sword and a dissolution of the compact; and that it ought to be established under the general rather than under the local governments, or, to speak more properly, that it could be safely established under the first alone, is a position not likely to be combated.

If we try the Constitution by its last relation to the authority by which amendments are to be made, we find it neither wholly NATIONAL nor wholly FEDERAL. Were it wholly national, the supreme and ultimate authority would reside in the MAJORITY of the people of the Union; and this authority would be competent at all times, like that of a majority of every national society, to alter or abolish its established government. Were it wholly federal, on the other hand, the concurrence of each State in the Union would be essential to every alteration that would be binding on all. The mode provided by the plan of the convention is not founded on either of these principles. In requiring more than a majority, and principles. In requiring more than a majority, and particularly in computing the proportion by STATES, not by CITIZENS, it departs from the NATIONAL and advances towards the FEDERAL character; in rendering the concurrence of less than the whole number of States sufficient, it loses again the FEDERAL and partakes of the NATIONAL character.

The proposed Constitution, therefore, is, in strictness, neither a national nor a federal Constitution, but a composition of both. In its foundation it is federal, not national; in the sources from which the ordinary powers of the government are drawn, it is partly federal and partly national; in the operation of these powers, it is national, not federal; in the extent of them, again, it is federal, not national; and, finally, in the authoritative mode of introducing amendments, it is neither wholly federal nor wholly national.

PUBLIUS

3.2

WILLIAM H. RIKER

From *Federalism: Origin, Operation, Significance*

In this selection from his classic book on federalism, Riker offers a largely nega-
tive view of American federalism. While the benefits of federalism can be identi-
fied in theory, the costs have been steep in actual practice: through the 1960s the
protection of privileged, wealthy minorities by state governments resulted in the
oppression of poor, previously enslaved minorities.

IS THE FEDERAL BARGAIN WORTH KEEPING?

Up to this point this interpretation of federalism has been as simply descriptive as I have been able to keep it. The questions of whether or not federalism is superior to its contemporary alternative, unitary government, or its previous alternative, imperialism; of whether or not federalism makes for good government or the good life; of whether or not federalism is an effective instrument of political integration—all these I have tried to keep out of the discussion in order to concentrate on the descriptive questions: What occasions federalism and what maintains it?

But most of the interest in federalism, both academic and popular, is about the further question: Is federalism worth keeping? And so in this final chapter we shall consider this moral question, not attempting to answer it but rather attempting to indicate some of the considerations that may properly enter into the answer.

Please note that I put the question "Is federalism worth keeping?" not "Is federalism worth starting?" If the argument has any validity at all, the latter question is trivial. In the drive for territorial expansion at the breakup of empire, one either needs to use the federal device to expand or one does not. Normative considerations presumably do not enter into calculation, once the decision to expand has been made. (Of course, that decision is itself normative; but, once it is made, the decision on the procedure of expansion is purely technical. Since the normative question is usually settled by unconscious consensus, the salient question at the beginning of federalisms is typically the technical one.) But even if the original question of adopting federalism is purely technical, still, once federalism has been established and once a federalism has reached that degree of centralization previously described as category B, the question of whether or not it ought to be maintained is open. Presumably a society with a federal government in category B has attained sufficient unity that it is no longer necessary to use the federal device to keep the expanded society viable. So at that point a normative judgment can be made about whether or not to keep the institutions that originally permitted the expansion.

Of course, the question of whether or not federalism is worth keeping seldom arises as a matter of complete constitutional revision (*e.g.*, in Austria and Germany after each of the world wars). More frequently, the question arises in a partial form; *i.e.*, "What attitude ought one to adopt on this measure that will tend to reinforce (or break down) the guarantees of federalism?" In mature and stable federalisms such as the United States or Australia, where complete constitutional revision seems unlikely in the foreseeable future, there is nevertheless a frequent opportunity to decide constitutional questions on the basis of an attitude toward federalism and this is where the partial form of the question arises.[1] Whether the question arises in its partial form or in a proposal for full-scale constitutional revision is, however, irrelevant to the considerations involved in the answer. Hence, the evaluation of whether or not federalism is worth keeping need not be restrained by the infrequency of constitutional conventions. Rather it is a question that politicians in a mature federalism, especially politicians in a category B federalism, must think about almost every day.

The considerations that commonly enter into decisions on these questions are the arguments advanced in favor of maintaining (or abrogating) the guarantees to constituent units. In the following sections, we shall therefore examine these arguments and some of the evidence adduced in support of them.

I. Federalism and Freedom—The Theoretical Argument for Retention

Probably the commonest argument in public debate for support of the guarantees to constituent units is the assertion that federalism is a guarantee of freedom, followed by the prescription that, in order to preserve freedom, one must preserve federalism. Assuming, as most of us would, that freedom (whatever it is) is worth preserving, the prescription nevertheless depends on a purportedly descriptive assertion, which may or may not be true. In what way is federalism related to freedom?

The political traditions of most federally governed societies predispose most of their citizens to believe that their constitutional form (*i.e.*, federalism) encourages a state of affairs (*i.e.*, freedom) that is almost universally approved. And in the traditions of both Anglo-American and Latin-American federalisms this predisposition has been reinforced by the identification of the spirit of federalism with the notion of local self-government, which in turn is often identified with freedom.

But despite these predispositions of the tradition, there are also some *a priori* reasons to be sceptical about the truth of the assertion that federalism encourages freedom. There are, for example, a number of societies that keep a high degree of freedom without the use of federalism and, on the other hand, a number of federalisms simultaneously have been dictatorships. Local self-government and personal freedom both coexist with a highly centralized unitary government in Great Britain and the Vargas dictatorship in Brazil managed to coexist with federalism.

In the United States, moreover, we have even more reasons to be sceptical about the truth of the assertion when we observe that the most persistent exponents of "states' rights"—a doctrine that makes much of the freedom-encouraging features of federalism—have been those who use the doctrine as a veiled defense first of slavery, then of civil tyranny. Here it seems that federalism may have more to do with destroying freedom than with encouraging it.

Clearly the relationship, if any, between federalism and freedom is not immediately clear and deserves further investigation.

The traditional argument, which derives from *The Federalist* papers and which has been reiterated continually by advocates of states' rights in all federal systems, is the assertion that concentrated power is dangerous, a position best expressed in Acton's aphorism that power tends to corrupt and absolute power corrupts absolutely. Federalism is said to be a device to prevent absolute power and therefore to prevent tyranny. I do not think we need to take this argument very seriously. It is based on a wise saw that has the same standing in the study of politics that weather wisdom has in the study of meteorology. The aphorism is not true—indeed, sometimes its opposite is.[2] And indeed, even if it were true, there is no assurance that separating power is the appropriate way to prevent tyranny. The separation may actually promote tyranny by its constant frustration of majorities which, in their frustration, come to behave tyrannically.[3] So let us leave aside the traditional argument, which is at best folk wisdom, and examine the relationship between federalism and freedom *de novo*.

Of course, though we know fairly well what "federalism" means, we have at best a confused notion of what "freedom" means. So before we can go further, the word "freedom" must be defined. And many volumes have been written on this subject without conspicuous success in reaching agreement. Owing to the tradition of controversy over the meaning of this word, we do know, however, that one of the variables involved in the notion is the specific reference to persons. That is, one elementary question about freedom is: "freedom for whom?"

The question arises in this way: Given a society with a multiplicity of goals (and surely all societies with federal governments satisfy this assumption) and given the possibility that the achievement of goal A renders the achievement of another goal, B, unlikely or impossible. Then, when one speaks of freedom, one must specify whether one means freedom for the supporters of goal A or for those of goal B. If political life were conveniently arranged so that all feasible goals were compatible with one another, then this question could not arise. But usually we do not find such neat dovetailing of aspirations. And so in the presence of conflicting goals, a definition of freedom must always specify freedom for whom.

One convenient answer that some theories of freedom have offered is "the majority," which is unfortunately a highly artificial creation of rules of voting. Owing to this artificiality, therefore, other theories of freedom have suggested that freedom involves liberty for minorities to achieve their goals. The first kind of answer solves the problem in a somewhat arbitrary fashion, whereas the second kind begs the question completely.

But since this reading has no space to pursue the problem of the meaning of freedom, we shall merely assume the existence of two kinds, majoritarian and minoritarian, and then inquire whether or not it is theoretically true that federalism is a guarantee of either kind.

Considering, first, majoritarian freedom, it seems fairly obvious that federalism cannot at all be a guarantee of this kind of freedom; but rather can actually be an impediment. The effect of allowing ultimate decision at two different levels of government (which is the essence of the federal relationship) is that the losers at the national level may reverse the decision at the constituent level. Thus, the losers nationally may become the winners locally which of course negates the national decision in at least portions of the federal nation. Thereby, of course, the freedom of the national majority is infringed upon by local majorities.

A notorious example of such negation is the reversal of decision on civil rights for Negroes in the Southern and border states. The original national decision, taken by a narrow majority in the Civil War era, was soon reversed by local decisions in the South and along the border—where, of course, most Negroes lived. As a consequence, the Civil War decisions were thoroughly negated for most Negroes until sufficient numbers migrated northward and reawakened interest in again enforcing the old and, in recent years, frequently reaffirmed national decision.

To one who believes in the majoritarian notion of freedom, it is impossible to interpret federalism as other than a device for minority tyranny. At the present time in the United States (*i.e.*, from roughly 1954 to that future time, if it ever comes, when most Negroes have full citizen rights) the chief question of public morals is whether or not the national decision will be enforced. To those who wish to enforce it, the plea for states' rights or for maintaining the guarantees of federalism is simply a hypocritical plea for the special privilege to disregard the national majority and, of course, to permit one minority, segregationist Southern whites, to tyrannize over another minority, the Southern Negroes. When freedom is defined as the right of self-direction for majorities, then the assertion that federalism promotes freedom is simply a hypocritical falsehood.

Considering, in the second place, minoritarian freedom, which is usually presented as the freedom of a minority to preserve its civil rights against a tyrannical majority, it is apparent, I shall argue, that for this kind of freedom federalism is, if not an impediment, still quite irrelevant.

Minoritarian freedom can be interpreted either as (1) the right of minorities to have a chance to become majorities and thus to make policy or (2) the right of minorities to make policy without becoming majorities. The first interpretation; *i.e.*, the right to the chance to make policy, is in practice the maintenance of civil liberties so that prospective majorities will not be destroyed before they become such. The latter interpretation, though often set forth as the abstract ideal of freedom, is of course simply a rationale of confusion. Given, as previously, the existence of conflicting social goals, then the guarantee of the right of minorities to make policy merely assures the simultaneous existence of contradictory policies.

If minoritarian freedom is the right to have a chance to make policy, then federalism is undoubtedly an impediment to freedom in many circumstances and irrelevant to it in others. Federalism is a guarantee to constituent units of the *right* to make policy, not of the *chance* to make policy. Thus it grants far more than is necessary for freedom. The analysis works out as follows: Suppose the constituent unit granted the right to make policy agrees for the most part with the kind of policy that would be made by the national officials. Then the right to make policy means relatively little and in general federalism is irrelevant to the maintenance of freedom. Suppose, however, that the constituent unit does not so agree; then the right to make policy allows it to impinge on the right of local minorities to become majorities. This is exactly what has happened in the American South where, under its freedom to make policy, the local majority (which is a minority nationally) has deprived the local minority of its civil rights (even though that local minority has close links with the national majority). In short, federalism that grants *more* local autonomy than is necessary for freedom and civil liberty encourages local tyranny, even when freedom is narrowly interpreted as the grant of the right to minorities to have a chance to become majorities.

If, on the other hand, minoritarian freedom is the right to make policy; *i.e.*, to allow minorities to create confusion, then federalism is again irrelevant to freedom in some circumstances and a positive hindrance to freedom in others. One may distinguish the circumstances according to whether or not it costs the society more to obtain uniformity than uniformity is worth. Consider an instance in which the cost of uniformity is greater than the reward: women's clothing. At numerous times in many societies sumptuary laws and laws against nudity have been passed and frequently they have been enforced only briefly. Presumably in such instances of laxity the cost of enforcement against numerous minorities of one is greater than the reward of uniformity. When enforcement costs more than the reward, federalism is irrelevant to freedom. If freedom is the grant to minorities of one of the right to decide, *e.g.*, on physical decoration, then the right of constituent units to make policy they probably will not care to enforce against minorities is a meaningless grant. In such an instance, federalism has nothing to do with freedom, although it may guarantee tyranny.

But when national uniformity is worth more than confusion, then federalism is an impediment to freedom because it deprives the national majority of the chance to eliminate the excess costs of confusion. Consider, for example, the matter of civil rights for Negroes in the United States. The grant to constituent units to make policy on this question has meant at least the following consequences: For the last century approximately 10 percent of the people have been denied civil rights. Those so denied have been a kind of *lumpenproletariat* and hence a drain on the whole society. In short, the grant of autonomy to local majorities to create confused policies has resulted in a cost to the whole society that is probably greater than the cost of uniformity. At least, so the present restiveness of the national majority toward Southern whites' practices of tyranny so indicates. In such an instance, we may infer that, when the costs of the consequences of federalism are greater than the costs of enforcing uniformity, local tyrannies are also national tyrannies because they prevent national majorities from reducing costs. For example, the national costs of putting up with the consequences of Southern bigotry are so great that the permission to enforce bigotry locally constitutes a cost on the whole nation, a cost which is presumably greater than the cost of enforcing desegregation. In this instance, therefore, federalism is an impediment to the freedom of everybody except segregationist whites in the South.

In summary, the abstract assertion that federalism is a guarantee of freedom is undoubtedly false. If this assertion is intended as a description of nature, then it is manifestly false, as shown by counterinstances of the coexistence of federalism and dictatorship. If it is, however, intended as a theoretical assertion about an abstract relationship undisturbed by other institutional arrangements, then it is still false. If freedom is interpreted in a majoritarian way, then the assertion is invariably false, for federalism is an impediment to freedom. If freedom is interpreted in a minoritarian way, then either federalism has nothing to do with freedom or federalism is again an impediment to freedom.

II. The High Cost of Uniformity—The Practical Argument for Retention

The most frequently presented practical argument for the maintenance of the federal guarantees to the constituent units is that the cost of national decision making is greater than the reward that might be obtained from it. This argument is usually presented as a defense of expediency (*e.g.*, that it would cost more in prospective civil disturbance to integrate the schools of Mississippi than can presently be gained from this action). But sometimes it is also presented as a moral good (*e.g.*, that a positive value is obtained from diversity of culture). (The latter was a favorite argument of Justice Holmes, who interpreted the states as laboratories for solving public problems.) In either form, however, this argument is essentially an economic one involving a kind of cost analysis of constitutional forms.[4]

National decision making is in the abstract more efficient than local decision making on every issue. That is, assuming uniformity is itself costless, it is cheaper on any subject of legislation to have a uniform rule, which is made by a majority, than not to have uniformity. There are at least two strong theoretical reasons for this circumstance. For one thing there is some saving in uniformity; and for another, there is less likelihood of a minority imposing high external costs on the majority. Considering the first and lesser reason, it is apparent that there is some saving in personal learning to have something like nationally uniform rules of the road. If a red light meant different things in different localities it is highly likely that the cost of enforcement of road rules would increase enormously. But the more important saving through uniformity is the minimization of the external costs imposed on individuals when minorities are allowed to legislate a minority policy. These costs are, of course, very high when two minority policies are in direct conflict. But even when they do not seem to be in direct conflict, external costs may still be inordinately high. Consider the sum of the costs to individuals when there are different minimum wages in different localities. There is then much likelihood of capital flow from the high-wage localities to the low-wage localities for all those industries in which labor represents a high proportion of the cost. Aside from the imposition of a nationally uniform minimum wage, the only way that high-wage localities may counter this capital flow is by reducing the minimum wage level. Thus the localities with the low minimum wage are permitted to set this wage nationally. For all the localities that would like to have the high wage, the imposition of the low wage is, of course, a high external cost. Since only the lowest-wage locality will be satisfied, all other localities will suffer these external costs. The obvious way to reduce this cost is to impose a national policy. It is this possibility that accounts for the greater efficiency of uniform rules. The only circumstances in which the uniform policy would not reduce external costs over local policies would be when the low-wage locality constituted a national majority. But in this case, the supposedly local policy is in fact imposed by a national majority and is thus a uniform policy. Hence in all cases a uniform policy is cheaper from the point of view of external costs than a non-uniform policy.

Or consider the savings from uniformity in the regulation of morality rather than the regulation of the economy. Given the possibility of variation in divorce codes among constituent units, divorce may be easier to obtain in one jurisdiction than in another. Then, so long as some provision like the full faith and credit clause of the United States Constitution exists—and all federalisms have something like it—it follows that the code that will in fact regulate is the one with easiest divorce. We have an excellent example of this in the United States, where the national scandal of excessively large numbers of divorces and the concomitant scandal of ill-considered marriages are both the consequences of a variation in divorce codes. The existence of a few jurisdictions that grant divorces on the most trivial grounds and after only the briefest periods of residence are sufficient to render nugatory the more restrictive grounds and longer residence requirements of most other states. Thus the different moral standards of a few states, the codes of which seem to have been motivated more by a concern for tourist business than by any convictions one way or another about family stability, have the effect of imposing easy divorce on all jurisdictions. The external costs of the existence of what most citizens of most states regard as low moral standards are thus very high for the probably overwhelming majority that opposes easy divorce. Uniformity of divorce laws could materially lighten these costs for the majority, although it might raise costs for Nevada lawyers.

It seems clear on the basis of both theory and example that uniform national decision making is invariably more efficient, *i.e.*, less costly in undesired impositions on other people, than is local decision making. This is simply to say that decisions made by a majority hurt fewer people than do decisions made by minorities. Since constituent governments are invariably minorities in the nation, the maintenance of federal guarantees to constituent units assures that the whole society must bear some extra and unnecessary external costs.

So far, however, we have considered the cost of decision making only in a vacuum. Even if national decision making is clearly more efficient in decreasing external costs, it still may be more expensive than local decision making because of (1) costs of decision making and (2) costs of enforcement.

Costs of decision making are those incurred in the process of assembling a coalition of the size necessary to make a decision. As the requirements increase from minorities (*e.g.*, majorities in a constituent unit) to majorities (*i.e.*, a national majority), the cost of making side-payments to reluctant members (*i.e.*, logrolling) and of negotiating with all prospective members increases greatly. The cost of national decision making may well be greater than the rewards obtained from eliminating anarchy. Consider, for example, standards of beach clothing for females. Possibly a majority of people in the United States are offended by the appearance of bikinis and, were the decision costless, they would be glad to prohibit them. But, in fact, the decision is not costless. Some effort must be expended on defining what is offensive and what is not; more effort must be expended on finding the people who make up this majority; and finally additional effort must be expended on bringing them together in a group for action. In this imaginary example, the cost of decision is clearly very high, whereas the sum of the rewards to the majority is probably relatively low. Quite possibly the decision costs exceed the rewards.

Costs of enforcement are those incurred in the process of enforcing a majority decision against a recalcitrant minority. These costs vary with (1) the relative size of the minority, (2) the intensity of feeling of the minority, and (3) the ability of the minority to resist enforcement. It makes a difference for the existence of a national policy of prohibition, for example, whether or not most of the people are convinced teetotalers. In the United States during the prohibition era, the minority of regular users of alcohol was almost as large as the group of teetotalers, if indeed not larger. Hence enforcement was exceptionally costly. In India, on the other hand, where a much larger proportion of the population consists of teetotalers and where the indigenous pharmacopoeia includes a variety of drugs with physiological and social effects similar to those of alcohol, the enforcement of prohibition is relatively less costly. Again it makes a difference for the existence of a national policy of assessing an income tax whether or not the prosperous and the rich believe deeply that they should not be taxed. Thus, in the United States, the prosperous and the rich accept the basic notion of the tax and hence usually obey the exact letter of the law. The existence of this attitude means that enforcement officers are freed to pursue the minority of dishonest taxpayers. Hence the income tax works pretty well as the basic tax of the nation. In India, on the other hand, the justice of the tax is not as widely acknowledged by the prosperous and rich. Hence enforcement agents must spend most of their efforts on what would elsewhere be regarded as ordinary collection. As a consequence, enforcement is costly and the income tax cannot be used as the basic tax system. Finally, it makes a difference for the existence of a national policy of civil rights for depressed classes whether or not those who oppress them can successfully defend the oppression both practically and philosophically. Again compare India and the United States, in both of which national decisions have repeatedly condemned the oppression of in one case the Scheduled Castes and in the other case Negroes. In both cases there are good practical devices to avoid enforcement; *e.g.*, the relative unanimity of the rural upper classes on the desirability of resistance. In both cases there are also good philosophical grounds to resist enforcement; *e.g.*, the doctrine of states' rights in the United States and the doctrines of Hinduism in India. But the outlook for enforcement of the national policy is much better in the United States than in India simply because (1) the unanimity of the rural upper classes is nationwide in India whereas in the United States it is breaking down and indeed is limited to two or three very recalcitrant states and (2) the doctrine of states' rights is increasingly regarded as a sham for oppression whereas, owing to the new nationalism, the doctrines of Hinduism are held to even more tenaciously than before. Negroes are likely to obtain civil rights sooner than untouchables simply because the ability of their oppressors to resist enforcement is less.

In this analysis of the costs of national decision making in relation to decision making by constituent units, we have thus identified three kinds of charges:

1. the profits of uniformity, symbolized by "U"; which are invariably positive in sign because majority decision is always better than anarchy;
2. the costs of making decisions, symbolized by "D," which are invariably negative in sign because it is more costly to assemble a majority than a minority; and

3. the costs of enforcement of decisions, symbolized by "E," which are
   also invariably negative in sign because the existence of a majority
   implies the existence of a minority that must be coerced.

The practical argument in favor of maintaining the federal guarantees to
the constituent units is that $U+D+E \leq 0$. Of course, this argument cannot be
uttered generally for it would mean the desirability of the dissolution of the
federalism. Rather, it must be uttered in particular instances and where it is
asserted after a rough assessment of the values of U, D, and E. Since the argument cannot be asserted generally except as a proposal for civil war, one wonders about what kind of instances it seems reasonable in. In short, what kinds
of circumstances minimize the sum of U, D, and E?

It is impossible, of course, to offer an exhaustive list; but one can specify
some typical circumstances. As for minimizing U, which of course increases
the likelihood that the inequation $U+D+E \leq 0$ will hold, the most important
circumstance probably is that the policy field will be fairly low on the preference schedules of most of the members of the prospective majority. If most
people don't care much whether or not policy in a specific area (*e.g.*, women's
beachwear) is anarchic, then the positive value of U will be low. The issue of
whether or not to maintain the federal guarantee to constituent units does
not, however, arise when U is low, for to say U is low is to say it concerns something to which most people are close to indifferent. So the problem is: In what
circumstances, when U is high, is—$(D+E)$ higher?

What minimizes D is the existence of numerous territorial minorities, each
of whose schedules of preference is quite different from others. The fact that
these minorities are territorially based gives them some strength to insist on
obtaining their preferences and the fact that their preference schedules are different renders the bargaining process expensive. India is a federalism in which,
a priori, one might expect D to be very low in many areas of public policy.

What minimizes E is the intensity of feeling of a minority, a defensive sense
that their separateness is both under attack and worth preserving. Coupled
with this sense of separateness must also be a large territorial and population
base so that the minority actually has some strength to resist enforcement.
Canada is a federalism in which, *a priori*, one might expect E to be very low in
many areas of public policy.

The practical argument for the maintenance of the federal guarantees to the
constituent units, *viz.*, that $U+D+E \leq 0$, is clearly dependent upon the calculations of politicians and citizens about the magnitudes of U, D, and E in particular sets of circumstances. In general, if there are numerous areas *of importance*
in which it is agreed that the inequation $U+D+E \leq 0$ holds, then the argument
in favor of maintaining the guarantees is good. If not, then the argument fails.
For me, the argument is reasonable and impressive with respect to such federalisms as Canada and India, but it is specious and unreasonable with respect
to such federalisms as the United States, Germany, Austria, and Australia.

III. Abrogating the Guarantees

The main theoretical argument in favor of abrogating the federal guarantees to constituent units has already been developed in connection with arguments for maintaining them: Decisions made by constituent units are invariably minority decisions that impose high external costs on the national majority. This assertion is wholly irrefutable on the level of theory, although it may be shown, as I have also indicated, that in particular instances it may cost more to remove the external costs than is saved with uniformity. But even though the assertion is theoretically irrefutable some effort has been expended in showing that it is not necessarily true in all circumstances. Cohen and Grodzins, for example, have attempted to show that state fiscal policies in the United States do not always conflict with national policies.[5] And they did indeed show that the state policies are less sharply in conflict with national policy than had previously been believed.[6] But to show that the anarchy of numerous minority decisions does not impose external costs as high as Hansen and Perloff believed is also to admit that external costs do exist. Indeed, the chief significance of Cohen and Grodzins' work is that they found a way to measure them. The existence of external costs is an invitation to eliminate them, which is the chief theoretical argument in favor of abrogating the guarantees.

Unfortunately the theoretical arguments, though theoretically decisive, are practically uncertain because of the uncertainty surrounding the magnitudes of U, D, and E. Hence, to decide in particular instances whether or not to abrogate the guarantees it is necessary to examine the cultural and institutional setting of the constitution. The appropriate questions are: Who benefits by the imposition of external costs on others? or, What minority is allowed by the federal device to impose its rules on the majority? According as one disapproves or approves of the values and purposes of these minorities, one favors or opposes the abrogation of the guarantees. One does not decide on the merits of federalism by an examination of federalism in the abstract, but rather on its actual meaning for particular societies.

What minorities benefit from the grant to make policy in:

The United States?

The main beneficiary throughout American history has been the Southern whites, who have been given the freedom to oppress Negroes, first as slaves and later as a depressed caste. Other minorities have from time to time also managed to obtain some of these benefits; *e.g.*, special business interests have been allowed to regulate themselves, especially in the era from about 1890 to 1936, by means of the judicial doctrine of dual federalism, which eliminated both state and national regulation of such matters as wage rates and hours of labor. But the significance of federal benefits to economic interests pales beside the significance of benefits to the Southern segregationist whites. The judgment to be passed on federalism in the United States is therefore a judgment on the values of segregation and racial oppression.

Canada?

The main beneficiary in Canada from the beginning has been the French-speaking minority, whose dissidence was the original occasion for adopting federalism and is the justification for retaining it today. Secondarily, as in the United States, commercial interests have also benefited by escaping regulation. But since the French Canadians have no particular alliance with business, economic conservatives have benefited less in Canada than in the United States (where Southern segregationists have a tacit alliance with economic conservatives). That is, the French speakers have seen less reason to rig the competitive market to the advantage of owners (as against workers or consumers) because very few French Canadians have been owners.

Brazil?

The most significant minority benefiting from Brazilian federalism is the class of large landowners, especially in the relatively underdeveloped north and east. Although Brazilian federalism lacks the tone of racism associated with federalism in the United States, the social consequences are the same: the maintenance of a class of poor and inefficient farm laborers for the presumed benefit of agrarian landlords.

India?

Indian federalism is probably too youthful to identify the main beneficiaries of the privilege of minority decision making. But two kinds of minorities have tended to emphasize states' rights: non-Hindi-speaking groups (who, together, are of course a majority) and landlords in the least-developed agricultural areas.

Australia?

Since no single minority has been able to exploit the advantages of minority decision exclusively or for long periods of time, it is difficult to identify the main beneficiary. Nevertheless, it seems that commercial interests have been granted freedom from regulation more than any other group.

Germany?

Originally, federalism was intended to grant the right of minority decision to the non-Prussian southwest. But the significance of this minority has declined in the successive transformations of German federalism so that today it is difficult to specify who, if anyone, benefits most.

The foregoing survey of several federal systems suggests the wide variety of kinds of minorities that may benefit especially from the privilege to legislate. The kind of minorities that appears most frequently on this list is business and agricultural owners. It is not difficult to understand why. In capitalistic

TABLE 1 Main Beneficiaries of Federalism

	Capitalists	Landlords	Linguistic minorities	Racists
United States	X	X		X
Canada	X		X	
Mexico		X		
Brazil	X	X		
Argentina	X	X		
Australia	X			
India		X	X	
Switzerland	X		X	
Germany	X			
Yugoslavia			X	
Soviet Union			X	

nations conflicting economic interests are engaged constantly in an effort to rig the competitive system in their favor. Those groups which constitute national majorities, *e.g.*, workers, farm laborers, consumers, etc., are those which might be expected to benefit most from majoritarian decision processes. To allow minoritarian processes is, therefore, to deprive the very large groups of their chance to influence outcomes. Of course, the minority most likely to benefit from the chance to manipulate the market is that of the owners, business or agricultural according to whether the nation is primarily industrial or agrarian.

But it is not always or only the owners who benefit, for, as the brief survey indicates, linguistic or racist minorities may also thrive on federalism. One possible classification of federalism, especially appropriate for passing judgment on the desirability of retaining federalism, is by the main beneficiaries of the chance of minorities to legislate for the whole. A moral judgment must be passed in each instance and for comparative purposes I submit a list (Table 1) of the main characteristics of the main federalisms. It is notable that the federalism of the United States is unique in fostering racism.

IV. Is Federalism Worth Keeping?

One seldom has the opportunity to rewrite whole constitutions so the question of keeping or abandoning federalism can seldom arise. But a related question does frequently arise: What ought to be one's posture toward federalism? Should one always attempt to maintain or abrogate the guarantees to the constituent units?

In pure theory, the answer is that what one ought to seek to abrogate for federalism is a system of minority decision that imposes high external costs on everybody other than the minority. But practically the answer is not so clear, for the costs of decision and enforcement may outweigh the advantages of majoritarianism when the minority favored by federalism is passionate in its convictions.

Since the actual calculation of rewards and costs from abrogating federal guarantees is simply a rough "more or less" necessarily calculated by interested parties, one probably cannot even use a cost analysis in judging actual federalisms. Rather one must look to what they do and determine what minorities they favor. If one approves the goals and values of the privileged minority, one should approve the federalism. Thus, if in the United States one approves of Southern white racists, then one should approve of American federalism. If, on the other hand, one disapproves of the values of the privileged minority, one should disapprove of federalism. Thus, if in the United States one disapproves of racism, one should disapprove of federalism.

NOTES

1. For a concrete example of such an occasion, consider the creation (in 1935) of the unemployment insurance system as an adjunct to the social security system. President Roosevelt, apparently out of a concern for federalism, personally decided to assign the unemployment insurance and employment service to the states, at least so his advisor Tugwell tells us. (Rexford Tugwell, "The Experimental Roosevelt," *The Political Quarterly*, Vol. 21 (1950) pp. 239–62, at p. 241.) In turning down the advice of experts, Roosevelt personally preserved, at least in a small way, the constitutional guarantees of federalism. Whether or not he was wise to do so is, of course, another matter. Since the federal part of this system has been quietly and selectively administered, whereas the state part has been the center of much political turbulence and has often been charged with inefficiency, the experts were probably right from an administrative point of view. But constitutional considerations may be more important than administrative ones. What concerns us here, however, is not the correctness or incorrectness of Roosevelt's action, but simply the opportunity he had to decide a policy question on the basis of an interpretation of federalism.

2. See Arnold Rogow and Harold Lasswell, *Power, Corruption and Rectitude* (New York: Prentice-Hall, 1963).

3. See William H. Riker, *Democracy in the United States* (New York: Macmillan, 1953) Chapter 4.

4. An earlier attempt to apply a quasi-economic analysis to the costs of federalism is: J. Roland Pennock, "Federal and Unitary Government—Disharmony and Frustration," *Behavioral Science*, Vol. 4 (1959) pp. 147–57. This article contains an *ad hoc* and tendentious model from which calculations are made of the "harmony (or lessened frustration) which it is the peculiar genius of federalism to achieve." By conveniently ignoring what are here called external costs, *e.g.*, those imposed on the majority when the minority is permitted to make rules, the author finds that federalism lessens the frustrations of a minority, which, of course, no one has ever denied. The unanswered question is: At whose expense is the frustration relieved?

5. Jacob Cohen and Morton Grodzins, "How Much Economic Sharing in American Federalism," *American Political Science Review*, Vol. 57 (1963) pp. 5–23.

6. Alvin Hansen and Harvey Perloff, *State and Local Finance in the National Economy* (New York: Norton, 1944).

3.3

United States v. Lopez (1995)

In a relatively rare rebuke of the national government, the U.S. Supreme Court in this case decided in favor of state authority and against national authority in a case involving guns near schools. This decision is representative of the Court under Chief Justice William Rehnquist; in the Rehnquist era the Court limited the reach of national government regulation.

Chief Justice Rehnquist delivered the opinion of the Court.

In the Gun-Free School Zones Act of 1990, Congress made it a federal offense "for any individual knowingly to possess a firearm at a place that the individual knows, or has reasonable cause to believe, is a school zone." 18 U.S.C. 922(q). The Act neither regulates a commercial activity nor contains a requirement that the possession be connected in any way to interstate commerce. We hold that the Act exceeds the authority of Congress "[t]o regulate Commerce . . . among the several States. . . ." U.S. Const., Art. I, 8, cl. 3.

On March 10, 1992, respondent, who was then a 12th-grade student, arrived at Edison High School in San Antonio, Texas, carrying a concealed .38 caliber handgun and five bullets. Acting upon an anonymous tip, school authorities confronted respondent, who admitted that he was carrying the weapon. He was arrested and charged under Texas law with firearm possession on school premises. The next day, the state charges were dismissed after federal agents charged respondent by complaint with violating the Gun-Free School Zones Act of 1990.

A federal grand jury indicted respondent on one count of knowing possession of a firearm at a school zone, in violation of 922(q). Respondent moved to dismiss his federal indictment on the ground that 922(q) "is unconstitutional as it is beyond the power of Congress to legislate control over our public schools." The District Court denied the motion, concluding that 922(q) "is a constitutional exercise of Congress' well-defined power to regulate activities in and affecting commerce, and the 'business' of elementary, middle and high schools . . . affects interstate commerce." Respondent waived his right to a jury trial. The District Court conducted a bench trial, found him guilty of violating 922(q), and sentenced him to six months' imprisonment and two years' supervised release.

On appeal, respondent challenged his conviction based on his claim that 922(q) exceeded Congress' power to legislate under the Commerce Clause. The Court of Appeals for the Fifth Circuit agreed and reversed respondent's conviction. It held that, in light of what it characterized as insufficient congressional findings and legislative history, "section 922(q), in the full reach of its terms, is invalid as beyond the power of Congress under the Commerce Clause." Because of the importance of the issue, we granted certiorari, and we now affirm.

We start with first principles. The Constitution creates a Federal Government of enumerated powers. As James Madison wrote, "[t]he powers delegated by the proposed Constitution to the federal government are few and defined. Those which are to remain in the State governments are numerous and indefinite." The Federalist No. 45. This constitutionally mandated division of authority "was adopted by the Framers to ensure protection of our fundamental liberties." *Gregory v. Ashcroft* (1991). "Just as the separation and independence of the coordinate branches of the Federal Government serves to prevent the accumulation of excessive power in any one branch, a healthy balance of power between the States and the Federal Government will reduce the risk of tyranny and abuse from either front."

The Constitution delegates to Congress the power "[t]o regulate Commerce with foreign Nations, and among the several States, and with the Indian Tribes." The Court, through Chief Justice Marshall, first defined the nature of Congress' commerce power in *Gibbons v. Ogden* (1824):

> Commerce, undoubtedly, is traffic, but it is something more: it is intercourse. It describes the commercial intercourse between nations, and parts of nations, in all its branches, and is regulated by prescribing rules for carrying on that intercourse.

The commerce power "is the power to regulate; that is, to prescribe the rule by which commerce is to be governed. This power, like all others vested in Congress, is complete in itself, may be exercised to its utmost extent, and acknowledges no limitations, other than are prescribed in the constitution." The *Gibbons* Court, however, acknowledged that limitations on the commerce power are inherent in the very language of the Commerce Clause.

> It is not intended to say that these words comprehend that commerce, which is completely internal, which is carried on between man and man in a State, or between different parts of the same State, and which does not extend to or affect other States. Such a power would be inconvenient, and is certainly unnecessary.
>
> Comprehensive as the word "among" is, it may very properly be restricted to that commerce which concerns more States than one. . . . The enumeration presupposes something not enumerated; and that

something, if we regard the language or the subject of the sentence, must be the exclusively internal commerce of a State.

For nearly a century thereafter, the Court's Commerce Clause decisions dealt but rarely with the extent of Congress' power, and almost entirely with the Commerce Clause as a limit on state legislation that discriminated against interstate commerce. Under this line of precedent, the Court held that certain categories of activity such as "production," "manufacturing," and "mining" were within the province of state governments, and thus were beyond the power of Congress under the Commerce Clause.

In 1887, Congress enacted the Interstate Commerce Act, and in 1890, Congress enacted the Sherman Antitrust Act. These laws ushered in a new era of federal regulation under the commerce power. When cases involving these laws first reached this Court, we imported from our negative Commerce Clause cases the approach that Congress could not regulate activities such as "production," "manufacturing," and "mining." Simultaneously, however, the Court held that, where the interstate and intrastate aspects of commerce were so mingled together that full regulation of interstate commerce required incidental regulation of intrastate commerce, the Commerce Clause authorized such regulation.

In *A. L. A. Schecter Poultry Corp. v. United States* (1935), the Court struck down regulations that fixed the hours and wages of individuals employed by an intrastate business because the activity being regulated related to interstate commerce only indirectly. In doing so, the Court characterized the distinction between direct and indirect effects of intrastate transactions upon interstate commerce as "a fundamental one, essential to the maintenance of our constitutional system." Activities that affected interstate commerce directly were within Congress' power; activities that affected interstate commerce indirectly were beyond Congress' reach. The justification for this formal distinction was rooted in the fear that otherwise "there would be virtually no limit to the federal power and for all practical purposes we should have a completely centralized government."

Two years later, in the watershed case of *NLRB v. Jones & Laughlin Steel Corp.*, (1937), the Court upheld the National Labor Relations Act against a Commerce Clause challenge, and in the process, departed from the distinction between "direct" and "indirect" effects on interstate commerce. ("The question [of the scope of Congress' power] is necessarily one of degree"). The Court held that intrastate activities that "have such a close and substantial relation to interstate commerce that their control is essential or appropriate to protect that commerce from burdens and obstructions" are within Congress' power to regulate.

In *United States v. Darby* (1941), the Court upheld the Fair Labor Standards Act, stating:

The power of Congress over interstate commerce is not confined to the regulation of commerce among the states. It extends to those activities intrastate which so affect interstate commerce or the exercise of the power of Congress over it as to make regulation of them appropriate means to the attainment of a legitimate end, the exercise of the granted power of Congress to regulate interstate commerce.

In *Wickard v. Filburn*, the Court upheld the application of amendments to the Agricultural Adjustment Act of 1938 to the production and consumption of home-grown wheat. The *Wickard* Court explicitly rejected earlier distinctions between direct and indirect effects on interstate commerce, stating:

> [E]ven if appellee's activity be local and though it may not be regarded as commerce, it may still, whatever its nature, be reached by Congress if it exerts a substantial economic effect on interstate commerce, and this irrespective of whether such effect is what might at some earlier time have been defined as "direct" or "indirect."

The *Wickard* Court emphasized that although Filburn's own contribution to the demand for wheat may have been trivial by itself, that was not "enough to remove him from the scope of federal regulation where, as here, his contribution, taken together with that of many others similarly situated, is far from trivial."

Jones & Laughlin Steel, *Darby*, and *Wickard* ushered in an era of Commerce Clause jurisprudence that greatly expanded the previously defined authority of Congress under that Clause. In part, this was a recognition of the great changes that had occurred in the way business was carried on in this country. Enterprises that had once been local or at most regional in nature had become national in scope. But the doctrinal change also reflected a view that earlier Commerce Clause cases artificially had constrained the authority of Congress to regulate interstate commerce.

But even these modern-era precedents which have expanded congressional power under the Commerce Clause confirm that this power is subject to outer limits. In *Jones & Laughlin Steel*, the Court warned that the scope of the interstate commerce power "must be considered in the light of our dual system of government and may not be extended so as to embrace effects upon interstate commerce so indirect and remote that to embrace them, in view of our complex society, would effectually obliterate the distinction between what is national and what is local and create a completely centralized government." Since that time, the Court has heeded that warning and undertaken to decide whether a rational basis existed for concluding that a regulated activity sufficiently affected interstate commerce.

Similarly, in *Maryland v. Wirtz* (1968), the Court reaffirmed that "the power to regulate commerce, though broad indeed, has limits" that "[t]he Court has ample power" to enforce. In response to the dissent's warnings that the Court was powerless to enforce the limitations on Congress' commerce powers because "[a]ll activities affecting commerce, even in the minutest degree, [*Wickard*], may be regulated and controlled by Congress," (Douglas, J., dissenting), the *Wirtz* Court replied that the dissent had misread precedent as "[n] either here nor in *Wickard* has the Court declared that Congress may use a relatively trivial impact on commerce as an excuse for broad general regulation of state or private activities." Rather, "[t]he Court has said only that where a general regulatory statute bears a substantial relation to commerce, the de minimis character of individual instances arising under that statute is of no consequence."

Consistent with this structure, we have identified three broad categories of activity that Congress may regulate under its commerce power. First, Congress may regulate the use of the channels of interstate commerce. Second, Congress is empowered to regulate and protect the instrumentalities of interstate commerce, or persons or things in interstate commerce, even though the threat may come only from intrastate activities. Finally, Congress' commerce authority includes the power to regulate those activities having a substantial relation to interstate commerce, *Jones & Laughlin Steel*, i.e., those activities that substantially affect interstate commerce.

Within this final category, admittedly, our case law has not been clear whether an activity must "affect" or "substantially affect" interstate commerce in order to be within Congress' power to regulate it under the Commerce Clause. We conclude, consistent with the great weight of our case law, that the proper test requires an analysis of whether the regulated activity "substantially affects" interstate commerce.

We now turn to consider the power of Congress, in the light of this framework, to enact 922(q). The first two categories of authority may be quickly disposed of: 922(q) is not a regulation of the use of the channels of interstate commerce, nor is it an attempt to prohibit the interstate transportation of a commodity through the channels of commerce; nor can 922(q) be justified as a regulation by which Congress has sought to protect an instrumentality of interstate commerce or a thing in interstate commerce. Thus, if 922(q) is to be sustained, it must be under the third category as a regulation of an activity that substantially affects interstate commerce.

First, we have upheld a wide variety of congressional Acts regulating intrastate economic activity where we have concluded that the activity substantially affected interstate commerce. Examples include the regulation of intrastate coal mining, intrastate extortionate credit transactions, restaurants utilizing substantial interstate supplies, inns and hotels catering to interstate guests, and production and consumption of home-grown wheat. These examples are by no means exhaustive, but the pattern is clear. Where economic activity substantially affects interstate commerce, legislation regulating that activity will be sustained.

Even [*Wickard v. Filburn* (1942)], which is perhaps the most far reaching example of Commerce Clause authority over intrastate activity, involved economic activity in a way that the possession of a gun in a school zone does not. Roscoe Filburn operated a small farm in Ohio, on which, in the year involved, he raised 23 acres of wheat. It was his practice to sow winter wheat in the fall, and after harvesting it in July to sell a portion of the crop, to feed part of it to poultry and livestock on the farm, to use some in making flour for home consumption, and to keep the remainder for seeding future crops. The Secretary of Agriculture assessed a penalty against him under the Agricultural Adjustment Act of 1938 because he harvested about 12 acres more wheat than his allotment under the Act permitted. The Act was designed to regulate the volume of wheat moving in interstate and foreign commerce in order to avoid surpluses and shortages, and concomitant fluctuation in wheat prices, which had previously obtained. The Court said, in an opinion sustaining the application of the Act to Filburn's activity:

> One of the primary purposes of the Act in question was to increase the market price of wheat and to that end to limit the volume thereof that could affect the market. It can hardly be denied that a factor of such volume and variability as home-consumed wheat would have a substantial influence on price and market conditions. This may arise because being in marketable condition such wheat overhangs the market and, if induced by rising prices, tends to flow into the market and check price increases. But if we assume that it is never marketed, it supplies a need of the man who grew it which would otherwise be reflected by purchases in the open market. Home-grown wheat in this sense competes with wheat in commerce.

Section 922(q) is a criminal statute that by its terms has nothing to do with "commerce" or any sort of economic enterprise, however broadly one might define those terms. Section 922(q) is not an essential part of a larger regulation of economic activity, in which the regulatory scheme could be undercut unless the intrastate activity were regulated. It cannot, therefore, be sustained under our cases upholding regulations of activities that arise out of or are connected with a commercial transaction, which viewed in the aggregate, substantially affects interstate commerce.

Second, 922(q) contains no jurisdictional element which would ensure, through case-by-case inquiry, that the firearm possession in question affects interstate commerce. For example, in *United States v. Bass* (1971), the Court interpreted former 18 U.S.C. 1202(a), which made it a crime for a felon to "receiv[e], posses[s], or transpor[t] in commerce or affecting commerce . . . any firearm." The Court interpreted the possession component of 1202(a) to require an additional nexus to interstate commerce both because the statute was ambiguous and because "unless Congress conveys its purpose clearly, it will not be deemed to have significantly changed the federal-state balance." The *Bass* Court set aside the conviction because although the Government had demonstrated that Bass had possessed a firearm, it had failed "to show the requisite nexus with interstate commerce." The Court thus interpreted the statute to reserve the constitutional question whether Congress could regulate, without more, the "mere possession" of firearms. Unlike the statute in *Bass*, 922(q) has no express jurisdictional element which might limit its reach to a discrete set of firearm possessions that additionally have an explicit connection with or effect on interstate commerce.

Although as part of our independent evaluation of constitutionality under the Commerce Clause we of course consider legislative findings, and indeed even congressional committee findings, regarding effect on interstate commerce, the Government concedes that "[n]either the statute nor its legislative history contain[s] express congressional findings regarding the effects upon interstate commerce of gun possession in a school zone." We agree with the Government that Congress normally is not required to make formal findings as to the substantial burdens that an activity has on interstate commerce. But to the extent that congressional findings would enable us to evaluate the legislative judgment that the activity in question substantially affected interstate commerce, even though no such substantial effect was visible to the naked eye, they are lacking here.

The Government argues that Congress has accumulated institutional expertise regarding the regulation of firearms through previous enactments. We agree, however, with the Fifth Circuit that importation of previous findings to justify 922(q) is especially inappropriate here because the "prior federal enactments or Congressional findings [do not] speak to the subject matter of section 922(q) or its relationship to interstate commerce. Indeed, section 922(q) plows thoroughly new ground and represents a sharp break with the long-standing pattern of federal firearms legislation."

The Government's essential contention, in fine, is that we may determine here that 922(q) is valid because possession of a firearm in a local school zone does indeed substantially affect interstate commerce. The Government argues that possession of a firearm in a school zone may result in violent crime and that violent crime can be expected to affect the functioning of the national economy in two ways. First, the costs of violent crime are substantial, and, through the mechanism of insurance, those costs are spread throughout the population. Second, violent crime reduces the willingness of individuals to travel to areas within the country that are perceived to be unsafe. The Government also argues that the presence of guns in schools poses a substantial threat to the educational process by threatening the learning environment. A handicapped educational process, in turn, will result in a less productive citizenry. That, in turn, would have an adverse effect on the Nation's economic well-being. As a result, the Government argues that Congress could rationally have concluded that 922(q) substantially affects interstate commerce.

We pause to consider the implications of the Government's arguments. The Government admits, under its "costs of crime" reasoning, that Congress could regulate not only all violent crime, but all activities that might lead to violent crime, regardless of how tenuously they relate to interstate commerce. Similarly, under the Government's "national productivity" reasoning, Congress could regulate any activity that it found was related to the economic productivity of individual citizens: family law (including marriage, divorce, and child custody), for example. Under the theories that the Government presents in support of 922(q), it is difficult to perceive any limitation on federal power, even in areas such as criminal law enforcement or education where States historically have been sovereign. Thus, if we were to accept the Government's arguments, we are hard-pressed to posit any activity by an individual that Congress is without power to regulate.

Although Justice Breyer argues that acceptance of the Government's rationales would not authorize a general federal police power, he is unable to identify any activity that the States may regulate but Congress may not. Justice Breyer posits that there might be some limitations on Congress' commerce power such as family law or certain aspects of education. These suggested limitations, when viewed in light of the dissent's expansive analysis, are devoid of substance.

Justice Breyer focuses, for the most part, on the threat that firearm possession in and near schools poses to the educational process and the potential economic consequences flowing from that threat. Specifically, the dissent reasons that (1) gun-related violence is a serious problem; (2) that problem, in turn, has an adverse effect on classroom learning; and (3) that adverse effect on classroom learning, in turn, represents a substantial threat to trade and commerce. This analysis would be equally applicable, if not more so, to subjects such as family law and direct regulation of education.

For instance, if Congress can, pursuant to its Commerce Clause power, regulate activities that adversely affect the learning environment, then, a fortiori, it also can regulate the educational process directly. Congress could determine that a school's curriculum has a "significant" effect on the extent of classroom learning. As a result, Congress could mandate a federal curriculum for local elementary and secondary schools because what is taught in local schools has a significant "effect on classroom learning," and that, in turn, has a substantial effect on interstate commerce.

Justice Breyer rejects our reading of precedent and argues that "Congress . . . could rationally conclude that schools fall on the commercial side of the line." Again, Justice Breyer's rationale lacks any real limits because, depending on the level of generality, any activity can be looked upon as commercial. Under the dissent's rationale, Congress could just as easily look at child rearing as "fall[ing] on the commercial side of the line" because it provides a "valuable service—namely, to equip [children] with the skills they need to survive in life and, more specifically, in the workplace." We do not doubt that Congress has authority under the Commerce Clause to regulate numerous commercial activities that substantially affect interstate commerce and also affect the educational process. That authority, though broad, does not include the authority to regulate each and every aspect of local schools.

Admittedly, a determination whether an intrastate activity is commercial or noncommercial may in some cases result in legal uncertainty. But, so long as Congress' authority is limited to those powers enumerated in the Constitution, and so long as those enumerated powers are interpreted as having judicially enforceable outer limits, congressional legislation under the Commerce Clause always will engender "legal uncertainty." As Chief Justice Marshall stated in *McCulloch v. Maryland* (1819):

> The [federal] government is acknowledged by all to be one of enumerated powers. The principle, that it can exercise only the powers granted to it . . . is now universally admitted. But the question respecting the extent of the powers actually granted, is perpetually arising, and will probably continue to arise, as long as our system shall exist.

The Constitution mandates this uncertainty by withholding from Congress a plenary police power that would authorize enactment of every type of legislation. Congress has operated within this framework of legal uncertainty ever since this Court determined that it was the judiciary's duty "to say what the law is." *Marbury v. Madison* (1803). Any possible benefit from eliminating this "legal uncertainty" would be at the expense of the Constitution's system of enumerated powers.

In *Jones & Laughlin Steel*, we held that the question of congressional power under the Commerce Clause "is necessarily one of degree." To the same effect is the concurring opinion of Justice Cardozo in *Schecter Poultry*:

> There is a view of causation that would obliterate the distinction of what is national and what is local in the activities of commerce. Motion at the outer rim is communicated perceptibly, though minutely, to recording instruments at the center. A society such as ours "is an elastic medium which transmits all tremors throughout its territory; the only question is of their size."

These are not precise formulations, and in the nature of things they cannot be. But we think they point the way to a correct decision of this case. The possession of a gun in a local school zone is in no sense an economic activity that might, through repetition elsewhere, substantially affect any sort of interstate commerce. Respondent was a local student at a local school; there is no indication that he had recently moved in interstate commerce, and there is no requirement that his possession of the firearm have any concrete tie to interstate commerce.

To uphold the Government's contentions here, we would have to pile infer-ence upon inference in a manner that would bid fair to convert congressional authority under the Commerce Clause to a general police power of the sort retained by the States. Admittedly, some of our prior cases have taken long steps down that road, giving great deference to congressional action. See supra, at 8. The broad language in these opinions has suggested the possibility of additional expansion, but we decline here to proceed any further. To do so would require us to conclude that the Constitution's enumeration of powers does not presuppose something not enumerated, and that there never will be a distinction between what is truly national and what is truly local. This we are unwilling to do.

For the foregoing reasons the judgment of the Court of Appeals is Affirmed.

3.4

JONATHAN WALTERS AND DONALD F. KETTL

"The Katrina Breakdown"
From *On Risk and Disaster*

A close examination of the response to Hurricane Katrina in 2005 highlights the failures of multiple levels of government to communicate and coordinate their relief efforts. City, county, state, and national responses to the disaster often overlapped unnecessarily and were poorly coordinated, and thus ineffective and inefficient. This excerpt summarizes evaluations of the response to Katrina and emphasizes the value of effective intergovernmental cooperation.

When Hurricane Katrina hit New Orleans, only one thing disintegrated as fast as the earthen levees that were supposed to protect the city, and that was the intergovernmental relationship that is supposed to connect local, state and federal officials before, during and after such a catastrophe.

In sifting through the debris of the disaster response, the first question is why intergovernmental cooperation broke down so completely. While it's hard even at this point to get an official accounting of exactly what happened, clearly there were significant communication and coordination problems at all levels of government. At the moment, much time and effort is being spent assigning culpability—for a lack of preparation, delayed decision making, bureaucratic tie-ups and political infighting—to individuals and agencies. But in the end, such investigations may produce little that is of widespread practical use.

What is more critical, and has significant implications for the future of emergency management in the United States, is the need to explicitly and thoroughly define governments' roles and responsibilities so that officials in other jurisdictions don't suffer the same sort of meltdown in the next natural or man-made disaster. The lurching tactical responses to the terrorist attacks of 2001 and a rash of major hurricanes only underline the truly fundamental issue: how to sort out who should do what—and how to make sure the public sector is ready to act when the unexpected but inevitable happens.

It won't be easy. Some in the federal government clearly feel that if they're going to be blamed for failures—failures that they ascribe at least in part to state and local officials—then they'd prefer a system where the federal government has the option of being much more preemptive in handling large-scale domestic disasters. States as a whole, though, are not going to go along with any emergency management plan that involves the feds declaring something like martial law. They would much prefer that existing protocols be continued and the Federal Emergency Management Agency regain its independence from the Department of Homeland Security and be led by experienced professionals rather than political appointees.

■   ■   ■

LOCAL RESPONSE

. . . All emergencies are, initially at least, local—or local and state—events. "For the first 48 to 72 hours, it's understood that local and state first responders are principally responsible," says Bill Jenkins, director of the Homeland Security and Justice Issues Group, which is currently looking into the intergovernmental response to Katrina. "The feds come in as requested after that."

The extent to which the local-state-federal response ramps up depends on a host of factors, including the size of the incident and what plans and agreements are in place prior to any event. It also very much depends on the capacity of the governments involved. Some local and state governments have the ability to deal with disasters on their own and seem less inclined to ask for outside help. Others seem to hit the intergovernmental panic button more quickly. But whichever it is, say those on the front line of emergency response, how various governmental partners in emergency response and recovery are going to respond shouldn't be a surprise-filled adventure. Key players at every level of government should have a very good idea of what each will be expected to do or provide when a particular disaster hits.

Most important to the strength of the intergovernmental chain are solid relationships among those who might be called upon to work closely together in times of high stress. "You don't want to meet someone for the first time while you're standing around in the rubble," says Jarrod Bernstein, spokesman for the New York City Office of Emergency Management. "You want to meet them during drills and exercises." In New York, notes Bernstein, the city has very tight relationships with state and federal officials in a variety of agencies. "They're involved in all our planning and all our drills. They have a seat at all the tabletop exercises we do."

During those exercises, says Bernstein, federal, state and local officials establish and agree on what their respective jobs will be when a "big one" hits. Last summer, for example, the city worked with FEMA, the U.S. Department of Health and Human Services, the Federal Bureau of Investigation and New York State health and emergency response officials on an exercise aimed at collecting 8 million doses of medicine and distributing them throughout the city in a 48-hour window. "What we were looking at is how we'd receive medical stockpiles from the federal government, break them down and push them out citywide. There is a built-in federal component to that plan," Bernstein says.

NO PLAN B

While pre-plans and dry runs are all well and good, they're not much use if not taken seriously, however. In 2004, FEMA and Louisiana's Office of Homeland Security and Emergency Preparedness conducted a tabletop exercise, called Hurricane Pam, that simulated a Category 3 storm hitting and flooding New Orleans. It identified a huge gap in disaster planning: An estimated 100,000 people wouldn't be able to get out of the city without assistance. As is standard in emergency management practice, it is the locality's responsibility—at least initially—to evacuate residents, unless other partners are identified beforehand.

Critics of Mayor Ray Nagin say he failed to follow up aggressively on the finding. Last spring, the city floated the notion that it would rely primarily on the faith-based community to organize and mobilize caravans for those without cars or who needed special assistance getting out of the city. The faith-based community balked, however, citing liability issues. The city never came up with a Plan B.

Meanwhile, the Department of Homeland Security had great confidence in its 426-page "all-hazards" National Response Plan. Unveiled last January, it "establishes standardized training, organization and communications procedures for multi-jurisdictional interaction; clearly identifies authority and leadership responsibilities; enables incident response to be handled at the lowest possible organizational and jurisdictional level; ensures the seamless integration of the federal government when an incident exceeds state or local capabilities; and provides the means to swiftly deliver federal support in response to catastrophic incidents."

Katrina was its first test. And in the wake of the Category 4 storm and subsequent flooding, the city's vital resources—communications, transportation, supplies and manpower—were quickly overwhelmed. But DHS Secretary Michael Chertoff waited until 24 hours after the levees were breached to designate the hurricane as an "incident of national significance—requiring an extensive and well-coordinated response by federal, state, local, tribal and nongovernmental authorities to save lives, minimize damage and provide the basis for long-term community and economic recovery."

The nation—indeed the world—bore painful witness to its failure. "There are mechanisms and protocols set up as part of the National Response Plan, and those were not followed," says John R. Harrald, director of the Institute for Crisis, Disaster and Risk Management at George Washington University. Harrald notes that under the response plan, one of the first things that's supposed to happen is the rapid activation of a joint operations center to coordinate the intergovernmental response. In Louisiana, that didn't happen quickly enough, he says.

CALLING IN THE TROOPS

As a result of Katrina, and to a lesser extent Hurricanes Rita and Wilma, the general citizenry and elected leaders at all levels of government, as well as emergency responders up and down the chain of command, are demanding a comprehensive review of how local, state and federal governments work (or don't work) together.

Part of that discussion has to include what to do when a state or local government's ability to prepare, respond or to ask for help is either impaired or wiped out altogether. "The question is what do you do when state and local capacity fails for one reason or another, either because they're overwhelmed or they're incompetent," says GWU's Harrald. "Do we have a system that allows us to scale up adequately or do we need a system where we can bring the military in sooner but that doesn't give away state and local control?"

Bill Leighty, Virginia Governor Mark Warner's chief of staff, who volunteered to spend two weeks in Louisiana helping manage the state response to Katrina, says he thinks there needs to be a serious intergovernmental discussion about when, for example, it might be appropriate to involve the military more directly in a domestic crisis. It is a position born of watching FEMA in action, versus what he saw of the military while he was in New Orleans. FEMA's bureaucratic approach to every item it provided or action it took was, at times, brutally exasperating, says Leighty. "But when you tell the 82nd Airborne, 'Secure New Orleans,' they come in and they know exactly what to do and it gets done."

Even some longtime New Orleans residents, who watched helplessly as looters rampaged through parts of the city, say they wouldn't have minded at all if the military had stepped in to restore order. "There are times when people are overwhelmed," says Frank Cilluffo, director of the Homeland Security Policy Institute at George Washington University, "and they don't care what color uniform is involved in coming to the rescue—red, blue or green."

However, both Kathleen Babineaux Blanco, the Democratic governor of Louisiana, and Haley Barbour, the Republican governor of Mississippi, strenuously objected to requests from the White House to give the Pentagon command over their states' National Guard troops. And President George W. Bush's suggestion of a quick resort to the military in future disasters stunned many observers, including those in his own party. In a television address from New Orleans, he argued that only the armed forces were "capable of massive logistical operations on a moment's notice."

But governors were aghast at the idea that the military would become America's first responders. In a *USA Today* poll, 36 of 38 governors (including brother Jeb Bush) opposed the plan. Michigan Governor Jennifer Granholm put it bluntly: "Whether a governor is a Republican or Democrat, I would expect the response would be, 'Hell no.'" For one blogger, the worry was

"How long before a creek flooding in a small town in Idaho will activate the 82d Airborne Division?"

Bush grabbed the military option in part because of the poor performance of state and local governments. Indeed, everyone breathed a sigh of relief when Coast Guard Admiral Thad Allen arrived to assume command.

Part of the explanation also lies in public opinion polls. A Pew Research Center survey just after the storm revealed that nearly half of those surveyed believed state and local governments had done a fair or poor job—and there was no partisan difference on that conclusion. That meant the smart political play for Bush, although he didn't fare much better in the poll, was to suggest that the military might have to do what state and local governments could not.

That idea, of course, could scarcely be further from the strategy the Republicans had spent a generation building. The Richard Nixon–Ronald Reagan model of new federalism revolved around giving the states more autonomy and less money. But faced with the need to do something—and lacking any alternative—Bush reached back to Lyndon Johnson's Great Society philosophy of an expanded role for the federal government.

But Bush's plan to push the military into a first-response role was clearly less a broad policy strategy than a tactic to find a safe haven in the post-Katrina blame game. That became clear in November, when he announced his avian flu initiative. In that plan, he penciled in a heavy role for state and local public health officials.

CONTROL AND CONTENTION

Some believe there is a middle ground when it comes to issues of authority and autonomy. James A. Stever, director of the Center for Integrated Homeland Security and Crisis Management at the University of Cincinnati, says he and colleagues had forwarded a paper to the former head of Homeland Security, Tom Ridge, outlining the concept of "homeland restoration districts." The idea is to have established criteria for when a more robust federal disaster response might be appropriate. Recovery districts would allow for ad hoc federal takeovers of specific geographic areas when appropriate, says Stever, rather than creating some new, overriding national response protocol that calls for broad federal preemption of local and state authority.

But sifting through such ideas—and the others that are sure to surface—is going to mean rekindling the sort of conversation about intergovernmental coordination and cooperation that Washington hasn't seen in a long time.

▪   ▪   ▪

From hurricanes and pandemics and to earthquakes and terrorism, the United States is grappling with the prospect of a host of cataclysmic events. Taken individually, most communities face a small chance of being hit, but experts agree that its not a matter of "if" but "when" another large-scale disaster will occur somewhere in the United States. As Katrina so powerfully illustrated, a fragmented intergovernmental response can be disastrous.

BIBLIOGRAPHY

Federal Emergency Management Agency (FEMA). 2004 "Region VI. Hurricane Pam Exercise Concludes." Release date: July 23, 2004. Release number: R6-04-093. <http://www.fema.gov/newsrelease_print.fema?id13051>
U.S. Department of Homeland Security. 2004. *National Response Plan.* (December).

4

CIVIL RIGHTS AND CIVIL LIBERTIES

4.1

MICHAEL DAWSON

From *Behind the Mule: Race and Class in African-American Politics*

Dawson reminds us of what other scholars have found: that many individual African Americans believe that their fate is linked to the status of others who are similar. But similarity can mean different things. Do African Americans believe they have common political interests with others of similar economic class? Or do they believe they have common political interests with others of the same race? Using survey data, Dawson shows that race is more important than class in explaining African American political behavior.

This reading examines the tension—highlighted by these two images—between racial interests and class interests as factors shaping African-American politics. The tension arises from the historical legacy of racial and economic oppression that forged racial identity of African Americans. As bluesman Booker White suggests, the key to the historical origins of African-American social identity can be found "behind the mule." It is this legacy of a social identity in which racial and economic oppression have been intertwined for generations that has been the critical component in understanding not only the cultural basis of African-American politics, as Henry (1990) has argued, but also the material roots of black politics. As blues analyst Samuel Charters suggests, only when one "stripped away the misconception that the black society in the United States was simply a poor, discouraged version of the white" could one understand African-American society (Baker 1984). Although Charters was referring to the blues, his point is equally applicable to black politics. African-American politics, including political behavior, is *different*. It has been shaped by historical forces that produced a different pattern of political behavior from the pattern found among white citizens.[1]

■   ■   ■

THE PROBLEM: RACE AND CLASS AS COMPETING THEORIES OF AFRICAN-AMERICAN POLITICS

This study was motivated by a set of questions that have captured the attention of scholars such as W.E.B. Du Bois, Robert Dahl, and William Wilson. The central question, simply stated, is whether race or class is more important in shaping African-American politics. This question has been central both to the study of African-American society and to the study of ethnic politics. Both traditions have investigated when social scientists should expect racial and ethnic loyalties to decline, and when that decline is accompanied by a parallel decline in racially or ethnically oriented politics.

These questions are of general interest for two reasons. First, America is becoming racially and ethnically more diverse, and the effects of that diversity are being felt politically: rapidly growing Asian and Latino populations are reshaping politics in politically important states such as Florida and California, and, in addition, the increasing racial tensions that accompany increased diversity are sometimes played out in the political arena. Examples of the salience of racial tensions in the political arena during the 1980s and early 1990s include the 1983 mayoral races in Chicago and Philadelphia (won by Harold Washington and W. Wilson Goode, respectively), the strong showing among white voters in David Duke's 1991 gubernatorial race in Louisiana, and the English-only referenda in several states. Jesse Helms's 1990 Senate campaign, already mentioned, was a model of how to exploit racial fears, tensions, and outright racism.

Second, racial politics presents analysts of the American party system with several puzzles. One is the lack of diversity in African-American politics. Many scholars and political activists ask, Where are the black Republicans? Another puzzle is why the study of black politics has not become more central to the study of American political parties and other major American political institutions, despite the recognized importance of racial politics. Carmines and Stimson (1989) have argued that the party system has been transformed by racial politics, whereas Huckfeldt and Kohfeld (1989) argue that class politics has been submerged by racial politics.

■   ■   ■

Race

Most students of black politics generally, and of black political behavior specifically, argue that one should expect continued political homogeneity among African Americans. This position is based on the belief that the primary imperative in black politics is to advance the political interests of African Americans as a racial group (Barker 1988; Pinderhughes 1987; Walters 1988).

This belief, in turn, is based on studies by numerous observers showing that race is still a major social, economic, and political force in American society and a major shaper of African-American lives. Socially, scholars of this school argue, residential segregation is still a fact of American life and has major ramifications. Residential segregation, they argue, determines the quality of schooling available to African Americans; it means that the property of the black middle and working classes appreciates more slowly than the property of the white middle and working classes, contributing to the enormous gap in wealth between black and white Americans; and by concentrating poverty in black neighborhoods, it negatively affects the neighborhoods even of the black middle class, which is less able to escape neighborhoods with significant concentrations of poverty than it would be if residential segregation did not exist. These scholars also point to the apparent increase in violent racial incidents during the 1980s in cities and suburbs and on college campuses as a social factor that affects African Americans regardless of their class.

Within the economic sphere, adherents of this view argue, the entire class structure of black America is distorted by the legacy of racism. A black capitalist class does not fully exist. Further, the black middle class is economically vulnerable because of its extreme reliance on public sector and quasi-public sector employment. In addition, middle-class blacks own less wealth per family than poor whites. The median and mean levels of household wealth are less for black families that earn over $50,000 a year than for white families that earn under $10,000 a year.

Wealth is an often ignored but important indicator of life chances because it signifies the ability to transmit resources from one generation to the next, to produce income from resources, and to survive financial setbacks. Thus, the lack of wealth in the black middle class means that even affluent black families often find it difficult to pass resources to their children, that a pool of capital (often necessary for the survival of small businesses) is not available, and that many black middle-class families are, in Landry's words, "one paycheck from disaster" (Landry 1987). Glass ceilings (unspoken barriers to the promotion of minorities and women to partnership in firms and top managerial ranks) and other forms of inequity have also harmed the financial stability of the black middle and working classes.

Politically, these same scholars argue, race remains a major force in the lives of African Americans. The lack of competition between the two parties for the black vote, in combination with the recent shift to the right in American politics, reinforces the need for African-American political unity to continue. Whether one is talking about the cutback of means-tested programs of vital importance to the black poor or about the massive attack on the affirmative action programs that benefit the more affluent African Americans, these scholars conclude that the political interests of all African Americans are still bound by race.

According to this line of reasoning, because the social, economic, and political realities of whites and blacks differ substantially *because of race*, racial interests continue to override class interests (whether individual or family). And as long as this is true—as long as the political interests of African Americans are bound by race—one should expect high levels of political unity among African Americans *regardless of economic status*.

Class

There is, however, increasing support for the competing hypothesis that race is no longer the most salient factor in African-American lives because economic polarization within the black community is accelerating. University of Chicago sociologist William Wilson has been the most forceful proponent of the thesis that class has become the most salient social determinant of African Americans' life chances. In *The Declining Significance of Race* (1980) he makes three important claims. The first (the one that has given the book so much notoriety) is that discrimination is now less important in determining a person's life chances than social status or economic class. His second claim (which several scholars and politicians have embraced) is that the civil rights movement benefited mostly middle-class, well-trained, younger African Americans. Wilson's third claim is that to some degree the civil rights movement was consciously led by the black middle class mainly to benefit their own class interests.

Wilson's claims taken as a whole have profound implications for African-American politics. If it is true that in the 1960s American society changed so much that race ceased to be the overwhelming or even the major determinant of the fate of individual African Americans, one would expect African-American political behavior to reflect increasing diversity. As Dawson and Wilson (1991) have detailed, most major social science theories would predict that increased economic heterogeneity in a population would lead to increasing diversity in political behavior. Social theorist Robert Dahl, for example, in *Who Governs?* (1961), a sophisticated presentation of ethnic political development, certainly predicted this growing political diversity.

Some empirical evidence exists to support Wilson and like-minded scholars. Economic polarization among African Americans has indeed been increasing over the past twenty years. Both the black middle class and the group of economically marginalized African Americans have grown.

From 1960 to 1991, the black middle class more than doubled in size. Approximately one third of employed blacks now have middle-class occupations. (But when the unemployed and discouraged workers are added to the pool, the relative size of the black middle class shrinks to approximately 15 percent.) So on the one hand, there is a growing, if vulnerable, black middle class. Moreover, those such as Wilson would argue, despite glass ceilings, job and social segregation, residential segregation, and the like, this class has more opportunities than any group of African Americans in history. This is held to be particularly true of the new black middle class, which has grown as a result of advances in black civil rights—blacks whose economic status is based on employment in sectors not traditionally tied to the black community, such as multinational corporations, the media, predominantly white universities, and businesses that sell to predominantly white markets or to the government (Boston 1988; Landry 1987). In the future, the new black middle class may not identify as strongly with the black community, the Democratic party, or liberal causes.

On the other hand, the number of African Americans without stable employment is also growing. In the 1980s, black unemployment rates in states such as Illinois and Michigan were significantly higher than 20 percent. Among key age cohorts of black men—those who should be at the beginning or in the middle of their prime earning years—labor force participation rates have been decreasing. The result is that African Americans—adults and children alike—are three times more likely to live below the poverty line than whites. And when we look at families as opposed to individuals, as late as 1987, 30 percent of black families, containing 45 percent of black children, were below the poverty line. Nearly 70 percent of these poor families are headed by women. The lives of economically marginalized African Americans are dominated by the struggle for economic survival.

Many would argue that economic polarization within the black community will continue to increase throughout the 1990s and will bring in its wake increasing political polarization. African Americans already display an unusually high degree of class consciousness when compared with other Americans. Such consciousness is likely to grow, particularly among less affluent African Americans; as the objective importance of race in the lives of African Americans declines interests diverge. According to the proponents of the class thesis, the dire *economic* status of large numbers of African Americans, especially in contrast to the improved economic status of large numbers of other African Americans, dictates that class will supersede race as the most politically salient factor for African Americans.

A SOLUTION: A GROUP-INTERESTS PERSPECTIVE ON AFRICAN-AMERICAN POLITICS

This reading develops a framework for analyzing African-American political choice by testing whether race or class is the primary determinant of contemporary African-American political behavior and public opinion. This framework draws in recent work in the psychology of social groups to help explain how psychological processes are critical for the formation of social identity. Particularly the work of Turner (1987) is used to help develop a theory of African-American group interests that explains the continued political homogeneity of African Americans and describes the conditions under which African Americans will begin to display political diversity.

My framework is based on two assumptions. First, it is quite clear that, until the mid-1960s, race was the decisive factor in determining the opportunities and life chances available to virtually all African Americans, regardless of their own or their family's social and economic status. Consequently, it was much more efficient for African Americans to determine what was good for the racial group than to determine what was good for themselves individually, and more efficient for them to use the status of the group, both relative and absolute, as a proxy for individual utility. I call this phenomenon the *black utility heuristic*.[2] The black utility heuristic is the basis for my framework for analyzing micro black politics. It was more efficient to use group status as a proxy not only because a piece of legislation or a public policy could be analyzed relatively easily for its effect on the race but also because the information sources available in the black community—the media outlets, kinship networks, community and civil rights organizations, and especially the preeminent institution in the black community, the black church—would all reinforce the political salience of racial interests and would provide information about racial group status.

Second, I assume that cognitive psychological processes are critical in shaping perceptions of racial group status. Psychological theories of attribution and self-categorization suggest that psychological processes on the individual level would reinforce the salience of racial politics for African Americans. Information that either minimized intragroup differences or exaggerated intergroup differences would be accepted more easily than information that contradicted current images of the importance of race in politics. Errors in information processing and biases in decision making would tend to favor racial explanations of the social world. The salience of one's racial identity, or of any other group identity, is a function of the cognitive accessibility of information pertinent to that identity, and the fit of that identity with social reality. This fact suggests two ways in which racial identity can become less salient for African Americans. One way is if information about the political, economic, and social world of black America becomes less accessible, either because individual blacks do not live in the black community (some members of the black middle class are in fact moving out of black communities) or because social networks in the black community are breaking down, as has happened in some of the most economically devastated inner-city neighborhoods (Marable 1983; Wilson 1980, 1987). The other way, particularly for the new black middle class, is if race becomes less salient in individuals' own lives. This is essentially the process described by Wilson and Dahl.

If neither of those developments takes place—that is, if information does not become less accessible and race does not become less personally salient—we should expect the combination of the cognitive phenomenon of accessibility and fit to slow the growth of political diversity in the African

American community. And, in fact, exiting from their community is much harder for black Americans than it was for European ethnic groups earlier in the nation's history or for Asians or Latinos today. In addition, to the degree to which the political and social climate is still perceived to be racially hostile, economic information is counteracted, with the result that racial group politics remains salient for African Americans. It is upon these assumptions that my framework for analyzing African-American political choice is based.

▪   ▪   ▪

INTRODUCTION

Political and economic concerns have been at the forefront of African-American activism throughout American history. While either economic or political concerns may be more prominent during any given period in African-American history, politics and economics have been constant arenas for black struggle. Several scholars have documented the historical interplay between African Americans' efforts to achieve both racial and economic justice. . . . [3] The fierce Booker T. Washington-W.E.B. Du Bois debate was partly over the relative importance of economic and political strategies for black advancement. However, most African Americans, and Du Bois himself later in his career, have believed that advancement on both fronts is necessary and that the two types of progress are intertwined. The New Deal policies of Franklin D. Roosevelt confirmed the importance of the link between politics and economics for African Americans. As numerous scholars have shown for the white electorate, evaluations of the status of the American economy itself structure African-American individual-level as well as aggregate-level political choices and evaluations. Not surprisingly, however, *how* economic evaluations structure political decision making for blacks differs from how it does for whites. These interest-based evaluations of the economy powerfully structure African Americans' political behavior. Economic group interests directly and indirectly influence such basic political phenomena as African-American party identification, candidate evaluations, and voting behavior.

MEASURES OF CLASS AND THE AFRICAN-AMERICAN CLASS STRUCTURE

Wilson in *The Declining Significance of Race* (1980), calls class a "slippery concept." For African Americans the concept of class is even more problematic than usual because of the severe distortion of the African-American class structure due to the historical legacy of racism and exploitation. Several students of the American class structure have noted the extreme attenuation of the African-American class structure as compared with that of whites. Wright and colleagues (1982), working from a neo-Marxist framework, state that the black middle class is much smaller and the black working class is much larger than those of whites. According to Wright, for example, the black working class comprises 64 percent of the black population while the white working class comprises only 44 percent of the white population. Black managers are only 7 percent of the black population while white managers are 14 percent of the white population. Small-business owners (the Marxist petty bourgeoisie) and capitalists/employers combined only make up 3 percent of the black population as compared to 25 percent of whites. Boston (1988) finds similar divergence in his work on black social classes. He also argues that a black capitalist class with any social influence within the black community does not exist. He finds that the black middle class, when adjusted for the high rate of black unemployment, comprises 11 percent of the black population as opposed to an unemployment-adjusted white percentage of 27 percent.

This distortion of the African-American class structure is apparent whether one looks at various occupational structures, or looks at income and employment patterns. . . . Wilson (1980, ix) defines class as "any group of people who have more or less similar goods, services, or skills to offer for income in a given economic order and do therefore receive similar remuneration in the marketplace." This is the definition adopted here.

Several reasons—some theoretical, others pragmatic—support the adoption of Wilson's admittedly broad definition. First, it is flexible enough to accommodate both changes in the structure of the American political economy and changes in the African-American political economy. For many observers of African-American society, the stunning change in the African-American class structure that has occurred in the second half of the twentieth century is the creation of a new black middle class at the same time that many African-American workers became economically marginalized. This definition allows for the possibility that as the structure of the economy changes, new segments within classes may develop, or over time new classes may develop. Certainly, new structural opportunities have led to a situation in which a new segment has developed consisting of people whose income is less dependent on the black community and more dependent on traditionally white enterprises, both in the government and in the private sector. For Wilson, higher class means, among other things, greater life chances and higher income. Although Landry rejects a notion of class based on income or education, he argues that education is an enabling factor for higher class position while income is a reward for higher class position. Indeed, Boston argues that the new black middle class, in particular, is distinguished both by its members' possession of "scarce skills" and by their resulting relatively high salaries.

Boston and Wilson explicitly argue that different classes within the African-American population have different political interests. Of course, Wilson argues that race is declining in importance as a factor for determining African-American life chances and that class is an increasingly important factor. Boston, who directly challenges Wilson, still argues that within each class there are strata of African Americans who share similar class-based interests and political beliefs, even though for virtually all classes of African Americans, class positions have been influenced by racism. Consequently, he argues that if there is a social basis for the media pronouncements of a new black conservatism that were frequent during the Reagan administration, it is to be found in the new black middle class. This is because the financial well-being of the new black middle class is separate from that of the African-American community as a whole. Wilson (1987) would add that this class has also physically separated itself from the black community in a new suburban exodus from the inner city.

However, as Boston and others have pointed out, this class is so small as to be almost undetectable using social surveys. Research strategies such as participant observation or analysis of the social organizations of this new, up-and-coming black economic elite may be more fruitful in understanding the political beliefs of all classes of African Americans. Surveys, however, do provide tools with which to test the basic *political* proposition that as African Americans' station in life has improved in the late twentieth century, their political beliefs have become increasingly divergent from those of less affluent blacks. Most of the arguments advanced by scholars such as Boston and Wilson restate fairly directly the somewhat simplistic phrase "being determines consciousness." In other words, as *objective status* improves, African Americans become more conservative.

Jackman and Jackman (1983), however, argue that while individuals' perceptions of social class are highly correlated with income, education, and occupation, cultural beliefs are also important in all Americans' perceptions of class; for African Americans, they further contend that cultural beliefs are more important than objective criteria. They do argue that simple white collar-blue collar schemes of class, which ignore, for example, the routinized work of those such as secretaries, are inadequate for understanding even objective perceptions of class.[4] When exploring the "class consciousness" of African Americans, Jackman and Jackman found that working-class and middle-class blacks, unlike whites, exhibit higher degrees of racial identity than class identity. Those who are in a subordinate position seem to feel that they share a common fate, according to the Jackmans. Thus, racial identity cuts across class lines. However, because I am concerned in this reading to test Wilson's and others' thesis that *objective changes in the African-American class structure should lead to political divergence*, the objective measures of economic status are the ones that will be utilized here.

I also considered measures of occupation, income, and education. As previously mentioned, the new black middle class possess unprecedented educational opportunities and subsequent remuneration that allegedly follows their investment in "human capital." I also considered occupation, but the lack of variation among African Americans in their occupational attainment captured in social surveys limits the utility of occupation as a measure of class in this analysis. On the other hand, even those such as Landry who strongly prefer occupational measures state that one's education and income are closely related to one's class position. Further, the type of complex analysis of occupation and job content preferred by those influenced by the Marxist tradition such as Wright and colleagues (1982) is unsuitable for this analysis for two reasons. First, as Wright himself reports, the small number of African Americans falling into the petty bourgeois and employer categories makes any systematic analysis of how African-American political behavior and public opinion vary with class extremely difficult. Second, political surveys of African Americans do not contain the instrumentation necessary to probe the complex class positions suggested by Wright. Third, the concept of occupation itself becomes fuzzy when one examines a population such as African Americans in which a significant portion is either temporarily out of the labor force or has never been in the labor force.

More fundamentally, the concept of occupation imperfectly captures the shifts in the African-American class structure. Consider two black lawyers. One is a recent graduate from an elite law school who is working at a major corporation or law firm. She is earning an excellent salary that is at least somewhat on par with those of her white classmates. The other is an older lawyer who was not allowed to go to an elite law school and has a practice based in the black community. This lawyer's income hardly matches the salary of the other lawyer, but both share the same occupation. In this case, income better captures the disparities between class segments than does occupation. Income and education are the primary class measures used in this study.

COMPONENTS OF GROUP INTERESTS: MEASURES AND DATA

The central assumption of the black utility heuristic is that the more one believes one's own life chances are linked to those of blacks as a group, the more one will consider racial group interests in evaluating alternative political choices. This evaluation includes choosing between different public policies and evaluating candidates and parties, as well as engaging in other forms of political action. Such consideration of racial group interests contrasts with the use of other criteria for evaluating self-interest, particularly individual economic status. It has been argued that economic domination has been (and, many would argue, continues to be) an important aspect of African-American *political* reality over the past three centuries. Hence, a belief about the economic subordination of blacks is a component of racial group interests.

This theory is based to a significant degree on the self-categorization and social identity theories of Turner (1987). Individuals form their concepts of self at least in part by judging their similarities with and differences from others. This social identity theory allows for multiple self-concepts, prompted by different contexts, but the key to understanding the self-categorization process for African Americans is the fact that *the social category "black" in Ameri-*

can society cuts across multiple boundaries. African Americans and whites pray, play, and get paid differently.

Crucial to the formation of social identity is the active process of comparing in-group and out-group members. The more differences that are perceived between the in-group and the out-group on the salient social dimensions, the stronger the group identity of in-group members. A salient contrast between blacks and whites is the difference between black and white economic status. As a consequence of the process of comparison, black economic status shapes evaluations of the national economy. In the political domain, black evaluation of the political parties is based on African Americans' perceptions of how well the political parties serve black interests.

This approach is different from that of scholars who analyze social identity from the standpoint of group consciousness. While the concept of linked fate is similar to Conover's concept of interdependence and very close to Gurin's and colleagues' concept of common fate, it differs in that it explicitly links perceptions of self-interest to perceptions of racial group interests. Gurin's concept of group consciousness incorporates discontent with illegitimate social inequities, social comparisons, social identity, and collective action (Gurin, Hatchett, and Jackson 1989). Conover's definition also incorporates social identification, causal attributions concerning in-groups' and out-groups' status, and cognitive structures that incorporate affect as well as the other psychological attributes. While these definitions of group consciousness provide a useful measure of available psychological resources, the heuristic introduced here is intended to suggest a simpler mechanism by which the proposition that African-American political solidarity breaks down as economic polarization increases can be directly tested. Conover (1984) suggests that one's perceptions of group interests can become "personally relevant," but not "synonymous" with self-interest. My claim is somewhat different: the historical experiences of African Americans have resulted in a situation in which group interests have served as a useful proxy for self-interest.

MEASURES OF AFRICAN-AMERICAN RACIAL INTERESTS

Two components of group interests are critical to the political process for African Americans. For group interests to affect the political process, a significant number of African Americans must believe that what happens to the group as a whole affects their own lives. A construct of *linked fate* is needed to measure the degree to which African Americans believe that their own self-interests are linked to the interests of the race. Second, evaluations of relative group status, particularly economic status, are essential for understanding African-American perceptions of racial group interests.

The National Black Election Panel Study (NBES) of 1984–1988 demonstrates both the basic underpinnings of black group interests and the role they played in shaping African-American political behavior and political beliefs in 1984 and 1988. The study consisted of a national telephone survey in which 1,150 interviews were conducted with members of the adult African-American population. The NBES is one of the most extensive political surveys of the African-American population that has been conducted. . . .

The 1988 NBES survey provides both economic and general measures of absolute and relative group status. These measures allow us to compare the different hypotheses according to which the most important determinants of political choice are based on class, individual utility, evaluations of what is good for society, or racial group utility, respectively. Further, measures are provided that allow us to test the relative salience of both current and retrospective evaluations.

The concept of linked fate was measured in both 1984 and 1988. Survey participants were asked, "Do you think that what happens generally to the black people in this country will have something to do with what happens in your life?" Figure 1 shows the distribution of responses to this question. In 1984, 63 percent of the NBES sample responded affirmatively, and in 1988, the figure was 64 percent. Perceptions of economic subordination of blacks were also measured. The question was asked, "On the whole, would you say that the economic position of blacks is better, about the same, or worse than that of whites?" As shown in Figure 2, 65 percent of African Americans in both years of the sampling responded that blacks are in a worse economic position than whites.

FIGURE 1   Perceptions of linked fate, 1984 and 1988: "Do you think that what happens generally to the black people in this country will have something to do with what happens in your life?" Category values represent percentage of respondents responding in that category.

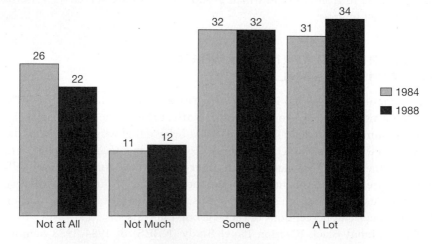

SOURCE: 1984–1988 National Black Election Panel Study.

FIGURE 2   Perceptions of economic subordination, 1984 and 1988: "On the whole, would you say that the economic position of blacks is better, about the same, or worse than that of whites?" Category values represent percentage of respondents responding in that category.

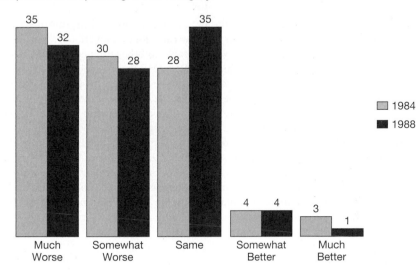

SOURCE: 1984–1988 National Black Election Panel Study.

Do perceptions of either linked fate or economic subordination vary with one's class position? To answer this question I look first at the . . . relationships between perceptions of linked fate and education. . . . Linked fate varies very slightly with socioeconomic variables. Variables associated with linked fate in 1984 were not associated with linked fate in 1988. . . .

A parallel analysis was conducted for perceptions of economic subordination. . . . There appears to be very little covariation between the socioeconomic measures and the measure of perceptions of economic subordination. Furthermore, occupation seems to add little information to that provided by education and income. Clearly, there is a relationship between socioeconomic status and perceptions of economic subordination. . . . This preliminary analysis suggests that those with more education and status are more likely than their less affluent cousins to believe that blacks as a group are in a poor economic state absolutely and relatively.

■   ■   ■

CONCLUSION

. . . Socioeconomic status only weakly influences perceptions of linked fate. The economic and political components of group interest have a major role in shaping perceptions of both economic well-being and relative group influence. . . . Throughout the 1980s, individual beliefs and perceptions constituted a firm basis for relatively unified group political behavior.

NOTES

1. By extension, the degree to which the politics of Latinos and Asian-Americans deviates from standard American politics also warrants an investigation.

2. This heuristic should in principle be applicable to other groups; the particular way it is manifest would depend on the historical context. For example, in many periods and places, a Jewish person's religious identity might well have dominated all other social identities; in the France of the 1980s, North Africans' identity and political struggles with other French were tied to the North Africans' belief in Islam. For African Americans, I shall argue, identity has been tied to subordinate economic status.

3. Marable's political economy approach to black politics is based partly on the political economy approach of Poulantzas (see Poulantzas 1974).

4. Thus, they argue, secretarial work is misclassified as white collar both because of the way the work has changed with the coming of large office pools, and because of the relatively low prestige ranking of secretarial, clerical, and related occupations that employ a significant percentage of women.

REFERENCES

Baker, Houston A., Jr. 1984. *Blues, ideology, and Afro-American literature: A vernacular theory.* Chicago: University of Chicago Press.

Barker, Lucius J. 1988. *Our time has come: A delegate's diary of Jesse Jackson's 1984 presidential campaign.* Urbana: University of Illinois Press.

Boston, Thomas D. 1988. *Race, class, and conservatism.* London: Unwin Hyman.

Carmines, Edward G., and James A. Stimson. 1989. *Issue evolution: Race and the transformation of American Politics.* Princeton: Princeton University Press.

Conover, Pamela Johnston. 1984. The influence of group identification on political perception and evaluation. *Journal of Politics* 46: 760–85.

Dahl, Robert A. 1961. *Who governs?* New Haven: Yale University Press.

Dawson, Michael C., and Ernest J. Wilson III. 1991. Paradigms and paradoxes: Political science and African American politics. In *Political science: Looking to the future,* ed. William Crotty, 1: 189–234.

Gurin, Patricia, Shirley Hatchett, and James S. Jackson. 1989. *Hope and independence: Blacks' response to electoral and party politics.* New York: Russell Sage Foundation.

Henry, Charles P. 1990. *Culture and African American politics.* Bloomington: Indiana University Press.

Huckfeldt, Robert R., and Carol Weitzel Kohfeld. 1989. *Race and the decline of class in American politics.* Urbana: University of Illinois Press.

Jackman, Mary R., and Robert W. Jackman. 1983. *Class awareness in the United States.* Berkeley: University of California Press.

Landry, Bart. 1987. *The new black middle class.* Berkeley: University of California Press.

Marable, Manning. 1983. *How capitalism underdeveloped black America: Problems in race, political economy, and society.* Boston: South End Press.

Pinderhughes, Dianne. 1987. *Race and ethnicity in Chicago politics.* Urbana: University of Illinois Press.

Poulantzas, Nicos. 1974. *Political power and social classes.* London: New Left Books.

Turner, John C. 1987. *Rediscovering the social group: A self-categorization theory.* Oxford: Basil Blackwell.

Walters, Ronald W. 1988. *Black presidential politics in America: A strategic approach.* Albany: State University of New York Press.

Wilson, William J. 1980. *The declining significance of race.* 2d ed. Chicago: University of Chicago Press.

———. 1987. *The truly disadvantaged: The inner city, the underclass, and public policy.* Chicago: University of Chicago Press.

Wright, Erik Olin, David Hachen, Cynthia Costello, and Joey Sprague. 1982. The American class structure. *American Sociological Review* 47: 709–26.

4.2

Brown v. Board of Education (1954)

In one of the most important Supreme Court cases in American history, the justices unanimously and emphatically overturned the precedent from Plessy v. Ferguson (1896), *which had upheld the right of local communities and states to maintain separate public facilities for the races. "[I]n the field of public education," the Court declared, "the doctrine of 'separate but equal' has no place." This 1954 decision started the American legal system down a new path of active intervention in the racial policies of government at all levels.*

Mr. Chief Justice Warren delivered the opinion of the Court.

These cases come to us from the States of Kansas, South Carolina, Virginia, and Delaware. They are premised on different facts and different local conditions, but a common legal question justifies their consideration together in this consolidated opinion.

In each of the cases, minors of the Negro race, through their legal representatives, seek the aid of the courts in obtaining admission to the public schools of their community on a nonsegregated basis. In each instance, they had been denied admission to schools attended by white children under laws requiring or permitting segregation according to race. This segregation was alleged to deprive the plaintiffs of the equal protection of the laws under the Fourteenth Amendment. In each of the cases other than the Delaware case, a three-judge federal district court denied relief to the plaintiffs on the so-called "separate but equal" doctrine announced by this Court in *Plessy v. Ferguson.* Under that doctrine, equality of treatment is accorded when the races are provided substantially equal facilities, even though these facilities be separate. In the Delaware case, the Supreme Court of Delaware adhered to that doctrine, but ordered that the plaintiffs be admitted to the white schools because of their superiority to the Negro schools.

The plaintiffs contend that segregated public schools are not "equal" and cannot be made "equal," and that hence they are deprived of the equal protection of the laws. Because of the obvious importance of the question presented, the Court took jurisdiction. Argument was heard in the 1952 Term, and reargument was heard this Term on certain questions propounded by the Court.

Reargument was largely devoted to the circumstances surrounding the adoption of the Fourteenth Amendment in 1868. It covered exhaustively consideration of the Amendment in Congress, ratification by the states, then-existing practices in racial segregation, and the views of proponents and opponents of the Amendment. This discussion and our own investigation convince us that, although these sources cast some light, it is not enough to resolve the problem with which we are faced. At best, they are inconclusive. The most avid proponents of the post-War Amendments undoubtedly intended them to remove all legal distinctions among "all persons born or naturalized in the United States." Their opponents, just as certainly, were antagonistic to both the letter and the spirit of the Amendments and wished them to have the most limited effect. What others in Congress and the state legislatures had in mind cannot be determined with any degree of certainty.

An additional reason for the inconclusive nature of the Amendment's history with respect to segregated schools is the status of public education at that time. In the South, the movement toward free common schools, supported by general taxation, had not yet taken hold. Education of white children was largely in the hands of private groups. Education of Negroes was almost nonexistent, and practically all of the race were illiterate. In fact, any education of Negroes was forbidden by law in some states. Today, in contrast, many Negroes have achieved outstanding success in the arts and sciences, as well as in the business and professional world. It is true that public school education at the time of the Amendment had advanced further in the North, but the effect of the Amendment on Northern States was generally ignored in the congressional debates. Even in the North, the conditions of public education did not approximate those existing today. The curriculum was usually rudimentary; ungraded schools were common in rural areas; the school term was but three months a year in many states, and compulsory school attendance was virtually unknown. As a consequence, it is not surprising that there should be so little in the history of the Fourteenth Amendment relating to its intended effect on public education.

In the first cases in this Court construing the Fourteenth Amendment, decided shortly after its adoption, the Court interpreted it as proscribing all state-imposed discriminations against the Negro race.[1] The doctrine of "separate but equal" did not make its appearance in this Court until 1896 in the case of *Plessy v. Ferguson*, involving not education but transportation.[2] American courts have since labored with the doctrine for over half a century. In this Court, there have been six cases involving the "separate but equal" doctrine in the field of public education. In *Cumming v. County Board of Education*, and *Gong Lum v. Rice*, the validity of the doctrine itself was not challenged. In more recent cases, all on the graduate school level, inequality was found in that specific benefits enjoyed by white students were denied to Negro students of the same educational qualifications. *Missouri ex rel. Gaines v. Canada, Sipuel v. Oklahoma, Sweatt v. Painter, McLaurin v. Oklahoma State Regents.* In none of these cases was it necessary to reexamine the doctrine to grant relief to the Negro plaintiff. And in *Sweatt v. Painter, supra,* the Court expressly reserved decision on the question whether *Plessy v. Ferguson* should be held inapplicable to public education.

In the instant cases, that question is directly presented. Here, unlike *Sweatt v. Painter,* there are findings below that the Negro and white schools involved have been equalized, or are being equalized, with respect to buildings, curricula, qualifications and salaries of teachers, and other "tangible" factors. Our decision, therefore, cannot turn on merely a comparison of these tangible factors in the Negro and white schools involved in each of the cases. We must look instead to the effect of segregation itself on public education.

In approaching this problem, we cannot turn the clock back to 1868, when the Amendment was adopted, or even to 1896, when *Plessy v. Ferguson* was written. We must consider public education in the light of its full development and its present place in American life throughout the Nation. Only in this way can it be determined if segregation in public schools deprives these plaintiffs of the equal protection of the laws.

Today, education is perhaps the most important function of state and local governments. Compulsory school attendance laws and the great expenditures for education both demonstrate our recognition of the importance of education to our democratic society. It is required in the performance of our most basic public responsibilities, even service in the armed forces. It is the very foundation of good citizenship. Today it is a principal instrument in awakening the child to cultural values, in preparing him for later professional training, and in helping him to adjust normally to his environment. In these days, it is doubtful that any child may reasonably be expected to succeed in life if he is denied the opportunity of an education. Such an opportunity, where the state has undertaken to provide it, is a right which must be made available to all on equal terms.

We come then to the question presented: Does segregation of children in public schools solely on the basis of race, even though the physical facilities and other "tangible" factors may be equal, deprive the children of the minority group of equal educational opportunities? We believe that it does.

In *Sweatt v. Painter,* in finding that a segregated law school for Negroes could not provide them equal educational opportunities, this Court relied in large part on "those qualities which are incapable of objective measurement but which make for greatness in a law school." In *McLaurin v. Oklahoma State Regents,* the Court, in requiring that a Negro admitted to a white graduate school be treated like all other students, again resorted to intangible considerations: ". . . his ability to study, to engage in discussions and exchange views with other students, and, in general, to learn his profession." Such considerations apply with added force to children in grade and high schools. To separate them from others of similar age and qualifications solely because of their race generates a feeling of inferiority as to their status in the community that may affect their hearts and minds in a way unlikely ever to be undone. The effect of this separation on their educational opportunities was well stated by a finding in the Kansas case by a court which nevertheless felt compelled to rule against the Negro plaintiffs: Segregation of white and colored children in public schools has a detrimental effect upon the colored children. The impact is greater when it has the sanction of the law, for the policy of separating the races is usually interpreted as denoting the inferiority of the negro group. A sense of inferiority affects the motivation of a child to learn. Segregation with the sanction of law, therefore, has a tendency to [retard] the educational and mental development of negro children and to deprive them of some of the benefits they would receive in a racial[ly] integrated school system.[3] Whatever may have been the extent of psychological knowledge at the time of *Plessy v. Ferguson,* this finding is amply supported by modern authority. Any language in *Plessy v. Ferguson* contrary to this finding is rejected.

We conclude that, in the field of public education, the doctrine of "separate but equal" has no place. Separate educational facilities are inherently unequal. Therefore, we hold that the plaintiffs and others similarly situated for whom the actions have been brought are, by reason of the segregation complained of, deprived of the equal protection of the laws guaranteed by the Fourteenth Amendment. This disposition makes unnecessary any discussion whether such segregation also violates the Due Process Clause of the Fourteenth Amendment.[4]

Because these are class actions, because of the wide applicability of this decision, and because of the great variety of local conditions, the formulation of decrees in these cases presents problems of considerable complexity. On reargument, the consideration of appropriate relief was necessarily subordinated to the primary question—the constitutionality of segregation in public education. We have now announced that such segregation is a denial of the equal protection of the laws. In order that we may have the full assistance of the parties in formulating decrees, the cases will be restored to the docket, and the parties are requested to present further argument on Questions 4 and 5 previously propounded by the Court for the reargument this Term.[5] The Attorney General of the United States is again invited to participate. The Attorneys General of the states requiring or permitting segregation in public education will also be permitted to appear as *amici curiae* upon request to do so by September 15, 1954, and submission of briefs by October 1, 1954.

It is so ordered.

NOTES

1. *Slaughter-House Cases,* 16 Wall. 36, 67–72 (1873); *Strauder v. West Virginia,* 100 U.S. 303, 307–308 (1880): It ordains that no State shall deprive any person of life, liberty, or property, without due process of law, or deny to any person within its jurisdiction the equal protection of the laws. What is this but declaring that the law in the States shall be

the same for the black as for the white; that all persons, whether colored or white, shall stand equal before the laws of the States, and, in regard to the colored race, for whose protection the amendment was primarily designed, that no discrimination shall be made against them by law because of their color? The words of the amendment, it is true, are prohibitory, but they contain a necessary implication of a positive immunity, or right, most valuable to the colored race—the right to exemption from unfriendly legislation against them distinctively as colored—exemption from legal discriminations, implying inferiority in civil society, lessening the security of their enjoyment of the rights which others enjoy, and discriminations which are steps towards reducing them to the condition of a subject race.

2. The doctrine apparently originated in *Roberts v. City of Boston*, 59 Mass.198, 206 (1850), upholding school segregation against attack as being violative of a state constitutional guarantee of equality. Segregation in Boston public schools was eliminated in 1855. Mass.Acts 1855, c. 256. But elsewhere in the North, segregation in public education has persisted in some communities until recent years. It is apparent that such segregation has long been a nationwide problem, not merely one of sectional concern.

3. A similar finding was made in the Delaware case: I conclude from the testimony that, in our Delaware society, State-imposed segregation in education itself results in the Negro children, as a class, receiving educational opportunities which are substantially inferior to those available to white children otherwise similarly situated.87 A.2d 862, 865.

4. See *Bolling v. Sharpe*, post, p. 497, concerning the Due Process Clause of the Fifth Amendment.

5. Assuming it is decided that segregation in public schools violates the Fourteenth Amendment, (a) would a decree necessarily follow providing that, within the limits set by normal geographic school districting, Negro children should forthwith be admitted to schools of their choice, or (b) may this Court, in the exercise of its equity powers, permit an effective gradual adjustment to be brought about from existing segregated systems to a system not based on color distinctions?

4.3

District of Columbia v. Heller (2008)

In the majority opinion from this controversial Supreme Court decision, Justice Antonin Scalia offers a view of the Second Amendment that interprets the right to bear arms as applying to individuals. He argues against the notion that the amendment was written to apply to the rights of collectives, like states or communities, to bear arms. Instead, the writers of the amendment intended the right to bear arms to be an individual right. Applying this reasoning, the Court struck down the Washington, D.C., law banning handguns as unconstitutional.

ON WRIT OF CERTIORARI TO THE UNITED STATES COURT OF APPEALS FOR THE DISTRICT OF COLUMBIA CIRCUIT

Justice Scalia delivered the opinion of the Court.

We consider whether a District of Columbia prohibition on the possession of usable handguns in the home violates the Second Amendment to the Constitution.

I

The District of Columbia generally prohibits the possession of handguns. It is a crime to carry an unregistered firearm, and the registration of handguns is prohibited. Wholly apart from that prohibition, no person may carry a handgun without a license, but the chief of police may issue licenses for one-year periods. District of Columbia law also requires residents to keep their lawfully owned firearms, such as registered long guns, "unloaded and dissembled or bound by a trigger lock or similar device" unless they are located in a place of business or are being used for lawful recreational activities.

Respondent Dick Heller is a D.C. special police officer authorized to carry a handgun while on duty at the Federal Judicial Center. He applied for a registration certificate for a handgun that he wished to keep at home, but the District refused. He thereafter filed a lawsuit in the Federal District Court for the District of Columbia seeking, on Second Amendment grounds, to enjoin the city from enforcing the bar on the registration of handguns, the licensing requirement insofar as it prohibits the carrying of a firearm in the home without a license, and the trigger-lock requirement insofar as it prohibits the use of "functional firearms within the home." The District Court dismissed respondent's complaint, The Court of Appeals for the District of Columbia Circuit, construing his complaint as seeking the right to render a firearm operable and carry it about his home in that condition only when necessary for self-defense, It held that the Second Amendment protects an individual right to possess firearms and that the city's total ban on handguns, as well as its requirement that firearms in the home be kept nonfunctional even when necessary for self-defense, violated that right. The Court of Appeals directed the District Court to enter summary judgment for respondent.

We granted certiorari.

II

We turn first to the meaning of the Second Amendment.

A

The Second Amendment provides: "A well regulated Militia, being necessary to the security of a free State, the right of the people to keep and bear Arms, shall not be infringed." In interpreting this text, we are guided by the principle that "[t]he Constitution was written to be understood by the voters; its words and phrases were used in their normal and ordinary as distinguished from technical meaning." *United States* v. *Sprague,* Normal meaning may of course include an idiomatic meaning, but it excludes secret or technical meanings that would not have been known to ordinary citizens in the founding generation.

The two sides in this case have set out very different interpretations of the Amendment. Petitioners and today's dissenting Justices believe that it protects only the right to possess and carry a firearm in connection with militia service. Respondent argues that it protects an individual right to possess a firearm unconnected with service in a militia, and to use that arm for traditionally lawful purposes, such as self-defense within the home.

The Second Amendment is naturally divided into two parts: its prefatory clause and its operative clause. The former does not limit the latter grammatically, but rather announces a purpose. The Amendment could be rephrased, "Because a well regulated Militia is necessary to the security of a free State, the right of the people to keep and bear Arms shall not be infringed." Although this structure of the Second Amendment is unique in our Constitution, other legal documents of the founding era, particularly individual-rights provisions of state constitutions, commonly included a prefatory statement of purpose.

Logic demands that there be a link between the stated purpose and the command. The Second Amendment would be nonsensical if it read, "A well regulated Militia, being necessary to the security of a free State, the right of the people to petition for redress of grievances shall not be infringed.' That requirement of logical connection may cause a prefatory clause to resolve an ambiguity in the operative clause. But apart from that clarifying function, a prefatory clause does not limit or expand the scope of the operative clause. Therefore, while we will begin our textual analysis with the operative clause, we will return to the prefatory clause to ensure that our reading of the operative clause is consistent with the announced purpose.

1. Operative Clause

a. "Right of the People." The first salient feature of the operative clause is that it codifies a "right of the people." The unamended Constitution and the Bill of Rights use the phrase "right of the people" two other times, in the First Amendment's Assembly-and-Petition Clause and in the Fourth Amendment's Search-and-Seizure Clause. The Ninth Amendment uses very similar terminology ("The enumeration in the Constitution, of certain rights, shall not be construed to deny or disparage others retained by the people"). All three of these instances unambiguously refer to individual rights, not "collective" rights, or rights that may be exercised only through participation in some corporate body.

Three provisions of the Constitution refer to "the people" in a context other than "rights"—the famous preamble ("We the people"), §2 of Article I (providing that "the people" will choose members of the House), and the Tenth Amendment (providing that those powers not given the Federal Government remain with "the States" or "the people"). Those provisions arguably refer to "the people" acting collectively—but they deal with the exercise or reservation of powers, not rights. Nowhere else in the Constitution does a "right" attributed to "the people" refer to anything other than an individual right.

This contrasts markedly with the phrase "the militia" in the prefatory clause. As we will describe below, the "militia" in colonial America consisted of a subset of "the people"—those who were male, able bodied, and within a certain age range. Reading the Second Amendment as protecting only the right to "keep and bear Arms" in an organized militia therefore fits poorly with the operative clause's description of the holder of that right as "the people."

We start therefore with a strong presumption that the Second Amendment right is exercised individually and belongs to all Americans.

b. "Keep and bear Arms." We move now from the holder of the right—"the people"—to the substance of the right: "to keep and bear Arms."

Before addressing the verbs "keep" and "bear," we interpret their object: "Arms." The eighteenth-century meaning is no different from the meaning today. The 1773 edition of Samuel Johnson's dictionary defined "arms" as "weapons of offence, or armour of defence." Timothy Cunningham's important 1771 legal dictionary defined "arms" as "any thing that a man wears for his defence, or takes into his hands, or useth in wrath to cast at or strike another."

We turn to the phrases "keep arms" and "bear arms." Johnson defined "keep" as, most relevantly, "[t]o retain; not to lose," and "[t]o have in custody."

Webster defined it as "[t]o hold; to retain in one's power or possession." No party has apprised us of an idiomatic meaning of "keep Arms." Thus, the most natural reading of "keep Arms" in the Second Amendment is to "have weapons."

"Keep arms" was simply a common way of referring to possessing arms, for militiamen and everyone else.

At the time of the founding, as now, to "bear" meant to "carry." When used with "arms," however, the term has a meaning that refers to carrying for a particular purpose—confrontation. In *Muscarello* v. *United States*, in the course of analyzing the meaning of "carries a firearm" in a federal criminal statute, Justice Ginsburg wrote that "[s]urely a most familiar meaning is, as the Constitution's Second Amendment . . . indicate[s]: 'wear, bear, or carry . . . upon the person or in the clothing or in a pocket, for the purpose . . . of being armed and ready for offensive or defensive action in a case of conflict with another person.'" We think that Justice Ginsburg accurately captured the natural meaning of "bear arms." Although the phrase implies that the carrying of the weapon is for the purpose of "offensive or defensive action," it in no way connotes participation in a structured military organization.

From our review of founding-era sources, we conclude that this natural meaning was also the meaning that "bear arms" had in the eighteenth century. In numerous instances, "bear arms" was unambiguously used to refer to the carrying of weapons outside of an organized militia. The most prominent examples are those most relevant to the Second Amendment: Nine state constitutional provisions written in the eighteenth century or the first two decades of the nineteenth, which enshrined a right of citizens to "bear arms in defense of themselves and the state" or "bear arms in defense of himself and the state." It is clear from those formulations that "bear arms" did not refer only to carrying a weapon in an organized military unit.

The phrase "bear Arms" also had at the time of the founding an idiomatic meaning that was significantly different from its natural meaning: "to serve as a soldier, do military service, fight" or "to wage war." But it *unequivocally* bore that idiomatic meaning only when followed by the preposition "against," which was in turn followed by the target of the hostilities.

In any event, the meaning of "bear arms" that petitioners and Justice Stevens propose is *not even* the (sometimes) idiomatic meaning. Rather, they manufacture a hybrid definition, whereby "bear arms" connotes the actual carrying of arms (and therefore is not really an idiom) but only in the service of an organized militia. No dictionary has ever adopted that definition, and we have been apprised of no source that indicates that it carried that meaning at the time of the founding. But it is easy to see why petitioners and the dissent are driven to the hybrid definition. Giving "bear Arms" its idiomatic meaning would cause the protected right to consist of the right to be a soldier or to wage war—an absurdity that no commentator has ever endorsed.

Petitioners justify their limitation of "bear arms" to the military context by pointing out the unremarkable fact that it was often used in that context—the same mistake they made with respect to "keep arms." It is especially unremarkable that the phrase was often used in a military context in the federal legal sources (such as records of congressional debate) that have been the focus of petitioners' inquiry. Those sources would have had little occasion to use it *except* in discussions about the standing army and the militia. Other legal sources frequently used "bear arms" in nonmilitary contexts. If one looks beyond legal sources, "bear arms" was frequently used in nonmilitary contexts.

Justice Stevens points to a study by *amici* supposedly showing that the phrase "bear arms" was most frequently used in the military context. Of course, as we have said, the fact that the phrase was commonly used in a particular context does not show that it is limited to that context, and, in any event, we have given many sources where the phrase was used in nonmilitary contexts. Moreover, the study's collection appears to include (who knows how many times) the idiomatic phrase "bear arms against," which is irrelevant. The *amici* also dismiss examples such as "'bear arms . . . for the purpose of killing game'" because those uses are "expressly qualified." That analysis is faulty. If "bear arms" means, as we think, simply the carrying of arms, a modifier can limit the purpose of the carriage. But if "bear arms" means, as the petitioners and the dissent think, the carrying of arms only for military purposes, one simply cannot add "for the purpose of killing game." The right "to carry arms in the militia for the purpose of killing game" is worthy of the mad hatter. Thus, these purposive qualifying phrases positively establish that "to bear arms" is not limited to military use.

Justice Stevens places great weight on James Madison's inclusion of a conscientious-objector clause in his original draft of the Second Amendment: "but no person religiously scrupulous of bearing arms, shall be compelled to render military service in person." He argues that this clause establishes that the drafters of the Second Amendment intended "bear Arms" to refer only to military service. In any case, what Justice Stevens would conclude from the deleted provision does not follow. It was not meant to exempt from military service those who objected to going to war but had no scruples about personal gunfights.

Finally, Justice Stevens suggests that "keep and bear Arms" was some sort of term of art, presumably akin to "hue and cry" or "cease and desist." Justice Stevens believes that the unitary meaning of "keep and bear Arms" is established by the Second Amendment's calling it a "right" (singular) rather than "rights" (plural). There is nothing to this. State constitutions of the founding period routinely grouped multiple (related) guarantees under a singular "right," and the First Amendment protects the "right [singular] of the people peaceably to assemble, and to petition the Government for a redress of grievances."

c. Meaning of the Operative Clause. Putting all of these textual elements together, we find that they guarantee the individual right to possess and carry weapons in case of confrontation. This meaning is strongly confirmed by the historical background of the Second Amendment. We look to this because it has always been widely understood that the Second Amendment, like the First and Fourth Amendments, codified a *pre-existing* right. The very text of the Second Amendment implicitly recognizes the pre-existence of the right and declares only that it "shall not be infringed." As we said in *United States v. Cruikshank*, "[t]his is not a right granted by the Constitution. Neither is it in any manner dependent upon that instrument for its existence. The Second Amendment declares that it shall not be infringed . . . ."

Between the Restoration and the Glorious Revolution, the Stuart Kings Charles II and James II succeeded in using select militias loyal to them to suppress political dissidents, in part by disarming their opponents. Under the auspices of the 1671 Game Act, for example, the Catholic James II had ordered general disarmaments of regions home to his Protestant enemies. These experiences caused Englishmen to be extremely wary of concentrated military forces run by the state and to be jealous of their arms. They accordingly obtained an assurance from William and Mary, in the Declaration of Right (which was codified as the English Bill of Rights), that Protestants would never be disarmed: "That the subjects which are Protestants may have arms for their defense suitable to their conditions and as allowed by law." This right has long been understood to be the predecessor to our Second Amendment. It was secured to them as individuals, according to "libertarian political principles," not as members of a fighting force.

And, of course, what the Stuarts had tried to do to their political enemies, George III had tried to do to the colonists. In the tumultuous decades of the 1760's and 1770's, the Crown began to disarm the inhabitants of the most rebellious areas. That provoked polemical reactions by Americans invoking their rights as Englishmen to keep arms.

There seems to us no doubt, on the basis of both text and history, that the Second Amendment conferred an individual right to keep and bear arms. Of course the right was not unlimited, just as the First Amendment's right of free speech was not. Thus, we do not read the Second Amendment to protect the right of citizens to carry arms for *any sort* of confrontation, just as we do not read the First Amendment to protect the right of citizens to speak for *any purpose*. Before turning to limitations upon the individual right, however, we must determine whether the prefatory clause of the Second Amendment comports with our interpretation of the operative clause.

2. Prefatory Clause

The prefatory clause reads: "A well regulated Militia, being necessary to the security of a free State . . . ."

a. "Well-Regulated Militia." In *United States* v. *Miller* (1939), we explained that "the Militia comprised all males physically capable of acting in concert for the common defense."

Petitioners take a seemingly narrower view of the militia, stating that "[m]ilitias are the state- and congressionally-regulated military forces described in the Militia Clauses." Although we agree with petitioners' interpretive assumption that "militia" means the same thing in Article I and the Second Amendment, we believe that petitioners identify the wrong thing, namely, the organized militia. Unlike armies and navies, which Congress is given the power to create the militia is assumed by Article I already to be *in existence*. Congress is given the power to "provide for calling forth the militia," §8, cl. 15; and the power not to create, but to "organiz[e]" it—and not to organize "a" militia, which is what one would expect if the militia were to be a federal creation, but to organize "the" militia, connoting a body already in existence. To be sure, Congress need not conscript every able-bodied man into the militia, because nothing in Article I suggests that in exercising its power to organize, discipline, and arm the militia, Congress must focus upon the entire body. Although the militia consists of all able-bodied men, the federally organized militia may consist of a subset of them.

Finally, the adjective "well-regulated" implies nothing more than the imposition of proper discipline and training.

b. "Security of a Free State." The phrase "security of a free state" meant "security of a free polity," not security of each of the several States as the dissent below argued. Joseph Story wrote in his treatise on the Constitution that "the word 'state' is used in various senses [and in] its most enlarged sense, it means the people composing a particular nation or community." Moreover, the other instances of "state" in the Constitution are typically accompanied by modifiers making clear that the reference is to the several States—"each state," "several states," "any state," "that state," "particular states," "one state," "no state." And the presence of the term "foreign state" in Article I and Article III shows that the word "state" did not have a single meaning in the Constitution.

3. Relationship between Prefatory Clause and Operative Clause

Does the preface fit with an operative clause that creates an individual right to keep and bear arms? It fits perfectly, once one knows the history that the founding generation knew and that we have described above. That history showed that the way tyrants had eliminated a militia consisting of all the able-bodied men was not by banning the militia but simply by taking away the people's arms, enabling a select militia or standing army to suppress political opponents.

The debate with respect to the right to keep and bear arms, as with other guarantees in the Bill of Rights, was not over whether it was desirable (all agreed that it was) but over whether it needed to be codified in the Constitution.

During the 1788 ratification debates, the fear that the federal government would disarm the people in order to impose rule through a standing army or select militia was pervasive in Antifederalist rhetoric. Federalists responded that because Congress was given no power to abridge the ancient right of individuals to keep and bear arms, such a force could never oppress the people. It was understood across the political spectrum that the right helped to secure the ideal of a citizen militia, which might be necessary to oppose an oppressive military force if the constitutional order broke down.

It is therefore entirely sensible that the Second Amendment's prefatory clause announces the purpose for which the right was codified: to prevent elimination of the militia. The prefatory clause does not suggest that preserving the militia was the only reason Americans valued the ancient right; most undoubtedly thought it even more important for self-defense and hunting. But the threat that the new Federal Government would destroy the citizens' militia by taking away their arms was the reason that right—unlike some other English rights—was codified in a written Constitution. Justice Breyer's assertion that individual self-defense is merely a "subsidiary interest" of the right to keep and bear arms, is profoundly mistaken. He bases that assertion solely upon the prologue—but that can only show that self-defense had little to do with the right's *codification;* it was the *central component* of the right itself.

B

Our interpretation is confirmed by analogous arms-bearing rights in state constitutions that preceded and immediately followed adoption of the Second Amendment. Four States adopted analogues to the Federal Second Amendment in the period between independence and the ratification of the Bill of Rights. Two of them—Pennsylvania and Vermont—clearly adopted individual rights unconnected to militia service.

We therefore believe that the most likely reading of all of these pre-Second Amendment state constitutional provisions is that they secured an individual right to bear arms for defensive purposes.

> [A]t least seven [states] unequivocally protected an individual citizen's right to self-defense is strong evidence that that is how the founding generation conceived of the right.

The historical narrative that petitioners must endorse would thus treat the Federal Second Amendment as an odd outlier, protecting a right unknown in state constitutions or at English common law, based on little more than an overreading of the prefatory clause.

C

Justice Stevens relies on the drafting history of the Second Amendment—the various proposals in the state conventions and the debates in Congress. It is dubious to rely on such history to interpret a text that was widely understood to codify a pre-existing right, rather than to fashion a new one. But even assuming that this legislative history is relevant, Justice Stevens flatly misreads the historical record.

It is true, as Justice Stevens says, that there was concern that the Federal Government would abolish the institution of the state militia. That concern found expression, however, *not* in the various Second Amendment precursors proposed in the State conventions, but in separate structural provisions that would have given the States concurrent and seemingly nonpreemptible authority to organize, discipline, and arm the militia when the Federal Government failed to do so. The Second Amendment precursors, by contrast, referred to the individual English right already codified in two (and probably four) State constitutions. The Federalist-dominated first Congress chose to reject virtually all major structural revisions favored by the Antifederalists, including the proposed militia amendments. Rather, it adopted primarily the popular and uncontroversial (though, in the Federalists' view, unnecessary) individual-rights amendments. The Second Amendment right, protecting only individuals' liberty to keep and carry arms, did nothing to assuage Antifederalists' concerns about federal control of the militia.

Justice Stevens thinks it significant that the Virginia, New York, and North Carolina Second Amendment proposals were "embedded . . . within a group of principles that are distinctly military in meaning," such as statements about the danger of standing armies. But so was the highly influential minority proposal in Pennsylvania, yet that proposal, with its reference to hunting, plainly referred to an individual right. Other than that erroneous point, Justice Stevens has brought forward absolutely no evidence that those proposals conferred only a right to carry arms in a militia.

D

We now address how the Second Amendment was interpreted from immediately after its ratification through the end of the nineteenth century.

1. Post-ratification Commentary

Three important founding-era legal scholars interpreted the Second Amendment in published writings. All three understood it to protect an individual right unconnected with militia service.

St. George Tucker's version conceived of the right as necessary for self-defense. He equated that right, absent the religious and class-based restrictions, with the Second Amendment. He grouped the right with some of the individual rights included in the First Amendment and said that if "a law be passed by congress, prohibiting" any of those rights, it would "be the province of the judiciary to pronounce whether any such act were constitutional, or not; and if not, to acquit the accused . . . ." It is unlikely that Tucker was referring to a person's being "accused" of violating a law making it a crime to bear arms in a state militia.

In 1825, William Rawle, a prominent lawyer who had been a member of the Pennsylvania Assembly that ratified the Bill of Rights, published an influential treatise.

Rawle clearly differentiated between the people's right to bear arms and their service in a militia. Rawle further said that the Second Amendment right ought not "be abused to the disturbance of the public peace," such as by assembling with other armed individuals "for an unlawful purpose"—statements that make no sense if the right does not extend to *any* individual purpose.

Joseph Story published his famous Commentaries on the Constitution of the United States in 1833. Justice Stevens suggests that "[t]here is not so much as a whisper" in Story's explanation of the Second Amendment that favors the individual-rights view. That is wrong. Story explained that the English Bill of Rights had also included a "right to bear arms," a right that, as we have discussed, had nothing to do with militia service.

Story's Commentaries also cite as support Tucker and Rawle, both of whom clearly viewed the right as unconnected to militia service. In addition, in a shorter 1840 work Story wrote: "One of the ordinary modes, by which tyrants accomplish their purposes without resistance, is, by disarming the people, and making it an offence to keep arms, and by substituting a regular army in the stead of a resort to the militia."

2. Pre–Civil War Case Law

The nineteenth-century cases that interpreted the Second Amendment universally support an individual right unconnected to militia service. In *Houston* v. *Moore*, this Court held that States have concurrent power over the militia, at least where not pre-empted by Congress. In the famous fugitive-slave case of *Johnson* v. *Tompkins*, Baldwin, sitting as a circuit judge, cited both the Second Amendment and the Pennsylvania analogue for his conclusion that a citizen has "a right to carry arms in defence of his property or person, and to use them, if either were assailed with such force, numbers or violence as made it necessary for the protection or safety of either."

Many early nineteenth-century state cases indicated that the Second Amendment right to bear arms was an individual right unconnected to militia service, though subject to certain restrictions.

An 1829 decision [*United States* v. *Sheldon*] by the Supreme Court of Michigan said:

> The constitution of the United States also grants to the citizen the right to keep and bear arms. But the grant of this privilege cannot be construed into the right in him who keeps a gun to destroy his neighbor. No rights are intended to be granted by the constitution for an unlawful or unjustifiable purpose.

In *Nunn* v. *State*, the Georgia Supreme Court construed the Second Amendment as protecting the *"natural* right of self-defence" and therefore struck down a ban on carrying pistols openly. Its opinion perfectly captured the way in which the operative clause of the Second Amendment furthers the purpose announced in the prefatory clause.

3. Post–Civil War Legislation

In the aftermath of the Civil War, there was an outpouring of discussion of the Second Amendment in Congress and in public discourse, as people debated whether and how to secure constitutional rights for newly free slaves. Since those discussions took place 75 years after the ratification of the Second Amendment, they do not provide as much insight into its original meaning as earlier sources. Yet those born and educated in the early nineteenth century faced a widespread effort to limit arms ownership by a large number of citizens; their understanding of the origins and continuing significance of the Amendment is instructive.

Blacks were routinely disarmed by Southern States after the Civil War. Those who opposed these injustices frequently stated that they infringed blacks' constitutional right to keep and bear arms. Needless to say, the claim was not that blacks were being prohibited from carrying arms in an organized state militia.

Congress enacted the Freedmen's Bureau Act on July 16, 1866. Section 14 stated:

> [T]he right . . . to have full and equal benefit of all laws and proceedings concerning personal liberty, personal security, and the acquisition, enjoyment, and disposition of estate, real and personal, including the constitutional right to bear arms, shall be secured to and enjoyed by all the citizens . . . without respect to race or color, or previous condition of slavery . . . .

The understanding that the Second Amendment gave freed blacks the right to keep and bear arms was reflected in congressional discussion of the bill, with even an opponent of it saying that the founding generation "were for every man bearing his arms about him and keeping them in his house, his castle, for his own defense."

It was plainly the understanding in the post–Civil War Congress that the Second Amendment protected an individual right to use arms for self-defense.

4. Post–Civil War Commentators

Every late-nineteenth-century legal scholar that we have read interpreted the Second Amendment to secure an individual right unconnected with militia service. The most famous was the judge and professor Thomas Cooley, who wrote a massively popular 1868 Treatise on Constitutional Limitations. Concerning the Second Amendment it said:

> Among the other defences to personal liberty should be mentioned the right of the people to keep and bear arms . . . . The alternative to a standing army is 'a well-regulated militia,' but this cannot exist unless the people are trained to bearing arms. How far it is in the power of the legislature to regulate this right, we shall not undertake to say, as happily there has been very little occasion to discuss that subject by the courts.

All other post–Civil War nineteenth-century sources we have found concurred with Cooley.

E

We now ask whether any of our precedents forecloses the conclusions we have reached about the meaning of the Second Amendment.

United States v. *Cruikshank*, in the course of vacating the convictions of members of a white mob for depriving blacks of their right to keep and bear arms, held that the Second Amendment does not by its own force apply to anyone other than the Federal Government. The opinion explained that the right "is not a right granted by the Constitution [or] in any manner dependent upon that instrument for its existence. The second amendment . . . means no more than that it shall not be infringed by Congress." The limited discussion of the Second Amendment in *Cruikshank* supports, if anything, the individual-rights interpretation.

Presser v. *Illinois* (1886) held that the right to keep and bear arms was not violated by a law that forbade "bodies of men to associate together as military organizations, or to drill or parade with arms in cities and towns unless authorized by law." Justice Stevens presses *Presser* into service to support his view that the right to bear arms is limited to service in the militia by joining *Presser*'s brief discussion of the Second Amendment with a later portion of the opinion making the seemingly relevant (to the Second Amendment) point that the plaintiff was not a member of the state militia. Unfortunately for Justice Stevens' argument, that later portion deals with the *Fourteenth Amendment;* it was the *Fourteenth Amendment* to which the plaintiff's nonmembership in the militia was relevant. Thus, Justice Stevens' statement that *Presser* "suggested that . . . nothing in the Constitution protected the use of arms outside the context of a militia," is simply wrong. *Presser* said nothing about the Second Amendment's meaning or scope, beyond the fact that it does not prevent the prohibition of private paramilitary organizations.

Justice Stevens places overwhelming reliance upon this Court's decision in *United States* v. *Miller* (1939) . "[H]undreds of judges," we are told, "have relied on the view of the amendment we endorsed there," and "[e]ven if the textual and historical arguments on both side of the issue were evenly balanced, respect for the well-settled views of all of our predecessors on this Court, and for the rule of law itself . . . would prevent most jurists from endorsing such a dramatic upheaval in the law," And what is, according to Justice Stevens, the holding of *Miller* that demands such obeisance? That the Second Amendment "protects the right to keep and bear arms for certain military purposes, but that it does not curtail the legislature's power to regulate the nonmilitary use and ownership of weapons."

Nothing so clearly demonstrates the weakness of Justice Stevens' case. *Miller* did not hold that and cannot possibly be read to have held that. The judgment in the case upheld against a Second Amendment challenge two men's federal convictions for transporting an unregistered short-barreled shotgun in interstate commerce, in violation of the National Firearms Act. It is entirely clear that the Court's basis for saying that the Second Amendment did not apply was *not* that the defendants were "bear[ing] arms" not "for . . . military purposes" but for "nonmilitary use." Rather, it was that the *type of weapon at issue* was not eligible for Second Amendment protection. Beyond that, the opinion provided no explanation of the content of the right.

Justice Stevens can say again and again that *Miller* did "not turn on the difference between muskets and sawed-off shotguns, it turned, rather, on the basic difference between the military and nonmilitary use and possession of guns," but the words of the opinion prove otherwise. The most Justice Stevens can plausibly claim for *Miller* is that it declined to decide the nature of the Second Amendment right.

It is particularly wrongheaded to read *Miller* for more than what it said, because the case did not even purport to be a thorough examination of the Second Amendment.

We conclude that nothing in our precedents forecloses our adoption of the original understanding of the Second Amendment. It should be unsurprising that such a significant matter has been for so long judicially unresolved. For most of our history, the Bill of Rights was not thought applicable to the States, and the Federal Government did not significantly regulate the possession of firearms by law-abiding citizens. Other provisions of the Bill of Rights have similarly remained unilluminated for lengthy periods. It is demonstrably not true that, as Justice Stevens claims, "for most of our history, the invalidity of Second-Amendment-based objections to firearms regulations has been well settled and uncontroversial." For most of our history the question did not present itself.

III

Like most rights, the right secured by the Second Amendment is not unlimited. Commentators and courts routinely explained that the right was not a right to keep and carry any weapon whatsoever in any manner whatsoever and for whatever purpose. Although we do not undertake an exhaustive historical analysis today of the full scope of the Second Amendment, nothing in our opinion should be taken to cast doubt on longstanding prohibitions on the possession of firearms by felons and the mentally ill, or laws forbidding the carrying of firearms in sensitive places such as schools and government buildings, or laws imposing conditions and qualifications on the commercial sale of arms.

IV

We turn finally to the law at issue here. As we have said, the law totally bans handgun possession in the home. It also requires that any lawful firearm in the home be disassembled or bound by a trigger lock at all times, rendering it inoperable.

As the quotations earlier in this opinion demonstrate, the inherent right of self-defense has been central to the Second Amendment right. The handgun ban amounts to a prohibition of an entire class of "arms" that is overwhelmingly chosen by American society for that lawful purpose. The prohibition extends, moreover, to the home, where the need for defense of self, family, and property is most acute. Under any of the standards of scrutiny that we have applied to enumerated constitutional rights, banning from the home "the most preferred firearm in the nation to 'keep' and use for protection of one's home and family," would fail constitutional muster.

Few laws in the history of our Nation have come close to the severe restriction of the District's handgun ban.

It is no answer to say, as petitioners do, that it is permissible to ban the possession of handguns so long as the possession of other firearms (*i.e.*, long guns) is allowed. It is enough to note, as we have observed, that the American people have considered the handgun to be the quintessential self-defense weapon. There are many reasons that a citizen may prefer a handgun for home defense: It is easier to store in a location that is readily accessible in an emergency; it cannot easily be redirected or wrestled away by an attacker; it is easier to use for those without the upper-body strength to lift and aim a long gun; it can be pointed at a burglar with one hand while the other hand dials the police. Whatever the reason, handguns are the most popular weapon chosen by Americans for self-defense in the home, and a complete prohibition of their use is invalid.

We must also address the District's requirement (as applied to respondent's handgun) that firearms in the home be rendered and kept inoperable at all times. This makes it impossible for citizens to use them for the core lawful purpose of self-defense and is hence unconstitutional.

In sum, we hold that the District's ban on handgun possession in the home violates the Second Amendment, as does its prohibition against rendering any lawful firearm in the home operable for the purpose of immediate self-defense. Assuming that Heller is not disqualified from the exercise of Second Amendment rights, the District must permit him to register his handgun and must issue him a license to carry it in the home.

We are aware of the problem of handgun violence in this country, and we take seriously the concerns raised by the many *amici* who believe that prohibition of handgun ownership is a solution. The Constitution leaves the District of Columbia a variety of tools for combating that problem, including some measures regulating handguns. But the enshrinement of constitutional rights necessarily takes certain policy choices off the table. These include the absolute prohibition of handguns held and used for self-defense in the home. Undoubtedly some think that the Second Amendment is outmoded in a society where our standing army is the pride of our Nation, where well-trained police forces provide personal security, and where gun violence is a serious problem. That is perhaps debatable, but what is not debatable is that it is not the role of this Court to pronounce the Second Amendment extinct.

We affirm the judgment of the Court of Appeals.

It is so ordered.

5

CONGRESS

5.1

DAVID MAYHEW

From *Congress: The Electoral Connection*

In this classic work on Congress, Mayhew asks, what would Congress look like, and how would members of Congress behave, if members were solely interested in one thing: getting reelected? Mayhew says they would posture and preen, but also occasionally produce valuable legislation. In other words, it would look like the Congress we actually observe in the United States.

Mostly through personal experience on Capitol Hill, I have become convinced that scrutiny of purposive behavior offers the best route to an understanding of legislatures—or at least of the United States Congress. In the fashion of economics, I shall make a simple abstract assumption about human motivation and then speculate about the consequences of behavior based on that motivation. Specifically, I shall conjure up a vision of United States congressmen as single-minded seekers of reelection, see what kinds of activity that goal implies, and then speculate about how congressmen so motivated are likely to go about building and sustaining legislative institutions and making policy. At all points I shall try to match the abstract with the factual.

I find an emphasis on the reelection goal attractive for a number of reasons. First, I think it fits political reality rather well. Second, it puts the spotlight directly on men rather than on parties and pressure groups, which in the past have often entered discussions of American politics as analytic phantoms. Third, I think politics is best studied as a struggle among men to gain and maintain power and the consequences of that struggle. Fourth—and perhaps most important—the reelection quest establishes an accountability relationship with an electorate, and any serious thinking about democratic theory has to give a central place to the question of accountability. The abstract assumption notwithstanding, I regard this venture as an exercise in political science rather than economics. Leaving aside the fact that I have no economics expertise to display, I find that economists who study legislatures bring to bear interests different from those of political scientists. Not surprisingly the public finance scholars tend to look upon government as a device for spending money. I shall give some attention to spending, but also to other governmental activities such as the production of binding rules. And I shall touch upon such traditional subjects of political science as elections, parties, governmental structure, and regime stability. Another distinction here is that economics research tends to be infused with the normative assumption that policy decisions should be judged by how well they meet the standard of Pareto optimality. This is an assumption that I do not share and that I do not think most political scientists share. There will be no need here to set forth any alternative assumption. . . .

My subject of concern here is a single legislative institution, the United States Congress. In many ways, of course, the Congress is a unique or unusual body. It is probably the most highly "professionalized" of legislatures, in the sense that it promotes careerism among its members and gives them the salaries, staff, and other resources to sustain careers. Its parties are exceptionally diffuse. It is widely thought to be especially "strong" among legislatures as a checker of executive power. Like most Latin American legislatures but unlike most European ones, it labors in the shadow of a separately elected executive. My decision to focus on the Congress flows from a belief that there is something to be gained in an intensive analysis of a particular and important institution. But there is something general to be gained as well, for the exceptionalist argument should not be carried too far. In a good many ways the Congress is just one in a large family of legislative bodies. I shall find it useful at various points in the analysis to invoke comparisons with European parliaments and with American state legislatures and city councils. I shall ponder the question of what "functions" the Congress performs or is capable of performing—a question that can be answered only with the records of other legislatures in mind. Functions to be given special attention are those of legislating, overseeing the executive, expressing public opinion, and servicing constituents. No functional capabilities can be automatically assumed.[1] Indeed the very term *legislature* is an unfortunate one because it confuses structure and function. Accordingly I shall here on use the more awkward but more neutral term *representative assembly* to refer to members of the class of entities inhabited by the United States House and Senate. Whatever the noun, the identifying characteristics of institutions in the class have been well stated by Loewenberg: it is true of all such entities that (1) "their members are formally equal to each other in status, distinguishing parliaments from hierarchically ordered organizations," and (2) "the authority of their members depends on their claim to representing the rest of the community, in some sense of that protean concept, representation."[2]

The following discussion will take the form of an extended theoretical essay. Perforce it will raise more questions than it answers. As is the custom in mono-causal ventures, it will no doubt carry arguments to the point of exaggeration; finally, of course, I shall be satisfied to explain a significant part of the variance rather than all of it. What the discussion will yield, I hope, is a picture of what the United States Congress looks like if the reelection quest is examined seriously.

■　　■　　■

The ultimate concern here is not how probable it is that legislators will lose their seats but whether there is a connection between what they do in office and their need to be reelected. It is possible to conceive of an assembly in which no member ever comes close to losing a seat but in which the need to be reelected is what inspires members' behavior. It would be an assembly with no saints or fools in it, an assembly packed with skilled politicians going about their business. When we say "Congressman Smith is unbeatable," we do not mean that there is nothing he could do that would lose him his seat. Rather we mean, "Congressman Smith is unbeatable as long as he continues to do the things he is doing." If he stopped answering his mail, or stopped visiting his district, or began voting randomly on roll calls, or shifted his vote record eighty points on the ADA scale, he would bring on primary or November election troubles in a hurry. It is difficult to offer conclusive proof that this last statement is true, for there is no congressman willing to make the experiment. But normal political activity among politicians with healthy electoral margins should not be confused with inactivity. What characterizes "safe" congressmen is not that they are beyond electoral reach, but that their efforts are very likely to bring them uninterrupted electoral success.

Whether congressmen think their activities have electoral impact, and whether in fact they have impact, are of course two separate questions. Of the former there can be little doubt that the answer is yes. In fact in their own minds successful politicians probably overestimate the impact they are having. Kingdon found in his Wisconsin candidates a "congratulation-rationalization effect," a tendency for winners to take personal credit for their victories and for losers to assign their losses to forces beyond their control. The actual impact of politicians' activities is more difficult to assess. The evidence on the point is soft and scattered. It is hard to find variance in activities undertaken, for there are no politicians who consciously try to lose. There is no doubt that the electorate's general awareness of what is going on in Congress is something less than robust. Yet the argument here will be that congressmen's activities in fact do have electoral impact. Pieces of evidence will be brought in as the discussion proceeds.

The next step here is to offer a brief conceptual treatment of the relation between congressmen and their electorates. In the Downsian analysis what national party leaders must worry about is voters' "expected party differential." But to congressmen this is in practice irrelevant, for reasons specified earlier. A congressman's attention must rather be devoted to what can be called an "expected incumbent differential." Let us define this "expected incumbent differential" as any difference perceived by a relevant political actor between what an incumbent congressman is likely to do if returned to office and what any possible challenger (in primary or general election) would be likely to do. And let us define "relevant political actor" here as anyone who has a resource that might be used in the election in question. At the ballot box the only usable resources are votes, but there are resources that can be translated into votes: money, the ability to make persuasive endorsements, organizational skills, and so on. By this definition a "relevant political actor" need not be a constituent; one of the most important resources, money, flows all over the country in congressional campaign years.

It must be emphasized that the average voter has only the haziest awareness of what an incumbent congressman is actually doing in office. But an incumbent has to be concerned about actors who do form impressions about him, and especially about actors who can marshal resources other than their own votes. Senator Robert C. Byrd (D., W.Va.) has a "little list" of 2,545 West Virginians he regularly keeps in touch with. A congressman's assistant interviewed for a Nader profile in 1972 refers to the "thought leadership" back in the district. Of campaign resources one of the most vital is money. An incumbent not only has to assure that his own election funds are adequate, he has to try to minimize the probability that actors will bankroll an expensive campaign against him. There is the story that during the first Nixon term Senator James B. Pearson (R., Kans.) was told he would face a well-financed opponent in his 1972 primary if he did not display more party regularity in his voting. Availability of money can affect strength of opposition candidacy in both primary and general elections.

Another resource of significance is organizational expertise, probably more important than money among labor union offerings. Simple ability to do electioneering footwork is a resource the invoking of which may give campaigns an interesting twist. Leut-hold found in studying ten 1962 House elections in the San Francisco area that 50 percent of campaign workers held college degrees (as against 12 percent of the Bay area population), and that the workers were more issue oriented than the general population. The need to attract workers may induce candidates to traffic in issues more than they otherwise would. Former Congressman Allard K. Lowenstein (D., N.Y.) has as his key invokable resource a corps of student volunteers who will follow him from district to district, making him an unusually mobile candidate.

Still another highly important resource is the ability to make persuasive endorsements. Manhattan candidates angle for the imprimatur of the *New*

York Times. New Hampshire politics rotates around endorsements of the *Manchester Union Leader*. Labor union committees circulate their approved lists. Chicago Democratic politicians seek the endorsement of the mayor. In the San Francisco area and elsewhere House candidates try to score points by winning endorsements from officials of the opposite party. As Neustadt argues, the influence of the president over congressmen (of both parties) varies with his public prestige and with his perceived ability to punish and reward. One presidential tool is the endorsement, which can be carefully calibrated according to level of fervor, and which can be given to congressmen or to challengers running against congressmen. In the 1970 election Senator Charles Goodell (R., N.Y.), who had achieved public salience by attacking the Nixon administration, was apparently done in by the resources called forth by that attack; the vice president implicitly endorsed his Conservative opponent, and the administration acted to channel normally Republican money away from Goodell.

What a congressman has to try to do is to insure that in primary and general elections the resource balance (with all other deployed resources finally translated into votes) favors himself rather than somebody else. To maneuver successfully he must remain constantly aware of what political actors' incumbent differential readings are, and he must act in a fashion to inspire readings that favor himself. Complicating his task is the problem of slack resources. That is, only a very small proportion of the resources (other than votes) that are conceivably deployable in congressional campaigns are ever in fact deployed. But there is no sure way of telling who will suddenly become aroused and with what consequence. For example, just after the 1948 election the American Medical Association, unnerved by the medical program of the Attlee Government in Britain and by Democratic campaign promises here to institute national health insurance, decided to venture into politics. By 1950 congressmen on record as supporters of health insurance found themselves confronted by a million-dollar AMA advertising drive, local "healing arts committees" making candidate endorsements, and even doctors sending out campaign literature with their monthly bills. By 1952 it was widely believed that the AMA had decided some elections, and few congressmen were still mentioning health insurance.

In all his calculations the congressman must keep in mind that he is serving two electorates rather than one—a November electorate and a primary electorate nested inside it but not a representative sample of it. From the standpoint of the politician a primary is just another election to be survived. A typical scientific poll of a constituency yields a congressman information on the public standing of possible challengers in the other party but also in his own party. A threat is a threat. For an incumbent with a firm "supporting coalition" of elite groups in his party the primary electorate is normally quiescent. But there can be sudden turbulence. And it sometimes happens that the median views of primary and November electorates are so divergent on salient issues that a congressman finds it difficult to hold both electorates at once. This has been a recurrent problem among California Republicans.

A final conceptual point has to do with whether congressmen's behavior should be characterized as "maximizing" behavior. Does it make sense to visualize the congressman as a maximizer of vote percentage in elections— November or primary or, with some complex trade-off, both? For two reasons the answer is probably no. The first has to do with his goal itself, which is to stay in office rather than to win all the popular vote. More precisely his goal is to stay in office over a number of future elections, which does mean that "winning comfortably" in any one of them (except the last) is more desirable than winning by a narrow plurality. The logic here is that a narrow victory (in primary or general election) is a sign of weakness that can inspire hostile political actors to deploy resources intensively the next time around. By this reasoning the higher the election percentages the better. No doubt any congressman would engage in an act to raise his November figure from 80 percent to 90 percent if he could be absolutely sure that the act would accomplish the end (without affecting his primary percentage) and if it could be undertaken at low personal cost. But still, trying to "win comfortably" is not the same as trying to win all the popular vote. As the personal cost (e.g. expenditure of personal energy) of a hypothetical "sure gain" rises, the congressman at the 55 percent November level is more likely to be willing to pay it than his colleague at the 80 percent level.

▪ ▪ ▪

Whether they are safe or marginal, cautious or audacious, congressmen must constantly engage in activities related to reelection. There will be differences in emphasis, but all members share the root need to do things— indeed, to do things day in and day out during their terms. The next step here is to present a typology, a short list of the *kinds* of activities congressmen find it electorally useful to engage in. The case will be that there are three basic kinds of activities. . . .

One activity is *advertising*, defined here as any effort to disseminate one's name among constituents in such a fashion as to create a favorable image but in messages having little or no issue content. A successful congressman builds what amounts to a brand name, which may have a generalized electoral value for other politicians in the same family. The personal qualities to emphasize are experience, knowledge, responsiveness, concern, sincerity, independence, and the like. Just getting one's name across is difficult enough; only about half the electorate, if asked, can supply their House members' names. It helps a congressman to be known. "In the main, recognition carries a positive valence; to be perceived at all is to be perceived favorably." A vital advantage enjoyed by House incumbents is that they are much better known among voters than their November challengers. They are better known because they spend a great deal of time, energy, and money trying to make themselves better known. There are standard routines—frequent visits to the constituency, nonpolitical speeches to home audiences, the sending out of infant care booklets and letters of condolence and congratulation. Of 158 House members questioned in the mid-1960s, 121 said that they regularly sent newsletters to their constituents; 48 wrote separate news or opinion columns for newspapers; 82 regularly reported to their constituencies by radio or television; 89 regularly sent out mail questionnaires. Some routines are less standard. Congressman George E. Shipley (D., Ill.) claims to have met personally about half his constituents (i.e. some 200,000 people). For over twenty years Congressman Charles C. Diggs, Jr. (D., Mich.) has run a radio program featuring himself as a "combination disc jockey-commentator and minister." Congressman Daniel J. Flood (D., Pa.) is "famous for appearing unannounced and often uninvited at wedding anniversaries and other events." Anniversaries and other events aside, congressional advertising is done largely at public expense. Use of the franking privilege has mushroomed in recent years; in early 1973 one estimate predicted that House and Senate members would send out about 476 million pieces of mail in the year 1974, at a public cost of $38.1 million—or about 900,000 pieces per member with a subsidy of $70,000 per member. By far the heaviest mailroom traffic comes in Octobers of even-numbered years. There are some differences between House and Senate members in the ways they go about getting their names across. House members are free to blanket their constituencies with mailings for all boxholders; senators are not. But senators find it easier to appear on national television—for example, in short reaction statements on the nightly news shows. Advertising is a staple congressional activity, and there is no end to it. For each member there are always new voters to be apprised of his worthiness and old voters to be reminded of it.

A second activity may be called *credit claiming,* defined here as acting so as to generate a belief in a relevant political actor (or actors) that one is personally responsible for causing the government, or some unit thereof, to do something that the actor (or actors) considers desirable. The political logic of this, from the congressman's point of view, is that an actor who believes that a member can make pleasing things happen will no doubt wish to keep him in office so that he can make pleasing things happen in the future. The emphasis here is on individual accomplishment (rather than, say, party or governmental accomplishment) and on the congressman as doer (rather than as, say, expounder of constituency views). Credit claiming is highly important to congressmen, with the consequence that much of congressional life is a relentless search for opportunities to engage in it.

Where can credit be found? If there were only one congressman rather than 535, the answer would in principle be simple enough. Credit (or blame) would attach in Downsian fashion to the doings of the government as a whole. But there are 535. Hence it becomes necessary for each congressman to try to peel off pieces of governmental accomplishment for which he can believably generate a sense of responsibility. For the average congressman the staple way of doing this is to traffic in what may be called "particularized benefits." Particularized governmental benefits, as the term will be used here, have two properties: (1) Each benefit is given out to a specific individual, group, or geographical constituency, the recipient unit being of a scale that allows a single congressman to be recognized (by relevant political actors and other congressmen) as the claimant for the benefit (other congressmen being perceived as indifferent or hostile). (2) Each benefit is given out in apparently ad hoc fashion (unlike, say, social security checks) with a congressman apparently having a hand in the allocation. A particularized benefit can normally be regarded as a member of a class. That is, a benefit given out to an individual, group, or constituency can normally be looked upon by congressmen as one of a class of similar benefits given out to sizable numbers of individuals, groups, or constituencies. Hence the impression can arise that a congressman is getting "his share" of whatever it is the government is offering. (The classes may be vaguely defined. Some state legislatures deal in what their members call "local legislation.")

In sheer volume the bulk of particularized benefits come under the heading of "casework"—the thousands of favors congressional offices perform for supplicants in ways that normally do not require legislative action. High school students ask for essay materials, soldiers for emergency leaves, pensioners for location of missing checks, local governments for grant information, and on and on. Each office has skilled professionals who can play the bureaucracy like an organ—pushing the right pedals to produce the desired effects. But many benefits require new legislation, or at least they require important allocative decisions on matters covered by existent legislation. Here the congressman fills the traditional role of supplier of goods to the home district. It is a believable role; when a member claims credit for a benefit on the order of a dam, he may well receive it. Shiny construction projects seem especially useful. In the decades before 1934, tariff duties for local industries were a major commodity. In recent years awards given under grant-in-aid programs have become more useful as they have become more numerous. Some quests for credit are ingenious; in 1971 the story broke that congressmen had been earmarking foreign aid money for specific projects in Israel in order to win favor with home constituents. It should be said of constituency benefits that congressmen are quite capable of taking the initiative in drumming them up; that is, there can be no automatic assumption that a congressman's activity is the result of pressures brought to bear by organized interests. Fenno shows the importance of member initiative in his discussion of the House Interior Committee.

A final point here has to do with geography. The examples given so far are all of benefits conferred upon home constituencies or recipients therein (the latter including the home residents who applauded the Israeli projects). But the properties of particularized benefits were carefully specified so as not to exclude the possibility that some benefits may be given to recipients outside the home constituencies. Some probably are. Narrowly drawn tax loopholes qualify as particularized benefits, and some of them are probably conferred upon recipients outside the home districts. (It is difficult to find solid evidence on the point.) Campaign contributions flow into districts from the outside, so it would not be surprising to find that benefits go where the resources are.

How much particularized benefits count for at the polls is extraordinarily difficult to say. But it would be hard to find a congressman who thinks he can afford to wait around until precise information is available. The lore is that they count—furthermore, given home expectations, that they must be supplied in regular quantities for a member to stay electorally even with the board. Awareness of favors may spread beyond their recipients, building for a member a general reputation as a good provider. "Rivers Delivers." "He Can Do More For Massachusetts." A good example of Capitol Hill lore on electoral impact is given in this account of the activities of Congressman Frank Thompson, Jr. (D., N.J., 4th district):

> In 1966, the 4th was altered drastically by redistricting; it lost Burlington County and gained Hunterdon, Warren, and Sussex. Thompson's performance at the polls since 1966 is a case study of how an incumbent congressman, out of line with his district's ideological persuasions, can become unbeatable. In 1966, Thompson carried Mercer by 23,000 votes and lost the three new counties by 4,600, winning reelection with 56% of the votes. He then survived a district-wide drop in his vote two years later. In 1970, the Congressman carried Mercer County by 20,000 votes and the rest of the district by 6,000, finishing with 58%. The drop in Mercer resulted from the attempt of his hard-line conservative opponent to exploit the racial unrest which had developed in Trenton. But for four years Thompson had been making friends in Hunterdon, Warren, and Sussex, busy doing the kind of chores that congressmen do. In this case, Thompson concerned himself with the interests of dairy farmers at the Department of Agriculture. The results of his efforts were clear when the results came in from the 4th's northern counties.

So much for particularized benefits. But is credit available elsewhere? For governmental accomplishments beyond the scale of those already discussed? The general answer is that the prime mover role is a hard one to play on larger matters—at least before broad electorates. A claim, after all, has to be credible. If a congressman goes before an audience and says, "I am responsible for passing a bill to curb inflation," or "I am responsible for the highway program," hardly anyone will believe him. There are two reasons why people may be skeptical of such claims. First, there is a numbers problem. On an accomplishment of a sort that probably engaged the supportive interest of more than one member it is reasonable to suppose that credit should be apportioned among them. But second, there is an overwhelming problem of information costs. For typical voters Capitol Hill is a distant and mysterious place; few have anything like a working knowledge of its maneuverings. Hence there is no easy way of knowing whether a congressman is staking a valid claim or not. The odds are that the information problem cuts in different ways on different kinds of issues. On particularized benefits it may work in a congressman's favor; he may get credit for the dam he had nothing to do with building. Sprinkling a district with dams, after all, is something a congressman is supposed to be able to do. But on larger matters it may work against him. For a voter lacking an easy way to sort out valid from invalid claims the sensible recourse is skepticism. Hence it is unlikely that congressmen get much mileage out of credit claiming on larger matters before broad electorates.

Yet there is an obvious and important qualification here. For many congressmen credit claiming on non-particularized matters is possible in specialized subject areas because of the congressional division of labor. The term "governmental unit" in the original definition of credit claiming is broad enough to include committees, subcommittees, and the two houses of Congress itself. Thus many congressmen can believably claim credit for blocking bills in subcommittee, adding on amendments in committee, and so on. The audience for transactions of this sort is usually small. But it may include important political actors (e.g. an interest group, the president, the *New York Times*, Ralph Nader) who are capable of both paying Capitol Hill information costs and deploying electoral resources. There is a well-documented example of this in Fenno's treatment of post office politics in the 1960s. The postal employee unions used to watch very closely the activities of the House and Senate Post Office Committees and supply valuable electoral resources (money, volunteer work) to members who did their bidding on salary bills. Of course there are many examples of this kind of undertaking, and there is more to be said about it.

The third activity congressmen engage in may be called *position taking*, defined here as the public enunciation of a judgmental statement on anything likely to be of interest to political actors. The statement may take the form of a roll call vote. The most important classes of judgmental statements are those prescribing American governmental ends (a vote cast against the war; a statement that "the war should be ended immediately") or governmental means (a statement that "the way to end the war is to take it to the United Nations"). The judgments may be implicit rather than explicit, as in: "I will support the president on this matter." But judgments may range far beyond these classes to take in implicit or explicit statements on what almost anybody should do or how he should do it: "The great Polish scientist Copernicus has been unjustly neglected"; "The way for Israel to achieve peace is to give up the Sinai." The congressman as position taker is a speaker rather than a doer. The electoral requirement is not that he make pleasing things happen but that he make pleasing judgmental statements. The position itself is the political commodity. Especially on matters where governmental responsibility is widely diffused it is not surprising that political actors should fall back on positions as tests of incumbent virtue. For voters ignorant of congressional processes the recourse is an easy one. The following comment by one of Clapp's House interviewees is highly revealing: "Recently, I went home and began to talk about the ———— act. I was pleased to have sponsored that bill, but it soon dawned on me that the point wasn't getting through at all. What was getting through was that the act might be a help to people. I changed the emphasis: I didn't mention my role particularly, but stressed my support of the legislation."

The ways in which positions can be registered are numerous and often imaginative. There are floor addresses ranging from weighty orations to mass-produced "nationality day statements." There are speeches before home groups, television appearances, letters, newsletters, press releases, ghostwritten books, *Playboy* articles, even interviews with political scientists. On occasion congressmen generate what amount to petitions; whether or not to sign the 1956 Southern Manifesto defying school desegregation rulings was an important decision for southern members. Outside the roll call process the congressman is usually able to tailor his positions to suit his audiences. A solid consensus in the constituency calls for ringing declarations; for years the late Senator James K. Vardaman (D., Miss.) campaigned on a proposal to repeal the Fifteenth Amendment. Division or uncertainty in the constituency calls for waffling; in the late 1960s a congressman had to be a poor politician indeed not to be able to come up with an inoffensive statement on Vietnam ("We must have peace with honor at the earliest possible moment consistent with the national interest"). On a controversial issue a Capitol Hill office normally prepares two form letters to send out to constituent letter writers—one for the pros and one (not directly contradictory) for the antis. Handling discrete audiences in person requires simple agility, a talent well demonstrated in this selection from a Nader profile:

> "You may find this difficult to understand," said Democrat Edward R. Roybal, the Mexican-American representative from California's thirtieth district, "but sometimes I wind up making a patriotic speech one afternoon and later on that same day an anti-war speech. In the patriotic speech I speak of past wars but I also speak of the need to prevent more wars. My positions are not inconsistent; I just approach different people differently." Roybal went on to depict the diversity of crowds he speaks to: one afternoon he is surrounded by balding men wearing Veterans' caps and holding American flags; a few hours later he speaks to a crowd of Chicano youths, angry over American involvement in Vietnam. Such a diverse constituency, Roybal believes, calls for different methods of expressing one's convictions.

Indeed it does. Versatility of this sort is occasionally possible in roll call voting. For example a congressman may vote one way on recommittal and the other on final passage, leaving it unclear just how he stands on a bill. Members who cast identical votes on a measure may give different reasons for having done so. Yet it is on roll calls that the crunch comes; there is no way for a member to avoid making a record on hundreds of issues, some of which are controversial in the home constituencies. Of course, most roll call positions considered in isolation are not likely to cause much of a ripple at home. But broad voting patterns can and do; member "ratings" calculated by the Americans for Democratic Action, Americans for Constitutional Action, and other outfits are used as guidelines in the deploying of electoral resources. And particular issues often have their alert publics. Some national interest groups watch the votes of all congressmen on single issues and ostentatiously try to reward or punish members for their positions; over the years some notable examples of such interest groups have been the Anti-Saloon League, the early Farm Bureau, the American Legion, the American Medical Association, and the National Rifle Association. On rare occasions single roll calls achieve a rather high salience among the public generally. This seems especially true of the Senate, which every now and then winds up for what might be called a "showdown vote," with pressures on all sides, presidential involvement, media attention given to individual senators' positions, and suspense about the outcome. Examples are the votes on the nuclear test-ban treaty in 1963, civil rights cloture in 1964, civil rights cloture again in 1965, the Haynsworth appointment in 1969, the Carswell appointment in 1970, and the ABM in 1970. Controversies on roll calls like these are often relived in subsequent campaigns, the southern Senate elections of 1970 with their Haynsworth and Carswell issues being cases in point.

Probably the best position-taking strategy for most congressmen at most times is to be conservative—to cling to their own positions of the past where possible and to reach for new ones with great caution where necessary. Yet in an earlier discussion of strategy the suggestion was made that it might be rational for members in electoral danger to resort to innovation. The form of innovation available is entrepreneurial position taking, its logic being that for a member facing defeat with his old array of positions it makes good sense to gamble on some new ones. It may be that congressional marginals fulfill an important function here as issue pioneers—experimenters who test out new issues and thereby show other politicians which ones are usable. An example of such a pioneer is Senator Warren Magnuson (D., Wash.), who responded to a surprisingly narrow victory in 1962 by reaching for a reputation in the area of consumer affairs. Another example is Senator Ernest Hollings (D., S.C.), a servant of a shaky and racially heterogeneous southern constituency who launched "hunger" as an issue in 1969—at once pointing to a problem and giving it a useful nonracial definition. One of the most successful issue entrepreneurs of recent decades was the late Senator Joseph McCarthy (R., Wis.); it was all there—the close primary in 1946, the fear of defeat in 1952, the desperate casting about for an issue, the famous 1950 dinner at the Colony Restaurant where suggestions were tendered, the decision that "Communism" might just do the trick.

NOTES

1. "But it is equally true, though only of late and slowly beginning to be acknowledged, that a numerous assembly is as little fitted for the direct business of legislation as for that of administration." John Stuart Mill, *Considerations on Representative Government* (Chicago: Regency, 1962), p. 104.

2. Gerhard Loewenberg, "The Role of Parliaments in Modern Political Systems," in Loewenberg (ed.), *Modern Parliaments: Change or Decline?* (Chicago: Aldine-Atherton, 1971), p. 3.

5.2

RICHARD F. FENNO, JR.

From *Home Style: House Members in Their Districts*

Fenno's study of members of Congress leads him to consider four groups of people that a typical representative considers subsets of his or her constituency: (1) all people in the district, (2) those who tend to vote for the representative in general elections, (3) those who ardently support and vote for the representative in primary elections, and (4) those who contribute money and time to the representative's reelection. These groups are like concentric circles surrounding the representative, and he or she has to pay careful attention to all four of these groups.

What does a House member see when looking at his or her constituency? Kaleidoscopic variety, no doubt. That is why there can be no one "correct" way of slicing up and classifying member perceptions—only "helpful" ways. Most helpful to me has been the member's view of a constituency as a nest of concentric circles. In one form or another, in one expression or another, in one degree or another, this bull's-eye perception is shared by all House members. It is helpful to us for the same reason it is common to them. It is a perception constructed out of the necessities of political life.

THE GEOGRAPHICAL CONSTITUENCY: THE DISTRICT

The largest of the concentric circles represents the House member's most encompassing view of his or her constituency. It is "the district," the entity to which, from which, and within which the member travels. It is the entity whose boundaries have been fixed by state legislative enactment or by court decision. It includes the entire population within those boundaries. Because it is a legal entity, we could refer to it as the legal constituency. We capture more of what the member has in mind when conjuring up "my district," however, if we think of it as the *geographical constituency*. We then retain the idea that the district is a legally bounded space, and emphasize that it is located in a particular place.

The Washington community is often described as a group of people all of whom come from somewhere else. The House of Representatives, by design, epitomizes this characteristic; and its members function with a heightened sense of their ties to another place. There are, of course, constant reminders. The member's district is, after all, "the Tenth District of *California*." Inside the chamber, he is "the gentleman from *California*." In the media, he is "Representative Smith (D. *California*)." So it is not surprising that when you ask a member, "What kind of district do you have?" the answer often begins with, and nearly always includes, a geographical, space-and-place perception. Thus, the district is seen as "the largest in the state, twenty-eight counties in the southeastern corner," or "three layers of suburbs to the west of the city, a square with the northwest corner cut out," or "a core district, the core of the city." If the boundaries have been changed by a recent redistricting, the geography of "the new district" will be compared to that of "the old district": "I picked up five northern counties and lost two on the eastern edge. The new district is a lot more spread out."

If one essential aspect of "the geographical constituency" is seen as its location and boundaries, another is its internal makeup. And House members describe their districts' internal makeup using political science's most familiar demographic and political variables: socioeconomic structure, ideology, ethnicity, residential patterns, religion, partisanship, stability, diversity, etc. Every congressman, in his mind's eye, sees his geographical constituency in terms of some special configuration of such variables.

■   ■   ■

THE REELECTION CONSTITUENCY: THE SUPPORTERS

Each congressman does perceive an explicitly political constituency nested within his geographical constituency. It is composed of those people in the district who he thinks vote for him. We shall call it his *reelection constituency*. But, because all members do not perceive their support in coalitional terms and because all members do see support in reelection terms, we shall use the more universal language.[1] As they move about "the district," House members continually draw the distinction between those people who vote for them and those who do not: "I do well here"; "I run poorly here"; "This group supports me"; "This group does not." By distinguishing supporters from nonsupporters, they articulate their fundamental political perception.

House members use two reference points—one cross-sectional, the other longitudinal—in shaping this perception. First, by a process of inclusion and exclusion, they come to a rough approximation of the upper and lower ranges of the reelection constituency. That is to say, there are some votes a member believes he nearly always gets. There are other votes he believes he almost never gets. Among those he thinks he usually gets, the perceived partisan component of the electorate is always a basic element. Every member begins with a perception of his partisan support—estimated by registration figures or poll data, and by political demography.

It's a good Democratic district now—59 percent registered Democrats. And for the first time I feel safe. . . . I used to brag that my old district was the wealthiest, best-educated district in the country represented by a Democrat. But I wasn't a bit sad to give up the wealthy part of the district and pick up all those poor, ill-educated good Democrats in the new part of the district.

When the partisan composition of the district is clearly insufficient for reelection, members express ideas about the nature of their cross-party supporters.

My district registers only 37 percent Republican. And they have no place else to go. My problem is, how can I get enough Democratic votes to win the general election. . . . Civil servants, bank clerks, insurance salesmen, bricklayers, carpenters, the craft unions; these have been the mainstream of my Democratic support—middle class and working class. . . . The hard hats are the people most likely to vote for me. That's my lucrative territory—not the liberal, intellectual wing [of the Democratic party].

Every member has some idea of the people most likely to join his reelection constituency, his "lucrative territory." During a campaign, these people will often be "targeted" and subjected to special recruiting or activating efforts.

A congressman's sense of the people least likely to join his reelection constituency is usually as well developed as his sense for his "lucrative territory." Comments like "I'll never carry this town"; "This part of the district is hopeless"; "I've never been able to crack these space industry guys"; "I'd love to get the pickup truck vote, but I never do" punctuate his travels in the district. If a member chooses to attack "the special interests" in his district, it is from these perceived never-supporters that the objects of his attacks will come.

■ ■ ■

Thinking about "last time's" electoral margin, if it was an apparently safe one, should assuage a good deal of a representative's uncertainty about his reelection constituency. And it does. But it does not produce certainty. Far from it. Most House members will have experienced, at some point in their careers, "the fight of my life"—a testing election they felt especially hard-pressed to win. When members recall their testing elections they dwell on the immense organizational and personal efforts required to win.

THE PRIMARY CONSTITUENCY: THE STRONGEST SUPPORTERS

In thinking about their political condition, House members make distinctions *within* their reelection constituency, thus giving us a third, still smaller perceptual circle. Having distinguished between their nonsupporters and their supporters, they further distinguish between their weak supporters and their strong supporters. Weak supporters come in both the routine and the temporary varieties. Routine supporters do no more than vote for the member, often simply following party identification. Temporary supporters back the member as the best available alternative "this time," as "the lesser of two evils." Strong supporters display an intensity capable of producing additional political activity, and they tender their support "through thick and thin," regardless of who the challenger may be. Within each reelection constituency, then, nests a smaller constituency perceived as "my strongest supporters," "my loyalists," "my true believers," "my political base," "my hard core," "my nucleus," "my tough nut," "my bread basket." We shall think of these people as the ones each congressman believes would provide his last line of electoral defense in a primary contest, and label them the *primary constituency.*[2] We do not mean this label to include all the people who vote for him in a primary, only those from whom he expects a special solidity of support in a primary election.

A protected congressional seat is one protected as much from primary defeat as from general election defeat. And a primary constituency is something every congressman must have one of.

■　　■　　■

THE PERSONAL CONSTITUENCY: THE INTIMATES

Within the primary constituency, House members perceive still a fourth, and final, concentric circle. These are the few individuals whose relationship with the member is so personal and so intimate that their relevance cannot be captured by any description of "very strongest supporters." Some of them are his closest political advisers and confidants. Others are people from whom he draws emotional sustenance for his political work. They are all people with whom the congressman has shared some crucial experience—usually early in his career, and often the "testing election." Times of relaxation are thick with reminiscence. Fellow feeling is heavily "we few, we happy few, we band of brothers." Sometimes a staff assistant is among these intimates; sometimes not. Sometimes the member's spouse is involved, but not always. These are the people, if any, to whom he has entrusted his political career. He can meet with all of them in one place, face to face, as he cannot with any of his other constituencies. He knows them by name, as individuals. He thinks of them as his friends. "A guy is lucky in politics," said one congressman. "He's carried here by his friends and he is kept here by his friends. That gives you a nice feeling." We shall think of these politically and emotionally supportive friends as the member's *personal constituency.*

■　　■　　■

CONCLUSION

Each member of Congress perceives four concentric constituencies: geographic, reelection, primary, and personal. This is not the only way a member sees his or her "constituency"; but it is one way. It is a set of perceptions that emphasizes the context in which, and the strategies by which, the House member seeks electoral support. It is a complicated context, one featuring varying scopes of support and varying intensities of support. The strategies developed for getting and keeping electoral support involve the manipulation of these scopes and intensities. . . .

A perceptual analysis of congressional constituencies both complicates and clarifies efforts of political science to understand the relationship between congressman and constituency. It complicates matters both conceptually and statistically. For example, political scientists have a heavy investment in role conceptions that distinguish between the "trustee" who follows his independent judgment and the "delegate" who follows the wishes of his constituency. But we now must ask, which constituency? And we cannot be content with a conceptual scheme that provides only two answers to this question: "the district" and "the nation."[3] More frequent, we think, than this kind of choice is one in which the congressman must choose among constituencies *within* the district. Also, when studies of party voting conclude that a member of Congress can vote independently because he or she "knows the constituency isn't looking,"[4] we need to ask again, which constituency? One of the several constituencies may very well be looking.

NOTES

1. John Kingdon, *Candidates for Office: Beliefs and Strategies* (New York: Random House, 1966), chap. 3. In her study of congressional challengers in New York, Linda Fowler finds that some did not perceive or think in terms of an electoral "coalition." Linda Fowler, "The Cycle of Defeat: Recruitment of Congressional Challengers," unpublished manuscript, University of Rochester, 1977. When asked to describe his "supporters," one congressman in my group answered, "That's very hard to evaluate. I never thought in terms of groups. . . . I never thought of my support as coming from groups. The middle group, I guess, homeowners. It's very hard to say." The importance of the reelection constituency is well argued (though not subsequently employed) in Aage Clausen, *How Congressmen Decide: A Policy Focus* (New York: St. Martin's, 1973), p. 126.

2. The term is from Leo Snowiss, "Congressional Recruitment and Representation," *American Political Science Review* 60 (September 1966): 629–639.

3. For example, see Roger Davidson, *The Role of the Congressman* (New York: Pegasus, 1973).

4. David Stokes and Warren Miller, "Party Government and the Saliency of Congress," *Public Opinion Quarterly* 26 (Winter 1962): 531–546.

5.3

MICHELE L. SWERS

From *The Difference* Women *Make*: *The Policy Impact of Women in Congress*

Does the gender of a member of Congress make a difference in legislative voting or in the kinds of policies that get prioritized? Swers argues that it does matter, and that congressional Democrats and moderate Republicans who are women pursue policies aimed at women, families, and children to a greater degree than men from either political party in Congress.

CONCLUSION: DOES ELECTING WOMEN MATTER? THE IMPACT ON POLICY DEVELOPMENT AND DEMOCRACY

Before women even gained the right to vote, Progressive Era women's groups lobbied their state and national government leaders to appoint women to school boards, public health agencies, and other community service entities (Skocpol 1992). Today, the approach of each election year finds women's groups, particularly feminist groups, donating money to women candidates, organizing candidate-training seminars for women, and actively campaigning for women candidates. When Americans go to the polls to cast their votes for a new representative, does it matter if the party nominee is a woman?

In addition to arguments based on equality, a close examination of members' legislative activity in the 103rd and 104th Congresses demonstrates that the personal identity of our representatives does have tangible policy consequences. These policy consequences affect our understanding of representational democracy, the congressional policy-making process, and relations between the political parties.

Issues of Representation: The Importance of Diversity

While the imperatives of reelection every two years dictate that legislators will pay close attention to the needs of their districts, the demands of the district constituencies are best viewed as guidelines for members' legislative activity rather than specific policy directives. Within the boundaries of constituency preferences, representatives are free to develop specific legislative priorities. In addition to pursuing programs for their districts and tending to committee responsibilities, personal interests based on politically significant social identities such as race and gender, occupational background, and individual experience will determine whether legislators focus their resources on breast cancer research or Parkinson's disease, violence against women or minimum mandatory sentences for drug offenders, a child-care tax credit or lowering capital gains tax rates. Thus, increasing membership diversity within the legislature will expand the range of issues and interests addressed by the congressional agenda.

The impact of social identities such as gender cannot be captured by a simple review of representatives' roll-call votes. Although two liberal Democrats may both take a feminist position on a roll-call vote concerning abortion, family and medical leave, or welfare reform, to understand fully how interests become incorporated into law, one must examine the entire policy-making process. The careful analysis of legislative activity . . . demonstrates that Democratic and moderate Republican congresswomen are more committed to the pursuit of women's interests than are their male partisan colleagues. They have focused attention on new issues, particularly feminist issues, and have helped define formerly private concerns such as child care and domestic violence as public policy problems. . . . [G]ender differences are greatest in the area of bill sponsorship. . . . [W]hen representatives are the least constrained by seniority, committee position, and the demands of party loyalty, they can most clearly express their unique policy priorities. Therefore, given the opportunity, female representatives will work to incorporate the interests of women, children, and families into the congressional agenda.

■   ■   ■

A member's level of commitment to women's issues is particularly important in the current era of budget politics in which Republicans and Democrats are competing to define themselves as the more fiscally responsible party. As individual programs compete for funding, one representative's wasteful pork barrel project is another's essential program. Politically significant social identities such as gender and race will play a more central role in the decision calculus of legislators when the results of the bill will have direct consequences for the representative's social group. As one Democratic congresswoman explained it, women are more active on issues like family planning, sexual harassment, and child-support enforcement because "women have the most at risk." . . .

The Congressional Policy-Making Process: The Influence of the Institutional and Political Contexts

Regardless of their abstract policy preferences, . . . the choices legislators make concerning which policies to pursue depends on the limitations of their positions within the institution and their assessment of the political context. For example, the analysis of the bill sponsorship patterns of representatives demonstrates that Democratic and Republican women initiate more social welfare proposals than did their male partisan colleagues only when they had access to the prerogatives of the majority party. Since the majority party controls the overall content and direction of the policy agenda, and social welfare issues make up a large portion of the legislation considered by the committees, congresswomen of both parties determined that the increased opportunity to influence policy on these issues justified the expense of political capital on developing and advocating social welfare policies.

While representatives campaign on promises to initiate legislation to provide prescription drug coverage for seniors and to reform the educational system, they have the most influence over policies within the jurisdiction of their committees. . . . [F]ew women command the seniority necessary to advance to leadership positions on the committees and subcommittees. Since the committee and subcommittee chairs draft the legislative vehicles that are subject to committee markups and their bills are the most likely to gain floor consideration and become law, congresswomen who want to influence policy on women's issues must convince the committee leaders to accept their proposals.

The examination of amending behavior in committees indicates that expanding the seats at the committee table to include more women will have an impact on the nature of the problems considered by the committees and expand the realm of legitimate solutions to a problem. In the 103rd Congress, Democratic women utilized their committee positions to encourage their Democratic colleagues to incorporate more gender-related proposals into committee legislation, while in the 104th Congress these women used their committee seats as a platform to vehemently oppose conservative Republican initiatives on women's issues. Similarly, in the 104th Congress, moderate Republican women sought to moderate their party's proposals on such issues as welfare reform by offering amendments to expand child-support enforcement and women's access to child care. Moreover, legislators and staff maintain that congresswomen bring a different perspective to committee deliberations on all issues. Clearly, a seat on a powerful committee provides a member of a politically significant minority group with the tools to fight for inclusion of his or her group's interests into the ultimate policy solution.

The Politics of Defection

Interest group advocates and media commentators often express disappointment that a legislator did not take a stand for principle on a particular issue or vote in the way one would expect them to vote as a representative of a particular social group. . . . [B]eyond the views of the district constituency, representatives carefully assess the nature of the political context before they decide to pursue priorities that are not in line with the views of the majority of their party caucus and important party interest group supporters.

Women's issues constitute an area where the preferences of moderate Republicans, particularly women, often diverge from their more conservative party colleagues. The analysis of the legislative behavior of moderate Republicans in the 103rd and 104th Congresses indicates that these representatives found it easier to pursue liberal stands on women's issues as members of the minority party. As minority party legislators, moderate Republicans were simply expected to bring along their contingent of votes; however, when they ascended to the majority they had to oppose their party colleagues more aggressively in order to incorporate their policy views into legislation or eliminate offending provisions. In addition, moderate Republicans had to take this more aggressive stance when their party commanded the stronger sanctions that come with majority power. Majority status yields opportunities for a representative to achieve action on their policy priorities on a wide range of issues. However, moderate Republicans who antagonized party colleagues and important party supporters such as social conservatives risked the retaliation of party and committee leaders. For example, leaders might refuse to incorporate funding for a cherished district project into the appropriations bills or they might exclude a representative's proposals on other issues from committee legislation. The costs of defection are exacerbated when a president of the same party occupies the White House. For example, moderate Republicans in the current Congress face additional pressure to support their party leader, President Bush.

. . . [E]vidence . . . shows that, as majority party members, moderate Republicans pursued their more liberal views on women's issues with a close eye on what party colleagues would bear. . . . [A]nalysis of the bill sponsorship patterns of legislators indicates that when moderate Republican women ascended to the majority in the 104th Congress, they shifted their resources from developing feminist proposals, which Republicans generally oppose, to a greater focus on social welfare initiatives. Furthermore, these women drastically reduced their support for liberal positions on women's issue roll-call votes and thus stayed closer to party lines.

At the same time that the pressure to support the party becomes more intense, members of a potentially strategic voting block will become the focus of more aggressive lobbying efforts from opposition interest groups. Thus, moderate Republicans, especially women, received more attention from liberal interest groups who viewed them as the last hope to preserve social welfare programs or eliminate conservative initiatives on reproductive rights. These moderates had to negotiate the competing pressures of working to achieve their policy goals on women's issues without damaging their credibility within the Republican conference by being perceived as advocates for Democratic interest groups. Therefore, as often as possible, moderates pursued their policy goals within the boundaries of what their natural allies, fellow Republicans, could accept and they lobbied their party colleagues to expand those boundaries by incorporating more gender-related concerns into party legislation.

Thus, the politics of defection is a complicated balancing act, the dynamics of which have far-reaching implications for our understanding of congressional policy making. This effort to balance contradictory policy preferences with party loyalty likely extends beyond moderate Republican women who support liberal positions on women's issues to pro-environment Republicans, fiscally conservative Democrats, and other legislators who espouse policy positions that contravene the prevailing view within their party caucus.

■   ■   ■

Conclusion

. . . [I]n addition to advocating for the needs of their districts, female legislators do exhibit a profound commitment to the pursuit of policies for women, children, and families. Both Democratic and moderate Republican women used their bill sponsorship and cosponsorship activity to focus attention on women's issues, and they championed gender-related proposals in their committee and floor activity. Congresswomen's consistent advocacy of women's issue initiatives, particularly feminist initiatives, demonstrates an intensity of commitment that could not be captured merely by a study of roll-call votes. Their unique policy priorities indicate that increasing the presence of women in Congress could open the congressional agenda to more gender-related concerns. Additionally, the important relationship between social identity and the intensity of commitment to issues that have a direct impact on their social group holds significant implications for understanding the influence of other politically significant social identities, including race and sexual orientation, on the policy priorities of individual legislators.

However, simply increasing the number of women and other minorities in Congress will not automatically lead to enhanced influence on policy design, since presence in the institution does not directly translate into power over legislative outcomes. While it is significant that increasing numbers of women are elected to Congress, . . . the ability of congresswomen to legislate on behalf of women is constrained by their position within the institution, particularly their level of seniority, access to committee positions, and status as a member of the majority/minority party.

▪ ▪ ▪

[U]nderstanding how politically significant social identities have an impact on the legislative behavior of representatives is not simply a matter of raw numbers in the legislature. The interplay of presence and power is complex. In the case of gender, the unique policy interests of women provide substantive support to those who call for the inclusion of more women in the cabinet choices of presidents and governors and the leadership ranks of Congress and the state legislatures. Electing women has important consequences for the quality of our representational system, thus making the call for more diversity in Congress more than a mere platitude. Presence, however, is only a first step. Power in Congress also depends on access to influential positions within the institution that allow members to exercise strategic influence over the shape of policy outcomes.

REFERENCE

Skocpol, Theda. 1992. *Protecting Soldiers and Mothers: The Political Origins of Social Policy in the United States.* Cambridge, Mass.: Harvard University Press.

5.4

GARY W. COX AND MATHEW D. McCUBBINS

From *Setting the Agenda: Responsible Party Government in the U.S. House of Representatives*

The majority party in the House of Representatives closely controls legislative business, but to do so the party needs the cooperation of its members. How do majority political parties in Congress keep their coalitions together to pass legislation? Cox and McCubbins argue that party leaders, first, offer plum committee assignments and pork barrel benefits to rank-and-file members, and second, keep tight control over the agenda to ensure that no bills are voted upon that would potentially divide the party.

PROCEDURAL CARTEL THEORY

> The job of speaker is not to expedite legislation that runs counter to the wishes of the majority of his majority.
>
> —Speaker Dennis Hastert (R-IL)[1]

In this chapter, we present and discuss the assumptions that undergird procedural cartel theory. To provide a context for comparison, however, we first briefly survey the literature on partisan legislative organization.

Theories of Partisan Legislative Organization

Much of the literature on legislative organization focuses on why political parties are created within legislatures in the first place. We divide extant explanations into those that hinge primarily on the internal legislative payoffs to forming parties and those that hinge primarily on the external electoral payoffs. We then turn to survey the literature on how parties are organized and what parties do.

Why are there parties in legislatures?

PARTIES ARE CREATED TO SOLVE INTERNAL COLLECTIVE ACTION PROBLEMS.   One line of theorizing about why parties exist is similar to the distributive line of argument regarding committees. Absent any organization (other than a voting rule for floor decisions), legislators face a chaotic and unpredictable agenda. They cannot be sure that the legislature will not vote tomorrow to strip them of benefits conferred today. Nor is it clear how to ensure that the benefits are conferred to begin with, given a world where any legislator can move any amendment at any time.

In order to deal with the unpredictability—and unprofitability—of the unorganized legislature, legislators form political parties to bind themselves together in durable coalitions. Gains from legislative trade that could not be accrued without parties are thus accrued.

PARTIES ARE CREATED TO SOLVE EXTERNAL COLLECTIVE ACTION PROBLEMS.   An alternative theory views legislative parties as being formed primarily to accrue electoral gains. Modern political parties facing mass electorates, similar to modern corporations facing mass markets, have a strong incentive to fashion and maintain a brand name. Such brand names are, however, public goods to all politicians running under the party's label. Thus, parties arise in order to ensure that the usual problems of providing and maintaining public goods are overcome—and in particular to internalize electoral externalities that would otherwise arise.

How are parties organized?

If parties exist to solve collective action problems, as seems the main tenet in the literature, then how do they organize to solve these problems? The literature has several suggestions, which we now survey.

PARTIES AS FIRMS.   Many scholars envision parties as being similar to the firms depicted in the literature on industrial organization (cf. Alchian and Demsetz 1972; Tirole 1988), in that they involve delegation to central agents (party leaders) in order to reduce transaction costs and ameliorate collective action problems. Scholars in this tradition implicitly accept the industrial organization literature's focus on hierarchical firms with single chief executive officers.

PARTIES AS PARTNERSHIPS.   In the case of the political party, we believe a more fruitful analogy is to partnerships, such as law or accountancy firms, in which various gradations of senior partners provide overall strategic and tactical direction to the firm. The "senior partners" in our story—at least as regards the majority party—will be committee and subcommittee chairs, majority party floor leaders, campaign finance committee chairs, and the like. Agenda-setting and other powers are distributed across the offices held by these senior partners rather than fully concentrated in the hands of the speaker, just as the right to recruit new clients and take on new jobs is distributed among the senior partners in a law or accountancy firm, rather than fully concentrated in the hands of the firm's president. Similarly, just as the job of ensuring that no senior partner's actions impinge too unfavorably on a law firm's overall reputation falls not just on the firm's president but also on the other senior partners collectively, so too the job of policing committee chairs falls partly to the speaker and partly to informal politics centered on the party caucus.

What do parties do?

Once organized, what do parties do to mitigate the collective action problems that are assumed to be the reason for their existence?

PARTIES AS FLOOR VOTING COALITIONS.   Some partisan theories view parties primarily as floor voting coalitions. In such theories, the central issue is the degree to which parties can discipline their members, ensuring a cohesive voting bloc on the floor, even when there are internal disagreements over policy.

The best-known model that seeks to explain variations in American parties' ability to discipline their members, and hence enact programs, is the conditional party government model of Aldrich (1995), Rohde (1991), and Aldrich and Rohde (2001). In this model, majority party backbenchers delegate more power to their party leaders, when preferences vary less within each party and more between the parties. Party government is thus conditional on a sufficient disagreement in preferences between the parties (relative to their internal disagreements) arising. When this condition is met, American parties act more in accord with the traditional model of responsible party government.

PARTIES AS PROCEDURAL COALITIONS.   Other partisan theories, including our own, view parties primarily as procedural coalitions. For such theories, the central issue is the majority party's ability to control the legislative agenda, defined as the set of bills considered and voted on the floor.

How do majority parties control the agenda?

Strict party discipline, at least on important votes, is one method for the majority party or coalition to control legislative outcomes. When party leaders have the means to impose discipline on their backbenchers, agenda control is attained by the extension of the will of the party leadership. But, where discipline is costly, other methods may be substituted. In considering these other methods, there is an important distinction to be made between positive and negative agenda power. Positive agenda power is the ability to push bills through the legislative process to a final-passage vote on the floor. Negative agenda power is the ability to block bills from reaching a final passage vote on the floor. Formal and informal models of legislative parties differ in whether they depict parties as controlling the agenda via the allocation of proposal rights (positive agenda power) or veto rights (negative agenda power).

PARTIES AS ALLOCATING PROPOSAL RIGHTS.   Two examples of theories in which proposal rights are the key resource allocated by parties to their members are Laver and Shepsle's (1996) model of ministerial government and Diermeier and Feddersen's (1998) model of the vote of confidence. In a common interpretation of Laver and Shepsle's model, multiparty coalition governments allocate ministerial portfolios to their various member parties, with each minister then possessing both positive and negative agenda power in his respective jurisdiction. Thus, each minister can make proposals directly to the assembly, without needing cabinet clearance. In Diermeier and Feddersen's model, coalitions of legislators allocate increased "recognition probabilities" to their members, thereby increasing their ability to make proposals. Once recognized, a given member of a coalition again needs no preclearance by other members of the coalition for his proposals: They go straight to a final-passage vote in the plenary.

PARTIES AS ALLOCATING VETO RIGHTS.   An alternative view of parties is that they allocate negative agenda power, or veto rights, among their members. Tsebelis (2002) takes this view of parliamentary coalitions. Rather than view individual parties as possessing both negative and positive agenda power across a range of issues (those under the jurisdiction of the party's ministers), Tsebelis views parties as possessing a general veto over the entire range of issues the coalition must face—therefore no coalition partner possesses unilateral proposal power. Similarly, Cox and McCubbins (2002) view majority parties primarily as allocating veto (or delaying) power to various offices held by their senior partners, such as committee chairs and speakers, thus necessarily lessening the proposal power of any given party member or subset of members.

Procedural Cartel Theory

In this section, we list the assumptions and motivating principles of procedural cartel theory. Assumptions 1–5 are from our previous book, *Legislative Leviathan*, and are defended at length in the second edition of that volume. Assumption 6 is new to this reading, and, accordingly, we expand on it here. . . . After elaborating the assumptions of our theory, we sketch some of the intuitions that have steered our research (. . .) and conclude. . . . In subsequent chapters, we will present and test simplified and formalized models consistent with the broader theory presented here.

> **Assumption 1:** Members of Congress seek reelection to the House, internal advancement within the House, good public policy, and majority status.

In our previous work (Cox and McCubbins 1993), our formal statement of members' goals included three of the motivations just discussed: reelection, internal advancement, and majority status.[2] Key to our approach was the assumption that majority status confers substantial benefits. In particular, advancement to committee chairs and other key posts in the House is possible only if one's party gains a majority, and advancement of one's legislative projects is greatly facilitated by majority status.[3] Thus, majority status is arguably an essential gateway to internal advancement and policy goals. The more substantial the benefits of majority status are, the more incentive they provide to the senior partners in a given party to pursue majority status—hence to undertake the sorts of agenda-setting actions that we describe in the remainder of the reading.

> **Assumption 2:** The reputation (or brand name) of a member's party affects both the member's personal probability of reelection and, more substantially, the party's probability of securing a majority.

We have discussed this premise at length in our previous work (see Cox and McCubbins 1993, Chapter 5). To the extent that this assumption holds, a political party's reputation is a *public good* to all candidates sharing the party's label. More specifically, if a party's reputation improves or worsens, all members benefit or suffer together, regardless of whether they contributed to the improvement or worsening.

> **Assumption 3:** A party's reputation depends significantly on its record of legislative accomplishment.

The policies with which a particular party and its leaders are associated—both those it promotes and those it opposes—can significantly affect the party's reputation. A recent example of this is the budget battle waged between Speaker of the House Newt Gingrich and President Bill Clinton in 1995. This battle led to the opening of the new fiscal year without a federal budget, causing the closure of nonessential government services. For present purposes, the important point about this budgetary stand-off is simply that it led to a sharp reduction in the popularity of congressional Republicans and their leaders, as measured by thermometer ratings in mass surveys (Jacobson 1996). In other words, in this instance a leader's legislative policy—that of refusing to compromise on the budget—led directly to a decline in the party's overall popularity.

We assume that this anecdote points to a more general phenomenon, in which legislative actions taken by various members of the party can affect the overall party's reputation on the margin. There is some disagreement about how much and how quickly party identification incorporates new events and evaluations. For our purposes, we need simply to assert a position similar to that adopted by V. O. Key (1966), in which parties' legislative actions *do* consequentially affect voters' behavior. Whether the path by which legislative actions influence votes is through party reputations (party identification) or through some shorter-term partisan pathways is less important.

> **Assumption 4:** Legislating—hence compiling favorable records of legislative accomplishment—is akin to team production and entails overcoming an array of cooperation and coordination problems.

Achieving their goals—reelection, internal advancement, and majority status—requires passage of legislation, yet legislators' ability to accomplish things on their own is quite limited. Legislation must be accepted by majorities in both houses of Congress and be signed by the president to become law.[4] To get through even one house, moreover, a bill needs to get scarce floor time and the support of a majority coalition, both of which are costly and difficult to achieve. Legislating thus requires that members somehow join forces, cooperate, and engage in "team production" (Alchian and Demsetz 1972).

Team production, however, means confronting and overcoming a variety of collective action and coordination problems. For example, all members would like to spend more money on their own districts than might be optimal from their party's perspective (Cox and McCubbins 1993); all members would like to have free access to floor time, but the result could be that nothing can get done reliably; divergent national, regional, and partisan interests might lead members to pursue different policies in the absence of some coordinating mechanism. Most important for our theory, as noted above, the party label itself is a public good (for party members) that is subject to free-rider problems. Managing the party label is the primary collective action problem that members of a party must solve, and their collective goal of solving this and other collective action problems is the sense in which they are members of a partnership.

> **Assumption 5:** The primary means by which a (majority) party regulates its members' actions, in order to overcome problems of team production in the legislative process, is by delegating to a central authority.

Though other solutions for collective action problems exist, the most common solution seems to be delegation to a central authority—an idea that appears in a wide variety of literatures.[5] Three common elements in all these works are that the central authority to whom power is delegated monitors individual behavior, controls carrots and sticks with which to reward and punish individuals, and is motivated to solve the collective action problem(s) faced by the group. Along these lines, the core point of our previous book (Cox and McCubbins 1993) is that majority party members delegate to party leaders the authority to manage legislative resources and the legislative process in order to solve the cooperation and coordination problems they face, including maintaining the value of the party label.[6]

How are party leaders motivated to use their delegated powers for collective, rather than purely personal, gain? We argue that members wishing to hold important offices in the House (such as the speakership and committee chairs) know that the only realistic route to getting these offices is for their party to attain a majority of seats and for them to be in sufficiently good standing with their caucus to be (re)nominated for such offices.[7] Thus, the more valuable are the top posts going to the majority party's senior members, the more motivated are those members to ensure the party's continued majority status (and their own good standing).

As noted in the previous chapter, we believe that political parties are more fruitfully analogized to legal or accountancy partnerships than to strictly hierarchical single-leader firms (or armies). Thus, when we speak of delegation to a central authority, we do not mean literally to a single person but instead to a group of "senior partners."

> **Assumption 6:** The key resource that majority parties delegate to their senior partners is the power to set the legislative agenda; the majority party forms a procedural cartel that collectively monopolizes agenda-setting power.

This is our key assumption, and our point of departure from most of the previous literature. A *procedural cartel* is a coalition of legislators who constitute a majority in the assembly, share a common label (at least in the United States), and cartelize the agenda via the following basic strategy. First, the cartel creates (or, more typically, inherits) a set of offices endowed with special agenda-setting powers. In the case of the U.S. House, the main agenda-setting offices are the committee chairs, slots on the Rules Committee, and the speakership.[8] Second, the cartel ensures that its members get all, or nearly all, of the agenda-setting offices.[9] Third, cartel members expect those appointed to agenda-setting offices to *always* obey "the first commandment of party leadership"—*Thou shalt not aid bills that will split thy party*—and to sometimes obey the second commandment—*Thou shalt aid bills that most in thy party like*. Fourth, cartel members expect rank-and-file members to support the agenda-setting decisions rendered by officeholders when those decisions are made in conformity to the expectations just noted. Fifth, the cartel's leadership takes action to maintain cooperation and coordination within the cartel.

We use the term "cartel" because procedural cartels, like economic cartels, seek to establish a collective monopoly on a particular resource (in this case, agenda-setting power), seek to restrict supply of products made with this resource (in this case, bills that are placed on the floor agenda), and face problems of free-riding (in this case, members reluctant to vote for a party measure when such a vote will not sell well back home, or members eager to use their delegated agenda powers for personal gain). We have also used the term "legislative leviathan" to describe party organizations within legislatures, in order to emphasize their sometimes considerable degree of centralized authority.[10] Indeed, even during their relatively decentralized periods, parties in the U.S. House have been more hierarchical and stable than the typical economic cartel. Even though neither term's connotations are fully satisfactory, in this reading we will refer to party organizations as forming procedural cartels (and we will stress the analogy of a group of senior partners directing a law or accountancy firm rather than of a CEO running a corporation or a general commanding an army).

How Does the Majority Cartelize the Agenda?

In this section, we reconsider the defining features of "procedural cartels," as mentioned in Assumption 6. At this point, we wish only to argue that these features *plausibly* characterize the modern (i.e., post-Reed) House of Representatives; we will return to them in greater detail later in the reading.

The structure of agenda-setting offices

An initial question is whether there exist offices endowed with special agenda-setting powers in the House and whether these offices' powers were in some sense chosen by the majority party. By "special agenda-setting powers," or agenda power for short, we refer to any *special* ability to determine which bills are considered on the floor and under what procedures. Because any member can participate in an attempt to discharge a bill, we would not count "the ability to participate in a discharge attempt" as an "agenda power" in our sense. Such an ability is not special; it is general. In contrast, only members of the Rules Committee can participate in fashioning special rules,[11] and only chairs can delay bills merely by not scheduling them—to mention two examples of agenda power as we define it.

Given this definition, there obviously do exist offices in the House endowed with agenda power. As noted previously, the most important of these include the committee and subcommittee chairs, the seats on the Rules Committee, and the speakership.

Did the majority party in some sense choose the level of agenda power delegated to the various agenda-setting offices? Yes, in two senses.

First, the House adopts rules anew in each Congress. These rules are proposed by the majority party and are usually adopted on a straight party-line vote. Thus, among other things, the majority chooses (or reaffirms) the delegation of agenda power in those rules.

Second, the modern structure of agenda power in the House was erected in the period 1880–94 to enable the majority party to legislate, even against the wishes of the minority. . . . We will show that the House's rules have not, since 1894, changed so as to erase the majority party advantages accrued in this period. In particular, the minority party's ability to delay has not been restored, nor has the central position of the Rules Committee been significantly altered.[12] The powers of the speaker have waxed and waned, but when they have changed, they have simply been redistributed within the majority party, not allocated to any minority party members. In this sense, the majority party chose the structure of agenda power and the majority's overall advantage has remained largely constant since the 1890s (a claim we defend at length. . . .

Who gets the agenda-setting offices?

A second question is whether the majority party sets up a procedure for select-ing the occupants of the agenda-setting offices that is likely to lead in principle, and does lead in practice, to its members winning most of the agenda-setting offices. The answer in practice is clear: the majority party secures all chairs, the speakership, and a super-proportional share of seats on the Rules Commit-tee. It also secures super-proportional shares on the major committees that enjoy privileged access to the floor and on conference committees (which also exercise special agenda-setting powers) (Cox and McCubbins 1993).

As for the procedures regulating access to the House's agenda-setting posts, they all include an initial stage in which each party decides on nominees for the various posts, followed by a choice between, or ratification of, the parties' nominees in the House. The choice of a speaker is largely unregulated, as this is the first vote in each Congress and occurs before the adoption of rules. The choice of all other agenda-setting posts—committee positions of various sorts—is regulated. In particular, since 1917 the procedure has been as fol-lows. First, the majority party informs the minority of how many seats each party will receive on each committee. Second, each party submits a slate specifying its nominees for its designated committee positions. Third, the two party slates are combined into a single resolution that is then voted up or down (since 1917 it has not been permissible to amend the slates on the floor). Given these procedures, it is not surprising that the majority party has never failed to secure a monopoly on chairs, the speakership, and a disproportion-ally large share of seats on the control and conference committees.[13]

Fiduciary behavior of officeholders

A third question is whether party members expect that party officeholders will exercise their official powers partly for the benefit of the party, rather than purely to pursue personal goals, and whether officeholders who do not act as expected are sanctioned in some way. Since agenda cartelization entails dele-gation of authority from party backbenchers to party leaders, cartelization creates the possibility of mischief by party leaders (i.e., not serving the collec-tive interests of the party). Much of the literature implicitly adopts a strict standard by which to judge when officeholders act in the interest of their party, according to which they must aid legislation favored by significant majorities of their party. For example, the well-known accounts of Judge Smith's ten-ure on the Rules Committee point out—quite accurately—that he frequently obstructed legislation desired by large portions of his own party, and they conclude from this that Smith was acting in pursuit of his own or his faction's interests, not his party's.

Delay or outright obstruction of bills that significant portions of one's party want to turn into "party issues" represents an agency loss, but it does not mean that the persons in question have utterly abandoned representing or serving their party. After all, the wets in Thatcher's government delayed and obstructed when they could, and many other examples of hard bargaining over tough issues in coalition governments involve such tactics. Are we to conclude from every instance of persistent obstruction by elements of the governing coalition that the coalition is entirely toothless?

We think that would be premature. There are less stringent standards that might serve as "lines in the sand" demarcating behavior that is minimally fiduciary from behavior that is treasonous. Here, we wish to characterize such a standard, one that we believe has been expected of officeholders in the House at least since the late nineteenth century. This standard focuses on crimes of commission—pushing legislation one's party mostly dislikes—not on crimes of omission—failing to aid (or actively blocking) legislation one's party mostly likes. Crimes of commission increase in seriousness (1) with the proportion of the party that dislikes it and (2) if the bill actually passes. As a specific benchmark, *we claim that officeholders are expected never to push bills that would pass despite the opposition of a majority of their party.* We call such an event—passage of a bill against the votes of a majority of a given party— a *roll* of that party. If the majority's officeholders are not held to even the minimal standard of not using their powers to roll their own party, then they do indeed look like nonpartisan figures willing (and able with impunity) to build shifting coalitions in support of their projects.

An example of a violator of our proposed standard is Representative Phil Gramm (D-TX) who, during the negotiations leading to the first Reagan budget, clearly used his position in a way intended to roll his own party. In this specific instance, Democratic party leaders branded Gramm's behavior as unconscionable after they discovered it and took quick actions to sanction him, including stripping him of the posts he had abused (Roberts 1983a).[14]

Other similar examples can be cited. In 1924, eight Republicans on the Rules Committee cooperated on the passage of a strengthened discharge procedure, which most majority party members opposed; six of them were removed from the committee in the next Congress (in which the offending rule was also eviscerated cf. Hasbrouck 1927: 163–4). In 1975, Chairman Richard Ichord of the Internal Security Committee, a longtime thorn in the side of liberal Democrats, found that the committee had essentially been disestablished, due largely to actions taken in the Democratic Caucus (Jacobs 1995). In all these cases, the majority party caucus essentially *denied renomination* to wayward officeholders. There was no House vote needed to ratify the majority's decision; moreover, it would have been difficult to reject those decisions in the House, given that each party's slate of committee nominations is unamendable under House rules. To the extent that threats to deny renomination are credible, they induce officeholders to abandon, or at least sweeten, bills that substantial portions of their party dislike.

Our position is that these anecdotes generalize. In any period of congressional history, an officeholder behaving as Gramm did would have met with comparable reactions. In any period, it would be common knowledge that the standard of "not conspiring, explicitly or implicitly, with the enemy to roll one's own party" would apply to officeholders and that violators of this standard could expect to lose their offices and/or face other sanctions.

Many in the congressional literature seem to believe that sanctions against officeholders, especially against committee chairs, were simply not feasible in the period from 1937 to 1960. If this were so, then one should expect that Southern Democrats in this period used their agenda powers with impunity to push bills that they and the Republicans agreed on. Such "conservative coalition" bills, moving policy rightward, would have provoked splits in committees chaired by Southerners—with Northern Democrats outvoted by a combination of Southern Democrats and Republicans. Moreover, such bills would easily have made it to the floor, with the help of a Rules Committee often seen as controlled by the conservative coalition in this period. Once on the floor, conservative coalition bills would have *both* split the majority party *and* passed. Passage would follow as long as the number of conservative Southern Democrats plus regular Republicans exceeded the number of Northern Democrats plus liberal Republicans. Put another way, as long as the policy being changed lay to the left of the House median, the conservative coalition would have outvoted a majority of the Democratic Party. We assess the impact of the conservative coalition in detail, and evaluate these predictions,. . . . For now, suffice it to say that we do not find significant evidence of Southern Democrats defecting from their party and joining with Republicans to successfully push an agenda unpalatable to Northern Democrats.

Loyalty from the rank and file

A final question is: how does a procedural cartel ensure that its rank-and-file members support the agenda-setting decisions of its officeholders, even though at least some members' short-term interests would be better served by voting against those decisions? A key to the answer is that votes taken on procedural decisions (e.g., a vote to ratify a special rule proposed by the Rules Committee or to sustain a decision rendered by the speaker) are more obscure to constituents than are ordinary substantive votes (cf. Froman and Ripley 1965). If a member votes for a bill her constituents oppose on final passage, she runs a clear risk. If she supports a special rule filled with arcane boilerplate that helps ensure the bill's success, she runs a smaller risk.[15] Thus, party pressures can affect members' decisions on procedure more than their decisions on substance, even though all legislators know that procedural motions directly affect substantive outcomes.[16]

Another key point is that the cartel does not need the loyalty of every member on every vote. Often, it needs only enough votes to snatch victory from the jaws of defeat on close and important votes (cf. King and Zeckhauser 2003). This is a much more limited and manageable task than enforcing some minimum standard of cohesion across the board, which some mistakenly take to be what any "partisan" model must predict.

Is there evidence that cartels in the U.S. House do demand loyalty? Alexander (1970 [1916]: 210) notes that, soon after Reed's elevation of the Rules Committee to its modern status, members chafed under the expectation that "one must support whatever the Rules Committee brought forward or become irregular." More recently, Republican Whip Tom DeLay (R-TX) has made the party's expectations regarding behavior on procedural motions clear to his freshmen (Burger 1995).

To buttress such anecdotal evidence that majority parties do expect loyalty on key procedural votes, one can also point to more systematic evidence that the majority party's rank and file support their officeholders' agenda-setting decisions, while minority party members oppose them. First, after the packing of the Rules Committee in 1961 (and especially after the procedural reforms of 1973), members have voted with their parties significantly more than would be expected on the basis of their left–right position on a wide range of procedural and organizational votes (Cox and Poole 2002).[17] Second, in the postreform Congress, majority party members have been prone to support special rules, even when they then vote against the bill in question, while minority party members have exhibited the opposite tendency (Sinclair 2002). Sinclair's interpretation of this evidence is that majority party members are supporting their leaders' agenda-setting decisions, even when they oppose the substance of the proposals aided by the special rule in question, while minority party members oppose the Rules Committee's resolutions, even when they support the measure being aided. Third, more evidence of parties' influence over their members' voting behavior is reviewed. . . .

In addition, party leaders reward party members' loyalty on key votes, and especially on "agenda votes" in which the leaders of the two parties take opposing positions.[18] More loyal members are more likely to be appointed to the most desirable committees and to have committee transfers granted than are less loyal party members (Cox and McCubbins 1993, Chapter 7).

In summary, majority party leaders make clear their expectations of loyalty on certain key procedural votes; there is evidence that party pressures are greater on such votes; and there is evidence that more loyal members get better committee assignments. These findings are all consistent with a picture in which majority party leaders both *expect* and *get* "loyalty on the margin," enough to make the difference between winning and losing on close votes (King and Zeckhauser 2003).

Nevertheless, it is the very costliness of enforcing discipline in the U.S. House that helps to explain why U.S. parties principally rely on controlling the legislative agenda to achieve their legislative goals. In the model of responsible party government (American Political Science Association 1950), parties ensure cohesive voting blocs through a combination of control over nominations and disciplining their members. U.S. parties, however, have relatively weak nominating powers. Similarly, discipline is weaker in the United States than in some other countries. This puts more emphasis on agenda control, or influencing the bills and motions on which members must vote, as the single most powerful mechanism by which legislative outcomes can be affected in the U.S. House. By using agenda control, the party can prevent votes on which its disciplinary abilities would be strained or broken.

What about quitting the party?

In the discussion of fiduciary behavior and loyalty . . . , we did not address the issue of why members of a cartel do not quit their party, join the other side, and form a new cartel (with a better share of the spoils for themselves). In particular, one might wonder why centrist members cannot extract a better deal. Why are not all the committee chairs centrists, for example? Alternatively, why are not centrist chairs free to exercise agenda power in any way they see fit, subject only to majoritarian and not specifically partisan constraints?

There are three points we would urge in answer to this line of inquiry. First, it is rare for a single member to be pivotal (Senator James Jeffords in May 2001 being the most notable exception). Typically several members must simultaneously switch parties in order to bring down the current cartel. Potential defectors must thus *coordinate*, not just in the sense of jumping at the same time but also in the sense of negotiating, *before* actually defecting, with their prospective new partners over the division of the spoils.[19]

Second, and more important, it is ex ante costly to switch parties. The Grenvillite faction in late eighteenth-century English politics could pivot freely, little constrained by electoral considerations, because they literally owned their seats. In the modern U.S. House, however, elections are partisan, and party labels count for a lot. When a member switches party labels, can he communicate that fact—and at what cost—to his constituents? How many voters in his former party will continue out of habit or loyalty to support that party? How many voters in the new party will remember that he used to be in the other party and refuse to support him on that ground? Among those voters who do learn of the member's switch, how many will view it as purely opportunistic, making the representative seem unreliable? Can he combat such ideas at low cost? How many names on the member's donor list will stop contributing? Who has been planning to run for the other party and how will they react to the incumbent's switch? All these questions about electoral ramifications—and more besides—would have to be considered by prospective defectors, at least if they are prudent.

Third, it is ex post costly to switch parties. Grose and Yoshinaka (2003) report "that incumbent legislators who switch parties have poorer showings after their switch in both general and primary election contests." Moreover, if one regresses the number of terms remaining in a legislator's career in Congress t on her seniority (i.e., the number of terms already served through Congress t) and a dummy variable equal to 1 if the member switched parties in Congress t, one finds the switched party dummy variable to have a statistically significant coefficient of roughly—3. In other words, by one crude estimate, the cost of switching parties is three fewer terms in the House than would otherwise be expected, given a member's current seniority.[20]

These various costs help explain why actual party switching has been rare in the House and Senate. To the extent that the exogenous electoral costs of switching are large, moreover, it would follow that the threat of switching parties would not be as effective as it would be in a pure spatial representation of politics.

Conclusion

. . . [W]e have laid out the main assumptions underpinning our theory of legislative parties. In our view, U.S. legislators seek not just reelection but also advancement in the internal hierarchy of posts within the House, good public policy, and majority status for their parties. Their parties compete in mass elections, as business firms compete in mass markets, by developing brand names. The value of a party's brand name depends on its legislative record of accomplishment. Thus, a key problem for majority parties is to manage the legislative process, in order to secure the best possible record, hence contributing to the best possible reputation.

This much was already evident in our original exploration of congressional organization, *Legislative Leviathan*. In this reading, we develop several additional themes.

First, we portray agenda control as the key to the majority party's influence over the legislative process. In the responsible party government model, the primary mechanisms by which a party overcomes collective action problems, so that it can enact a program, are screening candidates and disciplining legislators. In the U.S. context, however, both screening and discipline are—although utilized to some extent-relatively costly. This raises the importance of a third technique to manage conflicts between collective and individual goals; controlling the agenda so that the sharpest conflicts are never even considered on the floor.

How does a legislative majority party work to control the agenda? The mechanism is similar to that portrayed in *Legislative Leviathan*. Certain members of the party—whom we have here dubbed the "senior partners"—are given valuable offices wielding substantial agenda-setting powers. In order to secure their party's (re)nomination for these offices, senior partners are expected to obey a minimal commandment of party loyalty—namely, not using their official powers in order to promote bills that will, if considered on the floor, lead to serious splits in the party (operationalized as *rolls* in the coming chapters). The rank and file, meanwhile, are also expected to obey a minimal commandment of party loyalty—namely, supporting their officeholders' agenda-setting decisions, especially on the more procedurally arcane (yet substantively critical) votes. Their incentive to support such procedural maneuvers is the prospect of better internal advancement and a greater chance of majority status for the party as a whole.

Analogizing parties to partnerships is our second main point of departure from *Legislative Leviathan,* where we more often focused on the speaker and the top few leaders rather than the entire set of party members holding agenda-setting offices. Law and accountancy partnerships are designed to allow their senior partners considerable autonomy. By stressing the analogy to a partnership and the importance of agenda power, our approach naturally raises the question of how specific agenda powers are distributed among senior partners.

There are many theoretical possibilities, such as allocating *all* agenda power to the top party leader, allocating proposal power(s) to various senior partners, or allocating veto power(s) to various senior partners. We have argued that, whatever the details of agenda-power allocation, all majority parties in the U.S. House since adoption of Reed's Rules have structured agenda power in such a way that it is very difficult to roll them.

Closely related to the issue of what powers are distributed to which senior partners is the question of what standards of behavior those partners are expected to uphold. At one theoretical extreme, senior partners may have no fiduciary responsibilities to their parties. Agenda power is clearly allocated in these models but officeholders are then free to act in pursuit of their own interests, with neither formal checks (e.g., the necessity of securing their party's renomination) nor informal norms to constrain them. At the other theoretical extreme, senior partners may be expected completely to subordinate their personal goals to the party's. This is implicitly the case, for example, in Ranney's (1951) or the American Political Science Association's (1950) portrayal of responsible party government. Agenda power is not mentioned in such models, but officeholders are clearly enjoined to marshal their parties behind a coherent party platform.

We have opted for a theoretical middle ground of sorts, in which the norm to which senior partners are held depends on the internal homogeneity of the party. If the party is extremely heterogeneous (perhaps similar to a multiparty coalition government in other countries), then only a minimal standard can be realistically enforced: that of not using one's official powers to push legislation that will roll the party. As the party becomes more homogeneous, its senior partners are held to a higher standard, in which they must also use their official posts to help push legislation that most in the party support. Thus, for example, Jamie Whitten (D-MI) continued as chair of the powerful Appropriations Committee in the 1970s because he considerably increased his willingness to cooperate with the party leadership in pushing through Democratic priorities, even those he personally found distasteful (Crook and Hibbing 1985).

Why does the fiduciary standard become higher for more homogeneous parties? This prediction is entailed by our theory because procedural cartels, as we describe them, primarily distribute veto power among the senior partners of the party. Distributing veto power necessarily interferes with pushing through an ambitious program of legislation, as each senior partner with a veto in a particular policy area has to be brought on board. Thus, the ability of a procedural cartel to legislate necessarily depends on how similar their senior partners' preferences are.

Even when a majority's senior partners disagree on a wide range of issues, however, it becomes no easier to roll the majority party (i.e., pass bills that most majority party members dislike) because some senior partner or partners with relevant veto power will derail the bill. Thus, even internally divided majority parties do not surrender their *negative* agenda-setting power. They simply avoid bills that cannot be passed and move on to bills that can be passed, which tend to be less ideological and more porcine. The minority benefits from the internal divisions of the majority, in the sense that the bills the senior partners can agree on are less likely to have a clear ideological bite to them, hence less likely to roll the minority. But the minority is no more successful in dismantling the majority's previous accomplishments than before. Nor does it benefit by receiving a larger share of chairs, of staff, or of pork.

Because negative agenda power is the bedrock and "first story" of party government, in our view, most of this reading considers the consequences of such power. We return to the "second story" of party government, and discuss when a majority party might wish to build up such a story by readjusting the mix of positive and negative agenda power.

NOTES

1. Quoted in Babington (2004).

2. We did not there formally incorporate the third of Fenno's (1973) famous trio of goals: the pursuit of good public policy. . . . [H]owever, we adapt the standard spatial model of policy making for much of our argument, and this model is sufficiently abstract so that one can easily read personal policy goals into it. Thus, one can add the pursuit of policy as one of the goals that is consistent with the model we present here—although we do not insist on that interpretation.

3. As an example of the importance of majority status for members' legislative projects, consider the statements that Representative Ralph Hall made as he switched from being a member of the Democratic minority to being a member of the Republican majority: "This is the first time, I've just been zeroed out [by the Appropriations Committee]. . . . I've always said that if being a Democrat hurt my district, I'd either resign, retire or switch parties. . . . And it hurt my district this time [because I was denied funds]" (Wolf 2004).

4. Alternatively, of course, a bill can be vetoed, and the veto can be overridden by two thirds of both houses.

5. Among the other solutions suggested in the literature are preplay communication, repeated play, and property rights (Tirole 1988; Friedman 1971).

6. Describing the authority associated with party leadership, Dennis Hastert stated, "So I have two functions. One is governmental, the other political. The governmental function is to run the House, move legislation through, make sure the chairmen and the committees are all operating smoothly. . . . The other function is political. I have to recruit the best possible candidates for Congress and make sure they have the financial and other resources they need to run or, if they're already in Congress, to make sure they have enough to stave off potential challengers" (Hastert 2004: 181–2).

7. Speaker Dennis Hastert clearly recognized the importance of majority status and being in good standing with his party. He emphasized, "Stripped to its essentials, my job is to run the House and make sure we [Republicans] hold the House" (Hastert 2004: 181).

8. Although the speakership is a constitutional office, its agenda-setting powers, as well as those of the other offices mentioned, are stipulated in House rules and precedents. The cartel controls the allocation of agenda power to the various offices to the extent that it can control votes on the adoption of rules.

9. In the United States, the cartel ensures a near-monopoly on agenda-setting offices to the extent that it can control the relevant votes on the floor (on election of the speaker and appointment of committees). To aid in controlling these floor votes, the cartel establishes an intracartel procedure to decide on the nominee for speaker and on a slate of committee appointments.

10. The role of the majority party has also been analogized to former Soviet Congresses. Indeed, as Hastert (2004: 250) notes, "Representative David Obey . . . compares the way the House is run today to 'the old Soviet Congresses—stamp of approval and ratify' rather than using your own judgment. Well, Obey was here when Democrats ran the place. . . . Talk about rubber stamps and domination by a party that had lots of votes and squish room. They were ruthless. They did things like the old Soviet Congresses, such as removing offenders from their hideaway offices, grabbing their office furniture, and taking their parking spots away."

11. A "special rule" is a resolution reported by the Rules Committee that regulates the consideration of a bill or resolution.

12. We are talking here about the powers of the Rules Committee, not its membership.

13. Decrying this monopoly power of the majority party, Dennis Hastert stated, "The truth is that since the last time we had a majority in 1954 only one Republican, Missouri's Bill Emerson, had ever stood on the House Floor—and he stood there as a page. We [the Republicans] had been in the wilderness so long that nobody remembered anything about being in the leadership. We didn't even know where the special back rooms were; we didn't even know where the *keys* to those rooms were" (Hastert 2004: 118).

14. A number of his coconspirators, the so-called Boll Weevils, were also punished by then-Speaker Tip O'Neill. For example, John Breaux of Louisiana and Roy Dyson of Maryland failed to win spots on the Budget and Appropriations committees, respectively (Roberts 1983a). In Breaux's place, the Democratic Party awarded the Budget Committee position to Martin Frost, a Texas Democrat who had "proven himself to be a national Democrat" (Roberts 1983b). Although G. V. Montgomery of Mississippi was reelected chairman of Veterans' Affairs, he lost 53 votes in the party caucus and remarked that conservatives would henceforth likely be more cooperative with their party leaders in Congress (Roberts 1983a).

15. In Arnold's (1990) terms, procedural votes are less "traceable."

16. Nokken's (2004) analysis demonstrates that departing members of Congress in lame duck sessions increasingly vote with their party (as opposed to their constituency). The explanation for this phenomenon is that when constituency constraints are severed (as they are in this situation), members vote with their party in hopes that the party will reward them for their loyalty by aiding them in their future career moves.

17. Quantitatively, Cox and Poole estimate about five to 10 votes switching on key procedural votes, which is consistent with qualitative evidence regarding vest pocket votes.

18. Loyalty is always important in committee assignments, but during times of high homogeneity within the majority party, there may be an increased premium placed on legislative competence. High levels of intraparty homogeneity decrease the relative importance of high loyalty and increase the importance of competence (Wawro 2000, Crook and Hibbing 1985).

19. The Jeffords case is informative here, as it demonstrates the costs of negotiating a defection. The Democrats gave Senator Jeffords the chairmanship of the Environment and Public Works Committee as an inducement to switch parties, which required Harry Reid to give up his status as the ranking Democrat on the committee (Lancaster 2001).

20. The analysis covers only the 80th through 100th Congresses. It is a crude estimate for two main reasons. First, the (negative) correlation between whether a member switches parties and how long that member continues in the House may be only partly due to switching being bad pre se. Perhaps members who switched had very poor electoral prospects, had they remained in their parties, and switched for this reason. So far as we know, however, there is no systematic evidence that party switchers did face greater electoral risks than the typical nonswitching member. Indeed, Ansolabehere, Snyder, and Stewart (2001) find qualitative evidence that discomfort with being ideological misfits accounts for legislators' switching; however, Castle and Fett (2000: 236–7) find that switching is more likely the more ideologically out of step a member is with his copartisans, controlling for a measure of primary electoral risk. Second, our data do not include the full number of terms served by members whose careers continue past the 100th Congress. For these members, the number of terms remaining is coded as zero. As there were no members who switched parties in the 100th Congress, this defect of the data biases our estimate of the cost of switching downward. In other words, if we knew the correct total terms remaining for all members whose careers reached the 100th Congress, the difference between switchers and nonswitchers would be even larger than we report here.

BIBLIOGRAPHY

Alchian, Armen, and Harold Demsetz. 1972. "Production, Information Costs, and Economic Organization." *The American Economic Review* 62: 777–95.

Aldrich, John H. 1995. *Why Parties? The Origin and Transformation of Party Politics in America*. Chicago: University of Chicago Press.

Aldrich, John H., and David W. Rohde. 2001. "The Logic of Conditional Party Government." In *Congress Reconsidered*, 7th ed., eds. Lawrence C. Dodd and Bruce I. Oppenheimer. Washington, DC: Congressional Quarterly, pp. 269–92.

Alexander, DeAlva Stanwood. 1970 [1916]. *History and Procedure of the House of Representatives*. New York: Houghton Mifflin Company.

American Political Science Association. 1950. *Toward a More Responsible Party System, A Report*. New York: Rinehart.

Ansolabehere, Stephen, James Snyder, and Charles Stewart. 2001. "The Effects of Party and Preferences on Congressional Roll-Call Voting." *Legislative Studies Quarterly* 26: 533–72.

Arnold, R. Douglas. 1990. *The Logic of Congressional Action*. New Haven, CT: Yale University Press.

Babington, Charles. 2004. "Hastert Launches a Partisan Policy." Downloaded 11/27/04 from: www.washingtonpost.com.

Burger, Timothy. 1995. "After a Defeat, House Leaders Must Regroup." *Roll Call*, July 17.

Castle, David, and Patrick Fett. 2000. "Member Goals and Party Switching in the U.S. Congress." In *Congress on Display, Congress at Work*, ed. William T. Bianco. Ann Arbor: University of Michigan Press, pp. 231–42.

Cox, Gary W., and Mathew D. McCubbins. 1993. *Legislative Leviathan: Party Government in the House*. Berkeley: University of California Press.

2002. "Agenda Power in the U.S. House of Representatives, 1877 to 1986." In *Party, Process, and Political Change in Congress: New Perspectives on the History of Congress*, eds. David Brady and Mathew D. McCubbins. Stanford, CA: Stanford University Press.

Cox, Gary W., and Keith T. Poole. 2002. "On Measuring Partisanship in Roll-Call Voting: The U.S. House of Representatives, 1877–1999." *American Journal of Political Science* 46: 477–89.

Crook, Sara Brandes, and John R. Hibbing. 1985. "Congressional Reform and Party Discipline: The Effects of Changes in the Seniority System on Party Loyalty in the U.S. House of Representatives." *British Journal of Political Science* 15: 207–26.

Diermeier, Daniel, and Timothy J. Feddersen. 1998. "Cohesion in Legislatures and the Vote of Confidence Procedure." *American Political Science Review* 92: 611–21.

Fenno, Richard F. 1973. *Congressmen in Committees*. Boston: Little, Brown.

Friedman, James. 1971. "A Non-cooperative Equilibrium for Supergames." *Review of Economic Studies* 38: 1–12.

Froman, Lewis A., Jr., and Randall B. Ripley. 1965. "Conditions for Party Leadership: The Case of the House Democrats." *American Political Science Review* 59: 52–63.

Grose, Christian, and Antoine Yoshinaka. 2003. "The Electoral Consequences of Party Switching by Incumbent Members of Congress, Incumbent Legislators Who Switched Parties, 1947–2000." *Legislative Studies Quarterly* 27(1): 55–75.

Hasbrouck, Paul DeWitt. 1927. *Party Government in the House of Representatives*. New York: Macmillan.

Hastert, Dennis. 2004. *Speaker: Lessons from Forty Years in Coaching and Politics*. Washington, DC: Regnery.

Jacobs, John. 1995. *A Rage for Justice*. Berkeley: University of California Press.

Jacobson, Gary C. 1996. "The 1994 House Elections in Perspective." *Political Science Quarterly* 111: 203–23.

Key, V. O. 1966. *The Responsible Electorate*. Cambridge, MA: Harvard University Press.

King, David C., and Richard Zeckhauser. 2003. "Congressional Vote Options." *Legislative Studies Quarterly* 28: 387–411.

Lancaster, John. 2001. "Senate Republicans Try to Regroup: GOP Caucus Unites Behind Lott as Leader in the Wake of Jeffords's Defection," *The Washington Post*, May 26, p. A.18

Laver, Michael, and Kenneth A. Shepsle. 1996. *Making and Breaking Governments: Cabinets and Legislatures in Parliamentary Democracies.* Cambridge and New York: Cambridge University Press.

Nokken, Timothy P. 2004. "Roll Call Behavior in the Absence of Electoral Constraints: Shirking in Lan??? Duck Sessions of the House of Representatives, 1879–1933." Unpublished paper.

Ranney, Austin. 1951. "Toward A More Responsible Two-Party System: A Commentary." *American Political Science Review* 45: 488–99.

Roberts, Steven V. 1983a. "The Democrats Get Even." *New York Times*, January 9, p. E1.

1983b. "Democrats Reward Loyalty in Giving Assignments," *New York Times*, January 6, p. A25.

Rohde, David W. 1991. *Parties and Leaders in the Postreform House.* Chicago: University of Chicago Press.

Sinclair, Barbara. 2002. "Do Parties Matter?" In *Party, Process, and Political Change: New Perspectives on the History of Congress*, eds. David Brady and Mathew D. McCubbins. Stanford, CA: Stanford University Press, pp. 36–63.

Tirole, Jean. 1988. *The Theory of Industrial Organization.* MIT, Press: Cambridge, MA.

Tsebelis, George. 2002. *Veto Players: How Political Institutions Work.* Princeton, NJ: Princeton University Press.

Wawro, Gregory. 2000. *Legislative Entrepreneurship in the U.S. House of Representatives.* Ann Arbor: University of Michigan Press.

Wolf, Jim. 2004. "Veteran Texas Democrat Switches to Republicans." Washington, DC Reuters.

THE PRESIDENCY

6.1

RICHARD E. NEUSTADT

From *Presidential Power and the Modern Presidents: The Politics of Leadership from Roosevelt to Reagan*

In leading a vast executive branch with millions of employees, the president cannot monitor all those who work for him, nor can he or she compel many people to act. This excerpt from the famous book by Neustadt makes the simple point that presidents lead by persuading others that their interests coincide with the president's interests. According to Neustadt, presidential power ebbs and flows with each president's credibility as a persuader.

THE POWER TO PERSUADE

. . . The Constitutional Convention of 1787 is supposed to have created a government of "separated powers." It did nothing of the sort. Rather, it created a government of separated institutions *sharing* powers. "I am part of the legislative process," Eisenhower often said in 1959 as a reminder of his veto. Congress, the dispenser of authority and funds, is no less part of the administrative process. Federalism adds another set of separated institutions. The Bill of Rights adds others. Many public purposes can only be achieved by voluntary acts of private institutions; the press, for one, in Douglass Cater's phrase, is a "fourth branch of government." And with the coming of alliances abroad, the separate institutions of a London, or a Bonn, share in the making of American public policy.

What the Constitution separates our political parties do not combine. The parties are themselves composed of separated organizations sharing public authority. The authority consists of nominating powers. Our national parties are confederations of state and local party institutions, with a headquarters that represents the White House, more or less, if the party has a President in office. These confederacies manage presidential nominations. All other public offices depend upon electorates confined within the states. All other nominations are controlled within the states. The President and congressmen who bear one party's label are divided by dependence upon different sets of voters. The differences are sharpest at the stage of nomination. The White House has too small a share in nominating congressmen, and Congress has too little weight in nominating presidents for party to erase their constitutional separation. Party links are stronger than is frequently supposed, but nominating processes assure the separation.

The separateness of institutions and the sharing of authority prescribe the terms on which a President persuades. When one man shares authority with another, but does not gain or lose his job upon the other's whim, his willingness to act upon the urging of the other turns on whether he conceives the action right for him. The essence of a President's persuasive task is to convince such men that what the White House wants of them is what they ought to do for their sake and on their authority. (Sex matters not at all; for *man* read *woman*.)

Persuasive power, thus defined, amounts to more than charm or reasoned argument. These have their uses for a President, but these are not the whole of his resources. For the individuals he would induce to do what he wants done on their own responsibility will need or fear some acts by him on his responsibility. If they share his authority, he has some share in theirs. Presidential "powers" may be inconclusive when a President commands, but always remain relevant as he persuades. The status and authority inherent in his office reinforce his logic and his charm.

Status adds something to persuasiveness; authority adds still more. . . . In Walter Bagehot's charming phrase "no man can *argue* on his knees." Although there is no kneeling in this country, few men—and exceedingly few cabinet officers—are immune to the impulse to say "yes" to the President of the United States. It grows harder to say "no" when they are seated in his Oval Office at the White House, or in his study on the second floor, where almost tangibly he partakes of the aura of his physical surroundings. In Sawyer's case, moreover, the President possessed formal authority to intervene in many matters of concern to the secretary of commerce. These matters ranged from jurisdictional disputes among the defense agencies to legislation pending before Congress and, ultimately, to the tenure of the secretary, himself. . . .

A President's authority and status give him great advantages in dealing with the men he would persuade. Each "power" is a vantage point for him in the degree that other men have use for his authority. From the veto to appointments, from publicity to budgeting, and so down a long list, the White House now controls the most encompassing array of vantage points in the American political system. With hardly an exception, those who share in governing this country are aware that at some time, in some degree, the doing of *their* jobs, the furthering of *their* ambitions, may depend upon the President of the United States. Their need for presidential action, or their fear of it, is bound to be recurrent if not actually continuous. Their need or fear is his advantage.

A President's advantages are greater than mere listing of his "powers" might suggest. Those with whom he deals must deal with him until the last day of his term. Because they have continuing relationships with him, his future, while it lasts, supports his present influence. Even though there is no need or fear of him today, what he could do tomorrow may supply today's advantage. Continuing relationships may convert any "power," any aspect of his status, into vantage points in almost any case. When he induces other people to do what he wants done, a President can trade on their dependence now and later.

The President's advantages are checked by the advantages of others. Continuing relationships will pull in both directions. These are relationships of mutual dependence. A President depends upon the persons whom he would persuade; he has to reckon with his need or fear of them. They too will possess status, or authority, or both, else they would be of little use to him. Their vantage points confront his own; their power tempers his.

■   ■   ■

The power to persuade is the power to bargain. Status and authority yield bargaining advantages. But in a government of "separated institutions sharing powers," they yield them to all sides. With the array of vantage points at his disposal, a President may be far more persuasive than his logic or his charm could make him. But outcomes are not guaranteed by his advantages. There remain the counter pressures those whom he would influence can bring to bear on him from vantage points at their disposal. Command has limited utility; persuasion becomes give-and-take. It is well that the White House holds the vantage points it does. In such a business any President may need them all—and more.

I I

This view of power as akin to bargaining is one we commonly accept in the sphere of congressional relations. Every textbook states and every legislative session demonstrates that save in times like the extraordinary Hundred Days of 1933—times virtually ruled out by definition at midcentury—a President will often be unable to obtain congressional action on his terms or even to halt action he opposes. The reverse is equally accepted: Congress often is frustrated by the President. Their formal powers are so intertwined that neither will accomplish very much, for very long, without the acquiescence of the other. By the same token, though, what one demands the other can resist. The stage is set for that great game, much like collective bargaining, in which each seeks to profit from the other's needs and fears. It is a game played catch-as-catch-can, case by case. And everybody knows the game, observers and participants alike.

▪　▪　▪

In spheres of party politics the same thing follows, necessarily, from the confederal nature of our party organizations. Even in the case of national nominations a President's advantages are checked by those of others. In 1944 it is by no means clear that Roosevelt got his first choice as his running mate. In 1948 Truman, then the President, faced serious revolts against his nomination. In 1952 his intervention from the White House helped assure the choice of Adlai Stevenson, but it is far from clear that Truman could have done as much for any other candidate acceptable to him. In 1956 when Eisenhower was President, the record leaves obscure just who backed Harold Stassen's efforts to block Richard Nixon from renomination as vice president. But evidently everything did not go quite as Eisenhower wanted, whatever his intentions may have been. The outcomes in these instances bear all the marks of limits on command and of power checked by power that characterize congressional relations. Both in and out of politics these checks and limits seem to be quite widely understood.

Influence becomes still more a matter of give-and-take when Presidents attempt to deal with allied governments. A classic illustration is the long unhappy wrangle over Suez policy in 1956. In dealing with the British and the French before their military intervention, Eisenhower had his share of bargaining advantages but no effective power of command. His allies had their share of counterpressures, and they finally tried the most extreme of all: action despite him. His pressure then was instrumental in reversing them. But had the British government been on safe ground at home, Eisenhower's wishes might have made as little difference after intervention as before. Behind the decorum of diplomacy—which was not very decorous in the Suez affair— relationships among allies are not unlike relationships among state delegations at a national convention. Power is persuasion, and persuasion becomes bargaining. The concept is familiar to everyone who watches foreign policy.

In only one sphere is the concept unfamiliar: the sphere of executive relations. Perhaps because of civics textbooks and teaching in our schools, Americans instinctively resist the view that power in this sphere resembles power in all others. Even Washington reporters, White House aides, and congressmen are not immune to the illusion that administrative agencies comprise a single structure, "the" executive branch, where presidential word is law, or ought to be. . . . When a President seeks something from executive officials his persuasiveness is subject to the same sorts of limitations as in the case of congressmen, or governors, or national committeemen, or private citizens, or foreign governments. There are no generic differences, no differences in kind and only sometimes in degree. The incidents preceding the dismissal of MacArthur and the incidents surrounding seizure of the steel mills make it plain that here as elsewhere influence derives from bargaining advantages; power is a give-and-take.

Like our governmental structure as a whole, the executive establishment consists of separated institutions sharing powers. The President heads one of these; cabinet officers, agency administrators, and military commanders head others. Below the departmental level, virtually independent bureau chiefs head many more. Under midcentury conditions, federal operations spill across dividing lines on organization charts; almost every policy entangles many agencies; almost every program calls for interagency collaboration. Everything somehow involves the President. But operating agencies owe their existence least of all to one another—and only in some part to him. Each has a separate statutory base; each has its statutes to administer; each deals with a different set of subcommittees at the Capitol. Each has its own peculiar set of clients, friends, and enemies outside the formal government. Each has a different set of specialized careerists inside its own bailiwick. Our Constitution gives the President the "take-care" clause and the appointive power. Our statutes give him central budgeting and a degree of personnel control. All agency administrators are responsible to him. But they also are responsible to Congress, to their clients, to their staffs, and to themselves. In short, they have five masters. Only after all of those do they owe any loyalty to each other.

"The members of the cabinet," Charles G. Dawes used to remark, "are a president's natural enemies." Dawes had been Harding's budget director, Coolidge's vice president, and Hoover's ambassador to London; he also had been General Pershing's chief assistant for supply in World War I. The words are highly colored, but Dawes knew whereof he spoke. The men who have to serve so many masters cannot help but be somewhat the "enemy" of any one of them. By the same token, any master wanting service is in some degree the "enemy" of such a servant. A President is likely to want loyal support but not to relish trouble on his doorstep. Yet the more his cabinet members cleave to him, the more they may need help from him in fending off the wrath of rival masters. Help, though, is synonymous with trouble. Many a cabinet officer, with loyalty ill rewarded by his lights and help withheld, has come to view the White House as innately hostile to department heads. Dawes's dictum can be turned around.

A senior presidential aide remarked to me in Eisenhower's time: "If some of these cabinet members would just take time out to stop and ask themselves, 'What would I want if I were President?' they wouldn't give him all the trouble he's been having." But even if they asked themselves the question, such officials often could not act upon the answer. Their personal attachment to the President is all too often overwhelmed by duty to their other masters.

Executive officials are not equally advantaged in their dealings with a President. Nor are the same officials equally advantaged all the time. . . . The vantage points conferred upon officials by their own authority and status vary enormously. The variance is heightened by particulars of time and circumstance. In mid-October 1950, Truman, at a press conference, remarked of the man he had considered firing in August and would fire the next April for intolerable insubordination:

> Let me tell you something that will be good for your souls. It's a pity that you . . . can't understand the ideas of two intellectually honest men when they meet. General MacArthur . . . is a member of the Government of the United States. He is loyal to that Government. He is loyal to the President. He is loyal to the President in his foreign policy. . . . There is no disagreement between General MacArthur and myself.

MacArthur's status in and out of government was never higher than when Truman spoke those words. The words, once spoken, added to the general's credibility thereafter when he sought to use the press in his campaign against the President. And what had happened between August and October? Near victory had happened, together with that premature conference on postwar plans, the meeting at Wake Island.

If the bargaining advantages of a MacArthur fluctuate with changing circumstances, this is bound to be so with subordinates who have at their disposal fewer powers, lesser status, to fall back on. And when officials have no powers in their own right, or depend upon the President for status, their counterpressure may be limited indeed. White House aides, who fit both categories, are among the most responsive men of all, and for good reason. As a director of the budget once remarked to me, "Thank God I'm here and not across the street. If the President doesn't call me, I've got plenty I can do right here and plenty coming up to me, by rights, to justify my calling him. But those poor fellows over there, if the boss doesn't call them, doesn't ask them to do something, what *can* they do but sit?" Authority and status so conditional are frail reliances in resisting a President's own wants. Within the White House precincts, lifted eyebrows may suffice to set an aide in motion; command, coercion, even charm aside. But even in the White House a President does not monopolize effective power. Even there persuasion is akin to bargaining. A former Roosevelt aide once wrote of cabinet officers:

> Half of a President's suggestions, which theoretically carry the weight of orders, can be safely forgotten by a Cabinet member. And if the President asks about a suggestion a second time, he can be told that it is being investigated. If he asks a third time, a wise Cabinet officer will give him at least part of what he suggests. But only occasionally, except about the most important matters, do Presidents ever get around to asking three times.

The rule applies to staff as well as to the cabinet, and certainly has been applied *by* staff in Truman's time and Eisenhower's.

Some aides will have more vantage points than a selective memory. Sherman Adams, for example, as the assistant to the President under Eisenhower, scarcely deserved the appelation "White House aide" in the meaning of the term before his time or as applied to other members of the Eisenhower entourage. Although Adams was by no means "chief of staff" in any sense so sweeping—or so simple—as press commentaries often took for granted, he apparently became no more dependent on the President than Eisenhower on him. "I need him," said the President when Adams turned out to have been remarkably imprudent in the Goldfine case, and delegated to him, at least nominally, the decision on his own departure. This instance is extreme, but the tendency it illustrates is common enough. Any aide who demonstrates to others that he has the President's consistent confidence and a consistent part in presidential business will acquire so much business on his own account that he becomes in some sense independent of his chief. Nothing in the Constitution keeps a well-placed aide from converting status into power of his own, usable in some degree even against the President—an outcome not unknown in Truman's regime or, by all accounts, in Eisenhower's.

The more an officeholder's status and his powers stem from sources independent of the President, the stronger will be his potential pressure on the President. Department heads in general have more bargaining power than do most members of the White House staff; but bureau chiefs may have still more, and specialists at upper levels of established career services may have almost unlimited reserves of the enormous power which consists of sitting still.

▪   ▪   ▪

In the right circumstances, of course, a President can have his way with any of these people. Chapter 2 includes three instances where circumstances were "right" and a presidential order was promptly carried out. But one need only note the favorable factors giving those three orders their self-executing quality to recognize that as between a President and his "subordinates," no less than others on whom he depends, real power is reciprocal and varies markedly with organization, subject matter, personality, and situation. The mere fact that persuasion is directed at executive officials signifies no necessary easing of his way. Any new congressman of the Administration's party, especially if narrowly elected, may turn out more amenable (though less useful) to the President than any seasoned bureau chief "downtown." *The probabilities of power do not derive from the literary theory of the Constitution.*

III

There is a widely held belief in the United States that were it not for folly or for knavery, a reasonable President would need no power other than the logic of his argument. No less a personage than Eisenhower has subscribed to that belief in many a campaign speech and press-conference remark. But faulty reasoning and bad intentions do not cause all quarrels with Presidents. The best of reasoning and of intent cannot compose them all. For in the first place, what the President wants will rarely seem a trifle to the people he wants it from. And in the second place, they will be bound to judge it by the standard of their own responsibilities, not his. However logical his argument according to his lights, their judgment may not bring them to his view.

Those who share in governing this country frequently appear to act as though they were in business for themselves. So, in a real though not entire sense, they are and have to be. When Truman and MacArthur fell to quarreling, for example, the stakes were no less than the substance of American foreign policy, the risks of greater war or military stalemate, the prerogatives of Presidents and field commanders, the pride of a proconsul and his place in history. Intertwined, inevitably, were other stakes as well: political stakes for men and factions of both parties; power stakes for interest groups with which they were or wished to be affiliated. And every stake was raised by the apparent discontent in the American public mood. There is no reason to suppose that in such circumstances men of large but differing responsibilities will see all things through the same glasses. On the contrary, it is to be expected that their views of what ought to be done and what they then should do will vary with the differing perspectives their particular responsibilities evoke. Since their duties are not vested in a "team" or a "collegium" but in themselves, as individuals, one must expect that they will see things for themselves. Moreover, when they are responsible to many masters and when an event or policy turns loyalty against loyalty—a day-by-day occurrence in the nature of the case—one must assume that those who have the duties to perform will choose the terms of reconciliation. This is the essence of their personal responsibility. When their own duties pull in opposite directions, who else but they can choose what they will do?

When Truman dismissed MacArthur, the latter lost three posts: the American command in the Far East, the Allied command for the occupation of Japan, and the United Nations command in Korea. He also lost his status as the senior officer on active duty in the United States armed forces. So long as he held those positions and that status, though, he had a duty to his troops, to his profession, to himself (the last is hard for any man to disentangle from the rest). As a public figure and a focus for men's hopes he had a duty to constituents at home, and in Korea and Japan. He owed a duty also to those other constituents, the UN governments contributing to his field forces. As a patriot he had a duty to his country. As an accountable official and an expert guide he stood at the call of Congress. As a military officer he had, besides, a duty to the President, his constitutional commander. Some of these duties may have manifested themselves in terms more tangible or more direct than others. But it would be nonsense to argue that the last negated all the rest, however much it might be claimed to override them. And it makes no more sense to think that anybody but MacArthur was effectively empowered to decide how he himself would reconcile the competing demands his duties made upon him.

■   ■   ■

The essence of a President's persuasive task, with congressmen and everybody else, is to induce them to believe that what he wants of them is what their own appraisal of their own responsibilities requires them to do in their interest, not his. Because men may differ in their views on public policy, because differences in outlook stem from differences in duty—duty to one's office, one's constituents, oneself—that task is bound to be more like collective bargaining than like a reasoned argument among philosopher kings. Overtly or implicitly, hard bargaining has characterized all illustrations offered up to now. This is the reason why: Persuasion deals in the coin of self-interest with men who have some freedom to reject what they find counterfeit.

6.2

CHARLES M. CAMERON

"Bargaining and Presidential Power"

The president is the executive of the national government, but he has a key leg-
islative power that allows him to influence Congress: the veto. Cameron shows
how presidents can use the veto effectively to shape legislation. The threat of a
presidential veto can be enough; Congress will often write legislation specifically
to avoid a veto.

"Presidential power" is a deceptive phrase. It suggests that the capacity to
shape policy is an attribute of the *president*, and a single attribute at that. But
power is not an attribute of an individual, like her height or weight. Instead,
"power" describes something about the outcome of a strategic interaction (a
"game"). In particular, a president has power in a game when its outcome
resembles what the president wants and he causes the outcome to be that way.[1]

This way of thinking about power shifts attention from the attributes of
presidents to the characteristics of the games they play. Among these many
games are the Supreme Court nominations game, the veto game, the executive
order game, the treaty ratification game, the legislative leadership game, the
agency supervision and management game, the commander-in-chief game,
the staffing game, the executive reorganization game, the opinion leadership
game, and the impeachment game. *Understanding the presidency means under-*
standing these games. I am tempted to add, "and that is all it means," but that
would be too strong. Skill, personality, and charisma seem to matter, or so
many people believe. But they always operate within the confines of specific
games and strategic circumstances. Understanding the games presidents play
is fundamental for understanding presidential power.

Presidents participate in so many games that it is hard to characterize them
in a simple way. Broadly speaking, though, when presidents interact with Congress, they often play *coordination games* or *bargaining games*. Loosely speaking, coordination games require many players to act in one of several possible
ways if they are to benefit themselves. If they do not all act in the same way,
they work at cross-purposes. The politics of such games involve selecting the
"focal points" coordinating the players' actions. A majority party setting its
legislative agenda in Congress is a prime example of this situation, because
many players—across committees in both houses and in the leadership—
must focus on a few priorities if they are to accomplish much. Oft times, the

selection of focal points involves loose norms and improvisation rather than formal procedures specified in law or the Constitution; this lies outside what Neustadt called the "literary theory of the Constitution," though hardly outside the reach of social science.

In contrast, bargaining games require players to divide among themselves a "pie," or set of benefits. The politics of bargaining involves gambits increasing one's share of the pie. Examples include haggling over the content of laws, pulling and hauling to determine the direction and vigor of agency decisions, and bickering over the appointment of executive officials and judges. These activities all involve give-and-take across the branches of government. Many bargaining games in which the president participates are quite formal, with a structure specified by the Constitution, by law, or by norms of long-standing precedent.[2]

■   ■   ■

PRESIDENTIAL BARGAINING GAMES: WHAT DO WE KNOW?

Given the importance of bargaining games for the contemporary presidency, an obvious question is: What does the empirical record tell us about presidential bargaining games? This seems like it should be an easy question to answer, but unfortunately it is not. The problem is that data on the *process* of bargaining—the number of vetoes, of nominees rejected by Congress, the number of oversight hearings, the number of policy proposals in State of the Union messages, the number of bills introduced in Congress, the number of executive orders reversed by Congress, and so on—are relatively easy to collect but hard to interpret (I'll explain why shortly). Conversely, data on the *outputs* from bargaining games—for example, the number and content of important laws, executive orders, and treaties, the intensity and import of bureaucratic action, the ideological tenor and meaning of court decisions—are very hard to collect but much easier to interpret.

Why are process measures so much harder to interpret compared to output measures? The problem is that power in bargaining games often operates through *anticipation*. Congress anticipates a veto if it goes too far: in order to avoid the veto, it trims back a policy initiative. No veto occurs, but the president's preferences have altered what Congress would have done if could have operated without constraint. In other words, the game's structure allows the president to exercise power over the outcome, even absent a veto. As a second example, suppose the president anticipates a torrent of opposition if he nominates a controversial activist to head a regulatory agency. Accordingly, he eschews the controversial nominee in favor of a more moderate one, though he would prefer to put the activist in charge if he could do so without cost. The nomination then flies through Congress. In this case, the structure of the game allows Congress to exercise some power over the nominee's ideology even with no direct evidence of this in the public record.

Situations like this involve the "second face of power," power operating through anticipated response.[3] These situations are notoriously difficult to study using process measures since participants maneuver to avoid the most easily measured consequences of disagreement.

How can one find the traces of power when the second face of power is at work? There are two methods: the first direct, the second indirect. The direct method involves measuring policy outputs and relating them to the actors' preferences. If the president actually exercises power over the output, even without taking visible action, then a switch from a liberal president to a conservative one should result in a change in policy, *ceteris paribus*. If one collects data on policy outputs and proxies for preference changes (e.g., partisan affiliation of the president and key congressional actors), and the policy outputs change in a clear and simple way in response to changes in the preference proxies, then one has strong circumstantial evidence of power being exercised. Obviously, one needs to control for confounding influences, but the principle is clear enough.[4]

The indirect approach is more convoluted. It begins with process data, such as vetoes, rejected nominees, reversed executive orders, and blocked agency initiatives. The problem is interpreting such data. In order for events like vetoes to occur, there must be policy disagreement between the actors. But this is only a *necessary* condition. It is certainly not a *sufficient* condition, as arguments about the second face of power indicate. Instead, a process marker like a veto, a rejected nominee or treaty, or a reversed executive order, represents the impact of policy disagreement, *plus something else beyond mere disagreement*. Let us call this additional element "Factor X."[5] The essence of the indirect approach is to build an explicit model of bargaining *incorporating Factor X*. Using this model, one can interpret the process measures and even draw conclusions about presidential power. Absent such a model, all that can be concluded from process measures like counts of vetoes is that policy disagreement occurred—a very weak conclusion since policy disagreement may not trigger a veto without Factor X.[6]

■　　■　　■

The Indirect Approach: Studying Veto Bargaining

Absent a model of vetoes (actual vetoes, not just veto power), any number of vetoes is equally compatible with little, some, or a great deal of presidential power over legislative outputs. No vetoes may mean that Congress has capitulated to the president, or the president has capitulated to Congress; or that Congress has made some compromises before submitting the bill to the president, who compromises somewhat by accepting it. Many vetoes are equally ambiguous. The lesson is a general one—data on process measures simply do not speak for themselves. The idea of the indirect approach is to combine process measures with explicit models of bargaining, in the hope the data will speak more distinctly.

Veto threats

Matthews provides an elegant model of veto threats, beginning with a standard model of one-shot, take-it-or-leave-it bargaining over political issues.[7] Then he adds an explicit "Factor X"—congressional uncertainty about the president's policy preferences. In other words, Matthews assumes the president has a policy reputation, but the reputation is not so precise that Congress can predict with pinpoint accuracy the response of the president to every conceivable bill. Disagreement between the president and Congress, *plus* congressional uncertainty about how far it can push the president before triggering a veto, allows vetoes to occur within the model—they occur when the president turns out to be somewhat tougher (that is, more extreme) than Congress anticipated. Finally, Matthews allows the president to issue a veto threat before Congress writes a bill. Using quite sophisticated game theory, Matthews works out predictions about the behavior of Congress and president.

Within the confines of the model, one can evaluate the impact of the "institution" of the veto threat on presidential power. Broadly speaking, veto threats often enhance presidential power (relative to a world without veto threats), because they help the president and Congress strike bargains that they might not otherwise forge, for want of congressional concessions. Moreover, the concessions induced by threats often work to the advantage of the president.[8]

In our own research, my collaborators and I present systematic data on veto threats, congressional concessions after threats, and vetoes after threats, and use Matthews's model to interpret the data (and, to some extent, use the data to test the model).[9] The universe for the study consists of the 2,284 "nonminor" bills presented to the president between 1945 and 1992. We collected data on a random sample of 281 nonvetoed bills from the universe, stratified across three levels of "legislative significance" derived from an approach similar to Mayhew's. We also collected data on all vetoed bills in the universe, some 162 bills, for a total of 443 bills in all. We compiled data on threats and concessions from legislative histories of the bills, the public papers of the presidents, and newspaper accounts.

Statistical analysis of the data revealed the following patterns:

1. During unified government, veto threats rarely occur regardless of the significance of the legislation.
2. During divided government, veto threats occur frequently and increase in frequency with legislative significance. The frequency of veto threats for important legislation during divided government is surprisingly high: 34 percent of such bills received veto threats.
3. If a bill is not threatened, a veto is unlikely though not impossible.

4. If a bill is threatened, the probability of a veto increases dramatically, especially during divided government and at higher levels of legislative significance. But vetoes are not certain even after a threat.
5. Veto threats usually bring concessions.
6. Concessions deter vetoes. The bigger the concession the less likely a threatened bill is to be vetoed.

Although some of these findings lie outside the scope of Matthews's model (for example, the importance of legislative significance), for the most part these findings strongly resemble what the model predicts. Thus, the model "explains" the data, in the sense that it provides a detailed causal mechanism for the process. If one combines the import of the model—veto threats often enhance presidential power—with the data on the actual frequency of threats, one obtains a picture in which veto threats assume considerable importance in the armamentarium of presidents serving in periods of divided party government.

NOTES

1. This conclusion follows from the canonical definition of power: "power is a causal relationship between preferences and outcomes." For a thorough discussion, see Jack Nagal, *The Descriptive Analysis of Power* (New Haven, Conn.: Yale University Press, 1975).

2. The distinction I am drawing between coordination and bargaining is rooted more in presidential politics than abstract game theory. For example, there are bargaining games in which coordination is critical (e.g., Nash bargaining games, with a multitude of equilibria). So I am not drawing a logical or mathematical distinction but instead pointing to the character of different activities.

3. Peter Bachrach and Morton Baratz, "The Two Faces of Power," *American Political Science Review* (1962) 56: 947–952.

4. This method of studying power is laid out in the classics of the power literature, see Robert A. Dahl, *Modern Political Analysis*, 2nd ed. (Englewood Cliffs, N.J.: Prentice-Hall, 1970), and Jack Nagal, *The Descriptive Analysis of Power* (New Haven, Conn.: Yale University Press, 1975). It was first applied to studying presidential power in Terry Moe, "An Assessment of the Positive Theory of 'Congressional Dominance' of Bureaucracy," *Legislative Studies Quarterly* (1987) 12: 475, and Barry R. Weingast, and Mark J. Moran, "Bureaucracy Discretion or Congressional Control? Regulatory Policymaking by the Federal Trade Commission," *Journal of Political Economy* (1983) 91: 765–800.

5. For those who don't like suspense: "Factor X" often turns out to be some type of uncertainty, including uncertainty about what others will do (e.g., in the form of mixed strategies) or what they want (e.g., incomplete information about actors' preferences) and thus what they will do.

6. One cannot even conclude that vetoes are evidence of the most important or most intense disagreements. Drawing that conclusion requires a model of vetoes in which the statement is true; absent the model, it is not a valid inference.

7. Steven Matthews, "Veto Threats: Rhetoric in a Bargaining Game," *Quarterly Journal of Economics* (1989) 103: 347–369.

8. They don't always do so, for sometimes the concessions are inadequate to head off a veto. In this case, concessions don't actually advantage the president (neglecting veto overrides).

9. Charles M. Cameron, *Veto Bargaining: Presidents and the Politics of Negative Power* (New York: Cambridge University Press, 2000), and Charles Cameron, John S. Lapinski, and Charles Riemann, "Testing Formal Theories of Political Rhetoric," *Journal of Politics* (Winter 2000).

6.3

BRANDICE CANES-WRONE

From *Who Leads Whom? Presidents, Policy, and the Public*

Do presidents follow public opinion even when they believe it is wrong? Or do presidents do what they think is right even when doing so is unpopular? Canes-Wrone describes three important cases when presidents pandered; that is, they followed public opinion rather than do what they thought was the right thing to do. She argues that this happens often.

EXAMPLES OF POLICY PANDERING AND LEADERSHIP

Why did Jimmy Carter, a long-time proponent of expanding humanitarian assistance, suddenly propose to scale back the program? Why did Ronald Reagan, who was philosophically opposed to tax increases, recommend an unpopular one? And why did George H. W. Bush veto a bill extending unemployment benefits only to sign similar bills over the course of the following eight months?

. . . [T]he cases illustrate the behaviors of *policy pandering* and *policy leadership*. Pandering reflects circumstances in which a president supports a popular policy option despite the fact that he expects it to harm citizens' interests. Policy leadership, in comparison, occurs when a president endorses an unpopular option that he believes will advance societal welfare.

■ ■ ■

Case Selection

The primary motivation for developing the Conditional Pandering Theory was to assess the incentives of the president to pander to public opinion when forced to choose between endorsing a popular course of action or one he believes will produce a good outcome for society. Given this substantive aim, I focus the narrative analysis on executive decisions for which the president's beliefs regarding the optimal policy choice differed from those of the mass public. As previously discussed, the concept of policy pandering does not require that a president's beliefs regarding the optimal course of action are necessarily correct. Accordingly, in the cases, the fact that a president deemed the mass citizenry to be misguided does not mean that the reader will necessarily agree with the president's assessment.

The need to ascertain the president's beliefs in relation to public opinion made the selection of cases contingent on the availability of historical evidence on these factors. Even so, I imposed a number of additional restrictions regarding the selection. First, to illustrate how the theoretical predictions vary according to the president's popularity relative to that of his likely competition, I ensured that one case concerned a president far ahead of his likely competition, one a president far behind, and one a president who could expect a tight race. Using the language of chapter 5, at least one case involved a highly popular president, one an unpopular chief executive, and one a marginally popular president. Thus, in the narratives, presidential approval ratings are often employed as a proxy for a chief executive's popularity relative to that of his potential competition. Prior research establishes that this factor is correlated with a president's likelihood of retaining office (e.g., Brody and Sigelman 1983; Sigelman 1979). By comparison, trial heats are not particularly accurate assessments of a president's electoral prospects until the final months of a race; indeed, trial heats are not even routinely available throughout a president's term.

The second restriction is that the universe of potential cases was limited to the decisions of presidents since Nixon. The literature suggests that these presidents have been more likely than their predecessors to involve the mass public in policymaking (e.g., Kernell 1997; Skowronek 1993); the restriction enables showing that the Conditional Pandering Theory is germane to these presidencies. Third, to demonstrate that the theory is not limited in applicability to a given administration or personality, I selected a different chief executive for each case. Fourth, I chose only policy decisions that were significant enough to receive coverage in the *Congressional Quarterly Almanac*. This restriction was inspired by a desire to establish that the theory is relevant to relatively important policy decisions. Finally, the selection was influenced by the fact that presidents can more easily change public opinion in foreign as compared with domestic affairs. Because of this asymmetry, one might suppose that presidential pandering would be uncommon in foreign affairs and common in domestic matters. To demonstrate the relevance of the Conditional Pandering Theory across both domains, I illustrate the behavior of policy pandering with decisions involving foreign affairs and the behavior of policy leadership with decisions on domestic matters.

A substantial portion of each narrative is devoted to describing why seemingly plausible alternative explanations do not explain the sequence of events. This attention to alternative explanations is partially a function of the fact that one would not necessarily anticipate truth revelation by presidents and their advisors. Chief executives are not likely to admit, even in retrospect, that they followed public opinion despite having evidence suggesting the action would produce harmful effects. (Nor are presidents particularly likely to state that electoral motivations were what lead them to take an unpopular position, as occurs in the Conditional Pandering Theory when first-term presidents exercise policy leadership.) The narratives accordingly do not revolve around "smoking guns" of admissions by presidents but, instead, careful attention to their long-standing beliefs, public opinion, and possible alternative accounts.

President Carter and Foreign Aid: The Trustee Panders

Carter is reputed to have placed the public interest above other political objectives. For example, Erwin Hargrove (1988, 11) assesses in his biography of Carter: "The key of Carter's understanding of himself as a political leader was his belief that the essential responsibility of leadership was to articulate the good of the entire community rather than any part of it . . . Rather than being antipolitical or nonpolitical leadership, this was, for him, a different kind of leadership that eschewed the normal politician's preoccupation with representing private interests, bargaining, and short-term electoral goals." Similarly, Charles Jones (1988) characterizes Carter's regime as the "trusteeship presidency," in which the chief executive viewed himself as a trustee of the people and sought to enact policies he believed were in the public interest even when they were not politically expedient. Precisely because of this reputation, I illustrate the behavior of pandering with a case study that concerns President Carter. By establishing that the Conditional Pandering Theory has relevance for his policy decisions, I show it is applicable even to presidents who are not thought to cater to public opinion.

The case study focuses on Carter's budgetary proposal for the policy issue of humanitarian assistance in 1980, the year he ran for reelection. Upon taking office, Carter had pledged to switch U.S. policy toward communist containment in the Third World. Instead of responding militarily whenever conflicts over communism arose, Carter espoused a "preventive" approach. He sought to lessen the appeal of communism to the citizens of Third World nations by solving their underlying problems (e.g., Deibel 1987; Skidmore 1996). Development assistance comprised a key component of this preventive approach.

For the first three years of Carter's term, his proposals for humanitarian assistance, or economic aid, were consistent with this philosophy. In each year, Carter requested an increase and he invariably achieved one, even if not for the full amount he had requested. He pursued this expansion despite a lack of public support for the program; according to responses to the General Social Survey, throughout his administration over 65 percent of the populace believed the United States spent too much on foreign aid.[1]

Carter knew that his policy position was unpopular. He acknowledged as much during a call-in radio show he hosted during the first few months in office. Stating his policy stance to a caller, Carter began, "Well, John [the caller], I'm going to take a position that's not very popular, politically speaking."[2] Likewise, in a session with media representatives during the second year of the administration, Carter remarked, "I don't know of any issue that has less political support than that program itself, foreign aid in all its forms."[3]

Carter's lack of pandering over foreign aid during his first three years in office is consistent with his reputation for placing the public interest above other, more political objectives. His behavior also, however, comports with the Conditional Pandering Theory. The theory suggests that a president will not pander to public opinion if he does not soon face a contest for reelection or if he is highly popular or unpopular. In the early months of 1977 and 1978, when Carter submitted his foreign aid proposals as a part of his annual budgetary requests, the presidential election was relatively distant. By the outset of 1979, when Carter offered his humanitarian aid proposal for the following fiscal year, the electoral race was approaching but Carter's popularity was weak. His public approval ratings for the past year had averaged 43 percent, a very low level by historical standards. His decision to exercise policy leadership is thus consistent with the Conditional Pandering Theory.

Of course, that Carter's policymaking on foreign aid between 1977 and 1979 comports with the Conditional Pandering Theory does not eliminate the possibility that his actions were entirely the consequence of his character. For this reason, we focus on the humanitarian aid proposal Carter offered in 1980, when he reversed his previous position and recommended that the United States cut economic assistance. Specifically, in his budget of January 1980 (which was for fiscal year 1981), Carter proposed cutting economic assistance by 2 percent in nominal terms. The cut constituted a nominal decline of 26 percent relative to his recommendation in the previous budget. Moreover, given the inflation rate predicted by the administration, his request signified a real reduction of 11 percent from the appropriations of last year and 39 percent from his earlier proposal.

The descriptive summaries accompanying the numbers in Carter's budgets reflect the change in his policy position. The budget submitted in 1979 stated that it contained "increases in foreign aid with emphasis on long-term development of poor countries, and reducing widespread poverty." In contrast, the budget submitted in 1980 characterized the proposals for foreign affairs as "designed to help meet the near-term challenges to stability." This budget was also printed in the colors of Carter's reelection campaign, emphasizing the linkage between the document and election year politics (Hargrove 1988).

When Carter submitted his election-year budget, he had reason to believe the impending presidential race would be competitive. His approval ratings were respectable at 58 percent but not remarkably high by historical standards. Moreover, economists were forecasting an imminent recession that would cause double-digit inflation and an increase in unemployment. Carter knew that the recession, assuming it materialized, could cause him serious problems in his campaign for reelection. As a result, he very much wanted his budget to appeal to voters (Kaufman 1993, 168–69).

Carter's policy reversal on foreign aid helped to achieve this goal. By proposing a reduction in economic assistance, he ensured that his position on this program would be consonant with public opinion. According to a Roper survey taken the month before he submitted his budget, 72 percent of the population thought foreign assistance should be decreased.[4] Had Carter continued trying to expand economic aid, he would have handed challengers an easy issue on which to criticize him.

Thus consistent with the Conditional Pandering Theory, Carter switched his position in the direction of public opinion once he was marginally popular and soon faced a contest for reelection. He could reasonably expect that the effects of cutting economic assistance would not be known by voters before the election, particularly since appropriations bills are not typically enacted until summer at the earliest. Moreover, the anticipated competitiveness of the race meant that his policy choice might affect his likelihood of winning. As a result, Carter had an electoral incentive to take the popular position of cutting humanitarian assistance, even if he believed that increasing it was in America's long-term interest.

Among seemingly plausible alternative explanations, none receives support on careful examination. Perhaps the most natural justification, and one that would comport with Carter's reputation for pursuing the public interest, is that his beliefs about the value of humanitarian assistance had changed. In fact, as Michael Genovese (1994) observes, there is a good deal of evidence that Carter shifted from a "Wilsonian idealist" to a "Cold War confrontationist" as his term progressed. David Skidmore (1996) also describes this transformation in an analysis that is fittingly entitled *Reversing Course*. However, as these scholars acknowledge, the transformation began as early as 1978. Thus if the change in philosophy were the primary cause of Carter's policy reversal on foreign aid, the policy reversal should have occurred earlier.

Moreover, the budget that Carter proposed in his final month in office, after his electoral defeat, reiterated his commitment to a substantial growth in humanitarian assistance. He recommended increasing it by 26 percent in nominal terms, which, given the projected inflation rate, comprised a real increase of 12 percent. The justification Carter gave for this request in his Budget Message highlighted his continued belief in the importance of humanitarian assistance. He stated, "I believe in the need for higher levels of aid to achieve foreign policy objectives, promote economic growth, and help needy people abroad. Foreign aid is not politically popular and represents an easy target for budget reduction. But it is not a wise one." Carter's election-year proposal to decrease development assistance therefore cannot be attributed to a fundamental change in his convictions regarding the benefits of foreign aid.

Given that the policy shift cannot be ascribed to a change in Carter's convictions, I consider whether it can be attributed to factors specific to the time period in which it occurred. These alternative explanations include the macroeconomy, anticipated congressional behavior, and international events. I consider each in turn.

In January 1980, inflation was a major concern for President Carter and the public. During the past year, the consumer price index had increased by 12.4 percent and according to Gallup's Most Important Problem survey, 36 percent of citizens (a plurality of respondents) considered inflation to be the most important problem in the nation.[5] Carter accordingly designed his election-year budget with the goal of curbing inflation (Hargrove 1988, 102–3; Kaufman 1993, 168–69). One could therefore argue that he proposed to cut humanitarian aid in order to help reduce inflation.

The key problem with this argument is that Carter's overall budget was not all that fiscally conservative. As Hargrove (1988, 103) assesses, the budget reflected that Carter was "not, in the final analysis, a conservative prepared to launch a period of austerity." In fact, Carter's budget entailed real increases in other, more popular programs. For example, Carter proposed conspicuous growth in funding for federal health programs and ground transportation, issues on which a majority of the public supported higher spending.[6] It is therefore difficult to conclude that Carter's desire to curb inflation was the primary determinant of his decision to recommend reducing humanitarian assistance.

A separate potential explanation for the policy shift involves Carter's congressional relations. In 1979, Congress failed to enact a Foreign Aid Appropriations Bill. The funding for international assistance programs came from continuing resolutions, which appropriated almost 20 percent less than the president had requested for the programs. Given these events, one might conjecture that Carter's policy reversal resulted from a change in his bargaining strategy.

The evidence suggests, however, that Carter's proposal to reduce international assistance did not reflect a general adjustment in his approach to budgetary negotiations. In fact, in the same budget he proposed expanding programs for which Congress had in the previous year appropriated far less than he had requested. For example, in 1979 Carter obtained 23 percent less funding than he had proposed for the District of Columbia, but in 1980 he still requested 9 percent more than he had in the previous budgetary cycle. Likewise, Congress appropriated 9 percent less than Carter recommended for agricultural spending in 1979, yet in 1980 the president recommended an increase of 20 percent relative to his proposal of the previous year. Carter thus did not systematically lower his budgetary requests in response to previous failures to expand the programs.

In keeping with this evidence that Carter's legislative negotiations differed by policy area, I consider as a final rationale for his policy shift an explanation particular to foreign aid. Specifically, I examine the possibility that an international event induced the president to desire a lower level of humanitarian assistance. In 1979 there were two major international incidents that affected U.S. interests: the abduction of American hostages in Iran in November 1979 and the Soviet invasion of Afghanistan in the following month. Ostensibly, these incidents could have affected Carter's beliefs concerning the value of bilateral assistance to the Soviet Union and Iran.

Regardless of the president's beliefs about such bilateral assistance, however, his proposal to reduce humanitarian aid could not be the consequence of them. As documented in the 1981 *Country Report on Human Rights Practices* prepared by the State Department, the United States offered no bilateral assistance to the Soviet Union or Iran in 1979.[7] Thus, Carter could not recommend cutting assistance to these countries.[8] A related possibility is that the Soviet invasion of Afghanistan and the Iranian hostage crisis induced the president to disfavor the use of humanitarian aid as a means of solving the problems of the Third World. Yet, as previously discussed, soon after the 1980 elections, Carter proposed a massive increase in humanitarian assistance. Thus the international events seem to have, if anything, strengthened the president's belief that humanitarian assistance would promote U.S. interests.[9]

In sum, Carter's policy reversal on foreign aid in 1980 cannot be attributed to a change in his belief system, the state of the economy, congressional relations, or to the major foreign events of the day. Nor is the shift consistent with his subsequent policy proposals on foreign aid. The decision does, however, comport with the Conditional Pandering Theory. When the election was distant or Carter's approval ratings were low, he pursued the course of action he believed to be in the public interest. Yet when the election was near and his public standing was such that he seemed likely to face a tight race, the president pandered to public opinion.

President Bush and Unemployment Benefits: Policy Leadership from Ahead and Pandering

Throughout the summer of 1991, President Bush looked likely to sail to reelection. His approval ratings had hit historically high levels in the wake of the Gulf War victory earlier that year and still hovered in the high 60s and low 70s.[10] Front-runners for the Democratic nomination decided one after another not to challenge the president. By September, Al Gore, Richard Gephardt, and Jay Rockefeller IV had all dropped out of the race. As Robert E. Denton and Mary E. Stuckey (1994, 19) surmise, "Bush simply seemed unbeatable."

This popularity was noteworthy given the lackluster economy over which the president was presiding. The gross national product (GNP) had increased only 0.4 percent during the second quarter of 1991, and this relatively meager growth followed nine months of GNP retraction.[11] As of June, the unemployment rate was approaching 7 percent.[12] Much of the unemployment involved middle-management workers who had been downsized by corporations. These managers were having a particularly difficult time finding alternative employment; many remained jobless at the time their unemployment benefits expired. The unemployment rate thus reflected a substantial number of workers who were not only out of work but also not receiving government assistance. For instance, in July 1991 unemployment compensation expired for 350,000 jobless Americans (Cohen 1997, 218).

It was in this environment that Congress enacted a series of bills extending unemployment benefits. The first of these bills to reach Bush's desk was HR 3201, which arrived August 17. The legislation provided up to 20 weeks of extra benefits through July 1992 at an estimated cost of $5.3 billion. The legislation specified that for the compensation to be distributed, the president had to declare a state of emergency. Bush signed the bill but did not declare an emergency, thereby preventing the expenditure of the benefits.

The second unemployment bill to reach Bush's desk was S 1722, entitled the Emergency Unemployment Compensation Act of 1991. The bill, which was passed by Congress on October 1, again offered up to 20 weeks of extended benefits and had an estimated cost of $6.4 billion. Unlike the earlier legislation, S 1722 did not allow the president the option of signing the legislation without obligating the additional benefits. Bush could thus either veto the bill or enact the temporary extension.[13]

Surveys conducted around the time that Congress passed S 1722 suggest the bill was quite popular. A *Los Angeles Times* poll taken September 21 through 25 found that 63 percent of respondents favored the legislation strongly or at least somewhat, and only 33 percent opposed it.[14] Likewise, a Harris poll conducted September 27 through October 2 found that only 37 percent of respondents would rate the president's opposition to the bill as "excellent" or "pretty good."[15] These survey data suggest that to the extent Bush wished to placate the mass public, he had an incentive to endorse the legislation.

Bush's incentives were not straightforward, however, because he did not believe that the extension of unemployment benefits would promote a strong economy. As David Mervin (1996, 87) describes, the president was "particularly averse to government interference in the economy." This belief repeatedly put him in conflict with the Democratic-controlled Congress. Nicholas Calio, who was in charge of Bush's legislative relations, describes how the White House perceived congressional efforts to control the economy: "There were many things that, in our view, Congress got involved in [which] it really shouldn't—in micro managing markets . . . There were a lot of things we felt needed to be stopped."[16]

The legislation S 1722, the Emergency Unemployment Compensation Act, was apparently one of those things. While the legislation was being considered, Bush openly referred to it as part of "a bunch of garbage" that the Democrats were sending his way.[17] In a news conference, he argued that the measure would ultimately harm taxpayers. Furthermore, he exhorted citizens to implore their representatives to "do something that the President can sign that will help us with unemployment benefits but will also protect the other taxpayer."[18] On October 11, Bush vetoed S 1722, declaring in an accompanying memorandum that it would "threaten economic recovery and its associated job creation." He continued, "the Congress has . . . ignored my call for passage of measures that will increase the nation's competitiveness, productivity and growth.[19]

For all of this strong language, Bush agreed to a measure quite similar to S 1722, HR 3575, less than two months later. HR 3575 extended unemployment benefits for up to 20 weeks through mid-June at an estimated cost of $5.3 billion. When the president signed the bill on November 15, his electoral vulnerability was much greater than it had been when he had vetoed S 1722. Headlines from the preceding weeks had declared "Democrats Find Bush Is Vulnerable" and "Democrat Hopefuls See Bush Weakness."[20] Correspondingly, his popularity ratings had dropped to 56 percent.[21]

The possibility that Bush switched his policy position for electoral reasons did not go unnoticed at the time. For example, Senator George Mitchell of Maine, referring to Bush's apparent reversal, asserted the president was in "panic city."[22] The administration rebuked such criticism and claimed the legislative negotiations had in fact culminated in a victory for the president over the details of how the unemployment benefits would be funded. According to the administration, the bill that Bush had originally vetoed would have increased the deficit and thus violated the 1990 Budget Act, which required that any new program not add to the deficit. The bill he signed, in comparison, supposedly paid for itself through tax increases on the wealthy, the renewal of an employer tax, and a new policy of income confiscation from individuals who defaulted on school loans.[23]

Such a justification for Bush's action would have been more credible had the president not soon thereafter approved another temporary extension of unemployment benefits, HR 4095, which many believed would increase the deficit. Bush signed this subsequent legislation on February 7, 1992, after his popularity ratings had been hovering in the mid-40s for the past month.[24] HR 4095 provided an additional thirteen weeks of benefits, paying for them primarily through a "surplus" that the Office of Management and Budget (OMB) predicted would arise from 1991 tax bills.[25] The Congressional Budget Office (CBO) disputed the prediction of a surplus, and critics ridiculed the forecast.[26] For example, Representative Thomas J. Downey, a Democrat from Long Island, chided that "Only in the land of Oz could you take a $350 billion deficit and find $2 billion in savings."[27]

The claim that Bush did not switch his position seemed even more disingenuous in July 1992. On July 3, when the president was running neck-and-neck with Bill Clinton and Ross Perot in the pre-election polls, the president signed HR 5260, which permanently changed the unemployment system by allowing nonemergency benefits to take effect more easily during times of high unemployment. As recently as April, Bush had opposed making such permanent changes to the system.[28] Even the day before signing HR 5260, the president had threatened to veto the permanent expansion.[29] The champion of the bill in Congress, Representative Thomas J. Downey, offered an explanation for Bush's actions during the brief House debate over the legislation. He predicted, "The President is going to sign this bill for two reasons. Unemployment is up, and his popularity is down."[30]

Does the variation in Bush's policy decisions over unemployment benefits correspond to the predictions of the Conditional Pandering Theory? The theory suggests that a president will endorse policies that he believes are in the public interest when he is quite popular relative to his likely electoral competition, when he is relatively unpopular, or when he does not soon face a contest for reelection. In this case, Bush supported an unpopular policy that he believed would advance a strong economy so long as his electoral prospects were strong. Once he seemed vulnerable, however, he changed course and issued popular decisions that did not reflect his belief that preventing government interference in the economy would harm it and, by consequence, societal welfare. This variation in executive behavior is exactly what the Conditional Pandering Theory would predict.

Some readers may take issue with the notion that Bush was trying to advance societal welfare by vetoing unemployment benefits. It is accordingly worth reemphasizing that the Conditional Pandering Theory does not require that a president is actually advancing citizens' interests, only that he believes he is doing so; the president can be wrong in this assessment. The preceding description of events documented that Bush believed economic recovery, as well as long-term growth, would be best advanced by limiting government interference in the macroeconomy. The question of whether these beliefs were accurate, or whether they are in part a function of ideological biases, is not paramount to analyzing the predicative power of the theory. In the concluding section of this reading, I return to the issue of whether presidents are likely to have better information than citizens do about the expected consequences of policies. For now, I have a more precise goal, which is to show that the Conditional Pandering does a better job at predicting the variation in Bush's policy decisions than seemingly likely alternative explanations.

To realize this goal, four alternative rationales are evaluated, the last two of which are evaluated jointly. First, I examine whether Bush altered his policy beliefs in response to economic events. Second, the possibility that his claims of policy consistency were correct is considered. Third, I analyze executive-legislative negotiations that occurred after Clinton had taken a clear lead in order to assess whether Bush's likelihood of pandering was simply greater the sooner the election; and fourth, whether this likelihood was greater the lower his chances of retaining office.

During the course of the executive-legislative negotiations over the extension of unemployment benefits, the unemployment rate itself varied noticeably. When the president vetoed an extension of benefits in October 1991, the Labor Department had just announced that the rate had dropped a tenth of a percentage point to 6.7 percent. A month later, when Bush approved a temporary extension, the rate had risen back up to 6.8 percent. Furthermore, at the subsequent bill signings in February and July, the rate was estimated to be 7.1 percent and 7.8 percent respectively. It therefore seems plausible that changes in the economic situation caused Bush to believe greater government intervention in the economy was warranted.

Yet the evidence suggests otherwise. In June 1991 the unemployment rate was 6.9 percent and legislation temporarily extending compensation to the jobless was already making its way through Congress. Bush, who was enjoying approval ratings in the mid-70s, did not lend support to the bill. Then in July 1992, Bush threatened to veto a permanent expansion of unemployment benefits even after the Labor Department had announced that the unemployment rate was 7.8 percent, the highest level in eight years.[31]

Finally, Bush never intimated that he reversed course because of changes in the economy. Instead, he consistently stated that his willingness to approve extensions of compensation depended on whether they would increase the deficit. For example, during a news conference in August 1991, he promoted Senator Dole's proposed extension of unemployment benefits, which was less expensive than the Democratic proposals, claiming that the Dole plan had "fiscal integrity."[32] At a fundraising luncheon in November, the president expounded his position further, declaring that:

> The Democratic leaders know that I've been ready since August to sign an extension, but to sign one as proposed by most of the Republicans in the Senate and House that lives within the budget agreement. We don't have to add to the ever-increasing deficit and still do what is compassionate and correct. They passed a bill. They wanted to embarrass me politically. I vetoed that bill . . . Unemployed workers deserve this kind of support, but we need a change in the Congress if we're going to do it in a way that lives within the budget agreement.[33]

These assertions comport with the ones Bush gave eight months later with regards to permanently extending unemployment compensation. When the president was asked by Congressman Robert H. Michel, the Minority Leader of the House, whether he might veto such legislation, Bush responded that he had a "certain custodianship for trying to support reasonable expenditures." He continued, "If [Democratic congressional members] send me something that we view and the leadership here views as too expensive, we'll have to send it back and urge them to get one down there that we can support."[34]

In sum, Bush's actions as well as rhetoric indicate that changes in the unemployment rate did not alter his fundamental beliefs about the appropriateness of extending benefits to the jobless. The president's rhetoric highlights a separate alternative explanation, however, which is that substantive differences among the assorted bills explain the variation in his willingness to sign them. The president's decisions could accordingly be construed as an example of what Cameron (2000) terms "veto bargaining." This rationale for the seemingly disparate decisions has some merit. In fact, had the legislative matter ended after Bush's approval of the extension of benefits in November 1991, it would be relatively straightforward to argue that his policy actions reflected an aversion to increasing the deficit.

The president's behavior in February 1992 suggests that this alternative explanation cannot completely account for his behavior, however. As discussed previously, the extension Bush approved in February paid for itself only under highly disputed assumptions about unexpected revenues. In fact, during a congressional hearing on the legislation, Republican House members recommended that the unemployment trust fund be taken off-budget so that it could not affect the official deficit.[35] Bush's ostensible fiscal restraint thus not only entailed questionable assumptions about unexpected surpluses but also coincided with Republicans recommending score-keeping changes in the accounting of unemployment benefits. Given these circumstances, Bush's supposed fiscal responsibility appears more superficial than substantial. His desire for restraint may well have been sincere, but this desire appears to have been superseded by an impetus to enact a popular policy once he was facing a competitive electoral contest.

The final alternative hypotheses I consider are that Bush was simply more likely to pander to public opinion as the election neared, independent of his popularity; and that he was simply more likely to pander as his popularity declined, and thus would have pandered even if the preelection polls had indicated he was quite likely to lose reelection. The events described thus far do not allow one to distinguish between these explanations and the Conditional Pandering Theory. However, subsequent events shed light on the matter.

Clinton took a substantial lead in the polls following the Democratic Party Convention in mid-July. Throughout the remainder of the race, Bush was consistently the underdog, trailing the competition by as much as twenty-five points and sustaining approval ratings no higher than 40 percent.[36] While Congress did not enact other unemployment legislation during this period, the chambers did pass several bills that involved substantial government regulation of the private sector.

That legislation included the Family and Medical Leave Act of 1992 (S 5), which Congress enacted on September 10, and the Cable Television Consumer Protection and Competition Act of 1992 (S 12), which was sent to the president on September 22. The first bill granted workers up to twelve weeks of unpaid leave in order to care for a new baby or sick relative.[37] The second aided competitors to the cable industry, as well as bestowed the federal government with the power to set rates for the lowest-priced cable package.[38] Each of these bills appealed to popular sentiment. For instance, in a survey of registered voters, 63 percent of respondents stated that they would support a law requiring businesses to grant up to three months of unpaid leave for a new child or medical emergency, while only 31 percent opposed such a law.[39] Likewise, a Harris survey found that 87 percent of the national adult population believed most cable companies could overcharge customers owing to a lack of competition, and 70 percent favored allowing local telephone companies to provide cable services so that the cable industry would be more competitive.[40]

Despite the popularity of the policy issues, Bush vetoed the bills. In each case, his expressed rationale for doing so was consistent with his belief that government interference in the economy would harm it. The president professed that the Family and Medical Leave Act, if enacted, would become a "government-dictated mandate that increases costs and loses jobs."[41] He predicted the cable bill would "cost the economy jobs, reduce consumer programming choices, and retard the deployment of growth-oriented investment critical to the future of our Nation's communications infrastructure."[42]

Bush issued each veto within seven weeks of the election, by which time Clinton held a convincing lead in the preelection polls. When Bush delivered the Family Leave veto on September 22, Clinton maintained a ten percentage point advantage according to the Gallup trial heat.[43] At the time of the Cable Bill veto, on October 3, Bush trailed by eleven to twelve percentage points.[44] That the president vetoed the bills under these conditions suggests that he did not continually pander to public opinion as the election approached or as his popularity declined relative to his electoral competition.

Instead, as predicted by the Conditional Pandering Theory, Bush endorsed the policies he believed to be the right ones when he was unpopular compared with his electoral opposition. In combination with his decisions on unemployment legislation, Bush's behavior illustrates the theoretically predicted relationship between the likelihood of pandering and presidential popularity. When he was highly popular or unpopular relative to his competition, he supported the policies he believed would produce the best outcomes for the nation, despite the proximity of the presidential election. Only when he was in the midst of a seemingly tight race did he enact popular laws that he did not believe would ultimately advance citizens' interests.

Reagan and the Contingency Tax Proposal: Policy Leadership from Behind

In the beginning of 1983, Reagan's personal popularity was quite low. Throughout the month of January, his approval ratings hovered in the mid-30s.[45] This lack of popularity reflected the economic situation. In the previous year, the GNP had fallen 1.8 percent, the largest annual reduction since 1946.[46] Unemployment stood at 10.8 percent, the highest level since 1950.[47]

Many economists, including ones working in the executive branch, believed the projection of large deficits for years to come was holding back an economic recovery. As of January 1983, the projected deficits for the next five years were in the range of $185 to $300 billion, approximately 7 percent of GNP. In comparison, the deficit of the last full year before Reagan entered office was $60 billion, around 2 percent of GNP.[48] Paul Volcker, the Chairman of the Federal Reserve, publicly expressed his concerns about the projected deficits in January. He observed, "We are exposed to fears of 'out-of-control' structural

deficits, and the result is upward pressure on interest rates."[49] Martin Feldstein, chairman of the Council of Economic Advisors, agreed with Volcker
that the projection of large deficits was boosting interest rates and therefore
impeding an economic recovery, particularly in sectors dependent on borrowing, such as housing and automobiles.[50] Indeed, interest rates were quite high;
the prime rate was 11 percent and the rate for a conventional home loan was
13.25 percent.[51]

Reagan was deeply concerned about the economy and, moreover, realized
that he would not win reelection in 1984 unless conditions improved. He
acknowledged that if his administration could not move the country into
a recovery it "obviously . . . would be a sign" that he should retire after one
term.[52] Reagan also recognized the projected deficits as a problem. For
example, in an administration briefing in May 1982, he claimed that "the only
thing that's keeping the interest rates up and preventing a speedier recovery
is the lack of confidence on the part of the private sector that government will
stay the course" by progressing toward a balanced budget.[53]

Curbing the deficit was not a simple matter for the president, however.
He desired significant increases in defense spending and the preservation of
his recently enacted income tax cuts (e.g., Dallek 1984, 105; Feldstein 1994,
26 and 36–37). Furthermore, Reagan did not want to obtain the needed
reductions through changes to Medicare, Social Security, or federal employee
retirement programs, which together constituted a majority of the budget
(Dallek 1984, 72–73). The president was willing, indeed wanted, to decrease
spending on social welfare programs (e.g., Hogan 1990, 225), but congressional leaders had indicated that they would be unwilling to curtail these programs substantially.[54]

It was in this setting that Reagan proposed standby taxes that would be
triggered in a couple of years if the deficit did not decline by then; specifically,
the taxes were scheduled to take effect on October 1, 1985, if the estimated deficit for fiscal year 1986 turned out to be greater than 2½ percent of the gross
national product and Congress had approved the president's spending cuts.
The taxes included an excise fee on oil of approximately five dollars a barrel as
well as an increase in corporate and personal income tax payments of approximately 1 percent of taxable income.[55] Reagan promoted this proposal in his
State of the Union address, a radio address, and several targeted addresses
during the first two months of 1983.[56]

The evidence suggests that Reagan believed the policy was in citizens' interests because it would help to control the deficit and thereby improve the
economy by reducing interest rates. Martin Feldstein, who helped to design
the plan along with Reagan's domestic policy adviser Ed Harper, describes
how the president came to espouse the idea. Feldstein recounts that the president supported the policy over the objections of others within the White House
because, ultimately, he "recognized the need to project declining deficits and
an eventual budget balance" (Feldstein 1994, 28). The president's statements

support this assertion. For example, in remarks to the St. Louis Regional Commerce and Growth Association on February 1, the president promoted the standby tax proposal by claiming that "it will reassure many of those out in the money markets today that we do mean to control inflation and interest rates."[57]

Despite Reagan's public espousal of the policy, it was quite unpopular. In fact, survey data suggest it was even less popular than the option of eliminating Reagan's income tax reductions. When citizens were asked whether they would support "a standby program of increased personal and business taxes—as well as a special tax on oil" for the years 1986–88 in order to reduce the budget deficit, 60 percent opposed the proposal.[58] In comparison, only 39 percent of the population believed that "July's tax cut should be put into effect despite the size of the government deficit."[59]

Reagan's promotion of the contingency tax proposal is thus not a case of a president following public opinion. Instead, consistent with the Conditional Pandering Theory, Reagan advocated a policy he believed would serve the public interest even though it was unpopular. As documented earlier, the president knew that without an economic recovery, he would be unlikely to win reelection. He believed that the standby taxes, if enacted, would help the economy and thereby increase his likelihood of winning the upcoming race. His electoral incentive was therefore to promote the proposal despite its lack of popular support.

Of course, it remains plausible that Reagan's behavior was consistent with the Conditional Pandering Theory but that he promoted the proposal for other reasons. I discuss three plausible alternative explanations: that Reagan had a propensity to follow his policy beliefs regardless of the political circumstances; that the president was somehow catering to his conservative base; and that he was playing blame-game politics with the Democrats over who was responsible for the budget deficit. None of these explanations is corroborated under scrutiny.

A seemingly credible rationale for Reagan's behavior is that he generally advocated policies he thought were in the public interest, regardless of their popularity. Indeed, this claim receives some support from officials who worked for him. For example, Edwin Meese III, Reagan's attorney general from February 1985 through August 1988, observes that "Reagan was remarkably steadfast when pursuing his key objectives" (Meese 1992, 330). Martin Anderson, the chief domestic and policy adviser to the president in 1981 and 1982, similarly assesses that Reagan would "never alter his course" when he felt strongly about a decision (Pemberton 1997, 110).

Notwithstanding Reagan's dedication to his beliefs, there is evidence that he was not above catering to public opinion. For example, he was more than willing to fire agency heads who became unpopular while following his agenda. William Pemberton (1997, 121) notes that after the White House pressured Ann Gorsuch Burford to resign her post as head of the Environmental

Protection Agency, she "felt betrayed" by the president because he had "abandoned her when she came under fire for carrying out his policy." Likewise, when James Watt, Reagan's first Secretary of Interior, told the president that he probably have to fire Watt at some point because of the unpopular agenda Watt would be implementing, "Reagan, eyes sparkling with laughter, replied, 'I will'" (Pemberton 1997, 119).

Robert Dallek (1984, 33) reconciles the apparent tension between Reagan's faithfulness to his beliefs and capacity to make tactical modifications. "If Goldwater was ready to stand or fall on principle," Dallek observes, "Reagan, in his determination to be liked and to gain his personal goals, will compromise." As this assessment and Reagan's dealings with his officials imply, the president's support for the contingency taxes cannot be attributed to a universal unwillingness to take positions for purely political reasons.

Conclusion

The narratives on Carter's humanitarian assistance proposals, Bush's policy decisions on unemployment compensation, and Reagan's proposal for standby taxes establish that the Conditional Pandering Theory has explanatory power. In all of these analyses, the predictions of the theory were consistent with the president's policy decisions. Furthermore, the theory made sense of seemingly puzzling events; in each case a president switched positions and/or supported policies counter to his ideological leanings. In contrast, conventional explanations of presidential decision making—character, inside the beltway bargaining, and the appeasement of core constituencies, for example—did not account for the executive behavior.

NOTES

1. The survey asked, "We are faced with many problems in this country, none of which can be solved easily or inexpensively. I'm going to name some of these problems, and for each one I'd like you to tell me whether you think we're spending too much money on it, too little money, or about the right amount. Are we spending too much money, too little money, or about the right amount on foreign aid?"

2. Jimmy Carter, "'Ask President Carter' Remarks During a Telephone Call-in Program on the CBS Radio Network," March 5, 1977, *Public Papers of the Presidents of the United States, 1977 Book 1* (Washington, DC: Government Printing Office, 1977).

3. Jimmy Carter, "Remarks and a Question-and-Answer Session with a Group of Editors and News Directors," May 19, 1978, *Public Papers of the Presidents of the United States, 1978 Book 1* (Washington, DC: Government Printing Office, 1978).

4. Survey conducted December 1–8, 1979. The question wording is identical to that in footnote 1 of this chapter.

5. Survey conducted by the Gallup organization January 25–28, 1980. The survey asked the standard most important problem question, "What do you think is the most important problem in the nation today?" Responses were open-ended.

6. Carter proposed real increases of 9 percent in health programs and 4 percent in ground transportation. The public opinion data are from a Roper survey conducted

December 1–8, 1979. Respondents were asked the (by-now familiar) question, "We are faced with many problems in this country, none of which can be solved easily or inexpensively. I'm going to name some of these problems, and for each one I'd like you to tell me whether you think we're spending too much money on it, too little money or about the right amount." For health, the question ended with "improving and protecting the nation's health" and for ground transportation, it ended with "improving the public transportation." The responses suggest that 59 percent of adults believed the government was spending too little on health and that 50 percent believed too little was being spent on public transportation.

7. *Country Reports on Human Rights Practices,* report submitted to the Committee on Foreign Relations, U.S. Senate, and Committee on Foreign Affairs, U.S. House of Representatives, by the Department of State, February 2, 1981.

8. Carter did impose an embargo on the sale of grain to the Soviet Union, but this embargo did not affect appropriations for foreign assistance.

9. Nor did Carter shift his requests for humanitarian aid into security assistance; in nominal terms, Carter proposed a measly 0.002 percent increase in security aid.

10. Ragsdale (1998, 213).

11. Peter G. Gosselin, "Economy Rolling Again . . . But Slowly: Slight Gain in Gross National Product Worries Analysts," *Boston Globe,* July 27, 1991, 12.

12. U.S. Department of Labor, Bureau of Labor Statistics.

13. *Congressional Quarterly Almanac,* vol. 47 (1991), 304–8.

14. The question was: "Congress recently passed a bill to extend unemployment benefits beyond the regular 25-week period. To provide the 6.4 billion dollars needed to extend benefits, a budget emergency would have to be declared that President Bush says is not justified. Would you like to see Bush sign this bill into law, or do you think he should veto it?"

15. The question was: "Now let me ask you some specifics about President Bush. How would you rate him on . . . his opposition to a bill that would extend for 20 weeks unemployment insurance to unemployed workers whose benefits have run out . . . excellent, pretty good, only fair or poor?" The responses of "only fair" and "poor" are reported jointly by Harris, with 59 percent of the population assigning Bush one of these ratings.

16. Quoted in Mervin (1996, 114).

17. George Bush, "Remarks at a Republican Party Fundraising Dinner in East Brunswick, New Jersey," September 24, 1991, *Public Papers of the Presidents, 1991 Book 2* (Washington, DC: Government Printing Office, 1992).

18. George Bush, "The President's News Conference," October 4, 1991, *Public Papers of the Presidents, 1991 Book 2.*

19. George Bush, "Memorandum of Disapproval for the Emergency Unemployment Compensation Act of 1991," October 11, 1991, *Public Papers of the Presidents, 1991 Book 2.*

20. Andrew J. Glass, "Democrats Find Bush is Vulnerable," *Atlanta Journal and Constitution,* November 3, 1991, O5; Adam Pertman, "Democrat Hopefuls See Bush Weakness," *Boston Globe,* November 3, 1991, 213.

21. Ragsdale (1998, 213).

22. Michael Kranish, "Bush Bristles at Claims He Has Shifted," *Boston Globe,* November 17, 1991, 1.

23. *Congressional Quarterly Almanac,* vol. 48 (1992), 347–48.

24. Ragsdale (1998, 213).

25. *Congressional Quarterly Almanac*, vol. 48 (1992), 347.

26. Ibid.

27. To deal with the possibility that the additional unemployment compensation would add to the deficit, Congress voted to waive the 1990 Budget Act, which required that every new program pay for itself (*Congressional Quarterly Almanac*, vol. 48 [1992], 352).

28. Adam Clymer, "Bush Fights Long-Term Change in Jobless Benefits," *New York Times*, April 9, 1992, D20.

29. Adam Clymer, "Congress Passes Jobless Aid and Bush Says He Will Sign," *New York Times*, July 3, 1992, A13.

30. Ibid.

31. Jill Zuckman, "Bush Relents, Agrees to Sign Jobless Benefits Extension," *Congressional Quarterly Weekly*, July 4, 1992, 1961–62.

32. George Bush, "The President's News Conference," August 2, 1991, *Public Papers of the Presidents, 1991 Book 2.*

33. George Bush, "Remarks at a Bush-Quayle Fundraising Luncheon in New York City," November 12, 1991, *Public Papers of the Presidents, 1991 Book 2.*

34. George Bush, "Remarks and an Exchange with Reporters in a Meeting with the House Republican Conference on Health Care," July 2, 1992, *Public Papers of the Presidents, 1992–93 Book 1* (Washington, DC: Government Printing Office, 1993).

35. Ways and Means Committee Subcommittee on Human Resources Hearing. "Extending Unemployment Benefits." Panel of Congressional Witnesses, B-318 Rayburn House Office Building, January 23, 1992.

36. The 1992 Gallup Poll Presidential Candidate Trial Heats are available in the Roper Center for Public Opinion Research database on polls and surveys (commonly referred to as RPOLL). For Bush's approval ratings, see Ragsdale (1998, 213–14).

37. Jill Zuckman, "Family Leave Act Falls Again: Veto Override Fails in House," *Congressional Quarterly Weekly*, October 3, 1992, 3059.

38. Mike Mills, "Bush Asks for a Sign of Loyalty: Congress Changes the Channel," *Congressional Quarterly Weekly*, October 10, 1992, 3149–51.

39. NBC News and Wall Street Journal Poll conducted September 12–15, 1992. The survey asked: "Congress has passed a law that would require companies to give employees up to three months of unpaid leave for the birth or adoption of a child, or to care for a seriously ill family member, while protecting their job. Would you favor or oppose this law, even if it means additional costs for business?"

40. Harris survey conducted March 19–24, 1992. The first question was, "Here are some statements people have made about the cable television industry in American today. For each one, please tell me whether you agree or disagree . . . Because most cable T.V. companies have local monopolies, they can charge too much for the service they provide." The second question was, "Would you favor or oppose changing the regulations so that your telephone company could provide cable television service in competition with the company that provides now?"

41. George Bush, "Remarks and an Exchange with Reporters on Family Leave Legislation," September 16, 1992, *Public Papers of the Presidents, 1992–93 Book 2.*

42. George Bush, "Letter to Congressional Leaders on Cable Television Legislation," September 17, 1992, *Public Papers of the Presidents, 1992–93 Book 2.*

43. Each of the following trial heats, conducted September 17–20 of registered voters and those who could vote without having yet registered, gave Clinton a ten-point lead. The questions were "If the (1992) presidential election were being held today,

would you vote for the Republican ticket of George Bush and Dan Quayle or for the Democratic ticket of Bill Clinton and Al Gore? (If Perot (vol.)/Other (vol.)/Don't know/ Refused, ask:) As of today, do you lean more to Bush and Quayle, the Republicans, or to Clinton and Gore, the Democrats?" and "If the (1992) presidential election were being held today, would you vote for the Republican ticket of George Bush and Dan Quayle or for the Democratic ticket of Bill Clinton and Al Gore?" In the first case, Clinton received support from 50 percent of respondents, and in the second, he received support from 44 percent.

44. These trial heats were conducted by the Gallup Organization on October 1–3 using the questions in the format of footnote 55 of this chapter. The only difference in the questions is that Ross Perot was explicitly mentioned as a candidate, a result of the fact that he had reentered the race. In the survey that did not urge the leaners to make a choice, Clinton was favored by 47 percent of respondents and Bush by 35 percent. In the survey that pushed the leaners to choose a candidate, Clinton received support from 44 percent of the respondents and Bush from 33 percent.

45. Ragsdale (1998, 210).

46. Anantole Kaletsky, "GNP in U.S. Fell 1.8% Last Year," *Financial Times* (London ed.), January 20, 1983, I1.

47. "Unemployment Claims Rose at End of the Year," *New York Times*, January 14, 1983, D15.

48. Jonathan Fuerbringer, "Do Deficits Impede Recovery?" *New York Times*, January 20, 1983, D1.

49. Volcker's statement was made at a meeting of the American Council for Capital Formation. Kenneth B. Noble, "Deficits Criticized by Volcker," *New York Times*, January 21, 1983, D3.

50. Fuerbringer, "Do Deficits Impede Recovery?"

51. "Current Interest Rates," *New York Times*, January 10, 1983, D7; Kenneth R. Harney, "Interest Rates May Rise Along with Economy," *Washington Post*, January 15, 1983, F1.

52. Rich Jaroslovsky, "Economic Upturn Aids President's Popularity, but It Is Not Panacea," *Wall Street Journal*, April 28, 1983, 1. Cited in Kernell (1997, 224).

53. Ronald Reagan, "Meeting with Editors from the Midwestern Region," May 10, 1982, *Public Papers of the Presidents, 1982 Book 1* (Washington, DC: Government Printing Office, 1983).

54. Hedrick Smith, "Deficit in the $185 Billion Range Expected in 1984 Reagan Budget," *New York Times*, January 18, 1983, A1.

55. Robert D. Hershey Jr., "President to Seek Contingent Taxes," *New York Times*, January 26, 1983, A15.

56. These addresses include the State of the Union on January 25, a national radio address entitled "Fiscal Year 1984 Budget" on January 29, "Remarks and a Question-and-Answer Session at the St. Louis Regional Commerce and Growth Association" on February 1, "Remarks and a Question-and-Answer Session via Satellite to the Young Presidents Organization" on February 14. All of these addresses are in the *Public Papers of the Presidents, 1983 Book 1* (Washington, DC: Government Printing Office, 1984).

57. Ibid.

58. Cambridge Reports, Research International survey conducted in January of 1983. The full question was "Last month, in his State of the Union and Budget Messages to Congress, President (Ronald) Reagan proposed the following actions as ways

of reducing these budget deficits for the next few years. Please tell me whether you would favor or oppose each of them. . . . Putting in effect a standby program of increased personal and business taxes—as well as a special tax on oil—for the years 1986–88."

59. Roper survey conducted January 8–22, 1983. The full question was, "A 5% cut in income taxes took effect in October 1981, and another 10% cut in income taxes took effect this past July. An additional 10% cut in income taxes is due to take effect this coming July. Do you think next July's tax cut should be put into effect despite the size of the government deficit, or do you think next July's tax cut should be cancelled to help reduce the deficit?"

REFERENCES

Brody, Richard A., and Lee Sigelman. 1983. "Presidential Popularity and Presidential Elections: An Update and Extension." *Public Opinion Quarterly* 47: 325–28.

Cameron, Charles M. 2000. *Veto Bargaining: President and the Politics of Negative Power*. Cambridge, UK: Cambridge University Press.

Cohen, Jeffrey E. 1997. *Presidential Responsiveness and Public Policy-Making: The Public and the Policies that Presidents Choose*. Ann Arbor: University of Michigan Press.

Dallek, Robert. 1984. *Ronald Reagan: The Politics of Symbolism*. Cambridge, MA: Harvard University Press.

Deibel, Terry L. 1987. *Presidents, Public Opinion, and Power: The Nixon, Carter and Reagan Years*. New York: Foreign Policy Association.

Denton, Robert E., Jr., and Mary E. Stuckey. 1994. "A Communication Model of Presidential Campaigns: A 1992 Overview." In *The 1992 Presidential Campaign: A Communication Perspective*, ed. Robert E. Denton, Jr., 1–42. Westport, CT: Praeger.

Feldstein, Martin. 1994. Introductory chapter of *American Economic Policy in the 1980s*, ed. Martin Feldstein, 1–79. Chicago: University of Chicago Press.

Genovese, Michael A. 1994. "Jimmy Carter and the Age of Limits: Presidential Power in a Time of Decline and Diffusion." In *The Presidency and Domestic Politics of Jimmy Carter*, ed. Herbert D. Rosenbaum and Alexej Ugrinsky, 187–221. Westport, CT: Greenwood Press.

Hargrove, Erwin C. 1988. *Jimmy Carter as President: Leadership and the Politics of the Public Good*. Baton Rouge: Louisiana State University Press.

Hogan, Joseph. 1990. *The Reagan Years: The Record in Presidential Leadership*. Ed. Joseph Hogan. New York: Manchester University Press.

Jones, Charles O. 1988. *The Trusteeship Presidency: Jimmy Carter the United States Congress*. Baton Rouge: Louisiana State University Press.

Kaufman, Burton Ira. 1993. *The Presidency of James Earl Carter, Jr*. Lawrence: University Press of Kansas.

Kernell, Samuel. 1997. *Going Public: New Strategies of Presidential Leadership*, 3rd ed. Washington, DC: Congressional Quarterly Press.

Meese, Edwin III. 1992. *With Reagan: The Inside Story*. Washington, DC: Regnery Gateway.

Mervin, David. 1996. *George Bush and the Guardianship Presidency*. New York: St. Martin's Press.

Pemberton, William E. 1997. *Exit with Honor: The Life and Presidency of Ronald Reagan*. Armonk, NY: M. E. Sharpe.

Ragsdale, Lyn. 1998. *Vital Statistics on the Presidency: Washington to Clinton.* Washington, DC: Congressional Quarterly, Inc.

Sigelman, Lee. 1979. "Presidential Popularity and Presidential Elections." *Public Opinion Quarterly* 43: 532–34.

Skidmore, David. 1996. *Reversing Course: Carter's Foreign Policy, Domestic Politics, and the Failure of Reform.* Nashville, TN: Vanderbilt University Press.

Skowronek, Stephen. 1993. *The Politics Presidents Make: Leadership from John Adams to George Bush.* Cambridge, MA: Harvard University Press.

6.4

WILLIAM G. HOWELL

From *Power without Persuasion:*
The Politics of Direct Presidential Action

Presidents have increasingly used unilateral actions, such as executive orders, to make policy independent of Congress. Howell describes the trends in these unilateral actions and offers a historical explanation. Over the course of the twentieth century, both Congress and the Supreme Court permitted presidents more latitude because the problems they faced became more complicated.

PRESIDENTIAL POWER IN THE MODERN ERA

. . . Throughout the twentieth century, presidents have used their powers of unilateral action to intervene into a whole host of policy arenas. Examples abound:

- During World War II, Roosevelt issued dozens of executive orders that nationalized aviation plants, shipbuilding companies, thousands of coal companies and a shell plant—all clear violations of the Fifth Amendment's "taking" clause. The courts overturned none of these actions.
- With executive order 9066, Roosevelt ordered the evacuation, relocation, and internment of over 110,000 Japanese Americans living on the West Coast.
- In 1948, Truman desegregated the military via executive order 9981.
- After congressional efforts to construct a program that would send American youth abroad to do charitable work faltered three years in a row, Kennedy unilaterally created the Peace Corps and then financed it using discretionary funds.
- Johnson instituted the first affirmative action policy with executive order 11246.
- Preempting Congress, Nixon used an executive order to design the Environmental Protection Agency not as an independent commission, as Congress would have liked, but as an agency beholden directly to the president.
- By subjecting government regulations to cost-benefit analyses with executive order 12291, Reagan centralized powers of regulatory review.
- In 1992, George Bush federalized the National Guard and used its members to quell the Los Angeles riots.

While the majority of unilateral directives may not resonate quite so loudly in the telling of American history, a growing proportion involve substantive policy matters. Rather than being simply "daily grist-of-the-mill diplomatic matter," presidential directives have become instruments by which presidents actually set all sorts of consequential domestic and foreign policy (Paige 1977). . . .

Between 1920 and 1998, presidents issued 10,203 executive orders, or roughly 130 annually. As might be expected, presidents issued more civil service orders than orders in any other policy arena. On average, presidents issued thirty-three such orders, most of which dealt with the management of government personnel. This proportion, however, declined precipitously after World War II, when executive orders were no longer used to perform such trivial administrative practices as exempting individuals from mandatory retirement requirements.

Outside of those orders relating directly to the civil service, each year presidents issued on average thirty-two orders in foreign affairs, another eight on social welfare policy, sixteen on regulations of the domestic economy, and fully thirty-three that concerned the management of public lands and energy policy, though the number in this last category has declined markedly over the past few decades. The majority of orders, it seems, have substantive policy content, both foreign and domestic.

These figures only concern executive orders, which represent but one tool among many that presidents have at their disposal. When negotiating with foreign countries, presidents can bypass the treaty ratification process by issuing executive agreements; not surprisingly, the ratio of executive agreements to treaties, which hovered between zero and one in the nineteenth century, now consistently exceeds thirty (King and Ragsdale 1988). If presidents choose to avoid the reporting requirements Congress has placed on executive orders, they can repackage their policies as executive memoranda, determinations, administrative directives, or proclamations. And if they prefer to keep their decisions entirely secret, they can issue national security directives, which neither Congress nor the public has an opportunity to review (Cooper 2002).

The U.S. Constitution does not explicitly recognize any of these policy vehicles. Over the years, presidents have invented them, citing national security or expediency as justification. Taken as a whole, though, they represent one of the most striking, and underappreciated, aspects of presidential power in the modern era. Born from a truly expansive reading of Article II powers, these policy mechanisms have radically impacted how public policy is made in America today. The president's powers of unilateral action exert just as much influence over public policy, and in some cases more, than the formal powers that presidency scholars have examined so carefully over the past several decades.

■   ■   ■

If we want to account for the influence that presidents wield over the construction of public policy, we must begin to pay serious attention to the president's capacity to create law on his own.

"Presidential Power Is the Power to Persuade"

The image of presidents striking out on their own to conduct a war on terrorism or revamp civil rights policies or reconstruct the federal bureaucracy stands in stark relief to scholarly literatures that equate executive power with persuasion and, consequently, place presidents at the peripheries of the lawmaking process.

Richard Neustadt sets the terms by which every student of American politics has come to understand presidential power in the modern era. When thinking about presidents since FDR, Neustadt argues, "weak remains the word with which to start" (1991 [1960], xix). Presidents are much like Shakespearean kings, marked more by tragedy than grandeur. Each is held captive by world events, by competing domestic interests and foreign policy pressures, by his party, his cabinet, the media, a fickle public and partisan Congress. To make matters worse, the president exercises little control over any of these matters—current events and the political actors who inhabit them regularly disregard his expressed wishes. As a result, the pursuit of the president's policy agenda is marked more by compromise than conviction; and his eventual success or failure (as determined by either the public at the next election or historians over time) ultimately rests with others, and their willingness to extend a helping hand.

The public now expects presidents to accomplish far more than their formal powers alone permit. This has been especially true since the New Deal, when the federal government took charge of the nation's economy, commerce, and the social welfare of its citizens. Now presidents must address almost every conceivable social and economic problem, from the impact of summer droughts on midwestern farmers to the spread of nuclear weapons in the former Soviet Union. Armed with little more than the powers to propose and veto legislation and recommend the appointment of bureaucrats and judges, however, modern presidents appear doomed to failure from the very beginning. As one recent treatise on presidential. "greatness" puts it, "modern presidents bask in the honors of the more formidable office that emerged from the New Deal, but they find themselves navigating a treacherous and lonely path, subject to a volatile political process that makes popular and enduring achievement unlikely" (Landy and Milkis 2000, 197).

If a president is to enjoy any measure of success, Neustadt counsels, he must master the art of persuasion. Indeed, according to Neustadt, power and persuasion are synonymous. The ability to persuade, to convince other political actors that his interests are their own, defines political power and is the key to presidential achievement. Power is about bargaining and negotiating; about brokering deals and trading promises; and about cajoling legislators, bureaucrats, and justices to do things that the president cannot accomplish on his own. . . . The president wields influence when he manages to enhance his bargaining stature and build governing coalitions; and the principal way to accomplish as much, Neustadt claims, is to draw upon the bag of experiences, skills, and qualities that he brings to the office.

Intentionally or not, Neustadt set off a behavioral revolution. . . . Self-confidence, an instinct for power, an exalted reputation within the Washington community, and prestige among the general public were considered the foundations of presidential success. Without certain personal qualities, presidents could not hope to build the coalitions necessary for action. Power was contingent upon persuasion, and persuasion was a function of all the personal qualities individual presidents bore; and so, the argument ran, what the presidency was at any moment critically depended upon who filled the office.

By these scholars' accounts, a reliance on formal powers actually signals weakness. What distinguishes great presidents is not a willingness to act upon the formal powers of the presidency but an ability to rally support precisely when and where such formal powers are lacking. As Neustadt argues, formal powers constitute a "painful last resort, a forced response to the exhaustion of other remedies, suggestive less of mastery than of failure—the failure of attempts to gain an end by softer means" (1991 [1960], 24). Presidents who veto bill after bill (think Ford) do so because their powers to persuade have faltered. The presidents who effectively communicate (Reagan) or who garner strong professional reputations (Roosevelt) stand out in the eyes of history.

Although the notion of the personal presidency dominated the field for decades, its influence is on the decline. The principal reason is that it no longer matches up with the facts. The personal presidency became a popular theoretical notion just as the American presidency was experiencing tremendous growth and development as an institution: in its staffing, its budget, and the powers delegated to it by Congress. As time went on, it became increasingly clear that the field needed to take more seriously the formal structures and powers that define the modern presidency.

If the personal presidency literature is correct, executive power should rise and fall according to the personal qualities of each passing president. Presidential power should expand and contract according to the individual skills and reputations that each president brings to the office. The constituent elements of the personal presidency may be important. Prestige and reputation may matter. But if we are to build a theory of presidential power, it seems reasonable to start with its most striking developments during the modern era. And these developments have little to do with the personalities of the men who, since Roosevelt, have inhabited the White House.

By virtually any objective measure, the size and importance of the "presidential branch" has steadily increased over the past century (Hart 1995). According to Thomas Cronin, "for almost 150 years the executive power of the presidency has steadily expanded" (1989, 204). Edward Corwin echoes this sentiment, arguing that "taken by and large, the history of the Presidency is a history of aggrandizement" (1957, 238). How can such trends persist if presidential powers are fundamentally personal in nature? It cannot be that the caliber of presidents today is markedly higher than a century ago, and for that reason alone presidents have managed to exert more and more influence. Does it really make sense to say that successful twentieth-century presidents (e.g., the Roosevelts or Reagan) distinguish themselves from great nineteenth-century presidents (e.g., Jackson, Polk, or Lincoln) by exhibiting stronger personalities? And if not, how can we argue that the roots of modern presidential power are fundamentally personal in nature? While Neustadt may illuminate short-term fluctuations at the boundaries of presidential influence—skill in the art of persuasion surely plays some part in political power—he cannot possibly explain the general growth of presidential power.

During the past twenty years, scholars have revisited the more formal components of presidential power. Work on the institutional presidency has regained the stature it held in political science during the first half of the twentieth century. This work is far more rigorous than the personal presidency literature and, for that matter, the institutional literature's earlier incarnations. A science of politics is finally taking hold of presidential studies: empirical tests now are commonplace; theoretical assumptions are clearly specified; and hypotheses are subject to independent corroboration. Perhaps more important than its methodological contributions, though, the institutional literature has successfully refocused scholarly attention on the office of the presidency and the features that make it distinctly modern: its staff and budget, the powers and responsibilities delegated to it by Congress, and the growth of agencies and commissions that collect and process information within it.

Nothing in the institutional literature, however, fundamentally challenges Neustadt's original claim that "presidential power is the power to persuade" (1991 [1960], 11). Scholars continue to equate presidential power with an ability to bargain, negotiate, change minds, turn votes, and drive legislative agendas through Congress. Not surprisingly, the president remains secondary throughout this work. He continues to play second fiddle to the people who make real policy decisions: committee members writing bills, congressional representatives offering amendments, bureaucrats enforcing laws, judges deciding cases.

To legislate, to build a record of accomplishments about which to boast at the next election, and to find their place in history, presidents above all rely upon Congress—so the institutional literature argues. Without Congress's active support, and the endorsement of its members, presidents cannot hope to achieve much at all. . . . The struggle for votes is perennial; and success is always fleeting. Should Congress lock up, or turn away, the president has little or no recourse. Ultimately, presidents depend upon Congress to delegate authority, ratify executive decisions, and legislate when, and where, presidents cannot act at all.

■ ■ ■

Because of his unique position within a system of separated powers, the president has numerous opportunities to take independent action, with or without the expressed consent of either Congress or the courts. Sometimes he does so by issuing executive orders, proclamations, or executive agreements; other times by handing down general memoranda to agency heads; and still other times by dispensing national security directives. The number of these unilateral directives, and of opportunities to use them, has literally skyrocketed during the modern era (Moe and Howell 1999a, 1999b). While presidents freely exercise these powers during periods of national crises, as the events following September 11th have made clear, they also rely upon executive orders and executive agreements during periods of relative calm, effecting policy changes that never would survive the legislative process. And to the extent that presidents use these "power tools of the presidency" more now than they did a century ago, the ability to act unilaterally speaks to what is distinctively "modern" about the modern presidency (Cooper 1997, 2002).

Rather than hoping to influence at the margins what other political actors do, the president can make all kinds of public policies without the formal consent of Congress. While the growth of the presidency as an institution (its staffs, budgets, departments, and agencies) augments presidential power, it is the ability to set policy unilaterally that deserves our immediate and sustained attention.

■ ■ ■

Thinking about Unilateral Powers

From the beginning, it is worth highlighting what makes unilateral powers distinctive. For the ability to act unilaterally is unlike any other power formally granted the president. Two features stand out.

The most important is that the president moves policy first and thereby places upon Congress and the courts the burden of revising a new political landscape. Rather than waiting at the end of an extended legislative process to sign or veto a bill, the president simply sets new policy and leaves it up to Congress and the courts to respond. If they choose not to retaliate, either by passing a law or ruling against the president, then the president's order stands. Only by taking (or credibly threatening to take) positive action can either adjoining institution limit the president's unilateral powers.

. . . By moving first, and anticipating the moves of future actors, legislators of all stripes and in very different political systems influence the kinds of policies governments produce. . . . But gains to the president are twice over. While agenda setters in Congress only propose bills, the president moves first and creates legally binding public policies. And he does so without ever having to wait on coalitions subsequently forming, committee chairs cooperating, or party leaders endorsing.

The second important feature of unilateral powers is that the president acts alone. There is no need to rally majorities, compromise with adversaries, or wait for some interest group to bring a case to court. Rather than depending upon Congress to enact his legislative agendas, the president frequently can strike out on his own, occasionally catching even his closest advisors off guard (recall Clinton's unilateral decision to bomb Iraq in the fall of 1998, the day before his scheduled impeachment hearing in the House Judiciary Committee). As the chief of state, the modern president is in a unique position to lead, to define a national agenda, and to impose his will in more and more areas of governance.

■　　■　　■

The ability to move first and act alone, then, distinguishes unilateral powers from all other sources of influence. In this sense, Neustadt is turned upside-down, for unilateral action is the virtual antithesis of bargaining and persuading. Here, presidents just act; their power does not hinge upon their capacity to "convince [political actors] that what the White House wants of them is what they ought to do for their sake and for their authority" (Neustadt 1991 [1960], 30). To make policy, presidents need not secure the formal consent of Congress, the active support of bureaucrats, or the official approval of justices. Instead, presidents simply set public policy and dare others to counter. For as long as Congress lacks the votes (usually two-thirds of both chambers) to overturn him, the president can be confident that his policy will stand.

The presidency literature's traditional distinction between formal and informal powers does not contribute much insight here. Because the Constitution does not mandate them, powers of unilateral action cannot be considered formal. It is by reference to what presidents have done (or gotten away with) that these powers take form. But nor are these discretionary powers informal. They are not rooted in personal qualities that vary with each passing president. Rather, these powers emerge from specific institutional advantages within the office of the presidency itself: its structure, resources, and location in a system of separated powers. The promise of a sustained analysis of unilateral powers, then, is great. To the extent that presidents act unilaterally with increasing frequency and effect in the postwar era, an institutional theory of unilateral action enables scholars to see beyond Neustadt's original conception of presidential influence in the modern era.

The Tool Chest

. . . Presidents in . . . times have manufactured a number of policy instruments that give shape and meaning to . . . prerogative powers. The most common include executive orders, proclamations, national security directives, and executive agreements. There are few hard and fast rules about how policies are classified, affording presidents a fair measure of liberty to select the instrument that best serves their objectives. Still, some basic distinctions generally apply.

Among all unilateral directives, "executive orders combine the highest levels of substance, discretion, and direct presidential involvement" (Mayer 2001, 35). Executive orders, for the most part, instruct government officials and administrative agencies to take specific actions with regard to both domestic and foreign affairs. "Executive orders are directives issued by the president to officers of the executive branch, requiring them to take an action, stop a certain type of activity, alter policy, change management practices, or accept a delegation of authority under which they will henceforth be responsible for the implementation of law" (Cooper 2002, 16). But while presidents direct executive orders to subordinates within the executive branch, the impact of these orders is felt well beyond the boundaries of the federal government. . . . Through executive orders, presidents have dictated the terms by which government contractors hire and fire their employees, set restrictions on where American citizens can travel abroad, frozen the financial holdings of private parties, reset trade, tariffs, and determined the kinds of recreational activities that are allowed on public lands.

If executive orders are typically directed to officials within the federal government, presidential proclamations almost always target individuals and groups outside of the government. Because Article II of the Constitution does not endow the president with clear and immediate authority over private parties (as it does over the federal bureaucracy), it is not surprising that proclamations tend to be less consequential than executive orders, most involving ceremonial and commemorative affairs. There are, however, numerous exceptions, such as Nixon's 1971 proclamations and orders temporarily freezing all wages, rents, and prices as part of the national economic stabilization program; Ford's 1973 proclamation granting pardons to draft dodgers; and Carter's 1980 proclamations imposing new surcharges on imported oil.

■   ■   ■

Even the advent of the Cold War can be traced back to a national security directive. Issued in April 1950, N.S.C. 68 emphasized the historical importance of the mounting conflict between the United States and Soviet Union. The document, drafted by the director of the State Department's policy-planning staff, Paul Nitze, was a call to arms and defined the nation's military and political objectives as it waged an ongoing struggle against the world's only other superpower. . . . While it met some initial resistance within the Truman and Eisenhower administrations, N.S.C. 68, more than any other document, established the guiding doctrine for successive presidents' Cold War foreign policy.

Executive agreements stand apart from these other directives. While executive orders, proclamations, and (to a lesser degree) national security directives all are unilateral counterparts to legislation, executive agreements provide presidents with an alternative to the treaty ratification process. Rather than having to secure the consent of two-thirds of the Senate before entering into a bi- or multilateral agreement with foreign nations, presidents can use executive agreements to unilaterally commit the United States to deals involving such issues as international trade, ocean fishing rights, open air space, environmental standards, and immigration patterns. While most of these agreements concern very specific (and often technical) matters, the sheer number issued during the modern era has increased at such an astronomical rate that collectively they now constitute a vital means by which presidents unilaterally affect public policy.

When setting public policy, presidents frequently issue combinations of these various policy directives. To force the integration of schools in Little Rock, Arkansas, Eisenhower simultaneously issued a proclamation and an executive order. Carter relied upon a series of executive orders and executive agreements to negotiate the Iran Hostage Crisis. Presiding over World War II, the Korean War, and the Vietnam War, Roosevelt, Truman, Johnson, and Nixon all issued a wide array of secretive orders, national security directives and otherwise. Presidents frequently use executive orders, secretarial orders, and reorganization plans to create administrative agencies and then turn to other kinds of unilateral directives—for example, administrative directives, findings and determinations, and regulations—to monitor their behavior. The ease with which presidents can mix and match these unilateral directives to advance their policy goals is considerable.

The Legality of Unilateral Powers

The first Court challenge to a presidential order, *Little v. Barreme* (1804) concerned the legality of a seizure of a Danish ship, the *Flying Fish*. George Little, the captain of the *U.S.S. Boston*, had intercepted the ship at sea. At the time, Captain Little was complying with a John Adams presidential order that the Navy seize any and all ships sailing to or from French ports. Previously, however, Congress had only authorized the seizure of frigates sailing to French ports. Because the Danish brig was sailing *from* a French port and not *to* one (it was headed from Jérémie to St. Thomas), the Court for the first time had to resolve a discrepancy between a presidential order and congressional statute.

In a unanimous ruling written by Chief Justice John Marshall, the Court declared that had Adams' order stood alone, the Navy's actions would be constitutional. Because Congress had enacted a more restrictive statute, however, the Court was forced to rule in favor of the Danish captain. "Congressional policy announced in a statute necessarily prevails over inconsistent presidential orders. . . . Presidential orders, even those issued as Commander in Chief, are subject to restrictions by Congress." Marshall subsequently ordered Captain Little to pay damages. More importantly, though, Marshall established the clear principle that when an executive order blatantly conflicts with a law, the law prevails.

During the rest of the nineteenth century, the federal courts considered a host of challenges to unilateral directives issued by presidents, most of which involved military orders. It was not until the 1930s that the Supreme Court formally recognized the president's power to act unilaterally. Three cases—*United States v. Curtiss-Wright* (1936); *United States v. Belmont* (1937); and *United States v. Pink* (1942)—made the difference (Schubert 1973, 107).

Curtiss-Wright centrally involved the constitutionality of an executive agreement that forbade the sale of arms to countries involved in armed conflict. When it sold fifteen machine guns to the government of Bolivia, Curtiss-Wright Export Corporation was charged with violating the agreement. As part of its defense, the company argued that Congress had "abdicated its essential functions and delegated them to the Executive," and for that reason, the Court should overturn the executive agreement. Instead, the Supreme Court, in an oft-cited phrase, deemed the president the "sole organ of the federal government in the field of international relations" and upheld the constitutionality of this particular delegation of authority. Doing so, it formally recognized his legal right to issue executive agreements.

In *United States v. Belmont,* the Supreme Court extended this right to executive orders. When Russia reneged on debts owed to the United States in the 1930s, President Roosevelt seized Russian financial assets held in American banks. Arguing that Roosevelt's actions violated New York State law, a Russian investor asked the Court to overturn the executive order and to award compensation for his losses. The Court, however, refused. Doing so, it equated an executive order with federal law and reaffirmed its preeminence over state law.

The Supreme Court extended this reasoning to executive agreements in *United States v. Pink,* which again involved the seizure of Russian assets in American banks. This time, however, the focus concerned an exchange between the president and the Russian government known as the Litvinov Assignment. In a letter to Roosevelt, People's Commissar for Foreign Affairs Maxim Litvinov relinquished certain Russian claims to assets of Russian companies in New York banks. Roosevelt subsequently acknowledged the reassignment of property claims. In *Pink,* the question before the Court centered on the legal authority of this exchange. Ultimately, the Court ruled that because executive agreements have the same status as treaties, and because both override state laws, the plaintiffs could not use New York State law to try to recover their lost assets.

Collectively, *Curtiss-Wright, Belmont,* and *Pink* firmly established the president's authority to issue directives involving "external affairs." Their distinction between foreign and domestic policy, however, subsequently blurred. And for good reason. The list of exceptions to any definition of "foreign" or "domestic" policy is sufficiently long as to make the definitions themselves unworkable as elements of jurisprudence. "The original constitutional understanding that in domestic affairs Congress would make the law and presidents would see to its enforcement had never worked in practice and by the early 1990s it had largely been abandoned" (McDonald 1994, 314). The courts now fully recognize the president's power to issue executive orders and agreements that concern both foreign and domestic policy. Indeed, powers of unilateral action have become a veritable fixture of the American presidency in the modern era.

Writing Public Policy

Much can happen between the issuance of a presidential order and its implementation. Opportunities for shirking abound. Administrative agencies may read their mandates selectively; they may ignore especially objectionable provisions; they may report false or misleading information about initiatives' successes and failures. As we have already noted, the executive branch assuredly does not reduce to the president himself. Bureaucrats enjoy a fair measure of autonomy to do as they please.

Demanding a policy change does not make it so. As Neustadt himself forcefully argued, orders handed down from on high are not always self-executing (1991 [1960], 10–28). In 1948, for instance, Truman issued an executive order demanding the desegregation of the military, but decades passed before the outcome was finally realized. Presidents are engaged in a constant struggle to ensure compliance among members of the executive branch, and to advance the realization of their policy interests. Presidents appoint high-ranking officials who share their worldview, and whenever possible, presidents try to rally the support of their subordinates. This has important consequences for our understanding of presidential power; for when it comes to the implementation of public policy (whether enacted as a federal statute or issued as a unilateral directive), the power modern presidents wield very much depends upon their ability to persuade.

■   ■   ■

[W]hile presidents must build and sustain coalitions to pass laws, they can unilaterally issue policy directives over the vocal objections of congressional majorities. As one political observer instructs, "Forget Capitol Hill deliberations and back-room negotiations with industry titans. No need for endless debate and deal-making. For a president, an executive order can be as powerful as a law—and considerably easier to achieve." In the political fight over the content of public policy, presidents regularly exert power without persuasion.

■   ■   ■

7. CONCLUSION

■   ■   ■

Macrotrends in unilateral policy making

Since George Washington issued the Neutrality Proclamation in 1793, presidents have relied upon their unilateral powers to effect important policy changes. In the nineteenth century, Jefferson followed up with the Louisiana Purchase and Lincoln with the Emancipation Proclamation. In the early twentieth century, Theodore Roosevelt established the national parks system and Wilson issued more than 1,700 executive orders to guide the nation through World War I.

For the past fifty years, however, the trajectory of unilateral policy making has noticeably increased. While it was relatively rare, and for the most part inconsequential, during the eighteenth and nineteenth centuries, unilateral policy making has become an integral feature of the modern presidency. Presidents issue more unilateral directives today than ever before, steadily expanding their influence over all kinds of public policies, foreign and domestic. While there remain important fluctuations from year to year, and from administration to administration, the time-series of significant executive orders and executive agreements unmistakably rises.

In part, this is due to the overwhelming demands placed upon modern presidents. The public holds presidents responsible for all kinds of activities that previously either did not concern the federal government or rested solely within the domain of Congress. Presidents now develop policies on medical practices, racial discrimination, social welfare, labor and management relations, international trade, and education—areas that few presidents, prior to FDR, ever addressed. Indeed, it is difficult to think of a single area of governance that modern presidents can safely ignore. Modern presidents, in this sense, do more simply because the public expects them to.

In addition, presidential powers have expanded over the past half-century because the checks placed on them by Congress have subsided. As political parties have weakened, subcommittees have proliferated, and ideological divisions within Congress have heightened, Congress's ability to legislate has waned. So much so, in fact, that gridlock, while not constant, has become "a basic fact of U.S. lawmaking" (Krehbiel 1998, 4). This development has important implications for presidential power. As Congress weakens, the check it places on presidential power relaxes, and new opportunities arise for the president to strike out on his own. An expansion of presidential power then signals a shift in the overall division of powers—tipping the balance in favor of the president, and against Congress.

Two additional factors probably contributed to the overall increase in unilateral policy making during the latter half of the twentieth century. First, the time-series takes off in the late 1930s, just after the Supreme Court issued a series of rulings—*United States v. Curtiss-Wright* (1936); *United States v. Belmont* (1937); and *United States v. Pink* (1942)—that collectively fortified the president's legal authority to issue executive orders and executive agreements. With the official sanctioning of the Court, modern presidents proceeded with a greater measure of confidence when issuing executive orders and other unilateral directives. Second, many of these orders either created new administrative agencies or directed existing agencies to perform new functions. In this sense, the general trajectory of the significant executive order time-series maps the steady growth of the administrative state. Modern presidents did more simply because more needed to be done. Compared to their predecessors, modern presidents oversee more agencies that employ more employees that perform more tasks. As a consequence, it is little wonder that modern presidents rely upon the unilateral powers with greater frequency.

These trends, however, need not continue forever. There is nothing in the logic of the unilateral politics model that requires presidential power to increase monotonically over time. Quite the contrary, should a new consensus about policy matters emerge in Congress and legislative productivity displace gridlock, opportunities for presidents to act unilaterally may decline. Similarly, should executive actions attract heightened public scrutiny, judges may feel emboldened to overturn presidents with greater frequency.

BIBLIOGRAPHY

Cooper, Phillip. 2002. *By Order of the President: The Use and Abuse of Executive Direct Action*. Lawrence: University Press of Kansas.

———. 1997. "Power Tools for an Effective and Responsible Presidency." *Administration and Society* 29(5): 529–56.

Corwin, Edward. 1957. *The President, Office and Powers, 1787–1948: History and Analysis of Practice and Opinion*. New York: New York University Press.

Cronin, Thomas. 1989. *Inventing the American Presidency*. Lawrence: University of Kansas Press.

Hart, John. 1995. *The Presidential Branch From Washington to Clinton*. Chatham NJ: Chatham House Publishers, Inc.

King, Gary, and Lyn Ragsdale. 1988. *The Elusive Executive: Discovering Statistical Patterns in the Presidency*. Washington, DC: Congressional Quarterly Press.

Krehbiel, Keith. 1998. *Pivotal Politics: A Theory of U.S. Lawmaking*. Chicago: University of Chicago Press.

Landy, Marc, and Sidney Milkis. 2000. *Presidential Greatness*. Lawrence: University of Kansas Press.

Mayer, Kenneth. 2001. *With the Stroke of a Pen: Executive Orders and Presidentia Power*. Princeton, NJ: Princeton University Press.

McDonald, Forrest. 1994. *The American Presidency: An Intellectual History*. Lawrence: University of Kansas Press.

Moe, Terry, and William Howell. 1999a. "The Presidential Power of Unilateral Action." *Journal of Law, Economics and Organization* 15(1): 132–79.

————. 1999b. "Unilateral Action and Presidential Power: A Theory." *Presidential Studies Quarterly* 29(4): 850–72.

Neustadt, Richard E. 1991 [1960]. *Presidential Power and the Modern Presidents.* New York: Free Press.

Paige, Joseph. 1977. *The Law Nobody Knows: Enlargement of the Constitution—Treaties and Executive Agreements.* New York: Vantage Press.

Schubert, Glendon. 1973. *The Presidency in the Courts.* New York: Da Capo Press.

6.5

SAMUEL KERNELL

From *Going Public: New Strategies of Presidential Leadership*

Over the course of the twentieth century, American presidents increasingly spoke directly to the people rather than to news reporters or through press releases. Today, presidents spend a lot of their time giving public speeches, but this behavior was rare 100 years ago. Kernell argues that this increase has given presidents more leverage when bargaining with Congress and makes sense in an age with a more educated population and improved means of travel and communication.

INTRODUCTION: GOING PUBLIC IN THEORY AND PRACTICE

■　■　■

I call the approach to presidential leadership that has come into vogue at the White House "going public." It is a strategy whereby a president promotes himself and his policies in Washington by appealing directly to the American public for support. Forcing compliance from fellow Washingtonians by going over their heads to enlist constituents' pressure is a tactic that was known but seldom attempted during the first half of the century. Theodore Roosevelt probably first enunciated the strategic principle of going public when he described the presidency as the "bully pulpit." Moreover, he occasionally put theory into practice with public appeals for his Progressive Party reforms. During the next thirty years, other presidents also periodically summoned public support to help them in their dealings with Congress. Perhaps the most famous such instance is Woodrow Wilson's ill-fated whistle-stop tour of the country on behalf of his League of Nations treaty. Equally noteworthy, historically, is Franklin D. Roosevelt's series of radio "fireside chats," which were designed less to subdue congressional opposition than to remind politicians of his continuing national mandate for the New Deal.

These historical instances are significant in large part because they are rare. Unlike Richard Nixon, who thought it important "to spread the White House around" by traveling and speaking extensively,[1] these earlier presidents were largely confined to Washington and obliged to address the country through the nation's newspapers. The concept and legitimizing precedents of going public may have been established during these years, but the emergence

243

of presidents who *routinely* did so to promote their policies outside Washington awaited the development of modern systems of transportation and mass communications. Going public should be appreciated as a strategic adaptation to the information age.

The regularity with which recent presidents have sought public backing for their Washington dealings has altered the way politicians both inside and outside the White House regard the office. . . .

Presidential Theory

Going public has become routine. This was not always the case. After World War I Congress refused to support President Wilson's League of Nations, a peace treaty the president himself had helped negotiate. In this instance Congress determined to amend the treaty and a president equally determined to finalize the agreement the other countries had ratified left him with little choice but to go public to try to marshal public opinion to force the Senate's agreement. Today our information-age presidents opt to go public regardless of the political climate in Washington.

There is another reason to systematically study this leadership strategy. Compared with many other aspects of the modern presidency, scholarship has only recently directed its attention toward this feature of the president's repertoire. Although going public had not become a keystone of presidential leadership in the 1950s and 1960s, when much of the influential scholarship on the subject was written, sufficient precedents were available for scholars to consider its potential for presidential leadership in the future.

Probably the main reason traditional presidential scholarship short-changed going public is its fundamental incompatibility with bargaining. Presidential power is the "power to bargain," Richard E. Neustadt taught a generation of students of the presidency.[2] When Neustadt published his definitive study of presidential leadership in 1960, the "bargaining president" had already become a centerpiece of pluralist theories of American politics. Nearly a decade earlier, Robert A. Dahl and Charles E. Lindblom had described the politician in America generically as "the human embodiment of a bargaining society." They made a special point to include the president in writing that despite his possessing "more hierarchical controls than any other single figure in the government . . . like everyone else . . . the President must bargain constantly."[3] Since Neustadt's landmark treatise, other major works on the presidency have reinforced and elaborated this theme.[4]

■   ■   ■

Going public entails public posturing. To the extent that it fixes the president's bargaining position, posturing makes subsequent compromise with other politicians more difficult. Because negotiators must be prepared to yield some of their clients' preferences to make a deal, bargaining proverbially proceeds best behind closed doors. Consider the difficulty Ronald Reagan's widely publicized challenge "My tax proposal is a line drawn in dirt" posed for subsequent budget negotiations in Washington[5] Similarly, during his nationally televised State of the Union address in 1994, President Bill Clinton sought to repair his reputation as someone too willing to compromise away his principles by declaring to the assembled joint session of Congress, "If you send me [health care] legislation that does not guarantee every American private health insurance that can never be taken away, you will force me to take this pen, veto the legislation, and we'll come right back here and start all over again."[6] Not only did these declarations threaten to cut away any middle ground on which a compromise might be constructed, they probably stiffened the resolve of the president's adversaries, some of whom would later be needed to pass the administration's legislative program.

. . . [P]ossibly most injurious to bargaining, going public undermines the legitimacy of other politicians. It usurps their prerogatives of office, denies their role as representatives, and questions their claim to reflect the interests of their constituents. For a traditional bargaining stance with the president to be restored, these politicians would first have to reestablish parity, probably at a cost of conflict with the White House.[7]

Given these fundamental incompatibilities, one may further speculate that by spoiling the bargaining environment, going public renders the president's future influence ever more dependent upon his ability to generate popular support for himself and his policies. The degree to which a president draws upon public opinion determines the kind of leader he will be.

■   ■   ■

THE GROWTH OF GOING PUBLIC

■   ■   ■

Trends in Going Public

Going public can take a variety of forms. The most conspicuous is the formal, ceremonial occasion, such as an inaugural address or a State of the Union message, when official duty places the president prominently before the nation. Going public may, however, involve no more than a pregnant aside to a news reporter. This sort of casual, impromptu gesture eludes systematic analysis, but speeches, travel, and appearances—all of which take place in public view and therefore can be easily counted—form a good record of significant events with which to measure the rise of going public. Each of these nonexclusive activities can be further divided according to its locale or prominence.[8]

■   ■   ■

Figure 1 shows that until the 1960s, the average yearly numbers of major and minor addresses had grown steadily since Herbert Hoover's presidency. . . . The real explosion in presidential talk has occurred with minor addresses. Reagan, Carter, and Nixon on average surpassed Truman, Roosevelt, and Hoover by nearly fivefold in the use of such rhetoric. George H. W. Bush managed to

FIGURE 1 Presidential Addresses, 1929–2003 (Yearly Averages for First Three Years of First Term)

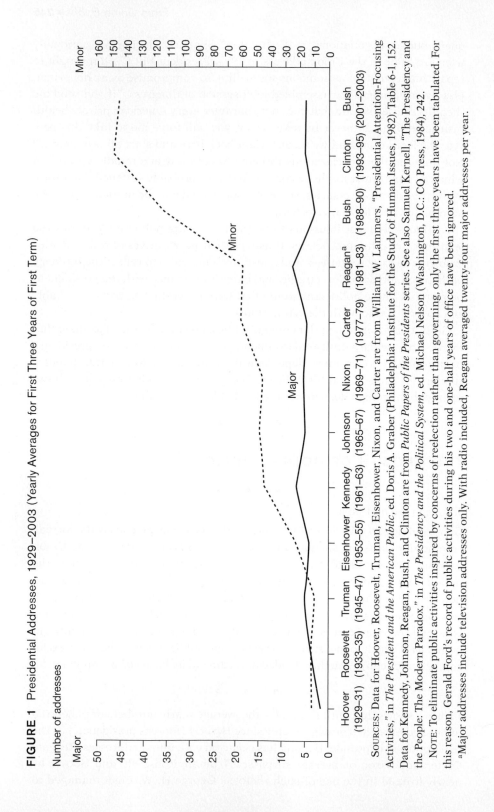

SOURCES: Data for Hoover, Roosevelt, Truman, Eisenhower, Nixon, and Carter are from William W. Lammers, "Presidential Attention-Focusing Activities," in *The President and the American Public*, ed. Doris A. Graber (Philadelphia: Institute for the Study of Human Issues, 1982), Table 6-1, 152. Data for Kennedy, Johnson, Reagan, Bush, and Clinton are from *Public Papers of the Presidents* series. See also Samuel Kernell, "The Presidency and the People: The Modern Paradox," in *The Presidency and the Political System*, ed. Michael Nelson (Washington, D.C.: CQ Press, 1984), 242.

NOTE: To eliminate public activities inspired by concerns of reelection rather than governing, only the first three years have been tabulated. For this reason, Gerald Ford's record of public activities during his two and one-half years of office have been ignored.

[a]Major addresses include television addresses only. With radio included, Reagan averaged twenty-four major addresses per year.

FIGURE 2 Public Appearances by Presidents, 1929–2003 (Yearly Averages for First Three Years of First Term)

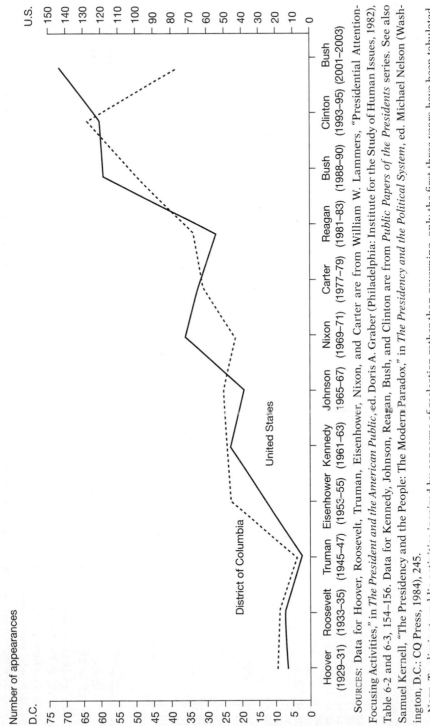

SOURCES: Data for Hoover, Roosevelt, Truman, Eisenhower, Nixon, and Carter are from William W. Lammers, "Presidential Attention-Focusing Activities," in *The President and the American Public*, ed. Doris A. Graber (Philadelphia: Institute for the Study of Human Issues, 1982), Table 6-2 and 6-3, 154–156. Data for Kennedy, Johnson, Reagan, Bush, and Clinton are from *Public Papers of the Presidents* series. See also Samuel Kernell, "The Presidency and the People: The Modern Paradox," in *The Presidency and the Political System*, ed. Michael Nelson (Washington, D.C.: CQ Press, 1984), 245.

NOTE: To eliminate public activities inspired by concerns of reelection rather than governing, only the first three years have been tabulated. For this reason, Gerald Ford's record of public activities during his two and one-half years of office have been ignored.

FIGURE 3 Days of Political Travel by Presidents, 1929–2003 (Yearly Averages for First Three Years of First Term)

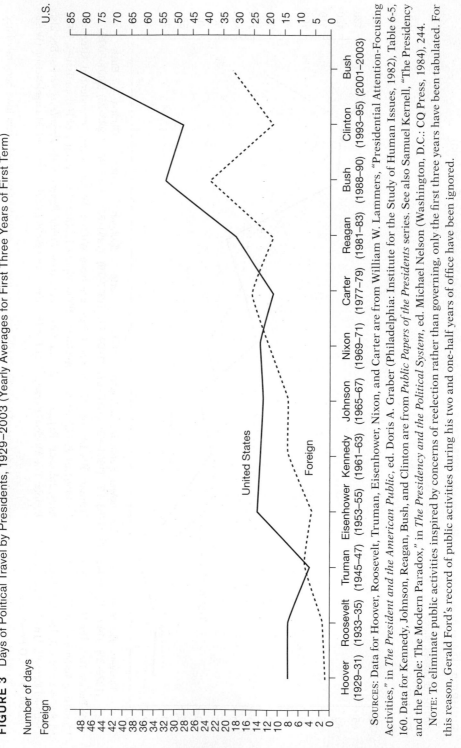

SOURCES: Data for Hoover, Roosevelt, Truman, Eisenhower, Nixon, and Carter are from William W. Lammers, "Presidential Attention-Focusing Activities," in *The President and the American Public*, ed. Doris A. Graber (Philadelphia: Institute for the Study of Human Issues, 1982), Table 6-5, 160. Data for Kennedy, Johnson, Reagan, Bush, and Clinton are from *Public Papers of the Presidents* series. See also Samuel Kernell, "The Presidency and the People," in *The Presidency and the Political System*, ed. Michael Nelson (Washington, D.C.: CQ Press, 1984), 244.

NOTE: To eliminate public activities inspired by concerns of reelection rather than governing, only the first three years have been tabulated. For this reason, Gerald Ford's record of public activities during his two and one-half years of office have been ignored.

double these already high levels of targeted addresses. During his first three years in office he averaged a minor address every three days. Clinton did Bush one better—a minor address nearly every other day, a pace almost matched by the younger Bush.

Public Appearances

Appearances are distinguished in Figure 2 by locale, those in Washington from those throughout the rest of the United States. The number of public appearances outside the city generally reflects the president's non-Washington origins and divided party control of government.

Conclusion

. . . [T]he degree to which presidents go public determines the kind of leaders they will be. Modern presidents rely upon public opinion for their leadership in Washington to an extent unknown in the early 1950s. This makes for a style of leadership in the White House that was unknown to Robert A. Dahl and Charles E. Lindblom when they described the president as "an embodiment of a bargaining society" in the early 1950s or a few years later when Richard E. Neustadt predicated presidential power exclusively on bargaining.[8]

This proposition, claiming a change in the degree of going public and inferring a change in the character of leadership, is subject to rejoinder on two fronts. Because every president since Theodore Roosevelt has sought at some moment to rally public opinion to his side, and each in his public activity has drawn on the precedents and departed only marginally from the base lines of his immediate predecessor, one can easily miss the striking degree to which presidents today go public compared with the presidents of the 1930s, 1940s, or even 1950s.

Moreover, I suspect that the increasing quantity of public activity has tended to be obscured by the varying quality of public rhetoric, which is always more memorable than the quantity. To those who compared Ronald Reagan's rhetorical talents with those of Franklin Roosevelt, little appears to have changed in the past fifty years.

■　　■　　■

Another counterargument accepts the trends examined in this chapter but holds that they have little bearing on the character of presidential leadership. The president may be a more familiar face on television, and he may spend more time on the road, but his public relations have not reduced the role of bargaining in presidential leadership.

NOTES

1. These categories of going public correspond to those developed by William W. Lammers, who was the first to systematically examine trends in presidents' public

activities (William W. Lammers, "Presidential Attention-Focusing Activities," in *The President and the American Public,* ed. Doris A. Graber [Philadelphia: Institute for the Study of Human Issues, 1982], 145–171).

To incorporate the research of Professor Lammers on the public activities of modern presidents, I adopted his coding scheme. I also consulted with him at the early stages of this study for his advice on how to code difficult cases. The present analysis, therefore, benefits from both his considerable research and good judgment.

1. The three general categories of public activities presented in Figures 1, 2, and 3 are intended to be neither mutually exclusive nor together an exhaustive classification of all public behavior. Press conferences . . . , purely ceremonial functions such as lighting the White House Christmas tree, vacation travel, and minor public activities such as White House receptions and brief remarks have been excluded from the analysis. The three categories of public activities are addresses, political travel, and appearances.

Addresses. Major addresses are those generally delivered in Washington, broadcast on television or radio, and focused on more than a narrow potential audience. Inaugural and State of the Union speeches are included in this group. Note that because of the extensive number of nationally broadcast radio addresses by President Reagan, I have separated his radio from his television addresses in Figure 1. The major address totals for Presidents Bush and Clinton also exclude radio addresses. Omitted from major addresses are presidential press conferences and purely ceremonial functions (for example, calls to astronauts and Christmas tree lighting ceremonies). . . . [Regarding] the decline in the use of press conferences: Minor addresses are all nonmajor statements made outside the White House in which the president spoke more than one thousand words. Question-and-answer sessions, even if conducted outside a formal press conference setting, are excluded.

Political travel. To distinguish purely vacation travel from work-related travel, only those travel days that involved public political activity are included in Figure 2. Moreover, to be coded as domestic political travel, the president must do more than engage in brief conversation with reporters. To be coded as political foreign travel, the travel day must include comments exceeding two hundred words, a meeting with a head of state, or attendance at an international conference, even if the president does not engage in public activity.

Appearances. Washington appearances take place away from the White House and the Executive Office Building and include all appearances in Washington and its surrounding suburbs. Brief comments with reporters are excluded from both Washington and U.S. appearances, but prepared remarks on arrival are included in the coding. Unlike Professor Lammers, who excluded President Carter's town meetings, I have coded them as constituting both days of travel and appearances.

2. As a cautionary note, in recent years the sources used to compile this list of television addresses appear to employ a more inclusive definition of "address to nation."

3. In Figures 1, 2, and 3, only the first three years have been tabulated in order to eliminate activities inspired by concerns for reelection rather than governing. Since Gerald Ford's tenure does not include three nonelection years, his record of public activities has been ignored.

4. Pierre Salinger, *With Kennedy* (New York Doubleday, 1966), 138–144. For a discussion of other presidents' concerns with overexposure, see Godfrey Hodgson, *All Things to All Men* (New York: Simon & Schuster, 1980), 188–189.

5. Newton N. Minow, John Bartlow Martin, and Lee M. Mitchell, *Presidential Television* (New York: Basic Books, 1973), 65–68.

6. J. F. terHorst and Col. Ralph Albertazzie provide a lively chronology of presidential air travel in *The Flying White House* (New York: Coward, McCann, and Geoghegan, 1979).

7. "Hoover, with 37 Radio Talks in Past Year, Made a Record," *New York Times,* December 28, 1930, 1.

8. See Robert A. Dahl and Charles E. Lindblom, *Politics, Economics, and Welfare* (New York: Harper and Row, 1960); and Richard E. Neustadt, *Presidential Power* (New York: John Wiley and Sons, 1980).

7

THE BUREAUCRACY

7.1

JAMES Q. WILSON

From *Bureaucracy: What Government Agencies Do and Why They Do It*

Wilson writes convincingly that bureaucracies can vary greatly in their effectiveness. He pokes holes in standard complaints about bureaucracies by indicating how some of the inefficiencies that people complain about are either unavoidable or by design.

BUREAUCRACY AND THE PUBLIC INTEREST

The German army beat the French army in 1940; the Texas prisons for many years did a better job than did the Michigan prisons; Carver High School in Atlanta became a better school under Norris Hogans. These successes were the result of skilled executives who correctly identified the critical tasks of their organizations, distributed authority in a way appropriate to those tasks, infused their subordinates with a sense of mission, and acquired sufficient autonomy to permit them to get on with the job. The critical tasks were different in each case, and so the organizations differed in culture and patterns of authority, but all three were alike in one sense: incentives, culture, and authority were combined in a way that suited the task at hand.

By now, . . . the reader may find all this painfully obvious. If [these points] are obvious to the reader, then surely they are obvious to government officials. Intellectually perhaps they are. But whatever lip service may be given to the lessons . . . the daily incentives operating in the political world encourage a very different course of action.

Armies

Though the leadership and initiative of field officers and noncoms is of critical importance, the Pentagon is filled with generals who want to control combat from headquarters or from helicopters, using radios to gather information and computers to process it. Though the skill of the infantryman almost always has been a key to military success, the U.S. Army traditionally has put its best people in specialized units (intelligence, engineering, communications), leaving the leftovers for the infantry.[1] Though it has fought wars since 1945 everywhere except in Europe, the army continues to devote most of its planning to big-tank battles on the West German plains.

Prisons

The success of George Beto in the Texas DOC was there for everyone to see, but many observers gave the most favorable attention to prison executives who seemed to voice the best intentions (rehabilitation, prisoner self-governance) rather than the best accomplishments (safe, decent facilities).

Schools

Especially in big cities, many administrators keep principals weak and teachers busy filling out reports, all with an eye toward minimizing complaints from parents, auditors, interest groups, and the press. Teachers individually grumble that they are treated as robots instead of professionals, but collectively they usually oppose any steps—vouchers, merit pay, open enrollment, strengthened principals—that in fact have given teachers a larger role in designing curricula and managing their classrooms. Norris Hogans received little help from the Atlanta school system; politically, extra resources had to go to all schools "equally" rather than disproportionately to those schools that were improving the most.

These generals, wardens, administrators, and teachers have not been behaving irrationally; rather, they have been responding to the incentives and constraints that they encounter on a daily basis. Those incentives include the need to manage situations over which they have little control on the basis of a poorly defined or nonexistent sense of mission and in the face of a complex array of constraints that seems always to grow, never to shrink. Outside groups—elected officials, interest groups, professional associations, the media—demand a voice in the running of these agencies and make that demand effective by imposing rules on the agencies and demanding that all these rules be enforced all of the time. Moreover, habitual patterns of action—the lessons of the past, the memories of earlier struggles, the expectations of one's co-workers—narrow the area within which new courses of action are sought.

Bureaucrats often complain of "legislative micromanagement," and indeed it exists. . . . with respect to the armed forces. There has been a dramatic increase in the number of hearings, reports, investigations, statutory amendments, and budgetary adjustments with which the Pentagon must deal.[2] But there also has been a sharp increase in presidential micromanagement. Herbert Kaufman notes that for a half century or more the White House has feared agency independence more than agency paralysis, and so it has multiplied the number of presidential staffers, central management offices, and requirements for higher-level reviews. Once you start along the path of congressional or White House control, the process acquires a momentum of its own. "As more constraints are imposed, rigidities fixing agencies in their established ways intensify. As a result, complaints that they do not respond to controls also intensify. Further controls, checkpoints, and clearances are therefore introduced."[3] Much the same story can be told with respect to the growing involvement of the courts in agency affairs.

With some conspicuous exceptions the result of this process has been to deflect the attention of agency executives away from how the tasks of their agencies get defined and toward the constraints that must be observed no matter what the tasks may be. Who then decides what tasks shall be performed? In a production agency with observable outputs and routinized work processes, the answer is relatively simple: The laws and regulations that created the agency also define its job. But in procedural, coping, and craft agencies, the answer seems to be nobody in particular and everybody in general. The operating-level workers define the tasks, occasionally by design, as in those cases where operator ideology makes a difference, but more commonly by accident, as in those instances where prior experiences, professional norms, situational and technological imperatives, and peer-group expectations shape the nature of the work.

From time to time a gifted executive appears at a politically propitious time and makes things happen differently. He or she creates a new institution that acquires a distinctive competence, a strong sense of mission, and an ability to achieve socially valued goals. The Army Corps of Engineers, the Social Security Administration, the Marine Corps, the Forest Service, the FBI: For many years after they were created, and in many instances still today, these agencies, along with a few others that could be mentioned, were a kind of elite service that stood as a living refutation of the proposition that "all bureaucrats are dim-witted paper-shufflers." And these are only the federal examples; at the local level one can find many school systems and police departments that have acquired a praiseworthy organizational character.

But one must ask whether today one could create from scratch the Marine Corps, or the FBI, or the Forest Service; possibly, but probably not. Who would dare suggest that a new agency come into being with its own personnel system (and thus with fewer opportunities for civil servants to get tenure), with a single dominant mission (and thus with little organizational deference to the myriad other goals outsiders would want it to serve), and with an arduous training regime designed to instill *esprit de corps* (and thus with less regard for those niceties and conveniences that sedentary people believe to be important)? Or how optimistic should we be that today we could organize a Social Security Administration in a way that would bring to Washington men and women of exceptional talent? Might not many of those people decide today that they do not want to risk running afoul of the conflict-of-interest laws, that they have no stomach for close media and congressional scrutiny, and that they would not accept the federal pay levels pegged to the salaries of members of Congress fearful of raising their own compensation?

It would be a folly of historical romanticism to imagine that great agencies were created in a golden age that is destined never to return, but it would be shortsighted to deny that we have paid a price for having emphasized rules and constraints to the neglect of tasks and mission. At the end of her careful review of the problems the SSA has had in managing disability insurance and supplemental security income, Martha Derthick makes the same point this way: "If the agencies repeatedly fall short, one ought at least to consider the possibility that there is a systematic mismatch between what they are instructed to do and their capacity to do it."[4] In recent years, when Congress has been creating new programs and modifying old ones at a dizzying rate, often on the basis of perfunctory hearings (or, as with the Senate's consideration of the 1988 drug bill, no hearings at all), a government agency capable of responding adequately to these endless changes would have to be versatile and adaptable, "capable of devising new routines or altering old ones very quickly." These qualities, she concludes, "are rarely found in large formal organizations."[5] I would only add that government agencies are far less flexible than formal organizations generally.

Things are not made much better by our national tendency to engage in bureaucrat-bashing. One has to have some perspective on this. It is true that bureaucracies prefer the present to the future, the known to the unknown, and the dominant mission to rival missions; many agencies in fact are skeptical of things that were "NIH"—Not Invented Here. Every social grouping, whether a neighborhood, a nation, or an organization, acquires a culture; changing that culture is like moving a cemetery: it is always difficult and some believe it is sacrilegious. It is also true, as many conservatives argue, that the government tries to do things that it is incapable of doing well, just as it is true, as many liberals allege, that the government in fact does many things well enough. As Charles Wolf has argued, both markets and governments have their imperfections; many things we might want to do collectively require us to choose between unsatisfactory alternatives.[6]

A Few Modest Suggestions That May Make a Small Difference

To do better we have to deregulate the government.[7] If deregulation of a market makes sense because it liberates the entrepreneurial energies of its members, then it is possible that deregulating the public sector also may help energize it. The difference, of course, is that both the price system and the profit motive provide a discipline in markets that is absent in non-markets. Whether any useful substitutes for this discipline can be found for public-sector workers is not clear, though I will offer some suggestions. But even if we cannot expect the same results from deregulation in the two sectors we can agree at a minimum that detailed regulation, even of public employees, rarely is compatible with energy, pride in workmanship, and the exercise of initiative. The best evidence for this proposition, if any is needed, is that most people do not like working in an environment in which every action is second-guessed, every initiative viewed with suspicion, and every controversial decision denounced as malfeasance.

James Colvard, for many years a senior civilian manager in the navy, suggests that the government needs to emulate methods that work in the better parts of the private sector: "a bias toward action, small staffs, and a high level of delegation which is based on trust."[8] A panel of the National Academy of Public Administration (NAPA), consisting of sixteen senior government executives holding the rank of assistant secretary, issued a report making the same point:

> Over many years, government has become entwined in elaborate management control systems and the accretion of progressively more detailed administrative procedures. This development has not produced superior management. Instead, it has produced managerial overburden. . . . Procedures overwhelm substance. Organizations become discredited, along with their employees. . . . The critical elements of leadership in management appear to wither in the face of a preoccupation with process. The tools are endlessly "perfected"; the manager who is expected to use these tools believes himself to be ignored. . . . Management systems are not management. . . . The attitude of those who design and administer the rules . . . must be reoriented from a "control mentality" to one of "how can I help get the mission of this agency accomplished."[9]

But how can government "delegate" and "trust" and still maintain accountability? If it is a mistake to foster an ethos that encourages every bureaucrat to "go by the book," is it not an equally serious problem to allow zealots to engage in "mission madness," charging off to implement their private versions of some ambiguous public goal? (Steven Emerson has written a useful account of mission madness in some highly secret military intelligence and covert-action agencies.)[10] Given everything we know about the bureaucratic desire for autonomy and the political rewards of rule making, is there any reason to suppose that anybody will find it in his or her interest to abandon the "control mentality" and adopt the "mission accomplishment" mentality?

Possibly not. But it may be worth thinking about what a modestly deregulated government might look like. It might look as it once did, when some of the better federal agencies were created. At the time the Corps of Engineers, the Forest Service, and the FBI were founded much of the federal government was awash in political patronage, petty cabals, and episodic corruption.

Organizing an elite service in those days may have been easier than doing so today, when the problems are less patronage and corruption than they are officiousness and complexity. But the keys to organizational success have not changed. The agencies were started by strong leaders who were able to command personal loyalty, define and instill a clear and powerful sense of mission, attract talented workers who believed they were joining something special, and make exacting demands on subordinates.

Today there is not much chance to create a new agency; almost every agency one can imagine already has been created. Even so, the lessons one learns from changing agencies confirm what can be inferred from studying their founding.

First: Executives should understand the culture of their organizations—that is, what their subordinates believe constitute the core tasks of the agency—and the strengths and limitations of that culture. If members widely share and warmly endorse that culture the agency has a sense of mission. This permits the executive to economize on scarce incentives (people want to do certain tasks even when there are no special rewards for doing it); to state general objectives confident that subordinates will understand the appropriate ways of achieving them; and to delegate responsibility knowing that lower-level decisions probably will conform to higher-level expectations.

A good executive realizes that workers can make subtle, precise, and realistic judgments, but only if those judgments refer to a related, coherent set of behaviors. People cannot easily keep in mind many quite different things or strike reasonable balances among competing tasks. People want to know what is expected of them; they do not want to be told, in answer to this question, that "on the one hand this, but on the other hand that."

In defining a core mission and sorting out tasks that either fit or do not fit with this mission, executives must be aware of their many rivals for the right to define it. Operators with professional backgrounds will bring to the agency their skills but also their biases: Lawyers, economists, and engineers see the world in very different ways. You cannot hire them as if they were tools that in your skilled hands will perform exactly the task you set for them. Black and Decker may make tools like that, but Harvard and MIT do not. Worker peer groups also set expectations to which operators conform, especially when the operators work in a threatening, unpredictable, or confrontational environment. You may design the ideal patrol officer or schoolteacher, but unless you understand the demands made by the street and the classroom, your design will remain an artistic expression destined for the walls of some organizational museum.

These advantages of infusing an agency with a sense of mission are purchased at a price. An agency with a strong mission will give perfunctory attention, if any at all, to tasks that are not central to that mission. Diplomats in the State Department will have little interest in embassy security; intelligence officers in the CIA will not worry as much as they should about counter-intelligence; narcotics agents in the DEA will minimize the importance of improper prescriptions written by physicians; power engineers in the TVA will not think as hard about environmental protection or conservation as about maximizing the efficiency of generating units; fighter pilots in the USAF will look at air transport as a homely stepchild; and navy admirals who earned their flag serving on aircraft carriers will not press zealously to expand the role of minesweepers.

If the organization must perform a diverse set of tasks, those tasks that are not part of the core mission will need special protection. This requires giving autonomy to the subordinate tasks subunit (for example, by providing for them a special organizational niche) and creating a career track so that talented people performing non-mission tasks can rise to high rank in the agency. No single organization, however, can perform well a wide variety of tasks; inevitably some will be neglected. In this case, the wise executive will arrange to devolve the slighted tasks onto another agency, or to a wholly new organization created for the purpose. Running multitask conglomerates is as risky in the public as in the private sector. There are limits to the number of different jobs managers can manage. Moreover, conglomerate agencies rarely can develop a sense of mission; the cost of trying to do everything is that few things are done well. The turf-conscious executive who stoutly refuses to surrender any tasks, no matter how neglected, to another agency is courting disaster; in time the failure of his or her agency to perform some orphan task will lead to a political or organizational crisis. Long ago the State Department should have got out of the business of building embassies. Diplomats are good at many things, but supervising carpenters and plumbers is not one of them. Let agencies whose mission is construction—the Army Corps of Engineers or the navy's Seabees—build buildings.

Second: Negotiate with one's political superiors to get some agreement as to which are the *essential* constraints that must be observed by your agency and which the marginal constraints. This, frankly, may be impossible. The decentralization of authority in Congress (and in some state legislatures) and the unreliability of most expressions of presidential or gubernatorial backing are such that in most cases you will discover, by experience if not by precept, that all constraints are essential all of the time. But perhaps with effort some maneuvering room may be won. A few agencies obtained the right to use more flexible, less cumbersome personnel systems modeled on the China Lake experiment, and Congress has the power to broaden those opportunities. Perhaps some enlightened member of Congress will be able to get statutory authority for the equivalent of China Lake with respect to procurement regulations. An executive is well advised to spend time showing that member how to do it.

Third: Match the distribution of authority and the control over resources to the tasks your organization is performing. In general, authority should be placed at the lowest level at which all essential elements of information are available. Bureaucracies will differ greatly in what level that may be. At one extreme are agencies such as the Internal Revenue Service or maximum-security prisons, in which uniformity of treatment and precision of control are so important as to make it necessary for there to be exacting, centrally determined rules for most tasks. At the other extreme are public schools, police departments, and armies, organizations in which operational uncertainties are so great that discretion must be given to (or if not given will be taken by) lower-level workers.

A good place in which to think through these matters is the area of weapons procurement. The overcentralization of design control is one of the many criticisms of such procurement on which all commentators seem agreed. Buying a new aircraft may be likened to remodeling one's home: You never know how much it will cost until you are done; you quickly find out that changing your mind midway through the work costs a lot of money; and you soon realize that decisions have to be made by people on the spot who can look at the pipes, wires, and joists. The Pentagon procures aircraft as if none of its members had ever built or remodeled a house. It does so because both it and its legislative superiors refuse to allow authority to flow down to the point where decisions rationally can be made.

The same analysis can be applied to public schools. As John Chubb and Terry Moe have shown, public and private schools differ in the locus of effective control.[11] At least in big cities, decisions in private schools that are made by headmasters or in Catholic schools that are made by small archdiocesan staffs are made in public schools by massive, cumbersome headquarters bureaucracies. Of course, there are perfectly understandable political reasons for this difference, but not very many good reasons for it. Many sympathetic critics of the public schools believe that the single most useful organizational change that could be made would be to have educational management decisions—on personnel, scheduling, and instructional matters—made at the school level.[12]

Fourth: Judge organizations by results. This reading has made it clear that what constitutes a valued result in government usually is a matter of dispute. But even when fairly clear performance standards exist, legislatures and executives often ignore them with unhappy results. William E. Turcotte compared how two state governments oversaw their state liquor monopolies. The state that applied clear standards to its liquor bureaucrats produced significantly more profit and lower administrative costs than did the state with unclear or conflicting standards.[13]

Even when results are hard to assess more can be done than is often the case. If someone set out to evaluate the output of a private school, hospital, or security service, he or she would have at least as much trouble as would someone trying to measure the output of a public school, hospital, or police department. Governments are not the only institutions with ambiguous products.

There are two ways to cope with the problem in government One . . . is to supply the service or product in a marketlike environment. Shift the burden of evaluation off the shoulders of professional evaluators and onto the shoulders of clients and customers, and let the latter vote with their feet. The "client" in these cases can be individual citizens or government agencies; what is important is that the client be able to choose from among rival suppliers.

But some public services cannot be supplied, or are never going to be supplied, by a market. We can imagine allowing parents to choose among schools but we cannot imagine letting them choose (at least for most purposes) among police departments or armies. In that case one should adopt the second way of evaluating a public service: carry out a demonstration project or conduct a field experiment. (I will use the two ideas interchangeably, though some scholars distinguish between them.)[14] An experiment is a planned alteration in a state of affairs designed to measure the effect of the intervention. It involves asking the question, "if I change X, what will happen to Y, having first made certain that everything else stays the same?" It sounds easy, but it is not.

A good experiment (bad ones are worse than no experiment at all) requires that one do the following: First, identify a course of action to be tested; call it the treatment. A "treatment" can be a police tactic, a school curriculum, or a welfare program. Second, decide what impact the treatment is intended to have; call this the outcome. The outcome can be a crime rate, an achievement score, a work effort, a housing condition, or an income level. Third, give the treatment to one group (the experimental group) and withhold it from another (the control group). A group might be a police precinct, a class of students, the tenants in a housing project, or people who meet some eligibility requirement (say, having low incomes). It is quite important how the membership in these groups is determined. It should be done randomly; that is, all eligible precincts, schools, tenants, or people should be randomly sorted into experimental and control groups. Random assignment means that all the characteristics of the members of the experimental and control groups are likely to be identical. Fourth, assess the condition of each group before and after the treatment. The first assessment describes the baseline condition, the second the outcome condition. This outcome assessment should continue for some time after the end of the treatment, because experience has shown that many treatments seem to have a short-term effect that quickly disappears. Fifth, make certain that the evaluation is done by people other than those providing the treatment. People like to believe that their efforts are worthwhile, so much so that perhaps unwittingly they will gather data in ways that make it look like the treatment worked even when it did not.[15]

The object of all this is to find out what works. Using this method we have discovered that tripling the number of patrol cars on a beat does not lower the crime rate; that foot patrol reduces the fear of crime but not (ordinarily) its incidence; and that arresting spouse-beaters reduces (for a while) future assaults more than does counseling the assaulters.[16] We have learned that giving people an income supplement (akin to the negative income tax) reduces work effort and in some cases encourages families to break up.[17] We have learned that giving special job training and support to welfare mothers, ex-offenders, and school drop-outs produces sizable gains in the employment records of the welfare recipients but no gain for the ex-offenders and school drop-outs.[18] We have learned that a housing allowance program increases the welfare of poor families even though it does not improve the stock of housing. We have learned that more flexible pay and classification systems greatly benefit the managers of navy research centers and improve the work atmosphere at the centers.

There also have been many failed or flawed management experiments. In the 1930s, Herbert Simon carried out what may have been the first serious such experiment when he tried to find out how to improve the performance of welfare workers in the California State Relief Administration. Though elegantly designed, the experimental changes proved so controversial and the political environment of the agency so unstable that it is not clear that any useful inferences can be drawn from the project.[19] The attempt to evaluate educational vouchers at Alum Rock was undercut by the political need to restrict participation by private schools. . . . There are countless other "studies" that are evaluations in name only; in reality they are self-congratulatory conclusions written by program administrators. The administrative world is a political world, not a scientific laboratory, and evaluators of administration must come to terms with that fact. Often there are no mutually acceptable terms. But where reasonable terms can be struck it is possible to learn more than untutored experience can tell us about what works.

Such dry and dusty research projects probably seem thin fare to people who want Big Answers to Big Questions such as "How can we curb rampant bureaucracy?" or "How can we unleash the creative talents of our dedicated public servants?" But public management is not an arena in which to find Big Answers; it is a world of settled institutions designed to allow imperfect people to use flawed procedures to cope with insoluble problems.

The fifth and final bit of advice flows directly from the limits on judging agencies by their results. All organizations seek the stability and comfort that comes from relying on standard operating procedures—"SOPs." When results are unknown or equivocal, bureaus will have no incentive to alter those SOPs so as better to achieve their goals, only an incentive to modify them to conform to externally imposed constraints. The SOPs will represent an internally defined equilibrium that reconciles the situational imperatives, professional norms, bureaucratic ideologies, peer-group expectations, and (if present) leadership demands unique to that agency. The only way to minimize the adverse effect of allowing human affairs to be managed by organizations driven by their autonomous SOPs is to keep the number, size, and authority of such organizations as small as possible. If none of the four preceding bits of advice work, the reader must confront the realization that there are no solutions for the bureaucracy problem that are not also "solutions" to the government problem. More precisely: All complex organizations display bureaucratic problems of confusion, red tape, and the avoidance of responsibility. Those problems are much greater in government bureaucracies because government itself is the institutionalization of confusion (arising out of the need to moderate competing demands); of red tape (arising out of the need to satisfy demands that cannot be moderated); and of avoided responsibility (arising out of the desire to retain power by minimizing criticism).

In short, you can have less bureaucracy only if you have less government. Many, if not most, of the difficulties we experience in dealing with government agencies arise from the agencies being part of a fragmented and open political system. If an agency is to have a sense of mission, if constraints are to be minimized, if authority is to be decentralized, if officials are to be judged on the basis of the outputs they produce rather than the inputs they consume, then legislators, judges, and lobbyists will have to act against their own interests. They will have to say "no" to influential constituents, forgo the opportunity to expand their own influence, and take seriously the task of judging the organizational feasibility as well as the political popularity of a proposed new program. It is hard to imagine this happening, partly because politicians and judges have no incentive to make it happen and partly because there are certain tasks a democratic government must undertake even if they cannot be performed efficiently. The greatest mistake citizens can make when they complain of "the bureaucracy" is to suppose that their frustrations arise simply out of management problems; they do not—they arise out of governance problems.

Bureaucracy and the American Regime

The central feature of the American constitutional system—the separation of powers—exacerbates many of these problems. The governments of the United States were not designed to be efficient or powerful, but to be tolerable and malleable. Those who devised these arrangements always assumed that the federal government would exercise few and limited powers. As long as that assumption was correct (which it was for a century and a half) the quality of public administration was not a serious problem except in the minds of those reformers (Woodrow Wilson was probably the first) who desired to rationalize government in order to rationalize society. The founders knew that the separation of powers would make it so difficult to start a new program or to create a new agency that it was hardly necessary to think about how those agencies would be administered. As a result, the Constitution is virtually silent on what kind of administration we should have. At least until the Civil War thrust the problem on us, scarcely anyone in the country would have known what you were talking about if you spoke of the "problem of administration."

Matters were very different in much of Europe. Kings and princes long had ruled; when their authority was captured by parliaments, the tradition of ruling was already well established. From the first the ministers of the parliamentary regimes thought about the problems of administration because in those countries there was something to administer. The centralization of executive authority in the hands of a prime minister and the exclusion (by and large) of parliament from much say in executive affairs facilitated the process of controlling the administrative agencies and bending them to some central will. The constitutions of many European states easily could have been written by a school of management.

Today, the United States at every level has big and active governments. Some people worry that a constitutional system well-designed to preserve liberty when governments were small is poorly designed to implement policy now that governments are large. The contrast between how the United States and the nations of Western Europe manage environmental and industrial regulation . . . is illuminating: Here the separation of powers insures, if not causes, clumsy and adversarial regulation; there the unification of powers permits, if not causes, smooth and consensual regulation.

I am not convinced that the choice is that simple, however. It would take another book to judge the advantages and disadvantages of the separation of powers. The balance sheet on both sides of the ledger would contain many more entries than those that derive from a discussion of public administration. But even confining our attention to administration, there is more to be said for the American system than many of its critics admit.

America has a paradoxical bureaucracy unlike that found in almost any other advanced nation. The paradox is the existence in one set of institutions of two qualities ordinarily quite separate: the multiplication of rules and the opportunity for access. We have a system laden with rules; elsewhere that is a sure sign that the bureaucracy is aloof from the people, distant from their concerns, and preoccupied with the power and privileges of the bureaucrats—an elaborate, grinding machine that can crush the spirit of any who dare oppose it. We also have a system suffused with participation: advisory boards, citizen groups, neighborhood councils, congressional investigators, crusading journalists, and lawyers serving writs; elsewhere this popular involvement would be taken as evidence that the administrative system is no system at all, but a bungling, jerry-built contraption wallowing in inefficiency and shot through with corruption and favoritism.

That these two traits, rules and openness, could coexist would have astonished Max Weber and continues to astonish (or elude) many contemporary students of the subject. Public bureaucracy in this country is neither as rational and predictable as Weber hoped nor as crushing and mechanistic as he feared. It is rule-bound without being overpowering, participatory without being corrupt. This paradox exists partly because of the character and mores of the American people: They are too informal, spontaneous, and other-directed to be either neutral arbiters or passionless Gradgrinds. And partly it exists because of the nature of the regime: Our constitutional system, and above all the exceptional power enjoyed by the legislative branch, makes it impossible for us to have anything like a government by appointed experts but easy for individual citizens to obtain redress from the abuses of power. Anyone who wishes it otherwise would have to produce a wholly different regime, and curing the mischiefs of bureaucracy seems an inadequate reason for that. Parliamentary regimes that supply more consistent direction to their bureaucracies also supply more bureaucracy to their citizens. The fragmented American regime may produce chaotic government, but the coherent European regimes produce bigger governments.

In the meantime we live in a country that despite its baffling array of rules and regulations and the insatiable desire of some people to use government to rationalize society still makes it possible to get drinkable water instantly, put through a telephone call in seconds, deliver a letter in a day, and obtain a passport in a week. Our Social Security checks arrive on time. Some state prisons, and most of the federal ones, are reasonably decent and humane institutions. The great majority of Americans, cursing all the while, pay their taxes. One can stand on the deck of an aircraft carrier during night flight operations and watch two thousand nineteen-year-old boys faultlessly operate one of the most complex organizational systems ever created. There are not many places where all this happens. It is astonishing it can be made to happen at all.

NOTES

1. Arthur T. Hadley, *The Straw Giant* (New York: Random House, 1986), 53–57, 249–52.

2. CSIS, *U.S. Defense Acquisition: A Process in Trouble* (Washington, D.C.: Center for Strategic and International Studies, March 1987), 13–16.

3. Herbert Kaufman, *The Administrative Behavior of Federal Bureau Chiefs* (Washington, D.C.: The Brookings Institution, 1981), 192.

4. Martha Derthick, *Agency Under Stress: The Social Security Administration and American Government* (Washington, D.C.: Brookings Institution, 1990).

5. Ibid., chap. 3.

6. Charles Wolf, Jr., *Markets or Governments: Choosing Between Imperfect Alternatives* (Cambridge, Mass.: MIT Press, 1988).

7. I first saw this phrase in an essay by Constance Horner, then director of the federal Office of Personnel Management: "Beyond Mr. Gradgrind: The Case for Deregulating the Public Sector," *Policy Review* 44 (Spring 1988): 34–38. It also appears in Gary C. Bryner, *Bureaucratic Discretion* (New York: Pergamon Press, 1987), 215.

8. James Colvard, "Procurement: What Price Mistrust?" *Government Executive* (March 1985): 21.

9. NAPA, *Revitalizing Federal Management: Managers and Their Overburdened Systems* (Washington, D.C.: National Academy of Public Administration, November 1983), vii, viii, 8.

10. Steven Emerson, *Secret Warriors* (New York: G. P. Putnam's Sons, 1988).

11. John E. Chubb and Terry M. Moe, "Politics, Markets, and the Organization of Schools," *American Political Science Review* 82 (1988): 1065–87.

12. Chester E. Finn, Jr., "Decentralize, Deregulate, Empower," *Policy Review* (Summer 1986): 60; Edward A. Wynne, *A Year in the Life of an Excellent Elementary School* (Lancaster, Pa: Technomic, 1993).

13. William E. Turcotte, "Control Systems, Performance, and Satisfaction in Two State Agencies," *Administrative Science Quarterly* 19 (1974): 60–73.

14. Richard P. Nathan, *Social Science in Government: Uses and Misuses* (New York: Basic Books, 1988), chap. 3.

15. Matters are, of course, a bit more complicated than this summary might suggest. There is a small library of books on evaluative research that go into these matters in more detail; a good place to begin is Richard P. Nathan, *Social Science in Government* (New York: Basic Books, 1988). On the political aspects of evaluation, see Henry J. Aaron, *Politics and the Professors* (Washington, D.C.: The Brookings Institution, 1978). On the technical side see Thomas D. Cook and Donald T. Campbell, *Quasi-Experimentation* (Chicago: Rand McNally, 1979). There is even a journal, *Evaluation Review*, specializing in these issues.

16. These projects were all done by the Police Foundation and are described in James Q. Wilson, *Thinking About Crime*, rev. ed. (New York: Basic Books, 1983).

17. See Joseph A. Pechman and P. Michael Timpane, eds., *Work Incentives and Income Guarantees* (Washington, D.C.: Brookings Institution, 1975); and R. Thayne Robson, ed., *Employment and Training R&D* (Kalamazoo, Mich.: Upjohn Institute for Employment Research, 1984).

18. Nathan, *Social Science*, chap. 5; and Manpower Demonstration Research Corporation, *Summary and Findings of the National Supported Work Demonstration* (Cambridge, Mass.: Ballinger, 1980).

19. Clarence E. Ridley and Herbert A. Simon, *Measuring Municipal Activities* (Chicago: International City Managers' Association, 1938).

7.2

MATHEW D. MCCUBBINS AND THOMAS SCHWARTZ

"Congressional Oversight Overlooked: Police Patrols versus Fire Alarms"

In this classic article, McCubbins and Schwartz compare two kinds of oversight of executive agencies by Congress. Under the police patrol model, Congress provides resources for constant monitoring of bureaucratic behavior. Under the fire alarm model, Congress waits for complaints from constituents and groups in society about the bureaucracies and then holds them accountable. The fire alarm model is often the more efficient method of oversight.

Scholars often complain that Congress has neglected its oversight responsibility: despite a large and growing executive branch, Congress has done little or nothing to oversee administrative compliance with legislative goals. As a consequence, we are told, Congress has largely lost control of the executive branch: it has allowed the executive branch not only to grow but to grow irresponsible. In popular debate as well as congressional scholarship, this neglect of oversight has become a stylized fact: widely and dutifully reported, it is often bemoaned, sometimes explained, but almost never seriously questioned.[1]

We question it. What has appeared to scholars to be a neglect of oversight, we argue, really is a preference for one form of oversight over another, less-effective form. In so arguing, we develop a simple model of congressional choice of oversight policy, offer evidence to support the model, and draw from it further implications regarding bureaucratic discretion and regulatory legislation. More generally, we model the choice by policy makers of an optimal enforcement strategy, given opportunity costs, available technology, and human cognitive limits.

THE MODEL

Congressional oversight policy concerns whether, to what extent, and in what way Congress attempts to detect and remedy executive-branch violations of legislative goals. Our model of congressional choice of oversight policy rests on a distinction between two forms or techniques of oversight:

Police-Patrol Oversight

Analogous to the use of real police patrols, police-patrol oversight is comparatively centralized, active, and direct: at its own initiative, Congress examines a sample of executive-agency activities, with the aim of detecting and remedying any violations of legislative goals and, by its surveillance, discouraging such violations. An agency's activities might be surveyed by any of a number of means, such as reading documents, commissioning scientific studies, conducting field observations, and holding hearings to question officials and affected citizens.

Fire-Alarm Oversight

Analogous to the use of real fire alarms, fire-alarm oversight is less centralized and involves less active and direct intervention than police-patrol oversight: instead of examining a sample of administrative decisions, looking for violations of legislative goals, Congress establishes a system of rules, procedures, and informal practices that enable individual citizens and organized interest groups to examine administrative decisions (sometimes in prospect), to charge executive agencies with violating congressional goals, and to seek remedies from agencies, courts, and Congress itself. Some of these rules, procedures, and practices afford citizens and interest groups access to information and to administrative decision-making processes. Others give them standing to challenge administrative decisions before agencies and courts, or help them bring alleged violations to congressmen's attention. Still others facilitate collective action by comparatively disorganized interest groups. Congress's role consists in creating and perfecting this decentralized system and, occasionally, intervening in response to complaints. Instead of sniffing for fires, Congress places fire-alarm boxes on street corners, builds neighborhood fire houses, and sometimes dispatches its own hook-and-ladder in response to an alarm.

The distinction between police-patrol and fire-alarm oversight should not be confused with the distinction that sometimes is drawn between *formal* and *informal* oversight, which differ in that formal oversight activities have oversight as their principal and official purpose, whereas informal oversight activities are incidental to other official functions, such as appropriations hearings. Both can involve direct and active surveillance rather than responses to alarms. (See Dodd and Schott, 1977; Ogul, 1977.)

Our model consists of three assumptions:

Technological Assumption

Two forms of oversight are available to Congress: police-patrol oversight and fire-alarm oversight. Congress can choose either form or a combination of the two, making tradeoffs between them in two circumstances: (1) When writing legislation, Congress can include police-patrol features, such as sunset review, or fire-alarm features, such as requirements for public hearings. (2) When it evaluates an agency's performance, Congress can either call oversight hearings to patrol for violations of legislative goals or else wait for alarms to signal potential violations.

Motivational Assumption

A congressman seeks to take as much credit as possible for the net benefits enjoyed by his potential supporters—by citizens and interest groups, within his constituency and elsewhere, whose support can help him win reelection. This means, in part, that a congressman seeks to avoid as much blame as possible for the net costs borne by his potential supporters.

Institutional Assumption

Executive agencies act as agents of Congress and especially of those subcommittees on which they depend for authorizations and appropriations.

The Motivational Assumption is closely tied to Mayhew's celebrated reelection model (1974) and to the blame-shirking model of Fiorina (1982a). The Institutional Assumption is found in Baldwin (1975), Ferejohn (1981), Joskow (1974), McCubbins (1982a,b), and Mitnick (1980). Although not previously stated, the Technological Assumption seems to us to be uncontroversial.

That cannot be said of the Motivational Assumption, which depicts congressmen as pure politicians, single-mindedly pursuing reelection. To this picture one might object that real congressmen are not just politicians but statesmen, pursuing justice and the public interest, acting according to various moral and ideological principles, even at some cost to their reelection prospects.

We will argue, however, that if the Motivational Assumption were replaced by the assumption that congressmen act strictly as statesmen, our conclusions regarding oversight would still be derivable, although in a somewhat different way. Our analysis has less to do with specific legislative goals than with optimal strategies for enforcing compliance with legislative goals of any sort.

CONSEQUENCES

Three important consequences follow from our model:

Consequence 1

To the extent that they favor oversight activity of any sort, congressmen tend to prefer fire-alarm oversight to police-patrol oversight.

Our argument for Consequence 1 is that a congressman's objective, according to the Motivational Assumption, is to take as much credit as possible for net benefits enjoyed by his potential supporters and that he can do so more efficiently under a policy of fire-alarm oversight than under a police-patrol policy, for three reasons:

First, congressmen engaged in police-patrol oversight inevitably spend time examining a great many executive-branch actions that do not violate legislative goals or harm any potential supporters, at least not enough to occasion complaints. They might also spend time detecting and remedying arguable violations that nonetheless harm no potential supporters. For this they receive scant credit from their potential supporters. According to the Motivational Assumption, then, their time is largely wasted, so they incur opportunity costs. But under a fire-alarm policy, a congressman does not address concrete violations unless potential supporters have complained about them, in which case he can receive credit for intervening. So a unit of time spent on oversight is likely to yield more benefit for a congressman under a fire-alarm policy than under a policy-patrol policy. As a result, a fire-alarm policy enables congressmen to spend less time on oversight, leaving more time for other profitable activities, or to spend the same time on more personally profitable oversight activities—on addressing complaints by potential supporters. Justly or unjustly, time spent putting out visible fires gains one more credit than the same time spent sniffing for smoke.

Second, under a realistic police-patrol policy, congressmen examine only a small sample of executive-branch actions. As a result, they are likely to miss violations that harm their potential supporters, and so miss opportunities to take credit for redressing grievances, however fair the sample. Under a fire-alarm policy, by contrast, potential supporters can in most cases bring to congressmen's attention any violations that harm them and for which they have received no adequate remedy through the executive or judicial branch.

Third, although fire-alarm oversight can be as costly as police-patrol oversight, much of the cost is borne by the citizens and interest groups who sound alarms and by administrative agencies and courts rather than by congressmen themselves. A congressman's responsibility for such costs is sufficiently remote that he is not likely to be blamed for them by his potential supporters.

Consequence 2

Congress will not neglect its oversight responsibility. It will adopt an extensive and somewhat effective (even if imperfect) oversight policy.

This is because one of the two forms of oversight—the fire-alarm variety—serves congressmen's interests at little cost. When his potential supporters complain of a violation of legislative goals, a congressman gains credit if he eliminates the cause of the complaint. By virtue of the Institutional Assumption, he often can be reasonably effective in eliminating such causes. Beyond establishing and perfecting the system and addressing some complaints, fire-alarm oversight is almost costless to congressmen: others bear most of the cost.

Consequence 3

Congress will adopt an extensive and somewhat effective policy of fire-alarm oversight while largely neglecting police-patrol oversight.

This just summarizes Consequences 1 and 2.

MISPERCEPTION

Faced with an apparent fact he finds puzzling, unfortunate, or otherwise worthy of attention, a scientist has two alternatives: (a) to accept the fact and try to explain it, or (b) to question the *apparent* fact and try to explain its appearance. In the case at hand, students of Congress have, for the most part, chosen (a): they have uncritically agreed that Congress neglects its oversight responsibility and have tried to explain this neglect.

Here are the three main explanations found in the literature, along with a brief critical comment on each:

Complexity

Because public-policy issues are so complex, Congress has had to delegate authority over them to a large, complex, technically expert bureaucracy, whose actions it is unable effectively to oversee (Lowi, 1969; Ogul, 1977; Ripley, 1969; Seidman, 1975; Woll, 1977).

Comment

Given sufficient incentives, as Fiorina (1982a) observes, Congress has found the capacity to tackle a number of complex issues itself. A striking example is the tax code (Jaffe, 1973, pp. 1189–90). What is more, there is no evident reason why Congress should respond to the complexity of issues by creating a large, expert bureaucracy without also creating a large, expert congressional staff—one sufficiently large and expert, not only to help decide complex issues, but to help oversee a large, expert bureaucracy.

Good Government

To serve the public interest, Congress has established regulatory and other executive-branch agencies based on expertise and divorced from politics. Because these agencies are designed to serve the public interest, whereas Congress is influenced by special-interest lobbies, oversight not only is unnecessary but might be regarded as political meddling in processes that ought to remain nonpolitical (Lowi, 1969).

Comment

Whatever the original intent, it is no longer plausible in most cases to suppose that the public interest is best served by a bureaucracy unaccountable to Congress and, therefore, unaccountable to the electorate.

Decentralization

Because congressional decisions are made, for the most part, by a large number of small, relatively autonomous subcommittees with narrow jurisdictions, general oversight committees tend to be weak (Dodd and Schott, 1979).

Comment

At most this explains why congressional oversight responsibilities are not centralized. It does not explain why they are neglected. If anything, subcommittee specialization should enhance congressional oversight over individual agencies. Subcommittees controlling authorizations and appropriations might be in a better position to do oversight than so-called oversight committees.

Regarding the apparent fact that Congress neglects oversight, we choose alternative (b) over (a): what appears to be a neglect of oversight can be explained as a preference by congressmen for fire-alarm over police-patrol oversight. We have already argued that congressmen have this preference. Scholars who decry the neglect of oversight have, we suggest, focused on an single form of oversight: they have looked only for police-patrol oversight, ignoring the fire-alarm alternative—and therewith the major part of actual oversight activity. Observing a neglect of *police-patrol* oversight, they have mistakenly concluded that *oversight* is neglected.

It has been suggested to us that scholars who have remarked congressional neglect of oversight were using the word more narrowly than we are—that they were *defining* "oversight" to mean police-patrol oversight, contrary to our Technological Assumption.

To this we have three replies: First, established usage equates oversight with the task of detecting and remedying violations of legislative goals by the executive branch.[2] No technique for accomplishing this task can be ruled out by definition. Second, the definitional equation of oversight with police-patrol oversight reflects the odd view that it is less important for Congress to make a serious attempt to detect and remedy violations of legislative goals than to employ a specific technique for doing so. Third, it would be odd to have a name for one way of detecting and remedying executive-branch violations of legislative goals but none for the general task of detecting and remedying such violations.

It has also been suggested to us that fire-alarm activities were never conceived or intended to be a form of oversight, whatever their effects.

We agree that congressmen rarely if ever refer to fire-alarm activities as "oversight," a term officially applied to subcommittees engaged in direct surveillance—in police-patrol oversight. Still, there is no evident reason for congressmen to engage in most fire-alarm activities unless they aim thereby to detect and remedy certain administrative violations of legislative goals.

Those who equate oversight with police-patrol oversight might argue that redressing grievances against the executive branch is not the same as enforcing compliance with congressional goals: the goals congressmen pursue in answering alarms related to particular laws need not be the goals they had in mind when they enacted those laws.

We see no reason to believe, however, that acts of legislation reflect well-defined or unalterable legislative goals—especially in view of the classical voting paradox and similar anomalies (Arrow, 1963; Plott, 1967; Schwartz, 1970, 1981, 1982a). Rather, legislative goals are refined, elaborated, and even changed over time in response to new problems—including complaints against executive agencies—and to changes in preferences and political alignments. In answering fire alarms, congressmen not only enforce compliance with legislative goals; they help decide what those goals are.

Possibly those who bemoan congressional neglect of oversight would agree that fire-alarm oversight is extensively practiced but argue that it is not *effective*.

We have argued already that fire-alarm oversight is likely to be somewhat effective. The evidence presented two sections hence supports this conclusion.

Even granting that fire-alarm oversight is extensively practiced and *somewhat* effective, hence that Congress does not *neglect* its oversight responsibility, one might still wonder which form of oversight is the *more* effective. To this question we now turn.

THE GREATER EFFECTIVENESS OF FIRE-ALARM OVERSIGHT

We will argue that fire-alarm oversight is likely to be more effective, on balance, than police-patrol oversight. But this requires two qualifications: First, we do not contend that the most effective oversight policy is likely to contain no police-patrol features, only that fire-alarm techniques are likely to predominate. Second, we do not contend that a predominantly fire-alarm policy is more likely than a predominantly police-patrol policy to serve the public interest, only that it is likely to secure greater compliance with legislative goals; whether such compliance serves the public interest depends on what those goals are.

A predominantly fire-alarm oversight policy is likely to be more effective—to secure greater compliance with legislative goals—than a predominantly police-patrol policy for two main reasons:

First, legislative goals often are stated in such a vague way that it is hard to decide whether any violation has occurred unless some citizen or group registers a complaint. Such a complaint gives Congress the opportunity to spell out its goals more clearly—just as concrete cases and controversies give courts the opportunity to elucidate legal principles that would be hard to make precise in the abstract.

Second, whereas a fire-alarm policy would almost certainly pick up any violation of legislative goals that seriously harmed an organized group, a police-patrol policy would doubtless miss many such violations, since only a sample of executive-branch actions would be examined.

One who agrees with this point might still argue, on behalf of the greater efficacy of police-patrol oversight, that the citizens harmed by violations of legislative goals are not always represented by organized groups and, hence, cannot always sound a loud enough alarm to secure a redress of grievances.

Our reply is fourfold: First, nowadays even "disadvantaged" groups often have public spokesmen. Second, as we show in the following section, sometimes Congress passes legislation, as part of its fire-alarm policy, that helps comparatively disorganized groups to act collectively. Third, congressmen's extensive constituent-service activities provide even individual citizens with an effective voice against administrative agencies: case work is part (but only part) of the fire-alarm system. Finally, if the point is merely that fire-alarm oversight can be biased in various ways, then the same is true of police-patrol oversight; and although a good enough police-patrol policy would avoid bias, so would a good enough fire-alarm policy.

To be sure, fire-alarm oversight tends to be *particularistic* in the sense of Mayhew (1974): it arguably emphasizes the interests of individuals and interest groups more than those of the public at large. This is an important difference—the essential difference, we think, between the respective products of police-patrol and fire-alarm oversight. But whether it is a shortcoming of fire-alarm oversight depends on one's ideological point of view: even if fire-alarm oversight deemphasizes some public-interest concerns, it gives special emphasis to a concern for the interests and rights of individual citizens and small groups—a concern well founded in American political values.

Although our model refers only to Congress, we hazard to hypothesize that as most organizations grow and mature, their top policy makers adopt methods of control that are comparatively decentralized and incentive based. Such methods, we believe, will work more efficiently (relative to accepted policy goals) than direct, centralized surveillance. This is sufficiently plausible that we wonder why students of Congress have generally assumed that congressional oversight must be of the direct, centralized police-patrol variety. Part of the reason, perhaps, is that Congress itself applies the label "oversight" to subcommittees charged with police-patrol responsibilities.

As we stated earlier, Consequences 1–3 do not depend on our Motivational Assumption, which depicts congressmen as pure politicians rather than statesmen. This is because statesmen, wishing to secure compliance with their legislative goals, would presumably adopt the most effective oversight policy, and that is likely to be one in which fire-alarm techniques predominate.

EVIDENCE

Evidence for Consequence 3—and therewith our model—is plentiful and well known. Scholars who bemoan congressional neglect of oversight have not ignored this evidence. Rather, they have missed its significance: lacking the concept of fire-alarm oversight, they have failed to see the details of our fire-alarm system as instances of oversight activity. Here is a brief summary of the available evidence:

1. Under a fire-alarm system, complaints against administrative agencies are often brought to the attention of congressional subcommittees by lobbyists for organized groups, and to the attention of administrative agencies by congressional subcommittees. The functioning of this "subgovernmental triangle" has been well documented (Dodd and Oppenheimer, 1977; Fenno, 1966, 1973a,b; Goodwin, 1970; Ornstein, 1975; Ripley, 1969; Huitt, 1973; Matthews, 1960; Ripley and Franklin, 1976).

2. Congress has passed legislation to help comparatively disorganized groups to press their grievances against the federal government. McConnell (1966) shows how the Agriculture, Labor, and Commerce Departments act as lobbyists for farm, labor, and small-business interests. Congress has also created new programs, such as the Legal-Services Corporation, to organize and press the claims of comparatively voiceless citizens.

3. Constituent-service activities are not limited to unsnarling procedural knots. As part of the fire-alarm system, district staff and casework help individuals and groups—some of them otherwise powerless—to raise and redress grievances against decisions by administrative agencies. This casework component of legislative policy making has been examined only recently, with a primary focus on the electoral connection (Cain, Ferejohn, and Fiorina, 1979a,b; Fenno, 1978; Fiorina, 1977a; Mayhew, 1974; Parker and Davidson, 1979) and with a secondary focus on policy consequences (Fiorina, 1977a, 1982b; Fiorina and Noll, 1978, 1979a,b).

4. Often the fire-alarm system allows for the redress of grievances by administrative agencies and courts; Congress itself need not always get involved. To facilitate such redress, Congress has passed several laws, notably the Administrative Procedures Act of 1946 and the Environmental Procedures Act of 1969, that have substantially increased the number of groups with legal standing before administrative agencies and district courts regarding bureaucratic controversies (Lowi, 1969).[3] Congress has also, as in sections 4–7 of the Toxic Substances Control Act of 1976, increased the courts' powers to issue injunctions in response to alarms and has required administrative agencies to hold hearings, publish information, and invite public comment on agency decision making (McCubbins, 1982a).

5. There are numerous cases in which violations of legislative goals were brought to the attention of Congress, which responded with vigorous remedial measures. For example, Congress dismantled the Area Redevelopment Administration (ARA) in 1963, even though it had just been authorized in 1961. The ARA was encouraging industries to relocate in redevelopment areas despite clear provisions in the law to the contrary. Congress also can redefine or reaffirm its goals by

redefining or explicating the jurisdictional authority of an administrative agency. This happened with the Federal Trade Commission when it first sought to regulate cigarette advertising, children's television, and funeral homes. Sometimes such congressional intervention is legislatively mandated. Before taking action on a pending case, for example, the National Labor Relations Board must consult with the appropriate congressional committees.

6. The general impression that Congress neglects oversight, we have argued, really is a perception that Congress neglects police-patrol over-sight. That impression and the evidence adduced to support it constitute further evidence for Consequences 1 and 3: they show that congressmen tend to prefer an oversight policy in which fire-alarm techniques predominate.

FURTHER IMPLICATIONS: HAS BUREAUCRATIC DISCRETION INCREASED?

Hand in glove with our stylized fact (neglect of oversight) goes another: Congress has increasingly relinquished its legislative authority to the executive branch, allowing the bureaucracy to make law (Dodd and Schott, 1979; Hess, 1976; Lowi, 1969; Woll, 1977).[4]

Although Congress may, to some extent, have allowed the bureaucracy to make law, it may also have devised a reasonably effective and noncostly way to articulate and promulgate its own legislative goals—a way that depends on the fire-alarm oversight system. It is convenient for Congress to adopt broad legislative mandates and give substantial rule-making authority to the bureaucracy. The problem with doing so, of course, is that the bureacracy might not pursue Congress's goals. But citizens and interest groups can be counted on to sound an alarm in most cases in which the bureaucracy has arguably violated Congress's goals. Then Congress can intervene to rectify the violation. Congress has not necessarily relinquished legislative responsibility to anyone else. It has just found a more efficient way to legislate.

When legislators try to write laws with sufficient detail and precision to preclude administrative discretion, they quickly run up against their own cognitive limits: beyond a certain point, human beings just cannot anticipate all the contingencies that might arise. The attempt to legislate for all contingencies can entail unintended (and undesired) consequences. In his classic study of Anglo-American judicial reasoning, Levi (1948) makes this point about judges (lawmakers of a sort), who lay down imprecise rules, which they subsequently and gradually elaborate in response to concrete legal disputes. Oakeshott (1973) makes a similar point about political activity of all sorts: it cannot be based on precise, detailed blueprints, and so policy formulations can at best be rough summaries of experience, requiring elaboration and judicious application case by case.

The ostensible shifting of legislative responsibility to the executive branch may simply be the responsible adoption of efficient legislative techniques and the responsible acceptance of human cognitive limits—both facilitated by the fire-alarm system.

FURTHER IMPLICATIONS: THE CHOICE OF REGULATORY POLICY

When it decides regulatory issues, Congress tends to choose one of two types of regulatory instrument: command-and-control instruments and incentive-based instruments. Congress faces a similar choice when it decides, not how to regulate society, but how to regulate the regulators—when it decides, in other words, on oversight policy. For police-patrol oversight is similar to command-and-control regulatory instruments, while fire-alarm oversight is similar to incentive-based instruments.

Offhand one might suppose that just as congressmen tend to prefer fire-alarm to police-patrol oversight policies, so they would tend to prefer incentive-based to command-and-control regulatory policies. Our observations, of course, do not support this supposition (Breyer, 1982; Fiorina, 1982a; Joskow and Noll, 1978; McCubbins, 1982a; McCubbins and Page, 1982; Schultze, 1977).

Paradoxically, Congress's very preference for fire-alarm oversight entails a preference for command-and-control regulatory policy. For command-and-control agencies are more susceptible of case-by-case congressional intervention in response to complaints, hence more susceptible of fire-alarm control, than are courts, taxing authorities, and private individuals and firms—the principal participants in incentive-based regulatory policy.

CONCLUSION

The widespread perception that Congress has neglected its oversight responsibility is a widespread mistake. Congressional scholars have focused their attention on police-patrol oversight. What has appeared to many of them to be a neglect of oversight is really a preference—an eminently rational one—for fire-alarm oversight. That a decentralized, incentive-based control mechanism has been found more effective, from its users' point view, than direct, centralized surveillance should come as no surprise.

Besides criticizing the received wisdom regarding congressional oversight, we hope to have highlighted a neglected way of looking at congressional behavior. Sometimes Congress appears to do little, leaving important policy decisions to the executive or judicial branch. But appearances can deceive. A perfectly reasonable way for Congress to pursue its objectives is by ensuring that fire alarms will be sounded, enabling courts, administrative agencies, and ultimately Congress itself to step in, whenever executive compliance with congressional objectives is called in question. In examining congressional policies and their impact, do not just ask how clear, detailed, or far-sighted congressional legislation is. Ask how likely it is that fire alarms will signal putative violations of legislative goals and how Congress is likely to respond to such alarms.

NOTES

1. See Bibby, 1966, 1968; Dodd and Schott, 1979; Fiorina, 1977a,b, 1982b; Hess, 1976; Huntington, 1973; Lowi, 1969; Mitnick, 1980; Ogul, 1976, 1977; Ripley, 1978; Scher, 1963; Seidman, 1975; Woll, 1977. The following remarks by Pearson (1975) succinctly exemplify this view: "Paradoxically, despite its importance, congressional oversight remains basically weak and ineffective" (p. 281). "Oversight is a vital yet neglected congressional function" (p. 288).

2. A 1977 report by the U.S. Senate Committee on Government Operations stated that "Oversight involves a wide range of congressional efforts to review and control policy implementation . . ." (pp. 4–5). According to Dodd and Schott (1979), "Oversight . . . involves attempts by Congress to review and control policy implementation" (p. 156). Ogul (1976) defines oversight as the process by which Congress determines, among other things, whether agencies are complying with congressional intent. See also Bibby, 1966; Harris, 1964; Lees, 1977; Lowi, 1969; Ripley, 1978; Woll, 1977.

3. Ferejohn (1974) provides a good example of how the decision-making procedures of the Army Corps of Engineers were expanded to include wilderness, wildlife, and environmental group interests by the passage of the 1969 Environmental Procedures Act.

4. On related points see Fiorina (1977b), Weingast and Moran (1981), McCubbins (1982a,b), and McCubbins and Page (1982). Weingast has argued that Congress employs a number of its constitutionally defined powers in a decentralized and often unobserved way in order to exercise control over the actions of administrative agencies (Calvert, Moran, and Weingast, 1982; Weingast and Moran, 1981).

REFERENCES

Arrow, Kenneth. 1963. *Social choice and individual values*. 2nd ed. New York: Wiley.
Baldwin, John. 1975. *The regulatory agency and the public corporation: The Canadian air transport industry*. Cambridge, Mass.: Ballinger.
Bibby, John. 1966. Committee characteristics and legislative oversight of administration. *Midwest Journal of Political Science*, 10 (February 1966): 78–98.
———. 1968. Congress' neglected function. In *Republican papers*, edited by Melvin Laird. New York: Praeger.
Breyer, Stephen. 1982. *Regulation and its reform*. Cambridge, Mass.: Harvard University Press.
Cain, Bruce, John Ferejohn, and Morris Fiorina. 1979a. The roots of legislator popularity in Great Britain and the United States. Social Science Working Paper No. 288, California Institute of Technology, Pasadena, Calif.
———. 1979b. Casework service in Great Britain and the United States. California Institute of Technology, Pasadena, Calif. Mimeo.

Calvert, Randall, Mark Moran, and Barry Weingast. 1982. Congressional influence over policymaking: The case of the FTC. Paper presented at the annual meeting of the American Political Science Association, Chicago, September 1982.

Dodd, Lawrence, and Bruce Oppenheimer, eds. 1977. *Congress reconsidered*. New York: Praeger.

Dodd, Lawrence, and Richard Schott. 1979. *Congress and the administrative state*. New York: Wiley.

Fenno, Richard, Jr. 1966. *The power of the purse*. Boston: Little, Brown.

———. 1973a. *Congressmen in committees*. Boston: Little, Brown.

———. 1973b. The internal distribution of influence: The house. In *The Congress and America's future*, 2nd ed, edited by David Truman, pp. 52–76. Englewood Cliffs, N.J.: Prentice-Hall.

———. 1978. *Home style*. Boston: Little, Brown.

Ferejohn, John. 1974. *Pork barrel politics*. Stanford, Calif.: Stanford University Press.

———. 1981. A note on the structure of administrative agencies. California Institute of Technology, Pasadena, Calif. Mimeo.

Fiorina, Morris, 1977a. *Congress: Keystone of the Washington establishment*. New Haven, Conn.: Yale University Press.

———. 1977b. Control of the bureaucracy: A mismatch of incentives and capabilities. Social Science Working Paper No. 182, California Institute of Technology, Pasadena, Calif.

———. 1982a. Legislative choice of regulatory forms: Legal process or administrative process? *Public Choice* 39 (September 1982): 33–66.

———. 1982b. Group concentration and the delegation of legislative authority. California Institute of Technology, Pasadena, Calif. Mimeo.

Fiorina, Morris, and Roger Noll. 1978. Voters, bureaucrats and legislators: A rational choice perspective on the growth of bureaucracy, *Journal of Public Economics* 9 (June 1978): 239–54.

———. 1979a. Voters, legislators and bureaucracy: Institutional design in the public sector. In *Problemi di administrazione publica, Centro di formazione e studi per il Messogiorno*, Naples, Italy, Formes 4 (2): 69–89.

———. 1979b. Majority rule models and legislative election. *Journal of Politics* 41: 1081–1104.

Goodwin, George, Jr. 1970. *The little legislatures*. Amherst: University of Massachusetts Press.

Harris, Joseph. 1964. *Congressional control of administration*. Washington, D.C.: Brookings.

Hess, Stephen. 1976. *Organizing the presidency*. Washington, D.C.: Brookings.

Huitt, Ralph. 1973. The internal distribution of influence: The Senate. In *The Congress in America's future*, 2nd ed., edited by David Truman, pp. 77–101. Englewood Cliffs, N.J.: Prentice-Hall.

Huntington, Samuel. 1973. Congressional responses to the twentieth century. In *The Congress in America's future*, 2nd ed., edited by David Truman, pp. 5–31. Englewood Cliffs, N.J.: Prentice-Hall.

Jaffe, Louis. 1973. The illusion of the ideal administration. *Harvard Law Review* 86: 1183–99.

Joskow, Paul. 1974. Inflation and environmental concern: Structural change is the process of public utility price regulation. *Journal of Law and Economics* 17 (October 1974): 291–327.

Joskow, Paul, and Roger Noll. 1978. Regulation in theory and practice: An overview. California Institute of Technology, Social Science Working Paper No. 213, Pasadena, Calif.

Lees, John D. 1977. Legislatures and oversight: A review article on a neglected area of research. *Legislative Studies Quarterly* (May 1977): 193–208.

Levi, Edward. 1948. *Legal reasoning*. Chicago: University of Chicago Press.

Lowi, Theodore. 1969. *The end of liberalism*. New York: Norton.

Matthews, Donald. 1960. *U.S. Senators and their world*. Chapel Hill: University of North Carolina Press.

Mayhew, David. 1974. *Congress: The electoral connection*. New Haven, Conn.: Yale University Press.

McConnell, Grant. 1966. *Private power and American democracy*. New York: Vintage Books.

McCubbins, Mathew. 1982a. Rational individual behavior and collective irrationality: The legislative choice of regulatory forms. Ph.D. dissertation, California Institute of Technology, Pasadena, Calif.

———. 1982b. On the form of regulatory intervention. Paper presented at the 1983 Annual Meeting of the Public Choice Society, Savannah, Ga., March 24–26, 1983.

McCubbins, Mathew, and Talbot Page. 1982. On the failure of environmental, health and safety regulation. Paper presented at the 1983 Annual Meeting of the Midwest Political Science Association, Chicago, Ill., April 20–23, 1983.

Mitnick, Barry. 1980. *The political economy of regulation*. New York: Columbia University Press.

Oakeshott, Michael. 1973. Political education. In *Rationalism in politics,* edited by Michael Oakeshott, pp. 110–36. New York: Basic Books, 1962. Reprinted in *Freedom and authority,* edited by Thomas Schwartz, 362–80. Encino, Calif.: Dickenson.

Ogul, Morris. 1976. *Congress oversees the bureaucracy*. Pittsburgh: University of Pittsburgh Press.

———. 1977. Congressional oversight: Structure and incentives. In *Congress reconsidered*, edited by Lawrence Dodd and Bruce Oppenheimer, pp. 207–221. New York: Praeger.

Ornstein, Norman, ed. 1975. *Congress in change*. New York: Praeger.

Parker, Glenn, and Roger Davidson. 1979. Why do Americans love their congressmen so much more than their Congress? *Legislative Studies Quarterly* 4 (February 1979): 53–62.

Pearson, James. 1975. Oversight: A vital yet neglected congressional function. *Kansas Law Review* 23: 277–88.

Plott, Charles. 1967. A notion of equilibrium and its possibility under majority rules. *American Economic Review* 57 (September 1967): 787–806.

Ripley, Randall 1969. *Power in the Senate*. New York: St. Martin's.

———. 1971. *The politics of economic and human resource development*. Indianapolis: Bobbs-Merrill.

———. 1978. *Congress: Process and policy*. 2nd ed. New York: Norton.

Ripley, Randall, and Grace Franklin. 1976. *Congress, the bureaucracy and public policy.* Homewood, Ill.: Dorsey.

Scher, Seymour. 1963. Conditions for legislative control. *Journal of Politics* 25 (August 1963): 526–51.

Schultze, Charles. 1977. *The public use of private interest*. Washington, D.C.: Brookings.

Schwartz, Thomas. 1970. On the possibility of rational policy evaluation. *Theory and Decision* 1 (October 1970): 89–106.

———. 1981. The universal-instability theorem. *Public Choice* 37 (3): 487–501.

———. 1982a. A really general impossibility theorem. *Quality and Quantity* 16 (December 1982): 493–505.

———. 1982b. The porkbarrel paradox. University of Texas, Austin, Tex. Mimeo.

Seidman, Harold. 1975. *Politics, position, and power: The dynamics of federal organization*. New York: Oxford.

U.S. Senate. Committee on Government Operations. 1977. *Study on federal regulation, vol. II, congressional oversight of regulatory agencies*. Washington, D.C.: Government Printing Office.

Weingast, Barry, and Mark Moran. 1981. Bureaucratic discretion of congressional control: Regulatory policymaking by the Federal Trade Commission. Washington University, St. Louis: Center of the Study of American Business. Mimeo.

Woll, Peter. 1977. *American bureaucracy*. New York: Norton.

7.3

DANIEL CARPENTER

From *The Forging of Bureaucratic Autonomy: Reputations, Networks, and Policy Innovation in Executive Agencies, 1862–1928*

Bureaucrats in the executive branch need some autonomy from politicians in order to do their work. Regulators of food and drugs, for example, should not be influenced by political pressure. After all, many of these bureaucrats have technical expertise or are in jobs that require impartial decisions. Carpenter argues that it took a long time for many bureaucratic positions to gain the appropriate amount of autonomy. Bureaucrats in the early twentieth century had to play their own political games to earn this autonomy, namely by cultivating their own loyal constituencies within industry and among the population.

Bureaucratic autonomy occurs when bureaucrats take actions consistent with their own wishes, actions to which politicians and organized interests defer even though they would prefer that other actions (or no action at all) be taken. Bureaucratic autonomy so defined is a common feature, though far from a universal one, of American government in the twentieth century. Agencies have at times created and developed policy with few, if any, constraints from legislative and executive overseers, and they have frequently coordinated organized interests as much as responded to them. To suggest that bureaucracies have policymaking autonomy may strike some readers as a controversial if not outlandish claim. Surely agencies lack the ability to take any action they desire in our system of representative government and rule of law. Yet I contend here that bureaucratic autonomy lies less in *fiat* than in *leverage*. Autonomy prevails when agencies can establish political legitimacy—a reputation for expertise, efficiency, or moral protection and a uniquely diverse complex of ties to organized interests and the media—and induce politicians to defer to the wishes of the agency even when they prefer otherwise. Under these conditions, politicians grant agency officials free rein in program building. They stand by while agency officials do away with some of their cherished programs and services. They even welcome agencies in shaping legislation itself.

■　　■　　■

CONCLUSION

The Politics of Bureaucratic Autonomy

Bureaucrats are politicians, and bureaucracies are organizations of political actors. Autonomy arises when bureaucrats successfully practice a politics of legitimacy. It occurs when agency leaders build reputations for their organizations—reputations for efficacy, for uniqueness of service, for moral protection, and for expertise. It occurs, further, when they ground this reputation in a diverse coalition wrought from the multiple networks in which they are engaged. These coalitions, suspended in beliefs and in networks, and uncontrollable by politicians, are the stuff of autonomous bureaucratic policy innovation. This, I submit, is the basic lesson of the forging of bureaucratic autonomy in the United States. *Bureaucratic autonomy is politically forged.*

Contemporary political science—including an entire literature on bureaucracy that depends on "principal-agent" models of bureaucratic politics—assumes that the linkages between voters and policies occur through parties, elections, representatives, and the legislature. Yet the decisive steps in forging bureaucratic autonomy occurred when federal bureaucrats broke free from the traditional model of politics and established links directly to citizens and the new associations that increasingly claimed their allegiance. Long before the "iron triangles" of the New Deal Era, bureaucracies began to aggregate citizens and voters precisely when parties and politicians were having a difficult time doing so.

Because some agencies did this more successfully than others, the state-building achievement of the Progressive Era was concrete but limited. What emerged in the 1910s and 1920s was not a uniformly more powerful bureaucracy than existed three decades earlier. In pockets of the American state, relative autonomy conditioned upon political legitimacy materialized. Most other agencies lay dormant. Therein lies the puzzle of American state building. Why was the Department of Agriculture able to establish a foothold in writing significant legislation? Why was the Interior Department, with authority over public lands and ties to numerous western interests, unable to capitalize on the movements for conservation and western reclamation? Why were reformers in the Post Office Department able to eliminate systematically the positions of strong Republican identifiers in fourth-class offices at the very time when Republicans enjoyed hegemony in electoral politics? Why were postal officials able to grab all of the moral policing powers they wanted and resist political control of their use? Why was the USDA able to take its newfound authority in food and drug regulation and turn its fire on the very firms who most supported Republicans during the Progressive period?

The answer lies in the organizational properties of executive agencies at the turn of the century. Bureaucratic autonomy cannot exist apart from the organizational characteristics of the agencies that experience it. If it exists, bureaucratic autonomy *must* be premised not upon the popularity of a policy, not upon occasional administrative fiat, not upon a single well-heeled lobby, but upon the stable political legitimacy of the bureaucracy itself. To focus on organizational reputations is not, as I have emphasized, to divorce bureaucracies from politics. Instead, it is to reconceive politics as a process of coalition building and to acknowledge that in some circumstances bureaucrats can take the decisive initiative (at times, the *only* initiative) in building them. It is to these reputations—and the capacities and coalitions that supported them—that autonomous bureaucracies in America owe their origins.

▪   ▪   ▪

The Poverty of Procedural Politics

The argument elaborated here poses several challenges to contemporary erudition on bureaucracies. Following the highly influential work of Mathew McCubbins, Roger Noll, and Barry Weingast, a generation of scholars has argued that an agency's "enacting coalition" of politicians can use administrative procedures to induce the agency to take exactly those actions that the coalition desires. These "procedural politics" theories suggest that most of the political action in bureaucratic politics occurs when the methods and processes for a given policy are set by politicians and the interests to which they respond. Hence bureaucratic politics does not really involve bureaucracies at all; "the administrative system is automatic."

The theory elaborated here suggests that procedural politics is unlikely to control agencies with stable political legitimacy. Agencies with esteemed officials who have publicly recognized capacity and expertise, and who have independent access to organized citizens, exercise power over the procedures of their agency. Autonomous agencies are powerful bargaining agents in procedural design. The more powerful constraint on administrative procedures is that legitimated agency officials can make it politically costly for politicians to constrain them. Partisans of the procedural-politics school of bureaucracy have discussed all sorts of mechanisms for controlling the bureaucracy without recognizing that these strategies have costs. In some respects, these amount to forfeiting the benefits of agency specialization. The argument here, however, is that when agencies have political legitimacy, the costs of control are *explicitly political and electoral*.

▪   ▪   ▪

Congress, the Media, and Multiplicity

The role of general beliefs about agencies in bureaucratic reputations points to important changes in Congress and the media that enabled agencies to erect reputations. The building of bureaucratic reputations between Congress and executive departments found fertile soil in the Progressive period. Not only were bureau chiefs serving longer tenures, but members of Congress were investing more and more time in committees. As a result, agency officials and their overseers in Congress began to develop a mutual familiarity. The institutional memory of Congress grew, the abilities and interests of bureaus became clearer and more consistent, and uncertainty over the bureaucracy declined. The stability of these relations gave bureau chiefs an incentive to cultivate the trust of committee chairs and congressional party leaders, and some Progressive-Era program leaders adopted this strategy to great advantage.[1]

Perhaps the most important venue of bureaucratic reputation lay in the rapidly expanding media. At a time when broadcast news remained only an imaginary possibility, Americans received their political information from a highly variegated print industry. In this market the critical split was between the larger urban newspapers and related syndicates and the rural farm weeklies. In the urban newspapers arose the "muckraking" of Progressive reformers, whereas farm editors remained committed to a mix of populist and pro-agrarian sentiments. In part because these papers depended increasingly on the USDA and the Post Office for information and rate classification, both agencies were treated with favor by urban and rural presses. Yet the network advantages of the two agencies transcended mere resource dependence. Numerous Agriculture Department officials were close acquaintances with one or more rural newspaper editors. And newspaper editors, urban and rural, interacted frequently with postal officials over matters of rate classification. As a result of these ties, Progressive-Era citizens were better (and more favorably) informed about the USDA and Post Office than any other agencies in American government.

Reputations for Neutrality and Moral Protection

Traditionally, political scientists have expected greater autonomy where agencies can lay claim to expertise—especially where agencies possess a monopoly on information in a given area. A more interesting case of "policy" in this book emerges from "moral politics" during the culturally conservative Progressive Era. A key component of both the USDA's and the Post Office's march to autonomy was their linkages to Victorian moral reformers and their anti-adulteration campaigns, both in the adulteration of food and the adulteration of morals (through pornography and gambling). The Interior Department lacked any such connection to anti-adulteration themes. These moral reputations, and the framing of policy campaigns in terms of "protection" from "the evils of adulteration," served to enhance the agencies' esteem for national service. A core component of strong agency reputations is the mien of neutrality, impartiality, or orientation toward the public good. Where an agency's innovations appear patently to serve its own interests or those of a selected group or region, the political legitimacy necessary for autonomy is less likely to emerge.

In the case of postal state building, coalition building combined moralist Progressives, media organizations, agrarians, and corporate business. Each of these interests sought something different from the Post Office. Progressive Victorians wanted moral policing in the form of Comstockery, agrarians wanted expanded services in rural America and an alternative to institutions dominated by corporate industry, and business interests and the media (for different reasons) wanted an efficient national communications infrastructure. Each saw their interests met in the same programs. Without all four (and more) of these organizational forces, programs such as rural free delivery, parcels post, and postal savings would not have marked Progressive change as they did. More critically, without Anthony Comstock, August Machen, John Wanamaker, and other postal officials to bridge these forces and to create a multifaceted coalition, the possibility of institutional change would have been trifling.

The logic of multifaceted coalitions was demonstrated nowhere more powerfully than in the Department of Agriculture. Republican presidents, women's organizations, conservationists, congressional committees, agrarian organizations—all of these interests converged to influence policy change in areas as diverse as pharmaceutical regulation, forest preservation, and agricultural extension. The central point, again, is that the coalitions were nursed and maintained not by elected politicians but by middle-level bureaucrats. Far more than in Herbert Hoover's Department of Commerce, the "associational state" in America was established in the early-twentieth-century USDA. Unlike Commerce, moreover, the USDA exerted an immense influence on the groups in its coalitions.

■   ■   ■

The organizational flourishing that was characteristic of Progressive society offers one reason that the patterns of bureaucratic autonomy witnessed in this book are less likely to be observed in contemporary politics. To be sure, modern America is rife with organizations in the formal sense. The day-by-day embedment of Americans in organizations has waned, not strengthened, over the last few decades. The challenge of contemporary American state building, in this view, may demand more than "reinventing" American government.

NOTE

1. Jonathan N. Katz and Brian R. Sala, "Careerism, Committee Assignments, and the Electoral Connection," *American Political Science Review* 90 (March 1996): 21.

THE JUDICIARY

8.1

GERALD N. ROSENBERG

From *The Hollow Hope: Can Courts Bring about Social Change?*

Rosenberg argues that courts in the United States are highly constrained in bringing about social change. Though many people think of the courts as "dynamic"— as drivers of social change—in Rosenberg's view, courts instead follow the other branches of government. They do not drive change but rather respond late to social changes and end up trying to catch up with trends in society.

INTRODUCTION

The Problem

■ ■ ■

To what degree, and under what conditions, can judicial processes be used to produce political and social change? What are the constraints that operate on them? What factors are important and why?

. . . Traditionally, most lawyers and legal scholars have focused on a related normative issue: whether courts *ought* to act. From the perspective of democratic theory, that is an important and useful question. Yet since much of politics is about who gets what, when, and how, and how that distribution is maintained, or changed, understanding to what extent, and under what conditions, courts can produce political and social change is of key importance.

. . . In the last several decades movements and groups advocating what I will shortly define as significant social reform have turned increasingly to the courts. Starting with the famous cases brought by the civil rights movement and spreading to issues raised by women's groups, environmental groups, political reformers, and others, American courts seemingly have become important producers of political and social change. Cases such as *Brown* (school desegregation) and *Roe* (abortion) are heralded as having produced major change. Further, such litigation has often occurred, and appears to have been most successful, when the other branches of government have failed to act. While officious government officials and rigid, unchanging institutions represent a real social force which may frustrate popular opinion, this litigation activity suggests that courts can produce significant social reform even when the other branches of government are inactive or opposed. Indeed, for many, part of what makes American democracy exceptional is that it includes the world's most powerful court system, protecting minorities and defending liberty, in the face of opposition from the democratically elected branches. Americans look to activist courts, then, as fulfilling an important role in the American scheme.[1] This view of the courts, although informed by recent historical experience, is essentially functional. It sees courts as powerful, vigorous, and potent proponents of change. I refer to this view of the role of the courts as the "Dynamic Court" view.

As attractive as the Dynamic Court view may be, one must guard against uncritical acceptance. Indeed, in a political system that gives sovereignty to the popular will and makes economic decisions through the market, it is not obvious why courts should have the effects it asserts. Maybe its attractiveness is based on something more than effects? Could it be that the self-understanding of the judiciary and legal profession leads to an overstatement of the role of the courts, a "mystification" of the judiciary? If judges see themselves as powerful; if the Bar views itself as influential, and insulated; if professional training in law schools inculcates students with such beliefs, might these factors inflate the self-importance of the judiciary? The Dynamic Court view may be supported, then, because it offers psychological payoffs to key actors by confirming self-images, not because it is correct.[2] And when this "mystification" is added to a normative belief in the courts as the guardian of fundamental rights and liberties—what Scheingold (1974) calls the "myth of rights"—the allure of the Dynamic Court view may grow.

Further, for all its "obviousness," the Dynamic Court view has a well-established functional and historical competitor. In fact, there is a long tradition of legal scholarship that views the federal judiciary, in Alexander Hamilton's famous language, as the "least dangerous" branch of government. Here, too, there is something of a truism about this claim. Courts, we know, lack both budgetary and physical powers. Because, in Hamilton's words, they lack power over either the "sword or the purse," their ability to produce political and social change is limited. In contrast to the first view, the "least dangerous" branch can do little more than point out how actions have fallen short of constitutional or legislative requirements and hope that appropriate action is taken. The strength of this view, of course, is that it leaves Americans free to govern themselves without interference from non-elected officials. I refer to this view of the courts as weak, ineffective, and powerless as the "Constrained Court" view.

The Constrained Court view fully acknowledges the role of popular preferences and social and economic resources in shaping outcomes. Yet it seems to rely excessively on a formal-process understanding of how change occurs in American politics. But the formal process doesn't always work, for social and political forces may be overly responsive to unevenly distributed resources. Bureaucratic inertia, too, can derail orderly, processional change. There is room, then, for courts to effectively correct the pathologies of the political process. Perhaps accurate at the founding of the political system, the Constrained Court view may miss growth and change in the American political system.

Clearly, these two views, and the aspirations they represent, are in conflict on a number of different dimensions. They differ not only on both the desirability and the effectiveness of court action, but also on the nature of American democracy. The Dynamic Court view gives courts an important place in the American political system while the older view sees courts as much less powerful than other more "political" branches and activities. The conflict is more than one of mere definition, for each view captures a very different part of American democracy. We Americans want courts to protect minorities and defend liberties, *and* to defer to elected officials. We want a robust political life *and* one that is just. Most of the time, these two visions do not clash. American legislatures do not habitually threaten liberties, and courts do not regularly invalidate the acts of elected officials or require certain actions to be taken. But the most interesting and relevant cases, such as *Brown* and *Roe*, occur when activist courts overrule and invalidate the actions of elected officials, or order actions beyond what elected officials are willing to do. What happens then? Are courts effective producers of change, as the Dynamic Court view suggests, or do their decisions do little more than point the way to a brighter, but perhaps unobtainable future? Once again, this conflict between two deeply held views about the role of the courts in the American political system has an obvious normative dimension that is worth debating.

■ ■ ■

THE DYNAMIC AND THE CONSTRAINED COURT

■ ■ ■

Structural Constraints: The Logic of the Constrained Court View

The view of courts as unable to produce significant social reform has a distinguished pedigree reaching back to the founders. Premised on the institutional structure of the American political system and the procedures and belief systems created by American law, it suggests that the conditions required for courts to produce significant social reform will seldom exist.

■   ■   ■

[T]he Constrained Court view holds that litigants asking courts for significant social reform are faced with powerful constraints. First, they must convince courts that the rights they are asserting are required by constitutional or statutory language. Given the limited nature of constitutional rights, the constraints of legal culture, and the general caution of the judiciary, this is no easy task. Second, courts are wary of stepping too far out of the political mainstream. Deferential to the federal government and potentially limited by congressional action, courts may be unwilling to take the heat generated by politically unpopular rulings. Third, if these two constraints are overcome and cases are decided favorably, litigants are faced with the task of implementing the decisions. Lacking powerful tools to force implementation, court decisions are often rendered useless given much opposition. Even if litigators seeking significant social reform win major victories in court, in implementation they often turn out to be worth very little. Borrowing the words of Justice Jackson from another context, the Constrained Court view holds that court litigation to produce significant social reform may amount to little more than "a teasing illusion like a munificent bequest in a pauper's will" (*Edwards* v. *California* 1941, 186).

Court Effectiveness: The Logic of the Dynamic Court View

The three constraints just presented are generated from the view of courts as unable to produce significant social reform. That view appears historically grounded and empirically plausible. Yet, on reflection, it has two main difficulties. First, it seems to overstate the limits on courts. After all, since the mid-twentieth century or so courts have been embroiled in controversies over significant social reform. Many lawyers, activists, and scholars have acted or written with the belief that the constraints are weak or non-existent and can easily be overcome. Indeed, the whole modern debate over judicial activism makes no sense if the Constrained Court view is correct. If courts are as impotent as the constraints suggest, then why has there been such political, academic, and judicial concern with the role of courts in modern America? Theory and practice are unaligned if the Constrained Court view is entirely correct. Second, examined carefully, its claim is that courts are *unlikely* to produce significant social reform; it does not deny the possibility. However, that doesn't help us understand when, and under what conditions, courts can produce significant social reform. The Constrained Court view is not the complete answer.

The Dynamic Court view may help. It maintains that courts can be effective producers of significant social reform. Its basic thrust is that not only are courts not as limited as the Constrained Court view suggests, but also, in some cases, they can be more effective than other governmental institutions in producing significant social reform.

Political, Institutional, and Economic Independence

■   ■   ■

The Dynamic Court view provides a powerful alternative to the view of courts as the "least dangerous branch." Pointing to pathologies in the other branches, it places courts in a unique position to act. Acknowledging, perhaps, that the Constrained Court view was accurate at the Founding and for part of American history, it maintains that great change has occurred over the last few decades and that courts now have the tools to effectively produce significant social reform. Unlike the Constrained Court view, it is congruent with judicial activism and the modern use of the courts to produce significant social reform. While courts cannot solve all problems, the Dynamic Court view does see them as powerful and effective, unconstrained by the concentrations of power and bureaucratic inertia that stymie self-initiated change in the other branches.

■   ■   ■

Yet for all their plausibility and surface appeal, and their seemingly accurate description of recent litigation, attempts to ground the Dynamic Court view empirically are not entirely satisfying. Unfortunately, studies of the sort referred to above neither completely validate it nor are particularly helpful in constructing hypotheses about courts' effectiveness in producing significant social reform. Often, they either focus on unrepresentative time periods, or on unimportant and noncontroversial cases, or they overstate their findings. In addition, many of the studies that support the Dynamic Court view are theoretical rather than empirical. They mistake what conceivably could happen with what actually has happened. Further, the empirical studies tend to examine only one case. The problem here, from the Constrained Court perspective, is that given the constraints on judges imposed by court rules and the legal culture, it is the rare judge who will become so actively engaged. Although the Dynamic Court view may be correct, the empirical evidence offered in its support does not seal the case.

■   ■   ■

With special masters, again, actual case studies do not bear out claims on behalf of the Dynamic Court view. For example, introducing an edited compilation of seven studies of school desegregation, Kalodner concludes that "Masters have seldom if ever been effective in the effort to find a solution that is both acceptable and constitutional" (Kalodner 1978, 9). Reviewing the use of masters in six school desegregation cases, Kirp and Babcock explicitly reject Aronow's optimistic conclusions (Kirp and Babcock 1981, 395). Finally, a lengthy and detailed study of institutional reform litigation points out that under court rules the use of special masters must "be the exception and not the rule. Consequently, there cannot be reference to masters as a matter of course" (Special Project 1978, 808). While special masters may be helpful in some cases, overall their record of use appears of limited effectiveness. And the crucial question of under what conditions special masters will be effective is left unanswered.

The Dynamic Court view, then, though in large part an effective retort to the unbending constraints of the Constrained Court view, does not get us very far in understanding the conditions under which courts can produce significant social reform. While its logic of independence and equal access makes good sense, its lack of generalizable empirical support is unhelpful. In sum, while courts may be more effective in producing significant social reform than the constraints of the Constrained Court view allow, the Dynamic Court view does not definitively demonstrate when, and under what conditions, court efficacy can be found.

Conditions for Court Efficacy

The thrust of the Dynamic Court view is that its competitor oversimplifies reality by *under*stating court effectiveness. However, it appears that the Dynamic Court view likewise oversimplifies, by *over*stating court effectiveness. Further, the views appear to be in conflict. For example, the Dynamic Court view proposes court action in the face of hostile or inert political institutions while the constraints of the Constrained Court view tell us that in such situations success is least likely. Along with conflict, however, each view appears to convey something of the truth. On an intuitive level, opposition from political elites is not conducive to court effectiveness. On the other hand, judicial isolation from many pressures allows courts to act when other institutions wish to but cannot. Surely it is naive to expect courts to be able to solve political and economic problems that the other branches cannot. But it appears equally short-sighted to deny that since mid-century courts have played an important role in producing significant social reform. It may well be that while each view captures part of the truth, neither is fine-grained enough to capture the conditions under which courts can effectively produce significant social reform.

■   ■   ■

I suggest that this is the case; the constraints of the Constrained Court view generally limit courts, but when political, social, and economic conditions have become supportive of change, courts can effectively produce significant social reform.

■   ■   ■

[T]he conditions enabling courts to produce significant social reform will seldom be present because courts are limited by three separate constraints built into the structure of the American political system:

1. The limited nature of constitutional rights . . .
2. The lack of judicial independence . . .
3. The judiciary's lack of powers of implementation . . .

However, when certain conditions are met, courts can be effective producers of significant social reform. These conditions occur when:

1. . . . There is ample legal precedent for change; *and,*
2. . . . There is support for change from substantial numbers in Congress and from the executive; *and,*
3. . . . There is either support from some citizens, or at least low levels
   of opposition from all citizens.

NOTES

1. Not everyone, however, thinks such liberal judicial activism is a good thing. It has
spawned a wave of attacks on the judiciary ranging from Nathan Glazer's warning of
the rise of an "imperial judiciary" to a spate of legislative proposals to remove court
jurisdiction over a number of issues. See Glazer (1975); *An Imperial Judiciary* (1979).
And, of course, Presidents Nixon and Reagan pledged to end judicial activism by
appointing "strict constructionists" to the federal courts.

2. As McCann (1986, 114) suggests, in the public-interest movement, lawyers are
"quite naturally the most ardent spokespersons" for the use of courts to produce change.

CASE REFERENCES

Edwards v. *California*, 314 U.S. 160 (1941).
Roe v. *Wade*, 410 U.S. 113 (1973).

REFERENCES

An imperial Judiciary: Fact or Myth? 1979. Washington, D.C.: American Enterprise
   Institute.
Aronow, Geoffrey F. 1980. "The Special Master in School Desegregation Cases: The
   Evolution of Roles in the Reformation of Public Institutions through Litigation." 7
   Hastings Const. L. Q. 739.
Glazer, Nathan. 1975. "Towards an Imperial Judiciary?" *The Public Interest* (Fall):
   104–23.
Kalodner, Howard I. 1978. Introduction. In *Limits to Justice.* Ed. Howard I. Kalodner,
   and James J. Fishman. Cambridge, Mass.: Ballinger. 1–24.
Kirp, David L., and Gary Babcock. 1981. "Judge and Company: Court Appointed Mas-
   ters, School Desegregation, and Institutional Reform. In "Symposium, Judicially
   Managed Institutional Reform." 32 *Alabama L. Rev.* 317.
McCann, Michael. 1986. *Taking Reform Seriously: Perspectives on Public Interest Liber-
   alism.* Ithaca: Cornell University Press.
Scheingold, Stuart A. 1974. *The Politics of Rights: Lawyers, Public Policy, and Political
   Change.* New Haven: Yale University Press.
Special Project. 1978. "The Remedial Process in Institutional Reform Litigation." 78
   Colum. L. Rev. 784.

8.2

Marbury v. Madison (1801)

This foundational Supreme Court decision was a bold move by the Court to establish its central role in the national government. In writing this opinion, Chief Justice John Marshall laid out the case in favor of the Supreme Court having the final say in determining whether a law or action of the government is constitutional. By declaring that "it is emphatically the province and duty of the judicial department to say what the law is," this opinion establishes judicial review as a fundamental aspect of American government.

Mr. Chief Justice MARSHALL delivered the opinion of the Court.

At the last term, on the affidavits then read and filed with the clerk, a rule was granted in this case requiring the Secretary of State to show cause why a mandamus should not issue directing him to deliver to William Marbury his commission as a justice of the peace for the county of Washington, in the District of Columbia.

No cause has been shown, and the present motion is for a mandamus. The peculiar delicacy of this case, the novelty of some of its circumstances, and the real difficulty attending the points which occur in it require a complete exposition of the principles on which the opinion to be given by the Court is founded.

These principles have been, on the side of the applicant, very ably argued at the bar. In rendering the opinion of the Court, there will be some departure in form, though not in substance, from the points stated in that argument.

If he has a right, and that right has been violated, do the laws of his country afford him a remedy?

The very essence of civil liberty certainly consists in the right of every individual to claim the protection of the laws whenever he receives an injury. One of the first duties of government is to afford that protection. In Great Britain, the King himself is sued in the respectful form of a petition, and he never fails to comply with the judgment of his court.

The Government of the United States has been emphatically termed a government of laws, and not of men. It will certainly cease to deserve this high appellation if the laws furnish no remedy for the violation of a vested legal right.

By the act concerning invalids, passed in June, 1794, the Secretary at War is ordered to place on the pension list all persons whose names are contained in a report previously made by him to Congress. If he should refuse to do so, would the wounded veteran be without remedy? Is it to be contended that where the law, in precise terms, directs the performance of an act in which an individual is interested, the law is incapable of securing obedience to its mandate? Is it on account of the character of the person against whom the complaint is made? Is it to be contended that the heads of departments are not amenable to the laws of their country?

Whatever the practice on particular occasions may be, the theory of this principle will certainly never be maintained. No act of the Legislature confers so extraordinary a privilege, nor can it derive countenance from the doctrines of the common law.

It follows, then, that the question whether the legality of an act of the head of a department be examinable in a court of justice or not must always depend on the nature of that act.

If some acts be examinable and others not, there must be some rule of law to guide the Court in the exercise of its jurisdiction.

In some instances, there may be difficulty in applying the rule to particular cases; but there cannot, it is believed, be much difficulty in laying down the rule.

The power of nominating to the Senate, and the power of appointing the person nominated, are political powers, to be exercised by the President according to his own discretion. When he has made an appointment, he has exercised his whole power, and his discretion has been completely applied to the case. If, by law, the officer be removable at the will of the President, then a new appointment may be immediately made, and the rights of the officer are terminated. But as a fact which has existed cannot be made never to have existed, the appointment cannot be annihilated, and consequently, if the officer is by law not removable at the will of the President, the rights he has acquired are protected by the law, and are not resumable by the President. They cannot be extinguished by Executive authority, and he has the privilege of asserting them in like manner as if they had been derived from any other source.

The question whether a right has vested or not is, in its nature, judicial, and must be tried by the judicial authority. If, for example, Mr. Marbury had taken the oaths of a magistrate and proceeded to act as one, in consequence of which a suit had been instituted against him in which his defence had depended on his being a magistrate; the validity of his appointment must have been determined by judicial authority.

So, if he conceives that, by virtue of his appointment, he has a legal right either to the commission which has been made out for him or to a copy of that commission, it is equally a question examinable in a court, and the decision of the Court upon it must depend on the opinion entertained of his appointment.

It is then the opinion of the Court:

That, by signing the commission of Mr. Marbury, the President of the United States appointed him a justice of peace for the County of Washington in the District of Columbia, and that the seal of the United States, affixed thereto by the Secretary of State, is conclusive testimony of the verity of the signature, and of the completion of the appointment, and that the appointment conferred on him a legal right to the office for the space of five years.

That, having this legal title to the office, he has a consequent right to the commission, a refusal to deliver which is a plain violation of that right, for which the laws of his country afford him a remedy.

It remains to be inquired whether, he is entitled to the remedy for which he applies.

With respect to the officer to whom it would be directed. The intimate political relation, subsisting between the President of the United States and the heads of departments, necessarily renders any legal investigation of the acts of one of those high officers peculiarly irksome, as well as delicate, and excites some hesitation with respect to the propriety of entering into such investigation. Impressions are often received without much reflection or examination, and it is not wonderful that, in such a case as this, the assertion by an individual of his legal claims in a court of justice, to which claims it is the duty of that court to attend, should, at first view, be considered [p170] by some as an attempt to intrude into the cabinet and to intermeddle with the prerogatives of the Executive.

It is scarcely necessary for the Court to disclaim all pretensions to such a jurisdiction. An extravagance so absurd and excessive could not have been entertained for a moment. The province of the Court is solely to decide on the rights of individuals, not to inquire how the Executive or Executive officers perform duties in which they have a discretion. Questions, in their nature political or which are, by the Constitution and laws, submitted to the Executive, can never be made in this court.

But, if this be not such a question; if so far from being an intrusion into the secrets of the cabinet, it respects a paper which, according to law, is upon record, and to a copy of which the law gives a right, on the payment of ten cents; if it be no intermeddling with a subject over which the Executive can be considered as having exercised any control; what is there in the exalted station of the officer which shall bar a citizen from asserting in a court of justice his legal rights, or shall forbid a court to listen to the claim or to issue a mandamus directing the performance of a duty not depending on Executive discretion, but on particular acts of Congress and the general principles of law?

If one of the heads of departments commits any illegal act under colour of his office by which an individual sustains an injury, it cannot be pretended that his office alone exempts him from being sued in the ordinary mode of proceeding, and being compelled to obey the judgment of the law. How then can his office exempt him from this particular mode of deciding on the legality of his conduct if the case be such a case as would, were any other individual the party complained of, authorize the process?

It is not by the office of the person to whom the writ is directed, but the nature of the thing to be done, that the propriety or impropriety of issuing a mandamus is to be determined. Where the head of a department acts in a case in which Executive discretion is to be exercised, in which he is the mere organ of Executive will, it is again repeated, that any application to a court to control, in any respect, his conduct, would be rejected without hesitation.

But where he is directed by law to do a certain act affecting the absolute rights of individuals, in the performance of which he is not placed under the particular direction of the President, and the performance of which the President cannot lawfully forbid, and therefore is never presumed to have forbidden—as for example, to record a commission, or a patent for land, which has received all the legal solemnities; or to give a copy of such record—in such cases, it is not perceived on what ground the Courts of the country are further excused from the duty of giving judgment that right to be done to an injured individual than if the same services were to be performed by a person not the head of a department.

This opinion seems not now for the first time to be taken up in this country.

It is true that the mandamus now moved for is not for the performance of an act expressly enjoined by statute.

It is to deliver a commission, on which subjects the acts of Congress are silent. This difference is not considered as affecting the case. It has already been stated that the applicant has, to that commission, a vested legal right of which the Executive cannot deprive him. He has been appointed to an office from which he is not removable at the will of the Executive, and, being so appointed, he has a right to the commission which the Secretary has received from the President for his use. The act of Congress does not, indeed, order the Secretary of State to send it to him, but it is placed in his hands for the person entitled to it, and cannot be more lawfully withheld by him than by another person.

This is a plain case of a mandamus, either to deliver the commission or a copy of it from the record, and it only remains to be inquired:

Whether it can issue from this Court.

The act to establish the judicial courts of the United States authorizes the Supreme Court to issue writs of mandamus, in cases warranted by the principles and usages of law, to any courts appointed, or persons holding office, under the authority of the United States.

The Secretary of State, being a person, holding an office under the authority of the United States, is precisely within the letter of the description, and if this Court is not authorized to issue a writ of mandamus to such an officer, it must be because the law is unconstitutional, and therefore absolutely incapable of conferring the authority and assigning the duties which its words purport to confer and assign.

The Constitution vests the whole judicial power of the United States in one Supreme Court, and such inferior courts as Congress shall, from time to time, ordain and establish. This power is expressly extended to all cases arising under the laws of the United States; and consequently, in some form, may be exercised over the present case, because the right claimed is given by a law of the United States.

In the distribution of this power. it is declared that the Supreme Court shall have original jurisdiction in all cases affecting ambassadors, other public ministers and consuls, and those in which a state shall be a party. In all other cases, the Supreme Court shall have appellate jurisdiction.

It has been insisted at the bar, that, as the original grant of jurisdiction to the Supreme and inferior courts is general, and the clause assigning original jurisdiction to the Supreme Court contains no negative or restrictive words, the power remains to the Legislature to assign original jurisdiction to that Court in other cases than those specified in the article which has been recited, provided those cases belong to the judicial power of the United States.

If it had been intended to leave it in the discretion of the Legislature to apportion the judicial power between the Supreme and inferior courts according to the will of that body, it would certainly have been useless to have proceeded further than to have defined the judicial power and the tribunals in which it should be vested. The subsequent part of the section is mere surplusage—is entirely without meaning—if such is to be the construction. If Congress remains at liberty to give this court appellate jurisdiction where the Constitution has declared their jurisdiction shall be original, and original jurisdiction where the Constitution has declared it shall be appellate, the distribution of jurisdiction made in the Constitution, is form without substance.

Affirmative words are often, in their operation, negative of other objects than those affirmed, and, in this case, a negative or exclusive sense must be given to them or they have no operation at all.

It cannot be presumed that any clause in the Constitution is intended to be without effect, and therefore such construction is inadmissible unless the words require it.

If the solicitude of the Convention respecting our peace with foreign powers induced a provision that the Supreme Court should take original jurisdiction in cases which might be supposed to affect them, yet the clause would have proceeded no further than to provide for such cases if no further restriction on the powers of Congress had been intended. That they should have appellate jurisdiction in all other cases, with such exceptions as Congress might make, is no restriction unless the words be deemed exclusive of original jurisdiction.

When an instrument organizing fundamentally a judicial system divides it into one Supreme and so many inferior courts as the Legislature may ordain and establish, then enumerates its powers, and proceeds so far to distribute them as to define the jurisdiction of the Supreme Court by declaring the cases in which it shall take original jurisdiction, and that in others it shall take appellate jurisdiction, the plain import of the words seems to be that, in one class of cases, its jurisdiction is original, and not appellate; in the other, it is appellate, and not original. If any other construction would render the clause inoperative, that is an additional reason for rejecting such other construction, and for adhering to the obvious meaning.

To enable this court then to issue a mandamus, it must be shown to be an exercise of appellate jurisdiction, or to be necessary to enable them to exercise appellate jurisdiction.

The authority, therefore, given to the Supreme Court by the act establishing the judicial courts of the United States to issue writs of mandamus to public officers appears not to be warranted by the Constitution, and it becomes necessary to inquire whether a jurisdiction so conferred can be exercised.

This original and supreme will organizes the government and assigns to different departments their respective powers. It may either stop here or establish certain limits not to be transcended by those departments.

The Government of the United States is of the latter description. The powers of the Legislature are defined and limited; and that those limits may not be mistaken or forgotten, the Constitution is written. To what purpose are powers limited, and to what purpose is that limitation committed to writing, if these limits may at any time be passed by those intended to be restrained? The distinction between a government with limited and unlimited powers is abolished if those limits do not confine the persons on whom they are imposed, and if acts prohibited and acts allowed are of equal obligation. It is a proposition too plain to be contested that the Constitution controls any legislative act repugnant to it, or that the Legislature may alter the Constitution by an ordinary act.

Between these alternatives there is no middle ground. The Constitution is either a superior, paramount law, unchangeable by ordinary means, or it is on a level with ordinary legislative acts, and, like other acts, is alterable when the legislature shall please to alter it.

If the former part of the alternative be true, then a legislative act contrary to the Constitution is not law; if the latter part be true, then written Constitutions are absurd attempts on the part of the people to limit a power in its own nature illimitable.

Certainly all those who have framed written Constitutions contemplate them as forming the fundamental and paramount law of the nation, and consequently the theory of every such government must be that an act of the Legislature repugnant to the Constitution is void.

This theory is essentially attached to a written Constitution, and is consequently to be considered by this Court as one of the fundamental principles of our society. It is not, therefore, to be lost sight of in the further consideration of this subject.

If an act of the Legislature repugnant to the Constitution is void, does it, notwithstanding its invalidity, bind the Courts and oblige them to give it effect? Or, in other words, though it be not law, does it constitute a rule as operative as if it was a law? This would be to overthrow in fact what was established in theory, and would seem, at first view, an absurdity too gross to be insisted on. It shall, however, receive a more attentive consideration.

It is emphatically the province and duty of the Judicial Department to say what the law is. Those who apply the rule to particular cases must, of necessity, expound and interpret that rule. If two laws conflict with each other, the Courts must decide on the operation of each.

So, if a law be in opposition to the Constitution, if both the law and the Constitution apply to a particular case, so that the Court must either decide that case conformably to the law, disregarding the Constitution, or conformably to the Constitution, disregarding the law, the Court must determine which of these conflicting rules governs the case. This is of the very essence of judicial duty.

If, then, the Courts are to regard the Constitution, and the Constitution is superior to any ordinary act of the Legislature, the Constitution, and not such ordinary act, must govern the case to which they both apply.

Those, then, who controvert the principle that the Constitution is to be considered in court as a paramount law are reduced to the necessity of maintaining that courts must close their eyes on the Constitution, and see only the law.

This doctrine would subvert the very foundation of all written Constitutions. It would declare that an act which, according to the principles and theory of our government, is entirely void, is yet, in practice, completely obligatory. It would declare that, if the Legislature shall do what is expressly forbidden, such act, notwithstanding the express prohibition, is in reality effectual. It would be giving to the Legislature a practical and real omnipotence with the same breath which professes to restrict their powers within narrow limits. It is prescribing limits, and declaring that those limits may be passed at pleasure.

That it thus reduces to nothing what we have deemed the greatest improvement on political institutions—a written Constitution, would of itself be sufficient, in America where written Constitutions have been viewed with so much reverence, for rejecting the construction. But the peculiar expressions of the Constitution of the United States furnish additional arguments in favour of its rejection.

The judicial power of the United States is extended to all cases arising under the Constitution.

Could it be the intention of those who gave this power to say that, in using it, the Constitution should not be looked into? That a case arising under the Constitution should be decided without examining the instrument under which it arises?

This is too extravagant to be maintained.

In some cases then, the Constitution must be looked into by the judges. And if they can open it at all, what part of it are they forbidden to read or to obey?

There are many other parts of the Constitution which serve to illustrate this subject.

It is declared that "no tax or duty shall be laid on articles exported from any State." Suppose a duty on the export of cotton, of tobacco, or of flour, and a suit instituted to recover it. Ought judgment to be rendered in such a case? ought the judges to close their eyes on the Constitution, and only see the law?

The Constitution declares that "no bill of attainder or *ex post facto* law shall be passed."

If, however, such a bill should be passed and a person should be prosecuted under it, must the Court condemn to death those victims whom the Constitution endeavours to preserve?

"No person," says the Constitution, "shall be convicted of treason unless on the testimony of two witnesses to the same overt act, or on confession in open court."

Here, the language of the Constitution is addressed especially to the Courts. It prescribes, directly for them, a rule of evidence not to be departed from. If the Legislature should change that rule, and declare one witness, or a confession out of court, sufficient for conviction, must the constitutional principle yield to the legislative act?

From these and many other selections which might be made, it is apparent that the framers of the Constitution contemplated that instrument as a rule for the government of courts, as well as of the Legislature.

Why otherwise does it direct the judges to take an oath to support it? This oath certainly applies in an especial manner to their conduct in their official character. How immoral to impose it on them if they were to be used as the instruments, and the knowing instruments, for violating what they swear to support!

The oath of office, too, imposed by the Legislature, is completely demonstrative of the legislative opinion on this subject. It is in these words: I do solemnly swear that I will administer justice without respect to persons, and do equal right to the poor and to the rich; and that I will faithfully and impartially discharge all the duties incumbent on me as according to the best of my abilities and understanding, agreeably to the Constitution and laws of the United States.

Why does a judge swear to discharge his duties agreeably to the Constitution of the United States if that Constitution forms no rule for his government? if it is closed upon him and cannot be inspected by him?

If such be the real state of things, this is worse than solemn mockery. To prescribe or to take this oath becomes equally a crime.

It is also not entirely unworthy of observation that, in declaring what shall be the supreme law of the land, the Constitution itself is first mentioned, and not the laws of the United States generally, but those only which shall be made in pursuance of the Constitution, have that rank.

Thus, the particular phraseology of the Constitution of the United States confirms and strengthens the principle, supposed to be essential to all written Constitutions, that a law repugnant to the Constitution is void, and that courts, as well as other departments, are bound by that instrument.

The rule must be discharged.

8.3

Lawrence v. Texas (2003)

In 2003, seventeen years after the Bowers *decision that let stand state laws against sodomy, the Supreme Court reversed itself and declared that a Texas law banning homosexual sodomy was unconstitutional. The majority decided that such state laws banning private sexual activity between consenting adults violated the constitutional right to privacy.*

Justice Kennedy delivered the opinion of the Court.

Liberty protects the person from unwarranted government intrusions into a dwelling or other private places. In our tradition the State is not omnipresent in the home. And there are other spheres of our lives and existence, outside the home, where the State should not be a dominant presence. Freedom extends beyond spatial bounds. Liberty presumes an autonomy of self that includes freedom of thought, belief, expression, and certain intimate conduct. The instant case involves liberty of the person both in its spatial and more transcendent dimensions.

I

The question before the Court is the validity of a Texas statute making it a crime for two persons of the same sex to engage in certain intimate sexual conduct.

In Houston, Texas, officers of the Harris County Police Department were dispatched to a private residence in response to a reported weapons disturbance. They entered an apartment where one of the petitioners, John Geddes Lawrence, resided. The right of the police to enter does not seem to have been questioned. The officers observed Lawrence and another man, Tyron Garner, engaging in a sexual act. The two petitioners were arrested, held in custody over night, and charged and convicted before a Justice of the Peace.

The complaints described their crime as "deviate sexual intercourse, namely anal sex, with a member of the same sex (man)." The applicable state law is Tex. Penal Code Ann. §21.06(a) (2003). It provides: "A person commits an offense if he engages in deviate sexual intercourse with another individual of the same sex." The statute defines "[d]eviate sexual intercourse" as follows:

"(A) any contact between any part of the genitals of one person and the mouth or anus of another person; or

"(B) the penetration of the genitals or the anus of another person with an object."

The petitioners exercised their right to a trial *de novo* in Harris County Criminal Court. They challenged the statute as a violation of the Equal Protection Clause of the Fourteenth Amendment and of a like provision of the Texas Constitution. Tex. Const., Art. 1, §3a. Those contentions were rejected. The petitioners, having entered a plea of *nolo contendere*, were each fined $200 and assessed court costs of $141.25.

The Court of Appeals for the Texas Fourteenth District considered the petitioners' federal constitutional arguments under both the Equal Protection and Due Process Clauses of the Fourteenth Amendment. After hearing the case en banc the court, in a divided opinion, rejected the constitutional arguments and affirmed the convictions. The majority opinion indicates that the Court of Appeals considered our decision in *Bowers v. Hardwick*, (1986), to be controlling on the federal due process aspect of the case. *Bowers* then being authoritative, this was proper.

We granted certiorari, to consider three questions:

1. Whether Petitioners' criminal convictions under the Texas "Homosexual Conduct" law—which criminalizes sexual intimacy by same-sex couples, but not identical behavior by different-sex couples—violate the Fourteenth Amendment guarantee of equal protection of laws?
2. Whether Petitioners' criminal convictions for adult consensual sexual intimacy in the home violate their vital interests in liberty and privacy protected by the Due Process Clause of the Fourteenth Amendment?
3. Whether *Bowers v. Hardwick*, should be overruled?

The petitioners were adults at the time of the alleged offense. Their conduct was in private and consensual.

II

We conclude the case should be resolved by determining whether the petitioners were free as adults to engage in the private conduct in the exercise of their liberty under the Due Process Clause of the Fourteenth Amendment to the Constitution. For this inquiry we deem it necessary to reconsider the Court's holding in *Bowers*.

There are broad statements of the substantive reach of liberty under the Due Process Clause in earlier cases, including *Pierce v. Society of Sisters*, (1925), and *Meyer v. Nebraska*, (1923); but the most pertinent beginning point is our decision in *Griswold v. Connecticut*, (1965).

In *Griswold* the Court invalidated a state law prohibiting the use of drugs or devices of contraception and counseling or aiding and abetting the use of contraceptives. The Court described the protected interest as a right to privacy and placed emphasis on the marriage relation and the protected space of the marital bedroom.

After *Griswold* it was established that the right to make certain decisions regarding sexual conduct extends beyond the marital relationship. In *Eisenstadt v. Baird*, (1972), the Court invalidated a law prohibiting the distribution of contraceptives to unmarried persons. The case was decided under the Equal Protection Clause; but with respect to unmarried persons, the Court went on to state the fundamental proposition that the law impaired the exercise of their personal rights. It quoted from the statement of the Court of Appeals finding the law to be in conflict with fundamental human rights, and it followed with this statement of its own:

> It is true that in *Griswold* the right of privacy in question inhered in the marital relationship. . . . If the right of privacy means anything, it is the right of the *individual*, married or single, to be free from unwarranted governmental intrusion into matters so fundamentally affecting a person as the decision whether to bear or beget a child.

The opinions in *Griswold* and *Eisenstadt* were part of the background for the decision in *Roe v. Wade*, (1973). As is well known, the case involved a challenge to the Texas law prohibiting abortions, but the laws of other States were affected as well. Although the Court held the woman's rights were not absolute, her right to elect an abortion did have real and substantial protection as an exercise of her liberty under the Due Process Clause. The Court cited cases that protect spatial freedom and cases that go well beyond it. *Roe* recognized the right of a woman to make certain fundamental decisions affecting her destiny and confirmed once more that the protection of liberty under the Due Process Clause has a substantive dimension of fundamental significance in defining the rights of the person.

In *Carey v. Population Services Int'l*, (1977), the Court confronted a New York law forbidding sale or distribution of contraceptive devices to persons under 16 years of age. Although there was no single opinion for the Court, the law was invalidated. Both *Eisenstadt* and *Carey*, as well as the holding and rationale in *Roe*, confirmed that the reasoning of *Griswold* could not be confined to the protection of rights of married adults. This was the state of the law with respect to some of the most relevant cases when the Court considered *Bowers v. Hardwick*.

The facts in *Bowers* had some similarities to the instant case. A police officer, whose right to enter seems not to have been in question, observed Hardwick, in his own bedroom, engaging in intimate sexual conduct with another adult male. The conduct was in violation of a Georgia statute making it a criminal offense to engage in sodomy. One difference between the two cases is that the Georgia statute prohibited the conduct whether or not the participants were of the same sex, while the Texas statute, as we have seen, applies only to participants of the same sex. Hardwick was not prosecuted, but he brought an action in federal court to declare the state statute invalid. He alleged he was a practicing homosexual and that the criminal prohibition violated rights guaranteed to him by the Constitution. The Court, in an opinion by Justice White, sustained the Georgia law. Chief Justice Burger and Justice Powell joined the opinion of the Court and filed separate, concurring opinions. Four Justices dissented. (opinion of Blackmun, J., joined by Brennan, Marshall, and Stevens, JJ.); (opinion of Stevens, J., joined by Brennan and Marshall, JJ.).

The Court began its substantive discussion in *Bowers* as follows: "The issue presented is whether the Federal Constitution confers a fundamental right upon homosexuals to engage in sodomy and hence invalidates the laws of the many States that still make such conduct illegal and have done so for a very long time." That statement, we now conclude, discloses the Court's own failure to appreciate the extent of the liberty at stake. To say that the issue in *Bowers* was simply the right to engage in certain sexual conduct demeans the claim the individual put forward, just as it would demean a married couple were it to be said marriage is simply about the right to have sexual intercourse. The laws involved in *Bowers* and here are, to be sure, statutes that purport to do no more than prohibit a particular sexual act. Their penalties and purposes, though, have more far-reaching consequences, touching upon the most private human conduct, sexual behavior, and in the most private of places, the home. The statutes do seek to control a personal relationship that, whether or not entitled to formal recognition in the law, is within the liberty of persons to choose without being punished as criminals.

This, as a general rule, should counsel against attempts by the State, or a court, to define the meaning of the relationship or to set its boundaries absent injury to a person or abuse of an institution the law protects. It suffices for us to acknowledge that adults may choose to enter upon this relationship in the confines of their homes and their own private lives and still retain their dignity as free persons. When sexuality finds overt expression in intimate conduct with another person, the conduct can be but one element in a personal bond that is more enduring. The liberty protected by the Constitution allows homosexual persons the right to make this choice.

Having misapprehended the claim of liberty there presented to it, and thus stating the claim to be whether there is a fundamental right to engage in consensual sodomy, the *Bowers* Court said: "Proscriptions against that conduct have ancient roots." In academic writings, and in many of the scholarly *amicus* briefs filed to assist the Court in this case, there are fundamental criticisms of the historical premises relied upon by the majority and concurring opinions in *Bowers*. We need not enter this debate in the attempt to reach a definitive historical judgment, but the following considerations counsel against adopting the definitive conclusions upon which *Bowers* placed such reliance.

At the outset it should be noted that there is no longstanding history in this country of laws directed at homosexual conduct as a distinct matter. Beginning in colonial times there were prohibitions of sodomy derived from the English criminal laws passed in the first instance by the Reformation Parliament of 1533. The English prohibition was understood to include relations between men and women as well as relations between men and men. Nineteenth-century commentators similarly read American sodomy, buggery, and crime-against-nature statutes as criminalizing certain relations between men and women and between men and men. The absence of legal prohibitions focusing on homosexual conduct may be explained in part by noting that according to some scholars the concept of the homosexual as a distinct category of person did not emerge until the late 19th century. Thus early American sodomy laws were not directed at homosexuals as such but instead sought to prohibit nonprocreative sexual activity more generally. This does not suggest approval of homosexual conduct. It does tend to show that this particular form of conduct was not thought of as a separate category from like conduct between heterosexual persons.

Laws prohibiting sodomy do not seem to have been enforced against consenting adults acting in private. A substantial number of sodomy prosecutions and convictions for which there are surviving records were for predatory acts against those who could not or did not consent, as in the case of a minor or the victim of an assault. As to these, one purpose for the prohibitions was to ensure there would be no lack of coverage if a predator committed a sexual assault that did not constitute rape as defined by the criminal law. Thus the model sodomy indictments presented in a 19th-century treatise, addressed the predatory acts of an adult man against a minor girl or minor boy. Instead of targeting relations between consenting adults in private, 19th-century sodomy prosecutions typically involved relations between men and minor girls or minor boys, relations between adults involving force, relations between adults implicating disparity in status, or relations between men and animals.

To the extent that there were any prosecutions for the acts in question, 19th-century evidence rules imposed a burden that would make a conviction more difficult to obtain even taking into account the problems always inherent in prosecuting consensual acts committed in private. Under then-prevailing standards, a man could not be convicted of sodomy based upon testimony of a consenting partner, because the partner was considered an accomplice. A partner's testimony, however, was admissible if he or she had not consented to the act or was a minor, and therefore incapable of consent. The rule may explain in part the infrequency of these prosecutions. In all events that infrequency makes it difficult to say that society approved of a rigorous and systematic punishment of the consensual acts committed in private and by adults. The longstanding criminal prohibition of homosexual sodomy upon which the *Bowers* decision placed such reliance is as consistent with a general condemnation of nonprocreative sex as it is with an established tradition of prosecuting acts because of their homosexual character.

The policy of punishing consenting adults for private acts was not much discussed in the early legal literature. We can infer that one reason for this was the very private nature of the conduct. Despite the absence of prosecutions, there may have been periods in which there was public criticism of homosexuals as such and an insistence that the criminal laws be enforced to discourage their practices. But far from possessing "ancient roots," American laws targeting same-sex couples did not develop until the last third of the 20th century. The reported decisions concerning the prosecution of consensual, homosexual sodomy between adults for the years 1880–1995 are not always clear in the details, but a significant number involved conduct in a public place.

It was not until the 1970's that any State singled out same-sex relations for criminal prosecution, and only nine States have done so. Post-*Bowers* even some of these States did not adhere to the policy of suppressing homosexual conduct. Over the course of the last decades, States with same-sex prohibitions have moved toward abolishing them.

In summary, the historical grounds relied upon in *Bowers* are more complex than the majority opinion and the concurring opinion by Chief Justice Burger indicate. Their historical premises are not without doubt and, at the very least, are overstated.

It must be acknowledged, of course, that the Court in *Bowers* was making the broader point that for centuries there have been powerful voices to condemn homosexual conduct as immoral. The condemnation has been shaped by religious beliefs, conceptions of right and acceptable behavior, and respect for the traditional family. For many persons these are not trivial concerns but profound and deep convictions accepted as ethical and moral principles to which they aspire and which thus determine the course of their lives. These considerations do not answer the question before us, however. The issue is whether the majority may use the power of the State to enforce these views on the whole society through operation of the criminal law. "Our obligation is to define the liberty of all, not to mandate our own moral code." *Planned Parenthood of Southeastern Pa. v. Casey,* (1992).

Chief Justice Burger joined the opinion for the Court in *Bowers* and further explained his views as follows: "Decisions of individuals relating to homosexual conduct have been subject to state intervention throughout the history of Western civilization. Condemnation of those practices is firmly rooted in Judeao-Christian moral and ethical standards." 478 U.S., at 196. As with Justice White's assumptions about history, scholarship casts some doubt on the sweeping nature of the statement by Chief Justice Burger as it pertains to private homosexual conduct between consenting adults. In all events we think that our laws and traditions in the past half century are of most relevance here. These references show an emerging awareness that liberty gives substantial protection to adult persons in deciding how to conduct their private lives in matters pertaining to sex. "[H]istory and tradition are the starting point but not in all cases the ending point of the substantive due process inquiry." *County of Sacramento v. Lewis,* (1998) (Kennedy, J., concurring).

This emerging recognition should have been apparent when *Bowers* was decided. In 1955 the American Law Institute promulgated the Model Penal Code and made clear that it did not recommend or provide for "criminal penalties for consensual sexual relations conducted in private." It justified its decision on three grounds: (1) The prohibitions undermined respect for the law by penalizing conduct many people engaged in; (2) the statutes regulated private conduct not harmful to others; and (3) the laws were arbitrarily enforced and thus invited the danger of blackmail. In 1961 Illinois changed its laws to conform to the Model Penal Code. Other States soon followed.

In *Bowers* the Court referred to the fact that before 1961 all 50 States had outlawed sodomy, and that at the time of the Court's decision 24 States and the District of Columbia had sodomy laws. Justice Powell pointed out that these prohibitions often were being ignored, however. Georgia, for instance, had not sought to enforce its law for decades.

The sweeping references by Chief Justice Burger to the history of Western civilization and to Judeo-Christian moral and ethical standards did not take account of other authorities pointing in an opposite direction. A committee advising the British Parliament recommended in 1957 repeal of laws punishing homosexual conduct. Parliament enacted the substance of those recommendations 10 years later.

Of even more importance, almost five years before *Bowers* was decided the European Court of Human Rights considered a case with parallels to *Bowers* and to today's case. An adult male resident in Northern Ireland alleged he was a practicing homosexual who desired to engage in consensual homosexual conduct. The laws of Northern Ireland forbade him that right. He alleged that he had been questioned, his home had been searched, and he feared criminal prosecution. The court held that the laws proscribing the conduct were invalid under the European Convention on Human Rights. Authoritative in all countries that are members of the Council of Europe (21 nations then, 45 nations now), the decision is at odds with the premise in *Bowers* that the claim put forward was insubstantial in our Western civilization.

In our own constitutional system the deficiencies in *Bowers* became even more apparent in the years following its announcement. The 25 States with laws prohibiting the relevant conduct referenced in the *Bowers* decision are reduced now to 13, of which 4 enforce their laws only against homosexual conduct. In those States where sodomy is still proscribed, whether for same-sex or heterosexual conduct, there is a pattern of nonenforcement with respect to consenting adults acting in private. The State of Texas admitted in 1994 that as of that date it had not prosecuted anyone under those circumstances.

Two principal cases decided after *Bowers* cast its holding into even more doubt. In *Planned Parenthood of Southeastern Pa. v. Casey,* the Court reaffirmed the substantive force of the liberty protected by the Due Process Clause. The *Casey* decision again confirmed that our laws and tradition afford constitutional protection to personal decisions relating to marriage, procreation, contraception, family relationships, child rearing, and education. In explaining the respect the Constitution demands for the autonomy of the person in making these choices, we stated as follows:

> These matters, involving the most intimate and personal choices a person may make in a lifetime, choices central to personal dignity and autonomy, are central to the liberty protected by the Fourteenth Amendment. At the heart of liberty is the right to define one's own concept of existence, of meaning, of the universe, and of the mystery of human life. Beliefs about these matters could not define the attributes of personhood were they formed under compulsion of the State. (Ibid.)

Persons in a homosexual relationship may seek autonomy for these purposes, just as heterosexual persons do. The decision in *Bowers* would deny them this right.

The second post-*Bowers* case of principal relevance is *Romer v. Evans,* (1996). There the Court struck down class-based legislation directed at homosexuals as a violation of the Equal Protection Clause. *Romer* invalidated an amendment to Colorado's constitution which named as a solitary class persons who were homosexuals, lesbians, or bisexual either by "orientation, conduct, practices or relationships," and deprived them of protection under state antidiscrimination laws. We concluded that the provision was "born of animosity toward the class of persons affected" and further that it had no rational relation to a legitimate governmental purpose.

As an alternative argument in this case, counsel for the petitioners and some *amici* contend that *Romer* provides the basis for declaring the Texas statute invalid under the Equal Protection Clause. That is a tenable argument, but we conclude the instant case requires us to address whether *Bowers* itself has continuing validity. Were we to hold the statute invalid under the Equal Protection Clause some might question whether a prohibition would be valid if drawn differently, say, to prohibit the conduct both between same-sex and different-sex participants.

Equality of treatment and the due process right to demand respect for conduct protected by the substantive guarantee of liberty are linked in important respects, and a decision on the latter point advances both interests. If protected conduct is made criminal and the law which does so remains unexamined for its substantive validity, its stigma might remain even if it were not enforceable as drawn for equal protection reasons. When homosexual conduct is made criminal by the law of the State, that declaration in and of itself is an invitation to subject homosexual persons to discrimination both in the public and in the private spheres. The central holding of *Bowers* has been brought in question by this case, and it should be addressed. Its continuance as precedent demeans the lives of homosexual persons.

The stigma this criminal statute imposes, moreover, is not trivial. The offense, to be sure, is but a class C misdemeanor, a minor offense in the Texas legal system. Still, it remains a criminal offense with all that imports for the dignity of the persons charged. The petitioners will bear on their record the history of their criminal convictions. Just this Term we rejected various challenges to state laws requiring the registration of sex offenders. We are advised that if Texas convicted an adult for private, consensual homosexual conduct under the statute here in question the convicted person would come within the registration laws of at least four States were he or she to be subject to their jurisdiction. This underscores the consequential nature of the punishment and the state-sponsored condemnation attendant to the criminal prohibition. Furthermore, the Texas criminal conviction carries with it the other collateral consequences always following a conviction, such as notations on job application forms, to mention but one example.

The foundations of *Bowers* have sustained serious erosion from our recent decisions in *Casey* and *Romer*. When our precedent has been thus weakened, criticism from other sources is of greater significance. In the United States criticism of *Bowers* has been substantial and continuing, disapproving of its reasoning in all respects, not just as to its historical assumptions. The courts of five different States have declined to follow it in interpreting provisions in their own state constitutions parallel to the Due Process Clause of the Fourteenth Amendment.

To the extent *Bowers* relied on values we share with a wider civilization, it should be noted that the reasoning and holding in *Bowers* have been rejected elsewhere. The European Court of Human Rights has followed not *Bowers* but its own decision in *Dudgeon v. United Kingdom*. Other nations, too, have taken action consistent with an affirmation of the protected right of homosexual adults to engage in intimate, consensual conduct. The right the petitioners seek in this case has been accepted as an integral part of human freedom in many other countries. There has been no showing that in this country the governmental interest in circumscribing personal choice is somehow more legitimate or urgent.

The doctrine of *stare decisis* is essential to the respect accorded to the judgments of the Court and to the stability of the law. It is not, however, an inexorable command. In *Casey* we noted that when a Court is asked to overrule a precedent recognizing a constitutional liberty interest, individual or societal reliance on the existence of that liberty cautions with particular strength against reversing course. The holding in *Bowers*, however, has not induced detrimental reliance comparable to some instances where recognized individual rights are involved. Indeed, there has been no individual or societal reliance on *Bowers* of the sort that could counsel against overturning its hold-ing once there are compelling reasons to do so. *Bowers* itself causes uncer-tainty, for the precedents before and after its issuance contradict its central holding.

The rationale of *Bowers* does not withstand careful analysis. In his dissent-ing opinion in *Bowers* Justice Stevens came to these conclusions:

> Our prior cases make two propositions abundantly clear. First, the fact that the governing majority in a State has traditionally viewed a particu-lar practice as immoral is not a sufficient reason for upholding a law prohibiting the practice; neither history nor tradition could save a law prohibiting miscegenation from constitutional attack. Second, indi-vidual decisions by married persons, concerning the intimacies of their physical relationship, even when not intended to produce offspring, are a form of "liberty" protected by the Due Process Clause of the Fourteenth Amendment. Moreover, this protection extends to intimate choices by unmarried as well as married persons. (footnotes and citations omitted)

Justice Stevens' analysis, in our view, should have been controlling in *Bowers* and should control here.

Bowers was not correct when it was decided, and it is not correct today. It ought not to remain binding precedent. *Bowers v. Hardwick* should be and now is overruled.

The present case does not involve minors. It does not involve persons who might be injured or coerced or who are situated in relationships where consent might not easily be refused. It does not involve public conduct or pros-titution. It does not involve whether the government must give formal recogni-tion to any relationship that homosexual persons seek to enter. The case does involve two adults who, with full and mutual consent from each other, engaged in sexual practices common to a homosexual lifestyle. The petitioners are entitled to respect for their private lives. The State cannot demean their exis-tence or control their destiny by making their private sexual conduct a crime. Their right to liberty under the Due Process Clause gives them the full right to engage in their conduct without intervention of the government. "It is a promise of the Constitution that there is a realm of personal liberty which the government may not enter." The Texas statute furthers no legitimate state interest which can justify its intrusion into the personal and private life of the individual.

Had those who drew and ratified the Due Process Clauses of the Fifth Amendment or the Fourteenth Amendment known the components of liberty in its manifold possibilities, they might have been more specific. They did not presume to have this insight. They knew times can blind us to certain truths and later generations can see that laws once thought necessary and proper in fact serve only to oppress. As the Constitution endures, persons in every generation can invoke its principles in their own search for greater freedom.

The judgment of the Court of Appeals for the Texas Fourteenth District is reversed, and the case is remanded for further proceedings not inconsistent with this opinion.

It is so ordered.

8.4

Bush v. Gore (2000)

The Supreme Court decided, in a narrow ruling, that the State of Florida had to stop its recount of votes in the 2000 presidential election. The majority of the Court reasoned that there was no way that the state could count those votes in a manner consistent with existing interpretation of the Equal Protection Clause of the Fourteenth Amendment that all votes when possible need to be treated equally under the law. The decision effectively handed the election to George W. Bush.

In a scathing dissenting opinion, which is included here at the end of the majority opinion below, Justice Ruth Bader Ginsburg argued that the case was actually about federalism and not about the Fourteenth Amendment, and that the majority's decision trampled on Florida's right to run its own elections as guaranteed in the U.S. Constitution.

CERTIORARI TO THE FLORIDA SUPREME COURT

I

On December 8, 2000, the Supreme Court of Florida ordered that the Circuit Court of Leon County tabulate by hand 9,000 ballots in Miami-Dade County. It also ordered the inclusion in the certified vote totals of 215 votes identified in Palm Beach County and 168 votes identified in Miami-Dade County for Vice President Albert Gore, Jr., and Senator Joseph Lieberman, Democratic Candidates for President and Vice President. The Supreme Court noted that petitioner, Governor George W. Bush asserted that the net gain for Vice President Gore in Palm Beach County was 176 votes, and directed the Circuit Court to resolve that dispute on remand. . . . The court further held that relief would require manual recounts in all Florida counties where so-called "undervotes" had not been subject to manual tabulation. The court ordered all manual recounts to begin at once. Governor Bush and Richard Cheney, Republican Candidates for the Presidency and Vice Presidency, filed an emergency application for a stay of this mandate. On December 9, we granted the application, treated the application as a petition for a writ of certiorari, and granted certiorari.

The proceedings leading to the present controversy are discussed in some detail in our opinion in *Bush v. Palm Beach County Canvassing Bd*. . . . (*Bush I*). On November 8, 2000, the day following the Presidential election, the Florida

Division of Elections reported that petitioner, Governor Bush, had received 2,909,135 votes, and respondent, Vice President Gore, had received 2,907,351 votes, a margin of 1,784 for Governor Bush. Because Governor Bush's margin of victory was less than "one-half of a percent . . . of the votes cast," an automatic machine recount was conducted under §102.141(4) of the election code, the results of which showed Governor Bush still winning the race but by a diminished margin. Vice President Gore then sought manual recounts in Volusia, Palm Beach, Broward, and Miami-Dade Counties, pursuant to Florida's election protest provisions. Fla. Stat. §102.166 (2000). A dispute arose concerning the deadline for local county canvassing boards to submit their returns to the Secretary of State (Secretary). The Secretary declined to waive the November 14 deadline imposed by statute. §§102.111, 102.112. The Florida Supreme Court, however, set the deadline at November 26. We granted certiorari and vacated the Florida Supreme Court's decision, finding considerable uncertainty as to the grounds on which it was based. . . . On December 11, the Florida Supreme Court issued a decision on remand reinstating that date.

On November 26, the Florida Elections Canvassing Commission certified the results of the election and declared Governor Bush the winner of Florida's 25 electoral votes. On November 27, Vice President Gore, pursuant to Florida's contest provisions, filed a complaint in Leon County Circuit Court contesting the certification. Fla. Stat. §102.168 (2000). He sought relief pursuant to §102.168(3)(c), which provides that "[r]eceipt of a number of illegal votes or rejection of a number of legal votes sufficient to change or place in doubt the result of the election" shall be grounds for a contest. The Circuit Court denied relief, stating that Vice President Gore failed to meet his burden of proof. He appealed to the First District Court of Appeal, which certified the matter to the Florida Supreme Court.

Accepting jurisdiction, the Florida Supreme Court affirmed in part and reversed in part. The court held that the Circuit Court had been correct to reject Vice President Gore's challenge to the results certified in Nassau County and his challenge to the Palm Beach County Canvassing Board's determination that 3,300 ballots cast in that county were not, in the statutory phrase, "legal votes."

The Supreme Court held that Vice President Gore had satisfied his burden of proof under §102.168(3)(c) with respect to his challenge to Miami-Dade County's failure to tabulate, by manual count, 9,000 ballots on which the machines had failed to detect a vote for President ("undervotes"). Noting the closeness of the election, the Court explained that "[o]n this record, there can be no question that there are legal votes within the 9,000 uncounted votes sufficient to place the results of this election in doubt." A "legal vote," as determined by the Supreme Court, is "one in which there is a 'clear indication of the intent of the voter.'" The court therefore ordered a hand recount of the 9,000 ballots in Miami-Dade County. Observing that the contest provisions vest broad discretion in the circuit judge to "provide any relief appropriate under such circumstances," Fla. Stat. §102.168(8) (2000), the Supreme Court further held that the Circuit Court could order "the Supervisor of Elections and the Canvassing Boards, as well as the necessary public officials, in all counties that have not conducted a manual recount or tabulation of the undervotes . . . to do so forthwith, said tabulation to take place in the individual counties where the ballots are located."

The Supreme Court also determined that both Palm Beach County and Miami-Dade County, in their earlier manual recounts, had identified a net gain of 215 and 168 legal votes for Vice President Gore. Rejecting the Circuit Court's conclusion that Palm Beach County lacked the authority to include the 215 net votes submitted past the November 26 deadline, the Supreme Court explained that the deadline was not intended to exclude votes identified after that date through ongoing manual recounts. As to Miami-Dade County, the Court concluded that although the 168 votes identified were the result of a partial recount, they were "legal votes [that] could change the outcome of the election." The Supreme Court therefore directed the Circuit Court to include those totals in the certified results, subject to resolution of the actual vote total from the Miami-Dade partial recount.

The petition presents the following questions: whether the Florida Supreme Court established new standards for resolving Presidential election contests, thereby violating Art. II, §1, cl. 2, of the United States Constitution and failing to comply with *3 U.S.C. § 5* and whether the use of standardless manual recounts violates the Equal Protection and Due Process Clauses. With respect to the equal protection question, we find a violation of the Equal Protection Clause.

II

A

The closeness of this election, and the multitude of legal challenges which have followed in its wake, have brought into sharp focus a common, if heretofore unnoticed, phenomenon. Nationwide statistics reveal that an estimated 2% of ballots cast do not register a vote for President for whatever reason, including deliberately choosing no candidate at all or some voter error, such as voting for two candidates or insufficiently marking a ballot. In certifying election results, the votes eligible for inclusion in the certification are the votes meeting the properly established legal requirements.

This case has shown that punch card balloting machines can produce an unfortunate number of ballots which are not punched in a clean, complete way by the voter. After the current counting, it is likely legislative bodies nationwide will examine ways to improve the mechanisms and machinery for voting.

B

The individual citizen has no federal constitutional right to vote for electors for the President of the United States unless and until the state legislature chooses a statewide election as the means to implement its power to appoint members of the Electoral College. U.S. Const., Art. II, §1. This is the source for the statement in *McPherson v. Blacker*, (1892), that the State legislature's power to select the manner for appointing electors is plenary; it may, if it so chooses, select the electors itself, which indeed was the manner used by State legislatures in several States for many years after the Framing of our Constitution. History has now favored the voter, and in each of the several States the citizens themselves vote for Presidential electors. When the state legislature vests the right to vote for President in its people, the right to vote as the legislature has prescribed is fundamental; and one source of its fundamental nature lies in the equal weight accorded to each vote and the equal dignity owed to each voter. The State, of course, after granting the franchise in the special context of Article II, can take back the power to appoint electors.

The right to vote is protected in more than the initial allocation of the franchise. Equal protection applies as well to the manner of its exercise. Having once granted the right to vote on equal terms, the State may not, by later arbitrary and disparate treatment, value one person's vote over that of another. It must be remembered that "the right of suffrage can be denied by a debasement or dilution of the weight of a citizen's vote just as effectively as by wholly prohibiting the free exercise of the franchise." *Reynolds v. Sims*, (1964).

There is no difference between the two sides of the present controversy on these basic propositions. Respondents say that the very purpose of vindicating the right to vote justifies the recount procedures now at issue. The question before us, however, is whether the recount procedures the Florida Supreme Court has adopted are consistent with its obligation to avoid arbitrary and disparate treatment of the members of its electorate.

Much of the controversy seems to revolve around ballot cards designed to be perforated by a stylus but which, either through error or deliberate omission, have not been perforated with sufficient precision for a machine to count them. In some cases a piece of the card—a chad—is hanging, say by two corners. In other cases there is no separation at all, just an indentation.

The Florida Supreme Court has ordered that the intent of the voter be discerned from such ballots. For purposes of resolving the equal protection challenge, it is not necessary to decide whether the Florida Supreme Court had the authority under the legislative scheme for resolving election disputes to define what a legal vote is and to mandate a manual recount implementing that definition. The recount mechanisms implemented in response to the decisions of the Florida Supreme Court do not satisfy the minimum requirement for non-arbitrary treatment of voters necessary to secure the fundamental right. Florida's basic command for the count of legally cast votes is to consider the "intent of the voter." This is unobjectionable as an abstract proposition and a starting principle. The problem inheres in the absence of specific standards to ensure its equal application. The formulation of uniform rules to determine intent based on these recurring circumstances is practicable and, we conclude, necessary.

The law does not refrain from searching for the intent of the actor in a multitude of circumstances; and in some cases the general command to ascertain intent is not susceptible to much further refinement. In this instance, however, the question is not whether to believe a witness but how to interpret the marks or holes or scratches on an inanimate object, a piece of cardboard or paper which, it is said, might not have registered as a vote during the machine count. The factfinder confronts a thing, not a person. The search for intent can be confined by specific rules designed to ensure uniform treatment.

The want of those rules here has led to unequal evaluation of ballots in various respects. As seems to have been acknowledged at oral argument, the standards for accepting or rejecting contested ballots might vary not only from county to county but indeed within a single county from one recount team to another.

The record provides some examples. A monitor in Miami-Dade County testified at trial that he observed that three members of the county canvassing board applied different standards in defining a legal vote. 3 Tr. 497, 499 (Dec. 3, 2000). And testimony at trial also revealed that at least one county changed its evaluative standards during the counting process. Palm Beach County, for example, began the process with a 1990 guideline which precluded counting completely attached chads, switched to a rule that considered a vote to be legal if any light could be seen through a chad, changed back to the 1990 rule, and then abandoned any pretense of a *per se* rule, only to have a court order that the county consider dimpled chads legal. This is not a process with sufficient guarantees of equal treatment.

An early case in our one person, one vote jurisprudence arose when a State accorded arbitrary and disparate treatment to voters in its different counties. The Court found a constitutional violation. We relied on these principles in the context of the Presidential selection process in *Moore v. Ogilvie,* (1969), where we invalidated a county-based procedure that diluted the influence of citizens in larger counties in the nominating process. There we observed that "[t]he idea that one group can be granted greater voting strength than another is hostile to the one man, one vote basis of our representative government."

The State Supreme Court ratified this uneven treatment. It mandated that the recount totals from two counties, Miami-Dade and Palm Beach, be included in the certified total. The court also appeared to hold *sub silentio* that the recount totals from Broward County, which were not completed until after the original November 14 certification by the Secretary of State, were to be considered part of the new certified vote totals even though the county certification was not contested by Vice President Gore. Yet each of the counties used varying standards to determine what was a legal vote. Broward County used a more forgiving standard than Palm Beach County, and uncovered almost three times as many new votes, a result markedly disproportionate to the difference in population between the counties.

In addition, the recounts in these three counties were not limited to so-called undervotes but extended to all of the ballots. The distinction has real consequences. A manual recount of all ballots identifies not only those ballots which show no vote but also those which contain more than one, the so-called overvotes. Neither category will be counted by the machine. This is not a trivial concern. At oral argument, respondents estimated there are as many as 110,000 overvotes statewide. As a result, the citizen whose ballot was not read by a machine because he failed to vote for a candidate in a way readable by a machine may still have his vote counted in a manual recount; on the other hand, the citizen who marks two candidates in a way discernable by the machine will not have the same opportunity to have his vote count, even if a manual examination of the ballot would reveal the requisite indicia of intent. Furthermore, the citizen who marks two candidates, only one of which is discernable by the machine, will have his vote counted even though it should have been read as an invalid ballot. The State Supreme Court's inclusion of vote counts based on these variant standards exemplifies concerns with the remedial processes that were under way.

That brings the analysis to yet a further equal protection problem. The votes certified by the court included a partial total from one county, Miami-Dade. The Florida Supreme Court's decision thus gives no assurance that the recounts included in a final certification must be complete. Indeed, it is respondent's submission that it would be consistent with the rules of the recount procedures to include whatever partial counts are done by the time of final certification, and we interpret the Florida Supreme Court's decision to permit this. This accommodation no doubt results from the truncated contest period established by the Florida Supreme Court in *Bush I*, at respondents' own urging. The press of time does not diminish the constitutional concern. A desire for speed is not a general excuse for ignoring equal protection guarantees.

In addition to these difficulties the actual process by which the votes were to be counted under the Florida Supreme Court's decision raises further concerns. That order did not specify who would recount the ballots. The county canvassing boards were forced to pull together ad hoc teams comprised of judges from various Circuits who had no previous training in handling and interpreting ballots. Furthermore, while others were permitted to observe, they were prohibited from objecting during the recount.

The recount process, in its features here described, is inconsistent with the minimum procedures necessary to protect the fundamental right of each voter in the special instance of a statewide recount under the authority of a single state judicial officer. Our consideration is limited to the present circumstances, for the problem of equal protection in election processes generally presents many complexities.

The question before the Court is not whether local entities, in the exercise of their expertise, may develop different systems for implementing elections. Instead, we are presented with a situation where a state court with the power to assure uniformity has ordered a statewide recount with minimal procedural safeguards. When a court orders a statewide remedy, there must be at least some assurance that the rudimentary requirements of equal treatment and fundamental fairness are satisfied.

Given the Court's assessment that the recount process underway was probably being conducted in an unconstitutional manner, the Court stayed the order directing the recount so it could hear this case and render an expedited decision. The contest provision, as it was mandated by the State Supreme Court, is not well calculated to sustain the confidence that all citizens must have in the outcome of elections. The State has not shown that its procedures include the necessary safeguards. The problem, for instance, of the estimated 110,000 overvotes has not been addressed, although Chief Justice Wells called attention to the concern in his dissenting opinion.

Upon due consideration of the difficulties identified to this point, it is obvious that the recount cannot be conducted in compliance with the requirements of equal protection and due process without substantial additional work. It would require not only the adoption (after opportunity for argument) of adequate statewide standards for determining what is a legal vote, and practicable procedures to implement them, but also orderly judicial review of any disputed matters that might arise. In addition, the Secretary of State has advised that the recount of only a portion of the ballots requires that the vote tabulation equipment be used to screen out undervotes, a function for which the machines were not designed. If a recount of overvotes were also required, perhaps even a second screening would be necessary. Use of the equipment for this purpose, and any new software developed for it, would have to be evaluated for accuracy by the Secretary of State, as required by Fla. Stat. §101.015 (2000).

The Supreme Court of Florida has said that the legislature intended the State's electors to "participat[e] fully in the federal electoral process," as provided in 3 *U.S.C. § 5.___* That statute, in turn, requires that any controversy or contest that is designed to lead to a conclusive selection of electors be completed by December 12. That date is upon us, and there is no recount procedure in place under the State Supreme Court's order that comports with minimal constitutional standards. Because it is evident that any recount seeking to meet the December 12 date will be unconstitutional for the reasons we have discussed, we reverse the judgment of the Supreme Court of Florida ordering a recount to proceed.

Seven Justices of the Court agree that there are constitutional problems with the recount ordered by the Florida Supreme Court that demand a remedy. The only disagreement is as to the remedy. Because the Florida Supreme

Court has said that the Florida Legislature intended to obtain the safe-harbor benefits of *3 U.S.C. § 5* Justice Breyer's proposed remedy-remanding to the Florida Supreme Court for its ordering of a constitutionally proper contest until December 18-contemplates action in violation of the Florida election code, and hence could not be part of an "appropriate" order authorized by Fla. Stat. §102.168(8) (2000).

None are more conscious of the vital limits on judicial authority than are the members of this Court, and none stand more in admiration of the Constitution's design to leave the selection of the President to the people, through their legislatures, and to the political sphere. When contending parties invoke the process of the courts, however, it becomes our unsought responsibility to resolve the federal and constitutional issues the judicial system has been forced to confront.

The judgment of the Supreme Court of Florida is reversed, and the case is remanded for further proceedings not inconsistent with this opinion.

Pursuant to this Court's Rule 45.2, the Clerk is directed to issue the mandate in this case forthwith.

It is so ordered.

Justice Ginsburg, with whom Justice Stevens joins, and with whom Justice Souter and Justice Breyer join as to Part I, dissenting.

I

The Chief Justice acknowledges that provisions of Florida's Election Code "may well admit of more than one interpretation." *Ante*, at 3. But instead of respecting the state high court's province to say what the State's Election Code means, The Chief Justice maintains that Florida's Supreme Court has veered so far from the ordinary practice of judicial review that what it did cannot properly be called judging. My colleagues have offered a reasonable construction of Florida's law. Their construction coincides with the view of one of Florida's seven Supreme Court justices. I might join The Chief Justice were it my commission to interpret Florida law. But disagreement with the Florida court's interpretation of its own State's law does not warrant the conclusion that the justices of that court have legislated. There is no cause here to believe that the members of Florida's high court have done less than "their mortal best to discharge their oath of office," *Sumner v. Mata*, (1981), and no cause to upset their reasoned interpretation of Florida law.

This Court more than occasionally affirms statutory, and even constitutional, interpretations with which it disagrees. For example, when reviewing challenges to administrative agencies' interpretations of laws they implement, we defer to the agencies unless their interpretation violates "the unambiguously expressed intent of Congress." *Chevron U.S. A. Inc. v. Natural Resources Defense Council, Inc.*, (1984). We do so in the face of the declaration in Article

I of the United States Constitution that "All legislative Powers herein granted shall be vested in a Congress of the United States." Surely the Constitution does not call upon us to pay more respect to a federal administrative agency's construction of federal law than to a state high court's interpretation of its own state's law. And not uncommonly, we let stand state-court interpretations of *federal* law with which we might disagree. Notably, in the habeas context, the Court adheres to the view that "there is 'no intrinsic reason why the fact that a man is a federal judge should make him more competent, or conscientious, or learned with respect to [federal law] than his neighbor in the state courthouse.'" *Stone v. Powell*, 35 (1976) (quoting Bator, Finality in Criminal Law and Federal Habeas Corpus For State (1963)). . . .

No doubt there are cases in which the proper application of federal law may hinge on interpretations of state law. Unavoidably, this Court must sometimes examine state law in order to protect federal rights. But we have dealt with such cases ever mindful of the full measure of respect we owe to interpretations of state law by a State's highest court. In the Contract Clause case, *General Motors Corp. v. Romein*, (1992), for example, we said that although "ultimately we are bound to decide for ourselves whether a contract was made," the Court "accord[s] respectful consideration and great weight to the views of the State's highest court." And in *Central Union Telephone Co. v. Edwardsville*, (1925), we upheld the Illinois Supreme Court's interpretation of a state waiver rule, even though that interpretation resulted in the forfeiture of federal constitutional rights. Refusing to supplant Illinois law with a federal definition of waiver, we explained that the state court's declaration "should bind us unless so unfair or unreasonable in its application to those asserting a federal right as to obstruct it."

In deferring to state courts on matters of state law, we appropriately recognize that this Court acts as an "'outside[r]' lacking the common exposure to local law which comes from sitting in the jurisdiction." *Lehman Brothers v. Schein*, (1974). That recognition has sometimes prompted us to resolve doubts about the meaning of state law by certifying issues to a State's highest court, even when federal rights are at stake. Notwithstanding our authority to decide issues of state law underlying federal claims, we have used the certification devise to afford state high courts an opportunity to inform us on matters of their own State's law because such restraint "helps build a cooperative judicial federalism."

Just last Term, in *Fiore v. White* (1999), we took advantage of Pennsylvania's certification procedure. In that case, a state prisoner brought a federal habeas action claiming that the State had failed to prove an essential element of his charged offense in violation of the Due Process Clause. Instead of resolving the state-law question on which the federal claim depended, we certified the question to the Pennsylvania Supreme Court for that court to "help determine the proper state-law predicate for our determination of the federal constitutional questions raised." The Chief Justice's willingness to *reverse* the Florida

Supreme Court's interpretation of Florida law in this case is at least in tension with our reluctance in *Fiore* even to interpret Pennsylvania law before seeking instruction from the Pennsylvania Supreme Court. I would have thought the "cautious approach" we counsel when federal courts address matters of state law, *Arizonans*, and our commitment to "build[ing] cooperative judicial federalism," *Lehman Brothers*, demanded greater restraint.

Rarely has this Court rejected outright an interpretation of state law by a state high court. *Fairfax's Devisee v. Hunter's Lessee*, (1813), *NAACP v. Alabama ex rel. Patterson*, (1958), and *Bouie v. City of Columbia*, (1964), cited by The Chief Justice, are three such rare instances. But those cases are embedded in historical contexts hardly comparable to the situation here. *Fairfax's Devisee*, which held that the Virginia Court of Appeals had misconstrued its own forfeiture laws to deprive a British subject of lands secured to him by federal treaties, occurred amidst vociferous States' rights attacks on the Marshall Court. The Virginia court refused to obey this Court's *Fairfax's Devisee* mandate to enter judgment for the British subject's successor in interest. That refusal led to the Court's pathmarking decision in *Martin v. Hunter's Lessee*, (1816). *Patterson*, a case decided three months after *Cooper v. Aaron*, (1958), in the face of Southern resistance to the civil rights movement, held that the Alabama Supreme Court had irregularly applied its own procedural rules to deny review of a contempt order against the NAACP arising from its refusal to disclose membership lists. We said that "our jurisdiction is not defeated if the nonfederal ground relied on by the state court is without any fair or substantial support." *Bouie*, stemming from a lunch counter "sit-in" at the height of the civil rights movement, held that the South Carolina Supreme Court's construction of its trespass laws—criminalizing conduct not covered by the text of an otherwise clear statute—was "unforeseeable" and thus violated due process when applied retroactively to the petitioners.

The Chief Justice's casual citation of these cases might lead one to believe they are part of a larger collection of cases in which we said that the Constitution impelled us to train a skeptical eye on a state court's portrayal of state law. But one would be hard pressed, I think, to find additional cases that fit the mold. As Justice Breyer convincingly explains, this case involves nothing close to the kind of recalcitrance by a state high court that warrants extraordinary action by this Court. The Florida Supreme Court concluded that counting every legal vote was the overriding concern of the Florida Legislature when it enacted the State's Election Code. The court surely should not be bracketed with state high courts of the Jim Crow South.

The Chief Justice says that Article II, by providing that state legislatures shall direct the manner of appointing electors, authorizes federal superintendence over the relationship between state courts and state legislatures, and licenses a departure from the usual deference we give to state court interpretations of state law. . . . The Framers of our Constitution, however, understood that in a republican government, the judiciary would construe the legislature's enactments. In light of the constitutional guarantee to States of a "Republican Form of Government," U.S. Const., Art. IV, §4, Article II can hardly be read to invite this Court to disrupt a State's republican regime. Yet The Chief Justice today would reach out to do just that. By holding that Article II requires our revision of a state court's construction of state laws in order to protect one organ of the State from another, The Chief Justice contradicts the basic principle that a State may organize itself as it sees fit. Article II does not call for the scrutiny undertaken by this Court.

   The extraordinary setting of this case has obscured the ordinary principle that dictates its proper resolution: Federal courts defer to state high courts' interpretations of their state's own law. This principle reflects the core of federalism, on which all agree. "The Framers split the atom of sovereignty. It was the genius of their idea that our citizens would have two political capacities, one state and one federal, each protected from incursion by the other." *Saenz v. Roe*, (1999). The Chief Justice's solicitude for the Florida Legislature comes at the expense of the more fundamental solicitude we owe to the legislature's sovereign. U.S. Const., Art. II, §1, cl. 2 ("Each *State* shall appoint, in such Manner as the Legislature *thereof* may direct," the electors for President and Vice President) (emphasis added).[1] Were the other members of this Court as mindful as they generally are of our system of dual sovereignty, they would affirm the judgment of the Florida Supreme Court.

II

I agree with Justice Stevens that petitioners have not presented a substantial equal protection claim. Ideally, perfection would be the appropriate standard for judging the recount. But we live in an imperfect world, one in which thousands of votes have not been counted. I cannot agree that the recount adopted by the Florida court, flawed as it may be, would yield a result any less fair or precise than the certification that preceded that recount.

   Even if there were an equal protection violation, I would agree with Justice Stevens, Justice Souter, and Justice Breyer that the Court's concern about "the December 12 deadline," is misplaced. Time is short in part because of the Court's entry of a stay on December 9, several hours after an able circuit judge in Leon County had begun to superintend the recount process. More fundamentally, the Court's reluctance to let the recount go forward-despite its suggestion that "[t]he search for intent can be confined by specific rules designed to ensure uniform treatment," *ante*, at 8–ultimately turns on its own judgment about the practical realities of implementing a recount, not the judgment of those much closer to the process.

   Equally important, as Justice Breyer explains, the December 12 "deadline" for bringing Florida's electoral votes into *3 U.S.C. § 5*'s safe harbor lacks the significance the Court assigns it. Were that date to pass, Florida would still be entitled to deliver electoral votes Congress *must* count unless both Houses find that the votes "ha[d] not been . . . regularly given." *3 U.S.C. § 15.* The statute identifies other significant dates. But none of these dates has ultimate significance in light of Congress' detailed provisions for determining, on "the sixth day of January," the validity of electoral votes. §15.

The Court assumes that time will not permit "orderly judicial review of any disputed matters that might arise." But no one has doubted the good faith and diligence with which Florida election officials, attorneys for all sides of this controversy, and the courts of law have performed their duties. Notably, the Florida Supreme Court has produced two substantial opinions within 29 hours of oral argument. In sum, the Court's conclusion that a constitutionally adequate recount is impractical is a prophecy the Court's own judgment will not allow to be tested. Such an untested prophecy should not decide the Presidency of the United States.

I dissent.

NOTES

1. "[B]ecause the Framers recognized that state power and identity were essential parts of the federal balance, see The Federalist No. 39, the Constitution is solicitous of the prerogatives of the States, even in an otherwise sovereign federal province. The Constitution . . . grants States certain powers over the times, places, and manner of federal elections (subject to congressional revision), Art. I, §4, cl. 1 . . . , and allows States to appoint electors for the President, Art. II, §1, cl. 2." *U.S. Term Limits, Inc. v. Thornton, 514 U.S. 779,* 841–842 (1995) (Kennedy, J., concurring).

9

PUBLIC OPINION

9.1

ARTHUR LUPIA AND MATHEW D. McCUBBINS

From *The Democratic Dilemma: Can Citizens Learn What They Need to Know?*

Some observers have concluded that Americans do not know enough about politics and government to make wise choices in voting and other political decisions. The "dilemma" in the title is that citizens are quite uninformed but are being asked to make weighty decisions, like who should be president. Lupia and McCubbins argue that most of the time, under normal conditions, citizens get enough information to make reasonable decisions.

> Knowledge will forever govern ignorance: And a people who mean to be their own Governors, must arm themselves with the power which knowledge gives. A popular Government, without popular information, or the means of acquiring it, is but a Prologue to a Farce or a Tragedy; or, perhaps both.
>
> —James Madison[1]

The founders of the American republic, and many of their contemporaries around the world, believed that democracy requires citizens to make reasoned choices. Reasoned choice, in turn, requires that people know the consequences of their actions.

Can voters, legislators, and jurors make reasoned choices? Many observers conclude that they cannot. The evidence for this conclusion is substantial—study after study documents the breadth and depth of citizen ignorance.

Making matters worse is the fact that many people acquire what little information they have from thirty-minute news summaries, thirty-second political advertisements, or eight-second sound bites. From this evidence, it seems very likely that "Men of factious tempers, of local prejudices, or of sinister designs, may, by intrigue, by corruption, or by any other means, first obtain the suffrages, and then betray the interests, of the people" (Madison, *Federalist* 10).

It is widely believed that there is a mismatch between the requirements of democracy and most people's ability to meet these requirements. If this mismatch is too prevalent, then effective self-governance is impossible. The *democratic dilemma* is that the people who are called upon to make reasoned choices may not be capable of doing so.

[W]e concede that people lack political information. We also concede that this ignorance can allow people "of sinister designs" to deceive and betray the underinformed. We do not concede, however, that democracy *must* succumb to these threats. Rather, we conclude that:

- Reasoned choice does not require full information; rather, it requires the ability to predict the consequences of actions. We define this ability as knowledge.[2]
- People *choose* to disregard most of the information they could acquire and base virtually all of their decisions on remarkably little information.
- People often *substitute* the advice of others for the information they lack. This substitution can give people the capacity for reasoned choice.
- Relying on the advice of others involves tradeoffs. Although it decreases the costs of acquiring knowledge, it also introduces the possibility of deception.
- A person who wants to gain knowledge from the advice of others must choose to follow some advice while ignoring other advice. People make these choices in systematic and predictable ways.
- Political institutions can help people choose which advice to follow and which advice to ignore. Institutions do this when they *clarify* the incentives of advice givers.
- Understanding how people learn not only helps us better identify when presumed democratic dilemmas are real but also shows us how we might begin to resolve these dilemmas. . . .

DEMOCRACY, DELEGATION, AND REASONED CHOICE

Democracy is a method of government based upon the choices of the people. In all modern democracies, the people elect or appoint others to represent them. Legislative assemblies, executives, commissions, judges, and juries are empowered by the people to make collective decisions on their behalf. These delegations form the foundation of democracy.

But there are dangers. As Dahl (1967: 21) warns, the principal danger is that uninformed decision makers, by failing to delegate well, will transform democracy into a *tyranny of experts:* "there are decisions that require me to *delegate* authority to others . . . but if I delegate, may I not, in practice, end up with a kind of aristocracy of experts, or even false experts?"

Must democracy become a tyranny of experts? Many observers answer yes, because those who delegate seem uninformed when compared with those to whom they delegate.

The principal democratic delegation, that of the people electing their governors, seems most susceptible to tyranny. Cicero's observation that "in the common people there is no wisdom, no penetration, no power of judgment" is an apt summary of modern voting studies (see Berelson 1952, Campbell et al. 1960, Converse 1964, Kinder and Sears 1985, Lane and Sears 1964, Luskin 1987, McClosky 1964, Neuman 1986, Schattschneider 1960, Schumpeter 1942, Zaller 1992, Zaller and Feldman 1992; for a survey, see Delli Carpini and Keeter 1996). Many scholars argue that voters, because of their obstinance or their inability to educate themselves, become the unwitting puppets of campaign and media puppet-masters (Bennett 1992, Sabato 1991). Iyengar (1987: 816) summarizes the literature on voting and elections: "the low level of political knowledge and the absence of ideological reasoning has lent credence to the charges that popular control of government is illusory." These studies suggest that voters who lack information cannot use elections to control their governors.

Other observers make similar arguments about elected representatives. Weber, for example, argues that legislators cannot control bureaucrats:

> Under normal conditions, the power position of a fully developed bureaucracy is always overtowering. The "political master" finds himself in the position of the "dilettante" who stands opposite the "expert," facing the trained official who stands within the management of administration. This holds whether the "master" whom the bureaucracy serves is a "people," equipped with the weapons of "legislative initiative," the "referendum," and the right to remove officials, or a parliament, elected on a more aristocratic or more "democratic" basis and equipped with the right to vote a lack of confidence, or with the actual authority to vote it. (Weber quoted in Gerth and Mills 1946: 232)

Niskanen (1971) continues that public officials' inability to contend with the complexities of modern legislation places them at the mercy of self-serving special interests and bureaucrats. Lowi (1979: xii) concludes, "actual policymaking will not come from voter preferences or congressional enactments but from a process of tripartite bargaining between the specialized administrators, relevant members of Congress, and the representatives of self-selected organized interests."

Jurors also seem to lack the information they need. Posner (1995: 52), for example, argues, "As American law and society become ever more complex, the jury's cognitive limitations will become ever more palpable and socially costly." Other observers characterize the legal system, not as a forum where citizens make reasoned choices, but as a stage for emotional appeals where style and deception overwhelm knowledge. As Abramson (1994: 3) laments,

> The gap between the complexity of modern litigation and the qualifica-
> tions of jurors has widened to frightening proportions. The average jury
> rarely understands the expert testimony in an anti-trust suit, a medical
> malpractice case, or an insanity defense. Nor do most jurors know the
> law or comprehend the judge's crash course of instructions on it. Trial
> by jury has thus become trial by ignorance.

Although the critiques of democracy's delegations are myriad and diverse, all have a common conclusion—*reasoned choice does not govern delegation.* As Schumpeter (1942: 262) argues, "the typical citizen drops down to a lower level of mental performance as soon as he enters the political field. He argues and analyzes in a way which he would readily recognize as infantile within the sphere of his real interests. He becomes a primitive again. His thinking is associative and affective. . . . [T]his may prove fatal to the nation."

If voters, legislators, and jurors lack the capability to delegate effectively, then democracy may be "but a prologue to a farce or a tragedy." Like the scholars just quoted, we find this possibility alarming. Unlike these scholars, however, we argue that the capabilities of the people and the requirements of democracy are not as mismatched as many critics would have us believe. In what follows, we will identify the conditions under which this mismatch does and does not exist.

A PREVIEW OF OUR THEORY

We argue that *limited information need not prevent people from making rea-
soned choices.* Of course, we are not the first analysts to make this type of argument. In the 1950s, for example, Berelson, Lazarfeld, and McPhee (1954) and Downs (1957) argued that voters rely on opinion leaders and political parties to overcome their information shortfalls. More recently, a generation of scholars has further countered the view that the "democratic citizen is expected to be well informed about political affairs" (Berelson, Lazarsfeld, and McPhee 1954: 308). Collectively, these scholars have demonstrated that voters can use a wide range of simple cues as substitutes for complex information. We concur with the basic insight of each of these studies—people can use substitutes for encyclopedic information.

However, we want to do more than argue that limited information need not prevent people from making reasoned choices. We want to argue that *there are specific conditions under which people who have limited information can make reasoned choices.* Therefore, in addition to showing that people *can* use cues, we want to answer questions about *when and how* people use cues, *when* cues are effective substitutes for detailed information, and *when* cues are detrimental. To understand who is (and who is not) capable of reasoned choice, we must be able to answer questions such as:

- When do people use simple cues?
- When do people ignore simple cues and seek more detailed information instead?
- When are simple cues sufficient for reasoned choice?
- When can people who offer simple cues manipulate or deceive those who use them?
- What factors determine why a person relies on some simple cues while ignoring many others?
- How do political institutions affect the use and effectiveness of simple cues?

To answer these questions, we construct theories of attention, persuasion, and delegation. . . . [O]ur theory has the rare advantage of being relevant to the usually separate debates on learning, communication, and choice held in cognitive science, economics, political science, and psychology. Next, we describe our theory and preview the answers it gives to the questions listed previously.

Knowledge and Information

We begin by developing a theory of attention. The purpose of our theory is to explain how humans cope with complexity and scarcity. As Simon (1979: 3) argues, "human thinking powers are very modest when compared with the complexities of the environments in which human beings live." Making matters worse is the fact that many of the resources people need to survive are scarce.

Ironically, for many political issues, information is not scarce; rather it is the cognitive resources that a person can use to process information that are scarce. For example, political information appears in the newspapers, in the mail, on community bulletin boards, and on television and radio and is relayed to us in person by friends and family. People often lack the time and energy needed to make sense of all this information. As a consequence, people often have only incomplete information. Fortunately, reasoned choice does not require complete information. Instead, it requires *knowledge: the ability to predict the consequences of actions.*[3]

Implicit in many critiques of democracy is the claim that people who lack *information* are incapable of reasoned choice. By contrast, we argue that people who lack information solve enormously complex problems every day.

They do so by making effective use of the information available to them, sorting that which is useful from that which is not.

Information is useful only if it helps people avoid costly mistakes. By contrast, if more information does not lead people to change their decisions, then it provides no instrumental benefit and they should ignore it. Indeed, ignoring useless information is necessary for humans and other species to survive and prosper (Churchland and Sejnowski 1992).

Those who find such statements surprising should consider the almost boundless range of actions, both mundane and grand, for which people ignore available information. For example, people take medication without knowing all of the conditions under which it might be harmful. They also buy houses based on limited information about the neighborhoods around them and with little or no information about the neighbors. People make choices in this way not because the information is unavailable but because the costs of paying attention to it exceed the value of its use.[4]

Although reasoned choice does not require complete information, it does require the ability to predict the consequences of actions. In many cases, simple pieces of information can provide the knowledge people need. For example, to navigate a busy intersection successfully, you must *know* where all of the other cars are going to be sure that you can avoid crashing into them. Advocates of complete information might argue that successful automotive navigation requires as much information as you can gather about the intentions of other drivers and the speed, acceleration, direction, and mass of their cars. At many intersections, however, there is a simple substitute for *all* of this information—a traffic signal. At these intersections, traffic signals are substitutes for more complex information and reduce the amount of information required to make a reasoned choice. At intersections without working traffic signals or other simple cues, reasoned choices require more information. Using similar logic, it follows that limited information precludes reasoned choice only if people are stuck at complex political intersections and lack access to effective political traffic signals.

Persuasion, Enlightenment, and Deception

People who want to make reasoned choices need knowledge. There are two ways to acquire knowledge. The first way is to draw from personal experience. People who exercise this option use their own observations of the past to derive predictions about the future consequences of their actions. The second way is to learn from others. People who exercise this option substitute other people's observations of the past for the personal experience they lack.

In many political settings, only the second option is available. This is true because politics is often abstract and its consequences are remote. In these settings, personal experience does not provide sufficient knowledge for reasoned choice. For many political decisions, reasoned choice requires learning from others.

There are many explanations of how people learn from others. Indeed, a generation of scholars, starting with Knight, Simon, Berelson et al. and Downs, suggest numerous heuristics—simple means for generating information substitutes.[5] . . .

Individually, each of these explanations of how we learn from others is valuable and enlightening. Each reveals a source of the judgmental shortcuts that people undoubtedly use. However, as Sniderman, Brody, and Tetlock (1991: 70) argue, "The most serious risk is that . . . every correlation between independent and dependent variables [is] taken as evidence of a new judgmental shortcut." We agree. We need a theory that explains when or how people choose among the shortcuts listed in the preceding paragraph. To understand how people learn from others, we must be able to explain *how people choose whom to believe.*

▪   ▪   ▪

[N]otice that any attempt to learn from others leads to one of three possible outcomes.

- The first outcome is *enlightenment*. When someone furnishes us with knowledge, we become enlightened. Enlightenment, then, is the process of becoming enlightened. If we initially lack knowledge sufficient for reasoned choice and can obtain such knowledge only from others, then we can make reasoned decisions only if others enlighten us.
- The second outcome is *deception*. Deception is the process by which the testimony we hear reduces our ability to predict accurately the consequences of our actions. For example, we are deceived when someone lies to us *and* we believe that individual.
- The third outcome is that we *learn nothing*. When we learn nothing, our beliefs go unchanged and we gain no knowledge.

Both enlightenment and deception, in turn, require *persuasion: a successful attempt to change the beliefs of another.* The key to understanding whether people become enlightened or deceived by the testimony of others is to understand the conditions under which they can persuade one another.

Most scholars of communication and politics, dating back to Aristotle, focus on a speaker's *internal character* (e.g., honesty, ideology, or reputation) as a necessary condition for persuasion. If a speaker lacks the right character, then these scholars conclude that the speaker will not be persuasive. [W]e present a different set of necessary and sufficient conditions for persuasion. We argue that persuasion need not be contingent upon personal character; rather, *persuasion requires that a listener perceive a speaker to be both knowledgeable and trustworthy*. Although a perception of trust can arise from a positive evaluation of a speaker's character, we show that *external forces can substitute for character* and can thus generate persuasion in contexts where it would not otherwise occur.

An example of an external force that generates trust and persuasion is a listener's observation of a speaker's costly effort. From this observation, the listener can learn about the intensity of a speaker's preferences. This particular condition is also very much like the adage that actions speak louder than words. When speaker costs have this effect, they can provide a basis for trust by providing listeners with a window to speaker incentives.

To see how costly effort affects persuasion, consider the following situation. First, suppose that a listener knows a speaker to have one of three possible motivations—he is a conservative with intense preferences, a conservative with non-intense preferences, or a liberal with non-intense preferences. Second, suppose that the listener does not know which of the three motivations the speaker actually has. Third, suppose that the listener can make a reasoned choice only if he or she knows whether the speaker is liberal or conservative. Fourth, suppose that if the listener observes that the speaker paid a quarter of his or her income to affect a policy outcome, then the listener can conclude that the speaker has intense preferences. If all four suppositions are true, then the speaker's costly effort persuades the listener. As a result, the listener can make a reasoned choice because she can infer that the speaker is a conservative.

Another example of a trust-inducing external force is a penalty for lying. Penalties for lying, whether explicit, such as fines for perjury, or implicit, such as the loss of a valued reputation, can also generate trust by revealing a speaker's incentives. That is, although a listener may believe that a speaker has an interest in deception, the presence of a penalty for lying may lead the listener to believe that certain types of lies are prohibitively costly, rendering certain types of statements very likely to be true.

Our conditions for persuasion show when forces such as costly effort and penalties for lying are, and are not, effective substitutes for a speaker's character.[6] These conditions reveal that you do not necessarily learn more from people who are like you, nor do you learn more from people you like. This is why most people turn to financial advisors, instead of their mothers, when dealing with mutual funds, and back to Mom when seeking advice about child rearing.

Unlike most well-known theories of persuasion and strategic communication, our conditions for persuasion also clarify how and when people suffer as a result of substituting simple cues for complex information. For example, our theory allows us to identify conditions under which a speaker can deceive a listener (i.e., conditions under which a speaker lies *and* a listener believes the lie). These conditions are important because many critics of democracy claim that uninformed citizens are ripe for manipulation at the hands of slick political salesmen.

■　　■　　■

More generally, our conditions for persuasion show why some statements are persuasive and others are not. The obvious reason for these differences is that statements vary in content. The less obvious reason is that the context under which a speaker makes a statement also affects persuasion considerably. Two people making precisely the same statement may not be equally persuasive if only one is subject to penalties for lying.

Our conditions for persuasion further imply that not everyone can persuade. People listen to some speakers and not others. They read some books and not others. They buy some products even though the manufacturers spend very little money on advertising while refusing to buy others supported by celebrity endorsements. Similarly, people respond to the advice of some experts or interest groups and not that of others. Our conditions for persuasion explain how people make these choices.

Our results also reveal the bounds on the effectiveness of the heuristics mentioned earlier. Consider, for example, the use of ideology as a heuristic. When there is a high correlation between a speaker's ideology and that speaker's knowledge and trustworthiness, then people are likely to find ideological cues useful. By contrast, when there is no clear correlation, ideology is useless. Similar arguments can be made about other heuristics, such as party, reputation, and likability. In sum, *concepts such as reputation, party, or ideology are useful heuristics only if they convey information about knowledge and trust. The converse of this statement is not true*—knowledge and trust are the fundamental factors that make cues persuasive; the other factors are not.

■　　■　　■

Successful Delegation and the Institutions of Knowledge

. . . Two reasons are commonly cited for the failure of delegation: principals and agents have *conflicting interests* over the outcome of delegation, and agents have *expertise* regarding the consequences of the delegation that principals do not. When delegation occurs under these conditions, agents are free to take any action that suits them, irrespective of the consequences for the principal, and the principal cannot cause them to do otherwise.

We find that delegation succeeds if two conditions are satisfied: the knowledge condition and the incentive condition. The knowledge condition is satisfied in one of two ways. First, it is satisfied when the principal's personal experience allows her to distinguish beneficial from detrimental agent actions. Second, it is satisfied when the principal can obtain this knowledge from others. Therefore, the knowledge condition does not require the principal to know everything the agent knows; it requires only that the principal know enough to distinguish welfare-enhancing from welfare-decreasing agent actions.

The incentive condition is satisfied when the agent and the principal have at least some goals in common. In many cases, satisfaction of the knowledge condition is sufficient for satisfaction of the incentive condition: A principal who becomes enlightened with respect to the consequences of delegation either can motivate the agent to take actions that enhance her welfare or can reject the agent's actions that do not enhance her welfare.

We find that the outcome of delegation is not determined by whether or not the principal can match the agent's technical expertise. Instead, it is determined by the principal's ability to use the testimony of others effectively. If the principal has this ability, then delegation can succeed despite the information she lacks. If the principal lacks information about the agent and lacks the ability to learn from others, then delegation is doomed.

Moreover, we argue that, if democratic principals can create the context in which knowledgeable and persuasive speakers can inform them of the consequences of their agent's actions, then they can facilitate successful delegation. We argue that institutions, such as administrative procedure, rules of evidence, and statutory law, provide the context in which principals can learn about their agent's actions. Institutions can, if properly structured, offer principals a way to better judge their agent's actions. When institutions are poorly designed, or the incentives they induce are opaque, then the political consequence of limited information is likely to be failed delegation. By contrast, when these institutions properly and clearly structure incentives, then they facilitate enlightenment, reasoned choice, and successful delegation even in complex circumstances.

Conclusion

The mismatch between what delegation demands and citizens' capabilities constitutes the democratic dilemma. If people are not capable of reasoned political choices, then effective self-governance is an illusion. After observing that voters, legislators, and jurors are ignorant of many of the details of the decisions they face, many scholars and political commentators conclude that the illusion is real and argue for some type of reform. If their conclusion is correct, then effective self-governance may indeed require political reform. If their conclusion is incorrect, their reforms may restrain the truly competent and do more harm than good.

Other scholars have argued that people are quite capable of making complex decisions with very little information. They point to instances in which people use heuristics and conclude that such heuristics are sufficient for reasoned choice. If these conclusions are correct, then successful delegation does not require reform and the critics mentioned previously are akin to democracy's Chicken Littles. If, however, these latter conclusions are incorrect, then the optimistic scholars are akin to democracy's

Pollyannas, advocating the perpetuation of ineffective and harmful systems of governance.

Both sides of this debate recognize that people are often ignorant about the details of the choices they make. They also both recognize the existence of information shortcuts, cues, and heuristics. What is missing from this debate is an understanding of when ignorance of details prevents reasoned choice, how people choose among potential heuristics, and when these heuristics provide effective substitutes for the detailed information people lack. Only when we have these understandings will we be able to make constructive use of the common observation that people lack information. At that point, we can separate the Chicken Littles from the Pollyannas and build effective solutions to the democratic dilemma.

NOTES

1. From Hunt (1910: 103). Madison expressed similar beliefs in *Federalist 57* and in a speech before the Virginia Ratifying Convention, where he argued that it is necessary that the people possess the "virtue and intelligence to select men of virtue and wisdom" (Riemer 1986: 40).

2. There exists a centuries-old debate about what democracy *should* do. This debate has involved many great minds, is wide ranging, and is totally unresolved. We do not believe ourselves capable of resolving this debate. However, we strongly believe that we can make the debate more constructive. We can do so by clarifying the relationship between what information people have and what types of decisions they can make. Our reading is firmly about determining the capabilities of people who lack political information. It is designed to resolve debates about how much information voters, jurors, and legislators need in order to perform certain tasks. So, although our reading may help to clarify debates about what democracy should do, it will not resolve these debates.

We mention this because our relationship to the debate about what democracy should do motivates our definition of reasoned choice. Our definition of reasoned choice allows the reader to define an amount of knowledge that is required for reasoned choice. Some readers may argue that a reasoned choice requires knowledge of very technical matters, whereas others may argue that a reasoned choice requires less knowledge. Note that the difference between these viewpoints reduces to different views on what democracy should do. Therefore, our definition of reasoned choice is purposefully precise with respect to the relationship between information, knowledge, and choice and is purposefully vague with respect to most normative debates about what democracies *should* do.

3. For example, knowing which of two products is "better" than the other is often sufficient for us to make the same choice we would have made had we been completely informed about each product.

4. Furthermore, beyond being useless, some types of information cause people to make the wrong (i.e., welfare-reducing) choices when they would have otherwise made the right (i.e., welfare-increasing) ones with less information. For example, a person who votes for Jones instead of Smith because a newspaper endorses Jones may regret having attended to this additional information when Jones later opposes a policy that both she and Smith support.

5. Also, see Key (1966) and Tversky and Kahneman (1974).

6. A third external force that can induce a listener to trust a speaker arises when the speaker's statements are subject to some chance of being externally verified.

REFERENCES

Abramson, Jeffrey. 1994. *We, the Jury: The Jury System and the Ideal of Democracy*. New York: Basic Books.

Bennett, W. Lance. 1992. *The Governing Crisis: Media, Money, and Marketing in American Elections*. New York: St. Martin's Press.

Berelson, Bernard. 1952. "Democratic Theory and Public Opinion." *Public Opinion Quarterly* XVI: 313–30.

Berelson, Bernard, Paul F. Lazarfeld, and William N. McPhee. 1954. *Voting: A Study of Opinion Formation in a Presidential Campaign*. Chicago: University of Chicago Press.

Campbell, Angus, Philip E. Converse, Warren E. Miller, and Donald E. Stokes. 1960. *The American Voter*. New York: Wiley.

Churchland, Patricia S., and Terrence J. Sejnowski. 1992. *The Computational Brain*. Cambridge, Mass.: MIT Press.

Converse, Philip E. 1964. "The Nature of Belief Systems in Mass Publics." In David E. Apter, ed., *Ideology and Discontent*. New York: Free Press.

Dahl, Robert A. 1967. *Pluralist Democracy in the United States: Conflict and Consent*. Chicago: Rand McNally.

Delli Carpini, Michael X., and Scott Keeter. 1991. "Stability and Change in the United States Public's Knowledge of Politics." *Public Opinion Quarterly* 55: 583–612.

Downs, Anthony. 1957. *An Economic Theory of Democracy*. New York: Harper.

Gerth, H. H., and C. Wright Mills, eds. 1946. *From Max Weber: Essays in Sociology*. New York: Oxford University Press.

Hunt, Gaillard, ed. 1910. *The Writings of James Madison*. New York: Putnam.

Iyengar, Shanto. 1987. "Television News and Citizens' Explanations of National Affairs." *American Political Science Review* 81: 815–32.

Key, V. O. 1966. *The Responsible Electorate: Rationality in Presidential Voting, 1936–1960*. Cambridge, Mass.: Belknap Press of Harvard University Press.

Kinder, Donald R., and David O. Sears. 1985. "Public Opinion and Political Participation." In G. Lindzey and E. Aronson, eds., *Handbook of Social Psychology*. Reading, Mass.: Addison-Wesley.

Lane, Robert E., and David O. Sears. 1964. *Public Opinion*. Englewood Cliffs, N.J.: Prentice-Hall.

Lowi, Theodore J. 1979. *The End of Liberalism: The Second Republic of the United States*. 2nd ed. New York: Norton.

Luskin, Robert C. 1987. "Measuring Political Sophistication." *American Journal of Political Science* 31: 856–99.

Madison, James. *Federalist*. In Clinton Rossiter, ed., *The Federalist Papers*. New York: Penguin.

McClosky, Herbert. 1964. "Consensus and Ideology in American Politics." *American Political Science Review* 58: 361–82.

Neuman, W. Russell. 1986. *The Paradox of Mass Politics: Knowledge and Opinion in the American Electorate*. Cambridge, Mass.: Harvard University Press.

Niskanen, William A. 1971. *Bureaucracy and Representative Government*. Chicago: Aldine-Atherton.

Posner, Richard. 1995. "Juries on Trial." *Commentary* 99: 49–52.

Riemer, Neal. 1986. *James Madison: Creating the American Constitution.* Washington, D.C.: Congressional Quarterly.

Sabato, Larry J. 1991. *Feeding Frenzy.* New York: Free Press.

Schattschneider, Elmer Eric. 1960. *The Semisovereign People: A Realist's View of Democracy in America.* New York: Holt, Rinehart and Winston.

Schumpeter, Joseph Alois. 1942. *Capitalism, Socialism, and Democracy.* New York: Harper.

Simon, Herbert A. 1979. *Models of Thought.* New Haven, Conn.: Yale University Press.

Sniderman, Paul M., Richard A. Brody, and Philip E. Tetlock. 1991. *Reasoning and Choice: Explorations in Political Psychology.* Cambridge: Cambridge University Press.

Tversky, Amos, and Daniel Kahneman. 1974. "Judgment under Uncertainty: Heuristics and Biases." *Science* 185: 1124–131.

Zaller, John. 1992. *The Nature and Origins of Mass Opinion.* Cambridge: Cambridge University Press.

Zaller, John, and Stanley Feldman. 1992. "A Simple Theory of the Survey Response: Answering Questions Versus Revealing Preferences." *American Journal of Political Science* 36: 579–616.

9.2

JOHN R. ZALLER

From *The Nature and Origins of Mass Opinion*

A large literature in political science examines what voters know and whether they have enough information to make informed choices in elections. Zaller proposes a model for how voters acquire information. Using this model, he argues that voters vary in the degree to which they are receptive to new information, depending on their underlying political predispositions and levels of knowledge about politics. His model lends insight into why some voters are swayed by public discourse and others stay firm in their attitudes.

HOW CITIZENS ACQUIRE INFORMATION AND CONVERT IT INTO PUBLIC OPINION

The comprehensive analysis of public opinion requires attention to two phenomena: how citizens learn about matters that are for the most part beyond their immediate experience, and how they convert the information they acquire into opinions.

. . . [I] propose a model of both phenomena. The model does not provide a fully accurate account of how people process information and form attitude statements. No model that is both parsimonious and testable on typical mass opinion data—the two most important constraints on my enterprise—could possibly do so. But the proposed model, as I hope to persuade the reader, does a plausible job of approximating what must actually occur, and a quite excellent job of accounting for the available survey evidence across a wide range of phenomena.

■ ■ ■

Some Definitions

I begin the statement of the model with definitions of primitive terms. The first is *consideration*, which is defined as any reason that might induce an individual to decide a political issue one way or the other.[1] Considerations, thus, are a compound of cognition and affect—that is, a belief concerning an object and an evaluation of the belief.

■ ■ ■

Second, I define two types of political messages: persuasive messages and cueing messages. Persuasive messages are arguments or images providing a reason for taking a position or point of view; if accepted by an individual, they become considerations, as the term was just defined. . . .

Note that there is nothing in this account that implies that either political messages or the considerations that result from them must be coldly rational. On the contrary, messages may involve subtle or even subliminal images, and considerations may involve feelings or emotions.

▪   ▪   ▪

Cueing messages, which are the second type of message carried in elite discourse, consist of "contextual information" about the ideological or partisan implications of a persuasive message. The importance of cueing messages is that, as suggested by Converse (1964), they enable citizens to perceive relationships between the persuasive messages they receive and their political predispositions, which in turn permits them to respond critically to the persuasive messages.

▪   ▪   ▪

The Model

The model itself consists of four assertions, or axioms, about how individuals respond to political information they may encounter. Each is stated first as a general theoretical position and then elaborated and justified in more precise terms.

▪   ▪   ▪

A1. *RECEPTION AXIOM. The greater a person's level of cognitive engagement with an issue, the more likely he or she is to be exposed to and comprehend—in a word, to receive—political messages concerning that issue.*[2]

The messages people may receive include all types: that is, persuasive messages and cueing messages.

▪   ▪   ▪

Although cognitive engagement is the right specification for my model, it is a cumbersome and somewhat precious phrase. Therefore, I will, through most of the analysis that follows, use a simpler phrase, namely *political attentiveness* or *political awareness*. But cognitive engagement, political attentiveness, and political awareness are meant to convey the same meaning.

▪   ▪   ▪

A2. RESISTANCE AXIOM. People tend to resist arguments that are inconsistent with their political predispositions, but they do so only to the extent that they possess the contextual information necessary to perceive a relationship between the message and their predispositions.

The key to resistance, in this formulation, is *information* concerning the relationship between arguments and predispositions, where the requisite information is carried in cueing messages. According to the Reception Axiom, the probability of individuals acquiring cueing information depends on their levels of awareness of each given issue. Thus, A1 and A2 together imply that the likelihood of resisting persuasive communications that are inconsistent with one's political predispositions rises with a person's level of political attentiveness. Or, to put it the other way, politically inattentive persons will often be unaware of the implications of the persuasive communications they encounter, and so often end up "mistakenly" accepting them.

∎ ∎ ∎

A3. ACCESSIBILITY AXIOM. The more recently a consideration has been called to mind or thought about, the less time it takes to retrieve that consideration or related considerations from memory and bring them to the top of the head for use.

Conversely, the longer it has been since a consideration or related idea has been activated, the less likely it is to be accessible at the top of the head; in the limit, a long unused set of considerations may be completely inaccessible, which is to say, forgotten.

This axiom appropriates for use in the model one of the best-established empirical regularities in cognitive psychology. General support for the basic idea is overwhelming and, as far as I can tell, undisputed. When an idea or concept has been recently used, seen, heard, or indirectly referenced, it is significantly more likely to be available for reuse than if it has not been recently activated.

∎ ∎ ∎

A4. RESPONSE AXIOM. Individuals answer survey questions by averaging across the considerations that are immediately salient or accessible to them.

This axiom, which completes the statement of my proposed model, implies that persons who have been asked a survey question do not normally canvass their minds for all considerations relevant to the given issue; rather, they answer the question on the basis of whatever considerations are accessible "at the top of the head." In some cases, only a single consideration may be readily accessible, in which case individuals answer on the basis of that consideration; in other cases, two or more considerations may come quickly to mind, in which case people answer by averaging across accessible considerations.

An important feature of the Response Axiom is that it permits different people to respond to issue questions on the basis of different considerations—one, for example, emphasizing ideological concerns, another gut-level likes and dislikes, and yet another self-interest.

▪ ▪ ▪

Perhaps the most apt description of a survey response within the proposed model is "opinion statement." This term implies that the expression of opinion is genuine without also implying that it either represents prior reflection or is destined for a long half-life. The phrase "attitude report" has similar virtues.

Opinion statements, as conceived in my four-axiom model, are the outcome of a process in which people *receive* new information, decide whether to *accept* it, and then *sample* at the moment of answering questions. For convenience, therefore, I will refer to this process as the Receive-Accept-Sample, or RAS, Model.

How the Model Is Used in This Book

The model I have outlined consists of four very general claims about how people acquire information from the political environment (in the form of persuasive arguments and cues) and transform that information into survey responses.

▪ ▪ ▪

The argument to be made from the RAS model may be previewed as follows. It follows from the Response Axiom that the probability that a person will support or oppose a given policy depends on the mix of positive and negative considerations available in the person's mind at the moment of answering a question about it. If, for the moment, we overlook the probability of nonresponse (which occurs when no considerations are immediately salient in memory), and assume also that every consideration a person has internalized is as likely to be sampled as any other, then the probability of a liberal response by a given person is

$$Prob(Liberal\ response) = \frac{L}{L + C}$$

where L and C refer to the number of liberal and conservative considerations available in the person's mind. (I reiterate that here, as elsewhere in this book, liberal and conservative are simply *labels* for the directional thrust of ideas; a person may use a liberal consideration as the basis for a liberal response even though she is not, in any deeper sense, "a liberal.")

The balance of liberal and conservative considerations in people's minds depends on both society-level and individual-level variables. The key societal variables are the intensities of liberal and conservative information flows in the political environment with respect to a given issue. The key individual variables are political awareness and political predispositions. More aware persons will be exposed to more political communications (via the Reception Axiom) but will be more selective in deciding which communications to internalize as considerations (via the Resistance Axiom). Thus, politically aware citizens will tend to fill their minds with large numbers of considerations, and these considerations will tend to be relatively consistent with one another and with the citizens' predispositions. Less aware persons will internalize fewer considerations and will be less consistent in doing so. As a result, more aware people will be more likely to be able to state opinions, and more likely to state opinions that are ideologically consistent with their predispositions.

NOTES

1. This term is a borrowing from Kelley (1983), who showed that individuals appear to make vote decisions in presidential elections on the basis of a net score across numerous competing "likes" and "dislikes" about the candidates, which he called "considerations."

2. These terms derive from McGuire, 1969.

REFERENCES

Converse, Philip. 1964. "The nature of belief systems in mass publics." In David Apter (ed.), *Ideology and Discontent* (pp. 206–61). New York: Free Press.

Kelley, Stanley, Jr. 1983. *Interpreting Elections*. Princeton, N.J.: Princeton University Press.

McGuire, William J. 1969. "The nature of attitudes and attitude change." In G. Lindzey and E. Aronson (eds.), *Handbook of Social Psychology*, 2d ed. (pp. 136–314). Reading, Mass.: Addison-Wesley.

9.3

BRYAN CAPLAN

From *The Myth of the Rational Voter: Why Democracies Choose Bad Policies*

Few questions elicit more discussion and less solid evidence among political scientists than the question, "Are voters rational?" In this excerpt, Caplan argues that voters often appear to vote for politicians who pursue policies that are against voters' material interests. Why? Voters choose politicians and parties based on the appeals that give them psychological benefits (such as confirmations of their own views and beliefs) but that are often illogical when those ideas are put into practice.

THE LANDSCAPE OF POLITICAL IRRATIONALITY

> Democracy is the theory that the common people know
> what they want, and deserve to get it good and hard.
> —*H. L. Mencken*[1]

Ordinary cynics—and most economists—compare voters to consumers who shrewdly "vote their pocketbooks." In reality, this is atypical. Empirically, there is little connection between voting and material interests. Contrary to popular stereotypes of the rich Republican and the poor Democrat, income and party identity are only loosely related. The elderly are if anything slightly less supportive of Social Security and Medicare than the rest of the population. Men are *more* pro-choice than women.[2]

If self-interest does not explain political opinion, what does? Voters typically favor the policies they perceive to be in the general interest of their nation. This is, however, no cause for democratic optimism. The key word is *perceive*. Voters almost never take the next step by critically asking themselves: "Are my favorite policies *effective means* to promote the general interest?" In politics as in religion, faith is a shortcut to belief.

What are the implications for democracy? Standard rational choice theory rightly emphasizes that politicians woo voters by catering to their preferences. But this means one thing if voters are shrewd policy consumers, and almost the opposite if, as I maintain, voters are like religious devotees. In the latter case, politicians have a strong incentive to do what is popular, but little to competently deliver results. Alan Blinder cuttingly refers to "a compliant Congress, disdainful of logic, but deeply respectful of public opinion polls."[3] If one politician fails to carry out the people's wishes, a competing politician will. Le Bon makes the same point in sweeping terms:

> The masses have never thirsted after truth. They turn aside from evidence that is not to their taste, preferring to deify error, if error seduce them. Whoever can supply them with illusions is easily their master; whoever attempts to destroy their illusions is always their victim.[4]

Thus, it is in *mind-set,* not practical influence, that voters resemble religious believers. Given the separation of church and state, modern religion has a muted effect on nonbelievers. Scientific progress continues with or without religious approval. Political/economic misconceptions, in contrast, have dramatic effects on everyone who lives under the policies they inspire—even those who see these misconceptions for what they are. If most voters think protectionism is a good idea, protectionist policies thrive; if most believe that unregulated labor markets work badly, labor markets will be heavily regulated.

■   ■   ■

[M]y story is voter-driven. Voters have beliefs—defensible or not—about how the world works. They tend to support politicians who favor policies that, in the voters' own minds, will be socially beneficial. Politicians, in turn, need voter support to gain and retain office. While few are above faking support for popular views, this is rarely necessary: Successful candidates usually sincerely share voters' worldview. When special interests woo politicians, they tailor their demands accordingly. They ask for concessions along policy margins where the voice of public opinion is silent anyway. The media, finally, do their best to entertain the public. Since scandalous behavior by politicians and interest groups is entertaining, the media are watchdogs. Like all watchdogs, though, the media have a subordinate role. If their coverage, however sound, conflicts with viewers' core beliefs, they change the channel.

■   ■   ■

Conclusion
In Praise of the Study of Folly

> It is hard . . . to claim that the same individuals act in
> a rational and forward-looking way as economic agents
> but become fools when casting their vote.
> —*Torsten Persson and Guido Tabellini,*
> Political Economics[5]

Democracies have a lot of apparently counterproductive policies. Economists emphasize the folly of protection and price controls. Experts in other fields have their own bones to pick. How are these policies possible? There are three basic responses.

Response 1: Defend the accused policies on their merits.
Response 2: Argue that politicians and special interests have subverted democracy.
Response 3: Explain how policies can be *both* popular *and* counterproductive.

Response 1 is rarely convincing. We would laugh if a professor spent hours poring over a failing exam scrawled in crayon, searching for its elusive wisdom. Why should we take the effort to rationalize misguided policies any more seriously? Their typical proponent has no subtle counterarguments. Most cannot *state the experts' main objections,* much less answer them.

Response 2 is more intellectually satisfying.[6] A policy with negative overall effects can still have big benefits for a small minority. But in spite of the academic attention this explanation has accumulated in recent decades, it suffers from two great flaws. First: Theoretically, there are many ways for the majority to cheaply reassert its dominance.[7] Second: Empirical public opinion research shows that the status quo—including and perhaps especially its counterproductive policies—enjoys broad popular support, and that politicians respond to changes in public opinion.[8]

These facts have led me to response 3. Yes, it seems paradoxical for policies to be popular yet counterproductive. Common sense tells us that people like the policies that work the best.[9] Economic training reinforces this presumption by analogizing democratic participation to market consumption: If the policy is so bad, why do voters keep putting it in their shopping cart?

But on closer examination, the paradox fades away. The analogy between voting and shopping is false: *Democracy is a commons, not a market.* Individual voters do not "buy" policies with votes. Rather they toss their vote into a big common pool. The social outcome depends on the pool's average content.

In common-pool situations, economists usually fear the worst. Heedless of the aggregate effect, people will foul the waters. The main reason that they are complacent about democracy, I suspect, is that the pollution is hard to visualize. It is not run-of-the-mill *physical* pollution. Democracy suffers from a more abstract externality: the *mental* pollution of systematically biased beliefs.

While economists rarely discuss the consumption value of beliefs, the idea is intuitively plausible and theoretically unobjectionable. Anything can be a "good," as far as economic theory is concerned. Daily experience tells us that one of the goods people care about is their worldview. Few of us relish finding out that our religious or political convictions are in error.

Once you grant this point, you only need to combine it with elementary consumer theory to get my model of rational irrationality. The quantity of irrationality demanded, like the quantity of pears demanded, decreases as its material price goes up. As is often the case in economics, however, this mundane assumption raises uncomfortable questions. In daily life, reality gives us material incentives to restrain our irrationality. But what incentive do we have to think rationally about politics?

Almost none. To threaten, "You will get bad policies unless you are rational" is a fallacy of composition. Democracy lets the individual enjoy the psychological benefits of irrational beliefs at no cost to himself. This of course does not deny the value of psychological benefits. But the trade-off is not socially optimal; democracy overemphasizes citizens' psychological payoffs at the expense of their material standard of living.

NOTES

1. Andrews (1993: 229).
2. For overviews of the empirical evidence on the self-interested voter hypothesis, see Mansbridge (1990), Sears and Funk (1990), Citrin and Green (1990), and Sears et al. (1980). On income and party identification, see Gelman et al. (2005), Luttbeg and Martinez (1990), and Kamieniecki (1985). On age and policy preferences, see Ponza et al. (1988). On gender and public opinion about abortion, see Shapiro and Mahajan (1986).
3. Blinder (1987: 89).
4. Le Bon (1960: 110).
5. Persson and Tabellini (2000: 419).
6. For an overview, see Grossman and Helpman (2001).
7. Wittman (1995, 1989).
8. See e.g. Caplan and Stringham (2005), Althaus (2003), Monroe (1998, 1983), Page and Shapiro (1992, 1983), Erikson, Wright, and McIver (1989), and Wright, Erikson, and McIver (1987).
9. For further discussion, see Wintrobe (1987).

REFERENCES

Althaus, Scott. 2003. *Collective Preferences in Democratic Politics: Opinion Surveys and the Will of the People.* Cambridge: Cambridge University Press.
Andrews, Robert, ed. 1993. *The Columbia Dictionary of Quotations.* New York Columbia University Press.
Blinder, Alan. 1987. *Hard Heads, Soft Hearts: Tough-Minded Economics for a Just Society.* Reading, MA: Addison-Wesley.
Caplan, Bryan, and Edward Stringham. 2005. "Mises, Bastiat, Public Opinion, and Public Choice: What's Wrong With Democracy." *Review of Political Economy* 17(1): 79–105.
Citrin, Jack, and Donald Green. 1990. "The Self-Interest Motive in American Public Opinion." *Research in Micropolitics* 3:1–28.
Erikson, Robert, Gerald Wright, and John McIver. 1989. "Political Parties, Public Opinion, and State Policy in the United States." *American Political Science Review* 83(3): 729–50.
Gelman, Andrew, Boris Shor, Joseph Bafumi, and David Park. 2005. "Rich State, Poor State, Red State, Blue State: What's the Matter with Connecticut?" www.stat.columbia.edu/~gelman/research/unpublished/redblue11.pdf.
Grossman, Gene, and Elhanan Helpman. 2001. *Special Interest Politics.* Cambridge: MIT Press.

Gruber, Jonathan. 2005. *Public Finance and Public Policy*. New York: Worth.

Hainmueller, Jens, and Michael Hiscox. 2005a. "Educated Preferences: Explaining Attitudes Toward Immigration in Europe." www.people.fas.harvard.edu/~hiscox/ EducatedPreferences.pdf.

Le Bon, Gustave. 1960. *The Crowd: A Study of the Popular Mind*. New York: Viking Press.

Luttbeg, Norman, and Michael Martinez. 1990. "Demographic Differences in Opinion." *Research in Micropolitics* 3:83–118.

Mansbridge, Jane, ed. 1990. *Beyond Self-Interest*. Chicago: University of Chicago Press.

Monroe, Alan. 1983. "American Party Platforms and Public Opinion." *American Journal of Political Science* 27(1): 27–42.

———. 1998. "Public Opinion and Public Policy, 1980–1993." *Public Opinion Quarterly* 62(1): 6–28.

Page, Benjamin, and Robert Shapiro. 1983. "Effects of Public Opinion on Policy." *American Political Science Review* 77(1): 175–90.

———. 1992. *The Rational Public: Fifty Years of Trends in Americans' Policy Preferences*. Chicago: University of Chicago Press.

Persson, Torsten, and Guido Tabellini. 2000. *Political Economics: Explaining Economic Policy*. Cambridge: MIT Press.

Ponza, Michael, Greg Duncan, Mary Corcoran, and Fred Groskind. 1988. "The Guns of Autumn? Age Differences in Support for Income Transfers to the Young and Old." *Public Opinion Quarterly.* 52(4): 441–66

Sears, David, and Carolyn Funk. 1990. "Self-Interest in Americans' Political Opinions." In Jane Mansbridge, ed., *Beyond Self-Interest*. Chicago: University of Chicago Press: 147–70.

Sears, David, Richard Lau, Tom Tyler, and Harris Allen. 1980. "Self-Interest vs. Symbolic Politics in Policy Attitudes and Presidential Voting." *American Political Science Review* 74(3): 670–84.

Shapiro, Robert, and Harpreet Mahajan. 1986. "Gender Differences in Policy Preferences: A Summary of Trends From the 1960s to the 1980s." *Public Opinion Quarterly* 50(1): 42–61.

Wintrobe, Ronald. 1987. "The Market for Corporate Control and the Market for Political Control." *Journal of Law, Economics, and Organization* 3(2): 435–48.

Wittman, Donald. 1995. *The Myth of Democratic Failure: Why Political Institutions Are Efficient*. Chicago: University of Chicago Press.

Wright, Gerald, Robert Erikson, and John McIver. 1987. "Public Opinion and Policy Liberalism in the American States." *American Journal of Political Science* 31(4): 980–1001.

10

PARTICIPATION

10.1

STEVEN ROSENSTONE AND JOHN MARK HANSEN

From *Mobilization, Participation, and Democracy in America*

People participate in politics for a variety of reasons. Rosenstone and Hansen emphasize several key factors in explaining why some types of people participate more than others. Simply put, those people who are easily mobilized and who tend to have similar preferences to the organizations that routinely mobilize are the ones most likely to participate. Rosenstone and Hansen's arguments put more emphasis on the attributes of mobilizing organizations than on the personal attributes of the people being mobilized.

Why do people get involved in politics? Why do some people participate in politics while others do not? Why are citizens deeply committed to participation in politics at some times and wholly passive at other times?

We offer two answers, one personal, one political. Working from one side, the personal, we trace participation to the individual characteristics of citizens. People participate in politics when they get valuable benefits that are worth the costs of taking part. Working from the other side, the political, we trace participation to the strategic choices of political leaders. People participate in politics when political leaders coax them into taking part in the game. Both sides are necessary: Strategic mobilization without individual motivation is impossible, and individual motivation without strategic mobilization is illogical.

The complex interaction of the personal and the political stems from the nature of democratic politics. We view democratic politics as a struggle for political power among competing political leaders. In such a system, citizen activism has *two* beneficiaries: It is a source of policy benefits for citizens and a source of political advantage for leaders. Accordingly, to understand political participation, we must appreciate how it is used, both by individual citizens and by their leaders.

In this [reading], we lay out the political logic of citizen activism in politics. First, working from the individual perspective, we lay out the benefits and costs of political participation and show how individual resources, interests, preferences, identifications, and beliefs determine the relative attractions of the benefits and the relative burdens of the costs. Next, we consider individuals in political society. We show how the social nature of political life affects the individual rewards of involvement. We show how the social nature of political life makes people accessible and amenable to the appeals of political leaders. And we show how the strategic choices of political leaders determine who participates and when.

Political participation, we conclude, cannot be explained entirely by the orientations and endowments of individual citizens. The competitive pressures of the democratic system encourage political leaders to mobilize their fellow citizens, and if we are to understand participation, we must also comprehend their choices.

INDIVIDUAL INFLUENCES ON POLITICAL PARTICIPATION

People participate in politics for a variety of personal reasons. Some people participate because it does not cost them much; some participate because they receive lots of benefits. As stated, this personal explanation of political activism is both obvious and tautological: It explains everything because it rules out nothing.

Even so, as political theorist Brian Barry noted, "it is still a quite potent tautology, because it can be combined with empirical assertions to produce significant implications." Our task in this section is to supply empirical linkages, to develop the implications of different resources for the relative costs of participation, and to develop the implications of different interests and attitudes for the relative benefits of participation.

Costs and Resources

Participation in politics puts demands on people's scarce resources. Working on a political campaign requires time; writing a letter requires verbal acuity; making a donation to a candidate requires money; signing a petition requires a sense of personal competence. Participation in politics, that is, has a price, a price that is some combination of money, time, skill, knowledge, and self-confidence.

Some people are better able to pay the price than others. In economic life people with greater resources can consume more of (almost) everything, from fancy meals to fast cars to flashy clothes. In social life people with greater resources can do more of (almost) everything, from entertaining friends to joining organizations to volunteering at schools, churches, and charities. So, too, in political life. People with abundant money, time, skill, knowledge, and self-confidence devote more resources to politics, not because politics gives them more in return (although it might) but because they can more easily afford it. Many of the most familiar empirical regularities in American politics follow from this simple observation.

First, the wealthy vote, write, campaign, and petition more than the poor. This should come as no surprise. Citizens with lots of income can simply afford to do more—of everything—than citizens with little money. The wealthy have discretionary income that they can contribute directly to political parties, candidates, political action committees, and other causes. Moreover, money is fungible—it can be freely converted into other political resources that make it easier for people to take part in politics. A car is not a necessary condition for political action, for example, but having one makes it much easier to get to a school board meeting, a political rally, or a candidate's campaign headquarters. Money can be used to hire someone to do the daily chores—to clean the house, buy the groceries, cook dinner, baby-sit the kids—and free up time for politics. Thus, if people want to participate in politics, money makes it easier for them to do so.

The costs of political activity can also be measured in opportunities forgone. Taking part in politics requires that people forfeit or postpone other activities, and these opportunity costs of participation are higher for some people than for others. Because the resources of the wealthy are more ample, they do not face the same hard tradeoffs that the poor face every day of their lives. As important and interesting as politics may be, its significance pales in comparison with paying the rent, maintaining the car, keeping the children in school, and putting food on the table. In short, for people whose resources are limited, politics is a luxury they often cannot afford, particularly when political outcomes may have only a modest impact on their own economic situations.

Second, the more educated are more likely to take part in politics than the less educated. Again, no surprise. In the United States, the educational experience fosters democratic values and nurtures a sense of citizen competence, both of which encourage participation. More important, however, education provides skills that facilitate participation in politics. As Wolfinger and Rosenstone argue, "education imparts information about politics and cognate fields and about a variety of skills, some of which facilitate political learning. . . . Schooling increases one's capacity for understanding and working with complex, abstract and intangible subjects, that is, subjects like politics. Skills in research, writing, and speaking, developed through education, help citizens to negotiate the maze of demands that participation places on them. To cast a ballot, citizens must figure out how to register to vote; they must make sense of the candidates and issues; they must locate polling places. To write a letter to a senator, citizens must compose a persuasive message once they have identified the senator and looked up her address. For the grade-school educated, these are daunting tasks; for the college educated, they are easy. The better educated have been better trained to participate in politics.

Finally, those with many years of formal schooling are substantially more likely to read newspapers, follow the news, and be politically informed, all of which makes them more aware of the opportunities to participate and more likely to possess information with which to do so.

This is not to say that politically useful knowledge and skills derive only from the classroom. Lessons picked up from the "school of hard knocks" can compensate for formal education, imparting equivalent knowledge, experience, and skills. With experience comes familiarity with the political process, familiarity with and increased attachment to the political parties and their candidates, and familiarity with the ins and outs of political action: what people need to do to take part and where people need to go to do it. Hence, older citizens vote, write, campaign, and petition more than young citizens who have had less experience in politics.

Finally, people with a sense of political efficacy are more likely to take a more active part in politics than those without this belief. By efficacy we mean both a sense of personal competence in one's ability to understand politics and to participate in politics (what political scientists call internal efficacy), as well as a sense that one's political activities can influence what the government actually does (external efficacy). Some people come to believe in their personal competence because they have been told again and again, by parents, teachers, and friends, that their efforts make a difference. Other people come to believe in their personal competence because they have acted and in fact found their actions consequential. As defined, it is already evident that efficacy is an important political resource. Working in a campaign or signing a petition involves some sense that the cause is not hopeless (even if the particular effort is). Participation is a waste of time if one does not believe that one's efforts make a material difference to political outcomes. Those who have confidence that their participation will make a difference are more likely to act than those who lack that basic confidence.

In summary, the costs of political activism affect different people in different ways, depending on their resources. For people with abundant money, time, knowledge, skills, and efficacy, involvement costs very little. Consequently, they participate more.

Rewards Interests, and Beliefs

People participate in politics because they get something out of it. The rewards take many forms. Participants sometimes enjoy *material benefits*, tangible rewards that are easily converted into money, like a government job or a tax break. Those active in politics can also receive *solidary benefits*, intangible rewards that stem from social interaction, like status, deference, and friendship. And participation can also yield *purposive benefits*, intrinsic rewards that derive from the act of participation itself, such as a sense of satisfaction from having contributed to a worthy cause.

This typology, suggested by James Q. Wilson, gives an idea of the great variety of possible benefits from participation, but for our purposes, the distinction between collective and selective rewards is more important. *Collective rewards*, on the one hand, benefit every resident of a particular place or every member of a particular group, whether she took part in politics or not. Most, but not all, are material. A clean air bill, for example, benefits every resident of Los Angeles, New York, or Denver. A residential parking ordinance benefits every resident of the neighborhoods surrounding a hospital. A mortgage interest deduction for homeowners benefits every homeowner, homebuilder, and realtor. An end to the ban on interstate sales of firearms benefits every gun owner and gun dealer. People receive collective rewards regardless of whether they participate. *Selective rewards*, on the other hand, benefit only those people who take part in politics. Some selective rewards are material: Government jobs in Brooklyn, for instance, may go exclusively to campaign workers. Others are solidary: Recognition as a leader falls only to neighborhood activists. Many are purposive: A sense of having done one's duty accrues only to those who have done their duty. Unlike collective rewards, people receive selective rewards because they participate; by the same token, people forgo selective rewards because they do not.

Each form of citizen participation in politics offers a unique mix of collective and selective benefits. Citizens find each combination of benefits more or less worthwhile depending on their interests, preferences, identifications, and beliefs. A man who works for the park district of the city of Chicago might view campaign work as a requirement of his job. A woman who lives on a farm in west Texas might see attendance at county commission meetings as a rare opportunity for visiting with friends and neighbors. A man who has been socialized with a deep sense of obligation to participate in the community might see voting as a way to live up to his duty. Depending on their needs, certain kinds of participation make more sense for certain people than other kinds of participation.

These observations help to structure our ideas about the role that interests, preferences, identifications, and beliefs play in promoting participation in politics.

First, people who have a direct stake in political outcomes are obviously more likely to participate in politics than people who do not have such an immediate stake. Parents who have children in public schools, for instance, are much more likely to attend school board meetings than other people, simply because the school board makes decisions that affect the welfare of their children directly, broadly, and consequentially. Although everybody in the community has an interest in the financial decisions that school boards make, only parents typically care very much about such matters as curricular requirements, athletics and activities, bus routes, crossing guards, and dress codes. People with direct interests anticipate greater material rewards, both collective and selective, from their actions.

Second, people who strongly prefer one political outcome to another are more likely to enter politics than people who have weaker preferences. Voters consistently complain that American elections offer no choices, only echoes. Their complaint, however, is not always on the mark. Some people see differences where others see none. For many Americans in 1948, Harry Truman and Thomas Dewey were Tweedledum and Tweedledee: Both supported the New Deal welfare state and both were anticommunist cold warriors. But for members of industrial labor unions the differences between them were clear: Truman was the defender of the National Labor Relations Act against the antiunion Republicans in Congress. Likewise, the system sometimes offers a real choice. Although voters might be forgiven for confusing Gerald Ford and Jimmy Carter in 1976, few could fail to discern the differences between Lyndon Johnson and Barry Goldwater in 1964 or Ronald Reagan and Walter Mondale in 1984.

The variations in preferences are important. Those who strongly prefer one candidate or one party or one policy to another anticipate greater policy benefits from the outcome than those whose preferences are weaker. Accordingly, they are more likely to get involved in politics.

Third, people who identify closely with political contenders are more likely to participate in politics than people whose psychological identifications are weaker. This may sound, on its face, like a restatement of the preceding point, but it is not. Before, we argued that strong preferences heighten the value of extrinsic rewards of participation, of material and solidary benefits that arise as a consequence of political action. Here, we argue that strong psychological attachments heighten the value of intrinsic rewards from participation, of the internal satisfactions that derive from taking part. Just as sports fans take pleasure in cheering on their favorite teams, so partisans take pleasure in acting on behalf of their favorite politicians, parties, or groups. The more committed the fans, the more lusty their cheers; the more committed the partisans, the more likely their participation.

Because of their psychological attachments, then, issue activists are more likely to write letters to their representatives in Congress. Because of their psychological attachments, likewise, strong Democrats and strong Republicans are more likely to be active in elections than independents or weak partisans. Political participation appeals more to the strongly than the weakly committed because the strongly committed derive greater personal satisfaction from it.

Finally, some people hold beliefs and preferences that motivate their participation internally. The most common is a sense of citizen duty. Because of their socialization by family, teachers, or friends, some people believe it is their responsibility to participate in politics—and in particular to vote—regardless of whether their participation has any effect on the outcome. Obviously, people who hold these beliefs are more likely to participate: Taking part makes them feel that they have discharged their obligations. The purposive rewards of participation are selective.

Thus, the benefits of political participation appeal to different people in different ways, depending on their interests, preferences, identifications, and beliefs. People who perceive more at stake in politics—because policies affect them more, identities beckon them more, options appeal to them more, or duty calls them more—participate more in politics.

People get involved in politics, then, in predictable ways: Because of their resources, some people can better afford politics than others; because of their interests, preferences, identifications, and beliefs, some people get more benefit from politics than others. Clearly, the two work together. No matter how valuable the benefits of participation, people cannot take part unless they have sufficient resources to do so. No matter how ample the resources, people will not take part unless they get more out of politics than other pursuits. Taken together, these considerations help to explain why some people take part in politics and others do not.

POLITICAL INFLUENCES ON PARTICIPATION: STRATEGIC MOBILIZATION

When applied to the question of *which* people participate in politics, the individual explanations of political activism that we have just discussed seem to satisfy. But when applied to the question of *when* people participate in politics, their inadequacies begin to show.

Suppose, for instance, that people participate in politics because of the solidary or the purposive benefits they receive—the approbations of their friends or the satisfactions from a duty performed. It stands to reason, then, that participation should not fluctuate very much from month to month or from year to year because fundamental social identifications and political beliefs change only slowly, if at all. The same people should turn out for politics time and time again.

Yet this prediction is wrong. . . . Both the level of political participation and the people who participate change significantly from month to month, year to year, and election to election. That being the case, we need to turn to the *political* circumstances that change over time and induce people to take part at one moment and not another: the personal qualities and policy stands of the candidates for office; the issues that appear and disappear on the political agenda; the actions of the politicians, parties, and interest groups that compete for political advantage. These considerations, in turn, lead to an explanation of political participation that emphasizes the collective benefits that people receive from political outcomes, such as military spending, abortion rights, tax breaks, and other public policies. But this line of thinking immediately runs up against two deadly logical conundrums.

Two Paradoxes: Participation and Rational Ignorance

The first difficulty is the famous "paradox of voting," or, more broadly, the "paradox of participation in politics.[1] If people are rational, the paradox holds, and if they receive only collective benefits, they will not turn out to vote, and for very good reason: The result of the election will be the same whether they participate or not. In any election, hundreds or thousands or millions of voters will cast ballots; the chance that a single ballot will determine the result is exceedingly small. In 1960, for example, the closest presidential election in the twentieth century, John F. Kennedy's victory over Richard M. Nixon hinged on 115,000 votes, only 0.2 percent of the total, but still a very large number. At the same time, casting a vote is costly. At a minimum, voters must spend time, energy, and money rousting themselves to polling places and marking their ballots. Thus, even if the outcome of the election really matters to people, trying to affect it does not make any sense. Rational people choose the most efficient means to achieve their goals; they do not knowingly waste their scarce resources. Voting, it follows, is irrational: It consumes resources but achieves no results that would not be achieved otherwise.

The same paradox holds with equal force for other forms of political activity. Objectively, the probability that any one person's one lonely act will determine a political outcome is vanishingly small. One more letter mailed to Congress, one more person attending a meeting, one more dollar sent to a campaign, one more person persuaded to vote will not make a bit of difference to the result, but it will cost the participant. If people receive only collective benefits from political outcomes, therefore, they will not participate in politics. Political action, if it occurs, is irrational.[2]

The second difficulty is "rational ignorance."[3] If political involvement is irrational, so, for much the same reason, is political learning. First, information about politics and government must be gathered, and its cost is far above zero. Washington is a distant place, government is a complicated business, and the press can be relied on to cover only a fraction of what the government is up to. Likewise, candidates for office are unfamiliar people, their records are voluminous, and the media are quite selective in their coverage of the campaigns. Second, the value of information, once obtained, is very small, precisely because of the paradox of participation in politics. Even if voters had lots of information about the issues debated in Washington and the issues contested in campaigns, what good would it do them? It makes no sense for them to act on it anyway: The outcome will be the same regardless. Thus, citizens have few incentives to inform themselves about politics. They stay "rationally ignorant."

Thus, the question of when people involve themselves in politics cannot be addressed solely within the context of individual motives and behaviors. One approach fails to provide an answer, and the other gets tangled in its own logic. Instead, the explanation of participation, to make any sense, must move beyond the worlds of individuals to include family, friends, neighbors, and co-workers, plus politicians, parties, activists, and interest groups.

The Social Nature of Political Life

With few exceptions, people are deeply embedded in a web of social relationships with family, friends, neighbors, and co-workers. Within these circles, people convey expectations to others about the kinds of behaviors, some political, that are appropriate and desirable. Sometimes they relate their expectations overtly: They ask acquaintances directly to do something. More often they relate their expectations subtly: They simply raise their concerns. What's more, people in these networks reward those who comply with expectations, and they sanction those who do not. They praise, esteem, and owe favors to those who do act, and reprove, shun, and take note of those who do not. Social networks, in short, create solidary rewards and bestow them, selectively, on those who act in the common interest.

For most people, the obligations and rewards of friendship, camaraderie, neighborliness, and family ties are very powerful. People want to be accepted, valued, and liked. As a consequence, social networks play a key role in overcoming the paradoxes of participation and rational ignorance.

Social networks address rational ignorance. They provide information. Participants in family, work, and friendship groups communicate, and in doing so they learn about politics from others in the group. They likewise reward contributions of information. Family, work, and friendship groups favor those who offer their knowledge to the collegium. Thus, because of social networks, each person bears the cost of collecting only a fraction of the political information she receives.

Too, social networks address the paradox of participation. People take part in family, work, and friendship groups on a regular and sustained basis. Consequently, members of social networks can identify readily those who comply with social expectations and those who do not, that is, those who vote and write and attend and otherwise participate in politics and those who do not. In turn, because members of social networks can distinguish participants from pikers, they can also selectively reward the one and sanction the other. Finally, because they can reward and sanction discerningly, they can also create and enforce expectations that many will act in concert. Although one letter to Congress is not likely to have any impact, one thousand letters is, and although one vote for governor is not likely to make a difference, one hundred thousand votes is. Social networks, the everyday groupings of friends, family, and associates, make effective, coordinated, political action possible.

They do not, however, make effective, coordinated, political action probable. Most citizens are not in positions to know what is occurring in politics, nor do they know anybody who is. Neither they nor their families, friends, and co-workers really know whether their interests are enough at stake at the moment to warrant political action—of whatever kind—being undertaken to advance or defend them.

Others in the system have such knowledge close at hand. Because they are in the thick of political battles, political leaders, be they candidates, party officials, interest groups, or activists, know exactly what is on the political agenda and exactly how it affects people. And because they are in the thick of political battles, they have a tangible incentive to convey such information to the people who can help them to win.

For politicians, political parties, interest groups, and activists, citizen involvement is an important political resource. In a democracy, the people's wants are supposed to matter. In elections, for example, candidates for office and their organized supporters need citizens' votes, money, and time. In national government, likewise, elected officials, interest groups, and activists want votes in Congress, favors from the White House, and rulings from the bureaucracy, and they can use citizens' letters, petitions, and protests to help get them. In local government, finally, neighborhoods want stop signs from city councils and parents want computer labs from school boards, and they can use citizens' contacts, presence, and pressures to try to get them. Citizen participation is a resource that political leaders use in their struggles for political advantage. We call their efforts to deploy it "mobilization."

Political Mobilization

Mobilization is the process by which candidates, parties, activists, and groups induce other people to participate. We say that one of these actors has *mobilized* somebody when it has done something to increase the likelihood of her participation.

We distinguish two types of mobilization. Leaders mobilize people *directly* when they contact citizens personally and encourage them to take action. Door-to-door canvasses by campaign organizations, direct mail solicitations by political agitators, televised appeals for aid by presidents, and grass-roots letter drives by interest groups are examples of direct mobilization. Leaders mobilize people *indirectly* when they contact citizens through mutual associates, whether family, friends, neighbors, or colleagues. When candidates solicit employers for campaign money and bosses in turn encourage their employees to give, when local activists push their friends to attend meetings and friends ask family to accompany them, when parties contact workers in a plant and the workers ask their co-workers to vote, that is indirect mobilization.

Direct mobilization

Through direct mobilization, political leaders provide opportunities for political action that citizens would not have otherwise. They build the organizations that give people the chance to contribute their time and money to political causes. They sponsor the meetings and rallies that give people the opportunity to attend. They circulate petitions that give people the chance to sign. They request contributions to causes that people may never have heard of until the moment of contact. The mobilization efforts of political leaders create the very opportunities for citizens to participate.

Through direct mobilization, likewise, political leaders subsidize political information. Because information is costly and because politics is far from the most pressing concern in most people's lives, few citizens know much about politics unless somebody tells them. People remain rationally ignorant. Through the mobilization efforts of political leaders, however, they are informed about the issues on the congressional agenda, alerted to the meetings of the school board, and reminded about the upcoming city council elections. In short, they are given information about the issues at stake and the opportunities to affect them. The mobilization efforts of political leaders help citizens to overcome their rational ignorance.

Through direct mobilization, finally, political leaders subsidize the costs of citizen activism. They distribute voter registration forms and absentee ballots. They drive people to the polls on election day. They provide child care to free parents to attend meetings and demonstrations. They supply people with the texts for letters to representatives and senators. By underwriting the costs of political participation, the mobilization efforts of political leaders help to overcome the paradox of participation.

Indirect mobilization

The impact of political mobilization, though, extends far beyond the effect it has on the limited number of people who are contacted directly. Membership in social networks makes people available to politicians, organizations, and activists. Membership in social networks makes people responsive to mobilization. Social networks, that is, convert direct mobilization into indirect mobilization. Political leaders mobilize citizens for political action through social networks.

For politicians, parties, interest groups, and activists, access to social networks reduces the costs of making contact. Leaders need not communicate with every person directly. Instead, leaders contact their associates, associates contact their colleagues and colleagues contact their friends, families, and co-workers. Through social networks, leaders get the word out, and citizens get the word. Social networks multiply the effect of mobilization: Direct mobilization reverberates through indirect mobilization.

Even more important, for politicians, parties, interest groups, and activists, access to social networks makes it possible to mobilize people to participate. Absent the involvement of social networks, leaders usually have only collective rewards to offer to potential participants: They hold out the prospect that favored candidates will win or that the government will formulate beneficial policies. Because rewards are collective, however, citizens receive them whether they act or not. Mobilization runs aground on the paradox of participation.

With the involvement of social networks, however, mobilization occasions the creation of selective rewards. When friends, neighbors, and co-workers present the opportunities to participate, they also convey social expectations about desirable courses of action. Citizens who comply and participate reap the rewards of social life. They enjoy the attentions and esteem of their friends and associates; they enjoy the instrinsic satisfactions of having helped their colleagues' cause. Citizens who fail to comply and refuse to participate receive no rewards; in fact, they may suffer social sanctions.

Indirect mobilization promotes participation, then, by allowing political leaders to exploit citizens' ongoing obligations to friends, neighbors, and social groups. Citizens feel an obligation to help people they like, people they identify with, people who are like them, and people who have helped them in the past—an obligation, that is, to help their friends, family, and daily associates. Likewise, citizens are more likely to contribute when they know that the people who expect them to help can tell whether or not they have done so. Political organizers have long thought personal, face-to-face contacts to be much more effective than impersonal mobilization through the mail or the media, and this is why.

Contact through social networks adds the power of social expectations to the message of mobilization.

Thus, by working through social networks, political leaders need not provide selective incentives themselves, need not coax, cajole, and persuade people to take part. Social networks do it for them. Family, friends, neighbors, and co-workers echo leaders' calls to action, and participants respond to please their neighbors and co-workers and to honor their obligations to friends. Working through social networks, politicians, parties, interest groups, and activists piggyback political action onto the everyday hum of social relationships.

The Strategy of Political Mobilization

Of course, mobilization is not a universal or a constant occurrence. Political leaders do not try to mobilize everybody, and they do not try to mobilize all of the time. Mobilization, after all, is not their real goal; they have little interest in citizen activism per se. Rather, they seek to use public involvement to achieve other ends: to win elections, to pass bills, to modify rulings, to influence policies. Mobilization is one strategy they may use, but it is neither the only one nor, always, the best one. Alternatively, politicians, parties, interest groups, and activists might (among other things) incite other politicians, ally with other interest groups, compile facts and figures, muster experts, or even (we hope rarely) pay bribes. Because each strategy is costly, and because resources are scarce, political leaders simply cannot use every tool in their toolkit on every job.

Consequently, citizen participation is a resource that political leaders use selectively in their fights for political advantage. For maximum effect, they *target* their efforts on particular people, and they *time* them for particular occasions.

Targeting mobilization

Once political leaders decide to pursue a mobilization strategy, they want to get the most effective number of people involved with the least amount of effort. This simple—indeed obvious—criterion suggests four kinds of citizens whom leaders are most eager to contact.

First, politicians, parties, and other activists are most likely to mobilize the people they already know. For one thing, they are close at hand, easy to contact, and responsive to requests—because they are friends or associates. For another thing, they are familiar. Political leaders, naturally, want their allies to participate, not their enemies. Democrats want Democrats to vote, not Republicans, and abortion rights advocates want pro-choice voters to write letters, not pro-life voters. When leaders mobilize people they know, they have a good idea of how they are going to act.

Second, politicians, groups, and other activists are more likely to mobilize people who are centrally positioned in social networks. They are easier to identify, simply because they are more visible and because they know more people. More important, because they are in the middle of things they are in a good position to mobilize others. They turn direct mobilization into indirect mobilization.

Third, politicians, parties, groups, and agitators are more likely to mobilize the people whose actions are most effective at producing political outcomes. Like it or not, some citizens are more influential in politics than others, and legislators, executives, or bureaucrats like, fear, respect, or depend on them more. Because political leaders are interested in outcomes, they concentrate their mobilization efforts on the powerful.

Finally, politicians and activists are more likely to mobilize people who are likely to respond by participating. As we already argued earlier in this chapter, some people, because of their resources, interests, preferences, or beliefs, are more likely to participate in politics than other people. Because political leaders cannot afford to mobilize everyone, they concentrate their efforts on people they have the greatest chance of mobilizing.

A number of simple predictions follow from these observations.

First, people who are employed, especially in large workplaces, are more likely to be mobilized than people who are not; they are more likely, consequently, to participate. Their jobs make them visible. Political leaders know where to find them—at work—and know what they care about—their jobs. Their jobs make them powerful. Workplaces represent concentrations of numbers, wealth, and power, the currencies to which politicians respond. Finally, their jobs incline them toward participation. They have powerful incentives to act in defense of their livelihoods, and they have powerful incentives to live up to the expectations of their employers and co-workers.

Second, people who belong to associations are more likely to be mobilized and more likely to participate than people who do not belong. Group members are more visible. Labor unions, service clubs, and churches meet daily, weekly, or monthly, and their purposes often reveal their politics. Group members are more influential. In politics, organizations have the power of numbers, attentiveness, and singular purpose. Finally, through their organizations, group members get greater encouragement to participate. They voluntarily associate with people who share their identities and their interests; accordingly, they find it difficult to resist the entreaties of other members. Indeed, their very involvement in organizations signals their susceptibility to social expectations.

Third, leaders of organizations, businesses, and local governments are more likely to be mobilized: They are better known to political leaders, more likely to be effective, and more likely to participate, for the reasons we have already discussed. In addition, their positions atop organizations and institutions give them the ability to reach other people. Business owners have access to employees, union stewards to rank-and-file, club presidents to members, and church deacons to the faithful. They occupy the center of social networks. They turn direct mobilization into indirect mobilization.

Finally, the wealthy, the educated, and the partisan are more likely to be targeted for mobilization than the poor, the uneducated, and the uncommitted, which is part of the reason for their greater potential for political action. The advantaged are better known to political leaders because they travel in the same social circles. Politicians and activists are usually wealthier, better educated, and more partisan than ordinary citizens, and so are their friends and associates. Likewise, their actions are more likely to produce favorable political outcomes. Because of their social positions, they often know legislators, executives, and bureaucrats personally. Moreover, because of their status and wealth, they stand as benefactors of many politicians and government officials: campaign contributors, information sources, former and future employers. Consequently, political elites know them, like them, respect them, and depend on them. They, in short, have power. Finally, they are more likely to respond to political leaders' requests. They have more resources. They have the money, the leisure, and the skills to meet the demands that participation places on them. Likewise, they receive more rewards. Because of their social status they have a greater stake in political decisions, and because of their socialization they have a bigger psychological investment in political affairs. Perhaps most important, they are part of social networks that esteem, expect, and reward activism in politics; hence, they receive greater selective and solidary rewards from their activism. The greater propensity of the advantaged toward participation, that is, stems not only from their individual characteristics but also from their placement in the political system.

Thus, the strategic calculations of political leaders determine a lot about who participates. Intent on creating the greatest effect with the least effort, politicians, parties, interest groups, and activists mobilize people who are known to them, who are well placed in social networks, whose actions are effective, and who are likely to act. Their efforts to move the organized, the employed, the elite, and the advantaged into politics exacerbate rather than reduce the class biases in political participation in America.

Timing mobilization

Political leaders likewise identify favorable times to move citizens into politics. Sometimes mobilization of public participation is a worthwhile enterprise—it is likely to accomplish its purpose—and sometimes it is not.

Clearly, for mobilization of citizen activism to be an effective strategy, two conditions must obtain. First, people must be ready to follow their leaders into politics. If people are not interested in the issues or are distracted by other concerns, mobilization is wasted effort. Second, citizen participation must have a consequential effect on political outcomes. If important decisions are not on the docket, if political outcomes are foregone conclusions, or if public officials are unmoved by citizens' pleas, mobilization is wasted effort. Unless citizens are likely to act and action is likely to yield outcomes, leaders' resources are better spent on strategies other than mobilization.

These observations provide some perspective on when people are likely to be mobilized, and when in turn people are likely to participate in politics.

First, people participate in politics more when salient issues top the agenda. Leaders can only lead, after all, when the public is willing to follow. Big pocketbook issues, such as pensions and jobs, and big moral issues, such as prohibition and abortion, draw greater public attention than more arcane issues, such as deregulation of natural gas pipelines and accounting rules for capital depreciation. Salient issues affect more people more directly. Knowing that, political leaders adopt mobilization strategies when the issues excite people and adopt other strategies when they bore people. Because of their strategic calculations, citizens receive more pressure to participate when the issues are salient than when they are not.

Second, people participate more in politics when other concerns do not demand their attentions. As important as politics is, for most people other things come first: making a living, spending time with the family, and so forth. Leaders understand this, and they hesitate to mobilize citizen activism when more pressing needs dominate. On campus, for instance, college politicos rarely schedule political events during midterms and finals. In real politics, likewise, activists curb their efforts during holidays, when people want only to spend time with family, and during hard spells, when people want only to get back to work or to pay their bills. Because political leaders accommodate the more pressing concerns of the public, people feel less encouragement and pressure to participate when more important events distract them.

Third, people participate more in politics when important decisions are pending. Politics moves to its own distinctive rhythms. Elections, for example, are cyclic: Presidential elections occur every four years, House elections every two years, Senate elections every six years, and state and local elections idiosyncratically, some in presidential years, some in midterm years, and some in off years. Legislation, on the other hand, is seasonal: The U.S. Congress and the larger state legislatures formulate proposals in committees in the spring and summer, debate policies on the floor in the summer and fall, and recess in the winter. Cyclic or seasonal, calendars regulate the activities of political leaders. For maximum effect, these leaders mobilize citizens at the moment when conflicts near resolution. Because leaders are more likely to contact them when decisions are imminent, citizens respond to the rhythms of the calendar as well.

Fourth, people participate more in politics when outcomes hang in the balance. Some elections are so close that a few votes can make a difference, whereas others are so lopsided that hundreds of thousands could not affect them. Similarly, some legislative battles are so evenly matched that a burst of public involvement could clinch them, whereas others are so settled that nothing could perturb them. Given scarce resources, political leaders focus their efforts on the tight contests and forget about the cakewalks. Because leaders are more likely to contact them when decisions come down to the wire, citizens respond to political competition.

Finally, people are more likely to be mobilized to participate in politics when issues come before legislatures than when they come before bureaucracies and courts. The institutions of American government expose legislators to popular pressures, but they insulate bureaucrats and judges. Representatives, senators, county commissioners, and members of city councils submit regularly to the discipline of the voters, but bureaucrats and judges do not. Accordingly, public participation potentially has more impact when elected officials make decisions than when civil servants and judges do. Accordingly, politicians and activists pursue mobilization strategies when issues are before legislatures, but they favor other strategies when decisions are before agencies and courts. Because leaders are more likely to contact them when the outcomes they seek are laws, people participate more in legislative politics than in bureaucratic and judicial battles.

Thus, the strategic choices of political leaders determine a lot about when people are mobilized, and hence about when they participate. Eager to time their efforts so that they will have the greatest effect, candidates, parties, interest groups, and activists mobilize people when their efforts are most likely to be effective: when issues are salient, when distractions are few, when resolutions are imminent, when decisions are closely contested, and when decision makers depend on the evaluations of the public.

CONCLUSION

Political participation arises from the interaction of citizens and political mobilizers. Few people participate spontaneously in politics. Participation, instead, results when groups, political parties, and activists persuade citizens to take part. Personal characteristics—resources, perceived rewards, interests, and benefits from taking part in politics—define every person's predisposition toward political activity. The strategic choices of political leaders—their determinations of who and when to mobilize—determine the shape of political participation in America.

In mobilizing citizens for political action, political leaders intend only their own advantage. Seeking only to win elections, pass bills, amend rulings, or influence policies, they target their appeals selectively and time them strategically. Nevertheless, in doing so, they extend public involvement in political decision making. They bring people into politics at crucial times in the process. Their strategic choices impart a distinctive *political* logic to political participation.

Through mobilization of both kinds—direct contact, and indirect contact through social networks—political leaders supply information about politics that many citizens otherwise would not have. Politics is remote from the experience of most people. Absent mobilization, rational ignorance would defeat much citizen involvement in politics. Through mobilization of both kinds, moreover, political leaders create selective, solidary inducements to participate that many citizens otherwise would not have. Politics is not a priority for most people; absent mobilization, the paradox of participation would defeat much citizen involvement in politics.

People participate in politics for a host of reasons, but mobilization makes citizen participation both more common and more consequential. As Rosenau summarized,

> Most citizens . . . are not autonomous actors who calculate what ought to be done in public affairs, devise a strategy for achieving it, establish their own resources, and then pursue the course of action most likely to achieve their goals. Their instrumental behavior is often suggested, if not solicited, by others, either directly in face-to-face interactions or indirectly through the mass media; either explicitly through calls for support by mobilizers or implicitly through the statements of leaders, journalists and acquaintances that situations might be altered (or preserved) if

support were available. Thus, to conceive of the practices of citizenship as being largely sustained by independent action toward the political arena initiated by individuals is to minimize the relational context in which people participate in public affairs.[4]

NOTES

1. Downs, *An Economic Theory of Democracy*, chap. 14; Olson, *The Logic of Collective Action*, chap. 1; Barry *Sociologists, Economists and Democracy*, chap. 2.

2. On this more general point, see Olson, *The Logic of Collective Action*, chap. 1. See also Barry, *Sociologists, Economists and Democracy*, chap. 2.

3. Downs, *An Economic Theory of Democracy*, chaps. 12–13.

4. Rosenau, *Citizenship Between Elections*, p. 96.

REFERENCES

Barry, Brian. *Sociologists, Economists and Democracy*. London: Collier-Macmillan, 1970.

Downs, Anthony. *An Economic Theory of Democracy*. New York: Harper & Row, 1957.

Olson, Mancur, Jr. *The Logic of Collective Action*. Cambridge: Harvard University Press, 1965.

Rosenau, James N. *Citizenship Between Elections: An Inquiry into the Mobilizable American*. New York: Free Press, 1974.

10.2

NANCY BURNS, KAY SCHLOZMAN, AND SIDNEY VERBA

From *The Private Roots of Public Action*

Burns, Schlozman, and Verba offer the most comprehensive findings so far on comparing men and women in their political participation and engagement. Surveys indicate that men tend to pay more attention to politics and to be more interested in certain political issues, like international affairs, than women. Women, however, bring deeper religious sensibilities and greater concern for children and the poor to politics.

THE POLITICAL WORLDS OF MEN AND WOMEN

Political activity is embedded in a larger set of orientations to the political world. Behind what individuals do in politics is how they think and feel about it: whether they know or care about politics, feel capable of having an impact, have a taste for political participation and the gratifications it can provide, or harbor policy preferences they wish to communicate to public officials. . . . [W]e investigate gender differences with respect to a diverse set of predispositions that shape the motivation and propensity to take part. We first consider gender differences in the set of orientations toward political life that foster activity, including political interest, efficacy, and knowledge, as well as other indicators of affect toward politics. Second, we consider gender differences in what is sought from political action: the gratifications attendant to participation and the policy issues behind it.

Psychological Involvement with Politics

Participation is closely linked to a variety of psychological orientations that would make someone *want* to take part in political life. [W]e observed a noticeable but moderate participation gap between women and men. In this one, we see a wider gap in psychological involvement with politics. Data from the Citizen Participation Study confirm the findings of various studies to the effect that, compared with men, women are less interested in and less knowledgeable about politics and less likely to feel politically efficacious. Not only have differences in political involvement persisted over time, but similar relationships— of varying degrees of strength—have been observed in a number of democratic countries, especially countries in which Catholicism is the dominant religion. Table 1 presents data about gender differences in a number of aspects of

TABLE 1 Measures of Psychological Involvement with Politics

	Women		Men
POLITICAL INTEREST			
Very interested in politics (screener)	24%	⇔	29%
Very interested in national politics	29%	⇔	38%
Very interested in local politics	21%		22%
POLITICAL INFORMATION			
Mean number of correct answers (out of 10)	4.5	⇔	5.2
Correct answers to individual items			
Name of one U.S. senator	51%	⇔	67%
Name of second U.S. senator	30%	⇔	43%
Name of representative in Congress	32%	⇔	42%
Name of state representative	29%	⇔	34%
Name of head of the local public school system	40%	⇔	34%
Government spends more on NASA or Social Security	18%	⇔	40%
Meaning of Fifth Amendment	39%	⇔	52%
Origin of primaries—bosses or reformers	44%	⇔	49%
Meaning of civil liberties	77%	⇔	84%
Difference between democracy and dictatorship	85%	⇔	91%
Respondent above average in political information[a]	32%	⇔	42%
POLITICAL DISCUSSION			
Discuss national politics nearly every day	20%	⇔	31%
Discuss local politics nearly every day	16%	⇔	22%
Enjoy political discussion	26%	⇔	36%
SENSITIVITY TO POLITICAL CUES			
Say AARP takes stands in politics (AARP members)	79%		80%
Say clergy sometimes or frequently discuss political issues from pulpit (attenders)[b]	22%	⇔	28%
EXPOSURE TO THE MEDIA			
Watch news on television daily	57%		56%
Watch public affairs programs on television weekly	38%	⇔	45%
Read newspaper daily	55%	⇔	59%
Pay a great deal of attention to national politics	24%	⇔	40%
Pay a great deal of attention to local politics	36%		36%
POLITICAL EFFICACY			
Mean for efficacy scale	5.08	⇔	5.45
Government would pay some or a lot of attention			
National	40%		41%
Local	60%		64%

TABLE 1 (*continued*)

	Women		Men
Feeling of being able to influence some or a lot of governmental decisions (political voice)			
National	19%		17%
Local	46%	⇔	53%

SOURCES: Citizen Participation Study—Main Survey and Screener Survey.
a. Rating by interviewer.
b. Among those who attend religious services two or three times a month or more.
⇔ Difference between women and men is statistically significant at the .05 level.

psychological involvement with politics. A majority of these measures show statistically significant gender differences; in all but one of these cases women are less politically involved than men.

First, with respect to *political interest,* the data show men to have been somewhat more likely than women to report being very interested in national politics or, in the larger Screener sample, in politics in general. In a pattern that is repeated elsewhere in the table, there is no gender difference with respect to being very interested in local politics.

Political information differs from other aspects of political involvement in being an objective rather than a subjective measure. Thus the gender disparity in political knowledge cannot be the result of a masculine willingness to claim credit—although it might reflect differential willingness to guess and, therefore, to inflate scores. We measure political information with a ten-item scale, five asking the names of public officials and five testing knowledge of government and politics. As shown in Table 1, for nine of the ten items, men are more likely to provide a correct answer. Compared with women, men answered, on average, almost one additional item correctly across the whole test—an information gain roughly equivalent to that acquired from an additional 2¾ years of schooling.

Women are more likely than men to know the name of the head of the local school system. This single reversal is consistent with both what is known about political knowledge and what is known about women's experiences in politics. The ability to acquire political information is often domain specific and selective, based on preexisting information and the ease of incorporating new information. According to Shanto Iyengar, "people acquire information in domains about which they are already relatively informed." School politics is the political realm that has traditionally been defined as an appropriate one for women and that has been most welcoming to them. Before the enfranchisement of women in 1920, a number of states and even more locales extended a partial suffrage to women for participation in local elections, especially school elections. Moreover, school boards have traditionally been, and continue to be, the elected councils on which women have achieved their greatest representation. Furthermore, women legislators have traditionally been overrepresented on education committees. It is fully consistent with these patterns that women would be more likely than men to know the name of the head of the school system.

Although taking part in *political discussion* constitutes an action rather than a psychological state, it seems reasonable to examine it in this context as an indicator of psychological involvement with politics. Men are more likely than women to report that they discuss local and, especially, national politics every day or nearly every day. What is perhaps even more germane to our concerns, they were more likely to indicate enjoying, rather than avoiding, political discussion.

The data show relatively little disparity when it comes to whether, among individuals similarly situated, there is a gender difference in *sensitivity to political cues,* that is, in the likelihood of perceiving the political content of messages in the environment. AARP members, whether male or female, are equally likely to know that the organization takes stands in politics. Some evidence in the opposite direction might be the fact that among regular church attenders, women are less likely to report that clergy in their church sometimes or frequently discuss political issues from the pulpit.

In terms of *exposure to the media,* the data replicate patterns we have already seen. There is no gender gap in terms of either watching news on television or paying attention to newspaper stories about local politics and community affairs. However, men are somewhat more likely to report watching public affairs programs on television, reading a newspaper daily, or, especially, paying attention to stories about national and world politics in the newspaper.

Gender differences in *political efficacy* are well known. Our data, which focus on the respondent's perception of being able to have an impact on politics, or what is sometimes called "external efficacy," show a relatively small gender disparity, with men having higher average efficacy scores. However, when the four items in the scale are considered separately, the differences are not especially consistent and, in contrast to what we have seen for other measures, are more pronounced for local rather than for national politics.

We can highlight these findings about political orientations by focusing briefly on religion, a domain that we use throughout this reading as a counterpoint to the arena of politics. Data about gender differences in religious attitudes and orientations contrast strikingly with the data just reviewed about gender differences in political orientations. As we have mentioned, Americans are more deeply committed religiously than are people in the democracies of Europe; in turn, American women are more deeply committed religiously than are American men. For a series of measures of religious attitudes and orientations, Table 2 presents findings that are consistent with the higher level of religious practice—attendance at religious services and activity in religious institutions.

TABLE 2 Religious Attitudes and Orientations

	Women		Men
Express a Religious Preference	96%	⇔	90%
Religious Attitudes (among those expressing a preference)			
Say religion is very important	67	⇔	49
Think Bible is God's word	56	⇔	42
Have had a "born again" experience (among Protestants and Catholics)	39	⇔	32
Support Prayer in Schools	60	⇔	50
Reasons for Church Activity (among those active)			
Civic reasons			
Make the nation better	67		68
Influence government	6		5
Charitable reasons			
Lend a hand to people in need	77		73
Religious reasons			
To affirm religious faith	80	⇔	69
Further goals of religion	56	⇔	50

SOURCE: Citizen Participation Study—Main Survey.
⇔ Difference between women and men is statistically significant at the .05 level.

On each of several measures, women express greater depth of religious belief and concern about religious matters: they are more likely to report that religion is very important in their life, that the Bible is God's word, and, if Christian, that they have had a "born again" experience. In addition, they are more likely to support school prayer.

We also find an interesting pattern in the responses to a battery of questions posed to church activists about their reasons for being active in their churches. There was no significant difference between women and men with respect to civic reasons, such as making the nation a better place to live, or charitable reasons, such as lending a hand to those in need. However, women were more likely than men to mention religious reasons, affirming their faith or furthering the goals of their religion. The data reinforce our understanding that men and women direct their concerns in somewhat different directions.

Gender Consciousness and Experience of Gender Bias

With respect to politics, we have focused on general orientations—knowing and caring about politics, thinking that one could make a difference politically—that serve as a background to political participation. There is another set of political orientations, however, that deserves consideration. As members of a group that is disadvantaged in various ways, women may experience discrimination on the basis of sex. In addition, they may develop a sense of group consciousness. Either of these might be associated with political activity. These are not the easiest matters to probe in the context of a mass survey. Nevertheless, in the Citizen Participation Study we used a standard survey item in order to ask women and men whether they had ever experienced discrimination in jobs, school admissions, housing, or in other important things on the basis of their sex or gender. Because one individual might deem discriminatory an experience that another shrugs off, we consider this measure to be neither entirely objective nor entirely subjective. In addition, to measure gender consciousness for women, we asked them whether they felt closer to women than to men; whether they thought that there are problems of special concern to women that they need to work together to solve; and, if so, whether they thought that the government should be doing more about these problems. Analogous questions were posed to all respondents about discrimination on the basis of race or ethnicity. In addition, African-Americans and Latinos were asked questions about feeling close to other group members, thinking that they had joint problems, and the government's responsibility to assist in solving shared problems.

In Table 3 we present data about these group orientations. Because responses to these questions are difficult to interpret in isolation, for comparative purposes we include data about the parallel questions having to do with race or ethnicity. Not surprisingly, as shown in the top portion of Table 3, there are, overall, fewer reports of gender bias than of racial or ethnic bias from Blacks or Latinos respectively. Although women are more likely than men to have reported experiencing sex discrimination, only a small proportion of either group—11 percent of women and 6 percent of men—indicated experiencing this kind of discrimination. When it comes to racial or ethnic discrimination, as we would expect, compared with Anglo-Whites, minority group members are more likely to report having experienced bias, and African-Americans, especially African-American men, are more likely than Latinos to report having experienced racial or ethnic bias. In addition, Black women and Latina women each report at least twice as much racial or ethnic bias as gender bias.

In the bottom portion of Table 3, we report data on the three measures of group consciousness: whether respondents feel close to other group members; whether they think that there are problems of special concern to group members which they need to work together to solve; and, if so, whether the government should be doing more about these problems. In general, with respect to these measures, the similarities across groups are more striking than the differences. Only a modest proportion in each group report feeling particularly close to other group members.

Only a small minority of women say they feel especially close to other women, but 81 percent indicate that they believe women have common prob-

TABLE 3 Group Orientations: Experiences of Discrimination and Group Consciousness

A. Percentage Who Say They Experienced Discrimination on the Basis of Sex and Race or Ethnicity

	On Basis of Sex	On Basis of Race or Ethnicity	On Basis of Either or Both
Women	11%	6%	14%
Anglo-White women	11	3	13
Black women	10	20	23
Latina women	7	19	21
Men	6	9	11
Anglo-White men	6	7	9
Black men	6	30	31
Latino men	5	16	19

B. Expressions of Group Consciousness by Gender and Race or Ethnicity

	Feel Close to Others in the Group	Believe They Have Problems in Common	Government Should Help
Feel about Women			
All women	10%	81%	78%
Anglo-White women	10	81	77
Black women	11	84	86
Latina women	13	77	82
Feel about Blacks			
All Blacks	16	87	88
Black women	15	86	89
Black men	17	88	88
Feel about Latinos			
All Latinos	14	80	82
Latina women	14	82	84
Latino men	14	78	78

SOURCE: Citizen Participation Study—Main Survey.

lems and, of them, 78 percent believe that the government has some responsibility to help out. Similar proportions of African-Americans reported feeling especially close to other African-Americans and believing that African-Americans face joint problems. However, a somewhat higher proportion of African-Americans, 88 percent, indicated that the government should be involved in solving these problems.

Gender Differences in Political Voice?

We have examined gender differences with respect to a number of predispositions that provide background for political participation. Our next task is to get closer to political activity in order to explore the values and preferences that give to political activity its raison d'être. In this section, we consider gender differences in the rewards that activists seek in taking part and in the issue concerns they bring to their participation. We ask whether women and men derive different gratifications from their activity and whether their activity is inspired by different sets of policy priorities.

Over the past two decades, political scientists have cast considerable light on the question of whether there are gender differences in political voice. A number of theoretical perspectives have been developed with respect to the issue of whether we should expect women and men to display different orientations to politics. In terms of empirical findings, at the level of the mass public, scholars have focused upon gender differences in partisan identification and vote choices as well as in political attitudes.

In the aftermath of the 1980 election—when men gave 53 percent, and women gave 49 percent, of their votes to Ronald Reagan—scholars as well as observers in the media discovered the gender gap. Since then, women have consistently been somewhat more Democratic than men in both their electoral choices and their party leanings. This circumstance is ordinarily interpreted as the result of women's distinctive preferences. Longitudinal data, however, make clear that it is men's, not women's, partisanship and vote choices that have changed. While men have moved toward the Republicans, thus creating the gender gap, women's preferences have, in the aggregate, remained largely unchanged.

When it comes to attitudes on issues, the results of public opinion surveys, in which members of the mass public are asked to respond to a series of issues pre-selected by the researcher, have long shown interesting, and perhaps unexpected, patterns of gender difference. With respect to "women's issues"—that is, issues like women's rights, abortion, or during the 1970s, the Equal Rights Amendment (ERA) that affect men and women differently— the gender differences in opinion are narrow and inconsistent. The disparities in opinion are somewhat more marked with respect to what are sometimes called "compassion issues," such as support for government welfare guarantees. The differences are wider still and more consistent when it comes to a series of issues—ranging from gun control to support for military intervention in international conflicts—that involve violence or coercion.

We have also learned a great deal about gender differences in the orientations and agendas of political elites. Recent studies of public officials— especially legislators in both the state houses and the U.S. Congress—concur in finding that it makes a difference when women hold office. Compared with their male fellow partisans, female representatives tend to have distinctive attitudes: they are more liberal with respect not only to the issues on which there has traditionally been a gender gap in public opinion among citizens but also to a much broader array of policy concerns, including the relatively abbreviated list of issues that might be deemed women's issues. Moreover, their attitudes are reflected in their behavior and legislative priorities. Most notably, women legislators are more likely to support and to champion measures concerning women, children, and families.

Although political scientists have made substantial progress in probing the differences between men and women in the attitudes and choices of voters or political elites, we know much less about whether men and women speak with distinctive political voices when they participate as citizens and communicate to public officials about their needs, preferences, and priorities. Both the nature of the sample and the interview schedule of the Citizen Participation Study make it particularly useful for examining what activists seek when they take part. In contrast to ordinary random samples of the public, which net very few cases of those who undertake rare activities—respondents who, for example, have attended a protest or worked in a campaign within the recent past—the Citizen Participation Study deliberately oversampled activists. In addition, whenever a respondent indicated having been active in a particular way, we asked a series of questions designed to measure the relative importance of a range of possible rewards in animating the activity. We also inquired whether there was any issue or problem, "ranging from public policy issues to community, family, and personal concerns," that led to the activity. We later coded the verbatim answers into categories of issue concerns. These data permit us to investigate the roots of citizen activity in terms of the gratifications attendant to their participation and the issue concerns behind it.

The Rewards of Participation

The fact of political participation, for women or for men, is often considered a paradox. From a rational choice perspective, joint activity on behalf of shared objectives is, under ordinary circumstances, irrational. The logic is as follows: since governmental policies are collective goods—affecting citizens whether or not they are active in promoting or opposing them—the rational, self-interested individual has no incentive to invest scarce resources in political participation. Because the efforts of any single individual are unlikely to have a significant effect on whether the desired policy outcome is achieved, the rational individual will hitch a free ride on the activity of others and thus reap the benefits of the preferred policy without expending resources on its attainment. The result is that rational, self-interested individuals will refrain from taking part.

Nonetheless, millions vote and take part in other ways. Many solutions have been given to this puzzle; most of them focus on the range of selective, usually self-interested, gratifications that political activity can provide. In the Citizen Participation Study, we took a simple, somewhat novel, approach to this issue.

We looked at it from the perspective of the activists by asking them how *they* interpret their participation; in particular, how they recall the reasons for their activity.

Although we might entertain contradictory hypotheses about differences between women and men in their retrospective understandings of the reasons that led to activity, inferences from a variety of studies suggest that women would be more likely than men to cite civic concerns and less likely than men to indicate seeking material rewards. For example, in her study of delegates to the 1972 presidential nominating conventions, Jeane Kirkpatrick found women delegates in both parties to be less ambitious for elective office than their male counterparts. In addition, the literature on social feminism and women's involvements in the period just before the granting of suffrage emphasizes the extent to which that work was charitably oriented and motivated by community-spirited value orientations. Furthermore, in her study of state legislators, Kirkpatrick found women in the state houses to be more comfortable with a conception of politics as an arena characterized by problem solving in search of the common good rather than by self-interested conflict. Raymond Bauer, Ithiel de Sola Pool, and Louis Anthony Dexter echo this understanding of a distinctively female approach to politics in their patronizing 1963 characterization of "The Ladies from the League."

We consider four kinds of motivations: selective benefits of three types—material benefits, social gratifications, and civic gratifications—as well as the desire to influence a collective policy. *Selective gratifications* may be material or intangible. *Material benefits*, such as jobs, career advancement, or help with a personal or family problem, were the lubricant of the classic urban machine. They continue to figure importantly in contemporary discussions of congressional constituency service and incentives for joining organizations. *Social gratifications*, such as the enjoyment of working with others or the excitement of politics, cannot be enjoyed apart from the activity itself. Without taking part, there is no way to partake of the fun, gain the recognition, or enjoy other social benefits. Similarly, *civic gratifications*, such as satisfying a sense of duty or a desire to contribute to the welfare of the community also derive from the act itself. In this case, however, we are concerned that social norms give respondents an incentive to emphasize the desire for these psychological rewards in order to please the interviewer. Although there is no reason to expect respondents to exaggerate the social gratifications attendant to voluntary activity, they might overstate the extent to which they were motivated by civic concerns. *Collective outcomes* are the enactment or implementation of desired public policies or the election of a favored candidate.

■   ■   ■

In discussing voting, respondents—whether male or female—referred frequently to civic rewards and only rarely to material ones. With respect to the gratifications attendant to working in a campaign, social gratifications assume greater prominence—again for both women and men. What this means is that it is the nature of the act rather than the sex of the participant that determines the rewards associated with it. Since men and women choose to engage in the same kinds of participatory acts, the consequent rewards accruing to them are necessarily similar.

The Issue Agenda of Participation

One of the striking features of the data in Table 4 is the large proportion of activists, both women and men, who mention the chance to influence government policy as a reason for their activity—despite the fact that theories of rational choice would argue that it is irrational for them to do so. As we might expect, for most of those who contact a government official directly, there is some policy issue at stake. However, we also find that about half of the voters and campaign workers also mention a policy concern associated with their activity. In short, activists do hope to further a public purpose through their activity.

Our principal concern, of course, is whether men and women differ systematically in the issues and problems they bring into political life. Earlier we mentioned the results of studies of the gender differences among legislators with respect to their discretionary activities—cosponsoring bills, attending committee meetings, making speeches, and so forth. In contrast to casting roll-call votes, these are activities that afford a legislator considerable control over the issue agenda. With respect to these discretionary activities, studies show that women are more likely than men to place a high priority on issues relating to children, to families, and to women. These results seem especially germane to our concerns here because—like legislators undertaking discretionary activities, but unlike legislators casting roll-call votes or respondents to a public opinion poll, who must decide about a pre-selected set of issues— citizen activists choose freely the issue baskets in which to place their participatory eggs. In one respect, however, we might expect differences between citizens and legislators when it comes to the content of their discretionary agendas. Women legislators self-consciously assume that part of their legislative responsibility is to represent women. Presumably, most women activists do not feel a similar responsibility.

The scope of the agenda

Given women's traditional role within the family as well as the particularistic orientation to politics that has been ascribed to them since the Greeks, we might expect women to bring to politics more personal or family concerns. We can investigate this surmise by considering the scope of the issues behind political activity. Each time a respondent indicated having engaged in a particular activity, we inquired whether there was any particular issue or problem—"ranging from public policy issues to community, family, and personal concerns"—that led to the activity. Across the totality of more than

3,600 political acts discussed by our respondents, in 63 percent of cases respondents provided a comprehensible, "codable" answer about the policy concerns that animated the activity. Analyzing the substantive concerns behind this "issue-based activity" allows us to characterize the participatory input from various groups—including men and women.

Since we wish to assess whether women and men differ in the likelihood of mentioning a concern limited to the individual and the family rather than issues with a broader referent, we focus, at the outset, on contacts with public officials, the only activity for which sizable numbers of respondents said that their concern was narrowly personal. (With regard to all other participatory acts, for the overwhelming majority of activists, the referent was broader.) It turns out that there is remarkable similarity between men and women who get in touch with public officials with respect to whether the matter raised is germane only to themselves or their families or a policy issue of more general concern. Discussing their most recent contact, 22 percent of the men and 21 percent of the women indicated that the subject was a matter of particularized concern. Thirty-five percent of the female contactors indicated that the issue affects the whole community and 25 percent that it affects the entire nation (or the whole world); the analogous figures for male contactors are 38 percent and 22 percent respectively.

■   ■   ■

Participatory agendas: a further probe

We can probe further by considering the participatory agendas of men and women who differ in terms of their class and their family circumstances. We begin with socioeconomic advantage, and the findings are complex. In Table 4 we compare men and women who are relatively advantaged (who have had at least a year of college education and whose family incomes were $50,000 or more) with those who are much less advantaged (who have no more than a high school education and whose family incomes were no more than $20,000). Educational concerns figure importantly in the issue-based activity of both advantaged and disadvantaged respondents. Once again, however, they occupy greater space in women's activity than in men's. Abortion weighs more heavily in the issue-based activity of the advantaged, for whom there is no gender gap, than in the activity of the disadvantaged, for whom there is a gender disparity in abortion-related activity.

Disadvantaged respondents, both female and male, are more concerned with issues of basic human need. Among the advantaged there is no difference between women and men in the extent to which these issues figure in issue-based activity. In contrast, among the disadvantaged issues of basic human need occupy much more space in the bundle of issue concerns for women than for men. A similar pattern obtains for issues associated with drugs and crime. Concern about crime and drugs figures much more importantly on

TABLE 4   Socioeconomic Advantage and the Issues That Animate Political Participation[a]

	Advantaged[b]		Disadvantaged[c]	
	Women	Men	Women	Men
Basic Human Needs	9%	9%	27%	12%
Taxes	8	16	13	15
Economic Issues (except taxes)	14	15	4	5
Abortion	13	12	6	0
Social Issues (except abortion)	1	1	6	0
Education	24	14	17	8
Children or Youth (except education)	5	3	9	5
Crime or Drugs	8	5	15	6
Environment	5	10	0	4
Foreign Policy	7	9	2	4
Women's Issues	2	d	0	0
Number of Respondents	197	228	297	182
Number of Issue-Based Acts	326	338	113	72

SOURCE: Citizen Participation Study—Main Survey.

a. Entries are the proportion of issue-based participation motivated by concern about particular issues.

b. Advantaged: At least one year of college and family income at least $50,000.

c. Disadvantaged: No college education and family income less than $20,000.

d. Less than 1 percent.

the agenda of issues that inspire activity among disadvantaged women than among disadvantaged men or among the advantaged of either sex.

A special concern with single mothers led us to investigate the participatory agendas of parents with children living at home. In light of what we have seen so far, the findings in Table 5 are not unexpected. Consistent with the results we have already reviewed, concerns about education or about crime or drugs weigh less heavily—and concerns about taxes more heavily—in the activity of married fathers than of mothers, whether single or married. Reflecting their economic circumstances, single mothers are much more likely than their married counterparts to mention matters of basic need in connection with their issue-based activity. However, the most striking finding in Table 5 is not that public officials hear about different issues from single mothers than from married parents of either sex but rather that public officials hear so little from single mothers. The rate of issue-based activity among married mothers and fathers is nearly twice that among single mothers. In short, what is distinctive about the participation of single mothers is not its issue content but its rarity.

TABLE 5 Parenthood and the Issues That Animate Political Participation[a]

	Mothers		*Fathers*
	Single	*Married*	*Married*
Basic Human Needs	16%	6%	11%
Taxes	13	13	18
Economic Issues (except taxes)	12	6	11
Abortion	11	14	8
Social Issues (except abortion)	2	1	2
Education	22	25	13
Children or Youth (except education)	7	7	5
Crime or Drugs	16	10	5
Environment	4	6	8
Foreign Policy	7	3	7
Women's Issues	5	1	b
Number of Respondents	184	430	405
Number of Issue-based Acts	116	485	494

SOURCE: Citizen Participation Study—Main Survey.

a. Table lists the proportion of issue-based participation motivated by concern about particular issues.

b. Less than 1 percent.

Agendas for Women–Agendas for Men

Because we were struck at how little activity—pro or con, by women or by men—is animated by concern about women's issues, we decided to focus more explicitly on gender issues in the Follow-up study that we conducted in 1994. We asked two open-ended questions: one about whether there are any problems on which women need to work together in order to solve and an analogous one about problems men need to work together to solve. Because the question was open-ended, the issues mentioned came spontaneously from the respondents. However, the questions clearly directed the respondent to focus on gender. It is important to note that these data were collected a few years after those just reviewed, and the intervening years witnessed the Hill-Thomas hearings in the Senate, which brought attention to the issue of sexual harassment in the workplace, and the replacement of George H. W. Bush by Bill Clinton as president and, concomitantly, the replacement of Barbara Bush by Hillary Rodham Clinton as first lady.

The resulting data give us four possible sets of issues:

Issues that *women* believe require common action by *women;*
Issues that *men* believe require common action by *women;*
Issues that *women* believe require common action by *men;*
Issues that *men* believe require common action by *men.*

Not surprisingly, men and, especially, women see women as being more likely than men to have problems that they need to work together to solve: 64 percent of the men and 74 percent of the women mentioned an interpretable issue requiring joint action by women; in contrast, 49 percent of the men and 52 percent of the women mentioned an interpretable issue requiring joint action by men.

. . . Especially striking is the relative salience both to men and to women of matters pertaining to equality for women in the workplace—a category that includes reference to, for example, equal pay, sex discrimination on the job, unequal chances for advancement, and the glass ceiling. Thirty-five percent of the women and 26 percent of the men mentioned this issue as one on which women should work together—a quite high proportion for an open-ended question of so general a nature. No other issue draws this kind of spontaneous mention. In addition, a smaller, but still noticeable, number of both men and women referred to issues of sex discrimination and equal treatment for women without specifying a particular domain such as the workplace or the home.

Abortion was also mentioned frequently—by 14 percent of the women and 21 percent of the men—as a problem on which women should work together. Given the greater prominence of abortion on the participatory agendas of activists, it is notable that matters of workplace equality weigh more importantly in respondents' conceptions of what women need to work on together. A clue to the source of this seeming discrepancy may be in the extent to which the brief word bites describing concern about workplace equality are devoid of references to political solutions. Although the nature and implementation of civil rights laws have enormous potential consequences for the establishment of equal opportunity on the job, it may be that workplace discrimination—like child care and joblessness—are not fully politicized but are instead construed as problems that individuals can solve on their own. In contrast, both sides in the abortion controversy are only too aware of the political nature of the conflict.

Another subject that arose frequently is children and child care. In discussing problems of joint concern to women, women were especially likely to bring up child care and other issues concerning children: 15 percent of the women mentioned child care and 7 percent referred to other issues involving children as issues on which women should work together; 5 percent mentioned child care, and 1 percent brought up other children's issues, as concerns for men's joint action. Of the men, only 8 percent discussed child care and 1 percent referred to other child-related issues as something on which women ought to work together; 2 percent of the men mentioned child care, and 1 percent mentioned other children's issues, as matters on which men need to work together.

What is noteworthy is the extent to which these are deemed, by both men and women, as problems on which women, but not men, should work together. It is hardly surprising that abortion is considered a problem requiring joint action by women. After all, one side in the abiding political controversy frames the issue in terms of a "woman's right to choose." Similarly, with respect to equality for women, both men and women might reasonably assume that the burden for collective action in addressing inequality should be on the shoulders of the group that has the most to gain from it—the group seeking equality rather than the group that enjoys superior status. However, it is not clear why this principle should obtain for children, who are usually construed as being the joint responsibility of both parents.

The pattern continues when it comes to a final set of loosely related issues, various aspects of the relations between men and women. The issue of male violence or harassment of women—sexual harassment, spousal abuse, and other manifestations of violence against women, including rape—is, once again, more likely to be considered by both women and men as an issue on which women have to work together, even though it would seem that changing male behavior is the key to making progress. Only when it comes to men's "attitude problem"—the need for men to be more sensitive or less aggressive, to curb their egos, or to be less macho—is the problem construed as men's work. Thus to the extent that they think about these problems at all, men and women seem to view problems that men and women might be considered to share—issues surrounding children or relations between the sexes—as women's responsibility to solve.

Conclusion

We have found unmistakable gender differences in a variety of orientations toward politics. . . . We found that, in a variety of ways, men are more likely than women to register psychological involvement with politics, especially national politics: to be politically interested and informed; to feel that they can make a difference if they take part; to discuss politics on a regular basis; and to follow politics in the media. In contrast, women are more likely than men to manifest deep religious commitment and to consider religion to be important in their lives. . . .

With respect to matters more proximate to political activity—the rewards that derive from it and the issue concerns that animate it—we found much less evidence of a distinctive political voice. In terms of the gratifications attendant to participation, we found overall similarity between women and men. What was striking was not any systematic patterning by gender but rather the differences among political acts as well as the extent to which respondents cited civic and policy benefits in their retrospective understandings of their activity.

When we examined the issues that activists bring to their participation, we also found a great deal of similarity in the overall contours of men's and women's policy agendas. Both groups carry a diverse set of policy matters to their activity, and their relative priorities are quite similar. However, we also found evidence of subtle differences between women and men when it comes to the content of participation.

Where we found gender differences in the issue concerns that animate political activity, they come closer to replicating the distinctive policy priorities of men and women legislators than to mapping the issues on which there is the greatest gender disparity in the attitudes of the mass public. Educational issues, in particular, weigh more heavily in the concerns of women activists, a result that holds even when we consider groups defined by their socioeconomic and family circumstances. This finding mirrors that of the studies of the discretionary priorities of women in legislatures. Abortion also occupies greater space among the issue concerns of female than male activists. This is an issue that divides women—and men—resulting in polarized conflict between pro-life and pro-choice activists of both sexes, a pattern that differs from that among legislators, among whom men are distinctly more pro-life than women are.

REFERENCES

Jeane J. Kirkpatrick. 1974. *Political Woman*. New York: Basic Books.

Jeane J. Kirkpatrick. 1976. *The New Presidential Elite*. New York: Russell Sage.

Shanto Iyengar. 1990. "Shortcuts to political knowledge: selective attention and the accessibility bias," in John Ferejohn and James Kuklinski (eds.). *Information and Democratic Processes*. Champaign: University of Illinois Press.

10.3

ROBERT D. PUTNAM

From *Bowling Alone: The Collapse and Revival of American Community*

Social capital refers to networks of interpersonal interaction that support civic life and make democratic politics vibrant and meaningful. It is built, for example, when people participate in voluntary organizations. Putnam argues that there has been a steady decline in social capital in the United States since the 1960s, especially interactions occurring within social and political organizations. In this excerpt he describes the value of social capital and why its decline is worrisome.

. . . In recent years social scientists have framed concerns about the changing character of American society in terms of the concept of "social capital." By analogy with notions of physical capital and human capital—tools and training that enhance individual productivity—the core idea of social capital theory is that social networks have value. Just as a screwdriver (physical capital) or a college education (human capital) can increase productivity (both individual and collective), so too social contacts affect the productivity of individuals and groups.

Whereas physical capital refers to physical objects and human capital refers to properties of individuals, social capital refers to connections among individuals—social networks and the norms of reciprocity and trustworthiness that arise from them. In that sense social capital is closely related to what some have called "civic virtue." The difference is that "social capital" calls attention to the fact that civic virtue is most powerful when embedded in a dense network of reciprocal social relations. A society of many virtuous but isolated individuals is not necessarily rich in social capital.

■   ■   ■

By virtually every conceivable measure, social capital has eroded steadily and sometimes dramatically over the past two generations. The quantitative evidence is overwhelming. . . . Americans have had a growing sense at some visceral level of disintegrating social bonds.

Are we right? Does social capital have salutary effects on individuals, communities, or even entire nations? Yes, an impressive and growing body of research suggests that civic connections help make us healthy, wealthy, and wise. Living without social capital is not easy, whether one is a villager in southern Italy or a poor person in the American inner city or a well-heeled entrepreneur in a high-tech industrial district.

If we are to believe that social capital benefits individuals and communities, we must first understand how social capital works its magic. High levels of trust and citizen participation operate through a variety of mechanisms to produce socially desirable outcomes. Obviously the mechanism(s) at work will vary by the circumstance and outcome in question. But in general social capital has many features that help people translate aspirations into realities.

First, social capital allows citizens to resolve collective problems more easily. Social scientists have long been concerned about "dilemmas" of collective action. Such dilemmas are ubiquitous, and their dynamics are straightforward. People often might all be better off if they cooperate, with each doing her share. But each individual benefits more by shirking her responsibility, hoping that others will do the work for her. Moreover, even if she is wrong and the others shirk, too, she is still better off than if she had been the only sucker. Obviously if every individual thinks that the others will do the work, nobody will end up taking part, and all will be left worse off than if all had contributed.

Supporting government through a tax system is a dilemma of collective action. So is limiting lawn sprinklers and long showers during arid summers. These and other coordination challenges go by various names—"collective-action problems," "the prisoner's dilemma," "the free-rider problem," and "the tragedy of the commons," to name a few. But they all share one feature: They are best solved by an institutional mechanism with the power to ensure compliance with the collectively desirable behavior. Social norms and the networks that enforce them provide such a mechanism.

Second, social capital greases the wheels that allow communities to advance smoothly. Where people are trusting and trustworthy, and where they are subject to repeated interactions with fellow citizens, everyday business and social transactions are less costly. There is no need to spend time and money making sure that others will uphold their end of the arrangement or penalizing them if they don't. Economists such as Oliver Williamson and political scientists such as Elinor Ostrom have demonstrated how social capital translates into financial capital and resource wealth for businesses and self-governing units. Indeed, the Nobel Prize–winning economist Kenneth Arrow has concluded, "Virtually every commercial transaction has within itself an element of trust, certainly any transaction conducted over a period of time. It can be plausibly argued that much of the economic backwardness in the world can be explained by a lack of mutual confidence."[1]

A third way in which social capital improves our lot is by widening our awareness of the many ways in which our fates are linked. People who have active and trusting connections to others—whether family members, friends, or fellow bowlers—develop or maintain character traits that are good for the rest of society. Joiners become more tolerant, less cynical, and more empathetic to the misfortunes of others. When people lack connections to others, they are unable to test the veracity of their own views, whether in the give-and-take of casual conversation or in more formal deliberation. Without such an opportunity, people are more likely to be swayed by their worst impulses. It is no coincidence that random acts of violence, such as the 1999 spate of schoolyard shootings, tend to be committed by people identified, after the fact, as "loners."

The networks that constitute social capital also serve as conduits for the flow of helpful information that facilitates achieving our goals. For example, . . . many Americans—perhaps even most of us—get our jobs through personal connections. If we lack that social capital, economic sociologists have shown, our economic prospects are seriously reduced, even if we have lots of talent and training ("human capital"). Similarly, communities that lack civic interconnections find it harder to share information and thus mobilize to achieve opportunities or resist threats.

Social capital also operates through psychological and biological processes to improve individuals' lives. Mounting evidence suggests that people whose lives are rich in social capital cope better with traumas and fight illness more effectively. Social capital appears to be a complement, if not a substitute, for Prozac, sleeping pills, antacids, vitamin C, and other drugs we buy at the corner pharmacy. "Call me [or indeed almost anyone] in the morning" might actually be better medical advice than "Take two aspirin" as a cure for what ails us.

To clarify how these mechanisms operate in practice, consider the following stylized example, which, while technically fabricated, depicts reality for many parents. Bob and Rosemary Smith, parents of six-year-old Jonathan, live in an urban community that is full of both delights and troubles. Bob and Rosemary support public education in principle, and they would like their first-grader to be exposed to children from diverse backgrounds, an opportunity that the public schools provide. But the Smiths' local elementary school is a shambles: teachers are demoralized, paint is chipping off the walls, and there is no money for extracurricular activities or computer equipment. Worried about Jonathan's ability to learn and thrive in this environment, Bob and Rosemary have a choice. They can pull their child out of the public schools and pay dearly to put him in a private school, or they can stick around and try to improve the public school. What to do?

Let's suppose that the Smiths want to stick around and start a Parent-Teacher Association at Jonathan's school. The chances that they will be able to do so will depend upon two things: the existence of other concerned parents who are also likely to join; and the likelihood that such an association will be effective in improving conditions at the school. Here social capital comes in. The more the Smiths know and trust their neighbors, the greater their ability to recruit and retain reliable members of the new PTA. In cohesive neighborhoods filled with lots of overlapping connections, individuals more easily learn who can be counted on, and they can make better use of moral suasion to ensure continued attention to the problems at hand.

Let's assume the Smiths succeed in starting the PTA, and several months later it has an active membership of seventeen parents. What does this new institution, this addition to the stock of social capital, do for the individuals involved and for the community at large? For one, belonging to the PTA almost certainly inculcates civic skills in parents. People who might never have designed a project, given a presentation, lobbied a public official, or even spoken up at a meeting are pressed to do so. What's more, the PTA serves to establish and enforce norms of commitment and performance on the part of school officials, teachers, and perhaps even students. It also allows for the deepening of interpersonal bonds and "we-ness" between families and educators. On a more personal note, the PTA meetings are bound to establish, or strengthen, norms of reciprocity and mutual concern among parents. These connections will almost certainly pay off in myriad unexpected ways in the future. If Bob loses his job, he will now have fifteen other adults upon whom he can call for employment leads or even for simple moral support. If Rosemary decides to start a lobbying group to press for better child health facilities in the city, she will have fifteen other potential lobbyists to aid in her cause. At the very least, Bob and Rosemary will have another couple or two with whom they can catch a movie on Friday nights. All these gains—civic skills, social support, professional contacts, volunteer labor, moviegoing partners—arose because the Smiths wanted to put computers in their kid's school.

Community connectedness is not just about warm fuzzy tales of civic triumph. In measurable and well-documented ways, social capital makes an enormous difference in our lives. . . . Social capital makes us smarter, healthier, safer, richer, and better able to govern a just and stable democracy.

NOTE

1. Kenneth J. Arrow, "Gifts and Exchanges," *Philosophy and Public Affairs* 1 (summer 1972): 357.

11

INTEREST GROUPS

11.1

TERRY M. MOE

From *The Organization of Interests: Incentives and the Internal Dynamics of Political Interest Groups*

Moe builds on the work of Olson on the collective action problem (see Chapter 1). In this excerpt, Moe argues that interest group leaders use people's overestimation of their impact on group goals to persuade them to participate in group activities and lobbying.

THE DECISION TO JOIN

Because interest groups are comprised of members, it is only reasonable to begin an analysis of interest groups by asking why individuals choose to become members in the first place. What explains an individual's decision to join? Before *The Logic of Collective Action* first appeared, this question seemed to have a simple and obvious answer: people join groups because they agree with group goals. Indeed, the answer seemed so simple and so obvious that the question itself was not considered particularly interesting, and it was rarely the subject of inquiry. Olson changed all this. He did so by structuring his analysis of group membership around a theoretical concept that was essentially new to political scientists, but whose analytical value was recognized early on by writers in economics and public finance. This is the concept of a collective (or public) good.

For our purposes, this concept can be defined very simply. Any good can be viewed as a collective good for some set of individuals if, once it is supplied by one or more individuals in the set, it is automatically available for consumption by *all* individuals in the set.[1] A little reflection is enough to suggest that collective goods are widely sought and supplied in the political system. A public park is a collective good, for instance, because it can be enjoyed by everyone interested in using it, not just those persons who pay taxes and "supply" the park. Expenditures on national defense operate automatically to protect everyone in the nation, even though many individuals make no contributions at all.

These examples help to suggest why collective goods have such an intriguing theoretical role to play. In the first place, collective goods like public parks and national defense are often expensive to supply, while the average individual tends to gain an amount which, by comparison to the good's cost, is exceedingly small. If we think that an individual will typically be unwilling to contribute (pay) more than he stands to gain, then any contribution he could feasibly offer would constitute only a tiny portion of the total funds available to cover the necessary costs. It would appear to be a drop in the bucket, with little likelihood of making any noticeable difference in the good's supply. This should often serve as a major inhibitor of individual contributions. After all, if one persons fails to pay taxes, the national defense will not be impaired, nor will the public parks shut down. Moreover, this restraint on contributions is reinforced by a second factor that derives from the nature of the collective good itself: once it is supplied, the individual can enjoy the benefits even if he has shouldered none of the cost burden. As long as financial sources are found for public parks, national defense, and other collective goods, the individual can freely take advantage of them—without voluntarily throwing his money away on contributions that would, at any rate, have had no real impact in and of themselves.

This oversimplifies matters somewhat. But it should be clear that, when a collective good is at issue, the interesting question is why an individual would voluntarily want to pay something toward its supply. Olson's achievement is that he brought the analytical importance of collective goods to the full attention of political scientists. In effect, he shows how an "economic" concept can be transformed into a "political" concept, yielding a new and dramatically different perspective on the incentives for political action.

He does this by reconceptualizing the pluralist contention that individuals will act on the basis of common interests. He points out that, when individuals have a common interest in pursuing political goals—tax relief, civil rights legislation, farm subsidies, or minimum wage laws, to name only a few—these goals are typically collective goods for the "group" of individuals in question. If some of these people were willing to contribute toward the formation of a lobbying organization, and if this organization were successful in realizing the commonly held goals, all affected individuals would ultimately receive the benefits—noncontributors and contributors alike. This, along with the frequently high expense of political success, will clearly influence the willingness of individuals to contribute in the first place and thereby to "pursue their common interests." Thus, if we are to understand the conditions under which individuals will contribute toward interest group activity, the relationship between contributions and collective goods emerges as the fundamental consideration.

The Olson Theory

Olson's approach is straightforward. He proceeds by adopting a rational choice model and applying it to a group context which, from a pluralist standpoint, is ideally suited for the emergence of collective action: all individuals are taken to agree on the desirability of achieving a given political goal, viewed as a collective good. The question becomes: how much will rational individuals be willing to contribute toward the supply of a collective good that they have a common interest in obtaining?

Assumptions and basic conclusions

Olson is surprisingly vague about some of his assumptions, and a casual reading of his argument can easily lead to confusion about how conclusions are logically derived. This is particularly so with respect to individual values, since his intermittent reference to social pressure, ideology, and even altruism can leave the mistaken impression that a full range of values has been entered into the theory's premises. Because of such ambiguities, we will supplement Olson's explicit assumptions with others that are implicit in his analysis. The resulting set of assumptions, listed here, will be referred to as the Olson model. (*a*) Each individual is rational, perfectly informed, motivated by economic gain, and an independent decision maker. (*b*) The collective good is infinitely divisible.[2] (*c*) The marginal costs of providing the collective good are positive and increasing. (*d*) The marginal benefits of obtaining the good are positive and decreasing.

On the basis of assumptions corresponding to those presented here, Olson develops a mathematical analysis that justifies his conclusions about collective action. Given the task at hand, however, it is more instructive to forego a mathematical treatment and set out the elements of his argument diagrammatically.[3] Figure 1 consists of various marginal cost and marginal benefit curves expressed as a function of the level of collective good, X, supplied. For purposes of illustration, the "group" is assumed to have N "members," N minus two of whom derive equal benefits from increments of the collective good and have identical marginal benefit curves MB. The other two group members, j and k, are assumed to derive much greater benefit from the good, as shown by MB_j and MB_k. The group marginal benefit schedule, MB, is the sum of the curves of the N members. The MC curve expresses the marginal costs of supplying the collective good, and it is the same for everyone. It represents all the costs that are involved, organizational and otherwise, in achieving each additional increment.

Each individual, in deciding how much to contribute, must take into account how much it costs to supply each increment of the good, how much he stands

FIGURE 1

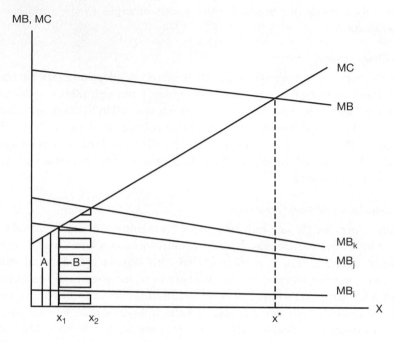

to gain from each increment, and how much of the good has already been supplied (if any). Because he acts independently, he does not try to "game" his decision, nor does he enter into any cooperative agreements. This being so, he will contribute up to the point where the marginal costs of providing the good are equal to the marginal benefits he derives. At this level he is maximizing his net benefits. Assuming none of the good is as yet provided, it is to k's advantage to supply x_2, to j's advantage to supply x_1, and to everyone else's advantage to contribute nothing. Based on their incentives to contribute, we will refer to j and k as "Large Members" and to the rest as "Small Members," as does Olson.

What is the total contribution? Although j and k have an incentive to contribute amounts A and AB, respectively,[4] the total contribution is not $2AB$. This is where the "prevailing level of supply" factor comes into play. For if k contributes first—which he might do, since he is not gaming the situation— then the new level of supply becomes a fact which, by assumption, is immediately known by j. Acting rationally, j will then ask himself, How much should I contribute given that x_2 has already been provided? The answer is that he should contribute nothing: at x_2, the costs to j of providing more of the good are greater than any benefits he will derive. Hence, in this case only x_2 will be provided, and even though everyone gains when the good is made available, k will have paid the entire cost.

If, on the other hand, j contributes first, then x_1 of the good is provided for the group and k must ask himself: How much should I contribute given that x_1, is already supplied? His optimal solution is to contribute an amount B sufficient to move the group from x_1 to x_2. In this case, j and k split the cost of x_2 while again the other members pay nothing. But in either case, and thus regardless of who contributes first, only x_2 is provided, the Large Members pay for all of it, and the Small Members get a "free ride"—illustrating what Olson calls "the exploitation of the great by the small."

This outcome is suboptimal for the group. We can see this by viewing the group as a "superindividual" with marginal benefit curve MB. Such an individual would contribute beyond x_2 until x^* is reached. At each point between x_2 and x^*, the gains to the group as a whole outweigh the costs. Because there is an aggregate surplus, it is clear that our superindividual could distribute the costs and benefits among members so that each gains at least as much as he is required to pay. When the group moves from x_2 to x^*, then, everyone can be made at least as well off as before.

Such a move cannot occur within the model because it requires some sort of coordination, which violates the assumption of independence. As the situation stands, group members have no incentive to provide themselves with anything more than x_2. The group must remain at a level of provision that is "too low," with the cost load shared unevenly. Moreover, when individuals are added to the group (and k remains the largest member), the suboptimality increases. As N grows, the group's MB curve increases and pushes x^* farther out, thus widening the gap between x^* and x_2.

One final point: if all individuals in the group are Small Members, then no one will contribute and none of the collective good will be supplied. This conclusion is obvious enough, but it is especially important from Olson's perspective, because he makes the empirical argument that the Large Member phenomenon is very rare and thus many interest groups cannot turn to this source for any political support whatever.[5]

Bargaining and selective incentives

These aspects of the theory paint a bleak picture indeed. Yet interest groups are not necessarily doomed to failure or even to inadequate resources. This is because there are two basic mechanisms for circumventing, at least to some degree, the problem of contributions.[6]

The first is member cooperation through bargaining. This mechanism violates the assumption of independence, but it can be viewed as a "solution" of sorts if its relevance is allowed to turn on an empirical point—that the likelihood of effective bargaining varies with group size. In very large groups, the costs of communication and coordination tend to be prohibitive; each individual tends to see his own participation as unnecessary to a successful bargain; and, not least, each individual will get the benefits anyway if he lets the other members do the cooperating. As the group gets smaller—in particular, as it gets small enough to enable face-to-face interaction—members can become personally acquainted, aware of each other's interests, and in a position to predict and react to each other's behavior. It is more likely, then, that they will recognize their mutual dependence and calculate accordingly.

Small groups thus are different from large groups, in that they facilitate certain behavior—strategic behavior—that Olson's model assumes away. Even in very small groups, however, there remains a major obstacle to the success of bargaining agreements: as long as members are economically self-interested, and as long as they are bargaining over the supply of a collective good, the free-rider incentive is inherent in individual decision-making, including bargaining activities. Each member knows that if the *other* members (or some of them) do the cooperating and contributing, then he will get the benefits anyway. This makes bargaining agreements more difficult to arrange and constantly threatens the cohesion of any agreements that are actually arrived at. Additionally, the free-rider incentive should work to the disadvantage of Large Members, just as it does in the absence of bargaining, since they have an incentive to contribute even if the others do not, and they stand to lose a great deal if they hold back.

In sum, even for small groups in which bargaining occurs, the free-rider incentive continues to inhibit contributions and encourage the exploitation of the great by the small. The theoretical importance of bargaining is not that it solves the contributions problem, but that it holds out the possibility that small groups will be able to supply themselves with more of the collective good than independent behavior would lead us to expect. In view of this, Olson correctly suggests that his model is more usefully applied to large interest groups. It is here that individuals are most likely to make their decisions independently, and here that his theory's pessimistic conclusions are most likely to be borne out. Thus while bargaining is not actually incorporated into the model, its empirical relevance serves to qualify the model's range of applicability.[7]

There is another mechanism for increasing member contributions, however, that is entirely consistent with the original assumptions. This is what Olson calls a "selective incentive." Through the introduction of this crucial concept, he explains how large interest groups are able to attract financial support even when composed entirely of Small Members who calculate independently.

Selective incentives are private benefits which, precisely because they are private rather than collective in nature, can operate selectively on the membership as a whole: they can be conferred upon those who contribute and withheld from those who do not. For goods of this sort, there is no free-rider incentive. If a person wishes to obtain selective incentives, he cannot do so by waiting for others to shoulder the costs. He will have to "qualify" to receive them, which, in practice, ordinarily means paying dues and becoming a formal member.

This greatly expands the group's potential pool of inducements, for members will purchase anything of material value as long as they expect net benefits on the exchange. Information services, pension plans, group insurance—these are but a few of the most common selective incentives to be found in actual interest groups. Legal coercion is sometimes used as well; in these instances, the laws may be such that individuals are faced with fines, loss of employment, or loss of business if they do not join.

Herein lies the key to success for large groups. While the collective good itself is insufficient to induce member support, individuals who choose to pay for selective incentives are nonetheless contributing funds to group coffers, and leaders can use these funds to supply some of the collective good. Thus, even if no one has an incentive to supply any of the good at all, some of it may be provided as a by-product of the sale of selective incentives.

The Olson theory: Concluding comments

By recognizing that common interests typically take the form of collective goods and by making certain assumptions about individuals, Olson is able to arrive at basic conclusions about collective action. These he summarizes as follows:

> If the members of a large group rationally seek to maximize their per-sonal welfare, they will *not* act to advance their common or group objec-tives unless there is coercion to force them to do so, or unless some separate incentive, distinct from the achievement of common or group interest, is offered to the members of the group individually on the con-dition that they help bear the costs or burdens involved in the achieve-ment of the group objectives. . . .
>
> In small groups there may very well be some voluntary action in support of the common purposes of the individuals in the group, but in most cases this action will cease before it reaches the optimal level for the members of the group as a whole. In the sharing of the costs of efforts to achieve a common goal in small groups, there is however a surprising tendency for the "exploitation" of the *great* by the *small*.[8]

Olson's logic has quite a bit to say about politics. Above all, it subverts the traditional pluralist notion that common interests give rise to collective action, demonstrating that there are certain obstacles inherent in the situation that inhibit the average individual from "doing his part." Indeed, the irony is that the only way vast numbers of individuals can be induced to contribute their share is to offer them something different from, and perhaps entirely unre-lated to, the group's goals.

This result has implications for a host of pluralist notions, because once the motivational connection between common interests and member support is undermined, a good part of the pluralist perspective on politics is called into question. For instance, Olson's analysis contradicts the notion that the effec-tiveness of a group, or at least its resource base, is a function of its degree of support in society. Widespread and enthusiastic agreement on a political goal may give rise to no contributions at all for its organizational sponsor—while other groups, enjoying far less support, may be better financed and more effective as a result of selective incentives, or perhaps the presence of a few Large Members. Thus, in terms of the impact on public policy, a political pluralism of groups may severely distort the underlying social pluralism of interests.

To take another example: we can see that a group's formal membership is not a valid indicator of its political support. This is particularly true of mass-based groups that successfully organize large numbers of average individuals. In such groups—like the Farm Bureau, the Chamber of Commerce, or Common Cause—Olson's theory points to selective incentives, not political goals, as the explanation of large size. Formal membership indicates that the group is successful at selling selective incentives, not that it is politically popular. Indeed, since selective incentives need have nothing whatever to do with the group's goals, there is no guarantee that any dues-payers even agree with those goals. What could be further from pluralist preconceptions?

A Revision: Imperfect Information

Olson's theory is a major contribution to the study of interest groups. It contradicts traditional ways of thinking about political groups, their connection to the social system, and their roles in politics. Moreover, it does this by employing new concepts—collective good, selective incentive—which, while previously accorded almost no systematic attention in political science, are clearly of the greatest relevance for political behavior and promise exciting new directions for theoretical inquiry.

Yet Olson's model is not the only way of constructing a rational theory of interest groups, nor are his dramatic conclusions the only ones implied by the assumption of rationality. What rationality "entails" depends upon the nature of the other assumptions operating in conjunction with it, and, when these are allowed to vary, different rational models are created along with different sets of conclusions. We have already shown this to be so for the assumption of independence. In this section, we will see that the same sort of thing happens when the assumption about perfect information is relaxed.

Olson assumes that individuals are perfectly informed about marginal costs, marginal benefits, and the amount supplied by others. We can now drop this restriction and assume instead that individuals are imperfectly informed, that they arrive at estimates of each curve, and that their rational choices derive from these estimates. The question becomes: under what perceptual conditions will they have an incentive to contribute?

The most general relationships between perceptions and incentives are apparent if we mentally allow the curves in Figure 2 to undergo basic shifts (and disregard any effects of attitudes toward risk). Consider individual i, who, given his present perceptions, is like Olson's Small Member in that he

FIGURE 2

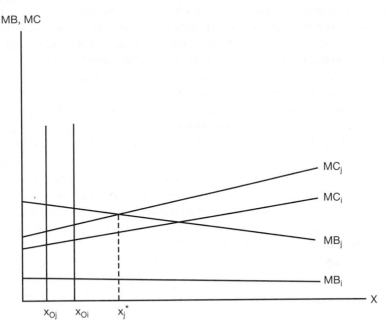

has no incentive to contribute. It is obvious from the figure that any upward shift in his estimated gains from the collective good, as well as any downward shift in the amount he thinks additional increments cost, enhances the likelihood that his marginal cost and benefit curves will intersect at some point to the right of x_{oi}, the amount of X he expects others to supply. When this occurs, he has every incentive to contribute—and the amount he wants to contribute will then vary inversely with any changes in his estimate x_{oi}. Now consider individual j, who, like Olson's Large Member, has an incentive to contribute as things stand. Because his marginal cost and benefit curves already intersect to the right of x_{oi}, even the slightest changes in his estimates will alter his rational choice. The amount of the collective good he chooses to supply, $x_j^* x_{oj}$, will vary directly with his estimated marginal benefits, inversely with his estimated marginal costs, and inversely with the amount of X he expects others to supply. And his contribution will adjust accordingly.[9]

The actual estimates people rely on and the way their perceptions are determined are, of course, empirical questions. The point to be stressed here is a logical one: that behavioral expectations are contingent in specific ways upon perceptions. This yields a perspective on interest groups that is very different from Olson's. Above all, whereas Olson claims that the vast majority of individuals can have no incentive to contribute toward collective goods, the revised model implies that anyone can have an incentive to contribute, depending upon his subjective estimates of the relevant quantities. Generally speaking, an individual is more likely to contribute the higher his estimate of marginal benefits, the lower his estimate of marginal costs, and the lower his estimate of the total level of supply. These estimates in effect lead him to think that his contribution will make a difference in bringing about net personal gains. They lead him, in other words, to have a perception of personal efficacy. The efficacious individual can have a rational incentive to contribute whether or not his efficacy is justified by the objective context.

It follows that interest organizations, even in the complete absence of selective incentives, are better able to recruit members and amass contributions to the extent that these estimates are characteristic of individuals in their sectors. Individuals will then join and quit for political reasons and, accordingly, a group's size and resource base should tend to be more strongly linked to its underlying political support. Thus, perceptions of efficacy among members and potential members suggest an organizational setting that may be roughly consistent with pluralist expectations and is certainly more conducive to political action than Olson's theory would imply.

Additionally, we should recognize that a model in which information about costs, benefits, and the level of supply is assumed to be less than perfect intrinsically contains a new tool for group leaders: some of that information can purposely be manipulated in order to attract members and contributions. This is all the more potent a device given that leaders are in an ideal position to possess (or claim to possess) such information, while the average individual has very few facts on which to base his estimates, other than what the leaders say. Thus, leaders need not simply leave the estimation process to chance, but can play an active role in shaping how individuals arrive at their decisions.

The Role of Efficacy: An Empirical Aside

It might be claimed that Olson's model is the "central tendency," since individuals are as likely to underestimate as to overestimate their true efficacy, and that this modification of his theory is uncalled for. Two basic responses are in order. First, it is an empirical question whether individuals are as likely to underestimate as to overestimate, and there is some basis for believing that overestimation is actually more common. There is now a good deal of research, for example, to indicate that efficacy plays a role in explaining individual involvement in various types of political activity—even when, as in voting, the objective likelihood that the individual's contribution will affect the outcome is infinitesimally small. Why should membership in interest groups be any different? Empirical work also indicates that subjective efficacy is not entirely derived from factors intrinsic to the decisional context itself. In many Western democracies, and certainly in the United States, individuals tend to be socialized to political efficacy by their experiences (e.g., childhood schooling experiences) within the prevailing political culture. They thus come to specific political contexts with certain "efficacy predispositions"—which, in coloring perceptions of the objective context, enhance the likelihood that they will think that their contributions make a difference. In democratic nations, then, perceptual errors by potential members may not be anywhere near randomly distributed about the true cost, benefit, and level of supply curves. The vast majority of individuals may well tend to err in the direction of greater efficacy. This expectation is only reinforced by the informational roles that leaders doubtless play in shaping perceptions.[10]

Second, even if individual estimates are distributed randomly, those who sufficiently overestimate their efficacy will have an incentive to join for political reasons because of it. Depending upon the size of the sector, this could translate into large numbers of people who join in support of group goals; and, especially if selective incentives are not too valuable, it is perfectly possible that most of any given group's formal members (as opposed to those individuals who might have joined but did not) are attracted because of its goals. Thus, even if Olson's model is the central tendency (and it probably is not), informational variations are still basic to an understanding of group membership—and, as we will see . . . , they play major organizational roles as well.

Conclusion

In this reading, we began with Olson's model of the individual's decision to join, relaxed the assumption of perfect information, and arrived at a more general but still quite simple revised theory. From this perspective, the key to group membership does not rest solely with the congruence of member interests and group goals, as the pluralists contend; nor does it rest with the singular role of economic selective incentives, as Olson claims. Instead, we find that both group goals and selective incentives can serve as membership inducements for ordinary members, regardless of their economic size. . . .

These inducements come into play in different ways. Selective incentives are direct member inducements which the individual receives in exchange for his contribution; in deciding whether to buy, he is concerned with whether his gain from selective incentives exceeds their cost. If an individual is to be attracted purely on the basis of group goals, by contrast, he must perceive that his contribution makes a difference for the group's political success, resulting in net gains for himself. As a modification of Olson's analysis, this efficacy requirement opens the door for the inducement value of group goals; but it also represents a condition which many individuals may not satisfy even if they place very high value on the collective good itself. Thus, the introduction of imperfect information does not eliminate the "Olson problems" intrinsic to the individual's collective goods calculus. But it does imply a wider range of (perceptual) conditions under which these problems are overcome.

Selective incentives therefore retain their basic advantage over group goals as member inducements, but this advantage is now of less significance than Olson's original model contends. For any given group, the relative salience of the two types of inducements can vary depending upon the perceptual characteristics of potential members and upon the value of the selective incentives supplied. Some groups may be able to form by offering nothing more than political goals with which enough individuals agree. Other groups may have to supplement political goals with selective incentives in order to attract sufficient support. And still others may find that their goals have no inducement value at all, and that they can form only by relying entirely upon selective incentives. While we have a logical basis for highlighting the importance of selective incentives, then, both types of inducements play special roles in attracting members to the group—and both will take on distinctive organizational roles in the analysis that follows.

NOTES

1. For more technical definitions and discussions of the various dimensions and "degrees" of collective goods, see Paul A. Samuelson, "The Pure Theory of Public Expenditure," *Review of Economics and Statistics* 36 (November 1954): 387–90; "Diagrammatic Exposition of a Theory of Public Expenditure," Ibid., 37 (November 1955): 350–56; "Aspects of Public Expenditure Theories," Ibid., 40 (November 1958): 332–38; Richard Musgrave, *The Theory of Public Finance* (New York: McGraw-Hill, 1959); John G. Head, "Public Goods and Public Policy," *Public Finance* 17, no. 3 (1962): 197–219.

2. We are assuming, with Olson, that various levels or amounts of the collective good can be achieved, and that the provision of the good is not simply an all-or-nothing proposition. Were we to assume the latter, a slightly different analysis would be required.

3. Some of the more technically oriented readers would doubtless prefer a mathematical presentation and will consider this sort of diagrammatical exposition too primitive. An adequate mathematical analysis, however, would eventually become quite involved. One suitable method, given the kinds of substantive issues we are concerned with in this reading, would be to interpret the decisional problem as one of maximization subject to nonlinear constraints and to arrive at optimal solutions by applying the Kuhn-Tucker conditions. An analysis along these lines is set out in Terry M. Moe, "A Calculus of Group Membership," Working Paper No. 7, Public Policy and Political Studies Center, Michigan State University, November 1978. Because most readers would probably find such approaches too technical to be very enlightening, it seems preferable simply to illustrate diagrammatically how Olson's model can be employed and modified to generate conclusions about individual behavior. In this way, at least, it is quite apparent why we have certain expectations about the bases for membership, since it is actually possible to "see" the various theoretical components at work.

4. Solely for purposes of illustration, the implicit assumption here is that fixed costs are zero; were they nonzero, the area under the marginal cost curve would not represent the entire amount necessary for supplying any specified level of X. This simplification does not affect the general conclusions that follow.

5. For simplicity, income effects are assumed to be zero and multiple time periods are not considered. Were these two factors taken into account, the ceiling on provision would be somewhat greater than x_2 and the precise sharing of costs between j and k would be affected. But the basic conclusions outlined in the text would still hold. For a dynamic analysis of collective action that incorporates income effects, see, e.g., John Chamberlin, "Provision of Collective Goods as a Function of Group Size," *American Political Science Review* 68 (June 1974): 707–16. See also Mancur Olson and Richard

Zeckhauser, "An Economic Theory of Alliances," *Review of Economics and Statistics* 43 (August 1966): 66–79.

6. Olson develops these parts of his analysis with the aid of a three-fold typology of groups: privileged, intermediate, and latent. These categories are unnecessary and we will not rely upon them here.

7. Olson also seems to assume that Large Members will emerge only in small groups and that this, too, gives them advantages over large groups. What makes someone a Large Member, however, is the relationship between his marginal cost and benefit curves, and neither of these logically depends on the size of the group. Thus, it seems preferable to say that Large Members can be present in groups of any size and to stress that the advantages of small groups derive from strategic interaction.

8. Olson, *The Logic of Collective Action*, pp. 2–3.

9. Two general points about x_{om}, the amount that any individual m expects others to supply. First, the individual's estimate x_{om} is not necessarily altered when others contribute, since he may be entirely unaware of their behavior. Second, the relationship between x_{om} and contributions will be attenuated when income effects are taken into account: a decrease in x_{om} will have a less positive impact and an increase in x_{om} will have a less negative impact. (In effect, his marginal benefit curve becomes contingent upon x_{om} and shifts when the latter shifts.)

10. On political efficacy, see, e.g., Gabriel A. Almond and Sidney Verba, *The Civic Culture* (Princeton, N.J.: Princeton University Press, 1963); Sidney Verba and Norman H. Nie, *Participation in America: Political Democracy and Social Equality* (New York: Harper and Row, 1972); David Easton and Jack Dennis, "The Child's Acquisition of Regime Norms: Political Efficacy," *American Political Science Review* 61 (March 1967): 25–38; Robert Weissberg, "Political Efficacy and Political Illusion," *Journal of Politics* 37 (May 1975): 469–87; and, for a review of studies of efficacy, Paul R. Abramson, *The Political Socialization of Black Americans: A Critical Evaluation of Research on Efficacy and Trust* (New York: Free Press, 1977).

11.2

KEN KOLLMAN

From *Outside Lobbying: Public Opinion and Interest Group Strategies*

Kollman contrasts two types of lobbying, inside and outside. The inside game is more private and is played among people in Washington. The outside game is played by interest group leaders who bring people from outside Washington into the business of persuading members of Congress. Outside lobbying both signals existing public opinion to lawmakers and tries to shape that public opinion to an interest group's advantage.

INTRODUCTION

Outside lobbying is defined as attempts by interest group leaders to mobilize citizens outside the policymaking community to contact or pressure public officials inside the policymaking community. It represents a viable and effective strategy for many interest groups trying to influence representative government between elections. What better way is there to win favorable legislation in Congress, for example, than to mobilize a significant number of constituents to contact key legislators? Old-fashioned inside lobbying, the personal access and contact with legislators so necessary for maintaining good relations with government, may have only limited effectiveness today. Just as elected officials in Washington feel the need to monitor and assuage public opinion through polls and public relations, modern lobbying increasingly requires sophisticated methods of public mobilization. Lobbying in Washington is not just a game among well-paid lawyers, ideological activists, and legislators in the Capitol. The outside public is increasingly involved.

Mass expressions of public concern directed toward the federal government are rarely spontaneous. Behind most telephone calls, letters, faxes, and E-mails to members of Congress, behind marches down the Mall in Washington, D.C., and behind bus caravans to the Capitol, there are coordinating leaders, usually interest group leaders, mobilizing a select group of citizens to unite behind a common message. At the most basic level, an interest group leader seeks to persuade policymakers that what the members of the group want (as specified by the leader) is good public policy and/or good politics. And the leader uses outside lobbying to demonstrate first, that the members of the group are in fact united behind the leader, and second, that many other constituents agree with what the group leader wants. Faced with organized groups of constituents making noise about this or that policy issue, not many members of Congress could afford to ignore these efforts completely. Any leader who can organize thousands of citizens to write letters to their congressional representative, for example, can with some probability organize a good number of voters on election day to support or oppose the incumbent. For all the apparent benefits of outside lobbying to an interest group—sending a strong message to policymakers or reinforcing to voters that the group represents a credible source of political information—it is surprising nonetheless that outside lobbying is not undertaken more often by groups with an interest in controversial policy issues.

Outside lobbying, however, is in fact applied selectively, and lobbyists and interest group leaders spend precious hours and resources crafting careful public campaigns of persuasion. On some policy issues, groups on all sides use outside lobbying intensively. On other policy issues, only groups on one side of the issue use outside lobbying. There are many issues, even those considered extremely important to specific interest groups, where no groups use outside lobbying. And of course, groups try to time their public appeals for maximum effect. As every lobbyist (or salesperson, parent, or leader) knows, persuasion is a subtle business, and careless lobbying strategies can backfire. It is not always the case that outside lobbying, even when it generates a substantial public response, wins over the policymakers targeted.

The selective application and timing of outside lobbying strategies raises important questions. Obviously, outside lobbying is not always influential, even when interest group leaders on only one side of an issue use it. Who or what captures the attention of Washington policymakers? When are demonstrations of popular support effective in influencing policymakers? How do outside lobbying campaigns compare to financial donations or inside lobbying in influencing policymakers? V. O. Key raised similar questions nearly four decades ago, and he found answers difficult to come by. In the 1961 book *Public Opinion and American Democracy*, he expresses doubts about the influence of outside lobbying activities. "Their function in the political process," he writes in reference to "propagandizing campaigns" by interest groups, "is difficult to divine" (528). Outside lobbying activities are "rituals in obeisance to the doctrine that public opinion governs" and are "on the order of the dance of the rainmakers. . . . Sometimes these campaigns have their effects—just as rain sometimes follows the rainmakers' dance. Yet the data make it fairly clear that most of these campaigns do not affect the opinion of many people and even clearer that they have a small effect by way of punitive or approbative feedback in the vote" (528).

Why and when, Key is really asking, do policymakers pay attention to outside lobbying? Certainly many organizational leaders consider outside lobbying potentially influential; otherwise, they would not do it. The leaders of the major labor unions, peak business organizations, and civil rights and environmental groups use outside lobbying regularly enough to indicate that they believe outside lobbying is more than the dancing of rainmakers. Even corporate leaders use outside lobbying occasionally. And policymakers admit that organized groups of constituents influence their decisions. One congressional staff member justified his boss's vote to repeal catastrophic health insurance in 1990, little more than a year after voting for the insurance bill, by explaining, "It was a no-brainer. He got over five thousand letters for the repeal of the insurance, and literally eight letters in favor of the current insurance. He didn't have much choice really. He had to vote for repeal."

But beyond the relatively uninteresting claims that interest group leaders consider outside lobbying effective and that policymakers sometimes consider it influential, the topic deserves more attention than it receives. If, as most observers claim, interest groups wield considerable power in Washington, and if interest groups spend resources using outside lobbying fairly regularly, then outside lobbying should be an important part of the process by which these groups wield their power. Precisely when, why, or how outside lobbying operates to enhance group influence, however, is not well understood.

Our evaluations of the normative effects of outside lobbying are similarly imprecise. We know very little about whether outside lobbying serves to improve the correspondence between what constituents want and what their representatives do or whether it merely confuses representatives with meaningless information or reinforces inequalities in access to representatives that accrue from campaign contributions and other less edifying activities of interest groups. Surprisingly, many depictions of outside lobbying in the national press are as unfavorable as those of lobbying in general. The image of fat-cat lobbyists shoving money in the pockets of legislators has been supplemented by negative images of farmers, teachers, truckers, or public employees demonstrating at the Capitol or flooding Congress with telephone calls for a bigger slice of the budgetary pie, or of business lobbyists spending money to generate so-called astroturf (in contrast to real grass-roots support) to save a valuable tax provision. The press depiction of interest group activities has had either a large influence on Americans or has tapped into deeply negative sentiments among the general population. Recent polls show that a vast majority of Americans are cynical about the power of special interests. In the 1992 American National Election Study (ANES), when asked whether "the government is pretty much run by a few big interests looking out for themselves or [if] it is run for the benefit of all the people," 78 percent of those offering a response answered, "a few big interests." Common wisdom, it appears, holds that some interest groups have their way in Washington, and that outside lobbying either reinforces existing inequalities in access or is irrelevant to the real game of special interest lobbying.

The cynicism of the press and the general public toward interest groups is not shared by many political scientists. Studies have tended to describe a more sanguine climate of bargaining and information gathering between interest groups and policymakers in Washington. Descriptions of interest group activities and influence from the last four decades range from the near impotence of business lobbyists during legislative conflicts over free trade to subtle forms of persuasion and pressure that influence legislation marginally. Many studies of policymaking or interest groups have concluded that other pressures on policymakers besides interest group lobbying—colleagues in the House or Senate, public opinion in the district, the White House, party leaders—were more important in determining policy. Even those who ascribe considerable power to special interests suggest that that power is wielded subtly or silently, without the intense lobbying activity so common in Washington.

One reason the press and the general public may tend to exaggerate the influence of interest groups is that the news overemphasizes dramatic instances of graft, exploited campaign finance loopholes, or extraordinary pressure exerted on members of Congress by organizations like the National Rifle Association. Successful outside lobbying campaigns and increasingly large campaign contributions due to the reporting of the Federal Election Commission attract attention and are visible manifestations of group power. Inside lobbying in the form of interpersonal contacts, while an everyday occurrence for nearly all interest groups, is harder for the mass media to observe on a regular basis and has more of the flavor of relationship building and coordination among lobbyists and legislators than of outright pressure. Thus, the media fail to report adequately on the effects of inside strategies, and if they were to do so, it would probably bring the popular evaluation of interest group power more into balance.

In contrast, some of the conclusions of political scientists about the muted influence of interest groups may have something to do with the lack of research on outside lobbying. Researchers have tended to focus on inside lobbying, campaign contributions, and especially organizational formation. For each of these subjects, conclusions of researchers have highlighted the limitations of organized interests. Inside lobbying rarely changes legislators' positions on policy issues. Campaign contributions seem to correlate only weakly with legislative or electoral success. And groups are hard to form because of collective action problems. Given all the obstacles interest groups presumably face, one wonders why there are more than seven thousand registered organizations in Washington, and why so many of them spend precious resources trying to influence policymakers. Interest groups work hard to influence legislation, and it is difficult to believe that their money and efforts go to waste.

Part of the problem for political scientists may be that they fail to see the role that outside lobbying serves in enhancing the inside lobbying of interest groups. Interest groups choose lobbying strategies at the same time policymakers are trying to please constituents. Groups thus choose strategies intended to convince policymakers that group goals align with constituent goals. If successfully wielded, these strategies can enable interest group leaders to be quite influential in shaping public policies. While this seems apparent, outside lobbying does not get the attention it deserves in interest group research. Simply put, outside lobbying has rarely been studied systematically. The kinds of interest group activities the mass media tend to highlight are precisely those that political scientists tend to understudy, and the differences in coverage among the two affect conclusions about interest group power. This reading, in attempting to answer three questions—Why do groups use outside lobbying? When does outside lobbying work? Who benefits from outside lobbying?—is an effort to rectify the imbalance in interest group research.

Of course, interest group leaders are not the only ones who find it in their interests to mobilize citizens to pressure American policymakers. Political party leaders, politicians (especially the president), and even newspapers and mass media personalities actively encourage citizens to contact their elected representatives. The question of when it is advantageous in a democracy to mobilize citizens to pressure policymakers is considerably more general than the more specific question of when interest groups should do so. Many of the ideas in this reading about outside lobbying by interest groups should certainly apply to other actors in the political system.

Overview

Outside lobbying is important because it is a common means (perhaps the most common means except for elections) for elite policymakers to experience pressure in the form of popular participation. Were it not for outside lobbying from interest groups, many policy decisions would take place solely among a relatively insulated group of Washington insiders. Instead, interest group leaders call upon people outside of Washington to remind policymakers that a sizable portion of their constituents is paying attention. At least potentially, outside lobbying can pressure policymakers to adopt more popularly supported policies than they would in the absence of outside lobbying.

Outside lobbying accomplishes two tasks simultaneously. First, at the elite level it communicates aspects of public opinion to policymakers. The many forms of outside lobbying—publicizing issue positions, mobilizing constituents to contact Congress, protesting or demonstrating—have the common purpose of trying to show policymakers that the people the group claims to represent really do care about some relevant policy issue. These tactics say, in effect, "See, we told you constituents were angry about policy X, and now you can hear it from them."

I refer to this role for outside lobbying as *signaling* because it has many characteristics of basic signaling models in game theory. An interest group (the sender) tries to signal its popular support (its type) to a policymaker (the receiver). . . . When do the signals sent by interest group leaders actually influence policymakers' behavior?

The noteworthy characteristic of outside lobbying, however, is that it is not just an elite-level phenomenon. It is intended to influence members of the mass public as well. The second role for outside lobbying is to influence public opinion by changing how selected constituents consider and respond to policy issues. I shall call this its *conflict expansion* role in reference to the theoretical legacy of Schattschneider, who wrote in 1960 that the "most important strategy of politics is concerned with the scope of the conflict. . . . Conflicts are frequently won or lost by the success that the contestants have in getting the audience involved in the fight or in excluding it, as the case may be" (3–4). As Schattschneider emphasized, political elites, when faced with intransigent opposition, can bring attention to their cause, invite constituents to participate in the policy process, and hope to swing momentum to their side.

For both of these roles, the salience of policy issues to constituents, an often-overlooked characteristic of public opinion, lies at the center of interest group politics. It is not the popularity of policies that is mostly communicated or altered through outside lobbying. For one, the popularity of policies tends to stay relatively fixed over long periods of time, even given the outside lobbying activities of interest groups. But even more important, policymakers tend to have good information on the popularity of policies, primarily through opinion polls, but also because such popularity stays relatively constant and they can learn about it over time. Salience, however, defined as the relative importance people attach to policy issues, is an aspect of public opinion that policymakers perpetually running for reelection want to know but cannot learn about from ordinary opinion polls and experience. Policymakers want to know what proportion of constituents, when voting in the next election, will weigh the actions of their elected representatives on a particular policy issue. More salient policy issues will weigh more heavily on voting decisions than will less salient policy issues, and policymakers rely to a considerable extent on interest groups for current information on which issues rank high on salience. Because they can mobilize constituents to speak for themselves and can occasionally increase the salience of issues to those constituents, interest group leaders have a comparative advantage in sending credible signals on this precious information.

In sum, interest group leaders can turn their informational and leadership advantages into policy influence. They can try through inside lobbying to convince policymakers that voters care about an issue and are on the side of their group on the issue. But outside lobbying goes a step further in making a costly, public demonstration that, one, the issue is in fact salient to voters and, two, the interest group can make the issue even more salient.

The distinction between the two roles can be quite fuzzy, especially in practice. Consider two analogous situations. An opposition leader in an authoritarian regime wants to hold a large rally in the capital. The rally, if it successfully gathers hundreds of thousands of people as planned, accomplishes the two tasks just specified. It both communicates to the current regime the swelling sentiment among the population that the current regime is offensive *and* coordinates or mobilizes the opposing citizens on a particular course of action: support the opposition leader and work to topple the current government. To the government the rally signals the status of the opposition, and to the citizens in the rally it reinforces the notion that the effort to topple the regime is important and worthy of risky collective action.

Outside lobbying is also similar to the marketing behavior of business entrepreneurs promoting new product ideas to consumers and investors at the same time. Entrepreneurs do their own brand of inside lobbying among investors, hawking their product ideas and wooing support among a small group of people. At the same time, they gauge consumer demand for their products, communicate that level of demand to potential investors, and even try to stimulate more demand among consumers. Success among one audience (consumers) will likely lead to success among the other audience (investors). Just as investors try to assess potential consumer response to the entrepreneur's marketing efforts because future investments will succeed or fail based on consumer behavior, elected officials look to constituents' responses to outside lobbying because reelection efforts may hinge on the interest group success in mobilizing constituents. For interest groups, as with entrepreneurs, there are two audiences in mass marketing, but the overall goals converge because one audience relies very much on the other audience. . . .

The duality of purpose makes outside lobbying a powerful tool in the hands of interest groups. It can simultaneously fan the flames of constituent anger and bring the heat of those flames to the attention of representatives far away, whose job it is to put out or contain the fire. However, while the two roles can get mixed together in practice, there are important conceptual distinctions between them. In the signaling role, the salience of a policy issue must be considered *exogenous* in that there is something fixed and unknown to policymakers about salience that the group claims to be able to demonstrate through outside lobbying. Perhaps it is the potential salience of an issue that interest groups want to communicate. In this case, the "fixed" element of public opinion being communicated is the latent salience of an issue. The group is confident it can expand the conflict to a certain point, and it wants to communicate that confidence through outside lobbying. In the conflict expansion role, the salience of a policy issue is *endogenous*, in that the strategy is intended to influence the very characteristic of public opinion that is being communicated in the signaling role.

▪   ▪   ▪

Communication costs in particular are relevant to the study of outside lobbying because the costs of successful outside lobbying are related systematically to the existing state of public salience on an issue. Precisely because outside lobbying is costly, and the strategies of interest groups conditional on those costs offer clues to the underlying public salience groups are trying to communicate, outside lobbying can influence policymakers. Policymakers learn about salience by making inferences from the revealed efforts of interest groups.

When group leaders are confident they can expand the conflict—raise public awareness of an issue or frame issues in different ways to their advantage—

additional considerations besides the advantages of signaling to policymakers become important. What information should a group present to constituents to convince them the issue is worth costly collective action? When in the course of legislation should conflict expansion happen for maximum impact? How should a group frame the advantages of one policy over another policy? In general, when there are opportunities to expand the conflict, decision making over strategies turns on how potential increases in salience (or sometimes popularity) will benefit interest group goals, rather than on how the current level of popular support will play with policymakers.

As a first cut at understanding conflict expansion, we might think it benefits groups that do not have ready access to policymakers. Much of our understanding of this comes from Schattschneider. Schattschneider believed not only that outsider groups would want to outside lobby, but also that such groups tend to have advantages in the realm of public opinion. According to Schattschneider, "It is the weak who want to socialize conflict, i.e., to involve more and more people in the conflict until the balance of forces is changed" (1960, 40), the assumption being that groups with concentrated wealth or power would eschew politics involving broad popular participation and do not stand to gain from increased salience.

Schattschneider's ideas, however, do not completely square with contemporary interest group politics. In an age when all kinds of organizations, including large corporations, wealthy trade associations, and professional groups outside lobby on policy issues of great concern to millions of Americans, clearly there are times when the strong and those groups with considerable inside access want to expand the scope of the conflict as well. . . .

Two aspects of the policy context that influence outside lobbying are discussed in detail in that chapter: the stage of legislation and the policy alternatives confronting policymakers. The stage of legislation—whether a policy problem is just being introduced to the government or whether well-defined alternatives are being considered by legislators—will have a large effect on both signaling and conflict expansion decisions (Kingdon 1984). In decisions over lobbying strategies or tactics, groups facing policies in earlier stages, when they merely try to raise consciousness on a new policy issue, will be less concerned about popular support for their policy positions than will groups facing policies in later stages, when they fight to swing a few key votes in a congressional committee. The stage of legislation shapes the way public opinion constrains interest group strategies mostly by varying the benefits groups attain in signaling the current salience of an issue versus in trying to increase the salience of that issue or the popularity of specific policies.

Policy alternatives, or more specifically the relative popularity of policy alternatives, matter a great deal because they also determine whether increasing salience is a good idea for a group. What may not be overwhelmingly popular—say, needle exchange programs—may be more popular than the most prominent policy alternative, increased spending on drug rehabilitation programs. Thus, as for influencing outside lobbying decisions, the popularity of policies must be regarded as relative, not absolute, a consideration that carries implications about whether a group benefits from conflict expansion.

■   ■   ■

Most us would presumably like to see outside lobbying coming from groups supporting popular policies on salient issues. Instead, the empirical conclusions of this study are mixed. I find that outside lobbying, contrary to the view that most of it produces phony grass-roots support, is far from artificial. It is actually a good way for policymakers to learn what their constituents care about. My data show that outside lobbying on average works as a policymaker might hope: it communicates fairly accurately the salience of policy issues to large numbers of constituents, and it often influences the salience of policy issues to benefit the more popular side of an issue. At the same time, however, and more often than we would like, outside lobbying springs forth from intense groups pursuing relatively unpopular policies (especially early in the legislative process), and in this regard, it falls somewhat short in reinforcing the majority's preferences. Outside lobbying, in sum, does not distort the policymaking process nearly as much as many people like to claim, but it does a better job in communicating salience information than in bolstering popular pressure for majoritarian policies.

■   ■   ■

TACTICS AND STRATEGIES

The Story of the Hat Trick

One beautiful August morning in 1989, Leona Kozien took the bus from near her home in Chicago to the Copernicus Center for senior citizens on the city's northwest side. Kozien, who was sixty-nine years old, had no idea at the time that she was going to become a brief media star and a figure of political lore. All she knew was that she was angry with the politicians in Washington. In particular, she felt betrayed by her congressman, Dan Rostenkowski, chairman of the Ways and Means Committee of the House of Representatives. Kozien was upset by a new policy from Washington that caused her husband to pay a surtax for catastrophic health care insurance. In her mind, it was an unfair attempt by the federal government to make senior citizens pay unreasonably for health care.

Rostenkowski knew many seniors were angry, but he did not know the extent of the anger. Since the unveiling of the policy a year earlier, a policy that he and the largest seniors lobby, the American Association of Retired Persons (AARP), had sponsored and supported all through the legislative process, he had been reluctant to meet with smaller senior citizens' groups, even those from his own district. National groups separate from the AARP, especially the National Committee to Preserve Social Security and Medicare, run by James Roosevelt, son of President Franklin D. Roosevelt, had been mobilizing grass-roots opposition to the policy for more than a year. The AARP then decided to oppose the new policy. Partly as a concession and partly as a compromise, Rostenkowski had agreed to meet with a few of the leaders of local senior citizens groups. The meeting was held at the Copernicus Center, right in the heart of Rostenkowski's district.

After prodding by her husband (who could not attend), Kozien joined approximately one hundred seniors who waited in the main hall of the center for Rostenkowski to emerge from the meeting with the group leaders. She and other seniors had been given signs to wave at Rostenkowski. The signs indicated displeasure with the current policy: Congressman Rostenkowski, Don't Tax the Seniors and Read My Lips: Catastrophic Act Is a Seniors Tax.

While Rostenkowski met with group leaders, Kozien and her own group were holding a meeting of their own in the main hall. Participants were taking turns telling the rest of the group why the catastrophic health policy was bad for seniors. The group waiting for Rostenkowski agreed that the catastrophic "tax" had to go, but they also agreed on something else. They wanted Rostenkowski to speak to them in person.

"A lot of people felt they were owed something," one local interest group leader recalls. "They just wanted to see him. He was right there, and they felt this was their opportunity [to tell him what they thought of the policy]."

Rostenkowski emerged from his meeting and headed for the exit. The group waiting for him booed and hissed. Before the congressman could get to the door, a television crew stopped him to ask questions about events in Poland, a topic of keen interest to many of his constituents. This pause gave a small group of seniors enough time to run out of the building and surround Rostenkowski's car. Kozien led the charge.

Kozien shouted, "Where's his car parked? I'm going to make him talk to us!"

A small mob followed Kozien outside, and pretty soon there were fifteen to twenty seniors surrounding the congressman's car, while television crews stood nearby. Rostenkowski, meanwhile, fought through the crowd and got in the car.

"Coward!" "Shame!" "Impeach Rottenkowski!" The seniors stood in front of the car and waved placards. The congressman's driver honked the horn and moved the car a few inches. The front bumper brushed against Kozien's thigh, and she staggered a bit. Some man shouted, "You knocked her down! You hurt her!" This same man then turned to Kozien and said quietly, "Lay down under the car."

"Are you crazy? No way, he'd run me over!" retorted Kozien, who was barely over five feet tall. The car moved again, and this time Kozien fell on the hood of the car. Her face was inches from Rostenkowski's, with glass separating them. She was still carrying her placard, and from inside the car, Rostenkowski saw her placard, her face, and her body sprawled across the windshield.

"Killer! Killer!" the crowd shouted.

Rostenkowski then got out of the car and ran through a parking lot while angry seniors chased after him. The driver maneuvered through the crowd, drove around the block, and caught up with Rostenkowski down the street from the center. Rostenkowski jumped in, and the car sped off.

"It was a funny picture," recalled one local politician present, "because it was a true chase. The seniors would move faster, and Rosty would move faster. He gets in the car, and they stand in front of the car."

The scene made for dramatic television. The Chicago film crews, delighted with the footage, distributed it immediately to the national networks. All three major television news shows carried the story prominently that evening, earning the interest group leaders what they call "a hat trick," in reference to a hockey player scoring three goals in one game.

Kozien, meanwhile, the activist and agitator for that day, was an unlikely hero. She had never before been active in politics. She knew little about the seniors groups at the Copernicus Center. Her relatives called that evening, expressing amazement at their "crazy Aunt Leona." Over the next several years politicians, prior to speaking at senior citizen events, would ask her to accompany them onstage. She always refused.

She likewise downplayed her heroism. "We just wanted answers. Had he answered our questions, there would have been no incident." Yet the incident was a bonanza for the leaders of the interest groups. The image of Kozien on the hood of Rostenkowski's car was used for years afterward on network news to symbolize the potency of the senior citizen lobby.

The catastrophic insurance program, which had passed the House in June 1988 by a vote of 328 to 72, was soon after repealed. The vote was not even close. The House voted 360 to 66 in favor of repeal in October 1989. Incidentally, Rostenkowski stood firm, voting to oppose repeal.

Many members of Congress had heard from people like Kozien, though presumably not from atop the hoods of their cars. Two Florida legislators reported getting more than seventy-five thousand pieces of mail, each opposing the policy. One staffer reported to me that his boss received more than two thousand mail pieces in favor of repeal, and eight mail pieces against repeal. The turn of events on catastrophic health insurance had people shaking their heads.

To some, the outside lobbying gave a large voice to a small number of people. "It was a case of the House of Representatives being stampeded by a small, vocal group of seniors," said Pete Stark, a Democratic congressman from California. "Ambushed is how a lot of people here feel now," Tim Penny, a Democrat from Minnesota, said at the time. "Every member of Congress was getting accosted at town meetings," said Senator John McCain, Republican from Arizona.

Others were more positive about the outcome, preferring to think that the outside lobbying tapped into a widespread sentiment. "We made a mistake last year [in 1988]," said Brian Donnelly, a Democratic congressman from Massachusetts. "This time, we listened to the voters."

Significance of the Story

The story of the Rostenkowski incident in north Chicago, while hardly typical of stories of outside lobbying, is useful for several reasons. For one, it shows in dramatic fashion how interest groups can instigate or facilitate collective action through outside lobbying. Contrary to what interest group leaders were claiming afterward, the mobbing of Rostenkowski was not all that spontaneous. The meeting between Rostenkowski and the interest group leaders was set up by the interest group leaders, and seniors from around the neighborhood were encouraged to attend by the interest group leaders. The interest groups leaders, not Rostenkowski's staff, had invited the networks to the meetings at the Copernicus Center. Rostenkowski's staff wanted to avoid media attention. And the interest group leaders made the placards and distributed them to Kozien and other seniors.

Interest group leaders also knew that the seniors attending were unusually angry about the new policy, and the leaders wanted to communicate that anger forcefully and make it seem less than fully staged. The seniors at the Copernicus Center were to represent the tip of the iceberg of constituent opinion. As for the seniors, their reactions could not have been better for the group leaders. The leaders provided a small, low-cost spark and let it turn into a conflagration. The behavior of Kozien and others was spontaneous and chaotic enough to indicate that the seniors were just plain mad. After all the preparations, events got out of control at the right time and at the right level. "Just barely out of control" might be the optimum level of behavioral response interest group leaders want from constituents in an outside lobbying campaign.

Therefore, what was communicated loudly and clearly to policymakers was the ease with which interest group leaders mobilized Kozien and her fellow seniors. The low costs involved for the interest groups to get hundreds of seniors to stampede the car of a powerful committee chairman counted for much more than the stampede itself. In trying to signal the "true" level of public salience over an issue, an interest group that succeeds with little effort can gain credibility. I shall discuss this important point in more detail in the next chapter.

Most of the conflict expansion on the issue had occurred well before that fateful day. National seniors organizations like the Gray Panthers and the National Committee to Preserve Social Security and Medicare had been running advertisements for months, and they had successfully framed the issue as one of unfair taxation for all seniors as opposed to one of health care benefits for a vast majority of seniors. By one reasonable interpretation, through the summer of 1989 interest groups had increased the level of salience among seniors on the issue. Then, as the salience of the issue peaked in late summer, interest group leaders had only to signal to policymakers the salience of the issue among those seniors who opposed the new policy. The Rostenkowski incident was timed perfectly. The conflict had been expanded, and the time had come to let policymakers know about it.

The story also neatly illustrates the roles assumed by the main players described in the previous chapter. Interest group leaders, the ones who had invited people like Kozien in the first place, set the stage for the famous confrontation (though they got lucky when it succeeded beyond their expectations). A policymaker, in this case a powerful House committee chairman, found himself the target of outside lobbying efforts by interest group leaders and constituents. And the ordinary constituents like Kozien, who behaved in both an organized and disorganized manner, made the lives of policymakers more difficult through simple expressions of anger.

The story is useful as well for highlighting the potential influence of outside lobbying. The renegade senior citizens groups, those distinguishing themselves early on from the AARP on the catastrophic health care policy, appear to have had an effect on Rostenkowski's colleagues in the House. As Table 1 indicates, 240 members of the House switched their votes from supporting catastrophic coverage in June 1988 to supporting repeal of catastrophic coverage sixteen months later. This is a remarkable instance of collective reconsideration. Only 124 members, or approximately half of the number that switched votes, voted the "same" way for both bills—that is, 124 either voted against the original bill and for repeal, or they voted for the original bill and against repeal. The latter vote, on the amendment to repeal the Catastrophic Coverage Act, was the first time Congress had ever voted to repeal a major social benefit it had created.

"An event of about 150 elderly people changed the tide of the thing," recalled Jan Schakowsky, at the time a leader of the Illinois State Council of Senior Citizens, one of the groups that mobilized seniors on that day. "It was a pivotal event." It was pivotal not because it changed Rostenkowski's mind (which it

TABLE 1 Reconsidering Catastrophic Health Insurance: Number of Members of the House of Representatives Voting For or Against Original Bill and Repeal

	Original Bill	
Repeal	*Yea*	*Nay*
Yea	240	64
Nay	60	1

NOTE: This takes into account turnover from the 100th to 101st Congress, in that only members who voted on both bills are included. One member, Larry Hopkins, a Republican from Kentucky, voted against the original proposal and against repeal. The original bill was HR 2470, Catastrophic Health Insurance/Rule. The repeal was HR 3299, Amendment to Budget Reconciliation, Repealing Catastrophic Health Insurance Surtax.

did not), but because it had such an influence on his colleagues. As the story and its aftermath remind us, a well-publicized event among a small number of people can send very strong signals about, and enhance the reputation of, a group numbering many thousands or even millions of people. More than five years later, members of Congress referred to the Rostenkowski incident as cementing the reputation of the senior citizens lobby. This, according to people in Washington who are inclined to slight hyperbole, is one group in the population they do not want to cross.

Another revealing aspect of the story is that the Rostenkowski event happened because of a grave miscalculation on the part of the chairman and his colleagues. They enacted the original policy because they were led to believe that seniors were behind it, but they gambled and lost when interest groups tapped into a undiscovered level of antipathy among certain groups of seniors.[1] In general, legislators try to estimate the policy preferences and issue salience among their constituents, yet these estimates are shots in the dark on many controversial issues. They never know how some groups will respond, or which issues their next electoral opponent will use against them. They need to do the near impossible: anticipate how latent constituent opinion will manifest itself in the coming years. Rostenkowski was probably warned when he led his committee to recommend the original policy. Like anyone facing a difficult decision, however, he listened to the people who had previously established a credible reputation for electoral power, the AARP. Yet until Kozien and her fellow seniors let him know loudly and clearly their preferences, he could not have been certain about the consequences of his previous actions. The response among seniors led Rostenkowski and other policymakers to move toward repeal.

The Rostenkowski story is unusual, of course. Rarely are outside lobbying efforts as successful. Famous examples, such as this one, become lore around the Capitol. Another example from the early 1980s still generates discussion around Washington. During the successful outside lobbying efforts in 1982 by the American Bankers Association to repeal tax withholding from interest-bearing accounts, 22 million postcards from depositors flooded into Congress within days of the passage of the tax bill containing the provision. Every congressional district responded, according to the staff of Robert Dole, the chair of the Senate Finance Committee at the time. The marvel is that bankers, of all people, were able to make an issue more salient through conflict expansion, and at the same time were able to signal that salience to policymakers with a successful outside lobbying campaign. They did all of this without hiding their identities as bankers, indicating that latent salience among constituents is a great resource for all groups, not just for those with popular images or credibility as electoral powerhouses.

NOTE

1. In truth, even the AARP was caught off guard. Dissident elderly groups, those opposed to the policy all along, began stirring opposition until the AARP changed its policy on the issue. Then, once the AARP was opposed to the policy, it galvanized further action by the dissident elderly groups.

BIBLIOGRAPHY

Key, V. O. 1961. *Public Opinion and American Democracy.* New York: Alfred Knopf.

Kingdon, John. 1984. *Agendas, Alternatives, and Public Policies.* Boston: Little, Brown.

Schattschneider, E. E. 1960. *The Semi-Sovereign People.* Hinsdale, Illinois: Dryden Press.

11.3

KATHERINE CRAMER WALSH

From *Talking about Race: Community Dialogues and the Politics of Difference*

Conflict among racial and ethnic groups has bedeviled communities in the United States for a long time. In many cities around the United States, city governments have instituted intergroup dialogues, which are forums for people to share their concerns about problems related to, among other things, interracial tension and lost opportunities for cooperation. Walsh summarizes her study of these intergroup dialogues and concludes that these groups have been effective at leading to practical solutions worked out after fruitful periods when people have been able to talk with each other in respectful, if at times tense, settings. This reading provides a revealing look at settings where interest groups can interact with the intention of settling differences.

CHOOSING THE ACTION OF TALK

Communities across the United States . . . turn to intergroup dialogue programs on race out of a need to pursue social justice as well as, if not more than, out of a desire to foster individual self-actualization. . . .

If people are intent on promoting social justice, it is a bit of a mystery why they pursue civic dialogue as a strategy. The politics of unity would predict that instead of *talking* about race relations, people would choose to build bridging social capital by working together on a common project, in a cooperative, not combative, fashion.[1] Talking about conflict directly might exacerbate tensions, but working on a common project supposedly diverts attention away from conflict.

Pursuing talk about race is also a bit of a mystery because public talk is not easy.[2] It seems antithetical to most Americans' preference for democracy that requires only their occasional interest, not their active participation,[3] and it seems contrary to the widespread desire to avoid conflict[4] and conversation with people who hold opposing political opinions.[5] More to the point, public talk *particularly about race* is notoriously difficult. It runs the risk of dwelling on one's own role in perpetuating intergroup conflict and discrimination. It has the potential to bring painful memories to the surface. It also creates a space for people to say out loud damaging stereotypes—thereby possibly legitimating racist talk.[6] Many people seem to prefer to avoid the topic of race because "the issue is simply too complex and painful.[7]

■   ■   ■

This [reading] examines why individuals choose to implement dialogue groups and analyzes what their reasons suggest about the functions and uses of such groups. . . .

I . . . pay attention to this . . . little understood dimension—the meaning people in particular social settings ascribe to their political actions. We value public talk as the enactment of public life, but what do people *mean* by it? . . . The purpose . . . is not to reveal what actually causes people to pursue intergroup dialogue programs but to understand and give coherence to the explanations people offer for pursuing this form of public talk. I listen to the reasons people give and take these reasons for what they are—subjective understandings of oneself and the value of a particular action.[8] The reasons people give for their actions—their "vocabularies of motive"—reveal what is meaningful to them. They can therefore help us understand what active citizens believe are sufficient justifications for public talk and therefore help us make sense of a surprising form of political action that is valued in democracies but little understood.

There are a variety of common assumptions about the choice to pursue talk as a strategy for addressing public problems. . . . For one, it is commonly assumed that dialogue fills a higher-order individual need such as self-development or self-actualization. Talk that emphasizes listening is perceived as "touchy-feely" or "therapeutic." Second, interracial dialogue about race is expected to be multiculturalist, reifying subgroup categories over the common good, and is expected to be promoted particularly by intellectuals. Third, insofar as talk is justified as a form of action, it is a way to appease people, a kind of compromise, a strategy that people rely on because no others are feasible. Listening as action is widely perceived as not radical or intended to bring about social justice, but as passive. Fourth, if dialogue is explained as related to political action, it is used as a way to forge common ground, a common identity, or shared concerns, or another form of unity in the sense of similarity. Finally, we expect that people pursue talk as a means of addressing public problems when the situation is amenable to talk—when it is not adversarial or saturated with long-standing conflicts.[9] And if it is implemented in order to contest the status quo, we expect it to be pursued by activists, not government employees.

. . . I interviewed fifty-five state and local government officials and nonprofit organization employees in thirty-eight medium-sized Census-designated central cities, and ten such people in nine larger metropolitan areas. . . . They were selected to represent medium-sized cities in states throughout the continental United States, and represent programs that vary in type (i.e., SCRC, Honest Conversations, etc.), government sponsorship, and racial heterogeneity of the population. . . .

I use various labels to refer to the interviewees. I use the term "practitioner" to refer to people who were administrating dialogue programs, regardless of whether they were employed by an NGO or a government. To refer to employees of NGOs, I use the term "activist" or "NGO administrator." I use the term "public official" to refer to government employees and elected officials. (I specify when I am referring specifically to nonelected government employees or to elected officials.) Of the sixty-five people interviewed, five were elected officials, twenty-three were government employees but not elected officials (including four police officers), and thirty-seven were volunteers or employees of nongovernmental organizations.

▪ ▪ ▪

Dialogue as a Way to Be Who They Are

Why do people choose to improve race relations through intergroup dialogue programs? The reasons I encountered . . . stress the role of personal history and a perspective on civic life that values relationships and stresses dialogue as a necessary complement to other forms of action. . . . [T]heories of dialogue challenge many scholars' conceptions of the place of talk in everyday democracy.

For one thing, practitioners' conceptions do not suggest that listening-focused talk is primarily about self-development or self-actualization. They talk about it as serving a political function: action. They tend not to talk about it as a passive action, a compromise strategy, or a strategy they turned to because they knew it would pass approval. Instead, they treat it as an integral component of eliminating racism, attaining racial equality, and doing their jobs. Many practitioners rooted their conceptions in a lifetime of concern with social justice in which talk and action were intertwined.

These conceptions have credibility because if these practitioners were pursuing this talk as primarily a means of self-development, postmaterialist theory suggests that they would readily say so. Postmaterialism holds that people *value* self-development and self-actualization. Therefore, if postmaterialism were at work, social desirability would bias their remarks in favor of emphasizing self-actualization.

Although many practitioners talked about recognizing difference as an essential part of moving their communities forward, their words and behaviors seldom fit the common stereotypes of multiculturalism. . . . [P]ublic opinion research suggests that multiculturalism is supported by only a small portion of the public, feeding claims that privileging racial group differences is elitist. But it would be incorrect to say that civic dialogue is a function of just a fringe element in these communities. It is true that just a small minority of people in a given community participate in these programs (with a few rare exceptions).[10] However, the rosters of people involved do not support the idea that this form of public talk is pursued by people with extremist political agendas. Participants include elected officials, city government department heads, government employees, fire and safety officials, librarians, public school teachers, local business leaders, maintenance workers, retirees, full-time parents, and other ordinary citizens. Moreover, even those who assert the most intense injunctions to focus on difference commonly also talked about the need to identify similarities.

And contrary to some treatments, the perceptions among people conducting dialogue do not support the idea that contexts have to be sufficiently unitary, in the sense of consensus over interests, for public talk to be feasible.[11] The question that concerns these practitioners is not whether we have enough in common or sufficient friendship for *deliberation* to work, but whether or not we have the right kind of communication in place for *democracy* to work.

Also, the justifications for the choice to engage in dialogue that center on the necessity of dealing with conflict stand in contrast to prescriptions of contact hypothesis research that fruitful intergroup contact involves working on common projects together in a noncompetitive manner. Dialogue practitioners suggest that if the people who are attempting to forge productive relationships are embedded in a context of longstanding conflict, people need to confront that conflict head-on, not avoid it.[12]

Finally, it is not just activists who advocate contestation. We see it among government employees, and even elected officials. The way these officials as well as NGO practitioners are conceptualizing talk is at odds with a belief that when public talk is used to contest the status quo, public officials will distance themselves from it.

As a practical answer to the challenges these people face in doing their jobs and improving race relations, their conceptions of these programs reveal some weaknesses. In some contexts, it seems that dialogue was allowed because it was perceived to be innocuous. Others explicitly say that they do not wish for it to be connected to action. And yet others talk about wanting to focus specifically on race, implying that attention to related issues such as immigration detracts from the job they perceive they need to do.

■   ■   ■

Nelson, Kaboolian, and Carver propose an "investment theory" of collective action to explain the emergence of concord organizations. In contrast to conventional conceptions of collective action, in which actors' choices are understood as a function of a cost-benefit analysis, they find that individuals behaved as though they were investors. The "goods" involved seemed to be values-based rather than economics-based; the conflicts were about identities and beliefs, and thus were not solvable by dividing up the goods among the groups in conflict. Instead, what people valued was watching the relationships and the trust they established through their investment ripple out to positively influence community life and future conflicts.

The interviews and site visits I conducted support many of the claims of this investment theory. People who founded programs in their communities often did conceptualize the need for dialogue as arising from values-based conflicts. They simultaneously had concerns with economic, social, and political inequality alongside a perception that fundamental intergroup misunderstandings needed to be resolved. No one emphasized economic benefits over social ones, and no one expected dialogue would be a quick remedy. Many expected—and believed that they achieved—ripple effects in the sense that graduates from the program would behave differently. They expected participants would use their newfound courage to stop everyday discriminatory behavior, such as racist jokes and discrimination in workplace hiring practices.

However, one aspect of practitioners' explanations for why they chose to do this work is not encompassed by the investment theory. When people explained their involvement, they did not describe it as a choice, or as one alternative among many in which they decided to invest their resources. They talked about it as the obvious thing to do. They explained it as a necessary part of *any* action toward improved race relations or social justice.

NOTES

1. For example, see David. W. Johnson, Roger Johnson, and Geoffrey Maruyama, "Goal Interdependence and Interpersonal Attraction in Heterogeneous Classrooms," In *Groups in Contact: The Psychology of Desegregation*, ed. Norman Miller and Marilyn B. Brewer (Orlando: Academic Press, 1984).

2. As David Ryfe notes, "an insight . . . is slowly becoming apparent in the broader literature on the practice of deliberative democracy, namely that deliberation is hard work: it is not easily undertaken, and once undertaken, it is not easily pursued" ("Narrative and Deliberation in Small Group Forums," *Journal of Applied Communication Research* 34 (2006): 73). See also Molly Patterson, "Structuration and Deliberation: A Theory of Power for Deliberative Democracy," paper presented to the Midwest Political Science Association, Chicago, April 7–10, 2005.

3. John Hibbing and Elizabeth Theiss-Morse, *Stealth Democracy: Americans' Belief about How Government Should Work* (Cambridge: Cambridge University Press, 2002).

4. Nina Eliasoph, *Avoiding Politics: How Americans Produce Apathy in Everyday Life* (Cambridge: Cambridge University Press, 1998); Jane Mansbridge, *Beyond Adversary Democracy* (Chicago: University of Chicago Press, 1983), chap. 6; Hibbing and Theiss-Morse, *Stealth Democracy*.

5. Diana Mutz and Paula Martin, "Facilitating Communication Across Lines of Difference," *American Political Science Review* 95 (2005); Paul Beck, "Voters' Intermediation Environments in the 1988 Presidential Contest," *Public Opinion Quarterly* 55 (1991); see also Mutz, "Cross-Cutting Social Networks: Testing Democratic Theory in Practice," *American Political Science Review* 96 (2002); Stacy Ulbig and Carolyn Funk, "Conflict Avoidance and Political Participation," *Political Behavior* 21 (1999). People also appear to interact with people whom they believe have similar political leanings (Robert Huckfeldt and John Sprague, *Citizens, Politics, and Social Communication: Information and Influence in an Election Campaign* [Cambridge: Cambridge University Press, 1995], 135–136),

and the pool of potential discussion partners is influenced by lifestyle choices that are themselves associated with political preferences (Mutz, *Hearing the Other Side: Deliberative versus Participatory Democracy* [Cambridge: Cambridge University Press], 44–48).

6. Lawrie Balfour, "'A Most Disagreeable Mirror': Race Consciousness as Double Consciousness," *Political Theory* 26 (1998): 366n; see also Kimberlé Crenshaw, "Color-blind Dreams and Racial Nightmares: Reconfiguring Racism in the Post–Civil Rights Era," in *Birth of a Nation 'hood: Gaze, Script, and Spectacle in the O.J. Simpson Case*, ed. Toni Morrison and Claudia Brodsky Lacour (New York: Pantheon, 1997).

7. Richard Merelman, "The Mundane Experience of Political Culture," *Political Communication* 15 (1998): 529.

8. C. Wright Mills, "Situated Actions and Vocabularies of Motive," *American Sociological Review* 5 (1940).

9. Jane Mansbridge, *Beyond Adversary Democracy* (Chicago: Chicago University Press, 1983).

10. For example, a study circles program in Lima, Ohio, has reportedly involved over 5,000 people, or 12.5 percent of the 2000 Census population. Matt Leighninger, "How Have Study Circles Made an Impact? Organizers Report on Their Successes," *Focus*, Fall 2000.

11. Mansbridge, *Beyond Adversary Democracy*.

12. See also Mohammed Abu-Nimer, *Dialogue, Confict Resolution, and Change: Arab-Jewish Encounters in Israel* (Albany: State University of New York Press, 1999).

BIBLIOGRAPHY

Abu-Nimer, Mohammed. *Dialogue, Conflict Resolution, and Change: Arab-Jewish Encounters in Israel*. Albany: State University of New York Press, 1999.

Balfour, Lawrie. "'A Most Disagreeable Mirror': Race Consciousness as Double Consciousness." *Political Theory* 26 (1998): 346–69.

Beck, Paul Allen. "Voters' Intermediation Environments in the 1988 Presidential Contest." *Public Opinion Quarterly* 55 (1991): 371–94.

Crenshaw, Kimberlé Williams. "Color-blind Dreams and Racial Nightmares: Reconfiguring Racism in the Post-Civil Rights Era." In *Birth of a Nation 'hood: Gaze, script, and Spectacle in the O.J. Simpson Case*, edited by Toni Morrison and Claudia Brodsky Lacour, 97–168. New York: Pantheon, 1997.

Eliasoph, Nina. *Avoiding Politics: How Americans Produce Apathy in Everyday Life*. Cambridge: Cambridge University Press, 1998.

Hibbing, John R., and Elizabeth Theiss-Morse. *Stealth Democracy: Americans' Beliefs about How Government Should Work*. Cambridge: Cambridge University Press, 2002.

Huckfeldt, Robert, and John Sprague. *Citizens, Politics, and Social Communication: Information and Influence in an Election Campaign*. Cambridge: Cambridge University Press, 1995.

Johnson, David W., Roger Johnson, and Geoffrey Maruyama. "Goal Interdependence and Interpersonal Attraction in Heterogeneous Classrooms: A Metanalysis." In *Groups in Contact: The Psychology of Desegregation*, edited by Norman Miller and Marilynn B. Brewer, 187–212. Orlando: Academic Press. 1984.

Leighninger, Matt. "How Have Study Circles Made an Impact? Organizers Report on Their Successes." *FOCUS*, Fall 2000.

Mansbridge, Jane J. *Beyond Adversary Democracy.* Reprint with new preface. Chicago: University of Chicago Press, 1983.

Merelman, Richard M. "The Mundane Experience of Political Culture." *Political Communication* 15 (1998): 515–35.

Mills, C. Wright. "Situated Actions and Vocabularies of Motive." *American Sociological Review* 5 (1940): 904–13.

Mutz, Diana C. "Cross-Cutting Social Networks: Testing Democratic Theory in Practice." *American Political Science Review* 96 (2002): 111–26.

———. *Hearing the Other Side: Deliberative versus Participatory Democracy.* Cambridge: Cambridge University Press.

Mutz, Diana C., and Paul S. Martin. "Facilitating Communication Across Lines of Difference: The Role of Mass Media." *American Political Science Review* 95 (2001): 97–114.

Patterson, Molly A. "Structuration and Deliberation: A Theory of Power for Deliberative Democracy." Paper presented to the annual meetings of the Midwest Political Science Association, Chicago, April 7–10, 2005.

Ryfe, David M. "Narrative and Deliberation in Small Group Forums." *Journal of Applied Communication Research* 34 (2006): 72—93.

Ulbig, Stacy G., and Carolyn L. Funk. "Conflict Avoidance and Political Participation." *Political Behavior* 21 (1999): 265–82.

12

POLITICAL PARTIES

12.1

JOHN H. ALDRICH

From *Why Parties? The Origin and*
Transformation of Party Politics in America

Political parties are multifaceted organizations, and scholars have struggled to
describe them and their functions in ways that make sense across eras and
across countries. In this important piece Aldrich writes that, above all, parties are
designed to serve the needs of ambitious politicians seeking public office. Accord-
ing to Aldrich, parties have to be understood as solutions to a variety of collec-
tive dilemmas. Parties help government officials coordinate their actions so they
can make public policy, they help candidates coordinate their behavior to win
office, and they help voters overcome their collective action problems during
elections.

POLITICS AND PARTIES IN AMERICA

... My basic argument is that the major political party is the creature of the
politicians, the ambitious office seeker and officeholder. They have created and
maintained, used or abuse, reformed or ignored the political party when doing
so has furthered their goals and ambitions. The political party is thus ... an
institution shaped by these political actors. Whatever its strength or weakness,
whatever its form and role, it is the ambitious politicians' creation. These politicians do not have partisan goals per se. Rather, they have more fundamental
goals, and the party is only the instrument for achieving them. Their goals are
several and come in various combinations. Following Richard Fenno (1973),
they include most basically the desire to have a long and successful career in

political office, but they also encompass the desire to achieve policy ends and to attain power and prestige within the government. These goals are to be sought in government, not in parties, but they are goals that at times have best been realized *through* the parties.

Ambitious politicians turn to the political party to achieve such goals only when parties are useful vehicles for solving problems that cannot be solved as effectively, if at all, through other means. Thus I believe that the political party must be understood not only in relation to the goals of the actors most consequential for parties, but also only in relation to the electoral, legislative, and executive institutions of the government. Fiorina was correct: only given our institutions can we understand political parties.

The third major force shaping the political party is the historical setting. Technological changes, for instance, have made campaigning for office today vastly different than it was only a few decades ago, let alone in the nineteenth century. Such changes have had great consequences for political parties. In the nineteenth century, political parties were the only feasible means for organizing mass elections. Today television, air travel, and the computer allow an individual member of Congress to create a personal, continuing campaign organization, something that was technologically impossible a century ago. There is more to the historical context than technology, of course.

Normative understandings have changed greatly. Even Ronald Reagan, who claimed that "government is not the solution to our problems, government *is* the problem," also held to the value of a "social safety net" provided by the government that is far larger than even the most progressive politician of the nineteenth century could have imagined. Ideas, in short, matter a great deal. Founders had to overcome antipathy verging on disgust over the very idea of political parties in order to create them in the first place, and Martin Van Buren's ideas about the nature and value of the "modern mass party" greatly shaped the nature of Jacksonian democracy and political parties generally for at least a century.

History matters in yet another way, beyond the ideas, values, and technological possibilities available at any given historical moment. The path of development matters as well. Some call the partisan alignment—realignment path the fundamental dynamic of American political history (albeit perhaps in the past tense). Once a set of institutional arrangements is in place, the set of equilibrium possibilities is greatly reduced, and change from the existing equilibrium path to a new and possibly superior one may be difficult or impossible. In other words, that there are now two major parties induces incentives for ambitious politicians to affiliate with one party or the other, and some of these incentives emerge only because of the prior existence of these two parties.

The combination of these three forces means that the fundamental syllogism for the theory of political parties to be offered here is just what Rohde and Shepsle (1978) originally offered as the basis for the rational-choice-based new institutionalism: political outcomes—here political parties—result from actors' seeking to realize their goals, choosing within and possibly shaping a given set of institutional arrangements, and so choosing within a given historical context.

■   ■   ■

Previous Approaches to the Study of American Political Parties

Parties as diverse coalitions

There are three basic views or understandings of major political parties in America.[1] The first is most often associated with V. O. Key Jr. (e.g., 1964), Frank Sorauf (1964; now Beck and Sorauf 1991), Samuel Eldersveld (1964, 1982), and others. The major American party, to them, is a broad and encompassing organization, a coalition of many and diverse partners, that is commonly called umbrella-like. In seeking to appeal to a majority of the public, the two parties are based on similar values, roughly defining the "American creed." McClosky (1969) said of political (which is to say partisan) elites, "The evidence suggests that it is the [political elites] rather than the public who serve as the major repositories of the public conscience and as the carriers of the Creed. Responsibility for keeping the system going, hence, falls most heavily upon them" (p. 286). His basic finding was that such elites share most elements of this "creed."

On many policy issues, however, there are clear and sometimes sharply drawn lines between the two parties. What Benjamin I. Page (1978) referred to as "partisan cleavages" are possible, even likely.

■   ■   ■

Each party is a coalition of many and diverse groups. This is most evident in the New Deal coalition Roosevelt forged in creating a working Democratic majority in the 1930s. It consisted of the then solid South, cities, immigrants, blacks, ethnic and religious groups of many types, the working class and unions, and so on. Over half a century later this "coalition of minorities" has frayed considerably; some parts of it have exited from the coalition entirely, and the remnants are no longer capable of reaching majority size in presidential elections. Although some elements have left entirely or their loyalties have weakened, they have been replaced by others. For example, the Democratic coalition may no longer be home to as much of the South or as many blue-collar voters, but teachers' unions, women's groups, and organizations representing blacks, Hispanics, gays, environmentalists, and many others have been added since the 1960s to the panoply of voices seeking to be heard at their national convention. The Republican party may once have been defined more easily by what wasn't included in the New Deal coalition, but it too has attracted a range of groups and interests. At Republican conventions one can find both Wall Street and Main Street fiscal conservatives, westerners who seek to remove government interference in their lives (and lands), and social conservatives, such as pro-life groups, fundamentalist Christians, and so on, who seek active government intervention in behalf of their central concerns.

Although there are good reasons why these groups are allied with their particular party, there is still great diversity within each party. There are even apparent contradictions latent—and at critical moments active—within each party. Blacks and white southerners may have found alliance comfortable when both were so deeply affected by the depression; but when civil rights made it onto the agenda, the latent tensions in their respective views become active and divisive. Recent Republican conventions may have been noncontroversial, but "yuppies," fundamentalists, Main Street business leaders, or others may well find that latent disagreements will become just as divisive when circumstances and the political agenda change—as their 1992 convention perhaps foreshadows.

In this view James Madison was correct. There is no small set of fixed interests; there are, rather, many and diverse interests in this extended Republic. He argued that a fundamental advantage of the new Constitution in creating a stronger federation was that the most evident and serious concern about majority rule—that a cohesive majority could tyrannize any minority—would be alleviated because there could be no cohesive majority in an extended republic. So too could no political party, no matter how large, rule tyrannically, because it must also be too diverse.

In a truly diverse republic, the problem is the opposite of majority tyranny. The problem is how to form *any* majority capable of taking action to solve pressing problems. A major political party, then, aggregates these many and varied interests sufficiently to appeal to enough voters to form a majority in elections and to forge partisan-based, majority coalitions in government. In this view, parties are intermediaries that connect the public and the government. Parties also aggregate these diverse interests into a relatively cohesive, if typically compromise, platform,[2] and they articulate these varied interests by representing them in government. The result, in this view, is that parties parlay those compromise positions into policy outcomes, and so they—a ruling, if nonhomogeneous and shifting, government majority—can be held accountable to the public in subsequent elections.

■   ■   ■

The responsible party thesis

The second view of parties is tighter. Instead of a theory of what actually is, it is a doctrine—that of responsible parties—and is thus inherently normative. No one believes that American parties are consistent with the responsible party thesis, except on rare occasions. But the doctrine is more than a lament about what it would be nice to have; it is also an ideal type or standard by which to measure the adequacy and strength of the major political parties at any given time. Their thesis is most directly associated with E. E. Schattschneider (1942) and the Committee for a more Responsible Two-Party System, sponsored by the American Political Science Association, that he chaired (1950). But this view has deeper historical roots. Woodrow Wilson's *Congressional Government* (1881), for example, included a plea for parties more in the responsible party mold, and as Ranney (1975) and Epstein (1986) report, prominent political scientists at the turn of the century were much enamored of this doctrine.

Ranney (1975, p. 43) lists four criteria that define responsible parties. Such parties: (1) make policy commitments to the electorate; (2) are willing and able to carry them out when in office; (3) develop alternatives to government policies when out of office; and (4) differ sufficiently between themselves to "provide the electorate with a proper range of choice between alternative actions."[3] This doctrine derives from an idealized (and more closely realized) form of the British system, what Lijphart (1984) calls the "Westminster model." As a normative standard, it has several obvious defects. For example, it reduces choices for the public to exactly two. If the United States is a diverse and extended Madisonian republic, it is not obvious that the public would find its views as adequately articulated by exactly two options, no matter how clear and distinct. A mélange of compromise proposals may be more suitable. Alternation of parties in office may also make policy trajectories shift dramatically back and forth. And if one party does capture a longtime working majority, majority tyranny could follow. This is a normative standard that thus places great weight on the accountability of elected officials, through their party's control of office, and less weight on interest articulation. In more practical terms, it is an idealization that fits more readily with a unified, essentially unicameral assembly that combines the legislative and executive branches and that is elected all at once. It fits more poorly with a government designed around the principles of separated but intermingled powers, with officials elected at different times from differently defined constituencies for the Madisonian purpose of making ambition check ambition.

■   ■   ■

When the parties' candidates do address issues, it is often felt, they are too similar. The parties are at times like Tweedledum and Tweedledee, or as George Wallace claimed in his third-party presidential campaign in 1968, "there ain't a dime's worth of difference" between them. It was not always so. In other eras parties were stronger, and they were stronger in the sense of responsible parties. At the very least they were sufficiently united in office to "be willing and able to carry out" whatever policy commitments the majority party chose. They may not have been truly responsible parties, consistent with that doctrine, but they once were stronger, more effective, and more easily held accountable. Perhaps they can be again.

■ ■ ■

Parties and electoral competition

The third view of parties focuses on the importance of this competition for office. Of course both earlier views also saw electoral competition as a central characteristic of partisan politics. But this third view sees competition for office as the singular, defining characteristic of the major American political party. The most rigorous advocates of this position are Anthony Downs (1957) and Joseph A. Schlesinger (1991; see also Demsetz 1990). Both are rational choice theorists, positing that actors are goal seekers and that their actions, and eventually the institutional arrangements they help shape, are the product of their attempts to realize their goals. At the center of their theory are the partisan elites, the aspiring office seekers and the successful officeholders. Their theories rest, moreover, on a simple assumption about the goal of each such partisan elite; office seeking and holding per se. That is, party leaders are motivated to win elections. As a result a party is, in the words of Downs (1957, p. 25), "a team seeking to control the governing apparatus by gaining office in a duly constituted election." The political party therefore is the organization that team uses to realize its goals. Electoral victory is paramount; other motives are at most secondary. Most important, as Downs puts it, parties formulate policies to win elections rather than winning elections to promulgate policies. In a two-party system, the "health" of the system is measured by how competitive the two parties are for a wide range of elective offices over a long period. As we will see below, Schlesinger (1991) argues strongly against the decline of parties thesis precisely because the two parties are capable of competing effectively for so many offices in every region. The hallmark of a party, in his view, is its ability to channel the competing career ambitions of its potential and actual officeholders, forming them into an effective electoral machine. More accurately, Schlesinger argues that each office and its partisan seeker serves as one "nucleus" of a party, and a strong party is one that has many strong organizational nuclei connected to each other in supporting its ambitious partisan office seekers.

The genius of democracy, in this view, is rather like the genius Adam Smith found in the free market. In Smith's case individuals acting in their own self-interest turn out to be guided, as if by some unseen hand, to act in the economic interests of the collective. In Schlesinger's case ambitious politicians, seeking to have a long and successful career, are all led by the necessity of winning broad support in the face of stiff competition to reflect the desires of those citizens who support them. Without competition for office—without strong political parties—career ambition is not necessarily harnessed to reflect the desires of the public. In elections, political parties serve the Madisonian principle of having ambition clash with, and thereby check, ambition. Seeking popular support in the face of competition yields officeholders who find it in their self-interest to respond to the wishes of the public so that that public will continually reelect then, thereby satisfying their career ambition. All else about parties flows from this Schumpeterian view. Office seekers will try to create a strong electoral machine for mobilizing the electorate, but only if competition forces them to do so. Thus will the party-as-organization flow from competition for office. So too will the party-in-government flow naturally from electoral competition—but only so long as it is in the long-term career interests of office seekers and holders to do so. Only so long, that it, as there is a shared, collective interest in working together in office, and doing so to remain in office.[4] And that collective interest must come from a common electoral fate.

These, then, are the three major views or understandings of political parties. I will offer a fourth. . . . [I]t will be one that takes career ambitions of elective office seekers and holders as one of its central building blocks. It will differ, however, in seeing office seeking as only one of several goals held by those with political ambitions. To be sure, winning elections is an intermediary end in addition to being an end in itself. Motivations for policy ends and for power and prestige in office require electoral victory. But for many winning office per se is not the end of politics but the beginning. As we will see, this leads naturally and inevitably to drawing from the other views of parties, and it will be necessary to trace the historical . . . path of development.

▪　　▪　　▪

A Theory of Political Parties

As diverse as are the conclusions reached by these and other astute observers, all agree that the political party is—or should be—central to the American political system. Parties are—or should be—integral parts of all political life, from structuring the reasoning and choice of the electorate, through all facets of campaigns and seemingly all facets of the government, to the very possibility of effective governance in a democracy.

How is it that such astute observers of American politics and parties, writing at virtually the same time and looking at much the same evidence, come to such diametrically opposed conclusions about the strength of parties? Eldersveld provided an obvious answer. He wrote that "political parties are complex institutions and processes, and as such they are difficult to understand and evaluate" (1982, p. 407). As proof, he went on to consider the decline of parties thesis. At one point he wrote, "The decline in our parties, therefore, is difficult to demonstrate, empirically or in terms of historical perspective" (p. 417). And yet he then turned to signs of party decline and concluded his book with the statement: "Despite their defects they continue today to be the major instruments for democratic government in this nation. With necessary reforms we can make them even more central to the governmental process and to the lives of American citizens. Eighty years ago, Lord James Bryce, after studying our party system, said, 'In America the great moving forces are the parties. The government counts for less than in Europe, the parties count for more. . . .' If our citizens and their leaders wish it, American parties will still be the 'great moving forces' of our system" (Eldersveld, 1982, pp. 432–33).

The "fundamental equation" of the new institutionalism applied to parties

That parties are complex does not mean they are incomprehensible. Indeed complexity is, if not an intentional outcome, at least an anticipated result of those who shape the political parties. Moreover, they are so deeply woven into the fabric of American politics that they cannot be understood apart from either their own historical context and dynamics or those of the political system as a whole. Parties, that is, can be understood only in relation to the polity, to the government and its institutions, and to the historical context of the times.

The study of political parties, second, is necessarily a study of a major pair of political *institutions*. Indeed, the institutions that define the political party are unique, and as it happens they are unique in ways that make an institutional account especially useful. Their establishment and nature are fundamentally extralegal; they are nongovernmental political institutions. Instead of statute, their basis lies in the actions of ambitious politicians that created and maintain them. They are, in the parlance of the new institutionalism, *endogenous institutions*—in fact, the most highly endogenous institutions of any substantial and sustained political importance in American history.

By endogenous, I mean it was the actions of political actors that created political parties in the first place, and it is the actions of political actors that have shaped and altered them over time. And political actors have chosen to alter their parties dramatically at several times in our history, reformed them often, and tinkered with them constantly. Of all major political bodies in the United States, the political party is the most variable in its rules, regulations, and procedures—that is to say, in its formal organization—and in its informal methods and traditions. It is often the same set of actors who write the party's rules and then choose the party's outcomes, sometimes at nearly the same time and by the same method. Thus, for example, one night national party conventions debate, consider any proposed amendments, and then adopt their rules by a majority vote of credentialed delegates. The next night these same delegates debate, consider any proposed amendments, and then adopt their platform by majority vote, and they choose their presidential nominee by majority vote the following night.

Who, then, are these critical political actors? Many see the party-in-the-electorate as comprising major actors. To be sure, mobilizing the electorate to capture office is a central task of the political party. But America is a republican democracy. All power flows directly or indirectly from the great body of the people, to paraphrase Madison's definition. The public elects its political leaders, but it is that leadership that legislates, executes, and adjudicates policy. The parties are defined in relation to this republican democracy. Thus it is political leaders, those Schlesinger (1975) has called "office-seekers"—*those who seek and those who hold elective office*—who are the central actors in the party.[5]

Ambitious office seekers and holders are thus the first and most important actors in the political party. A second set of important figures in party politics comprises those who hold, or have access to, critical resources that office seekers need to realize their ambitions. It is expensive to build and maintain the party and campaign organizations necessary to compete effectively in the electoral arena. Thomas Ferguson, for example, has made an extended argument for the "primary and constitutive role large investors play in American politics" (1983, p. 3; see also Ferguson 1986, 1989, 1991). Much of his research emphasizes this primary and constitutive role in party politics in particular, such as in partisan realignments. The study of the role of money in congressional elections has also focused in part on concentrations of such sources of funding, such as from political action committees (e.g., Sorauf 1988) which political parties are coming to take advantage of (see Hernnson 1988; Kayden and Mayhe 1985). Elections are also fought over the flow of information to the public. The electoral arm of political parties in the eighteenth century was made up of "committees of correspondence," which were primarily lines of communication among political elites and between them and potential voters, and one of the first signs of organizing of the Jeffersonian Republican party was the hiring of a newspaper editor. . . . The press was first a partisan press, and editors and publishers from Thomas Ritchie . . . to Horace Greeley long were critical players in party politics. Today those with specialized knowledge relevant to communication, such as pollsters, media and advertising experts, and computerized fund-raising specialists, enjoy influence in party, campaign, and even government councils that greatly exceeds their mere technical expertise (see Aldrich 1992).

In more theoretical terms, this second set of party actors include those Schlesinger (1975) has called "benefit seekers," those for whom realization of their goals depends on the party's success in capturing office. Party activists shade from those powerful figures with concentrations, of, or access to, money and information described above to the legions of volunteer campaign activists who ring doorbells and stuff envelopes and are, individually and collectively, critical to the first level of the party—its office seekers. All are critical because they command the resources, whether money, expertise, and information or merely time and labor, that office seekers need to realize their ambitions. As a result, activists' motivations shape and constrain the behavior of office seekers, as their own roles are, in turn, shaped and constrained by the office seekers. . . . [T]he changed incentives of party activists have played a significant role in the fundamentally altered nature of the contemporary party, but the impact of benefit seekers will be seen scattered throughout this account.

Voters, however, are neither office seekers nor benefit seekers and thus are not a part of the political party at all, even if they identify strongly with a party and consistently support its candidates.[6] Voters are indeed critical, but they are critical as the targets of party activities. Parties "produce" candidates, platforms, and policies. Voters "consume" by exchanging their votes for the party's product (see Popkin et al. 1976). Some voters, of course, become partisans by becoming activists, whether as occasional volunteers, as sustained contributors, or even as candidates. But until they do so, they may be faithful consumers, "brand name" loyalists a it were, but they are still only the targets of partisans' efforts to sell their wares in the political marketplace.

Why, then, do politicians create and recreate the party, exploit its features, or ignore its dictates? The simple answer is that it has been in their interests to do so. That is, this is a *rational choice* account of the party, an account that presumes that rational, elective office seekers and holders use the party to achieve their ends.

I do not assume that politicians are invariably self-interested in a narrow sense. This is not a theory in which elective office seekers simply maximize their chances of election or reelection, at least not for its own sake. They may well have fundamental values and principles, and they may have preferences over policies as means to those ends. They also care about office, both for its own sake and for the opportunities to achieve other ends that election and reelection make possible. In chapters 3–5, I recount several historical cases in some detail. None of these make sense under the assumption of a single-minded office-seeking goal. All are understandable as the rational actions of goal-seeking politicians using the political party to help achieve their ends. Their ends are simply more numerous, interesting, and political than mere careerism. Just as winning elections is a means to other ends for politicians (whether career or policy ends), so too is the political party a means to these other ends.[7]

Why, then, do politicians turn to create or reform, to use or abuse, partisan institutions? The answer is that parties are designed as attempts to solve problems that current institutional arrangements do not solve and that politicians have come to believe they cannot solve. These problems fall into three general and recurring categories.[8]

The problem of ambition and elective office seeking

Elective office seekers, as that label says, want to win election to office. Parties regulate access to those offices. If elective office is indeed valuable, there will be more aspirants than offices, and the political party and the two-party system are means of regulating that competition and channeling those ambitions. Major party nomination is necessary for election, and partisan institutions have been developed—and have been reformed and re-reformed—for regulating competition. Intra-institutional leadership positions are also highly valued and therefore potentially competitive. There is, for example, a fairly well institutionalized path to the office of Speaker of the House. It is, however, a Democratic party institution. Elective politicians, of course, ordinarily desire election more than once. They are typically careerists who want a long and productive career in politics. Schlesinger's ambition theory (1966), developed and extended by others (see especially Rohde 1979), is precisely about this general problem. Underlying this theory, though typically not fully developed, is a problem. The problem is that if office is desirable, there will be more, usually many more, aspirants than there are offices to go around. When stated in rigorous form, it can be proved that in fact there is no permanent solution to this problem.[9] And it is a problem that can adversely affect the fortunes of a party. In 1912 the Republican vote was split between William Howard Taft and Theodore Roosevelt. This split enabled Woodrow Wilson to win with 42 percent of the popular vote. Not only was Wilson the only break in Republican hegemony of the White House in this period, but in that year Democrats increased their House majority by sixty-five additional seats and captured majority control of the Senate. Thus failure to regulate intraparty competition cost Republicans dearly.

For elective office seekers, regulating conflict over who holds those offices is clearly of major concern. It is ever present. And it is not just a problem of access to government offices but is also a problem internal to each party as soon as the party becomes an important gateway to office.

The problem of making decisions for the party and for the polity

Once in office, partisans determine outcomes for the polity. They propose alternatives, shape the agenda, pass (or reject) legislation, and implement what they enact. The policy formation and execution process, that is, is highly partisan. The parties-in-government are more than mere coalitions of like-minded individuals, however; they are enduring institutions. Very few incumbents change their partisan affiliations. Most retain their partisanship throughout their career, even though they often disagree (i.e., are not uniformly likeminded) with some of their partisan peers. When the rare incumbent does change parties, it is invariably to join the party more consonant with that switcher's policy interests. This implies that there are differences between the two parties at some fundamental and enduring level on policy positions, values, and beliefs. Thus, parties are institutions designed to promote the achievement of collective choices—choices on which the parties differ and choices reached by majority rule. As with access to office and ambition theory, there is a well-developed theory for this problem: *social choice theory*. Underlying this theory is the well-known problem that no method of choice can solve the elective officeholders' problem of combining the interests, concerns, or values of a polity that remains faithful to democratic values, as shown by the consequences flowing from Arrow's theorem (Arrow 1951). Thus, in a republican democracy politicians may turn to partisan institutions to solve the problem of collective choice. In the language of politics, parties may help achieve the goal of attaining policy majorities in the first place, as well as the often more difficult goal of maintaining such majorities.

The problem of collective action

The third problem is the most pervasive and thus the furthest-ranging in substantive content. The clearest example, however, is also the most important. To win office, candidates need more than a party's nomination. Election requires persuading members of the public to support that candidacy and mobilizing as many of those supporters as possible. This is a problem of collective action. How do candidates get supporters to vote for them—at least in greater numbers than vote for the opposition—as well as get them to provide the cadre of workers and contribute the resources needed to win election? The political party has long been the solution.

As important as wooing and mobilizing supporters are, collective action problems arise in a wide range of circumstances facing elective office seekers. Party action invariably requires the concerted action of many partisans to achieve collectively desirable outcomes. Jimmy Carter was the only president in the 1970s and 1980s to enjoy unified party control of government. Democrats in Congress, it might well be argued, shared an interest in achieving policy outcomes. And yet Carter was all too often unable to get them to act in their shared collective interests. In 1980 not only he but the Democratic congressional parties paid a heavy price for failed cooperation. The theory here, of course, is the *theory of public goods* and its consequence, the *theory of collective action*.

The elective office seekers' and holders' interests are to win

Why should this crucial set of actors, the elective office seekers and officeholders, care about these three classes of problems? The short answer is that these concerns become practical problems to politicians when they adversely affect their chances of winning. Put differently, politicians turn to their political party—that is, use its powers, resources, and institutional forms—when they believe doing so increases their prospects for winning desired outcomes, and they turn from it if it does not.[10]

Ambition theory is about winning per se. The breakdown of orderly access to office risks unfettered and unregulated competition. The inability of a party to develop effective means of nomination and support for election therefore directly influences the chances of victory for the candidates and thus for their parties. The standard example of the problem of social choice theory, the "paradox of voting," is paradoxical precisely because all are voting to win desired outcomes, and yet there is no majority-preferred outcome. Even if there happens to be a majority-preferred policy, the conditions under which it is truly a stable equilibrium are extremely fragile and thus all too amenable to defeat. In other words, majorities in Congress are hard to attain and at least as hard to maintain. And the only reason to employ scarce campaign resources to mobilize supporters is that such mobilization increases the odds of victory. Its opposite, the failure to act when there are broadly shared interests—the problem of collective action—reduces the prospects of victory, whether at the ballot box or in government. Scholars may recognize these as manifestations of theoretical problems and call them "impossibility results" to emphasize their generic importance. Politicians recognize the consequences of these impossibility results by their adverse effects on their chances of winning—of securing what it is in their interests to secure.

So why have politicians so often turned to political parties for solutions to these problems? Their existence creates incentives for their use. It is, for example, incredibly difficult to win election to major office without the backing of a major party. It is only a little less certain that legislators who seek to lead a policy proposal through the congressional labyrinth will first turn to their party for assistance. But such incentives tell us only that an ongoing political institution is used when it is useful. Why form political parties in the first place? . . . A brief statement of three points will give a first look at the argument.

First, parties are institutions. This means, among other things, that they have some durability. They may be endogenous institutions, yet party reforms are meant not as short-term fixes but as alterations to last for years, even decades. Thus, for example, legislators might create a party rather than a temporary majority coalition to increase their chances of winning not just today but into the future. Similarly, a long and successful political career means winning office today, but it also requires winning elections throughout that career. A standing, enduring organization makes that goal more likely.

Second, American democracy chooses by plurality or majority rule. Election to office therefore requires broad-based support wherever and from whomever it can be found. So strong are the resulting incentives for a two-party system to emerge that the effect is called Duverger's law (Duverger 1954). It is in part the need to win vast and diverse support that has led politicians to create political parties.

Third, parties may help officeholders win more, and more often, than alternatives. Consider the usual stylized model of pork barrel politics. All winners get a piece of the pork for their districts. All funded projects are paid for by tax revenues, so each district pays an equal share of the costs of each project adopted, whether or not that district receives a project. Several writers have argued that this kind of legislation leads to "universalism," that is, adoption of a "norm" that every such bill yields a project to every district and thus passes with a "universal" or unanimous coalition. Thus everyone "wins." Weingast proved the basic theorem (1979). His theorem yields the choice of the rule of universalism over the formation of a simple majority coalition, because in advance each legislator calculates the chances of any simple majority coalition's forming as equal to that of any other. As a result, expecting to win only a bit more than half the time and lose the rest of the time, all legislators prefer consistent use of the norm of universalism.[11] But consider an alternative. Suppose some majority agree to form a more permanent coalition, to control outcomes now and into the future, and develop institutional means to encourage fealty to this agreement. If they successfully accomplish this, they will win regularly. Members of this institutionalized coalition would prefer it to universalism, since they always win a project in either case, but they get their projects at lower cost under the institutionalized majority coalition, which passes fewer projects.[12] Thus, even in this case with no shared substantive interests at all, there are nonetheless incentives to form an enduring voting coalition—to form a political party. And those in the excluded minority have incentives to counterorganize. United, they may be more able to woo defectors to their side. If not, they can campaign to throw those rascals in the majority party out of office.

In sum, these theoretical problems affect elective office seekers and officeholders by reducing their chances of winning. Politicians therefore may turn to political parties as institutions designed to ameliorate them. In solving these theoretical problems, however, from the politicians' perspective parties are affecting who wins and loses and what is won or lost. And it is to parties that politicians often turn, because of their durability as institutionalized solutions, because of the need to orchestrate large and diverse groups of people to form winning majorities, and because often more can be won through parties. Note that this argument rests on the implicit assumption that winning and losing hang in the balance. Politicians may be expected to give up some of their personal autonomy only when they face an imminent threat of defeat without doing so or only when doing so can block opponents' ability to build the strength necessary to win.

This is, of course, the positive case for parties, for its specifies conditions under which politicians find them useful. Not all problems are best solved, perhaps even solved at all, by political parties. Other arrangements, perhaps interest groups, issue networks, or personal electoral coalitions, may be superior at different times and under different conditions (see Hansen 1991, for example). The party may even be part of the problem. In such cases politicians turn elsewhere to seek the means to win.[13] Thus this theory is at base a theory of ambitious politicians seeking to achieve their goals. Often they have done so through the agency of the party, but sometimes, this theory implies, they will seek to realize their goals in other ways.

The political party has regularly proved useful. Their permanence suggests that the appropriate question is not When parties? but How much parties and how much other means? That parties are endogenous implies that there is no single, consistent account of the political party—nor should we expect one. Instead, parties are but a (major) part of the institutional context in which current historical conditions—the problems—are set, and solutions are

sought with permanence only by changing that web of institutional arrangements. Of these the political party is by design the most malleable, and thus it
is intended to change in important ways and with relatively great frequency.
But it changes in ways that have, for most of American history, retained major
political parties and, indeed, retained two major parties.

NOTES

1. I resist calling these theories, largely because some of them (especially the first
view) are collections of sometimes quite different perspectives of particular scholars.
For example, if the first view sees parties as "umbrella-like" organizations, including
within them many and diverse views, so too are the scholars and their theoretical
understandings many and diverse in this category I have constructed. This is less true
of the responsible party scholars, and the competitive-party category is more uniform,
consisting primarily of rational choice theories.

2. I use the term "platform" figuratively, as a set of policies proposed to be enacted
in office.

3. Ranney is quoting Polsby and Wildavsky (1971, p. 225).

4. That is, collective interests as partisans are necessary for there to be a strong
party-in-government. Such interests are not a sufficient condition, however, owing to
the collective action problem. . . .

5. The justification for partisan use of political power, then, is that it is consistent with
the republican principle. All power flows directly or indirectly from the great body of the
people through elective office seekers and into the hands of the party. To be sure, partisan powers are often highly indirect and not very democratic. Indeed, major reforms
of the political party are often sought to make the party a more republican-democratic
institution in its own right. Thus was the invention of the convention system justified in
the 1820s as more representative than "King Caucus," and thus was the primary election
method of nomination so justified (see Aldrich 1989). Today, the nearly exclusive reliance
on primary elections is rooted in the belief that all power should flow into the party
more directly from the great body of the people. Nonetheless, primary voters do not
choose party rules, platforms, organizations, or virtually any other form of outcome.
They choose the leaders, but it is the leaders who will then choose the outcomes.

6. Office seekers, in Schlesinger's account, seek the private good of holding office,
whereas benefit seekers, in addition to any value they, like office seekers, might obtain
from good public policy, seek private preferments that come from the capture of office
per se. Note that this distinction makes the most sense when speaking of benefit seekers
in terms of the high-level resource providers or of the political machine, which had
many private goods to allocate to its activists. The distinction becomes much less
clear when discussing volunteer activists in general and especially the (purely) policy-
motivated activist. . . .

7. In chapter 4 I give a detailed account of Van Buren's idea of the importance of the
political party, above and beyond that of any individual (himself included). Even here,
though, the reason for desiring this form of political party (and those who subsequently
subscribed to this view of the political party throughout the "party period," see McCormick 1979; Silbey 1985; and various places throughout this text) was not for the party
above all, even if for a party above men, but for the desirable effects such party would
have for democracy.

8. The reason these problems are recurring will be developed in the next chapter.

9. The allocation of n k aspirants to n offices, at least for pure office-seeking candidates, defines an n-person, zero-sum game that, as such, lacks a core.

10. Riker's pathbreaking study of coalition formation (1962) that introduced many to rational choice theory began with a strong argument for the importance of winning in politics. Clearly, Schlesinger's ambition theory (1966) and its many related studies, such as those that follow Mayhew's emphasis on the importance of reelection in understanding Congress (1974) or those that follow Downs's accounts of elections (1957), place winning just as centrally as Riker does.

11. This result does not seem to depend heavily on the assumption that the alternative to universalism is the formation of minimal winning majority coalitions. What does seem to be crucial is the assumption that all coalitions are equally likely a priori.

12. At least they prefer this majority coalition to universalism if the costs of forming and maintaining it are less than the savings from not giving the minority any projects.

13. Once parties have organized, the current institutional arrangements will include those current partisan arrangements. Thus it may be that partisan institutions are part, even much, of the problem. By definition, these current partisan arrangements are at least insufficient to solve that problem. These three recurring problems share at their base something like an impossibility result. That is, no institutional arrangements, partisan or otherwise, that are consistent with republican democracy can solve any of these problems in all circumstances. This logical consequence is the reason partisan institutions are always threatened by, or in a state of, crisis. The party is designed to solve what cannot be permanently solved. The solution is thus contingent. That is, it is the solution that works for the particular set of circumstances currently faced; the same arrangements may not work adequately under other conditions. And in a purely logical sense, any given set of partisan institutions will necessarily fail at some time, if these are indeed true impossibility results. It is in part for this reason that the historical context is so important for understanding political parties.

REFERENCES

Aldrich, John H. 1989. Power and order in Congress. In *Home style and Washington work: Studies in congressional politics,* ed. Morris P. Fiorina and David W. Rohde, pp. 219–52. Ann Arbor: University of Michigan Press.

———. 1992. Presidential campaigns in party- and candidate-centered eras. In *Under the watchful eye: Managing presidential campaigns in the television era,* ed. Mathew D. McCubbins, pp. 59–82. Washington, D.C.: CQ Press.

Aldrich, John H., and William T. Bianco. 1992. A game-theoretic model of party affiliation of candidates and office holders. *Mathematical and Computer Modelling* 16 (8–9): 103–16.

Arrow, Kenneth J. 1951. *Social choice and individual values.* New York: Wiley.

Beck, Paul Allen, and Frank J. Sorauf. 1991. *Party politics in America.* 7th ed. New York: HarperCollins.

Demsetz, Harold. 1990. Amenity potential, indivisibilities, and political competition. In *Perspectives on political economy,* ed. James E. Alt and Kenneth A. Shepsle, pp. 144–60. New York. Cambridge University Press.

Downs, Anthony. 1957. *An economic theory of democracy.* New York: Harper & Row.

Duverger, Maurice. 1954. *Political parties: Their organization and activities in the modern state.* New York: Wiley.

Eldersveld, Samuel J. 1964. *Political parties: A behavioral analysis.* Chicago: Rand McNally.

———. 1982. *Political parties in American society.* New York: Basic Books.

Epstein, Leon D. 1986. *Political parties in the American mold.* Madison: University of Wisconsin Press.

Fenno, Richard F. 1973. *Congressmen in committees.* Boston: Little, Brown.

Ferguson, Thomas. 1983. Party realignment and American industrial structures: The investment theory of political parties in historical perspective. In *Research in political economy*, vol. 6, ed. Paul Zarembka, pp. 1–82. Greenwich, Conn.: JAI Press.

———. 1986. Elites and elections, or: What have they done to you lately? In *Do elections matter?* ed. Benjamin Ginsberg and Alan Stone, pp. 164–88. Armonk, N.Y.: Sharpe.

———. 1989. Industrial conflict and the coming of the New Deal: The triumph of multinational liberalism in America. In *The rise and fall of the New Deal order, 1930–80*, ed. Steve Fraser and Gary Gerstle, pp. 3–31. Princeton, N.J.: Princeton University Press.

———. 1991. An unbearable lightness of being—party and industry in the 1988 Democratic primary. In *Do elections matter?* 2d ed., ed. Benjamin Ginsberg and Alan Stone, pp. 237–54. Armonk, N.J.: Sharpe.

Hansen, John Mark. 1991. *Gaining access: Congress and the farm lobby.* Chicago: University of Chicago Press.

Herrnson, Paul S. 1988. *Party campaigning in the 1980s.* Cambridge: Harvard University Press.

Kayden, Xandra, and Eddie Mayhe Jr. 1985. *The party goes on: The persistence of the two-party system in the United States.* New York: Basic Books.

Key, V. O., Jr. 1964. *Politics, parties, and pressure groups.* 5th ed. New York: Crowell.

Lijphart, Arend. 1984. *Democracies: Patterns of majoritarian and consensus government in twenty-one countries.* New Haven, Conn.: Yale University Press.

Mayhew, David R. 1974. *Congress: The electoral connection.* New Haven, Conn.: Yale University Press.

McClosky, Herbert. 1969. Consensus and ideology in American politics. In *Empirical democratic theory*, ed. Charles F. Cnudde and Deane E. Neubauer, pp. 268–302. Chicago: Markham, 1969. Originally published in *American Political Science Review* 58 (June 1964): 361–82.

McCormick, Richard L. 1979. The party period and public policy: An exploratory hypothesis. *Journal of American History* 66 (September): 279–98.

Page, Benjamin I. 1978. *Choices and echoes in presidential elections: Rational man and electoral democracy.* Chicago: University of Chicago Press.

Polsby, Nelson W., and Aaron B. Wildavsky. 1971. *Presidential elections: Strategies of American electoral politics.* 3d ed. New York: Scribner.

Popkin, Samuel, John W. Gorman, Charles Phillips, and Jeffrey A. Smith. 1976. Comment: What have you done for me lately? Toward an investment theory of voting. *American Political Science Review* 70 (September): 779–805.

Ranney, Austin. 1975. *Curing the mischiefs of faction: Party reform in America.* Berkeley and Los Angeles: University of California Press.

Riker, William H. 1962. *The theory of political coalitions.* New Haven, Conn.: Yale University Press.

Rohde, David W. 1979. Risk-bearing and progressive ambition: The case of the United States House of Representatives. *American Journal of Political Science* 23 (February): 1–26.

Rohde, David W., and Kenneth A. Shepsle. 1978. Thinking about legislative reform. In *Legislative reform: The policy impact,* ed. Leroy N. Rieselbach. Lexington, Mass.: Lexington Books.

Schattschneider, E. E. 1942. *Party government.* New York: Rinehart.

Schlesinger, Joseph A. 1966. *Ambition and politics: Political careers in the United States.* Chicago: Rand McNally.

———. 1975. The primary goals of political parties: A clarification of positive theory. *American Political Science Review* 69 (September): 840–49.

———. 1984. On the theory of party organization. *Journal of Politics* 46 (May): 369–400.

———. 1985. The new American political party. *American Political Science Review* 79 (December): 1152–69.

———. 1991. *Political parties and the winning of office.* Chicago: University of Chicago Press.

Silbey, Joel H. 1985. *The partisan imperative: The dynamics of American politics before the Civil War.* New York: Oxford University Press.

Sorauf, Frank J. 1964. *Party politics in America.* Boston: Little, Brown.

———. 1984. *Party politics in America.* 5th ed. Boston: Little, Brown.

———. 1988. *Money in American elections.* Glenview, Ill.: Scott, Foresman/Little, Brown.

Weingast, Barry R. 1979. A rational choice perspective on congressional norms. *American Journal of Political Science* 23 (May): 245–62.

Wilson, Woodrow. 1881. *Congressional government: A study in American society.* Baltimore: Johns Hopkins University Press.

12.2

ANGUS CAMPBELL, PHILIP E. CONVERSE, WARREN E. MILLER,
AND DONALD E. STOKES

From *The American Voter*

In this selection from the classic book The American Voter, *the authors depict partisanship as a deep psychological attachment to one of the two major parties, an attachment that largely determines individual voting decisions and shapes the way individuals evaluate policies and politicians. The authors demonstrate a way to measure partisanship in the population using surveys. Even though the original book was published in 1960, this conceptualization of partisanship and the method of measuring it are still widely used by scholars all over the world.*

THE IMPACT OF PARTY IDENTIFICATION

A general observation about the political behavior of Americans is that their partisan preferences show great stability between elections. . . . Often a change of candidates and a broad alteration in the nature of the issues disturb very little the relative partisanship of a set of electoral units, which suggests that great numbers of voters have party attachments that persist through time.

The fact that attachments of this sort are widely held is confirmed by survey data on individual people. In a survey interview most of our citizens freely classify themselves as Republicans or Democrats and indicate that these loyalties have persisted through a number of elections. Few factors are of greater importance for our national elections than the lasting attachment of tens of millions of Americans to one of the parties. These loyalties establish a basic division of electoral strength within which the competition of particular campaigns takes place. And they are an important factor in assuring the stability of the party system itself.

The Concept and Measurement of Party Identification

Only in the exceptional case does the sense of individual attachment to party reflect a formal membership or an active connection with a party apparatus. Nor does it simply denote a voting record, although the influence of party allegiance on electoral behavior is strong. Generally this tie is a psychological identification, which can persist without legal recognition or evidence of formal membership and even without a consistent record of party support. Most Americans have this sense of attachment with one party or the other. And for the individual who does, the strength and direction of party identification are facts of central importance in accounting for attitude and behavior.

The importance of stable partisan loyalties has been universally recognized in electoral studies, but the manner in which they should be defined and measured has been a subject of some disagreement. In keeping with the conception of party identification as a psychological tie, these orientations have been measured in our research by asking individuals to describe their own partisan loyalties. Some studies, however, have chosen to measure stable partisan orientations in terms of an individual's past voting record or in terms of his attitude on a set of partisan issues. We have not measured party attachments in terms of the vote or the evaluation of partisan issues precisely because we are interested in exploring the *influence* of party identification on voting behavior and its immediate determinants. When an independent measure of party identification is used, it is clear that even strong party adherents at times may think and act in contradiction to their party allegiance. We could never establish the conditions under which this will occur if lasting partisan orientations were measured in terms of the behavior they are thought to affect.

Our measurement of party identification rests fundamentally on self-classification. Since 1952 we have asked repeated cross sections of the national population a sequence of questions inviting the individual to state the direction and strength of his partisan orientation.[1] The dimension presupposed by these questions appears to have psychological reality for virtually the entire electorate. The partisan self-image of all but the few individuals who disclaim any involvement in politics permits us to place each person in these samples on a continuum of partisanship extending from strongly Republican to strongly Democratic. The sequence of questions we have asked also allows us to distinguish the Independents who lean toward one of the parties from those who think of themselves as having no partisan coloration whatever.

The measure these methods yield has served our analysis of party identification in a versatile fashion. To assess both the direction and intensity of partisan attachments it can be used to array our samples across the seven categories shown in Table 1, which gives the distribution of party identification in the electorate during the years from 1952 to 1958.

In using these techniques of measurement we do not suppose that every person who describes himself as an Independent is indicating simply his lack of positive attraction to one of the parties. Some of these people undoubtedly are actually repelled by the parties or by partisanship itself and value their position as Independents. Certainly independence of party is an ideal of some currency in our society, and it seems likely that a portion of those who call themselves Independents are not merely reporting the absence of identification with one of the major parties.

Sometimes it is said that a good number of those who call themselves Independents have simply adopted a label that conceals a genuine psychological commitment to one party or the other. Accordingly, it is argued that a per-

TABLE 1   The Distribution of Party Identification

	Oct. 1952	Sept. 1953	Oct. 1954	Apr. 1956	Oct. 1956	Nov. 1957	Oct. 1958
Strong Republicans	13%	15%	13%	14%	15%	10%	13%
Weak Republicans	14	15	14	18	14	16	16
Independent Republicans	7	6	6	6	8	6	4
Independents	5	4	7	3	9	8	8
Independent Democrats	10	8	9	6	7	7	7
Weak Democrats	25	23	25	24	23	26	24
Strong Democrats	22	22	22	19	21	21	23
Apolitical, don't know	4	7	4	10	3	6	5
Total	100%	100%	100%	100%	100%	100%	100%
Number of cases	1614	1023	1139	1731	1772	1488	1269

son's voting record gives a more accurate statement of his party attachment than does his own self-description. Our samples doubtless include some of these undercover partisans, and we have incorporated in our measure of party identification a means of distinguishing Independents who say they lean toward one of the parties from Independents who say they do not. We do not think that the problem of measurement presented by the concealed partisan is large. Rather it seems to us much less troublesome than the problems that follow if psychological ties to party are measured in terms of the vote.

This question can be illuminated a good deal by an examination of the consistency of party voting among those of different degrees of party identification, as is done in Table 2. The proportion of persons consistently supporting one party varies by more than sixty percentage points between strong party identifiers and complete Independents. For the problem of the undercover partisan, the troublesome figure in Table 2 is the 16 per cent of full Independents who have voted for the candidates of one party only. The importance of this figure diminishes when we remember that some of these persons have voted in very few presidential elections and could have supported one party consistently because of the way their votes fell, free of the influence of a genuine party tie.

■　■　■

The measurement of party identification in the period of our research shows how different a picture of partisan allegiance voting behavior and self-description can give. Despite the substantial Republican majorities in the

TABLE 2 Relation of Strength of Party Identification to Partisan Regularity in Voting for President, 1956[a]

	Strong Party Identifiers	Weak Party Identifiers	Independents Leaning to Party	Independents
Voted always or mostly for same party	82%	60%	36%	16%
Voted for different parties	18	40	64	84
Total	100%	100%	100%	100%
Number of cases	546	527	189	115

[a]The question used to establish party consistency of voting was this: "Have you always voted for the same party or have you voted for different parties for President?"

elections of 1952 and 1956, the percentages of Table 1 make clear that the Democratic Party enjoyed a three-to-two advantage in the division of party identification within the electorate in these same years. Moreover, Table 1 documents the stability of this division of party loyalty in a period whose electoral history might suggest widespread change. Except for the shifting size of the group of respondents refusing to be assigned any position on the party scale, there is not a single variation between successive distributions of party identification that could not be laid to sampling error.

The great stability of partisan loyalties is supported, too, by what we can learn from recall data about the personal history of party identification. We have asked successive samples of the electorate a series of questions permitting us to reconstruct whether an individual who accepts a party designation has experienced a prior change in his party identification. The responses give impressive evidence of the constancy of party allegiance.

The fact that nearly everyone in our samples could be placed on a unitary dimension of party identification and that the idea of prior movements on this dimension was immediately understood are themselves important findings about the nature of party support within the electorate. In view of the loose, federated structure of American parties it was not obvious in advance that people could respond to party in these undifferentiated terms. Apparently the positive and negative feelings that millions of individuals have toward the parties are the result of orientations of a diffuse and generalized character that have a common psychological meaning even though there may be a good deal of variation in the way party is perceived.

Party Identification and Political Attitude

The psychological function of party identification undoubtedly varies among individuals. Our interest here centers primarily on the role of party as a supplier of cues by which the individual may evaluate the elements of politics. The fact that most elements of national politics are far removed from the world of the common citizen forces the individual to depend on sources of information from which he may learn indirectly what he cannot know as a matter of direct experience. Moreover, the complexities of politics and government increase the importance of having relatively simple cues to evaluate what cannot be matters of personal knowledge.

In the competition of voices reaching the individual the political party is an opinion-forming agency of great importance. This is not to say that party leaders are able as a matter of deliberate technique to transmit an elaborate defense of their position to those in the electorate who identify with the party. To the contrary, some of the most striking instances of party influence occur with only the simplest kind of information reaching the party's mass support. For example, a party undoubtedly furnishes a powerful set of cues about a political leader just by nominating him for President. Merely associating the party symbol with his name encourages those identifying with the party to develop a more favorable image of his record and experience, his abilities, and his other personal attributes. Likewise, this association encourages supporters of the opposite party to take a less favorable view of these same personal qualities. Partisans in each camp may incorporate into their view of the candidates whatever detailed information they can, and the highly-involved may develop an elaborate and carefully-drawn portrait. But the impact of the party symbol seems to be none the less strong on those who absorb little of politics and whose image of the candidates is extremely diffuse.

Apparently party has a profound influence across the full range of political objects to which the individual voter responds. The strength of relationship between party identification and the dimensions of partisan attitude suggests that responses to each element of national politics are deeply affected by the individual's enduring party attachments.

▪ ▪ ▪

In the period of our studies the influence of party identification on attitudes toward the perceived elements of politics has been far more important than the influence of these attitudes on party identification itself. We are convinced that the relationships in our data reflect primarily the role of enduring partisan commitments in shaping attitudes toward political objects. Our conviction on this point is rooted in what we know of the relative stability and priority in time of party identification and the attitudes it may affect. We know that persons who identify with one of the parties typically have held the same partisan tie for all or almost all of their adult lives. But within their experience since coming of voting age many of the elements of politics have changed.

■   ■   ■

What is more, even the elements of politics that carry over from one election to another may be evaluated anew in later campaigns by part of the electorate. The involvement of many Americans in politics is slight enough that they may respond *de novo* to issues and personalities that have been present in earlier elections but that are salient to them only at the height of a presidential campaign. For many voters the details of the political landscape may be quite blurred until they are brought more into focus during the campaign period. The formative influence of party identification on these re-evaluations would not be essentially different from its influence on responses to newer elements of politics.

Because the influence of party identification extends through time, its workings cannot be fully disclosed by the relationships seen at a particular moment. For this reason, our statement of causal priorities is in the end an inference, but one for which the evidence is strong. If the inference is correct, the differences in attitude between those of differing partisan loyalties enlarge considerably our understanding of the configuration of forces leading to behavior.

■   ■   ■

Our hypothesis that party identification influences the voting act by influencing attitudes toward the objects to which this act relates needs to be modified for the person who has only the faintest image of these objects. If someone has little perception of the candidates, of the record of the parties, of public issues or questions of group interest, his attitudes toward these things may play a less important intervening role between party identification and the vote. Like the automobile buyer who knows nothing of cars except that he prefers a given make, the voter who knows simply that he is a Republican or Democrat responds directly to his stable allegiance without the mediating influence of perceptions he has formed of the objects he must choose between.

Party Identification and Electoral Choice

The role of general partisan orientations in molding attitudes toward the elements of politics is thus very clear. As a consequence of this role, party identification has a profound impact on behavior. . . . From the strength and direction of attitudes toward the various elements of politics we could order the individuals in our samples according to the probability of their voting Republican. That is, we could form an array extending from those most likely to vote Democratic to those most likely to vote Republican. Let us now make explicit the impact party identification has on behavior through its influence on attitude, by showing a separate array for each of five groups defined by our party identification scale. For each of the distributions shown in Fig. 1 the

FIGURE 1   Probable Direction of Vote by Party Identification Groups, 1956

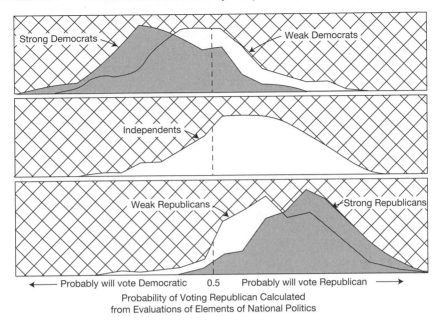

◀—— Probably will vote Democratic   0.5   Probably will vote Republican ——▶

Probability of Voting Republican Calculated
from Evaluations of Elements of National Politics

horizontal dimension is the probability an individual will vote Republican; to the left this probability is low (that is, the likelihood the individual will vote Democratic is high), and to the right the probability that the individual will vote Republican is high. The effect of party is seen at once in the changing location of the distributions along this probability dimension as we consider successively Strong Democrats, Weak Democrats, Independents, Weak Republicans, and Strong Republicans. The moving positions of these arrays show clearly the impact of party identification on the forces governing behavior.

NOTE

1. The initial question was this: "Generally speaking, do you think of yourself as a Republican, a Democrat, an Independent, or what?" Those who classified themselves as Republicans or Democrats were also asked, "Would you call yourself a strong (Republican, Democrat) or a not very strong (Republican, Democrat)?" Those who classified themselves as Independents were asked this additional question: "Do you think of yourself as closer to the Republican or Democratic Party?" The concept itself was first discussed in George Belknap and Angus Campbell, "Political Party Identification and Attitudes toward Foreign Policy," *Public Opinion Quarterly*, XV (Winter 1952), 601–623.

13

ELECTIONS

13.1

STEPHEN ANSOLABEHERE AND JAMES M. SNYDER, JR.

From *The End of Inequality: One Person, One Vote and the Transformation of American Politics*

The Supreme Court's decision in Baker v. Carr *(1963) was monumental, establishing that the Fourteenth Amendment required the principle of "one person, one vote" to be applied to all American elections. This meant that electoral districts at the state and national levels from that point onward had to be of equal population size. The Court's decision fundamentally altered political representation at all levels in the United States, with profound consequences for governments and for public policies. This excerpt summarizes the consequences of that decision.*

A QUIET REVOLUTION

■   ■   ■

The End of Inequality

. . . The [*Baker v. Carr* (1963)] decision itself reads as quite limited. The majority opinion by Brennan stated that voters had the right to sue under the Fourteenth Amendment . . . But it offered no solution, no remedy, no path forward for other plaintiffs or other states. The ruling merely sent the case back to the Tennessee courts to be decided in a way consistent with state law. That, however, was enough. Brennan's opinion set in motion a chain of events and decisions that would lead to one unavoidable conclusion—that all legislative districts must have equal populations. The only questions were how quickly the transformation would occur and how painfully.

The rapidity of the revolution surprised even its architects. Within a year, the Justices established a new interpretation of the Fourteenth Amendment to the Constitution.[1] Equal protection before the law requires equal representation—one person, one vote. One more cycle of the Court's calendar would pass before the meaning of the *Baker* decision would finally come clear. On June 15, 1964, the Supreme Court handed down six decisions requiring the states to apportion both chambers of the legislature so that all districts had equal populations; a week later, the Court declared unconstitutional state legislative apportionments in a dozen other states. Every legislative chamber in every state had to comply with the new standard of mathematical equality. No exceptions were permitted. By 1970, all states had brought their legislative and U.S. House district boundaries into alignment with the new legal criteria. Only the U.S. Senate was beyond the scope of the line of cases following *Baker v. Carr*, and that was because the Senate enjoys special protection in the Constitution.[2] *Baker v. Carr* led in short order to the equalization of voting power in the U.S. House, in every state legislature, in every city council. The Court's success was immediate, complete, and stunning.

Earl Warren later wrote in his *Memoirs* that *Baker v. Carr* stands as the most important decision of the U.S. Supreme Court in his fifteen-year tenure as Chief Justice[3]—more important than *Gideon v. Wainwright* and the cases protecting the rights of accused in the criminal system; more important than *New York Times v. Sullivan* and the cases that redefined the First Amendment rights of the press; more important even than *Brown v. Board of Education* and the subsequent decisions that forced American society to end racial segregation of schools and other public facilities. Like these other landmark cases, *Baker v. Carr* would ultimately establish a fundamental right—the right to an equal voice in representative government—and it asserted the authority of the Court in protecting that right. But more than any other modern Supreme Court case, *Baker* profoundly altered the balance of political power in the United States.

Here was a brilliant solution to one of the oldest and most vexing problems of representative democracy. For centuries, political theorists have pointed to legislative districting as one of the fundamental flaws of self-rule.[4] The legislature expresses the will of the people and, as such, acts as the sovereign that determines the laws governing the society. The problem arises because the legislature, as the sovereign, writes the laws that govern elections. An obvious conflict of interest arises: the sitting legislature determines the rules of elections, especially the districts, under which future legislatures will be chosen. And district boundaries must change; they cannot remain static. As populations move, legislative district boundaries must accommodate the changing demography, or representation will become skewed. Inevitably, the responsibility falls to the legislature to craft new constituencies. This moment—the moment at which districts are created—turns democratic representation back upon itself, because at this moment the legislators choose their constituents rather than the constituents choosing their legislators.

It is a fundamental law of politics that those in power will do what they can to remain in power. Nowhere is the impulse and opportunity for self-preservation greater than in the creation of election districts. Districting becomes a tool through which the sitting legislators can sustain themselves in office, even long after they no longer represent the majority of the people. England, from which the United States inherited its electoral institutions, labored under this malady for centuries. America adopted the English system of representation with all of its strengths and flaws. By the middle of the twentieth century, malapportionment had become acute in the American states as well.

The U.S. Supreme Court broke the vicious legislative cycle that sustained unequal representation. The Justices asserted a new right to an equal vote and their own authority to check the power of the legislature. The Warren Court has been criticized for anointing itself chancellors, "guardians of American democracy." However, the solution that Brennan fashioned worked precisely through the means that Frankfurter desired, by allowing—no, forcing—the normal political process to work. The judges did not draw the lines. Rather, they put the onus on the legislature to accomplish the task of forming new districts subject to the requirement that districts have equal populations.

On its face, the requirement that all districts have equal populations seems like a simple and not very restrictive rule. However, in order to comply with the rule, state legislatures have to alter the boundaries of nearly every district with each decennial census. Americans move—a lot. As a result, districts must be adjusted merely to accommodate such shifts in population. Most districts experience relatively small net changes in population, but some have two to three times as many people as they ought to, and in others the population either fails to keep pace with overall state population growth or even shrinks. Redistricting would be an easy task if one could reallocate people from one district to another or change just one line to fix population inequities. But a change in one boundary has a ripple effect. The populations of neighboring districts change, and alterations in those districts' boundaries, in turn, affect other districts' populations. Changes in populations also affect the balance of partisans in the districts, leading state legislators to demand further jiggling of the lines to replace the supporters they lost. Compliance with one person, one vote, then, forces the state legislatures to craft a completely new set of district lines.

The new districting process is politics at work. Legislative leaders must accommodate the interests of individual incumbents, of parties, of factions and interest groups, and of disparate communities and disadvantaged minorities. They must also, in the end, satisfy the courts. The Supreme Court's decisions in the reapportionment cases have, by and large, spared the judges from actually performing the legislative role. Unlike the school desegregation cases, in which the courts have had to write plans for school busing and, in some extreme instances, decide which students go to which schools, the judges have, by and large, not had to draw district boundaries. The legislatures have now taken up that responsibility, one that they had avoided for decades.

Therein lies a great irony of the *Baker* decision. The majority's decision turned Felix Frankfurter's political-thicket doctrine on its head. Justice Frankfurter reasoned, rightly, that the legislatures must draw the lines, as only they can balance the many competing interests. Only the push and pull of a political process could lead to proper districts. It was on that basis that Frankfurter argued that courts ought not to enter the political thicket. The flaw in his argument, though, was that politics were not happening. Legislatures simply failed to reapportion, even when their state constitutions required it. Nothing could force the legislatures to act, and the political-thicket doctrine removed a critical check on the legislature—the courts. The majority's ruling in *Baker* allowed the normal politics to work. Court-ordered reapportionment forced legislatures to find a political solution to the districting problem. In the process, the Court opened a new era of political equality in the United States, one founded on the simple principle of one person, one vote and the periodic renewal of that idea through regular redistricting.[5]

The Transformation of American Politics

This was the beginning of a great transformation of American politics. Court-ordered reapportionment swept aside decades-old, and in some states centuries-old, political deals grounded in a society that no longer existed. For most of American history, legislators served towns and counties. This arrangement made sense in a nation where almost all people lived on farms or in small towns, and counties contained fairly similar populations. Agrarian America, however, faded fast as the nineteenth century gave way to the twentieth. By 1920, just over half of all Americans lived in urban areas, and by 1960, seven in ten Americans lived in urban and suburban communities. Rural counties and towns, however, held a majority of the state legislative seats in every region of the country, and they were unwilling to surrender power. Most state legislatures, dominated by rural interests, followed the path of least resistance. They left old boundaries in place, with the result that enormous inequities in representation worsened as metropolitan areas continued to grow.

Baker v. Carr forced the states to plough under long-established legislative districts and with them the ancien régime. By 1967, just five years after the decision, nearly every state had complied with the Supreme Court's edicts.

With the reapportionment revolution, the era of rural political power receded. Rural politicians, many of whom had dominated state politics for decades, saw their base of political power evaporate as the courts' edicts eliminated thousands of rural legislative seats and gave them to the densely populated metropolitan areas. Long muted by malapportionment, city and suburb enjoyed a newfound political voice, and a new generation of urban and suburban politicians emerged in American politics. They would prove effective advocates of the interests of their constituents and would shift the balance of political power decidedly toward the metropolitan areas.

Reapportionment reshaped the ideological topography of American governments. It raised up political interests and ideas weighed down by malapportionment, and it leveled those whose popular base had long since eroded but who had held on simply from the inertia of the past. Within the legislatures and within the political parties, the centers of political gravity shifted to the left or right, depending on the circumstance. Democrats emerged as a party firmly rooted in urban America, while Republicans shifted away from their rural base and toward the suburbs. The effects differed markedly across the regions of the country, creating new political divisions in the nation.

In the Northeast and Midwest, malapportionment heavily favored the Republicans, especially rural Republicans. Malapportionment inflated the number of state legislative seats won by Republicans across a wide swath of the United States, from Maine and New Jersey to North Dakota and Kansas, and in these states the majority of Republicans represented rural counties. One person, one vote decimated the ranks of rural Republican legislators and shifted the party toward a new type of Republican voter, ones living in the rapidly growing suburban fringe around major cities. This shift also recast the ideological orientation of the Republican Party, as its rural base consisted of its most conservative voters. Reapportionment, then, cost Republicans in the Northeast and Midwest, and it replaced conservative rural Republicans with moderate suburban Republicans.

Across these regions, urban Democrats ascended to power. By 1960, northeastern and midwestern Democrats already drew a majority of their support from those in cities, and northern urban Democrats were the most liberal voters in the country, strong supporters of unions, economic regulation, and expansions of welfare spending and economic redistribution. Reapportionment pushed the Republicans out of their majority status throughout the Northeast and Midwest and either made these regions highly competitive or brought Democrats to power. The net effect was to move politics in the Northeast to the left.

The shift in the South ran along a parallel cleavage, but in the opposite direction. Democrats dominated public life in the South. Unlike their counterparts in the North, the southern Democratic parties were rooted in the staunchly conservative rural areas. The conservatism of southern Democrats concerned civil rights more than economics, though they also disliked unions and expansion of federal powers generally. Reapportionment eliminated large numbers of rural Democratic seats and gave them to urban Democrats, dramatically changing the face and ideology of the Democratic parties in southern state legislatures. The loss of rural seats was not enough to hand majorities to Republicans in the short term, but it likely contributed to the steady decline in the Democratic Party in the region. As the new urban

Democrats pulled the party to the left, new opportunities emerged for the Republicans.

Reapportionment gave Republicans an important political foothold in the southern state legislatures. Republicans had little presence in South before the 1960s. They won precious few seats in southern state legislatures, but their strongest support came from cities and the socially and economically conservative suburbs. Reapportionment created, overnight, several dozen suburban Republican seats scattered throughout the region. As suburbanization expanded in the South, these seats grew in number and importance, and the Republican Party in the South and in the nation found in them a new political base that, by the 1990s, would supplant the more moderate northeasterners as the bedrock of Republicanism.

From local school boards to the U.S. Congress, the principle of equality became the foundation for a new political landscape. Huge inequities that once defined American government were leveled. . . .

A Natural Experiment

■   ■   ■

The political inequalities that marked the American electoral landscape before *Baker v. Carr* distorted democratic representation and skewed political power strongly toward those areas and interests that were overrepresented in American legislatures. One person, one vote led to a rapid leveling of our politics and a shift in political power of a magnitude rarely seen in any society.

The reapportionment revolution . . . is for political scientists what an earthquake is for geologists. Most of what we see lies only on the surface and reflects the gradual shifts that occur naturally over time. Typically, it is hard to detect the fundamental forces at work. Upheavals lay bare the raw structure and reveal how the thing itself operates.

Such is the case with the reapportionment of American legislatures in the 1960s. The sudden, surprising shift in representation exposed the simple mechanics of democratic politics. Some voters saw their voting power greatly reduced, while others were raised up. The country moved from a system of unequal representation rooted in old state constitutions to equal representation, enforced by the courts and implemented by the legislatures. This transformation—from unequal to equal—allows us to see in clear relief how representation shapes political power. Revisiting the political history leading up to the decision and the years following speaks directly to one of the most fundamental questions concerning representative democracy: what is the value of the vote?

Two basic and fundamentally different theories of political power in democratic societies clashed in the great debate over *Baker v. Carr*.

Behind the . . . rationale of the Warren Court lay a simple equation: votes equal power. The bargaining that happens within the legislature, however complex, yields outcomes roughly proportionate to people's representation. Those with more power will get more from government, and equal political rights produce fair divisions of the public weal.

Those who defended the ancien régime set forth a very different view of political power: the large and wealthy interests will dominate the small. If given their proportionate representation, the large cities and the interests that govern them will find common ground and create a formidable voting bloc that the diffuse rural voters could not resist or ward off. Those with greater wealth or concentrated interests will dominate the poor or those with diffuse and unorganized interests. Such fears found voice in the writings of a wide spectrum of political theorists of the day—conservatives,[6] pluralists,[7] and radicals[8] alike. Only mixed representation or overrepresentation of rural areas would combat the tyranny of the majority—or worse, the tyranny of urban wealth and organization.

The conflict between these two views of power cuts to the core of our understanding of democratic representation. If the levelers were right, then equalizing representation in the state legislatures would equalize the political power of all voters, regardless of what sort of community they lived in. As a consequence, reapportionment would bring public policy in line with the electorate's wishes. However, if the liberals held a naïve and incorrect understanding of political power, they would permanently empower wealthier and more concentrated urban interests at the expense of the nation's poorer rural areas, magnifying further social inequalities. History, in the end, would prove Warren and the liberals on the Court right.

The effects of reapportionment on these different aspects of politics all point to a singular conclusion: equal votes mean equal power. The equalization of representation led directly to an equalization of the distribution of public expenditures—who got what. It also restored the political balance among competing ideologies and drew state policy back in line with the wants of the typical voter, who was in most states moderate. Votes equal power. This simple equation emerges in full from the great transformation produced by the reapportionment cases, and it carries broad lessons for democracies throughout the world, including our own.

The reapportionment revolution reveals the value of the vote in two distinct and important domains of government: money and ideology. The first of these—money—is the crudest but most direct indicator of power. Power, in Harold Laswell's famous definition, reduces to who gets what, and distribution of public money has long served as the metric of the ability of various interests and constituencies to get their way in the political arena. Every constituency pushes for its own share of the public weal; party or ideology plays little part. Constituencies who have more representation than they would under an equitable apportionment have a greater chance to win in the complicated bargaining over the division of public money. The second—ideology— is more subtle. Most laws reflect the balance between competing views of the role of government—the balance between left and right, Democrat and Republican. Constituencies who have more representation than they would under an equitable apportionment have a stronger voice in determining the overall ideological balance of the legislature. Reapportionment brought the laws the legislatures passed into closer alignment with the beliefs of the typical voter.[9]

■　■　■

The equalization of representation in the United States was brought about not by popular rule or through the legislature, but by the least democratic branch of government—the courts. The *Baker* decision ultimately led to a new districting process, one that requires the state legislatures to redistrict periodically under the watchful eye of the courts. The political cognoscenti overwhelmingly dislike this new process, and they blame the courts for making the electoral process even worse than before the 1960s; indeed, many legal scholars and even some Justices now echo Frankfurter's sentiment—that the judges should stay out of political matters.[10]

Looking back over the span of decades before *Baker* and across the nearly half-century since, we can assess whether the Court's intervention in fact aggravated other political problems. The provocative answer . . . runs completely contrary to the received wisdom. It is certainly the case that the Court succeeded in its immediate aim, of eliminating population disparities in legislative districts. The new districting process also appears to have lessened other forms of political manipulation, especially partisan gerrymandering. The great lesson of *Baker v. Carr,* then, is not just the tremendous value of the vote, but also the power of the American political process, when engaged to the fullest extent, to yield fair outcomes.

NOTES

1. The case was *Gray v. Sanders,* 372 U.S. 368 (1963). It concerned the county unit-vote in the selection of Georgia's governor, not its state legislature.

2. Article 5 of the Constitution states that "no state, without its consent, shall be deprived of its equal suffrage in the Senate." The provisions for constitutional amendments stipulate that no amendment can change the representation of the states in the Senate. This proviso protected the Connecticut Compromise, a political deal struck by Roger Sherman of Connecticut to satisfy smaller states, which wanted to keep the equal representation of states under the Articles of Confederation, and larger states, which wanted representation of population. Without this compromise, it seems doubtful that the U.S. Constitution would have been ratified by Congress.

3. Earl Warren, *The Memoirs of Earl Warren* (Garden City, NY: Doubleday, 1977), 306.

4. The problem dates back at least to 1690 and was described by the great English philosopher John Locke in his *Second Treatise on Government,* chap. XIII, sec. 157.

5. See Bruce Cain, "Assessing the Partisan Effects of Redistricting," *American Political Science Review* 79, no. 2 (June, 1985): 320–33.

6. Oliver Wendell Holmes, cited in Elliott, *Rise of Guardian Democracy,* 67.

7. Robert Dahl, *A Preface to Democratic Theory* (Chicago: University of Chicago Press, 1963).

8. Alfred deGrazia, *Apportionment and Representative Government* (New York: Praeger, 1962). See Robert Dixon, *Democratic Representation: Reapportionment in Law and Politics* (New York: Oxford University Press, 1968), for a thorough discussion of the competing arguments surrounding the reapportionment cases.

9. Anthony Downs provides the classic characterization of ideological politics in *An Economic Theory of Democracy* (New York: Harper, 1957).

10. Alan Ehrenhalt, "Frankfurter's Curse," *Governing* (January 2004), www.governing.com/archive/2004/jan/assess.txt. James A. Gardner, "What Is 'Fair' Partisan Representation, and How Can It Be Constitutionalized? The Case for a Return to Fixed Election Districts," *Marquette Law Review* 90, no. 3 (Spring 2007): 555–92. *Vieth v. Jubelirer*, 541 U.S. 267 (2004).

13.2

Citizens United v. Federal Election Commission (2010)

Justice Anthony Kennedy's majority opinion in this controversial Supreme Court decision establishes the key precedent that in matters of political speech, all organizations, including corporations and unions, are accorded First Amendment rights similar to those granted to individuals. Campaign finance regulations that treat corporations and unions as different from people and other kinds of organizations are at odds with the intent of the First Amendment. Thus, this decision strikes down portions of a campaign finance law that makes distinctions among the types of political organizations that can air political advertisements.

Justice Kennedy delivered the opinion of the Court:

Federal law prohibits corporations and unions from using their general treasury funds to make independent expenditures for speech defined as an "electioneering communication" or for speech expressly advocating the election or defeat of a candidate. Limits on electioneering communications were upheld in *McConnell* v. *Federal Election Comm'n*. The holding of *McConnell* rested to a large extent on an earlier case, *Austin* v. *Michigan Chamber of Commerce*, (1990). *Austin* had held that political speech may be banned based on the speaker's corporate identity.

In this case we are asked to reconsider *Austin* and, in effect, *McConnell*. It has been noted that "*Austin* was a significant departure from ancient First Amendment principles," *Federal Election Comm'n* v. *Wisconsin Right to Life, Inc.* (2007) *(WRTL)*. We agree with that conclusion and hold that *stare decisis* does not compel the continued acceptance of *Austin*. The Government may regulate corporate political speech through disclaimer and disclosure requirements, but it may not suppress that speech altogether. We turn to the case now before us.

Citizens United is a nonprofit corporation. It brought this action in the United States District Court for the District of Columbia. A three-judge court later convened to hear the cause. The resulting judgment gives rise to this appeal.

Citizens United has an annual budget of about $12 million. Most of its funds are from donations by individuals; but, in addition, it accepts a small portion of its funds from for-profit corporations.

In January 2008, Citizens United released a film entitled *Hillary: The Movie.* We refer to the film as *Hillary.* It is a 90-minute documentary about then-Senator Hillary Clinton, who was a candidate in the Democratic Party's 2008 Presidential primary elections. *Hillary* mentions Senator Clinton by name and depicts interviews with political commentators and other persons, most of them quite critical of Senator Clinton. *Hillary* was released in theaters and on DVD, but Citizens United wanted to increase distribution by making it available through video-on-demand.

Video-on-demand allows digital cable subscribers to select programming from various menus, including movies, television shows, sports, news, and music. The viewer can watch the program at any time and can elect to rewind or pause the program. In December 2007, a cable company offered, for a payment of $1.2 million, to make *Hillary* available on a video-on-demand channel called "Elections '08." Some video-on-demand services require viewers to pay a small fee to view a selected program, but here the proposal was to make *Hillary* available to viewers free of charge.

To implement the proposal, Citizens United was prepared to pay for the video-on-demand; and to promote the film, it produced two 10-second ads and one 30-second ad for *Hillary.* Each ad includes a short (and, in our view, pejorative) statement about Senator Clinton, followed by the name of the movie and the movie's Website address.

Citizens United desired to promote the video-on-demand offering by running advertisements on broadcast and cable television.

Before the Bipartisan Campaign Reform Act of 2002 (BCRA), federal law prohibited—and still does prohibit—corporations and unions from using general treasury funds to make direct contributions to candidates or independent expenditures that expressly advocate the election or defeat of a candidate, through any form of media, in connection with certain qualified federal elections.

BCRA §203 amended §441b to prohibit any "electioneering communication" as well. An electioneering communication is defined as "any broadcast, cable, or satellite communication" that "refers to a clearly identified candidate for Federal office" and is made within 30 days of a primary or 60 days of a general election. The Federal Election Commission's (FEC) regulations further define an electioneering communication as a communication that is "publicly distributed."

Corporations and unions are barred from using their general treasury funds for express advocacy or electioneering communications. They may establish, however, a "separate segregated fund" (known as a political action committee, or PAC) for these purposes. The moneys received by the segregated fund are limited to donations from stockholders and employees of the corporation or, in the case of unions, members of the union.

Citizens United wanted to make *Hillary* available through video-on-demand within 30 days of the 2008 primary elections. It feared, however, that both the film and the ads would be covered by §441b's ban on corporate-funded independent expenditures, thus subjecting the corporation to civil and criminal penalties under §437g. In December 2007, Citizens United sought declaratory and injunctive relief against the FEC. It argued that (1) §441b is unconstitutional as applied to *Hillary;* and (2) BCRA's disclaimer and disclosure requirements, BCRA §§201 and 311, are unconstitutional as applied to *Hillary* and to the three ads for the movie.

The District Court denied Citizens United's motion for a preliminary injunction. The court held that §441b was facially constitutional under *McConnell*, and that §441b was constitutional as applied to *Hillary* because it was "susceptible of no other interpretation than to inform the electorate that Senator Clinton is unfit for office, that the United States would be a dangerous place in a President Hillary Clinton world, and that viewers should vote against her." The court also rejected Citizens United's challenge to BCRA's disclaimer and disclosure requirements. It noted that "the Supreme Court has written approvingly of disclosure provisions triggered by political speech even though the speech itself was constitutionally protected under the First Amendment."

As the foregoing analysis confirms, the Court cannot resolve this case on a narrower ground without chilling political speech, speech that is central to the meaning and purpose of the First Amendment. It is not judicial restraint to accept an unsound, narrow argument just so the Court can avoid another argument with broader implications. Indeed, a court would be remiss in performing its duties were it to accept an unsound principle merely to avoid the necessity of making a broader ruling. Here, the lack of a valid basis for an alternative ruling requires full consideration of the continuing effect of the speech suppression upheld in *Austin*.

Citizens United stipulated to dismissing count 5 of its complaint, which raised a facial challenge to §441b, even though count 3 raised an as-applied challenge. The Government argues that Citizens United waived its challenge to *Austin* by dismissing count 5. We disagree.

First, even if a party could somehow waive a facial challenge while preserving an as-applied challenge, that would not prevent the Court from reconsidering *Austin* or addressing the facial validity of §441b in this case. And here, the District Court addressed Citizens United's facial challenge. In rejecting the claim, it noted that it "would have to overrule *McConnell* " for Citizens United to prevail on its facial challenge and that "[o]nly the Supreme Court may overrule its decisions." The District Court did not provide much analysis regarding the facial challenge because it could not ignore the controlling Supreme Court decisions in *Austin* or *McConnell*. Even so, the District Court did " 'pas[s] upon' " the issue. Furthermore, the District Court's later opinion, which granted the FEC summary judgment, was "[b]ased on the reasoning of [its] prior opinion," which included the discussion of the facial challenge. After the District Court addressed the facial validity of the statute, Citizens United raised its challenge to *Austin* in this Court. In these circumstances, it is necessary to consider Citizens United's challenge to *Austin* and the facial validity of §441b's expenditure ban.

Second, throughout the litigation, Citizens United has asserted a claim that the FEC has violated its First Amendment right to free speech. All concede that this claim is properly before us. Citizens United's argument that *Austin* should be overruled is "not a new claim." Rather, it is—at most—"a new argument to support what has been [a] consistent claim: that [the FEC] did not accord [Citizens United] the rights it was obliged to provide by the First Amendment."

Third, the distinction between facial and as-applied challenges is not so well defined that it has some automatic effect or that it must always control the pleadings and disposition in every case involving a constitutional challenge. The distinction is both instructive and necessary, for it goes to the breadth of the remedy employed by the Court, not what must be pleaded in a complaint. The parties cannot enter into a stipulation that prevents the Court from considering certain remedies if those remedies are necessary to resolve a claim that has been preserved.

Citizens United has preserved its First Amendment challenge to §441b as applied to the facts of its case; and given all the circumstances, we cannot easily address that issue without assuming a premise—the permissibility of restricting corporate political speech—that is itself in doubt. As our request for supplemental briefing implied, Citizens United's claim implicates the validity of *Austin*, which in turn implicates the facial validity of §441b.

When the statute now at issue came before the Court in *McConnell*, both the majority and the dissenting opinions considered the question of its facial validity. The holding and validity of *Austin* were essential to the reasoning of the *McConnell* majority opinion, which upheld BCRA's extension of §441b. *McConnell* permitted federal felony punishment for speech by all corporations, including nonprofit ones, that speak on prohibited subjects shortly before federal elections.

The *McConnell* majority considered whether the statute was facially invalid. An as-applied challenge was brought in *Wisconsin Right to Life, Inc.* v. *Federal Election Comm'n*, and the Court confirmed that the challenge could be maintained. Then, in *WRTL*, the controlling opinion of the Court not only entertained an as-applied challenge but also sustained it. Three Justices noted that they would continue to maintain the position that the record in *McConnell* demonstrated the invalidity of the Act on its face. The controlling opinion in *WRTL*, which refrained from holding the statute invalid except as applied to the facts then before the Court, was a careful attempt to accept the essential elements of the Court's opinion in *McConnell*, while vindicating the First Amendment arguments made by the *WRTL* parties.

As noted above, Citizens United's narrower arguments are not sustainable under a fair reading of the statute. In the exercise of its judicial responsibility, it is necessary then for the Court to consider the facial validity of §441b. Any other course of decision would prolong the substantial, nation-wide chilling effect caused by §441b's prohibitions on corporate expenditures. Consideration of the facial validity of §441b is further supported by the following reasons.

First is the uncertainty caused by the litigating position of the Government. As discussed above, see Part II–D, *supra*, the Government suggests, as an alternative argument, that an as-applied challenge might have merit. This argument proceeds on the premise that the nonprofit corporation involved here may have received only *de minimis* donations from for-profit corporations and that some nonprofit corporations may be exempted from the operation of the statute. The Government also suggests that an as-applied challenge to §441b's ban on books may be successful, although it would defend §441b's ban as applied to almost every other form of media including pamphlets. The Government thus, by its own position, contributes to the uncertainty that §441b causes. When the Government holds out the possibility of ruling for Citizens United on a narrow ground yet refrains from adopting that position, the added uncertainty demonstrates the necessity to address the question of statutory validity.

Second, substantial time would be required to bring clarity to the application of the statutory provision on these points in order to avoid any chilling effect caused by some improper interpretation. It is well known that the public begins to concentrate on elections only in the weeks immediately before they are held. There are short timeframes in which speech can have influence. The need or relevance of the speech will often first be apparent at this stage in the campaign. The decision to speak is made in the heat of political campaigns, when speakers react to messages conveyed by others. A speaker's ability to engage in political speech that could have a chance of persuading voters is stifled if the speaker must first commence a protracted lawsuit. By the time the lawsuit concludes, the election will be over and the litigants in most cases will have neither the incentive nor, perhaps, the resources to carry on, even if they could establish that the case is not moot because the issue is "capable of repetition, yet evading review." Here, Citizens United decided to litigate its case to the end. Today, Citizens United finally learns, two years after the fact, whether it could have spoken during the 2008 Presidential primary—long after the opportunity to persuade primary voters has passed.

Third is the primary importance of speech itself to the integrity of the election process. As additional rules are created for regulating political speech, any speech arguably within their reach is chilled.

This regulatory scheme may not be a prior restraint on speech in the strict sense of that term, for prospective speakers are not compelled by law to seek an advisory opinion from the FEC before the speech takes place. As a practical matter, however, given the complexity of the regulations and the deference courts show to administrative determinations, a speaker who wants to avoid threats of criminal liability and the heavy costs of defending against FEC enforcement must ask a governmental agency for prior permission to speak. These onerous restrictions thus function as the equivalent of prior restraint by giving the FEC power analogous to licensing laws implemented in 16th- and 17th-century England, laws and governmental practices of the sort that the First Amendment was drawn to prohibit.

This is precisely what *WRTL* sought to avoid. *WRTL* said that First Amendment standards "must eschew 'the open-ended rough-and-tumble of factors,' which 'invit[es] complex argument in a trial court and a virtually inevitable appeal.'" Yet, the FEC has created a regime that allows it to select what political speech is safe for public consumption by applying ambiguous tests. If parties want to avoid litigation and the possibility of civil and criminal penalties, they must either refrain from speaking or ask the FEC to issue an advisory opinion approving of the political speech in question. This is an unprecedented governmental intervention into the realm of speech.

The ongoing chill upon speech that is beyond all doubt protected makes it necessary in this case to invoke the earlier precedents that a statute which chills speech can and must be invalidated where its facial invalidity has been demonstrated.

The First Amendment provides that "Congress shall make no law . . . abridging the freedom of speech." Laws enacted to control or suppress speech may operate at different points in the speech process.

The law before us is an outright ban, backed by criminal sanctions. Section 441b makes it a felony for all corporations—including nonprofit advocacy corporations—either to expressly advocate the election or defeat of candidates or to broadcast electioneering communications within 30 days of a primary election and 60 days of a general election. Thus, the following acts would all be felonies under §441b: The Sierra Club runs an ad, within the crucial phase of 60 days before the general election, that exhorts the public to disapprove of a Congressman who favors logging in national forests; the National Rifle Association publishes a book urging the public to vote for the challenger because the incumbent U. S. Senator supports a handgun ban; and the American Civil Liberties Union creates a Web site telling the public to vote for a Presidential candidate in light of that candidate's defense of free speech. These prohibitions are classic examples of censorship.

Section 441b is a ban on corporate speech notwithstanding the fact that a PAC created by a corporation can still speak. A PAC is a separate association from the corporation. Even if a PAC could somehow allow a corporation to speak—and it does not—the option to form PACs does not alleviate the First Amendment problems with §441b. PACs are burdensome alternatives; they are expensive to administer and subject to extensive regulations. For example, every PAC must appoint a treasurer, forward donations to the treasurer promptly, keep detailed records of the identities of the persons making donations, preserve receipts for three years, and file an organization statement and report changes to this information within 10 days.

PACs have to comply with these regulations just to speak. This might explain why fewer than 2,000 of the millions of corporations in this country have PACs.

Section 441b's prohibition on corporate independent expenditures is thus a ban on speech. As a "restriction on the amount of money a person or group can spend on political communication during a campaign," that statute "necessarily reduces the quantity of expression by restricting the number of issues discussed, the depth of their exploration, and the size of the audience reached." Were the Court to uphold these restrictions, the Government could repress speech by silencing certain voices at any of the various points in the speech process. If §441b applied to individuals, no one would believe that it is merely a time, place, or manner restriction on speech. Its purpose and effect are to silence entities whose voices the Government deems to be suspect.

Speech is an essential mechanism of democracy, for it is the means to hold officials accountable to the people. The right of citizens to inquire, to hear, to speak, and to use information to reach consensus is a precondition to enlightened self-government and a necessary means to protect it. The First Amendment "'has its fullest and most urgent application' to speech uttered during a campaign for political office."

For these reasons, political speech must prevail against laws that would suppress it, whether by design or inadvertence. Laws that burden political speech are "subject to strict scrutiny," which requires the Government to prove that the restriction "furthers a compelling interest and is narrowly tailored to achieve that interest."

Premised on mistrust of governmental power, the First Amendment stands against attempts to disfavor certain subjects or viewpoints. Prohibited, too, are restrictions distinguishing among different speakers, allowing speech by some but not others. As instruments to censor, these categories are interrelated: Speech restrictions based on the identity of the speaker are all too often simply a means to control content.

By taking the right to speak from some and giving it to others, the Government deprives the disadvantaged person or class of the right to use speech to strive to establish worth, standing, and respect for the speaker's voice. The Government may not by these means deprive the public of the right and privilege to determine for itself what speech and speakers are worthy of consideration. The First Amendment protects speech and speaker, and the ideas that flow from each.

The Court has upheld a narrow class of speech restrictions that operate to the disadvantage of certain persons, but these rulings were based on an interest in allowing governmental entities to perform their functions. The corporate independent expenditures at issue in this case, however, would not interfere with governmental functions, so these cases are inapposite. These precedents stand only for the proposition that there are certain governmental functions that cannot operate without some restrictions on particular kinds of speech.

By contrast, it is inherent in the nature of the political process that voters must be free to obtain information from diverse sources in order to determine how to cast their votes. At least before *Austin*, the Court had not allowed the exclusion of a class of speakers from the general public dialogue.

We find no basis for the proposition that, in the context of political speech, the Government may impose restrictions on certain disfavored speakers. Both history and logic lead us to this conclusion.

The Court has recognized that First Amendment protection extends to corporations. Under the rationale of these precedents, political speech does not lose First Amendment protection "simply because its source is a corporation." The Court has thus rejected the argument that political speech of corporations or other associations should be treated differently under the First Amendment simply because such associations are not "natural persons."

At least since the latter part of the 19th century, the laws of some States and of the United States imposed a ban on corporate direct contributions to candidates. Yet not until 1947 did Congress first prohibit independent expenditures by corporations and labor unions in §304 of the Labor Management Relations Act 1947. In passing this Act Congress overrode the veto of President Truman, who warned that the expenditure ban was a "dangerous intrusion on free speech."

In its defense of the corporate-speech restrictions in §441b, the Government notes the antidistortion rationale on which *Austin* and its progeny rest in part, yet it all but abandons reliance upon it. It argues instead that two other compelling interests support *Austin*'s holding that corporate expenditure restrictions are constitutional: an anticorruption interest, and a shareholder-protection interest.

The Government contends that *Austin* permits it to ban corporate expenditures for almost all forms of communication stemming from a corporation. If *Austin* were correct, the Government could prohibit a corporation from expressing political views in media beyond those presented here, such as by printing books.

Political speech is "indispensable to decision making in a democracy, and this is no less true because the speech comes from a corporation rather than an individual." This protection for speech is inconsistent with *Austin*'s antidistortion rationale. *Austin* sought to defend the antidistortion rationale as a means to prevent corporations from obtaining "'an unfair advantage in the political marketplace'" by using "'resources amassed in the economic marketplace.'" But *Buckley* rejected the premise that the Government has an interest "in equalizing the relative ability of individuals and groups to influence the outcome of elections." *Buckley* was specific in stating that "the skyrocketing cost of political campaigns" could not sustain the governmental prohibition. The First Amendment's protections do not depend on the speaker's "financial ability to engage in public discussion."

The rule that political speech cannot be limited based on a speaker's wealth is a necessary consequence of the premise that the First Amendment generally prohibits the suppression of political speech based on the speaker's identity.

Either as support for its antidistortion rationale or as a further argument, the *Austin* majority undertook to distinguish wealthy individuals from corporations on the ground that "[s]tate law grants corporations special advantages—such as limited liability, perpetual life, and favorable treatment of the accumulation and distribution of assets."

Austin's antidistortion rationale would produce the dangerous, and unacceptable, consequence that Congress could ban political speech of media corporations. Media corporations are now exempt from §441b's ban on corporate expenditures. Yet media corporations accumulate wealth with the help of the corporate form, the largest media corporations have "immense aggregations of wealth," and the views expressed by media corporations often "have little or no correlation to the public's support" for those views. Thus, under the Government's reasoning, wealthy media corporations could have their voices diminished to put them on par with other media entities. There is no precedent for permitting this under the First Amendment.

Austin interferes with the "open marketplace" of ideas protected by the First Amendment. It permits the Government to ban the political speech of millions of associations of citizens. Most of these are small corporations without large amounts of wealth. This fact belies the Government's argument that the statute is justified on the ground that it prevents the "distorting effects of immense aggregations of wealth." It is not even aimed at amassed wealth.

The censorship we now confront is vast in its reach. The Government has "muffle[d]" the voices that best represent the most significant segments of the economy." By suppressing the speech of manifold corporations, both for-profit and nonprofit, the Government prevents their voices and viewpoints from reaching the public and advising voters on which persons or entities are hostile to their interests. Factions will necessarily form in our Republic, but the remedy of "destroying the liberty" of some factions is "worse than the disease."

The purpose and effect of this law is to prevent corporations, including small and nonprofit corporations, from presenting both facts and opinions to the public. When that phenomenon is coupled with §441b, the result is that smaller or nonprofit corporations cannot raise a voice to object when other corporations, including those with vast wealth, are cooperating with the Government. That cooperation may sometimes be voluntary, or it may be at the demand of a Government official who uses his or her authority, influence, and power to threaten corporations to support the Government's policies. Those kinds of interactions are often unknown and unseen. The speech that §441b forbids, though, is public, and all can judge its content and purpose. References to massive corporate treasuries should not mask the real operation of this law. Rhetoric ought not obscure reality.

Even if §441b's expenditure ban were constitutional, wealthy corporations could still lobby elected officials, although smaller corporations may not have the resources to do so. And wealthy individuals and unincorporated associations can spend unlimited amounts on independent expenditures. Yet certain disfavored associations of citizens—those that have taken on the corporate form—are penalized for engaging in the same political speech.

When Government seeks to use its full power, including the criminal law, to command where a person may get his or her information or what distrusted source he or she may not hear, it uses censorship to control thought. This is unlawful. The First Amendment confirms the freedom to think for ourselves.

What we have said also shows the invalidity of other arguments made by the Government. For the most part relinquishing the antidistortion rationale, the Government falls back on the argument that corporate political speech can be banned in order to prevent corruption or its appearance. In *Buckley* , the Court found this interest "sufficiently important" to allow limits on contributions but did not extend that reasoning to expenditure limits. When *Buckley* examined an expenditure ban, it found "that the governmental interest in preventing corruption and the appearance of corruption [was] inadequate to justify [the ban] on independent expenditures."

The *Buckley* Court, nevertheless, sustained limits on direct contributions in order to ensure against the reality or appearance of corruption. That case did not extend this rationale to independent expenditures, and the Court does not do so here.

The anticorruption interest is not sufficient to displace the speech here in question. Indeed, 26 States do not restrict independent expenditures by for-profit corporations. The Government does not claim that these expenditures have corrupted the political process in those States.

For the reasons explained above, we now conclude that independent expenditures, including those made by corporations, do not give rise to corruption or the appearance of corruption.

The Government contends further that corporate independent expenditures can be limited because of its interest in protecting dissenting shareholders from being compelled to fund corporate political speech. This asserted interest, like *Austin* 's antidistortion rationale, would allow the Government to ban the political speech even of media corporations. Assume, for example, that a shareholder of a corporation that owns a newspaper disagrees with the political views the newspaper expresses. Under the Government's view, that potential disagreement could give the Government the authority to restrict the media corporation's political speech. The First Amendment does not allow that power. There is, furthermore, little evidence of abuse that cannot be corrected by shareholders "through the procedures of corporate democracy."

Those reasons are sufficient to reject this shareholder-protection interest; and, moreover, the statute is both underinclusive and overinclusive. As to the first, if Congress had been seeking to protect dissenting shareholders, it would not have banned corporate speech in only certain media within 30 or 60 days before an election. A dissenting shareholder's interests would be implicated by speech in any media at any time. As to the second, the statute is overinclusive because it covers all corporations, including nonprofit corporations and for-profit corporations with only single shareholders. As to other corporations, the remedy is not to restrict speech but to consider and explore other regulatory mechanisms. The regulatory mechanism here, based on speech, contravenes the First Amendment.

Our precedent is to be respected unless the most convincing of reasons demonstrates that adherence to it puts us on a course that is sure error.

For the reasons above, it must be concluded that *Austin* was not well reasoned. The Government defends *Austin*, relying almost entirely on "the quid pro quo interest, the corruption interest or the shareholder interest," and not *Austin*'s expressed antidistortion rationale.

Austin is undermined by experience since its announcement. Political speech is so ingrained in our culture that speakers find ways to circumvent campaign finance laws. Our Nation's speech dynamic is changing, and informative voices should not have to circumvent onerous restrictions to exercise their First Amendment rights. Speakers have become adept at presenting citizens with sound bites, talking points, and scripted messages that dominate the 24-hour news cycle. Corporations, like individuals, do not have monolithic views. On certain topics corporations may possess valuable expertise, leaving them the best equipped to point out errors or fallacies in speech of all sorts, including the speech of candidates and elected officials.

Rapid changes in technology—and the creative dynamic inherent in the concept of free expression—counsel against upholding a law that restricts political speech in certain media or by certain speakers. Today, 30-second television ads may be the most effective way to convey a political message. Soon, however, it may be that Internet sources, such as blogs and social networking Web sites, will provide citizens with significant information about political candidates and issues. Yet, §441b would seem to ban a blog post expressly advocating the election or defeat of a candidate if that blog were created with corporate funds. The First Amendment does not permit Congress to make these categorical distinctions based on the corporate identity of the speaker and the content of the political speech.

Due consideration leads to this conclusion: *Austin* should be and now is overruled. We return to the principle established in *Buckley* and *Bellotti* that the Government may not suppress political speech on the basis of the speaker's corporate identity. No sufficient governmental interest justifies limits on the political speech of nonprofit or for-profit corporations.

Given our conclusion we are further required to overrule the part of *McConnell* that upheld BCRA §203's extension of §441b's restrictions on corporate independent expenditures. The *McConnell* Court relied on the antidistortion interest recognized in *Austin* to uphold a greater restriction on speech than the restriction upheld in *Austin* , and we have found this interest unconvincing and insufficient. This part of *McConnell* is now overruled.

Modern day movies, television comedies, or skits on Youtube.com might portray public officials or public policies in unflattering ways. Yet if a covered transmission during the blackout period creates the background for candidate endorsement or opposition, a felony occurs solely because a corporation, other than an exempt media corporation, has made the "purchase, payment, distribution, loan, advance, deposit, or gift of money or anything of value" in order to engage in political speech. Speech would be suppressed in the realm where its necessity is most evident: in the public dialogue preceding a real election. Governments are often hostile to speech, but under our law and our tradition it seems stranger than fiction for our Government to make this political speech a crime. Yet this is the statute's purpose and design.

Some members of the public might consider *Hillary* to be insightful and instructive; some might find it to be neither high art nor a fair discussion on how to set the Nation's course; still others simply might suspend judgment on these points but decide to think more about issues and candidates. Those choices and assessments, however, are not for the Government to make. "The First Amendment underwrites the freedom to experiment and to create in the realm of thought and speech. Citizens must be free to use new forms, and new forums, for the expression of ideas.

The judgment of the District Court is reversed with respect to the constitutionality of 2 U. S. C. §441b's restrictions on corporate independent expenditures.

It is so ordered.

13.3

NOLAN McCARTY, KEITH POOLE, AND HOWARD ROSENTHAL

From *Polarized America: The Dance of Ideology and Unequal Riches*

McCarty, Poole, and Rosenthal link together several crucial topics to improve our understanding of the relationship between elections and policy outcomes. Two of these topics are from earlier chapters: political parties and political participation. The third topic is income inequality among Americans. They show evidence that in recent elections the two major political parties have polarized in terms of the types of citizens they target and that this has been mostly driven by the increasing income gap between voters supporting each party. Furthermore, nonvoting by the poorest citizens (especially immigrants who cannot vote) has diminished pressures on both parties (but especially the Democrats) to propose redistributive policies that would benefit the poor.

THE CHOREOGRAPHY OF AMERICAN POLITICS

In the middle of the twentieth century, the Democrats and the Republicans danced almost cheek to cheek in their courtship of the political middle. Over the past thirty years, the parties have deserted the center of the floor in favor of the wings. In the parlance of punditry and campaign rhetoric circa 2004, American politics have "polarized." Scarcely a day went by without headlines such as the *San Francisco Chronicle's* "Where did the middle go? How polarized politics and a radical GOP have put a chill on measured debate."[1] Story after story attempted to explain the seemingly unbridgeable divide between red and blue states. Was the country divided on moral issues, national security, or NASCAR? Even the First Lady offered her diagnosis, as the Associated Press reported: "First Lady Laura Bush thinks the news media is increasingly filled with opinions instead of facts, and suggested . . . that journalists are contributing to the polarization of the country."[2]

What public commentators missed, however, was that polarization was not a solo performer but part of a tight ensemble. Polarization's partners were other fundamental changes in the American society and economy. Most important, just as American politics became increasingly divisive, economic fortunes diverged. Middle- and high-income Americans have continued to benefit from the massive economic growth experienced since the Second World War. But material well-being for the lower-income classes has stagnated. For each story about successful people like Bill Gates and Sam Walton, there are contrasting stories about low-wage, no-benefit workers.

That Wal-Mart is the center of both the good news and the bad underscores how unequally America's economic growth has been allocated. To put some hard numbers on the disparities, in 1967 a household in the 95th percentile of the income distribution had six times the income of someone in the 25th percentile. By 2003 the disparity had increased to 8.6 times.[3]

It is important to note that inequality rose in a period of increasing prosperity, with the added riches going much more to the haves than to the have-nots. Households with an annual income of over $100,000 (year 2000 dollars) increased from under 3 percent in 1967 to over 12 percent in 2000. Even the middle of the income distribution was more prosperous. In year 2000 dollars, median income increased from $31,400 in 1967 to $42,200 in 2000. Inequality probably had a real (versus perceived) bite on consumption only at the very bottom of the income distribution. This increase in riches, albeit unequal, is likely to have contributed to polarization.

Economists, sociologists, and others have identified a number of factors behind the shift to greater inequality. Returns to education have increased, labor union coverage has declined, trade exposure has increased, corporate executives have benefited from sharp increases in compensation and stock options, and family structure has changed through rising rates of divorce, late marriage, and two-income households. An additional factor helping tie our ensemble together is the massive wave of immigration, legal and illegal, since the 1960s.

The new immigrants are predominantly unskilled. They have contributed greatly to the economy by providing low-wage labor, especially in jobs that American citizens no longer find desirable. They also provide the domestic services that facilitate labor market participation by highly skilled people. On the other hand, immigrants have also increased inequality both directly, by occupying the lowest rungs of the economic ladder, and indirectly, through competition with citizens for low-wage jobs. Yet as noncitizens they lack the civic opportunities to secure the protections of the welfare state. Because these poor people cannot vote, there is less political support for policies that would lower inequality by redistribution.

[W]e trace out how these major economic and social changes are related to the increased polarization of the U.S. party system. We characterize the relationships as a "dance"—that is, relationships with give and take and back and forth, where causality can run both ways. On the one hand, economic inequality might feed directly into political polarization. People at the top might devote time and resources to supporting a political party strongly opposed to redistribution. People at the bottom would have an opposite response. Polarized parties, on the other hand, might generate policies that increase inequality through at least two channels. If the Republicans move sharply to the right, they can use their majority (as has been argued for the tax bills of the first administrations of Ronald Reagan and George W. Bush) to reduce redistribution. If they are not the majority, they can use the power of the minority in American politics to block changes to the status quo. In other words, polarization in the context of American political institutions now means that the political process cannot be used to redress inequality that may arise from nonpolitical changes in technology, lifestyle, and compensation practices.

Measuring Political Polarization

Before laying the groundwork for our argument that political polarization is related to economic inequality, we need to discuss how we conceptualize and measure political polarization. What do we mean by "polarization"? Polarization is, for short, a separation of politics into liberal and conservative camps. We all recognize that members of Congress can be thought of as occupying a position on a liberal-conservative spectrum. Ted Kennedy is a liberal, Dianne Feinstein a more moderate Democrat, Joe Lieberman even more so; Olympia Snowe is a moderate Republican and Rick Santorum a conservative Republican. The perception of conservativeness is commonly shared. There is a common perception because a politician's behavior is predictable. If we know that Olympia Snowe will fight a large tax cut, we can be fairly certain that all or almost all the Democrats will support her position.

There are two complementary facets to the polarization story. First, at the level of individual members of Congress, moderates are vanishing. Second, the two parties have pulled apart. *Conservative* and *liberal* have become almost perfect synonyms for *Republican* and *Democrat.*

Because we are social scientists and not journalists or politicians, we need to nail these shared impressions with precise operational definitions. When two of us (the two not in high school at the time) published "The Polarization of American Politics" in 1984, we measured polarization with interest group ratings. Each year, a number of interest groups publish ratings of members of Congress. Among the many groups are the United Auto Workers (UAW), the Americans for Democratic Action (ADA), the National Taxpayers Union (NTU), the American Conservative Union (ACU), and the League of Conservation Voters (LCV). Each interest group selects a fairly small number of roll call votes, typically twenty to forty, from the hundreds taken each year. A senator or representative who always votes to support the interest group's position is rewarded with a score of 100. Those always on the "wrong" side get a score of 0. Those who support the group half the time get a score of 50, and so on.

To see that moderates had vanished by 2003, consider the ratings of the Americans for Democratic Action for that year. The possible ADA ratings rose in five-point steps from 0 to 100. Of the twenty-one possible ratings, nine were in the range 30 through 70. Yet only eleven of the hundred senators (McCain, AZ; Campbell, CO; Lieberman, CT; Breaux, LA; Landrieu, LA; Collins, ME; Snowe, ME; Nelson, NE; Reid, NV; Edwards, NC; and Chafee, RI) fell in one of the nine middle categories. In contrast, ten Democrats got high marks of 95 or 100 and fourteen Republicans got 5 or 0. That is, more than twice as many senators (24) fell in the four very extreme categories as fell in the nine middle categories (11).

Our 1984 article documented two findings about the scores of the ADA and other interest groups. First, the interest groups gave out basically the same set of ratings or the mirror image of that set. If a general-purpose liberal interest group like the ADA gave a rating of 100 to a representative, the representative would nearly always get a very high rating from another liberal interest group, such as the LCV, even when the interest group focused on a single policy area, like the environment. Similarly, a 100 ADA rating made a very low rating from a conservative group like ACU or NTU a foregone conclusion. This agreement across interest groups meant that interest groups were evaluating members of Congress along a single, liberal-conservative dimension. Individual issue areas, such as race, no longer had a distinctive existence. Second, the interest groups were giving out fewer and fewer scores in the moderate range in the 40s, 50s, and 60s. Moderates were giving way to more extreme liberals and conservatives. Put simply, the interest groups had little difficulty placing Ted Kennedy and Jesse Helms as ideological opposites, and they were finding fewer and fewer Jacob Javitses and Sam Nunns to put in the middle. The change we noted occurred in the last half of the 1970s; indeed, our data went only through 1980.

We summarized our findings by combining all the ratings to give a single liberal-conservative score to each member.[4] We then measured polarization in a variety of technical ways, which we explain more fully in chapter 2. One measure was simply how much the scores for members of the two political parties overlapped. If moderates were abundant in both parties, there would be substantial overlap, or low polarization. If the Democrats had only liberals and the Republicans only conservatives, there would be no overlap, or high polarization. We found that the overlap had shrunk.

Using interest group ratings only, however, has two limitations. First, interest groups select only a small number of roll call votes. The ADA, for example, uses just twenty per year. But each house of Congress conducts hundreds of roll calls each year. ADA's selections might be a biased sample of this richer universe.[5] Second, interest group ratings became common only in the second half of the twentieth century. We cannot do a long-run study of polarization, inequality, and immigration just on the basis of interest group ratings. So we developed NOMINATE, a quantitative procedure that would score politicians directly from their roll call voting records, using all of the recorded votes. To locate the politicians' positions, these techniques use information on who votes with whom and how often. For example, if Arlen Specter votes with both Hillary Clinton and Bill Frist much more frequently than Clinton and Frist vote together, then these techniques position Specter as moderate, in between those more extreme senators. Using this algorithm over millions of individual choices made by thousands of legislators on tens of thousands of roll calls allows us to develop quite precise measures of each member's position on the liberal-conservative spectrum. . . .

The Common Trajectory of Polarization and Inequality

Our measure of political polarization closely parallels measures of economic inequality and of immigration for much of the twentieth century. We show this correlation with three plots of time series.

One measure of income inequality is the Gini coefficient of family income calculated by the Bureau of the Census. The Gini coefficient shows how the entire distribution of income deviates from equality. When every family has the same income, the Gini is zero. When one family has all the income, the Gini is one. In figure 1, we show the Gini and polarization in the post-World War II period.[6] Income inequality falls from 1947 through 1957 and then bounces up and down until 1969. After 1969, income inequality increases every two years, with a couple of slight interruptions. Polarization bounces at a low level until 1977, and thereafter follows an unbroken upward trajectory.

We stress an important aspect of the timing of the reversal in inequality and polarization. In some circles, both of these phenomena are viewed as the consequence of Ronald Reagan's victory in the 1980 elections. Both reversals, however, clearly predate Reagan and Reaganomics. Reagan conservatism

FIGURE 1   Income Inequality and House Polarization

SOURCE: Gini index from the U.S. Census Bureau (2005).

NOTE: Polarization is measured as the difference between the Democratic and Republican Party mean NOMINATE scores in the U.S. House. The Gini and polarization measures correspond to the first year of each biennial congressional term.

was a product sitting on a shelf in the political supermarket. In 1980, customers switched brands, arguably the result of a preference shift marked by rising inequality and party polarization.[7]

▪   ▪   ▪

Piketty and Saez used income tax returns to compute the percentage share of income going to the richest of the rich. In figure 2, we plot the share going to the top one percent of the income distribution. This longer series matches up nicely with our polarization measure over the entire twentieth century.

The decline in polarization throughout the first seventy years of the twentieth century is echoed by much of the literature written toward the end of the decline or just after. During this period, Americans were seen as having grown closer together politically. In 1960, the sociologist Daniel Bell published *The End of Ideology: On the Exhaustion of Political Ideas in the Fifties*. A year later, the political scientist Robert Dahl pointed to a nation moving from oligarchy to pluralism (Dahl 1961). Similarly, the new "rational choice" school in political science emphasized Tweedle-dee/Tweedle-dum parties focused on the median voter (Downs 1957), members of Congress largely concerned with constituency service (Fiorina 1978), and universalism in pork-barrel politics

FIGURE 2   Top One Percent Income Share and House Polarization

SOURCE: Income shares from Piketty and Saez (2003), table II.

(Weingast, Shepsle, and Johnsen 1981). What these authors were pointing to was echoed in analyses of roll call voting patterns in the House and Senate. Put simply, the fraction of moderates grew and the fraction of extreme liberals and extreme conservatives fell from 1900 to about 1975 (Poole and Rosenthal 1997; McCarty, Poole, and Rosenthal 1997). By the beginning of the twenty-first century, the extremes had come back.

The corresponding story for immigration is told by figure 3. Immigration is captured by looking at the percentage of the population that is foreign-born. (This is the only measure available before the Census Bureau began biennial collection of data on citizenship in 1972. From 1972 on, we will look, in chapter 4, at the percentage of the population represented by those who claim to be noncitizens.) For comparison, we have taken the polarization period back to 1880, the first census after the modern Democrat-Republican two-party system formed upon the end of Reconstruction following the elections of 1876.

Until World War I, the percentage of foreign-born living in the United States was very high, hovering in the 13–15 percent range. With the curtailing of

FIGURE 3 Percent Foreign-Born and House Polarization

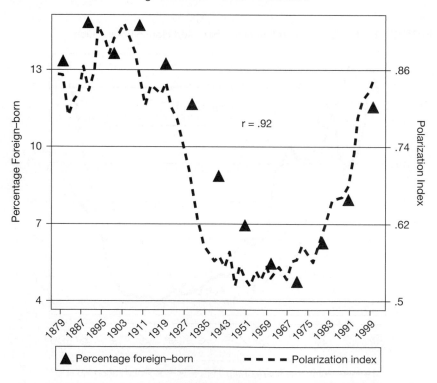

NOTE: Each observation of foreign-born population corresponds to a U.S. decennial census.

immigration, first by the war and then by the restrictive immigration acts of the 1920s, the percentage of foreign-born falls continuously until the 1970 census, just after immigration was liberalized by the 1965 reforms. The percentage of foreign-born thereafter increases sharply, exceeding 11 percent in the census of 2000. In 1970, a majority of the foreign-born had become naturalized citizens. By 2000, a substantial majority of the foreign-born was formed by noncitizens. Parallel to the track of immigration, polarization hovers at a high level until 1912 and then declines until 1967, with the exception of the uptick in the 1940s. The immigration series, like the income series, largely parallels our polarization measure.[8]

When we ourselves first saw figures 1, 2, and 3, we realized that major indicators of the politics, the economics, and the demographics of the United States had followed very similar trajectories over many decades. . . .

A Focus on Income

[W]e look at income and other components of economic well-being as an important variable in defining political ideology and voter preferences. We do not, however, discount the importance of such other factors as race and "moral values." We chose to emphasize economics partly because we seek to redress an imbalance in political science: income has been largely ignored, and race-ethnicity and class (as measured by occupation rather than income) receive more attention. We chose economics also because many public policies are defined largely in terms of income. Certainly the tax bills of 1993, 2001, and 2003 were among the most important domestic policy changes of the Clinton and George W. Bush administrations. Indeed, the overwhelming majority of congressional roll calls are over taxes, budgets, and economic policies, especially after the issue of *de jure* political rights for African-Americans left the congressional agenda at the end of the 1960s. Most importantly, income is closely related to how people vote, to whether they participate in politics by either voting or making campaign contributions, and to whether they are eligible to vote as United States citizens.

Race does appear to be related to the current absence of redistribution in the United States (Alesina and Glaeser 2004) and to the absence of public spending in local communities (Alesina, Baqir, and Easterly 1999; Alesina and La Ferrara 2000, 2002). The claim that welfare expenditures in the United States are low because of race has been made by many authors, including Myrdal (1960), Quadagno (1994), and Gilens (1999). The basic claim of this literature is that the correlation with poverty lowers the willingness of voters to favor public spending for redistribution. But it is hard to see racism as hardening in the last quarter of the twentieth century when inequality was increasing. Racism and racial tension seem to have been rife when inequality was falling: recall the lynchings and race riots in the first half of the century and the urban riots of the 1960s. (Similarly, with regard to occupation or class, unionization has been declining since the 1950s.) We do explicitly consider race when treating ideological polarization in Congress and income polarization in the mass public, but it does, in historical perspective, appear appropriate to make income and economics our primary focus.

The Dance Card

... Polarization has increased for two reasons. First, Republicans in the North and South have moved sharply to the right. Second, moderate Democrats in the South have been replaced by Republicans. The remaining, largely northern, Democrats are somewhat more liberal than the Democratic Party of the 1960s.

The movements we observe tell us only about the relative positioning of politicians. We say that Republicans have moved to the right because newly elected Republicans have, on the whole, voted in a more conservative manner than the Republicans who remain in Congress. Northern Democrats, in contrast, don't look sharply different from the Democrats of old.

At the same time, however, how policy issues map onto liberal-conservative preferences may have changed. The Republicans have moved sharply away from redistributive policies that would reduce economic inequality. The Democrats as analyzed by John Gerring (1998), a political scientist at Boston University, have moved their platforms away from general welfare issues to issues based on ascriptive characteristics (race, gender, and sexual preference) of individuals. For example, figure 4, drawn from Gerring, shows that the Democrats increased emphasis on general welfare through the 1960s but then deemphasized it in the 1970s. The turn in platforms thus matches the reversals in economic inequality and polarization. Parallel to Gerring's results, we show that race as an issue has been absorbed into the main redistributive dimension of liberal-conservative politics. Taxes, minimum wages, and other traditional redistributive policy areas continue to be liberal-conservative issues; they have been joined by issues related to ascription.

IMMIGRATION, INCOME, AND THE VOTERS' INCENTIVE TO REDISTRIBUTE

Economic inequality in the United States has increased sharply. At the same time, income differences have become more important in determining where a congressional district's representative is likely to fall on the liberal-conservative dimension and how voters identify with parties and make voting decisions in presidential elections. Why has the increased importance of income not translated into policies that would curtail the sharp growth in inequality? At least in part, noncitizens who are ineligible to vote are concentrated at the bottom of the income distribution, so politicians feel little pressure to respond to their interests. Although economic inequality has increased, the relative income of the vast majority of *voters* has not markedly deteriorated.

■　　■　　■

In 1972, noncitizens were a small fraction of the United States population. They were also relatively well-to-do. In fact, the median income of a noncitizen was actually higher than that of citizens reporting themselves as having not voted in the presidential race between Nixon and McGovern. Noncitizens today are growing in number, and they tend to be at the bottom of the income distribution. In contrast, the relative economic position of voters and nonvoters shows little change since 1972.

The changing economic position of noncitizens is politically relevant. It is likely to contribute to the failure of the political process in the United States to generate redistribution that would eliminate growing disparities in wage and income inequality. As we said, the income of the median voter has *not* declined relatively over the past thirty years. How has the median voter's economic position been sustained, while that of the median family has declined? Part of the answer, as we show, is that lower-income people are increasingly likely to be noncitizens. The median income of noncitizens has shifted sharply downward, and the fraction of the population that is noncitizen has increased dramatically. From 1972 to 2000, the median family income of noncitizens fell from 78 percent of the median income of voters to 59 percent, while the fraction of the population that is noncitizen rose from 2.6 percent to 7.8 percent.[9]

One of the main reasons for the dramatic change in the number and poverty of noncitizens is federal legislation that has opened the doors to increased legal immigration while doing little to control illegal immigration. During the late nineteenth and early twentieth centuries, immigration was made more difficult for Europeans, and the Chinese and Japanese were excluded entirely. The immigration acts of 1921, 1924, and 1929 set up permanent quotas by national origin that both restricted total immigration and favored the relatively wealthy people of northwestern Europe. The barriers of the 1920s were only broken down by the 1965 amendments to the Immigration and Nationality Act of 1952. The amendments largely ended discrimination on the basis of national origin. Annual immigration quotas were greatly increased by the Immigration Act of 1990.

Economists have recognized that immigration, through low wage competition, has had an effect on inequality. But how big is the effect? . . .

We stress that the direct economic effects must be combined with the indirect political effects. Changes in such public policies as minimum wages, income taxation, and estate taxation have, on balance, held the median voter's relative position in place. More redistributive policies would have occurred, we conjecture, had there been a sharp deterioration in the position of voters in the middle of the income distribution.

There is a large literature, including the references above, that focuses on immigration. In contrast, this chapter emphasizes citizenship because many immigrants eventually become naturalized citizens and are then eligible to vote. Our results suggest that naturalized immigrants are likely to look, in terms of income, much like native citizens. At least, it is clear that the relative income of the median voter has not greatly declined during the wave of poor, naturalized immigrants. In contrast, as some immigrants have become naturalized, they have more than been replaced by the continuing surge of poor immigrant noncitizens.

The analysis is all in terms of relative incomes. Only these, and not the real levels, matter in the economic model of redistribution. [O]ver the period of our study real median income has in fact increased. To the extent that redistribution accomplished by the political process is social insurance (such things as unemployment benefits, old-age benefits, and medical benefits), the increase in real income should diminish support for redistribution, complementing the results of this chapter.[10] The effects of income inequality, however, are all on relative incomes.

We explore the relationship between income and voting in a way that differs from the standard approach taken by political scientists. The usual approach is to see if the rich in fact vote more than the poor. We take a different approach, comparing characteristics of the income distribution of voters to the same characteristics for nonvoters and noncitizens. We ask how the income characteristics have changed over time. In the standard approach, one is also concerned with verifying that income has an effect when one controls for other demographics. We are less concerned with this issue because public policy depends less on covariates than on income. A person's taxes are not lower because he or she is a college graduate, an African American, or an evangelical. (One's labor market experience may differ, however.) Taxes may be slightly less if a person is over 65, but the monthly social security check still depends on lifetime earnings and not race, education, or gender. So if we want to study redistribution, we should start with income, at least as a first cut.

In most political economy models, the income inequality that has arisen since the 1970s would have self-equilibrated. As inequality increased, there would be more pressure to redistribute. . . . As inequality, defined as a decrease in the ratio of median voter income to mean income, went up, more redistribution should have occurred. In the United States, however, public policy veered in the opposite direction. . . .

Other industrial nations have been exposed to the same technological change or opportunities as the United States. Although economic inequality might be driven by technological change, the responses elsewhere have not been the same. For example, Piketty and Saez (2003) show that during the last three decades of the twentieth century, the share of national income going to the top 0.1 percent of the population remained unchanged in France but sharply increased in the United States. We also note, in keeping with the theme of this chapter, that France has had a dramatically different experience with noncitizenship. From 1975 to 1999, roughly the period of our study, French government statistics show that the percentage of noncitizens decreased, falling from 6.5 percent of the population to 5.6 percent.[11] France and the United States, thus, have had contrasting trends in income inequality and in citizenship. How might these trends have been reflected in political processes?

To answer this question, we return to the Bolton and Roland (1997) model and focus on median/mean ratios. From the perspective of that model, noncitizenship has both a *disenfranchisement* effect and a *sharing* effect.[12]

The *disenfranchisement effect* can be viewed as a change in the numerator of the median/mean ratio. The median income of voters is higher than that of all families. This fact reflects not just that voters have higher incomes than eligible nonvoters, but also that voters have higher incomes than noncitizens. The effect of disenfranchising non-citizens will increase either if noncitizens become more numerous or if they become poorer.

If all citizens voted, the appropriate ratio would be median citizen income/mean family income. If all those over 18 voted, the appropriate ratio would be median family income/mean family income. By comparing these ratios to median voter income/mean family income, we can study how much "disenfranchisement" is due to nonvoting by citizens and how much to the ineligibility of noncitizens.

The presence of noncitizens in the population not only affects the numerator of the median/mean ratio, it also changes the denominator. Because noncitizens are poorer than citizens, mean family income is less than mean citizen income. Noncitizens thus increase the ratio, making redistribution less attractive to the median voter. Noncitizens shrink the per capita pie that has to be shared equally with all residents. The sharing of benefits with noncitizens has, of course, become a political hot potato. To assess the *sharing effect*, we will compare redistribution when mean family income for citizens is substituted for mean family income in the ratio. This counterfactual presumes that mean citizen income is unaffected by the presence of noncitizens. Although citizen income may well be affected by immigration, it is hard to argue that it would fall below realized mean family income. Some sharing effect must be present.

The sharing effect will drive all citizens to be less favorable to redistribution. The disenfranchisement effect decreases the political influence of relatively low-income families and increases the influence of higher-income families. We focus, for convenience, on median incomes, but our findings can be viewed as indicative of the incentives to redistribute that face a large segment of the electorate with incomes not very distant from the median. The main point of this chapter is that the relative income of the median income *voter* in the United States is in fact not worse today than it was thirty years ago. The disenfranchisement effect and the sharing effect have contributed to lessening voter support for redistribution despite increasing income inequality.

Although the ratio of family income of the median *individual* to mean family income has indeed fallen in the United States over the past thirty years, the ratio of the family income of the median *voter* to mean family income has been remarkably constant. The political process does appear to have equilibrated in the sense that the median voter is not worse off compared to the mean.

How has this distinction between the median voter and the median individual arisen?

First, not every eligible individual votes. United States citizens who do not vote have lower incomes than those who do. This income difference has always been the case, and it does not appear to have shifted much over the past thirty years.[13] An argument that it may have shifted originates in the observation that many states bar voting by convicted felons and that convictions and incarcerations have trended sharply upwards. Convicted felons—Bernie Ebbers, Michael Milken, and Martha Stewart aside—tend to be poor. Making felons ineligible might make nonvoters disproportionately poor. But we don't see such effects in our data. It is possible that the Census Bureau undersamples convicted felons and therefore consistently overestimates the incomes of nonvoters. But it is also possible that people susceptible to felony convictions always had very low turnout, so changing conviction rates and eligibility would have minimal impact on the income distribution of nonvoters. In any event, the impact of ineligible felons has to be small relative to that of noncitizens. McDonald and Popkin (2001), for example, estimate that, in 2000, noncitizens outnumbered ineligible felons by over five to one. Uggen and Manza (2002) estimate that 2.3 percent of the adult population was ineligible felons in 2000, in contrast to the 7.8 percent of the CPS sample that is noncitizen.

Second, and more important, the percentage of residents who are noncitizens has risen sharply, tripling between 1972 and 2000. Moreover, as emphasized by Bean and Bell-Rose (1999) and Borjas (1999), noncitizens are increasingly low-wage and poor. Our most striking observation is the rapid decline of the median income of noncitizens relative to the median income of voters. In a nutshell, continuing immigration has created a large population of noncitizens. These noncitizens appear to be a leading cause of the fall of median family income relative to mean income. Voters are doing as well as they have ever done.

We have a second interesting finding. There is a midterm cycle in the income of nonvoters. The median income of nonvoters increases in off years and declines in presidential years. In other words, marginal voters who vote in presidential elections but not in off years have higher incomes than persistent nonvoters. The smaller set of citizens who vote in neither presidential nor off-year elections have particularly low incomes. In presidential elections, then, the median family income of a voter is sharply higher than that of the median income of a nonvoter and much, much higher than that of a noncitizen.

■　　■　　■

Conclusion

The median income *voter*'s incentive to redistribute has not increased as over-all economic inequality has risen in the United States. The reason is partly that the rise in inequality has been offset by immigration, which has changed the location of citizens in the income distribution. Those ineligible to vote are substantially poorer than the eligible. Moreover, poorer citizens have not become increasingly apathetic, at least as measured by the tendency to vote. Most citizens, and voters in particular, have been "bumped up" by the dis-enfranchisement of poorer noncitizens. At the same time, a voter of a given income is less eager to redistribute if that redistribution has to be shared with the noncitizen poor.

In any event, immigration cannot have been a driving force in the onset of the increase in income inequality and political polarization. In the early 1970s, noncitizens were quite a small share of the population of the United States, and their income profiles were close to those of citizens. Increasingly, however, noncitizens became a larger, poorer share of the population. From 1990 on, this change placed a number of ineligibles at the bottom of the income distribution, sufficient to make a substantial impact on the redistrib-utive preferences of the median income voter. Even if immigration occurred too late to have produced the increases in inequality and polarization, it may well be contributing to the blocking of efforts to redress these trends.

Our results argue against the claim of Lijphart (1997) in his American Political Science Association presidential address that low voter participa-tion is responsible for the much greater inequality in the United States than in Europe. Lijphart's claim may make sense in terms of contemporary cross-national comparisons, but it does not hold up in the time series. Piketty and Saez (2003) present evidence that inequality fell in the United States just as much as in France and Britain from the First World War until 1970. During this period, there was considerably lower turnout in the United States than in France. Since 1970, the three nations have diverged in inequality, but turn-out of eligible citizens in the United States has not fallen. Turnout in France fell, but inequality has remained in check. It is true that turnout of *residents* of the United States over 18 has fallen, but few would be prepared to extend the right to vote to noncitizens. Compulsory voting for citizens, proposed by Lijphart, might indeed lead to more redistribution, but the absence of com-pulsory voting cannot by itself explain the rise in inequality in the United States in the past thirty years. The explanation is likely to be more closely related to the rise in noncitizenship. The increase reflects two political out-comes. First, immigration reforms in the 1960s and 1990s permitted a large increase in legal immigration. Second, the United States did little to contain illegal immigration. The two outcomes have changed the relationship of income to voting.

NOTES

1. October 24, 2004. Quoted at http://www.sfgate.com/cgi-bin/article.cgi?file/chronicle/archive/2004/10/10/RVG1T9289T1.DTL.

2. Story of August 24, 2004, found at http://www.editorandpublisher.com/eandp/news/article_display.jsp?vnu_content_id1000592440.

3. Computed from www.census.gov/hhes/income/histinc/h01ar.html.

4. We used the least squares unfolding procedure of Poole (1984).

5. On this point, see Snyder (1992).

6. The Census Bureau series does not cover earlier years.

7. A number of commentators date the conservative Republican movement from organizational initiatives, including the formation of think tanks that arose in the early 1970s following the Goldwater candidacy in the 1964 election. See Perlstein (2001) and a *New York Times* opinion article by former New Jersey senator Bill Bradley. See www.nytimes.com/2005/03/30/opinion/30bradley.html. Downloaded April 3, 2005.

8. It is difficult to pinpoint the switch from a decline in polarization to a surge. The turning point occurred somewhere between the late 1960s (following the passage of the Great Society program of the Johnson administration and the immigration amendments of 1965) and the mid to late 1970s. The statistical correlations between polarization, income inequality, and immigration are all slightly sensitive to measurement. The polarization measure will change if the sample period used for DW-NOMINATE changes (end the series in 2000 or 2004), if Senate rather than House polarization is used, if a two-dimensional rather than one-dimensional measure is used, etc. Similarly, income inequality will change if one switches from a Gini to various income shares, etc., and the immigration measure will change if one uses percentage noncitizens (chapter 4) rather than percentage foreign born. The substantive tenor of our results is quite robust to these variations.

9. Our computations are from the November Current Population Survey. The November CPS family income series includes single adult households but does not combine the incomes of unmarried individuals with the same residence.

10. Welch (1999) finds that inequality has increased much less when one looks within the population that remains in the labor force in two periods or within age cohorts. This also reinforces the main claim of this chapter—that the median voter's incentive to redistribute has not increased. Voters may take into account where they stand in the life cycle when making voting decisions.

11. See www.insee.fr/fr/ffc/chifcle_fiche.asp?ref_idNATTEF02131&tab_id339, viewed on December 7, 2004. We equate *"étrangers"* to noncitizens. Immigrants, comprising both noncitizens and naturalized (*"acquisition"*) citizens rose slightly from 9.1% to 9.6%. We should point out that France counts citizens of other EU nations as noncitizens even though there is free mobility of labor within the EU. The EU "noncitizens" would have had, until the recent admission of former Soviet bloc nations, a very different skill mix from that of the largely unskilled Latin American, Caribbean, and Asian immigrants who have come to the United States.

12. We thank Patrick Bolton for suggesting this decomposition.

13. Brady (2004, p. 692) presents evidence, like ours drawn from the CPS, that there has been little change in voter turnout by income quintile over the past thirty years. Summarizing the data in terms of the ratio of turnout in the top quintile to the bottom quintile, he finds no trend in midterm elections and an increasing trend in presidential elections. Some of the trend may reflect inaccuracies engendered by how Brady formed

quintiles from the categorical data. Brady does not indicate whether he excluded non-citizens in forming the quintiles.

REFERENCES

Alesina, Alberto, Reza Baqir, and William Easterly. 1999. "Public Goods and Ethnic Divisions." *Quarterly Journal of Economics* 114(4): 1243–1284.

Alesina, Alberto, and Edward L. Glaeser. 2004. *Fighting Poverty in the U.S. and Europe.* New York: Oxford University Press.

Alesina, Alberto, and Eliana La Ferrara. 2000. "Participation in Heterogeneous Communities." *Quarterly Journal of Economics* 115(3): 847–904.

Alesina, Alberto, and Eliana La Ferrara. 2002. "Who Trusts Others?" *Journal of Public Economics* 85(2): 207–234.

Bean, Frank D., and Stephanie Bell-Rose. 1999. "Introduction" in Frank Bean and Stephanie Bell-Rose, eds. *Immigration and Opportunity: Race, Ethnicity, and Employment in the United States.* New York: Russell Sage Foundation, 1–28.

Bolton, Patrick, and Gerard Roland. 1997. "The Breakup of Nations." *Quarterly Journal of Economics* 112(4): 1057–1090.

Borjas, George J. 1999. *Heaven's Door: Immigration Policy and the American Economy.* Princeton, NJ: Princeton University Press.

Brady, Henry. 2004. "An Analytical Perspective on Participatory Inequality and Income Inequality." In Kathy Neckerman, ed. *Social Inequality.* New York: Russell Sage Foundation.

Dahl, Robert A. 1961. *Who Governs: Democracy and Power in an American City.* New Haven, CT: Yale University Press.

Downs, Anthony. 1957. *An Economic Theory of Democracy.* New York: Harper and Row.

Fiorina, Morris. 1978. *Congress: Keystone of the Washington Establishment.* New Haven, CT: Yale University Press.

Gerring, John. 1998. *Party Ideologies in America, 1828–1996.* New York: Cambridge University Press.

Gilens, Martin. 1999. *Why Americans Hate Welfare: Race, Media, and the Politics of Antipoverty Policy.* Chicago: University of Chicago Press.

Lijphart, Arend. 1997. "Unequal Participation: Democracy's Unresolved Dilemma." *American Political Science Review* 91(1): 1–14.

McCarty, Nolan, Keith T. Poole, and Howard Rosenthal. 1997. *Income Redistribution and the Realignment of American Politics.* Washington, DC: American Enterprise Institute.

McDonald, Michael P., and Samuel Popkin. 2001. "The Myth of the Vanishing Voter." *American Political Science Review* 95(4): 963–974.

Myrdal, Gunnar. 1960. *Beyond the Welfare State: Economic Planning and its International Implications.* New Haven, CT: Yale University Press.

Perlstein, Rick. 2001. *Before the Storm: Barry Goldwater and the Unmaking of the American Consensus.* New York: Hill and Wang.

Piketty, Thomas, and Emmanuel Saez. 2003. "Income Inequality in the United States, 1913–1998." *Quarterly Journal of Economics* 118(1): 1–39.

Poole, Keith T. 1984. "Least Squares Metric, Unidimensional Unfolding." *Psychometrica* 49: 311–323.

Poole, Keith T., and Howard Rosenthal. 1997. *Congress: A Political-Economic History of Roll Call Voting.* New York: Oxford University Press.

Quadagno, Jill S. 1994. *The Color of Welfare: How Racism Undermined the War on Poverty*. Oxford: Oxford University Press.

Snyder, James. 1992. "Artificial Extremism in Interest Group Ratings." *Legislative Studies Quarterly* 17(3): 319–345.

Uggen, Christopher, and Jeff Manza. 2002. "Democratic Contraction? Political Consequences of Felon Disenfranchisement in the United States." *American Sociological Review* 67(6): 777–803.

U.S. Census Bureau. 2005. "Table F–4. Gini Ratios for Families, by Race and Hispanic Origin of Householder: 1947 to 2003." Accessed at http://www.census.gov/hhes/income/histinc/f04.html.

Weingast, Barry R., Kenneth A. Shepsle, and Christopher Johnsen. 1981. "The Political Economy of Benefits and Costs: A Neoclassical Approach to Distributive Politics." *Journal of Political Economy* 89(4): 642–664.

Welch, Finnis. 1999. "In Defense of Inequality." *American Economic Review: Papers and Proceedings* 89(2): 1–17.

THE MEDIA

14.1

MATTHEW A. BAUM

From *Soft News Goes to War: Public Opinion and American Foreign Policy in the New Media Age*

Soft news refers to mass media programming that is primarily intended to entertain rather than provide news, but that also includes—as a by-product of the entertainment—information about politics and international events. Baum analyzes the degree to which people who are relatively uninterested in politics receive information about politics from soft news sources. He finds that international crises especially find their way into "water cooler" conversations—and thus the public's broader consciousness—because people learn about these events from soft news.

SUMMARY AND HYPOTHESES

Driven by market competition and the relatively low cost of producing soft news, broadcasters are finding human interest and other entertainment values in places where their predecessors saw only dry news. One implication is that soft news, as opposed to traditional news programming, may actually increase the likelihood that typical individuals—particularly those not normally interested in politics—will be exposed to information about at least *some* of the major issues of the day, especially those that become water-cooler events, albeit in a format that is less public-policy-oriented and less apt to provide a context for understanding an issue.

Under normal, everyday circumstances, these developments might not result in a public more attuned to political issues than were earlier generations. Given well-documented increases in political apathy and cynicism about politics, it is not surprising to find that typical individuals are no more interested in politics than their parents or grandparents were. This suggests that individuals have reacted to the explosion of available information by becoming increasingly selective regarding what information warrants their attention. Most of the time, the highly segmented modern television marketplace presumably allows individuals to *escape* news and information more effectively than in prior decades. Soft news programs, for instance, generally avoid such "mundane" political topics as foreign affairs, in favor of more salacious issues like celebrity sex scandals, murder trials, and fashion shows. Hence, with minimal effort, television viewers can remain blissfully uninformed about the day-to-day political issues facing the nation, including foreign policy.

When, however, potential water-cooler events emerge—and cross over from network evening newscasts to the soft news media—a far broader audience will likely confront such issues, albeit perhaps as the subject of an entertainment-oriented talk show or entertainment newsmagazine show. Moreover, unlike the relatively arcane or complex presentation of political information offered by traditional news outlets, soft news programs will focus on aspects of such issues of interest to their particular niche of the viewing audience.

For instance, during the Persian Gulf War, while CNN and the major networks filled the airwaves with graphic images of precision bombs and interviews with military experts, the daytime talk shows hosted by Oprah Winfrey, Geraldo Rivera, and Sally Jesse Raphael, as well as the original tabloid TV newsmagazine, *A Current Affair,* focused on episodic stories of the personal hardships faced by spouses of soldiers serving in the Gulf and on the psychological trauma suffered by families of Americans being held prisoner in Iraq as "human shields." In this context, learning about the war was an incidental by-product of seeking entertainment (e.g., human drama or a fight between good and evil). War-related information was effectively piggybacked to entertainment-oriented information, and thereby made available to viewers at virtually no additional cost. In other words, when *The Oprah Winfrey Show* presented a program dealing with the Gulf War, substantive information about the war was "piggybacked," via cheap framing (e.g., human impact and injustice), to information presented primarily for its entertainment value. In choosing to watch Oprah, viewers also, at no additional cost, received substantive information about the Persian Gulf War.[1]

The incidental nature of soft news coverage of foreign crises in illustrated in the following comment by Barry Berk of *Access Hollywood,* regarding that program's rationale for covering some foreign crisis issues, despite the program's primary mission of providing their audience with information about movies and celebrities:

> I think rather than just say [to a celebrity], "Why did you like that script?" or "Why do you want to make this movie?" . . . it's a way to get

to know the celebrities better. And let [the audience] know there's another level there; that they [celebrities] do have opinions; that they're citizens and they're parents, and they have concerns. And they get very upset about the prospect that we're bombing Iraq. Or "good for them, I'm glad we're going in there." You know, they have opinions. I think people find that interesting.[2]

Hence, when a foreign crisis emerges, the numerous programming formats that comprise the modern television marketplace may focus their diverse lenses upon a single issue, albeit varying aspects of that issue. When the mass media unify their focus, I expect the contemporary public, in the aggregate, to be significantly more attentive to such an issue, compared to the publics of prior decades. In today's news environment, when an issue crosses over from traditional news outlets to the soft news media, politically uninterested citizens are far more likely to be exposed and pay attention to the issue—as an incidental by-product of seeking entertainment—relative to most typical political issues, which rarely reach beyond traditional news programming.

Most importantly, this mechanism does not depend on any overall increase in the public's interest in or knowledge about politics or foreign affairs.[3] Indeed, the basis for predicting increased attentiveness is entirely independent of the expected benefit for typical individuals of political information in general or information about foreign affairs in particular. Once someone is exposed to an issue in her preferred programming format, her cost-benefit calculus for paying attention to additional information about the issue is altered. For such an individual, this issue is no longer a typical mundane, and perhaps baffling, political news item.

■　■　■

WHAT ARE CRISES AND WHEN DO THEY BECOME WATER-COOLER EVENTS?

■　■　■

[D]ue in part to the increasing prevalence of soft news outlets, foreign military crises—as well as some other issues which are decidedly not "high politics"— are increasingly likely to attract the attention of typical individuals. In general, issues that can be readily framed in stark and dramatic terms, thereby priming widely accessible frames, without generating significant cognitive conflict between simultaneously accessible yet contradictory causal narratives, are most likely to be covered by the soft news media. Such issues are thereby most likely to attract the attention of even politically uninterested individuals. These are the issues that occasionally become water-cooler events.

A direct marketing revolution in television has systematically altered the cost-benefit calculus for a large segment of the public, which is not predisposed to follow politics. By transforming mundane political coverage into entertainment, the soft news media have successfully employed piggyback-ing and cheap framing strategies in order to capture a substantial segment, or niche, of the television audience. This has the perhaps unintended effect of increasing the likelihood that politically uninterested individuals will be exposed to information about those political issues that cross over from hard to soft news outlets.

. . . [T]he class of issues most likely to become water-cooler events [are] "dra-matic crises" because these events typically possess the several characteris-tics necessary to appeal to the soft news media. Nonetheless, not all crises, nor even all dramatic crises, are covered by the soft news media or become water-cooler events. Indeed, it seems unlikely that there exists any foolproof formula for determining ex ante which issues will pass this attentiveness threshold. Rather, given the extraordinary complexity of the modern political, media, and public opinion environments, perhaps the best we can hope for in the near term is an improved understanding of the various factors that raise or lower the probability that a given issue or event will capture the public's imagination.

NOTES

1. The contrast between war coverage on *The Oprah Winfrey Show* and the emphasis of traditional news programming on military tactics and precision bombing cam-paigns also illustrates the increasing niche orientation of the traditional and soft news media. The former orientation may be intended, in part, to have a greater appeal for the largely female audience that typically watches *The Oprah Winfrey Show*, while the latter type of coverage has traditionally held greater appeal for a male audience.

2. Barry Berk, interview with author, Los Angeles, Calif., June 20, 2000.

3. I do, however, present some evidence in the concluding chapter that exposure to soft news outlets can enhance some individuals' knowledge about particular foreign crisis events.

14.2

SHANTO IYENGAR

From *Media Politics: A Citizen's Guide*

In this selection, Iyengar discusses how new forms of media, such as the Internet, social media, and cell phones, are changing American politics. He evaluates claims by scholars about the nature of those changes. Some scholars suggest that the new media only highlight and enhance partisan difference among people. Others focus on how new media lead to the creation of small groups of people intensely interested in isolated topics. And still others argue that the new media perpetuate inequalities among people in how much they pay attention to politics. While there are differences among scholars, all agree that the new media have opened up new ways for politicians to raise money.

NEW MEDIA, NEW FORMS OF CAMPAIGNING

■   ■   ■

The revolution in information technology has altered not only the form of the media landscape but also the very concept of communication. The traditional forms of communication were either *point-to-point* (between a single sender and recipient) or *broadcast* (between a single sender and multiple recipients). Most senders did not have ready access to broadcast forms of communication and could not reach a significant audience. Traditional media were also limited to a single form (print, audio, or video).

The development of the Internet permitted simultaneous point-to-point and broadcast forms of communication for the first time and provided individual users with easy access to an unlimited audience. Every individual on the network of computers making up the World Wide Web is both a sender and a receiver. Any user of the Internet can direct e-mail messages to individual recipients and at the same time communicate with a worldwide audience by hosting a website, writing a message on Facebook, uploading a video to YouTube, or posting on a blog. Moreover, unlike with conventional media, Internet-based communication is multichannel, allowing the free transmission of text, voice, still images, and video.

■   ■   ■

FIGURE 1   Percentage of US Population with Broadband Connections At Home

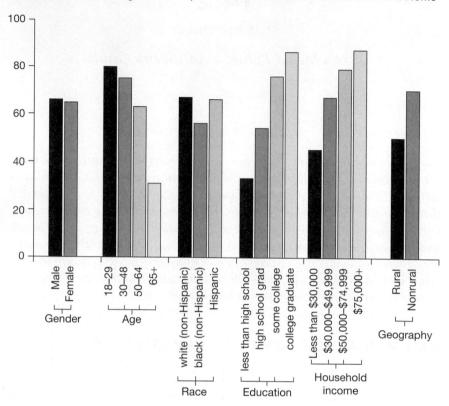

SOURCE: Data from Pew Research Center, 2010.

THE DIFFUSION OF TECHNOLOGY

■   ■   ■

News represents a tiny sliver of the information available online; the Internet provides access to everything from vital health information to job listings. Internet access has become so important in today's world that it's now labeled a "fundamental human right" in several countries, including Estonia, France, Finland, and Greece, and these countries have passed legislation to ensure Internet access for all. A related issue concerns access to bandwidth.

Those with regular access to broadband Internet have a tremendous advantage over those with a slower, less stable connection. In the United States, as shown in Figure 1, there are wide gaps in broadband access between the young and the old, the less and the more educated, and the rich and the poor, as well as between urban and rural dwellers.

EFFECTS OF NEW MEDIA ON CONSUMERS

There are two schools of thought concerning the potential impact of new media on the end user. *Optimists* see technology as a means of revitalizing the public sphere. By providing direct and immediate access to diverse political perspectives, the Internet should enhance the ability of ordinary people to follow events and to participate in the political process. The hope is that even modest levels of online news consumption will build civic awareness and engagement. Vice President Al Gore (1994) epitomized this view when he declared that the coming Internet would bring about "robust and sustainable economic progress, strong democracies, better solutions to global and local environmental challenges, improved health care, and—ultimately—a greater sense of shared stewardship of our small planet."

Skeptics, on the other hand, warn that information technology is no panacea for the limitations of conventional news programming and the weak demand for political information. If serious news coverage cannot attract television viewers, why should it draw people online? If Americans are not used to reading or watching foreign media, is there any reason to suppose that they will suddenly access the BBC or the Press Trust of India just because it's possible to do so? Skeptics think not. They believe that the Internet will actually discourage consumers from devoting time to news programming (whether Internet or conventional) in favor of more engaging pursuits, such as online shopping, dating, or keeping in touch. As people become more fluent in the ways of the Web, they may become more personally isolated, preferring surfing alone over community involvement or social interaction. Quite possibly, the net effect of technology could be to weaken community and civic engagement.

Quite apart from the question of whether Internet technology will increase or decrease the average time devoted to public affairs content is the question of whether the Internet will, in practice, be used to broaden users' political horizons. Although an infinite variety of information is available, individuals may well sample selectively, limiting their exposure to news or sources that they expect to find agreeable. There is no doubt that the Internet makes available an ample supply of news that is not screened for accuracy or objectivity. By turning to biased but favored providers, consumers may be able to "wall themselves off from topics and opinions that they would prefer to avoid" (Sunstein, 2001, pp. 201–202). The end result could be a less informed and more polarized electorate.

INTERNET USE AND CIVIC ENGAGEMENT

Representing the optimists, some scholars believe that the Internet will expand the universe of political participation by reducing costs. Rather than having to write a check, address an envelope, find a stamp, and mail a political donation, one can simply go online and pay with a credit card. And it's not

only making a financial contribution that is easier; creating membership rosters, sending out announcements of upcoming meetings, and signing petitions
are all simplified.

Optimists also cite the potential of the Internet to draw in individuals who
hold a wide variety of ideas and perspectives. Unlike the mainstream news
media, which is constrained by the norms of professional journalism and
consumer demand, websites can target smaller audiences with more specialized interests making it possible to create greater numbers of online networks
and discussion groups.

Not only does technology facilitate conventional forms of participation but
it has also spawned new forms of civic engagement. People can contribute
comments to blogs, view and post YouTube videos, and reach out to like-
minded others on Facebook and Twitter. These innovations are already influencing the conduct of campaigns. During the 2008 presidential primaries,
CNN sponsored candidate debates in which Internet users across the country
submitted questions to the candidates over YouTube.

Despite the potential of the Internet to foster new forms of political engagement, the skeptics respond that the Internet has had little impact on the
actual level of political participation. A recent meta-analysis (a quantitative
research methodology that summarizes past research findings) found that
Internet use has exerted little positive effect overall (Boulianne, 2009).

FIGURE 2   Group Differences in Participation

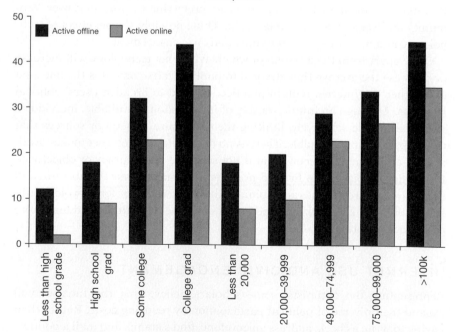

SOURCE: Data from Smith, Schlozman, Verba, Brady, 2009.

A parallel debate concerns the potential impact of technology on inequalities in civic participation. Optimists assumed that the Internet would draw in hitherto inactive groups and level the playing field. Pessimists, however, argued that the costs of going online, in terms of both money and skills, would only exacerbate existing disparities in participation. Since technology use is significantly correlated with social class, it is unlikely that the voices of the poor and less educated will be heard online. In fact, as shown in Figure 2, the evidence shows that online activists, like their offline counterparts, are drawn disproportionately from high-status groups. For instance, the participation gap between college and high school graduates is almost identical (around 25 percent higher for college graduates) for offline and online participation (Smith, Schlozman, Verba, Brady, 2009; Bimber, 2003).

The overrepresentation of higher status groups as online activists suggests that new forms of participation simply replicate the old. But some skeptics go even further and argue that Internet use can displace conventional forms of civic life and lower the overall level of participation. Just as the advent of television made people cancel their subscriptions to visually oriented magazines such as *Life*, these scholars argue that surfing the Web will gradually diminish face-to-face social interaction. We might become sufficiently preoccupied with our private technological spaces to have few opportunities to visit with the neighbors, write letters to the editor, or even converse with anybody. Because technology use is an inherently isolated rather than a social experience, it has the potential to weaken the bonds between the individual and the community.

To date, the scholarly verdict on the question of displacement is inconclusive. . . . Thus, at the level of individuals' self-reported exposure to conventional media and other discretionary activities, the consequences of increased Internet use are unclear. For some, Internet use may free up time for other activities; for others, the effect may be the opposite.

For one group in particular, however, it is clear that the Internet has dramatically increased participation. Young adults are the least likely to engage in traditional forms of political activity but the most likely to take advantage of technologically enhanced forms of participation. The young, for instance, are more likely to post comments on blogs and organize for political causes through social networking sites. . . . [T]he age gap in the use of social networking sites for political purposes favors those between the ages of eighteen and thirty-four by a margin of 32 percentage points. College students are especially likely to participate in online political networks.

Overall, with the notable exception of the young, the advent of new technologies has done little to raise the overall level of involvement in civic or community affairs. Civic participation requires motivation, and the motivated are more likely to take advantage of both new and old forms of participation.

■ ■ ■

Given the availability of so much information and so many news providers, the audience must make choices or be overwhelmed. Exactly how do Internet users decide whether the information they're getting is worth considering or should be passed over?

There are three main possibilities. First, as we have just seen with the question of civic engagement, exposure to political information online may be simply a matter of generic political interest (the *attentive public hypothesis*). Political junkies will seek out news and political commentary, whereas the apolitical majority simply tunes out all things political, except when major events generate a torrent of coverage that is impossible to ignore. From this perspective, multiplying the number of information sources only widens the information gap between the more and the less interested. Second, among those with some level of political interest, people may prefer to encounter information that they find supportive or consistent with their political beliefs (the *partisan polarization hypothesis*). For example, Republicans may tune in to Fox News, Democrats to *The Rachel Maddow Show*. We use the blogosphere as a case study of polarization; the great majority of bloggers participate in completely homogeneous (in-party) discussion networks. Third, people may seek information not on the basis of their anticipated agreement with the message but because of their interest in particular issues (the *issue public hypothesis*). For example, the elderly seek out information bearing on Social Security or healthcare legislation simply because these policies have an immediate impact on their welfare.

In Focus: Hypotheses of Selectivity

- *Attentive public.* People interested by politics tune in to all forms of news, whereas the apolitical majority pays very little attention to news in any medium.
- *Partisan polarization.* People prefer to encounter information that supports their beliefs and avoid information that is inconsistent with those beliefs.
- *Issue public.* People seek out information about subjects that are particularly important or interesting to them and tune out information about other subjects.

IMPACT OF THE INTERNET ON CAMPAIGN ORGANIZATIONS

▪ ▪ ▪

In principle, campaigns can harness the immense networking power of the Internet to accomplish multiple campaign objectives, including fund-raising, producing and distributing information that increases the candidate's visibility and likability, and, most critically, recruiting and mobilizing a cadre of activists. To date, the impact of new media has been greatest on the goal of mobilization. Although other facets of the campaign remain grounded in conventional (especially broadcast) media because there are still more voters to be reached in front of their television sets than at their computers, the development of video-sharing sites and the rapidity with which campaign videos now circulate around the Web means that candidates can deliver campaign messages at their own discretion. . . . Nonetheless, as described in a minute, the ability to organize and communicate with online networks of supporters has transformed the conduct of campaigns.

Before the Internet, candidates recruited volunteers and raised money by making phone calls, sending mass mailings, or going door to door. These old-fashioned forms of mobilization and fund-raising were both capital and time intensive; successful campaigns had an existing organization, professional (paid) staff, and access to phone banks or mailing lists of prospective supporters. Candidates themselves might spend long hours on the phone with prospective donors. The amount of time between the initial contact and receipt of a financial contribution might take weeks or even months. These infrastructure costs made it nearly impossible for lesser-known candidates to develop and manage a hard-core group of activists.

By lowering the cost of communication, the Internet has opened up the political arena by enabling any campaign, no matter how large its electoral constituency, to assemble a network of supporters. Any candidate with the ability to mount a basic website can instantly sign up volunteers and send them assignments for upcoming events, thus developing the nucleus of a viable field organization. Once formed, these groups become smart mobs—capable of acting in a coordinated manner, despite the absence of any face-to-face contact (for examples of smart mobs in action, see Rheingold, 2002). In effect, the Internet lowered the eligibility requirements for groups to engage in collective action. For large and small campaigns alike, the Internet is a public good that can be exploited with minimal marginal costs.

The first campaign to take advantage of the Internet to organize its supporters was Jesse Ventura's 1998 run for governor of Minnesota. As the Reform Party candidate, Ventura was heavily outspent by his Republican and Democratic opponents (Norm Coleman and Hubert H. Humphrey III, respectively). But Ventura's campaign launched a website in early 1998 (at a monthly cost of under thirty dollars) and began to develop a statewide e-mail list of volunteers. The list was used to publicize information about local organizational meetings; one such meeting drew a standing-room-only crowd of more than 250 people.

Despite being outspent and outstaffed by his opponents (the campaign had only one paid staff member, the campaign manager), Ventura was elected governor. It is difficult to say precisely how much difference Ventura's use of technology made to the upset victory. After all, his unusual persona and career as a professional wrestler combined to make him a highly visible candidate, and his antigovernment, populist platform resonated well in a state with a long history of supporting progressive reformers. In one respect, however, the payoff of using technology was clear: young people, who are most likely to be reached online, turned out to vote in large numbers. Over half of them voted for Ventura—more than enough to account for the margin of his victory.

The success of the Ventura campaign made it clear to campaign operatives that the Internet could and should be exploited for political action. By 2000, all reputable candidates had elaborate, interactive websites and e-mail lists of prospective supporters. Among the presidential contenders, it was John McCain who became the poster boy for use of the Internet. Capitalizing on McCain's special appeal to the young, his campaign went online to recruit some fifteen hundred volunteers in advance of the 2000 New Hampshire primary. The campaign scheduled regular online chat encounters with the candidate. In one such session, five hundred people each paid a hundred dollars for the privilege of submitting an e-mail question to McCain. The McCain campaign set a new record (four million dollars) for electronic fund-raising.

Despite McCain's stunning victory in the New Hampshire primary, his candidacy proved short-lived. George W. Bush rebounded from New Hampshire and soundly defeated McCain in South Carolina. Shortly thereafter, McCain withdrew from the race. But once again, an insurgent candidate had demonstrated competitiveness with the help of a relatively modest investment in new media.

It was during the 2004 campaign that Internet campaigning came into its own. Governor Howard Dean tied his presidential candidacy inextricably to the Internet. Although Dean was eventually forced to withdraw from the campaign for lack of support, his campaign's innovative use of technology contributed to his meteoric rise from the relatively unknown governor of a small state to the front-running contender for the Democratic nomination.

■   ■   ■

The 2008 Presidential election was, in the words of the *Wall Street Journal*, "the first real Internet election" (Rhoads, 2008). And no one used the power of the Web more effectively than Barack Obama's campaign. According to Joe Trippi, the architect of Dean's ground-breaking campaign in 2004, "the tools [for elections] changed between 2004 and 2008. Barack Obama won every single caucus state that matters, and he did it because of those tools, because he was able to move thousands of people to organize." From the day he declared his candidacy in Springfield (February 10, 2007), the campaign's sensitivity to online marketing was evident. . . .

In contrast with previous presidential campaigns, all of which had maintained separate organizations corresponding to online and traditional efforts, the Obama campaign integrated the new and old media teams into one overarching organization under the control of its campaign manager, David

Plouffe. Both forms of the campaign operated under the same priorities and emphasized similar themes. . . .

Given the interactive nature of online communication, the Obama campaign was able to compile a massive database of supporters by requesting e-mail addresses and phone numbers whenever a person visited the website. Using cookies, the campaign tracked the Web browsing behavior of online supporters. Based on the browsing profile of a particular voter, the campaign would have a good idea of that voter's interests and e-mail her messages or banner ads of likely interest.

In developing a vast network of supporters and volunteers, Obama's use of the Internet was no different from other candidates. But where the campaign broke new ground was its systematic use of online campaign communication. The video-sharing site YouTube played a critical role in the dissemination of campaign messages. The ability to reach a large Internet audience made it possible to counteract or rebut critical media commentary.

▪ ▪ ▪

What was truly astonishing about Obama's campaign was its ability to raise money online. Obama raised about half a billion dollars through his online efforts, an amount equal to the combined fund-raising of the Bush and the Kerry campaigns in 2004. Three million donors contributed $6.5 million, $6 million of which arrived in donations of less than $100. In one month alone— September 2008—Obama raised $150 million, 75 percent of which came from online donations (Vargas, 2008).

▪ ▪ ▪

CONCLUSION

The scholarly evidence concerning the emerging role of the Internet in American public life suggests that the audience for news is becoming more fragmented. Given the availability of unlimited choice, Americans with limited interest in politics prefer to avoid news coverage entirely. For those who care about politics, the amount of information and increased availability of news sources forces them to exercise choice. [And] increasingly, online media choices reflect partisan values. In the case of the blogosphere, what people see or read is driven primarily by the desire to encounter opinions with which they are likely to agree. In the case of news sources, partisan choices are limited to cable outlets, and the level of motivated exposure to news is not nearly as extensive as in the case of the audience for blogs.

Even though partisans still encounter objective, nonpartisan news coverage from mainstream news organizations, they are apt to ignore or discount highly publicized facts when these facts are at odds with their political preferences. In 2004, for instance, Republicans refused to acknowledge that

President Bush's decision to go to war in Iraq was based on inaccurate intelligence, despite an avalanche of news stories calling the intelligence reports into question. . . .

Quite apart from the ambiguous verdict of the scholarly literature concerning the effects of the Internet on civic engagement or exposure to diverse points of view, there is a different reason to feel optimistic about the potential impact of technology on the political process. We have already documented that media-based campaigns fail to deliver substantive information. In place of the candidates' positions and past performance on the issues, news coverage gravitates inevitably toward the more entertaining facets of the campaign: the horse race, the strategy, and, whenever possible, instances of scandalous or unethical behavior. Against this backdrop, technology at least makes it possible for voters to bypass or supplement media treatment of the campaign and access information about the issues that affect them.

Rather than waiting (typically in vain) for news organizations to report on the issues they care about, voters can take matters into their own hands and seek out information about the candidates' positions on these issues. This form of motivated exposure is hardly an impediment to deliberation: paying attention to what the candidates have to say on the issues facilitates issue-oriented voting; paying attention to the media circus does not. Thus, there is some reason to hope that the spread of new forms of unmediated communication will provide a better way to inform and engage voters.

FURTHER READINGS

Bimber, B. (2003). *Information and American democracy: Technology in the evolution of political power.* New York: Cambridge University Press.

Boulianne, S. (2009). Does Internet use affect engagement? A meta-analysis of research. *Political Communication, 26,* 193–211.

Gore, A. 1994. *Remarks prepared for delivery by Vice President Al Gore, International Telecommunications Union, Monday March 21, 1994.* Retrieved October 7, 2005, from www.ifla.org/documents/infopol/us/goregji.txt.

Rheingold, H. (2002). *Smart mobs: The next social revolution.* Cambridge MA: Basic Books.

Rhoads, C. (2008, October 18) Web data offer new slant on traditional horse race. *Wall Street Journal,* p. A5.

Smith, A., Schlozman, K. L., Verba, S., Brady, H. (2009). The Internet and civic engagement. Pew Research Center, Washington, DC.

Sunstein, C. (2001). *Republic.com.* Princeton, NJ: Princeton University Press.

Vargas, J. A. (2008, November 20). Obama raised half a billion online. *The Washington Post.* Retrieved August 20, 2010, from http://voices.washingtonpost.com/44/2008/11/20/obama_raised_half_a_billion_on.html.

15

ECONOMIC POLICY

15.1

JOHN MAYNARD KEYNES

From *The General Theory of Employment, Interest, and Money*

Keynes's classic book emphasizes the role that governments play to stabilize the economy and reduce unemployment. Contrary to the standard view among classical economists that governments get in the way of efficient markets, Keynes's view is that markets, if left on their own, will lead to debilitating fluctuations in employment. Government fiscal spending should be used during difficult economic times to promote employment.

I

. . . [T]he volume of employed resources is duly determined, according to the classical theory, by the two postulates. The first gives us the demand schedule for employment, the second gives us the supply schedule; and the amount of employment is fixed at the point where the utility of the marginal product balances the disutility of the marginal employment.

It would follow from this that there are only four possible means of increasing employment:

(*a*) An improvement in organization or in foresight which diminishes "frictional" unemployment;

(*b*) a decrease in the marginal disutility of labour, as expressed by the real wage for which additional labour is available, so as to diminish "voluntary" unemployment;

(c) an increase in the marginal physical productivity of labour in the wage-goods industries (to use Professor Pigou's convenient term for goods upon the price of which the utility of the money-wage depends);

or (d) an increase in the price of non-wage-goods compared with the price of wage-goods, associated with a shift in the expenditure of non-wage-earners from wage-goods to non-wage-goods.

■   ■   ■

II

Is it true that the above categories are comprehensive in view of the fact that the population generally is seldom doing as much work as it would like to do on the basis of the current wage? For, admittedly, more labour would, as a rule, be forthcoming at the existing money-wage if it were demanded.[1] The classical school reconcile this phenomenon with their second postulate by arguing that, while the demand for labour at the existing money-wage may be satisfied before everyone willing to work at this wage is employed, this situation is due to an open or tacit agreement amongst workers not to work for less, and that if labour as a whole would agree to a reduction of money-wages more employment would be forthcoming. If this is the case, such unemployment, though apparently involuntary, is not strictly so, and ought to be included under the above category of "voluntary" unemployment due to the effects of collective bargaining, etc.

■   ■   ■

The traditional theory maintains . . . *that the wage bargains between the entrepreneurs and the workers determine the real wage*; so that, assuming free competition amongst employers and no restrictive combination amongst workers, the latter can, if they wish, bring their real wages into conformity with the marginal disutility of the amount of employment offered by the employers at that wage. If this is not true, then there is no longer any reason to expect a tendency towards equality between the real wage and the marginal disutility of labour.

■   ■   ■

Now the assumption that the general level of real wages depends on the money-wage bargains between the employers and the workers is not obviously true. Indeed it is strange that so little attempt should have been made to prove or to refute it. For it is far from being consistent with the general tenor of the classical theory, which has taught us to believe that prices are governed by marginal prime cost in terms of money and that money-wages largely govern marginal prime cost. Thus if money-wages change, one would have expected the classical school to argue that prices would change in almost the same proportion, leaving the real wage and the level of unemployment practically the same as before, any small gain or loss to labour being at the expense or profit of other elements of marginal cost which have been left unaltered.[2] They seem, however, to have been diverted from this line of thought, partly by the settled conviction that labour is in a position to determine its own real wage and partly, perhaps, by preoccupation with the idea that prices depend on the quantity of money. And the belief in the proposition that labour is always in a position to determine its own real wage, once adopted, has been maintained by its being confused with the proposition that labour is always in a position to determine what real wage shall correspond to *full* employment, *i.e.* the *maximum* quantity of employment which is compatible with a given real wage.

To sum up: there are two objections to the second postulate of the classical theory. The first relates to the actual behavior of labour. A fall in real wages due to a rise in prices, with money-wages unaltered, does not, as a rule, cause the supply of available labour on offer at the current wage to fall below the amount actually employed prior to the rise of prices. To suppose that it does is to suppose that all those who are now unemployed though willing to work at the current wage will withdraw the offer of their labour in the event of even a small rise in the cost of living. Yet this strange supposition apparently underlies Professor Pigou's *Theory of Unemployment,* and it is what all members of the orthodox school are tacitly assuming.

But the other, more fundamental, objection, which we shall develop in the ensuing chapters, flows from our disputing the assumption that the general level of real wages is directly determined by the character of the wage bargain. In assuming that the wage bargain determines the real wage the classical school have slipt in an illicit assumption. For there may be *no* method available to labour as a whole whereby it can bring the wage-goods equivalent of the general level of money-wages into conformity with the marginal disutility of the current volume of employment. There may exist no expedient by which labour as a whole can reduce its *real* wage to a given figure by making revised *money* bargains with the entrepreneurs.

▪   ▪   ▪

The State will have to exercise a guiding influence on the propensity to consume partly through its scheme of taxation, partly by fixing the rate of interest, and partly, perhaps, in other ways. Furthermore, it seems unlikely that the influence of banking policy on the rate of interest will be sufficient by itself to determine an optimum rate of investment. I conceive, therefore, that a somewhat comprehensive socialisation of investment will prove the only means of securing an approximation to full employment; though this need not exclude all manner of compromises and of devices by which public authority will cooperate with private initiative. But beyond this no obvious case is made out for a system of State Socialism which would embrace most of the economic life of the community. It is not the ownership of the instruments of production which it is important for the State to assume. If the State is able to determine the aggregate amount of resources devoted to augmenting the instruments and the basic rate of reward to those who own them, it will have accomplished all that is necessary. Moreover, the necessary measures of socialisation can be introduced gradually and without a break in the general traditions of society.

Our criticism of the accepted classical theory of economics has consisted not so much in finding logical flaws in its analysis as in pointing out that its tacit assumptions are seldom or never satisfied, with the result that it cannot solve the economic problems of the actual world. But if our central controls succeed in establishing an aggregate volume of output corresponding to full employment as nearly as is practicable, the classical theory comes into its own again from this point onwards. If we suppose the volume of output to be given, *i.e.* to be determined by forces outside the classical scheme of thought, then there is no objection to be raised against the classical analysis of the manner in which private self-interest will determine what in particular is produced, in what proportions the factors of production will be combined to produce it, and how the value of the final product will be distributed between them. Again, if we have dealt otherwise with the problem of thrift, there is no objection to be raised against the modern classical theory as to the degree of consilience between private and public advantage in conditions of perfect and imperfect competition respectively. Thus, apart from the necessity of central controls to bring about an adjustment between the propensity to consume and the inducement to invest, there is no more reason to socialise economic life than there was before.

▪ ▪ ▪

Whilst, therefore, the enlargement of the functions of government, involved in the task of adjusting to one another the propensity to consume and the inducement to invest, would seem to a nineteenth-century publicist or to a contemporary American financier to be a terrific encroachment on individualism, I defend it, on the contrary, both as the only practicable means of avoiding the destruction of existing economic forms in their entirety and as the condition of the successful functioning of individual initiative.

For if effective demand is deficient, not only is the public scandal of wasted resources intolerable, but the individual enterpriser who seeks to bring these resources into action is operating with the odds loaded against him. The game of hazard which he plays is furnished with many zeros, so that the players *as a whole* will lose if they have the energy and hope to deal all the cards. Hitherto the increment of the world's wealth has fallen short of the aggregate of positive individual savings; and the difference has been made up by the losses of those whose courage and initiative have not been supplemented by exceptional skill or unusual good fortune. But if effective demand is adequate, average skill and average good fortune will be enough.

The authoritarian state systems of today seem to solve the problem of unemployment at the expense of efficiency and of freedom. It is certain that the world will not much longer tolerate the unemployment which, apart from brief intervals of excitement, is associated—and, in my opinion, inevitably associated—with present-day capitalistic individualism. But it may be possible by a right analysis of the problem to cure the disease whilst preserving efficiency and freedom.

NOTES

1. *Cf.* the quotation from Prof. Pigou in the *Economics of Welfare* (4th ed. p. 127) (my italics): "Throughout this discussion, except when the contrary is expressly stated, the fact that some resources are generally unemployed against the will of the owners is ignored. *This does not affect the substance of the argument*, while it simplifies its exposition." Thus, whilst Ricardo expressly disclaimed any attempt to deal with the amount of the national dividend as a whole, Prof. Pigou, in a book which is specifically directed to the problem of the national dividend, maintains that the same theory holds good when there is some involuntary unemployment as in the case of full employment.

2. This argument would, indeed, contain, to my thinking, a large element of truth, though the complete results of a change in money-wages are more complex.

15.2

MILTON FRIEDMAN

From *Capitalism and Freedom*

In contrast to Keynes, Friedman's famous argument suggests that government spending to stimulate the economy is almost always a mistake. Instead, according to this view, government spending drains the private economy of resources that would be more efficiently allocated through unfettered markets. Private companies and individuals will, through their buying, selling, and investing decisions, allocate money in the society much more efficiently than government, and smaller government will benefit society overall.

GOVERNMENT AS RULE MAKER AND UMPIRE

It is important to distinguish the day-to-day activities of people from the general customary and legal framework within which these take place. The day-to-day activities are like the actions of the participants in a game when they are playing it; the framework, like the rules of the game they play. And just as a good game requires acceptance by the players both of the rules and of the umpire to interpret and enforce them, so a good society requires that its members agree on the general conditions that will govern relations among them, on some means of arbitrating different interpretations of these conditions, and on some device for enforcing compliance with the generally accepted rules. As in games, so also in society, most of the general conditions are the unintended outcome of custom, accepted unthinkingly. At most, we consider explicitly only minor modifications in them, though the cumulative effect of a series of minor modifications may be a drastic alteration in the character of the game or of the society. In both games and society also, no set of rules can prevail unless most participants most of the time conform to them without external sanctions; unless that is, there is a broad underlying social consensus. But we cannot rely on custom or on this consensus alone to interpret and to enforce the rules; we need an umpire. These then are the basic roles of government in a free society: to provide a means whereby we can modify the rules, to mediate differences among us on the meaning of the rules, and to enforce compliance with the rules on the part of those few who would otherwise not play the game.

The need for government in these respects arises because absolute freedom is impossible. However attractive anarchy may be as a philosophy, it is not feasible in a world of imperfect men. Men's freedoms can conflict, and when they do, one man's freedom must be limited to preserve another's—as a Supreme Court Justice once put it, "My freedom to move my fist must be limited by the proximity of your chin."

The major problem in deciding the appropriate activities of government is how to resolve such conflicts among the freedoms of different individuals. In some cases, the answer is easy. There is little difficulty in attaining near unanimity to the proposition that one man's freedom to murder his neighbor must be sacrificed to preserve the freedom of the other man to live. In other cases, the answer is difficult. In the economic area, a major problem arises in respect of the conflict between freedom to combine and freedom to compete. What meaning is to be attributed to "free" as modifying "enterprise"? In the United States, "free" has been understood to mean that anyone is free to set up an enterprise, which means that existing enterprises are not free to keep out competitors except by selling a better product at the same price or the same product at a lower price. In the continental tradition, on the other hand, the meaning has generally been that enterprises are free to do what they want, including the fixing of prices, division of markets, and the adoption of other techniques to keep out potential competitors. Perhaps the most difficult specific problem in this area arises with respect to combinations among laborers, where the problem of freedom to combine and freedom to compete is particularly acute.

A still more basic economic area in which the answer is both difficult and important is the definition of property rights. The notion of property, as it has developed over centuries and as it is embodied in our legal codes, has become so much a part of us that we tend to take it for granted, and fail to recognize the extent to which just what constitutes property and what rights the ownership of property confers are complex social creations rather than self-evident propositions. Does my having title to land, for example, and my freedom to use my property as I wish, permit me to deny to someone else the right to fly over my land in his airplane? Or does his right to use his airplane take precedence? Or does this depend on how high he flies? Or how much noise he makes? Does voluntary exchange require that he pay me for the privilege of flying over my land? Or that I must pay him to refrain from flying over it? The mere mention of royalties, copyrights, patents; shares of stock in corporations; riparian rights, and the like, may perhaps emphasize the role of generally accepted social rules in the very definition of property. It may suggest also that, in many cases, the existence of a well specified and generally accepted definition of property is far more important than just what the definition is.

Another economic area that raises particularly difficult problems is the monetary system. Government responsibility for the monetary system has long been recognized. It is explicitly provided for in the constitutional provision which gives Congress the power "to coin money, regulate the value thereof, and of foreign coin." There is probably no other area of economic activity with respect to which government action has been so uniformly accepted. This habitual and by now almost unthinking acceptance of governmental responsibility makes thorough understanding of the grounds for such respon-sibility all the more necessary, since it enhances the danger that the scope of government will spread from activities that are, to those that are not, appropriate in a free society, from providing a monetary framework to deter-mining the allocation of resources among individuals. . . .

In summary, the organization of economic activity through voluntary exchange presumes that we have provided, through government, for the main-tenance of law and order to prevent coercion of one individual by another, the enforcement of contracts voluntarily entered into, the definition of the mean-ing of property rights, the interpretation and enforcement of such rights, and the provision of a monetary framework.

■   ■   ■

FISCAL POLICY

Ever since the New Deal, a primary excuse for the expansion of governmental activity at the federal level has been the supposed necessity for government spending to eliminate unemployment. The excuse has gone through several stages. At first, government spending was needed to "prime the pump." Tem-porary expenditures would set the economy going and the government could then step out of the picture.

When the initial expenditures failed to eliminate unemployment and were followed by a sharp economic contraction in 1937–38, the theory of "secu-lar stagnation" developed to justify a permanently high level of government spending. The economy had become mature, it was argued. Opportunities for investment had been largely exploited and no substantial new opportunities were likely to arise. Yet individuals would still want to save. Hence, it was essential for government to spend and run a perpetual deficit. The securi-ties issued to finance the deficit would provide individuals with a way to accumulate savings while the government expenditures provided employ-ment. This view has been thoroughly discredited by theoretical analysis and even more by actual experience, including the emergence of wholly new lines for private investment not dreamed of by the secular stagnationists. Yet it has left its heritage. The idea may be accepted by none, but the government programs undertaken in its name, like some of those intended to prime the pump, are still with us and indeed account for ever-growing government expenditures.

More recently, the emphasis has been on government expenditures neither to prime the pump nor to hold in check the specter of secular stagnation but as a balance wheel. When private expenditures decline for any reason, it is said, governmental expenditures should rise to keep total expenditures stable; conversely, when private expenditures rise, governmental expenditures should decline. Unfortunately, the balance wheel is unbalanced. Each recession, how-ever minor, sends a shudder through politically sensitive legislators and administrators with their ever present fear that perhaps it is the harbinger of another 1929–33. They hasten to enact federal spending programs of one kind or another. Many of the programs do not in fact come into effect until after the recession has passed. Hence, insofar as they do affect total expenditures, on which I shall have more to say later, they tend to exacerbate the succeeding expansion rather than to mitigate the recession. The haste with which spending programs are approved is not matched by an equal haste to repeal them or to eliminate others when the recession is passed and expansion is under way. On the contrary, it is then argued that a "healthy" expansion must not be "jeopardized" by cuts in governmental expenditures. The chief harm done by the balance-wheel theory is therefore not that it has failed to offset recessions, which it has, and not that it has introduced an inflationary bias into governmental policy, which it has done too, but that it has continuously fostered an expansion in the range of governmental activities at the federal level and prevented a reduction in the burden of federal taxes.

In view of the emphasis on using the federal budget as a balance wheel, it is ironic that the most unstable component of national income in the postwar period is federal expenditure, and the instability has not at all been in a direction to offset movements of other expenditure components. Far from being a balance wheel offsetting other forces making for fluctuations, the federal budget has if anything been itself a major source of disturbance and instability.

Because its expenditures are now so large a part of the total for the economy as a whole, the federal government cannot avoid having significant effects on the economy. The first requisite is therefore that the government mend its own fences, that it adopt procedures that will lead to reasonable stability in its own flow of expenditures. If it would do that, it would make a clear contribution to reducing the adjustments required in the rest of the economy. Until it does that, it is farcical for government officials to adopt the self-righteous tones of the schoolmaster keeping unruly pupils in line. Of course, their doing so is not surprising. Passing the buck and blaming others for one's own deficiencies are not vices of which governmental officials have a monopoly.

Even if one were to accept the view that the federal budget should be and can be used as a balance wheel—a view I shall consider in more detail below— there is no necessity to use the expenditure side of the budget for this purpose. The tax side is equally available. A decline in national income automatically reduces the tax revenue of the federal government in greater proportion and thus shifts the budget in the direction of a deficit, and conversely during a boom. If it is desired to do more, taxes can be lowered during recessions and raised during expansions. Of course, politics might well enforce an asymmetry here too, making the declines politically more palatable than the rises.

If the balance-wheel theory has in practice been applied on the expenditure side, it has been because of the existence of other forces making for increased governmental expenditures; in particular, the widespread acceptance by intellectuals of the belief that government should play a larger role in economic and private affairs; the triumph, that is, of the philosophy of the welfare state. This philosophy has found a useful ally in the balance-wheel theory; it has enabled governmental intervention to proceed at a faster pace than would otherwise have been possible.

How different matters might now be if the balance-wheel theory had been applied on the tax side instead of the expenditure side. Suppose each recession had seen a cut in taxes and suppose the political unpopularity of raising taxes in the succeeding expansion had led to resistance to newly proposed governmental expenditure programs and to curtailment of existing ones. We might now be in a position where federal expenditures would be absorbing a good deal less of a national income that would be larger because of the reduction in the depressing and inhibiting effects of taxes.

■ ■ ■

I should like to discuss the view, now so widely held, that an increase in governmental expenditures relative to tax-receipts is necessarily expansionary and a decrease contractionary. This view, which is at the heart of the belief that fiscal policy can serve as a balance-wheel, is by now almost taken for granted by businessmen, professional economists, and laymen alike. Yet it cannot be demonstrated to be true by logical considerations alone, has never been documented by empirical evidence, and is in fact inconsistent with the revelant empirical evidence of which I know.

The belief has its origin in a crude Keynesian analysis. Suppose governmental expenditures are raised by $100 and taxes are kept unchanged. Then, goes the simple analysis, on the first round, the people who receive the extra hundred dollars will have that much more income. They will save some of it, say one-third, and spend the remaining two-thirds. But this means that on the second round, someone else receives an extra $66⅔ of income. He in turn will save some and spend some, and so on and on in infinite sequence. If at every stage one-third is saved and two-thirds spent, then the extra $100 of government expenditures will ultimately, on this analysis, add $300 to income. This is the simple Keynesian multiplier analysis with a multiplier of three. Of course, if there is one injection, the effects will die off, the initial jump in income of $100 being succeeded by a gradual decline back to the earlier level. But if government expenditures are kept $100 higher per unit of time, say $100 a year higher, then, on this analysis, income will remain higher by $300 a year.

This simple analysis is extremely appealing. But the appeal is spurious and arises from neglecting other relevant effects of the change in question. When these are taken into account, the final result is much more dubious: it may be anything from no change in income at all, in which case private expenditures will go down by the $100 by which government expenditures go up, to the full increase specified. And even if money income increases, prices may rise, so real income will increase less or not at all. . . .

In the first place, nothing is said in the simple account about what the government spends the $100 on. Suppose, for example, it spends it on something that individuals were otherwise obtaining for themselves. They were, for

example, spending $100 on paying fees to a park which paid the cost of atten-
dants to keep it clean. Suppose the government now pays these costs and
permits people to enter the park "free." The attendants still receive the same
income, but the people who paid the fees have $100 available. The govern-
ment spending does not, even in the initial stage, add $100 to anyone's income.
What it does is to leave some people with $100 available to use for purposes
other than the park, and presumably purposes they value less highly. They
can be expected to spend less out of their total income for consumer goods
than formerly, since they are receiving the park services free. How much less,
it is not easy to say. Even if we accept, as in the simple analysis, that people
save one-third of additional income, it does not follow that when they get one
set of consumer goods "free," two-thirds of the released money will be spent
on other consumer goods. One extreme possibility, of course, is that they
will continue to buy the same collection of other consumer goods as they did
before and add the released $100 to their savings. In this case even in the
simple Keynesian analysis, the effect of the government expenditures is completely offset: government expenditures go up by $100, private down by $100.
Or, to take another example, the $100 may be spent to build a road that a
private enterprise would otherwise have built or the availability of which may
make repairs to the company's trucks unnecessary. The firm then has funds
released, but presumably will not spend them all on what are less attractive
investments. In these cases, government expenditures simply divert private
expenditures and only the net excess of government expenditures is even
available at the outset for the multiplier to work on. From this point of view,
it is paradoxical that the way to assure no diversion is to have the government
spend the money for something utterly useless—this is the limited intellectual content to the "filling-holes" type of make-work. But of course this itself
shows that there is something wrong with the analysis.

In the second place, nothing is said in the simple account about where the
government gets the $100 to spend. So far as the analysis goes, the results
are the same whether the government prints extra money or borrows from
the public. But surely which it does will make a difference. To separate fiscal
from monetary policy, let us suppose the government borrows the $100 so
that the stock of money is the same as it would have been in the absence of
the government expenditure. This is the proper assumption because the stock
of money can be increased without extra government expenditure, if that is
desired, simply by printing the money and buying outstanding government
bonds with it. But we must now ask what the effect of borrowing is. To analyze this problem, let us assume that diversion does not occur, so in the first
instance there is no direct offset to the $100 in the form of a compensating
drop in private expenditures. Note that the government's borrowing to spend
does not alter the amount of money in private hands. The government borrows $100 with its right hand from some individuals and hands the money
with its left hand to those individuals to whom its expenditures go. Different
people hold the money but the total amount of money held is unchanged.

The simple Keynesian analysis implicitly assumes that borrowing the money does not have any effects on other spending. There are two extreme circumstances under which this can occur. First, suppose people are utterly indifferent to whether they hold bonds or money, so that bonds to get the $100 can be sold without having to offer a higher return to the buyer than such bonds were yielding before. (Of course, $100 is so small an amount that it would in practice have a negligible effect on the required rate of return, but the issue is one of principle whose practical effect can be seen by letting the $100 stand for $100 million or $100 ten-million.) In Keynesian jargon, there is a "liquidity trap" so people buy the bonds with "idle money." If this is not the case, and clearly it cannot be indefinitely, then the government can sell the bonds only by offering a higher rate of return on it. A higher rate will then have to be paid also by other borrowers. This higher rate will in general discourage private spending on the part of would-be borrowers. Here comes the second extreme circumstance under which the simple Keynesian analysis will hold: if potential borrowers are so stubborn about spending that no rise in interest rates however steep will cut down their expenditures, or, in Keynesian jargon, if the marginal efficiency schedule of investment is perfectly inelastic with respect to the interest rate.

I know of no established economist, no matter how much of a Keynesian he may regard himself as being, who would regard either of these extreme assumptions as holding currently, or as being capable of holding over any considerable range of borrowing or rise in interest rates, or as having held except under rather special circumstances in the past. Yet many an economist, let alone noneconomist, whether regarding himself as Keynesian or not, accepts as valid the belief that a rise in governmental expenditures relative to tax receipts, even when financed by borrowing, is *necessarily* expansionist, though as we have seen, this belief implicitly requires one of these extreme circumstances to hold.

If neither assumption holds, the rise in government expenditures will be offset by a decline in private expenditures on the part either of those who lend funds to the government, or of those who would otherwise have borrowed the funds. How much of the rise in expenditures will be offset? This depends on the holders of money. The extreme assumption, implicit in a rigid quantity theory of money, is that the amount of money people want to hold depends, on the average, only on their income and not on the rate of return that they can get on bonds and similar securities. In this case, since the total stock of money is the same before and after, the total money income will also have to be the same in order to make people just satisfied to hold that money stock. This means that interest rates will have to rise enough to choke off an amount of private spending exactly equal to the increased public expenditure. In this extreme case, there is no sense at all in which the government expenditures are expansionary. Not even money income goes up, let alone real income. All that happens is that government expenditures go up and private expenditures down.

16

SOCIAL POLICY

16.1

FRANK R. BAUMGARTNER AND BRYAN D. JONES

From *Agendas and Instability in American Politics*

Why do certain social problems arise on the agenda of the national government, leading to demands by the public for new social policies? Baumgartner and Jones compare two theories. One predicts that issues like pesticides or smoking burst onto the scene due to negative media publicity, but then slowly fade from the government's agenda as the public loses attention. The other predicts that, once an issue is on the agenda, interest groups push for a government response, usually a set of regulations or agency actions, that forever transform the issue. A new set of interest groups need to keep that issue on the agenda. The authors find support for the latter theory.

TWO MODELS OF ISSUE EXPANSION

The Dual Mobilization Theories of Downs and Schattschneider

In his classic article "Up and Down with Ecology," Anthony Downs (1972) argues that public attention to political issues typically follows a cyclical pattern. In Downs's approach, a preproblem stage is characterized by low attention. Then a state of alarmed discovery and euphoria generates much attention, followed by a realization of the costs of solving the problem and a gradual decline in public interest. This is a decidedly pessimistic view of the agenda-setting process. According to Downs, hitting the agenda is of little policy relevance, for the public and the national political leaders are likely soon to reach the conclusion that action is futile, that the costs of solving the problem are too high, or that some other problem requires their attention even more urgently. Taken to its logical conclusion, this view of agenda-setting implies a never-ending series of "alarmed discoveries" during which the public suddenly focuses on an issue, but after which serious action may never take place. Attention simply fades as the difficulties of action become clear or as some new crisis pushes the old one out of the limelight.

Certainly some issues have followed the pattern described by Downs, but on the other hand, some issues remain on the agenda for quite some time. Now twenty years after his discussion of "ecology," environmental issues remain much higher on the national political agenda than they were at any time before Downs wrote about them, for example. So the cyclical pattern described by Downs is not the only possible outcome of the agenda-setting process. Agenda dynamics have important policy consequences; they are not simple exercises in futility. Some issues remain high on the public agenda for considerable periods of time, and some problems really do get solved, surprising as this might sound.

▪ ▪ ▪

When public attention focuses on some new problem in the way described by Downs, feelings of optimism lead policymakers to fund the research or to implement the programs of specialists who claim to have a solution. Specialists with potential solutions of course waste no time in asking for programs to be implemented, and, as John Kingdon (1984) describes, policies then result from the combinations of the problems that interest political leaders and the solutions proposed by the bureaucratic and other experts. The institution of new programs, policies, and agencies is thus strongly associated with the agenda-setting process.

Down's theory of cycles may be approximately correct when dealing with public attention to problems that lack a feasible solution. Attention surges, declines, as the futility of action becomes clear. Where solutions are present in the form of existing governmental programs, initiatives, and institutions, however, a surge in public attention to a problem may lead to the enactment of new programs and to the growth of new institutions. . . .

Consider the development and breakup of the civilian nuclear power subsystem in the United States. That issue went through at least two distinct periods of emergence on the national political agenda, each associated with opposite results for the industry. A period of enthusiasm for the potentials of nuclear power led government leaders to create an extremely favorable set of institutions in order to support and develop the industry. In the pages to come we call such a mobilization of enthusiasm a Downsian mobilization. In such mobilizations, government is called on to solve problems or take advantage of new technologies.

Public attention to nuclear power then faded, as the plants took years to build, as cost overruns multiplied, and as other issues came to the forefront of the nation's political agenda. But the institutional subsystem remained, and it worked quietly for about two decades implementing the new policy of encouraging greater use of nuclear power, building and ordering more nuclear plants in the United States than in any other country in the world. So the period of optimism and positive mobilization did not last for long, but it left a tremendous institutional legacy.

Nuclear power of course is no longer associated with the positive image it enjoyed in the early postwar years. Neither has it receded permanently from the agenda. Its reemergence on the political agenda in the 1970s was certainly not associated with enthusiasm, but with fear, mistrust, complaints, and criticism. We call this a Schattschneider mobilization since it often stems from the efforts of opponents of the status quo to expand the scope of conflict (Schattschneider 1960). Here the government is already involved in the solution, and some have begun to see the solution as the problem. Hence the issue must be expanded beyond the confines of the existing policymaking system.

▪   ▪   ▪

Just as the Downsian mobilization led to the creation of the favorable institutional structure that the industry enjoyed for decades, the Schattschneider mobilization led to the destruction of these favorable structures. Two waves of mobilization, one positive for the industry, one negative, led to the emergence of the issue on the public agenda twice during the postwar period, each time with important institutional and policy changes. In between these periods of emergence, changes in nuclear power policy were mostly incremental. The system appeared to be near equilibrium during each period of low public attention, but this apparent equilibrium was punctuated by the emergence of the issue on the public agenda, when dramatic policy changes occurred.

▪   ▪   ▪

Smoking and Tobacco Policies in the Twentieth Century

The tobacco industry in the United States benefits from a series of favorable institutional arrangements centering on agricultural subsidies to farmers. At the same time, the government is active in antismoking campaigns. When we look at the history of public attention and government action toward smoking since the turn of the century, we develop a better understanding of how these diverse governmental reactions came to be. Tobacco once generated almost no coverage in the media, and government actions were almost entirely supportive of the agricultural subsidy program. Tobacco, like wheat or corn, was seen as an important crop that generated export earnings, supported millions of farmers, and on which whole communities and even some state economies were dependent. With tobacco seen as an economic issue, the role of political leaders was clear: they should defer to experts and allow the agricultural subsystem to run its course. This is precisely what happened during the entire first half of the century.

FIGURE 1 Annual Coverage of Smoking in the *Readers' Guide* and Tobacco
Consumption, 1900–1986

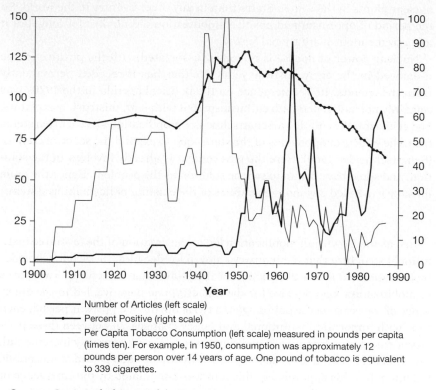

Number of Articles (left scale)
Percent Positive (right scale)
Per Capita Tobacco Consumption (left scale) measured in pounds per capita
(times ten). For example, in 1950, consumption was approximately 12
pounds per person over 14 years of age. One pound of tobacco is equivalent
to 339 cigarettes.

SOURCE: *Statistical Abstract of the United States.*

As can be seen in figure 1, media attention to smoking and tobacco questions has varied widely during the century. A total of 2,020 articles has
appeared in the *Readers' Guide,* but these have been distributed very unevenly
across the years. Coverage during the pre- 1950 period averaged only about
6 articles per year, but annual articles on smoking averaged 38 in the 1950s,
62 in the 1960s, 31 in the 1970s, and 58 from 1980 to 1987. In 1964 alone, the
year of the surgeon general's report on smoking, there were 136 articles listed
in the *Readers' Guide,* more than twenty times the prewar average.

Smoking received scant press coverage prior to the 1950s, and what coverage it received was decidedly mixed in tone. Press attention to cigarettes and
smoking during World War Two was overwhelmingly positive, focusing on
the use of cigarettes as barter by GIs in Europe, on shortages and rationing,
on the size of the tobacco crop, and on other items that could not be considered bad for industry. Essentially, figure 1 shows that smoking has never been
seen with great enthusiasm in the national media, but it was mostly a nonissue for the first fifty years of this century. A few negative articles might have
appeared each year, but so did a few positive ones.

Figure 1 also shows how media attention to smoking and tobacco questions seems to have been related to the behavior itself. During the postwar years, the industry and the habit were glamorized in popular culture. Per capita consumption of tobacco in the United States increased from about eight pounds per person during the 1930s to eleven or twelve pounds during the 1950s (figures are from the *Statistical Abstract* [Bureau of the Census 1991]). Smoking was not a new industry to be built from scratch after World War Two. Rather, a powerful subsystem was already in place before the war, centering on agricultural subsidies for tobacco farmers (Fritschler 1989; Ripley and Franklin 1991, 88–90). The buildup of the tobacco subsystem appears to have its roots before the turn of the century, so we cannot discuss it as we did for nuclear power. We can see its continued operation and expansion during the first half of the century, however, and we can certainly observe its demise.

The dramatic increases in levels of coverage of smoking issues in the media that occurred in the years following World War Two were driven almost exclusively by negatives. Health warnings had always been a part of the media's coverage of this issue, but these suddenly became the dominant force during the 1960s. As more people began to smoke, health officials mobilized in an extremely effective manner. The number of articles we have coded as negative grew from an average of only 2 per year before 1950 to 20 during the 1950s, to 41 during the 1960s, 19 during the 1970s, and 44 during the 1980s. (There was also a slight increase in the number of positive stories on smoking, from 2 per year before 1950 to an average of 6 in the years from 1950 to 1987, but growth in the negatives far outstripped growth in the positives.) Following this explosion of emphasis on the health risks of smoking, per capita consumption of tobacco began its remarkable decline, which has continued unabated for three decades.

In the case of smoking, a Schattschneider mobilization was clearly evident: opponents of the industry were able to generate lots of bad news. This increase in public awareness led to a dramatic change in public behavior. Industry leaders had benefited from a long period of low public attention to the public health and public policy consequences of smoking policy during the prewar years and had benefited from a true glorification of smoking immediately after the war. This period of positive attention did not last, however, and the industry was not able to control the expansion of conflict once public attention shifted to public health questions.

▪   ▪   ▪

While smoking became part of the systemic agenda during the 1960s, and even to some extent during the 1950s, it was not until the mid-1970s that the issue burst onto the congressional agenda. When it did, however, it followed a pattern remarkably similar to the one we observed for nuclear power. As the total number of hearings increased, the hearings were held before an increasing number of different congressional bodies. During the period when there was little congressional attention to smoking and tobacco questions, a large

FIGURE 2   Congressional Hearings on Smoking

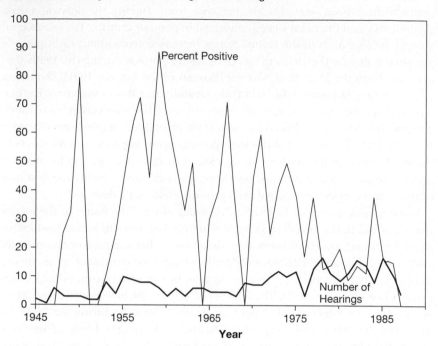

proportion of congressional hearings were relatively positive toward the indus-try; however, as participation expanded, this expansion was associated almost exclusively with criticism. Criticism did not come from previous allies chang-ing their minds; rather it stemmed from conflict expansion, as previously unin-volved persons began to assert themselves.

The percentage of topics that our coders coded as proindustry in the con-gressional hearings declined steadily as the number of hearings increased, as the bottom part of figure 2 shows. This is precisely the pattern we expect to be associated with a Schattschneider mobilization. Opponents of the indus-try are able to appeal to congressional allies to hold hearings and generate adverse publicity. The more they are successful in generating adverse public-ity and consideration on the systemic agenda, the more they are likely to be heard on the formal agenda. The more they are heard on the formal agenda, the more adverse publicity is likely to be generated in the media. So the Schattschneider mobilization process is a self-reinforcing mechanism, lead-ing to dramatic, not only incremental, change.

Pesticides

Beginning in the early part of the twentieth century, demand for pesticides began to increase dramatically as the size and variety of farms changed from family producers to large-scale commercial ventures (Bosso 1987). Compared to modern chemicals, of course, the first pesticides were extremely mild and ineffectual, but they did increase crop yields significantly, and their use spread rapidly. As the chemicals became popular, a great number of manufacturers entered the market, and farmers were presented with a confusing variety of products. The first problems associated with the pesticides industry stemmed mostly from farmers not knowing the harmful effects of combining two pesticides, or not knowing the toxicity to skin or from ingestion of the chemicals. By the first decade of this century there was considerable fraud in the industry, with poor labeling of products one of the main sources of problems. Congress first regulated the pesticides industry when it passed the Insecticide Act of 1910, mostly a truth-in-labeling act (Bosso 1987; Dunlap 1981). Enforcement was entrusted to the Bureau of Chemistry in the Department of Agriculture. Agriculture officials saw their mission as one of protecting the farmer from unsafe products even while encouraging the increased use of chemical pesticide. One small voice within the USDA, the Food and Drug Administration, was concerned with the residue levels of toxic agents left on food, but the FDA did not have jurisdiction over pesticide questions, and its studies were generally ignored by USDA officials.

Research during World War Two yielded a new generation of pesticides—synthetic organics such as DDT. These chemicals were stronger and more persistent than their predecessors, and were thought to be nontoxic to humans. Proponents made optimistic claims for the new generation of pesticides, claiming that they would end malaria, increase food production to the point of ending world hunger, and even completely eradicate those persistent pests, the housefly and the mosquito. These arguments should sound familiar to our readers by now. They had the same effect as those arguments in favor of nuclear power. They were also responsible for a later backlash against the industry. Just as in the case of nuclear power, the postwar years saw a great American enthusiasm for the progress of science, this time as represented in the pesticides industry. American science and industry would turn its efforts from the war in Europe and Japan to another war, this one with the purpose of eradicating world hunger and disease through increased use of pesticides.

The strength of this wave of enthusiasm for progress through chemistry is graphically depicted in figure 3. Like smoking, pesticides were mostly a nonissue throughout the beginning of the century, and what little attention they did receive in the popular press came mostly from farm magazines, where their virtues were almost uniformily extolled. Popular coverage of the issue shot up dramatically in the late war years and has remained higher ever since.

The wave of popular attention to the pesticides industry in the late war years was overwhelmingly positive in tone. In this environment Congress passed its second major piece of legislation concerning the industry. The Federal Insecticide, Fungicide, and Rodenticide Act of 1947 (FIFRA) passed with the strong support of both agricultural and chemical industry interests. Christopher Bosso writes that "the shared assumptions about pesticides as a

FIGURE 3 Annual Coverage of Pesticides in the *Readers' Guide*

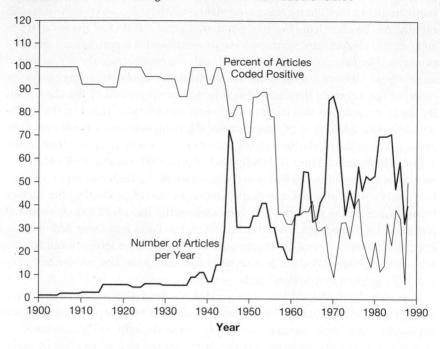

panacea, and the imperatives motivating their widespread use, provided the parameters for policy debate" (1987, 59). A cozy triangle governing pesticides (the Department of Agriculture; farm interests and chemical companies; and the congressional agriculture and appropriations committees) quickly controlled the regulation and use of these powerful new chemicals. Consumer interests, represented by the FDA, and environmental interests, basically unorganized, were excluded from participation. In other words, a Downsian mobilization took place in the late 1940s for pesticides. Great popular and official enthusiasm about the potentials of the industry to do good led government officials in Congress and the executive branch to facilitate the growth of the industry. They set up an institutional structure, based in the Agriculture Department, that promoted the industry for decades to come.

During the 1950s, the "golden age" of pesticides, widespread campaigns were developed to promote the use of pesticides, and local extension agents fanned out across the country encouraging and teaching farmers to increase their use of the chemicals. The degree of official optimism about the glories of pesticides is dramatically illustrated by two major policy disasters of the late 1950s. In 1957 the USDA launched two huge pest eradication campaigns, one in the Northeast, directed at the gypsy moth, and one in the South, aimed at the fire ant. Both involved massive aerial spraying; both resulted in huge fish kills, enormous crop damage, and the devastation of wildlife. Neither campaign was successful in eradicating the pest (see Bosso 1987). Figure 3 shows the decline in the positive tone of pesticide coverage in the press, coinciding exactly with the eradication programs—a decline in public image from which the industry never recovered. Another blow to the pesticides industry occurred in late 1959 when the FDA for the first time banned the sale of a crop because of pesticide residues. The cranberry scare, coming just before the holiday season, devastated annual sales of an entire crop, but more importantly it solidified the public's newly negative view of pesticides.

One simple example gives an idea of how small beginnings of criticism can be compounded through the interaction of image and venue. In reaction to the negative attention associated with the failed eradication campaigns in the late 1950s, of course a number of congressmen began to pay attention to pesticide issues where they had ignored them in the past. One of these was Rep. James Delaney, who became interested in the possible contamination of food through residues. The Delaney hearings in 1958, which led to the Food Additive Amendment, were home to a fierce battle among agricultural interests, health officials, and the food industry. The substantive legislative outcome of the hearings was a single important new rule: "no additive shall be deemed safe if it is found to induce cancer when ingested by man or animal" (Bosso 1987, 97). The institutional outcome of these debates was that the Food and Drug Administration, long the bureaucratic loser in its conflicts with Agriculture officials, was given expanded authority to restrict toxic residues in food. The cranberry scare, coming in 1959, could be seen as an adept piece of bureaucratic expansionism from a group that understood that increasing public attention to a problem in an especially dramatic way is one way to shift the issue from the bureaucratic institutions, where they continually lose, to the front pages of the papers and to congressional hearings, where their side might stand a better chance. From one change in levels of attention, new participants are called into a debate, then their participation leads to changes in the rules, leading to further changes in participation and public understanding of the issue: a pattern of self-reinforcement that we see again and again.

The golden age of pesticides in the United States was relatively short. The wave of popular enthusiasm about the benefits of the new industry lasted only from about 1945 until about 1956. After that, popular attention to the pesticide question was much more likely to focus on the problems than on the promises of the industry. However, our Downsian mobilization hypothesis implies that a powerful set of institutions may be set up during the initial period of popular enthusiasm, and this group of industry boosters may be powerful for years to come. This is exactly what occurred in the case of pesticides. It was several years before the Schattschneider mobilization of public outcry against the industry was able to make a significant difference.

The Schattschneider mobilization followed the abrupt reversal in the public image of pesticides that was associated with the three disasters of the late

1950s: the gypsy moth and fire ant campaigns and the cranberry scare. Attention did not reach its peak until the late 1960s, however. Rachel Carson's 1962 book, *Silent Spring* (parts of which were published in the 16, 23, and 30 June 1962 issues of *The New Yorker*), did not really change ideas about pesticides—the news was already bad for the industry, as can be seen in figure 3. Rather, it solidified a movement that had already gathered considerable steam. A rancorous debate between environmentalists and industry scientists ensued, a debate that went to the heart of the issue of scientific objectivity. Peak attention occurred in 1969, coinciding with the announcement of the banning of DDT, while the tone of media attention reached its all-time low of about 90 percent negative. Environmental groups pressed Congress, the courts, executive agencies, and state agencies during this time, with increased success, on air and water pollution, nuclear power, industrial wastes, and pesticides. In consequence, numerous major laws, regulations, and court decisions were issued during the late 1960s and early 1970s. Major revisions of pesticide regulation occurred in the National Environmental Policy Act (1969) and the Federal Environmental Pesticides Control Act (1972). Although the law was a result of compromises between the old agriculture-pesticides subsystem and environmentalists, it provided a new regulatory environment. The pesticides-Agriculture Department link was certainly not destroyed, but the Schattschneider mobilization of the late 1960s led to the breakup of much of the legacy of the Downsian mobilization of twenty years before.

For most of the history of pesticide policy, congressional attention has been low, and most hearings have been aimed at regulating and limiting the industry rather than promoting it. Unlike nuclear power or tobacco, the pesticides industry is not itself the center of a large body of government action. Rather, it is part of a large variety of agriculture policies centering on monoculture and price supports for a variety of crops. One example among many of how pesticide are heavily affected by government agriculture programs is the limitation of acreage in farm price-support programs. These limits encourage farmers to use more pesticides and fertilizers in order to maximize the yields from the land remaining under cultivation.

Because pesticides as such are rarely the exclusive focus of Congress in the normal process of administering programs, most hearings focusing specifically on pesticide issues are directed at problems in the industry. Figure 4 shows the levels and tone of congressional attention to pesticides during the twentieth century. Congress paid virtually no attention to pesticides until there were significant public worries about the industry in the 1960s. Despite passage of two major laws concerning the industry, in 1910 and 1947, there were almost no hearings before 1960. Congressional hearings seem to play an important role in the expansion of conflict, but Congress in its role of supporter or booster of an industry is not Congress in committees. Supportive laws seem to be passed with relatively limited discussion, while critical legislation tends to follow extensive hearings and debates.

FIGURE 4   Congressional Hearings on Pesticides

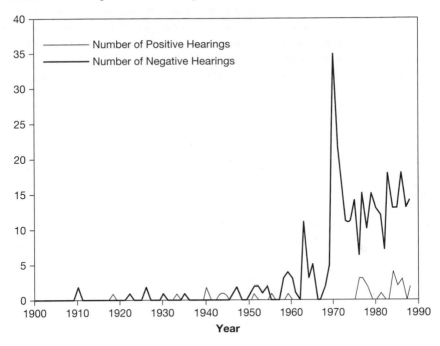

Between 1960 and 1975, no hearings could be classified as supportive of the pesticides industry. This is the period of *Silent Spring*, the DDT bans, and major environmental legislation. Congress acted as a venue of appeal for those interests not represented within the pesticide subsystem established after the 1947 legislation. Eventually, rules were changed to allow greater openness within that system of policymaking, and the result is considerably more conflict even within the pesticide policy community. Since 1975, Congress has held some hearings supportive of the industry, as actors on both sides now appeal to allies in the different committees and subcommittees. From a one-sided mobilization of interests centering on promoting the use of pesticides, Congress played a key role in expanding the opportunities for criticism. The once-powerful subsystem regulating and promoting the industry now is home to much more internal debate than was once the case.

The case of pesticides shows remarkable similarities to that of nuclear power. Both cases show tremendous growth of positive attention during the postwar period. Attention, as measured by press coverage, increased by factors of 10 to 20, as the industries were established and began to grow. The Downsian mobilization process worked almost identically in both cases. Attention dropped off after this initial surge, as the pesticides and nuclear power subsystems became firmly established. Later, the Schattschneider mobilization occurred. In both cases, we can note a second period of increased attention beginning in the 1960s and 1970s (slightly later for nuclear power than for pesticides), dominated by negative images. Pesticides and nuclear power emerged on the public agenda twice during the postwar period. The first time was the result of one-sided mobilization by proponents of the industry, as they sought and gained favorable government actions and institutionalized their control over these new industries. In the second phase of agenda access, however, the Schattschneider mobilization process led to major alterations in the proindustry subsystems.

■   ■   ■

Both Schattschneider and Downs are right, but only half right. There are clearly two types of agenda access, and the same issue studied over a relatively long period of time may show both. The remarkable element of each of these mobilizations, besides the tremendous policy implications that can follow from them, is their rapidity once they begin. Policymaking in many areas of American polities may not always be ruled by incrementalism, decreasing marginal returns, and slow changes (although these features remain important); rather, there are critical periods of mobilization of antagonists during which dramatic changes are put into effect. At any one time, there-may be little change, but periods of relative stability may be punctuated by fitful bursts of mobilization that change the structure of bias for decades to come. Institutions are the legacies of short periods of attention by the public to a given issue. They remain intact until attention increases at some later date to cause more institutional changes. Periods between agenda access may be characterized by stability, but this is not indicative of any equilibrium of values, tastes, or preferences. Rather, it is induced by the institutions that purposive entrepreneurs push through when they are able to take advantage of favorable conditions.

REFERENCES

Bosso, Christopher J. 1987. *Pesticides and Politics: The Life Cycle of a Public Issue.* Pittsburgh, Penn.: University of Pittsburgh Press.

Bureau of the Census. 1991. *Statistical Abstract of the United States.* Washington, D.C.: Department of Commerce.

Carson, Rachel. 1962. *Silent Spring.* Boston: Houghton Mifflin.

Downs, Anthony. 1972. Up and Down with Ecology: The Issue Attention Cycle. *Public Interest* 28: 38–50.

Dunlap, Thomas. 1981. *DDT: Scientists, Citizens, and Public Policy.* Princeton, N.J.: Princeton University Press.

Fritschler, A. Lee. 1989. *Smoking and Politics.* 4th ed. Englewood Cliffs, N.J.: Prentice-Hall.

Kingdon, John W. 1984. *Agendas, Alternatives, and Public Policies.* Boston: Little, Brown.

Ripley, Randall B., and Grace A. Franklin. 1991. *Congress, the Bureaucracy, and Public Policy.* 5th ed. Pacific Grove, Calif.: Brooks-Cole.

16.2

LARRY M. BARTELS

From *Unequal Democracy: The Political Economy of the New Gilded Age*

Bartels argues that the policies of the national government have had a major impact on income inequality in the United States. Income inequality has increased over the last three and half decades, with most of the increases occurring during Republican presidential administrations. Bartels argues that this reflects the different economic philosophies of the two major parties and the different political interests of partisan voters.

THE PARTISAN POLITICAL ECONOMY

> . . . as our economy grows, market forces work to provide the greatest rewards to those with the needed skills in the growth areas. . . . This trend . . . is simply an economic reality, and it is neither fair nor useful to blame any political party.
>
> —*Treasury Secretary Henry Paulson, 2006*[1]

The tendency to think of economic outcomes as natural and inevitable is politically significant because it discourages systematic critical scrutiny of their causes and consequences. If escalating inequality is "simply an economic reality," it seems pointless to spend too much energy worrying about how and why it arises. Moreover, if "there has always been extreme income inequality" under Republicans and Democrats alike, it seems pointless to hope that public policies might mitigate that inequality. As prominent policy analyst Lawrence Mead rather breezily put it, in a response to the report of the American Political Science Association's Task Force on Inequality and American Democracy, . . . "The causes [of growing economic inequality] are not well understood and have little tie to government."[2]

My aim . . . is to refute the notion that the causes of economic inequality in contemporary America "have little tie to government." Indeed, I suggest that the narrowly economic focus of most previous studies of inequality has caused them to miss what may be the most important single influence on the changing U.S. income distribution over the past half-century—the contrasting policy choices of Democratic and Republican presidents. Under Republican administrations, real income growth for the lower- and middle-income classes has consistently lagged well behind the income growth rate for the rich—and well behind the income growth rate for the lower and middle classes themselves under Democratic administrations.

. . . [T]he dramatic differences in patterns of income growth under Democratic and Republican presidents are quite unlikely to have occurred by chance; nor can they be attributed to oil price shocks or changes in the structure of the labor force or other purely economic factors, or to cyclical corrections by each party of the other party's policy excesses. Rather, they reflect consistent differences in policies and priorities between Democratic and Republican administrations. In the first half of the post-war era, these differences were expressed primarily in macroeconomic policies and performance, with Democrats presiding over significantly less unemployment and significantly more overall economic growth than Republicans. Since the 1970s some of these macroeconomic differences have been muted, but significant partisan differences in tax and transfer policies have continued to produce significant partisan disparities in patterns of post-tax income growth, with the middle class and, especially, the working poor experiencing significantly more income growth under Democratic presidents than under Republican presidents.

The cumulative effect of these partisan differences has been enormous. My projections based on the historical performance of Democratic and Republican presidents suggest that income inequality would actually have *declined* slightly over the past 50 years . . . had the patterns of income growth characteristic of Democratic administrations been in effect throughout that period. Conversely, continuous application of the patterns of income growth observed during periods of Republican control would have produced a much greater divergence in the economic fortunes of rich and poor people than we have actually experienced. . . .

■   ■   ■

The average rate of real income growth during 1948–2005 was higher for affluent families than for those lower in the income distribution. . . . What may be surprising is that this pattern of differential growth is entirely limited to periods in which Republicans controlled the White House.

. . . Figure 1 provides a graphical representation of . . . the starkly different patterns of income growth under Democratic and Republican administrations. . . . Under Democratic presidents, poor families did slightly better than richer families (at least in proportional terms), producing a modest net decrease in income inequality; under Republican presidents, rich families did vastly better than poorer families, producing a considerable net increase in income inequality. In both cases, the patterns are essentially linear over the entire range of family incomes represented in the figure (that is, for incomes ranging from about $25,000 to $200,000 in 2005).

■   ■   ■

FIGURE 1   Income Growth by Income Level under Democratic and Republican Presidents, 1948–2005

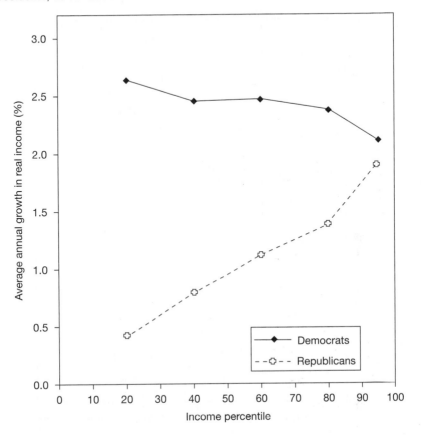

A Partisan Coincidence?

The partisan differences in characteristic rates of income growth documented in figure 1 would seem to be of immense economic and political significance—if they are real. They suggest that middle-class and poor families in the post-war era have routinely fared much worse under Republican presidents than they have under Democratic presidents. By this accounting, economic inequality in contemporary America is profoundly shaped by partisan politics.

But to what extent are these patterns really attributable to partisan politics rather than to accidental historical factors? One way to address this question is to examine their consistency across a range of presidents and circumstances. To that end, figure 2 shows the level of income inequality in each year of the post-war period as reflected in one standard measure of inequality, the ratio of incomes at the 80th percentile of the income distribution to those at the 20th percentile.

FIGURE 2 Income Inequality under Democratic and Republican Presidents, 1947–2005

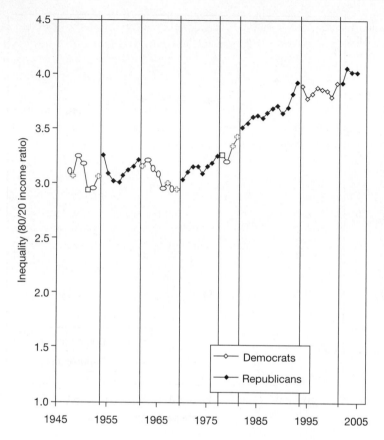

By this measure, income inequality was essentially constant from the late 1940s through the late 1960s, with families at the 80th percentile of the income distribution earning about three times as much as families at the 20th percentile. Inequality increased fairly steadily through the 1970s and 1980s before leveling off once again in the 1990s. These broad temporal trends reinforce the impression that growing inequality is significantly related to long-term technological and social changes.

Despite these long-term forces, distinguishing between Democratic and Republican administrations (the white circles and black diamonds in the figure, respectively) reveals the regularity with which Democratic presidents reduced and Republican presidents increased the prevailing level of economic inequality, regardless of the long-term trend. Indeed, the effect of presidential partisanship on income inequality turns out to have been remarkably consistent since the end of World War II. The 80/20 income ratio increased under each of the six Republican presidents in this period—Eisenhower, Nixon, Ford, Reagan, George H. W. Bush, and George W. Bush. In contrast, four of five Democratic presidents—all except Jimmy Carter—presided over declines in income inequality. If this is a coincidence, it is a very powerful one.[3] Even in the highly inegalitarian economic climate of the 1990s, Bill Clinton managed to produce slightly stronger income growth for families at the 20th percentile than at the 80th percentile, though families at the very top of the income distribution did even better.

The strikingly consistent partisan pattern of changes in income inequality in figure 2 seems hard to attribute to a mere coincidence in the timing of Democratic and Republican administrations.

▪   ▪   ▪

It may be tempting to suppose that the very different patterns of income growth under Democratic and Republican presidents in figure 1 reflect a cycle of partisan equilibration in which Democrats pursue expansionary policies in reaction to Republican contractions and Republicans produce contractions as

TABLE 1 The Impact of Partisan Turnover on Partisan Differences in Real Income Growth Rates, 1948–2005

Average annual real pre-tax income growth (%) for families at various points in the income distribution (with standard errors in parentheses). Partisan control measured from one year following inauguration to one year following subsequent inauguration. "Partisan turnover" refers to first-term Democrats who succeeded Republicans or first-term Republicans who succeeded Democrats.

	All Presidents	Democratic Presidents	Republican Presidents	Partisan Difference
Partisan turnover				
20th percentile	1.38 (.75)	2.28 (1.00)	.71 (1.08)	1.57 (1.52)
40th percentile	1.52 (.54)	2.07 (.75)	1.11 (.76)	.96 (1.09)
60th percentile	1.60 (.47)	2.00 (.63)	1.30 (.67)	.71 (.95)
80th percentile	1.80 (.45)	2.19 (.62)	1.51 (.63)	.68 (.91)
95th percentile	1.89 (.45)	1.93 (.69)	1.86 (.61)	.07 (.92)
N	28	12	16	28
No partisan turnover				
20th percentile	1.46 (.68)	2.95 (1.19)	.16 (.61)	2.80 (1.29)
40th percentile	1.56 (.56)	2.80 (.88)	.48 (.63)	2.31 (1.06)
60th percentile	1.86 (.51)	2.86 (.82)	.97 (.57)	1.89 (.98)
80th percentile	1.87 (.48)	2.55 (.78)	1.27 (.57)	1.28 (.95)
95th percentile	2.10 (.62)	2.28 (1.07)	1.95 (.70)	.34 (1.25)
N	30	14	16	30

Source: Calculations based on data from Census Bureau Historical Income Tables.

FIGURE 3   Post-Tax Income Growth under Democratic and Republican
Presidents, 1980–2003

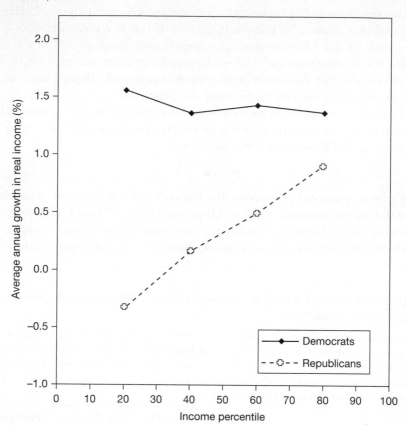

an antidote to Democratic expansions. However, a detailed analysis of the timing of partisan differences in income growth provides no support for that
notion. Table 1 provides tabulations of average income growth.

■   ■   ■

[T]he partisan differences in average growth rates at every income level were
about twice as large in terms with no partisan turnover as they were in the first
terms of new partisan regimes. Democratic presidents generally presided over
similar income growth rates for families in every part of the income distribution, regardless of whether they were in their first or second terms; but average
income growth was consistently higher (by a little more than half a percentage point) when Democrats succeeded Democrats than when Democrats succeeded Republicans. Conversely, most families (except the most affluent) did
better under first-term Republican presidents than in subsequent Republican
administrations; these differences, too, were on the order of half a percentage
point.

▪ ▪ ▪

[T]he partisan pattern of post-tax income growth in figure 3 is strikingly similar to the partisan pattern of pre-tax family income growth in figure 1. Households at every income level did about equally well under Carter and Clinton, with average growth rates ranging from 1.4% to 1.6%. On the other hand, Republican presidents presided over weaker income growth for households in the top half of the income distribution and little or no income growth for households in the bottom half of the income distribution. As with the partisan differences in pre-tax growth presented in figure 1, these partisan differences in post-tax growth are concentrated in the second year of each administration, when the policy initiatives adopted in the "honeymoon" period immediately following Inauguration Day are most likely to take effect.[4]

▪ ▪ ▪

Democrats, Republicans, and the Rise of Inequality

Economists associate the escalation of inequality over the past 30 years with important structural changes in the American economy, including demographic shifts, globalization, and technological change. I see no reason to doubt that these factors have played an important role in increasing the income gap between rich and poor people in the contemporary United States; but if this is "simply an economic reality," as Treasury Secretary Paulson asserted, it does not follow that nothing can be done to mitigate the economic and social consequences of that reality. Nor does the fact that "there has always been extreme income inequality," as Ben Stein observed, imply that presidents and their policy choices can have no significant effect on the extent of inequality at any given time.

The cumulative impact of these partisan policy choices is illustrated in figure 4. The dotted line in the center of the figure represents the actual course of inequality over the past half-century, as measured by the ratio of family incomes at the 80th and 20th percentiles of the income distribution. (This portion of the figure is simply repeated from figure 2.) The solid upper line represents the projected course of the 80/20 income ratio over the same period given the pattern of income growth that prevailed under Republican presidents during this period, while the lower line represents the projected course of the 80/20 income ratio under Democratic presidents. . . .

The projections in figure 4 imply that continuous Democratic control would have produced an essentially constant level of economic inequality over the past three decades, despite all the technological, demographic, and global competitive forces emphasized in economists' accounts of escalating inequality. In contrast, continuous Republican control would have produced a much sharper polarization between rich and poor than has actually occurred over the past 30 years, with the 80/20 income ratio reaching a level about one-third higher than it actually did.[5]

FIGURE 4 Projected Income Inequality under Republican and Democratic Presidents, 1947–2005

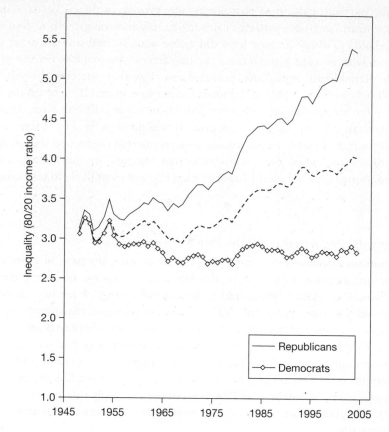

The projections presented in figure 4 are based on an arguably unrealistic assumption: that if either party had uninterrupted control of the White House, it would do all the time what it in fact does only half the time. It is impossible to know whether either party would actually have the political will or the political power to produce economic redistribution of the cumulative magnitude suggested by these projections. Nevertheless, the cumulative differences portrayed in figure 4 convey the fundamental significance of partisan politics in ameliorating or exacerbating economic inequality over the past half-century.

In the first 25 years of the post-war era, the partisan differences in income growth patterns documented [here] implied robust growth for middle-class and poor families under Democratic presidents and more modest growth under Republicans. In the less propitious economic circumstances prevailing in the early twenty-first century, not even a steady succession of Democratic presidents and policies would be likely to reproduce the robust broad-based income growth of the 1960s. However, that does not make the choice between Democrats and Republicans any less consequential.

NOTES

1. Remarks Prepared for Delivery by Treasury Secretary Henry H. Paulson at Columbia University, August 1, 2006, www.treas.gov/press/releases/hp41.htm.

2. Mead, "The Great passivity," Perspectives on Politics 2 (2004),671.

3. The probability of observing no more than one exception to the partisan pattern of increasing inequality under Republicans and decreasing inequality under Democrats in a random sequence of 11 increases and decreases would be $12 \div 2,048 = .006$.

4. In "honeymoon" years, the differences in average post-tax income growth between Democratic and Republican presidents range from 5.0% for households at the 20th percentile of the income distribution to 3.0% for households at the 80th percentile. The corresponding differences in nonhoneymoon years range from 0.9% to -0.3%.

5. The 80/20 income ratio increased by 27% between 1975 and 2005. The projections in figure 4 suggest that it would have increased by 45% under continuous Republican control but by only 3% under continuous Democratic control.

17

FOREIGN POLICY

17.1

WALTER RUSSELL MEAD

From *Special Providence: American Foreign Policy and How It Changed the World*

There are four strains of American foreign policy, Mead argues: Hamiltonian, Wilsonian, Jeffersonian, and Jacksonian. Contemporary American leaders invoke specific memories of American history related to one or more of these strains to justify their foreign policy decisions. Mead argues that foreign policy has had an enormous influence on domestic politics throughout American history, much more than is ordinarily supposed.

INTRODUCTION

. . . In little more than two hundred years, the United States has grown from a handful of settlements on the Atlantic seaboard to become the most powerful country in the history of the world. Both foreigners and Americans themselves take this remarkable development for granted. Throughout the U.S. rise to world power, most observers have believed that the country did not care very much about foreign policy and was not very good at it. Even today in the United States, most policy-makers and pundits think that foreign policy played only a very marginal role in American life before World War II, and that there is very little to be gained by studying the historical records of our past.

. . . I find myself increasingly drawn to question this conventional wisdom. I have wondered if American success in the rough-and-tumble contest of nations wasn't due just to dumb luck, the special providence for drunks,

539

fools, and the United States of America that Bismarck believed watched over us. I have also wondered if the American foreign policy system had a logic of its own, a different logic from the one that governed the foreign policy of the traditional great powers of Europe.

Two discrepancies led me to ask these questions. First, there was the odd fact that while much conventional discussion of foreign policy assumes at least tacitly that democracy is at best an irrelevance and at worst a serious obstacle in foreign affairs, in the twentieth century democratic states were generally more successful in foreign policy than either monarchies or dictatorships. The clearest examples come from Germany and Japan. Under nondemocratic regimes, both Germany and Japan followed risky, aggressive foreign policies that ultimately brought them to misery and ruin. Starting under much less favorable external circumstances after World War II, democratic German and Japanese governments made their countries rich, peaceful, and respected. Was it possible that something about democracy actually improves the ability of governments to conduct their foreign affairs?

Second, I could not escape the fact that the two most recent great powers in world history were what Europeans still sometimes refer to as "Anglo-Saxon" powers: Great Britain and the United States. Besides having a large number of cultural similarities, these two countries have historically looked at the world in a different way than have most of the European countries. The British Empire was, and the United States is, concerned not just with the balance of power in one particular corner of the world but with the evolution of what we today call "world order." A worldwide system of trade and finance made both Britain and the United States rich; those riches were what gave them the power to project the military force that ensured the stability of their international systems. Both Britain and the United States spent less time thinking about the traditional military security preoccupations of European power diplomacy and more time thinking about money and trade. "A nation of shopkeepers!" Napoleon scoffed about Britain—but the shopkeepers got him in the end.

Could it be that the British shopkeepers and American democrats know something about foreign policy that Napoleon and Bismarck didn't?

These questions have led me to the study of the history of American foreign policy. . . .

For one thing, . . . foreign policy has played a much more important role in American politics throughout our history than I expected. Our contemporary battles over the North American Free Trade Agreement (NAFTA) and the World Trade Organization (WTO) are the latest installments in a long line of American political contests over trade issues. Long before World War II or even World War I, foreign policy questions were deciding American elections, reshaping American politics, and driving the growth of the American economy.

Also . . . American thinking about foreign policy has been relatively stable over the centuries. The arguments over foreign policy in George Washington's administration—and some of the bitterest political battles Washington engaged in were over foreign policy—are clearly related to the debates of our own time.

Americans through the centuries seem to have had four basic ways of looking at foreign policy, which have reflected contrasting and sometimes complementary ways of looking at domestic policy as well. *Hamiltonians* regard a strong alliance between the national government and big business as the key both to domestic stability and to effective action abroad, and they have long focused on the nation's need to be integrated into the global economy on favorable terms. *Wilsonians* believe that the United States has both a moral obligation and an important national interest in spreading American democratic and social values throughout the world, creating a peaceful international community that accepts the rule of law. *Jeffersonians* hold that American foreign policy should be less concerned about spreading democracy abroad than about safeguarding it at home; they have historically been skeptical about Hamiltonian and Wilsonian policies that involve the United States with unsavory allies abroad or that increase the risks of war. Finally, a large populist school I call *Jacksonian* believes that the most important goal of the U.S. government in both foreign and domestic policy should be the physical security and the economic well-being of the American people. "Don't Tread on Me!" warned the rattlesnake on the Revolutionary battle flag; Jacksonians believe that the United States should not seek out foreign quarrels, but when other nations start wars with the United States, Jacksonian opinion agrees with Gen. Douglas MacArthur that "There is no substitute for victory."

These four schools have shaped the American foreign policy debate from the eighteenth century to the twenty-first. They are as important under George W. Bush as they were under George Washington and from everything that I can see, American foreign policy will continue to emerge from their collisions and debates far into the future.

. . . The long economic boom of the 1990s spawned some triumphalist literature about the American way of capitalism and the growth of American power. . . . After each of the three great wars of the twentieth century—the two world wars and the Cold War—many voices in America proclaimed an "end to history." With the powers of evil defeated, the United States and its allies, some argued each time, would go on in the postwar period to build a new world order of justice, peace, and democracy.

History, alas, has a way of hanging on. More than a decade after the Cold War, it now seems clear that the twenty-first century is bringing the United States new challenges and new problems. Not all countries will become democratic; not all democratic countries will agree with the United States about how the world should be run. Foreign policy will not become a field of dreams; our choices will sometimes be painful ones, and together with new opportunities and adventures this century may well bring new wars and new problems that are even worse than those of the bloody century just past.

. . . American foreign policy will not bring history to an end, but it has done a remarkably good job of enabling the United States to flourish as history goes on. I do not know how long the present moment of American supremacy will last, or if the world is due for a second American century. I am not even sure that another century of American global hegemony is what the American people should hope for. But the long and successful record of this country's unique—and uniquely complex—foreign policy system gives me solid grounds for believing that whatever else happens in the world, our foreign policy tradition offers the American people real hope for a prosperous and democratic future.

17.2

JOHN YOO

From *The Powers of War and Peace: The Constitution and Foreign Affairs after 9/11*

•

Yoo reacts to those who claim that the president has garnered too much power in foreign and military policy. It may be true, he says, that Congress is weaker than the president in these areas of policy, but this subordination of Congress was explicit in the Constitution. Powers of presidential initiative have been forged through experience. Congress has repeatedly shown the lack of political will to challenge presidential authority.

WAR POWERS FOR A NEW WORLD

. . . The Framers believed that separating the president's executive and commander-in-chief powers from Congress's powers over declaring war and funding would create a political system in which in each branch could use its own constitutional powers to develop foreign policy. A close reading of the constitutional text and structure shows that the original understanding of the war power is fully reflected in the Constitution. The Constitution's flexible warmaking system is especially pronounced when compared to other constitutional texts, and to the more formalistic processes established for other forms of government action.

This approach finds that the practice of the political branches in making war since the end of World War II has fallen within the constitutional design. While Congress never declared war in Korea or Vietnam, among many other places, it had every opportunity to control those conflicts through its funding powers. That it did not was a reflection of a lack of political will rather than a defect in the constitutional design. A more flexible approach also allows us to understand America's newest military interventions. Recent wars in Iraq, Afghanistan, and Kosovo were constitutional, even though in none of them was there a declaration of war and Kosovo received no statutory authorization, because Congress has had the full opportunity to participate in decisionmaking elsewhere.

■ ■ ■

War and the Constitutional Text

. . . Important and long-overlooked insights about the nature of the war power come to light through close examination of the text. First, it is apparent that

Congress's power to "declare war" is not synonymous with the power to begin military hostilities. Professor Ramsey's article in the *University of Chicago Law Review* best expresses the opposite view. He argues that the Framers understood the power to "declare war" as the giving Congress the sole power to decide on whether to commence military hostilities against other nations. Under international and domestic law at the time of the ratification, therefore, "declare war" must have been shorthand for "begin war" or "commence war" or "authorize war."[1] Only once Congress had issued this authorization could the president trigger his commander-in-chief authority and fight the war to its conclusion. At best, the president has a limited authority to use force without congressional consent only when the United States has suffered an attack. Thus, the Declare War Clause both expands Congress's war powers and restricts those of the president. As Glennon has written, the clause not only "empowers Congress to declare war," but also "serves as a limitation on executive war-making power, placing certain acts off limits for the President."[2]

The constitutional text, however, simply does not support such an expansive reading. First, the Constitution uses the word "declare" war, rather than "make," "begin," "authorize," or "wage" war. At the time of the Constitution's ratification, "declare" carried a distinct and separate meaning from "levy," "engage," "make," or "commence." Samuel Johnson's English dictionary (perhaps the definitive dictionary at the time of the framing) defined "declare" as "to clear, to free from obscurity"; "to make known, to tell evidently and openly": "to publish; to proclaim"; "to shew in open view"; or "to make a declaration, to proclaim some resolution or opinion, some favour or opposition."[3] This definition suggests that declaring war recognized a state of affairs— clarifying the legal status of the nation's relationship with another country— rather than authorized the creation of that state of affairs.

Second, if this view were correct, we would expect the Framers to have repeated the phrase "declare war" elsewhere in the Constitution when addressing the same subject. They did not. When discussing war in other contexts, the Constitution's phrasing indicates that declaring war referred to something less than the sole power to send the nation into hostilities. As we have seen, Article I, Section 10 declares that states may not "engage" in war. If "declare war" meant the same thing as initiate hostilities, Article I, Section 10 should have forbidden states from declaring war. Granting Congress the sole authority to "engage" the nation in war would have been a much clearer, direct method for vesting in Congress the power to control the actual conduct of war.

To take another example, Article III of the Constitution defines the crime of treason, in part, as consisting of "levying War" against the United States. Again, "levying" appears to be broader in meaning than merely declaring. If the Framers had used "levy War" in Article I, Section 8, they certainly would have made far clearer their alleged intention to grant Congress the sole power to decide on war. Conversely, if the step of declaring war were as serious as some believe, Article III ought to have defined treason to occur when a citizen "declares war" against the United States. To be sure, as Adrian Vermeule and

Ernest Young have argued, while there may be serious doubts about demanding a consistency in meaning between constitutional provisions, which have been added to the Constitution during different periods of time by different groups of legislators and delegates, this is not true of the original 1787 Constitution.[4] The unamended Constitution was drafted at one time and ratified at one time, and so it is not unreasonable to expect words used on the same subject to convey a common meaning throughout.

The structure of Article I, Section 10 deals an even heavier blow to the pro-Congress reading. It states:

> No State shall, without the Consent of Congress, lay any Duty of Tonnage, keep Troops or Ships of War in time of Peace, enter into any Agreement or Compact with another State, or with a foreign power, or *engage in War, unless actually invaded or in such imminent Danger as will not admit of delay.* (emphasis added)[5]

This provision creates the *exact* war powers process between Congress and the states that scholars critical of the presidency want to create between Congress and the president. It makes resort to force conditional on the "Consent of Congress," and it even includes an exception for defending against sudden attacks. Pro-Congress scholars have argued that the Framers understood the Declare War Clause to contain an unexpressed exception that permits the executive to use force in response to an attack without having to seek a declaration of war from Congress. Otherwise their strict interpretation would prevent the president from engaging in even defensive uses of force without congressional approval and have proven utterly unworkable in the real world. Article I, Section 10, however, shows the faults of this approach, because it requires us to believe that the Framers did not know how to express themselves in one part of the Constitution but did in another part of the Constitution on exactly the same subject.

Pro-Congress scholars have never attempted to account for the difference in language between Article I, Section 8 and Article I, Section 10.[6] If they assume that specific texts have specific meanings, they also must believe that different texts should be interpreted to have different meanings. If the pro-Congress reading were correct, the Framers naturally should have written a provision stating that "the President may not, without the Consent of Congress, engage in War, unless the United States are actually invaded, or in such imminent Danger as will not admit of delay." Or, Article I, Section 10 should have said that "no state shall, without the consent of Congress, declare war." Instead, the Constitution only allocates to Congress the declare war power and to the president the commander-in-chief power, without specifically stating—as it does in Article I, Section 10 with regard to the states—how those powers are to interact. The Constitution's creation of a specific, detailed war powers process at the state level, but its silence at the federal level, shows that the Constitution does not establish any specific procedure for going to war.

Two additional clues suggest that "declare war" served as a recognition of the legal status of hostile acts, rather than as a necessary authorization for hostilities. Congress's power to declare war does not stand alone, but instead is part of a clause that includes the power to "grant Letters of Marque and Reprisal" and to "make Rules concerning Captures on Land and Water."[7] Placement of the power to declare war alongside these other two is significant, because they clearly involve the power of Congress to recognize or declare the legal status and consequences of certain wartime actions, and not the power to authorize those actions. Ironically, the Marque and Reprisal Clause serves as the linchpin for some defenders of an expansive reading of Congress's war powers. Jules Lobel and Jane Stromseth, for example, who rely on the work of Charles Lofgren, argue that letters of marque and reprisal had come "to signify any intermediate or low-intensity hostility short of declared war."[8] In part, they respond to the history of the 1980s, in which presidents conducted "police actions," smaller conflicts, and convert activity that fall well short of World Wars I and II. When combined with Congress's control over declaring war, Stromseth, Lobel, and Lofgren argue, the Marque and Reprisal Clause provides Congress with full control over the initiation of all military hostilities, whether they be total war or covert actions.

Such interpretive moves, however, rip the constitutional text from its historical context. By the time of the framing, letters of marque and reprisal had come to refer to a fairly technical form of international reprisal, in which a government gave its permission to an injured private party to recover, via military operations, compensation from the citizens of a foreign nation. Without a letter of marque and reprisal, such actions—usually conducted on the high seas—would constitute piracy; with a letter, they were legitimate forms of privateering condoned by sovereign consent. While marque and reprisal certainly are one category of what we today might call "low-level conflict," it does not follow that marque and reprisal must refer to *all* forms of conflict short of war. Recent work suggests that, during the American Revolution, letters of marque and reprisal authorized a rather narrow form of commercial warfare that was conducted for profit and regulated by prize courts, in contrast to military actions by regular armed forces.[9] What seems fairly clear is that marque and reprisal did not refer to all forms of undeclared war, especially those with purely military and political goals, but rather with the legal implications of one species of commercial warfare.[10]

Other foundational documents of the period demonstrate that the Framers thought of the power to begin hostilities as different from the power to declare war. Under the Articles of Confederation, the nation's framework of government until the ratification. Congress operated as the executive branch of the United States.[11] As we have seen, Article IX vested Congress with "the sole and exclusive right and power of determining on peace and war."[12] Here the Framers (several of whom had served in the Continental Congress) had at hand a text that clearly and explicitly allocated to Congress the "sole and exclusive" authority to decide whether to fight a war. If the Framers had intended to grant Congress the power to commence military hostilities, they could easily have imported the phrase from the Articles of Confederation into the Constitution, as they did with other, related powers.[13] Instead, they changed Congress's power to "declare war" from "determining on peace and war." For the pro-Congress position to be correct, the Framers would have had to be clumsy draftsmen indeed.

Presidential critics also fail to take into account the next most important founding-era documents: the state constitutions. Most of the state constitutions did not explicitly transfer to their assemblies the power to initiate hostilities, but rather sought to control executive power by disrupting the structural unity of the executive branch.[14] One state, however chose to create exactly the type of arrangement contemplated by pro-Congress scholars. In its first 1776 constitution, South Carolina vested in its chief executive the power of commander in chief, but then declared that "the president and commander-in-chief shall have no power to make war or peace . . . without the consent of the general assembly and legislative council."[15] In its 1778 constitution. South Carolina reaffirmed its decision that the legislature first must authorize war by stating that "the governor and commander-in-chief shall have no power to commence war, or conclude peace" without legislative approval. South Carolina's 1776 and 1778 constitutions bear two important lessons. First, they show that the Framers did not understand the phrase "declare war" to amount to the power to "make war" or "commence war"—phrases the South Carolina constitution used to refer specifically to initiating war. Second, the South Carolina constitutions provide an example of constitutional language that clearly and explicitly created a legislature-dominated warmaking system—one that the Framers did not adopt.

Usage of these words during the late eighteenth century further supports the distinction between "declare" and "begin" or "commence." Recall that Article I. Section 10 uses the phrase "engage in War," and Article III uses "levying War." Johnson's dictionary, for example, defined "engage" as "to embark in an affair; to enter in an undertaking," or "to conflict; to fight." Johnson defined "levy" as "to raise, applied to war."[16] Other dictionaries of the period drew a similar distinction between "declare" and "engage" or "levy." Nathan Bailey's English dictionary defined "declare" as "to make known, to manifest, publish, or shew," while "engage" meant "to encounter or fight," and "levy" to "raise."[17] Thomas Sheridan's dictionary defined "declare" as "to make known," "engage" as "to conflict, to fight," and levy as "to raise, to bring together men."[18] All three defined "commence," as used by the South Carolina constitution, as "to begin." Even today, we commonly think of the statutes that establish public programs and mandates as "authorization" statutes (to be followed by appropriations), not "declaring" statutes. A declaration does not authorize or make, it recognizes and proclaims.

When the Framers employed "declare" in a constitutional context, they usually used it in a juridical manner, in the sense that courts "declare" the state of the law or the legal status of a certain event or situation. An example from early American political history—the Declaration of independence—illustrates this narrower meaning. The Declaration did not "authorize" military resistance to Great Britain. At the time that the Continental Congress met to draft the Declaration, hostilities had existed for more than a year, and Congress had been exercising sovereign powers—negotiating with Britain, sending representatives abroad, seeking aid—for at least two years.[19] Rather than authorize hostilities, the Declaration announced the legal relationship between the mother country and its former colonies. Thus, the Declaration of Independence appears in the form almost of a complaint, in which the revolutionaries recount their grievances (taxation without representation, suspension of the laws, use of bench trials), the remedy sought (independence), and the applicable law ("the Laws of Nature and of Nature's God"). The Declaration's importance was not in authorizing combat, but in transforming the legal status of the hostilities between Great Britain and her colonies from an insurrection to a war between equals. As historian David Armitage has observed, "in order to turn a civil war into a war between states, and thus to create legitimate corporate combatants out of individual rebels and traitors, it was essential to declare war and to obtain recognition of the legitimacy of such a declaration."[20] The Declaration of Independence was the nation's first declaration of war.

■　　■　　■

Declarations of war serve a purpose, albeit one that does not amount to the sole authority to initiate hostilities. Declarations do simply what they say they do: they declare. To use the eighteenth-century understanding, they make public, show openly, and make known the state of international legal relations between the United States and another nation. This is a different concept than whether the laws of war apply to the hostilities; two nations could technically not be at war, even though their forces might be engaged in limited combat (which would be governed by the laws of war). During the eighteenth century, declarations often took the form of a legal complaint in which a nation identified the grounds for waging war, explained the new rules that would apply to interaction between the two nations, and outlined the remedy. Declarations are also important for domestic constitutional purposes. Textually, a declaration of war places the nation in a state of total war, which triggers enhanced powers on the part of the federal government. The Fifth Amendment, for example, says that "[n]o person shall be held to answer for a capital, or otherwise infamous crime, unless on a presentment or indictment of a Grand Jury, except in cases arising in the land or naval forces, or in the Militia, when in actual service in time of War or public danger."

Congress has recognized the distinction between declared total wars and nondeclared hostilities by providing the executive branch with expanded domestic powers—such as seizing foreign property, conducting warrantless surveillance, arresting enemy aliens, and taking control of transportation systems, to name a few—only when war is declared.[21] Even the Supreme Court has suggested that in times of declared war, certain actions by the federal government would survive strict scrutiny but would certainly fail if attempted in peacetime. Thus, the terrible internment of Japanese Americans during World War II was justified only because the United States was in the midst of a war declared by Congress.[22] One doubts whether the courts would have allowed the wholesale internment of Panamanian Americans during the 1989 Panama War, or of Yugoslavs during the Kosovo conflict, or of all Iraqis Americans during the recent invasion and occupation of Iraq. Only a declaration of war from Congress could trigger and permit such extreme measures reserved only for total war.

▪　　▪　　▪

Practice and the Constitution

A more flexible approach to the allocation of war powers shows that, rather than violating the Constitution, the American way of war during the last decade has complied with the constitutional design. It is worth taking a closer look at recent conflicts to show that Congress has had an ample opportunity to consider and to check presidential initiatives in warmaking. In 2001 Afghanistan and 2003–4 Iraq, no declaration of war issued, that Congress did enact statutes "authorizing" the president to engage in armed combat. In response to the September 11, 2001 attacks, for example, Congress quickly enacted Senate Joint Resolution 23 "to authorize the use of the United States Armed Forces against those responsible for the recent attacks launched against the United States.[23] It found not only that the September 11 attacks constituted an "unusual and extraordinary threat to the national security and foreign policy of the United States" but also declared that "the President has authority under the Constitution to take action to deter and prevent acts of international terrorism against the United States," an admission, it seems of the president's inherent authority to use force without congressional permission. Congress then authorized the president to use military force against "those nations, organizations, or persons he determines planned, authorized, committed, or aided the terrorist attacks" of September 11, or "harbored such organizations or persons." In the course of enacting this legislation, Congress had a full opportunity to debate the merits of using military force abroad, particularly in Afghanistan.

Even if such legislation had never been considered, Congress had several other moments to block presidential efforts to wage war against al Qaeda. Military operations in Afghanistan have required additional funds, which President Bush initially requested as part of a $20 billion emergency appropriations bill in October of 2001, which was granted by Congress. The expense of modern war has required ongoing demands for appropriations, with another bill enacted on July 23, 2002 that appropriated more than $4 billion for continuing operations in Afghanistan. Even before the war in Iraq, military operations in Afghanistan and around the world generated approximately $2.5 billion in additional costs per month that require periodic supplemental appropriations to refill the Pentagon's coffers. In the fall of 2001, Congress also enacted a Defense Department authorization bill that determines the military's size, force structure, and weapons systems. If Congress had wanted to prevent the war in Afghanistan, or if it had disagreed with the continuing role of American troops there, it could have refused to provide the funds needed to pay for the personnel, material, and operational expenses of waging the war. War went ahead without a declaration, and Congress had every chance to consider the merits of the conflict and to prevent it.

Congress similarly had ample opportunity to prevent President Bush from ordering the invasion of Iraq.

■   ■   ■

One might respond that it is unreasonable to expect Congress to use its appropriations powers to cut off troops in the field. . . . We should not, however, mistake a failure of political will for a violation of the constitution.

NOTES

1. Michael D. Ramsey, *Textualism and War Powers*, 69 U. Chi. L. Rev. 1590–1609 (2002).

2. Michael J. Glennon, Constitutional Diplomacy 17 (1990).

3. I Samuel Johnson, A Dictionary of the English Language (W. Strahan ed., 1755).

4. Adrian Vermeule and Ernest Young, *Hercules, Herbert, and Amar: The Trouble with Intratextualism*, 113 Harv. L. Rev. 730 (2000). But see Akhil Reed Amar, *Intratextualism*, 112 Harv. L. Rev. 747 (1999).

5. U.S. Const. art. I, § 10.

6. I have had the pleasure of engaging (not declaring) in several direct, published exchanges with pro-Congress scholars on war powers. See, e.g., Ramsey, *supra* note 1; Louis Fisher, Presidential War Power 11 (1995). None of them has ever explained the difference in language between Article I, Section 8 and Article I, Section 10 other than to say that there is nothing wrong with using different language in different parts of the Constitution.

7. U.S. Const. art. I, § 8, cl. 11

8. Jane E. Stromseth, *Understanding Constitutional War Powers Today: Why Methodology Matters*, 106 Yale L.J. 845, 854 (1996) (quoting Jules Lobel, *Covert War and Congressional Authority: Hidden War and Forgotten Power*, 134 U. Pa. L. Rev. 1035, 1045 [1986]). See also Charles A. Lofgren, *War-Making under the Constitution: The Original Understanding*, 81 Yale L.J. 672 (1972).

9. Privateers sought to capture enemy merchant vessels with the object of selling their cargoes back home. As individualistic commercial entrepreneurs, they failed miserably at actual fighting and did not coordinate their efforts with the American navy. See C. Kevin Marshall, Comment, *Putting Privateers in Their Place: The Applicability of the Marque and Reprisal Clause to Undeclared Wars*, 64 U. Chi. L. Rev. 953, 974–81 (1997); John C. Yoo, *The Continuation of Politics by Other Means: The Original Understanding of War Powers*, 84 Cal. L. Rev. 167, 250–52 (1996).

10. The Declare War Clause also comes immediately after another provision that is directly about legal effect and consequence. The immediate clause before gives Congress the authority "To define and punish Piracies and Felonies committed on the high Seas, and Offenses against the Law of Nations." Like the declare war power, this clause vests Congress with the authority to "define" the legal status of certain actions that, in its mind, constitute piracy, felonies, or violations of international law. It may then enact legislation criminalizing those actions. Similarly, the Declare War Clause gives Congress the power to "declare" whether the a certain state of affairs legally constitutes a war, which then gives it the authority to enact wartime regulations of individual persons and property both within and outside the United States.

11. Jerrilyn Greene Marston, King and Congress: The Transfer of Political Legitimacy, 1774–1776, at 303 (1987) (arguing that "the executive and administrative responsibilities that had been exercised by or under the aegis of the king's authority were confided to the successor to his authority, the Congress").

12. Articles of Confederation art. IX (1777).

13. Article IX also gave Congress the power to "establish[ ] rules for deciding, in all cases, what captures on land or water shall be legal," and "of granting letters of marque and reprisal in times of peace." Articles of Confederation art. IX. Both provisions remained substantially unchanged in the Constitution, and, in fact, they appear in the same clause as the power to declare war. The Framers' alteration of Congress's authority from determining on peace and war to declaring war, while leaving the other provisions unchanged, indicates an intention to alter Congress's war power.

14. See Yoo, *supra* note 9, at 222–23; Willi Paul Adams, The First American Constitutions: Republican Ideology and the Making of the State Constitution in the Revolutionary Era 271 (Rita and Robert Kimber trans., 1980).

15. S.C. Const. art XXVI (1776), reprinted in The Federal and State Constitutions, Colonial Charters, and Other Organic Laws 3247 (Francis N. Thorpe ed., 1909).

16. Johnson, *supra* note 3.

17. Nathan Bailey, An Universal Etymological English Dictionary (Neill ed., 24th ed. 1782).

18. Thomas Sheridan, A General Dictionary of the English Language (Dodsley ed., 1780).

19. See David Armitage, *The Declaration of Independence and International Law*, 59 Wm. & Mary Q. 39 (2002).

20. Id. at 39.

21. See, e.g., 50 U.S.C. § 5(b)(I)(1994 & Supp. 1999) (seizure of foreign property); 50 U.S.C. § 1811 (1994) (electronic surveillance); 50 U.S.C. § 1829 (1994) (physical searches); 50 U.S.C. § 1844 (Supp. 1999) (trap and trace devices); 50 U.S.C. § 21 (1994) (seizure of aliens); 10 U.S.C. § 2644 (1994 & Supp. 1996) (seizure of transportation systems).

22. *Korematsu v. United States*, 323 U.S. 214, 216 (1944) (upholding racial classifications during World War II and noting that "legal restrictions which curtail the civil rights of a single racial group" may be justified by "[p]ressing public necessity").

23. Joint Resolution to Authorize the Use of United States Armed Forces against Those Responsible for the Recent Attacks against the United States, Pub. L. No. 107–40, 115 Stat. 224 (2001).

ACKNOWLEDGMENTS

John H. Aldrich: From *Why Parties* by John H. Aldrich. Reprinted with the permission of the University of Chicago Press.

Stephen Ansolabehere and James M. Snyder, Jr.: From *The End of Inequality: One Person, One Vote and the Transformation of American Politics* by Stephen Ansolabehere and James M. Snyder. Copyright © 2008 by W. W. Norton & Company, Inc. Used by permission of W. W. Norton & Company, Inc.

Larry M. Bartels: Bartles, Larry M; *Unequal Democracy.* Copyright © 2008 by Russell Sage Foundation. Published by Princeton University Press. Reprinted by permission of Princeton University Press.

Matthew A. Baum: Baum, Matthew; *Soft News Goes to War.* Copyright © 2003 by Princeton University Press. Reprinted by Permission of Princeton University Press.

Frank R. Baumgartner and Bryan D. Jones: "Two Models of Issue Expansion" from *Agendas and Instability in American Politics.* Copyright © 1993, 2009 by The University of Chicago. Reprinted with the permission of the University of Chicago Press.

Nancy Burns, Kay Schlozman, and Sidney Verba: "The Political Worlds of Men and Women" reprinted by permission of the publisher from *The Private Roots of Public Action: Gender, Equality and Political Participation* by Nancy Burns, Kay Lehman Schlozman, and Sidney Verba, pp. 99–133, Cambridge , Mass.: Harvard University Press, Copyright © 2001 by the President and Fellows of Harvard College.

Charles M. Cameron: From *Presidential Power* by Charles Cameron. Copyright © 2000 by Columbia University Press. Reprinted with permission of the publisher.

Angus Campbell: "The Impact of Party Identification" from *The American Voter: An Abridgement* by Angus Campbell, Phillip E. Converse, Warren Edward Miller, Donald E. Stokes. We have made diligent efforts to contact the copyright holder to obtain permission to reprint this selection. If you have information that would help us, please write to Permissions Department, W. W. Norton & Company, Inc., 500 Fifth Avenue, New York, NY 10110.

Brandice Canes-Wrone: From *Who Leads Whom?* by Brandice Canes-Wrone. Reprinted with the permission of the University of Chicago Press.

Bryan Caplan: Caplan, Bryan; *The Myth of the Rational Voter.* Copyright © 2007 by Princeton University Press. Reprinted by permission of Princeton University Press.

Daniel Carpenter: Carpenter, Daniel; *The Forging of Bureaucratic Autonomy.* Princeton University Press. Reprinted by permission of Princeton University Press.

Gary W. Cox and Mathew D. McCubbins: "Procedural Cartel Theory" from *Setting the Agenda: Responsible Party Governement in the U.S. House of Representatives.* Reprinted with the permission of Cambridge University Press.

Robert A. Dahl: From *How Democratic is the American Constitution* by Robert Dahl. Used by the permission of Yale University Press.

Michael Dawson: Dawson, Michael C. *Behind the Mule.* Copyright © 1994 Princeton University Press, 1995 paperback edition. Reprinted by permission of Princeton University Press.

Richard F. Fenno, Jr.: Excerpts from *Home Style* by Richard Fenno, pp. 1–28. Copyright © 2002 by Pearson Longman Publishing. Used by permission.

Milton Friedman: From *Capitalism and Freedom* by Milton Friedman. Reprinted with the permission of the University of Chicago Press.

Garrett Hardin: "The Tragedy of the Commons" from *Science*, Vol. 152, pp. 1243–1248 (1968). Reprinted with permission from AAAS.

William G. Howell: Howell, William G; *Power Without Persuasion.* Princeton University Press. Reprinted by permission of Princeton University Press.

Shanto Iyengar: From *Media Politics: A Citizen's Guide*, 2nd Edition by Shanto Iyengar. Copyright © 2012, 2007 by W. W. Norton & Company, Inc.

Samuel Kernell: From *Going Public: New Strategies of Presidential Leadership* by Samuel Kernell. Copyright © 1997 CQ Press, a division of SAGE Publications, Inc.

John Maynard Keynes: Excerpts from *The General Theory of Employment Interest and Money*, copyright © 1965 by John Maynard Keynes, reprinted by permission of Harcourt, Inc.

D. Roderick Kiewiet and Mathew McCubbins: From *Logic of Delegation* by Roderick Kiewiet and Mathew McCubbins. Reprinted by permission of the University of Chicago Press.

Ken Kollman: Kollman, Ken. From *Outside Lobbying: Public Opinion and Interest Group Strategies* by Ken Kollman. Copyright © 1998 by Princeton University Press. Reprinted by permission of Princeton University Press.

Arthur Lupia and Mathew D. McCubbins: Chapter 1, "Knowledge Democratic and the Foundation of Democracy" from *The Democratic Dilemma: Can Citizens Learn What They Need to Know?* By Arthur Lupia and Mathew D. McCubbins. Reprinted with the permission of Cambridge University Press.

David Mayhew: From *Congress: The Electoral Connection* by David Mayhew. Reprinted with the permission of Yale University Press.

Nolan McCarty, Keith Poole, and Howard Rosenthal: *Polarized America: The Dance of Ideology and Unequal Riches*, pp. 1–11, 115–138, plus associated Notes © 2006 Massachusetts Institute of Technology, by permission of The MIT Press.

Walter Russell Mead: From *Special Providence* by Walter Russell Mead, copyright © 2001 by The Century Foundation. Used by permission of Alfred A. Knopf, a division of Random House, Inc.

Terry M. Moe: From *The Organization of Interests* by Terry Moe. Reprinted with the permission of the University of Chicago Press.

Richard E. Neustadt: Reprinted with the permission of The Free Press, a Division of Simon and Schuster, Inc., from *Presidential Power and the Modern Presidents: The Politics of Leadership from Roosevelt to Reagan* by Richard E. Neustadt. Copyright © 1990 by Richard E. Neustadt. All rights reserved.

Mancur Olson, Jr.: "A Theory of Groups and Organizations," reprinted by permission of the publisher. From *The Logic of Collective Action: Public Goods and the Theory of Groups* by Mancur Olson, pp. 5–50, Cambridge Mass.: Harvard University Press. Copyright © 1965, 1971 by the President and Fellows of Harvard College.

Robert D. Putnam: Reprinted and edited with the permission of Simon & Schuster, Inc., from *Bowling Alone: The Collapse and Revival of American Community* by Robert D. Putnam. Copyright © 2000 by Robert D. Putnam. All rights reserved.

William H. Riker: "Chapter 6: Is the Federal Bargain Worth Keeping?" from *Federalism: Origin, Operation, Significance.* Reprinted by permission of the Estate of William Riker.

Gerald N. Rosenberg: From *The Hollow Hope*, 2nd Edition by Gerald Rosenberg. Reprinted by permission of the University of Chicago Press.

Steven Rosenstone and John Mark Hansen: Excerpts pp. 10–37 from *Mobilization, Participation, and Democracy in America* by Steven J. Rosenstone and John Mark Hansen. Copyright © 2003 by Pearson Education Inc. Reprinted by permission.

Michele L. Swers: From *The Difference Women Make* by Michele L. Swers. Reprinted by permission of the University of Chicago Press.

Katherine Cramer Walsh: From *Talking About Race* by Katherine Walsh. Reprinted by permission of the University of Chicago Press.

John Walters and Donald F. Kettl: "The Katrina Breakdown" from *On Risk and Disaster*, pp. 255, 257–261. Used by permission of the University of Pennsylvania Press.

James Q. Wilson: From *Bureaucracy* by James Wilson. Reprinted by permission of Basic Books, a member of the Perseus Books Group.

John Yoo: "Chapter 5: War Powers for a New World" from *Powers of War and Peace*, pp. 143–181. Reprinted by permission of the University of Chicago Press.

John R. Zaller: From *The Nature and Origins of Mass Opinion*. Copyright © 2005 by Gary W. Cox and Mathew D. McCubbins. Reprinted with the permission of Cambridge University Press.